INTERNATIONAL RELATIONS

Cooperation and Conflict

INTERNATIONAL RELATIONS

Cooperation and Conflict

CHARLES P. SCHLEICHER
University of Oregon

PRENTICE-HALL, INC.
Englewood Cliffs, N. J.

INTERNATIONAL RELATIONS: Cooperation and Conflict
formerly INTRODUCTION TO INTERNATIONAL RELATIONS

© 1954, 1962 by
PRENTICE-HALL, INC., Englewood Cliffs, N. J.

Library of Congress Catalog Card Number: 62-12975

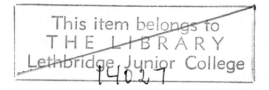
Third Printing ....*February, 1965*

Printed in the United States of America
47345—C

To
My Parents
in
Memory

Preface

This book is intended to present a comprehensive and accurate view of the nature of relations in contemporary international society. A difficult task in any age, it is especially so in one characterized by an increasing tempo of change. The study of international relations, however, has long since passed beyond the current events stage; nor can an assemblage of relatively unrelated topics touching on something called "international" pass as a serious treatment of the subject. Equally significant, there are today very few scholars in this complex field who believe that there is any one key factor—be it power, ideology, geography, geopolitics, or any other—capable of unlocking its mysteries.

These considerations impose certain responsibilities upon the writer of a comprehensive work on international relations intended for the beginning student and general reader. I have attempted to be as objective as is humanly possible, and to present more than one view where informed opinion is divided. Yet I have not hesitated to indicate my own stand when I believe facts, values, and reason so warrant. My principal aim, however, has been to present a systematic treatment, enabling the reader to separate the more enduring from the transient and to understand the basic factors behind the passing events of the day. In so doing, I have attempted to reflect the promising developments in research on this rapidly changing subject.

Building upon the frame of reference set forth in the two introductory chapters of Part I, I have endeavored to interweave fact and theory into a clear and orderly progression. A brief introductory statement precedes each of the subsequent parts. Part II is concerned with the principal dynamic forces operating in international society—nationalism, ideology, economics, and the security objective. This is followed, in Part III, by a consideration of the institutional forms and procedures—those of national governments and international organizations—through which these dynamic forces operate. Part IV begins by discussing and describing the resources of states and other entities (such as international organizations), whose resources in part determine their capacity to engage in international cooperation or conflict. It then treats the principal types of interaction, ranging from war to peaceful collaboration. The major factors which regulate the behavior of international decision-makers are the subject of Part V.

Finally, in Part VI, seven international relations "case studies" are presented against the background of the preceding chapters. In each instance, the United States is shown as an entity interacting with countries from a principal area of the world. To set the stage, an introductory chapter (21) discusses the objectives, resources, and internal factors which influence United States foreign policy, as well as the principal trends therein since 1945. The last seven of the eight chapters in Part VI have been written by distinguished experts on each of the seven areas. I have attempted to assure their integration with the book as a whole.

In addition to those special contributors, whose cooperation has greatly improved the quality of this book, there are many people who have helped me in its preparation. To my students through the years, both undergraduate and graduate, who have served both as guinea pigs and severe critics, I owe a great deal. Two of my graduate assistants in particular, Bhagwati Poddar and Carl Praktish, have helped with the bibliography, gathered data, checked numerous details, and criticized generally. Mrs. Charles Koburger has not only been an exceptionally fine typist, but has caught many a slip. To Al Goodyear of Prentice-Hall, and to members of the editorial staff, I am grateful for suggestions and encouragement.

Two persons who have been especially helpful and to whom I am deeply indebted and grateful are Mrs. W. Harold Dalgliesh of Salt Lake City and Fred A. Sondermann of Colorado College. Both of them have read the entire manuscript and offered suggestions of both a substantive and an editorial nature. I wish also to express my appreciation to those publishers and authors who have given me permission to reprint from their works. My family has endured my preparation of this book, as all families must. There are more to whom thanks are due, but they must go unnoted. I alone am responsible for the shortcomings of the book.

Charles P. Schleicher

Table of Contents

Tables, Charts, and Maps

I

THE FRAME
OF REFERENCE

1

How to Think About
International Relations

Two world wars within one generation, an almost countless number of limited wars, continued high tensions, a frightening armament race, the dire possibility of a total war which would surely destroy civilization and probably life itself—all of these raise grave doubts, not only as to the moral and intellectual capacity of man, but also the inherent soundness of his existing political institutions to cope with the great problems of the modern age. On the other hand, mastery of natural forces has allowed a third of mankind to enjoy a material standard of living previously un-attainable. Yet this achievement has incited an irrepressible demand among the nearly two billion people remaining—who are increasingly convinced that poverty and early death are no longer inevitable—to participate in the material progress from which they have hitherto been largely excluded. In short, while modern science and technology have made unprecedented resources available, there is a serious question whether we will use them to benefit or to destroy ourselves. The contrast between what is possible given a sane international order and what is probable without it produces alternating moods of pessimism and despair, optimism and hope.

That all the people of the world are increasingly dependent upon one another is a key fact of the contemporary era. The world is one big neighborhood, but unfortunately men are unable—or unwilling—to be good neighbors. With the fruits of the earth and human invention in-creasingly devoted to creating instruments of destruction (blandly called "weapons of peace") it is evident that human welfare and survival depend in large measure on the development of attitudes and institutions which will permit the diversion of resources to more productive and humane uses. Even if by some miracle world peace may be maintained through fear of mutual destruction, the material and moral burdens will be heavy. And if history takes its usual course, and the "weapons systems" through accident or deliberate decision are used without restraint in actual war, the worst fears of the pessimists are likely to be realized.

It is inherent in the democratic belief that men can and should understand and exercise a considerable measure of control over those forces which affect their lives. Yet so complex and bewildering are the events and forces of our time that many men despair of grappling with them successfully. Although they may reject the idea of fate as history preordained, they still view events as the "summary and unintended result of innumerable decisions of innumerable men. . . . There is no link between any one man's intentions and the summary result of innumerable intentions."[1]

The first requisite for refuting the notion of relentless fate is understanding what is involved in this basic dilemma. Yet expecting the average person to be capable of making intelligent judgments on details or even broad aspects of many complex problems (such as military policy, or the proper balance between military and development aid) is to expect more sophistication than even the expert possesses. Perhaps Professor Almond is correct in contending that the most effective approach to better understanding is a "selective and qualitative one" which should be aimed at enlarging what he calls the "attentive" public and educating the "elite." Teachers and clergymen, neither of whom he believes are at present adequately prepared to perform their tasks of leadership, are—among the elite groups—those capable of playing the most important role.[2]

INTERNATIONAL RELATIONS AS A FIELD OF STUDY

Just as the word "history" refers both to what actually happened and to what historians have written about the past, so also may we distinguish between International Relations as a subject and international relations as subject-matter—that is, as "an aspect of social reality."[3] The historian's purpose is to "recreate the past." The purpose of the international

---

[1] C. Wright Mills, *The Causes of World War Three* (New York: Simon & Schuster Inc., 1958), p. 12 ff.

[2] Gabriel A. Almond, *The American People and Foreign Policy* (New York: Harcourt, Brace & World, Inc., 1950); see in particular Chapter 10, "Consensus in a World of Crisis."

[3] Henceforth International Relations (capitalized) will be used to designate the subject and international relations the phenomena or subject matter.

relations student is to provide an accurate account of international reality. Men have thought about international relations for several thousand years, and a great many of their ideas have been expressed in writing. Today, words concerning international relations pour forth in an increasing torrent through a variety of media. As in the past, much of the effort is devoted to special pleading and propaganda; much of what purports to be educational is unsystematic and superficial.

In the development of academic disciplines some attention was devoted to the international as well as the domestic aspects of their subject matter.[4] Historians dealt with diplomatic history, economists with international trade and finance, political scientists with international law, organization, and politics. In recent years psychologists, sociologists, anthropologists, geographers, and philosophers have given increasing attention to the international field. Although their efforts are commendable, the results have generally been disappointing. In particular they have tended to overrate the significance of a single factor rather than to see it as only one aspect of a complex of personalities, forces, and situations.

It is obvious that a single discipline encompassing *all* aspects of international relations phenomena is hardly more feasible than one encompassing all of the relations within national societies. How then does one account for the development of a field of study called International Relations? Before World War I there was almost no organized study of international relations, either in American universities and colleges or elsewhere—although Paul S. Reinsch was pioneering in the field when in 1900 he lectured on world politics at the University of Wisconsin. His book on the subject was published the same year.[5] In the few courses that existed "these initial efforts were little more than unsystematic, and often superficial, attempts to discuss a wide variety of current problems which differed greatly in the level of their importance."[6]

The impact of World War I and its aftermath on the study and teaching of the subject was tremendous. The number of courses and writings multiplied. In the nineteen-twenties, courses in international organization, permeated with utopianism, became increasingly popular. With the decline of optimism in the thirties more attention was given to inter-

---

[4] See Quincy Wright, *The Study of International Relations* (New York: Appleton-Century-Crofts Inc., 1955), for the most ambitious attempt to date to describe and analyze the background and present status of the study of International Relations. For a survey of the teaching of International Relations in eight countries, see *The University Teaching of Social Science: International Relations*, a report prepared by C. A. W. Manning on behalf of the International Studies Conference (Paris: United Nations Educational Scientific and Cultural Organization, 1954).

[5] Paul S. Reinsch, *World Politics at the End of the Nineteenth Century as Influenced by the Oriental Situation* (New York: The Macmillan Co., 1900).

[6] See Grayson Kirk, *The Study of International Relations in American Colleges and Universities* (New York: Council on Foreign Relations, 1947), p. 2.

national politics, heavily colored by the so-called "realistic" or "power politics" approach. The advent of the cold war shortly after 1945 brought a renewed emphasis on power, or "the concept of interest defined in terms of power," as the central explanatory factor in the study of international relations or politics.[7]

In recent years many scholarly books and learned journals devoted to International Relations have been published. There has been an increased number of scholars and teachers specializing in this field, and new concepts and methods have developed. Perhaps the most promising contemporary trend is the building of conceptual frameworks which enable scholars and students to ask important questions, to seek out and organize the relevant data, and thus without prejudging to arrive at whatever generalizations evidence warrants.[8]

Scholars whose training has been in political science have been primarily responsible for this development. Increasingly, however, they draw from other fields such as psychology, sociology, philosophy, and geography. Although most academicians consider International Relations as a branch of political science, there is an increasing number who regard it as an emerging discipline, destined to join the established ones. The number of "majors" and departments of International Relations is growing. In terms of scope, unity, quantity and quality of literature, and recognized scholars, it compares favorably with many of the older disciplines. Yet specialists in International Relations are keenly aware of its serious shortcomings as they continue to search for newer and better foci, concepts, and methods.[9]

International Relations as a specialized study owes its existence to four interrelated factors: (1) In contrast to domestic society, the international society in which these relations take place is politically, legally, and psychologically decentralized and disintegrated. The political institutions and attitudes, on which orderly change and justice are based within states, are largely lacking in international society. (2) This first factor makes possible an area of concentration which is sufficiently distinct from that of other disciplines and which possesses the possibility of a focus and unity of its own. (3) Most of the existing disciplines, besides giving too little attention to the international aspects of their subjects, generally adopt as their model the integrated society, a practice which misrep-

---

[7] See Hans J. Morgenthau, *Politics Among Nations,* 3rd ed. (New York: Alfred A. Knopf, Inc., 1960), for a stimulating but controversial treatment from this point of view.

[8] See Stanley Hoffman, *Contemporary Theory in International Relations* (Englewood Cliffs, N.J.: Prentice-Hall, Inc., 1960), for a critical analysis of the principal empirical efforts.

[9] See Richard N. Swift, *World Affairs and the College Curriculum* (Washington, D.C.: American Council on Education, 1959), especially Chapter 1, "What are World Affairs?"

resents the setting under which international relations takes place.[10] This erroneous assumption is the source of many mistaken judgments and frustrations. (4) The development of an International Relations specialty facilitates the process of gathering and integrating data and focusing insights from all relevant fields of knowledge.

PURPOSES OF A CONCEPTUAL FRAMEWORK

Without understandable terms, concepts, and orderly ways of arranging and analyzing data, one is very much like the men described by Cardinal Newman. They had seen much of the world—even played a conspicuous part in it—without understanding what they had seen or done.

They abound in information and detail, curious and entertaining, about men and things; and, having lived under the influence of no very clear or settled principles . . . they speak of every one and everything, as only so many phenomena, which are complete in themselves, and lead to nothing, not discussing them, or teaching any truth, or instructing the hearer, but simply talking. . . .
Perhaps you are near such a man on a particular occasion, and expect him to be shocked or perplexed at something which occurs; but one thing is much the same to him as another, or, if he is perplexed, it is not knowing what to say, whether it is right to admire, or to ridicule, or to disapprove, while conscious that some expression or opinion is expected from him; for in fact he has no standard of judgment at all and no landmarks to guide him to a conclusion.[11]

The central aim of this chapter is to suggest standards of judgment and landmarks—in short, a conceptual framework, which has been described as

a sieve which helps to sort out, select, and reject observed facts; or a compass which indicates the direction in which research is moving; or a gauge which reports the state of development of a science at a particular time. . . . In place of the rigidity of a mechanical apparatus, it is flexible, in a state of constant flux. It is a body of theory which changes in the light of facts that it collects or that suggest it.
Less metaphorically, a conceptual framework consists of those theories and assumptions which an investigator uses in undertaking an analysis within a given field. . . . It is a system of working hypotheses, adopted and used only as long as it helps [to understand] . . . socially significant problems. . . .[12]

Briefly, a conceptual framework helps us gather, arrange, discern relationships among, and extract meaning from, data. It is a tool or set of tools, useful insofar as it contributes to understanding.

---

10 See Stanley H. Hoffman, "International Relations: The Long Road to Theory," *World Politics*, XI, (Apr. 1959), 46-47, for a discussion of this point.
11 John Henry Newman, *The Idea of a University*, new impression (London: Longmans, Green & Co., Ltd., 1912), pp. 135-36.
12 David Easton, *The Political System* (New York: Alfred A. Knopf, Inc., 1953), p. 57.

ESSENTIAL ELEMENTS
OF A CONCEPTUAL FRAMEWORK

International Relations is a social science concerned with certain aspects of human behavior in the international arena. Our task in constructing a conceptual framework is to devise a scheme to help us understand that behavior. In the analysis which follows we shall: (1) decide upon the entities, such as states, with whose relationships we are concerned; (2) classify interactions among these entities and determine which to include in our field; and (3) develop manageable categories for the classification of those factors which explain their international behavior and interactions.

Interacting Entities

International relations presumably consist of relations among things indicated by the term "national." But "national" is too vague to be a reliable guide. In making our selections here, two criteria will be used: manageability and importance. Although the terms per se are vague, involving value judgments of ends and empirical judgments of the significance of manageability, they will acquire substance and meaning in the ensuing parts of this chapter.

When we survey the international scene we have little difficulty in realizing that states are the principal entities involved. Some writers have even suggested that the discipline should be called *interstate* relations. But this would be unsatisfactory for three reasons: (1) the difficulty of changing long and firmly established usage; (2) the fact that *state* also refers to the major political subdivisions of federal systems such as those of the United States and Brazil; (3) states are not the only entities with which we are concerned. Herein, *state* will refer to so-called sovereign states (such as the United States) and not to geographical subdivisions within any governmental structure. While conceding that both usage and importance warrant concentration on "organized nation states," Professor Wright would have the term international relations refer to "relations between groups of major importance in the life of the world at any period of history. . . ."[13] Taken literally, this would include group relations within states, and surely this would be too ambitious to satisfy requisites of manageability, even if we were not concerned principally with focusing on the relations which occur in the kind of decentralized milieu so characteristic of international society.

A second type of entity—and one that appears to be of increasing importance—is an organization drawing its membership from a number of states. This we refer to as an international organization. In this instance

---

[13] Wright, *Study of International Relations*, p. 8.

we think immediately of the United Nations (UN) and its specialized agencies, as well as regional organizations such as the Organization of American States (OAS) and the European Coal and Steel Community (ECSC). Although other organizations, usually designated as alliances (the North Atlantic Treaty Organization [NATO] and the Warsaw Pact) differ in some basic aspects from those conventionally so-called international organizations, they are neverthless sufficiently similar to fit in the same category.

It is sometimes argued that these organizations are channels or instruments of state action rather than entities possessing purpose and policies of their own. From one point of view, national governments are also the means through which individuals and groups act on the national scene. Although governments possess legal authority and ordinarily command loyalty and obedience to a degree that differentiates them profoundly from international organizations, the latter are not entirely lacking in these characteristics. Furthermore, when confronted with conditions comparable to those of international society, governments—at least democratic ones—educate and persuade rather than coerce, as do international organizations. Whether regarded as interacting entities or as instruments of state action, various groupings of states both warrant and command the attention of those concerned with International Relations. In fact, international organization is a generally recognized subdivision of International Relations. It is argued here that these organizations are sufficiently important, both actually and potentially, to warrant inclusion among the entities of international society.

When we go beyond states and international organizations we are on less certain ground. If we look to practice, we find that relations between a governing state and its dependent peoples (usually in underdeveloped areas) have been treated in works devoted to International Relations, especially those dealing with international organization. Although according to general international law, colonies may be fully under the jurisdiction of the governing state, many self-governing peoples and areas have a distinct international status, such as protectorate or trusteeship. Moreover, from the Berlin Act of 1885, dealing with the Congo, to the UN Charter, colonial powers have accepted special obligations with respect to dependent people under their control. Aside from their legal status, most dependent people are ethnically distinct from the ruling group, and have loyalties which separate rather than join the rulers and the ruled into a common community. Since 1945, old-fashioned colonialism has almost disappeared, as a billion people have thrown off their colonial bonds and established some two score independent states. Although subject areas and peoples will be included herein and given some attention, it appears that within a short time only remnants will be left to remind us of once great empires.

In addition to those entities already indicated there are many groups of a private—or at least non-official—nature which could be included in our study. Individuals and national groups interested in religion, culture, labor, industry, finance, athletics, and politics have formed organizations transcending national boundaries. Undoubtedly, some of these—the International Chamber of Commerce, the International Federation of Free Trade Unions, and the Catholic Church, for example—are considerably more important than are some of the entities falling within any of the above categories. Nevertheless, they will be excluded on the grounds of manageability and that, on the whole, they are less important than the others. Accordingly, they can better be reserved for the consideration of other academic disciplines.[14] This does not mean that International Relations is not concerned with these private groups. It only means that they are among the many factors which must be considered as they influence interaction among the three major kinds of group entities.

Criteria for Classifying
Types of Interaction

One could select many criteria for classifying the myriad interactions among these group entities. For our purposes three appear to be of prime significance: (1) the role of the personnel involved; (2) the subject matter; and (3) the nature of the interaction.

Role of Personnel—Official and Private Relations. In considering the role of personnel involved, we may distinguish between "private" (unofficial or non-governmental) and official (or governmental) relations. Unofficial relations include all those among private individuals and groups of the interacting entities; they also include the private relations of officials. Thus, if the British Ambassador were to marry—or divorce— the daughter of the American Secretary of State, this would be an unofficial relationship. Since international organizations do not have subjects or citizens of their own, but only officials and employees, they can have private relations only in this limited respect. Private relations include those among business men, scientists, educators, labor leaders, and politicians, or groups in which they are represented. These relationships may be encouraged and controlled by officials, and they may be the subject-matter of official relations, as instanced by trade and cultural agreements.

International Relations does not focus on these private relationships; they are considered significant only as they affect official relations. This is not to deny them significance, nor to argue that they do not warrant

---

[14] See Georg Schwarzenberger, *Power Politics, A Study of International Society,* 2nd rev. ed. (New York: Frederick A. Praeger, Inc., 1951). Chapters 6, 7, and 8 deal with the "members of the international cast."

close study; but only that they fall principally within the province of other disciplines. Thus private international trade and finance is the proper domain of international economics, rather than of International Relations.

Official relations refer to those conducted by authorized leaders of states, international organizations, and dependent peoples. In the last, this concept presents a peculiar difficulty in that the governing power may insist that it is the only official spokesman for its dependent people and may regard their leaders as rebels and traitors. For example, although Gandhi and Nehru may have been the real leaders of the Indian people prior to 1947, only the British-dominated government of India, or the British government in London, could speak officially for India on the international scene. Nevertheless, India was a member of the League of Nations; and both India and the Philippines were members of the UN prior to independence.

The Subject Matter—Economic, Cultural, etc. Depending on the subject matter involved, one may speak of economic, financial, cultural, educational, religious, military, political, and other kinds of relationships. Because the focus of International Relations is on official interactions, the international behavior of private persons relating to these matters is only of indirect concern to a student of that subject. When *laissez faire* was at its height in the nineteenth century, this was a more important exception than it is now; but with the increasing concern with and participation of governments everywhere in economic and other activities, the danger is that the inclusion of all official relations may encompass too much within one discipline. If this be so, what, then, should be included? Some writers contend that the subject should be confined to political relations, and thus equate International Relations with international politics.

Nature of the Interaction Process—Cooperation and Opposition. All human relationships may be viewed as components of one of two broad patterns—cooperative or oppositional. No society would long exist if its individuals and groups could not agree on anything and were always in perpetual conflict. On the other hand, it is debatable whether progress would be as rapid and life as interesting if all were in complete agreement. The ideal of many men of good will is to minimize or, if possible, eliminate conflict. Yet most human relationships consist of varying amounts of cooperative and oppositional behavior. Because of the difference between international and domestic societies, conflict is likely to be more prevalent in the former.

The more common aims the members of a society have, the greater the similarities in their customs, expectations, historical experience, etc., the more likely it is that their relationships will be harmonious. Common aims, however, are not synonomous with like or similar aims. The former consist of ambitions and goals which can be maximized for all by common participation in their realization. No one gains at the expense of others.

Health, communication, navigation, and economic interests often—but not always—can be advanced for all by joint programs. It is otherwise, however, with many like but naturally incompatible aims. The United States and the Soviet Union, for example, whatever be the other causes of their animosities, seek security—each for itself—in a way that results in competition and conflict. Although it should be possible to develop institutions and practices whereby the security of all may be furthered, it is otherwise if one or more members of a society is inherently aggressive, or seeks to extend ideologies in basic conflict with other ideologies.

Oppositional behavior occurs whenever power is employed in human relationships. Whenever groups attempt to control each other by means of power, the relationship is *political,* as we shall use that term in studying international relations. Many writers who equate International Relations with international politics do not define their terms carefully. They usually regard politics as a form of intergroup struggle, or even as a "struggle for power." Yet, having indicated that this is their subject, they soon find themselves involved in matters which simply are not political in nature.

In this work the focus is on official relations among three types of entities, but it includes their cooperative nonpolitical as well as their oppositional or political behavior. It is therefore labeled International Relations rather than international politics. Although politics is a large and significant part of these relations, there is also considerable cooperation, and failure to give it commensurate treatment is a distortion of reality.

Components of Human Behavior

How one behaves depends on a combination of his own personality, the objectives he pursues, the situation in which the action takes place, and the resources at his disposal. Our purpose is to give content to these four components and apply them to official relationships among states, international organizations, and dependent peoples. Those who write about and conduct foreign policy seldom think in these neat categories. Nevertheless, because these are the factors which shape human behavior we can understand international relations only to the extent that we understand how they do so.

The Persons (Actors). That a state has a personality is fiction, but it does serve a useful purpose. Terms such as *France* and *Great Britain* are necessary human inventions whereby we can refer to organized collective entities. But *France* and *Great Britain* are not people who act in the international sphere. Those who do so are the representatives of their respective countries who act in an official capacity. In the case of a state, these may range from the foreign minister to an officer in charge of the armed forces. The President of the United States, or his authorized representative, is the sole official spokesman for the U.S. in international affairs. This does not mean that congressmen and other officials do not make vital decisions about foreign policy; it means only that they cannot enter into official relationship with other governments.

How these actors behave depends in part upon their personal characteristics. Their individual motivations, intellectual qualities, and ideological orientation shape their goals. These also shape, particularly, their interpretations of existing facts and their significance for policy. Although objective facts may determine the results of an action, they influence the taking of the action only as they are seen and interpreted by the subjective minds of men. Hitler, for example, decided when he launched his armies against the Soviet Union in 1941 that the facts justified his confidence in a quick victory. His poor judgment of the circumstances was one of his more grievous mistakes.

Objectives, conditions, and resources do not influence actions in a deterministic way; there is always the factor of human personality. A knowledge of human nature in general, and of statesmen in particular, should give us some basis for understanding and prediction. We assume a measure of rationality, which means that men attempt to select the most efficient means, under the circumstances as they see them, to achieve their goals. If this be so there should be a certain amount of order and predictability in international as in human behavior in general.

Objectives. An objective is a state of affairs an actor wishes to realize at some future time. It may be immediate or remote. A consideration of objectives requires an end-means analysis. Whether a particular state of affairs is regarded as an end or a means depends upon the perspective from which it is viewed. Let us assume that self-preservation of the state is an ultimate or non-contingent end of foreign policy, and that national security is a necessary means of self-preservation. Either national armaments or general disarmament may in turn be means to enhance national security. The preparation of plans, negotiations, and the establishment of control systems in order to obtain disarmament constitute subordinate means and ends in a hierarchy extending from a control system to national self-preservation. Self-preservation, although it may be the ultimate end of foreign policy, may be regarded either as a goal worthwhile in itself, as a condition for the realization of more basic values, or as both.

The selection of group goals is influenced by many factors. Although the personal goals of the actors may be included, the ends which they pursue as group leaders may be considerably different from those they would pursue in their personal capacities. Except for abstract ends (such as national security) on which there is likely to be consensus, most goals emerge from compromises among individuals and groups with different values and interests, from divergent views of the situation, and from estimates of capacity to realize the desired ends. It is particularly at the upper reaches of the ends-means series that basic or non-contingent values influence the selection of goals; yet views as to the morality or immorality of certain means, such as the use of force, presumably influence the selection of subordinate means and ends.

Resources. Actors vary greatly with respect to the resources available for pursuing the goals of the group. Most international organizations are quite limited in this respect and depend almost wholly on the support of the member states for their meager resources. Small states are not much better off, whereas the United States, accounting for about 30 per cent of the world's production, can put vast resources at the disposal of its foreign policy actors. Climate, soil, the technical and industrial machine, the nature of the economic and political system, the qualities and quantity of the population, and military forces are the major determinants of the resources potentially available to the policymakers.

Potential availability, however, may be considerably different from actual availability. In the Soviet Union—with only 40 per cent of U.S. production in the 1960's—resources devoted to military power, research, and non-military support of its foreign policy goals were comparable to those of the United States.

The amount and the kind of resources available to the actors are among the important determinants of both ends and means. Undoubtedly, Soviet use of propaganda immediately after the 1917 revolution was partially due to its lack of economic resources and military means. Similarly, its employment of economic means, after 1953, was an indication of their greater availability.

The reader should note the careful avoidance of reference to resources as being elements of power. Obviously they largely determine the power at the disposal of the actors; but they may also be used in a cooperative manner. *Whether they will be used to control or to cooperate with the actors of other entities depends upon the actors, the objectives they seek, the situation, and the extent and the nature of the resources themselves.*

Situation. Situation refers to those parts of the environment which at any given time the actors accept rather than try to change. In more technical language, they are the constants or parameters, in contrast to the variables. The conditions may be internal or external to the entity. The state of public opinion in the United States and constitutional and administrative arrangements are among the internal factors from the standpoint of American decision-makers. Viewed by the actors of other entities, however, they are external factors. The international society is an external factor from the standpoint of all the actors.

Rapid change is one of the chief characteristics of the present era. The major shifts in the distribution of power among states, the revolution in military technology, the nationalistic revolts among colonial and formerly colonial peoples, the development of vastly different and apparently irreconcilable ideologies, and the conquest of outer space, are among the major facts of our turbulent era. As has happened throughout human history, man's adaptability to new circumstances will largely determine his fate. The people of the United States, apparently rather content in their prosperity, and only recently forced to take an active part in world affairs, find adjusting to a rapidly changing world particularly difficult and unpleasant. Nevertheless, these changes are chiefly responsible for the revolution in American foreign policy since 1945.

The reader should be cautioned that the preceding discussion is an oversimplification. A more detailed and realistic inquiry would include a consideration of the following points:

1. The official actors, like private individuals, pursue not one end, but several ends, some of which may be incompatible. Basic objectives of American foreign policy, for example, may be both national security and the promotion of democracy abroad. Yet to promote national security it may be deemed necessary to support fascism in Spain and communism in Yugoslavia.

2. Because resources are usually limited it is often necessary to choose between ends, or at least to promote some less vigorously than others. *In a practical sense objectives may be regarded as the actual ends sought; these are the working objectives.* Who has not seriously pondered whether the United States has not undertaken objectives beyond its means?

Without the controlling principle that the nation must maintain its objectives and its power in equilibrium, its purposes within its means and its means equal to its purposes, its commitments related to its resources and its resources adequate to its commitments, it is impossible to think at all about foreign affairs. Yet the history of our acts and of our declarations in the past fifty years will show that rarely, and never consistently, have American statesmen and the American people been guided by the elementary principle of practical life.[15]

3. There are usually several alternative means, any one of which may be used to realize a given objective. There are also usually several different courses of action which may be followed simultaneously to promote the same end. A nation may work through the United Nations, build up its own military forces, enter into alliances, and strengthen the economic resources of its actual or potential allies in order to enhance its security. However, only if these means are compatible will it be sensible to employ them in combination. It is a grave question whether collective security through the UN and through alliances are compatible.

---

[15] Walter Lippmann, *U.S. Foreign Policy: Shield of the Republic* (Boston: Little, Brown & Co., 1943), p. 7.

Certainly one cannot pursue peace through disarmament and rearmament at the same time.

4. Several objectives may be pursued by the same means. A man saves money not only to buy a car but to feed himself and his family, to entertain guests, to play golf, and so forth. In like manner the Marshall plan was motivated by humanitarian, security, economic, and ideological considerations. It is sometimes said that money or wealth is to economics as power is to politics. That is, money may be used to satisfy a number of ends and power to further many goals. States may, therefore, desire a reserve of power, just as a person may want a financial reserve. Even though one may have no immediate need for money or power, the possession of both means a degree of psychological security.

5. Although an individual usually finds a way to integrate his own ends and economize his means, this process is much more difficult in the case of group action involving many individuals. These individuals may differ in their ends, as well as the value they place on similar goals. They are likely, especially in an integrated community, to differ even more on the reasonableness of the means to be employed. A democratic nation which is divided on both the ends and the means of foreign policy confronts those responsible for the conduct of that policy with exceedingly difficult problems.

TWO VANTAGE POINTS FOR
VIEWING INTERNATIONAL RELATIONS

One may attempt to envisage international society as a whole, to regard entities as parts of the system, and to concentrate on relationships. This is the system-oriented view. A second possibility is the entity-oriented approach. Here is the concentration is on the parts and on analysis of their purposes and structures, with perhaps only secondary attention given to the external situation. An examination of the most recent textbooks and the periodical literature on International Relations reveals an emphasis on the entity-oriented approach. Kenneth Thompson writes on this point:

Instead of beginning with the *international* structure and society, the new line of inquiry has emphasized the urgency of examining *national* goals and objectives as a logical point of departure. . . . The practices and policies of international organization are from this point of view no longer comprehended as abstract considerations. Instead they are conceived in the framework of national aims and aspirations, the points of conflict of these aspirations and their areas of compatibility and incompatibility.[16]

Each approach has its strengths and weaknesses. Some scholars con-

---

[16] Kenneth W. Thompson, "The Study of International Politics: A Survey of Trends and Developments," *Review of Politics*, XIV, No. 4 (Oct. 1952), 440.

tend that the system approach tends to overrate the importance of international law and organization and the international environment generally. Here the dynamic factors within states, and especially the differences among them, are neglected. States tend to be regarded as billiard balls, all of the same composition but varying in size. On the other hand, the entity approach leads to the opposite result of placing too great emphasis on the internal factors and national goals, so that the common international environment and the interactions or relations among the entities are in turn neglected. Specifically, the system approach is disposed to view the UN as an interacting entity whereas the entity emphasis is inclined to regard it as only an instrument of national policies and goals.

I have attempted to construct the preceding conceptual framework so as to accommodate the viewpoints of the actors, the private citizens of a country, and of those who conduct the business of the UN.

SUGGESTED READINGS

Bloomfield, Lincoln P. and Norman J. Padelford, "Three Experiments in Political Gaming," *American Political Science Review*, LIII (Dec. 1959), 1105-15.

Corbett, Percy E., "Objectivity in the Study of International Affairs," *World Affairs*, IV (July 1950), 257-63.

Deutsch, Karl W., "Game Theory and Politics: Some Problems of Application," *Canadian Journal of Economics and Political Science*, XX (Feb. 1954), 76-83.

———, "Toward an Inventory of Basic Trends and Patterns in Comparative and International Politics," *American Political Science Review*, LIV (Mar. 1960), 34-57.

———, ed., *Theoretical Aspects of International Relations*. Notre Dame, Ind.: University of Notre Dame Press, 1959.

Fox, William T. R. and Annette Baker Fox, "Teaching of International Relations in the United States," *World Politics*, XIII (Apr. 1961), 339-59.

Frankel, Joseph, "Toward a Decision-Making Model in Foreign Policy," *Political Studies*, VII (Feb. 1959), 1-11.

Gange, John, *University Research on International Affairs*. Washington, D.C.: American Council on Education, 1958.

Goodwin, Geoffrey L., ed., *The University Teaching of International Relations*. Oxford: Basil, Blackwell & Mott Ltd., 1951.

Hoffman, Stanley H., ed., *Contemporary Theory in International Relations*. Englewood Cliffs, N.J.: Prentice-Hall, Inc., 1960.

——————, "International Relations: The Long Road to Theory," *World Politics*, XI (Apr. 1959), 346-77.

Kaplan, Morton A., *System and Process in International Politics*. New York: John Wiley & Sons, Inc., 1957.

Kindleburger, C. P., "Scientific International Politics," *World Politics*, XI (Oct. 1958), 83-88.

Kirk, Grayson Louis, *The Study of International Relations in American Colleges and Universities*. New York: Council on Foreign Relations, Inc., 1947.

Knorr, Klaus and Sidney Verba, "The International System: Theoretical Essays," *World Politics*, XIV (Oct. 1961), entire issue. (Also available in clothbound edition.)

Kristof, Ladis K. D., "Political Laws in International Relations," *Western Political Quarterly*, XI (Sept. 1958), 598-606.

Lasswell, Harold D., "The Scientific Study of International Relations," *Year Book of World Affairs, 1958*, XII (1958), 1-28.

Liska, George, *International Equilibrium: A Theoretical Essay on the Politics and Organization of Security*. Cambridge: Harvard University Press, 1957.

Marchant, P. D., "Theory and Practice in the Study of International Relations," *International Relations*, I (Apr. 1955), 95-102.

Mathisen, Trygve, *Methodology in the Study of International Relations*. New York: The Macmillan Co., 1959.

McClosky, Herbert, "Concerning Strategies for a Science of International Politics," *World Politics*, VIII (Jan. 1956), 281-95.

Medicott, W. N., "The Scope and Study of International History," *International Affairs*, XXXI (1955), 413-26.

Rosenau, James N., ed., *International Politics and Foreign Policy: A Reader in Theory and Research*. New York: Free Press of Glencoe, Inc., 1961.

Schuman, Frederick L., "The Study of International Relations in the United States," UNESCO. *Contemporary Political Science*, p. 576. Paris, 1950.

Scott, Andrew M., "Challenge and Response: A Tool for the Analysis of International Affairs," *Review of Politics*, XVIII (Apr. 1956), 207-26.

Snyder, Richard C., "Toward Greater Order in the Study of International Politics," *World Politics*, VII (Apr. 1955), 461-78.

—————— and Glenn D. Paige, "The United States Decision to Resist Aggression in Korea: The Application of an Analytical Scheme," *Administrative Science Quarterly*, III (Dec. 1958), 341-78.

Sprout, Harold and Margaret, "Environmental Factors in the Study of International Politics," *Journal of Conflict Resolution*, I (1957), 309-28.

——————, *Man-Milieu Relationship Hypotheses in the Context of International Politics*. Princeton, N.J.: Center of International Studies, Princeton University, 1956.

Swift, Richard N., *World Affairs and the College Curriculum*. Washington, D.C.: American Council on Education, 1959.

Thompson, Kenneth W., "Toward a Theory of International Politics," *The American Political Science Review*, XLIX (Sept. 1955), 733-46.

Van Dyke, Vernon, ed., *Some Approaches and Concepts Used in the Teaching of International Politics*. Iowa City: State University of Iowa, 1957.

Wandyez, Piotr S., "The Theory of International Relations," *Review of Politics*, XVII (Apr. 1955), 189-205.

Williams, Benjamin H., "Scientific Method in Foreign Policy," *Bulletin of the Atomic Scientists*, XV (Dec. 1959), 419-21.

Wright, Quincy, *The Study of International Relations*. New York: Appleton-Century-Crofts, Inc., 1955.

2

Evolution and Nature
of International Society

So rapidly is the world changing that one may question the relevancy of history to an understanding of the present. J. Robert Oppenheimer holds that the "prevalence of newness, the changing scale and scope of change itself, . . ."[1] is one of the chief characteristics of contemporary society. Nevertheless, a knowledge of history should help us understand the road we have traveled to the present, as well as existing ideas and institutions which, however inadequate, are a legacy of the past. In this chapter, therefore, we shall trace in bold strokes the evolution of international society. Having done so, we shall indicate its chief characteristics as it stands in the seventh decade of the twentieth century, and conclude by a consideration of the adequacy of existing forms and institutions to enable men to cope with the present and emerging problems of a revolutionary age.

EVOLUTION OF INTERNATIONAL SOCIETY

Measured in the perspective of time that *Homo sapiens* has lived on earth, it was only yesterday that he developed what is called civilization. One of its chief characteristics is the division of the world into inhabited territorial areas ruled by groups of men with authority to suppress violence, maintain order, and protect it from outside invaders. Once resources and men are organized for defense, they are equally available to extend the boundaries of their area by negotiation, force, or guile.

---

[1] The Open Mind (New York: Simon & Schuster Inc., 1955), p. 141.

During the past six thousand years, practically all the inhabitable areas of the earth have been divided into political units known as city-states, states, and empires. The processes and methods by which the territorial boundaries of these units have been shaped and the governing authorities established have varied from place to place and from time to time. It is impossible to discern an orderly evolution; the comforting belief that there has been a steady development from the basic family unit through the tribe and the city-state to the modern state, and that the process is destined to continue inevitably until all mankind is included within one political unit, does not agree with the facts. The processes by which these developments have taken place have consisted of varying mixtures of consent and coercion, threat and promise, bribery and purchase, design and luck, as well as marriage—possibly for love, and certainly for purposes of state.

Pre-Modern Period

The earliest known civilizations, state systems, and empires developed some five thousand years ago in four different areas of the world—the basins of the Nile, the Euphrates, the Indus, and the Yellow rivers. Within each of these civilizations there was communication, intercourse, and wars of defense and conquest; but the means of travel and communication were such that relations among the systems were minimal. The life of men in the "non-Western" world continued with a minimum of intercourse with Western European society down to the fifteenth century. During most of that period the cultures of China, India, and the Middle East, as well as those of Mexico and parts of South America, were as highly developed, or even more so, than was that of Western Europe. It was Western European culture, however, that was to undergo a great transformation over the next five hundred years while these other societies changed but little until recently.

The breakdown of Western medieval society was marked by the development of independent states and relations among them. Because it was this system that eventually extended to the entire world, our account logically begins here. The roots of Western civilization, however, extend back through the medieval period to ancient Greece and Rome. The Greeks, despite a common origin and culture, were unable to achieve political unity. Divided into a number of city-states, relations among them bore a striking resemblance to those of state systems of the past and present. Alliances, temporary coalitions, exchanges of diplomatic representatives, "permanent" inter-city organizations, a system of law, arbitration for the peaceful settlement of disputes, wars among themselves and against the "barbarians," and eventual conquest by outside powers, characterize their history.

To the west the city-state of Rome had by 350 B.C. conquered the Italian peninsula. Beginning with the first Carthaginian War (264 B.C.), Rome embarked upon a series of conquests which, a century before the beginning of the Christian era, created an empire extending from North Africa to Scotland, and from the North Atlantic coast to the Caspian Sea and Persian Gulf. Thus, part of the ancient world, together with a new world in Europe, were drawn together in a unique political system. Although in the early period the international relations of Rome were similar to those of the Greeks, the Romans soon came to regard other people not as equals but as actual or potential subjects. As the Empire extended, the outlying areas became colonial dependencies. Peace—the *Pax Romana* imposed by arms and maintained by excellent administrative organization—prevailed throughout the empire. During the centuries following the passage of Roman control, the ideal of peace under a common political union—a restored Roman empire—persisted throughout Western Christendom.

Rome's greatest accomplishment and legacy is commonly held to be her system of law. One branch of that law, the *jus gentium,* originally a body of customs applied between non-Romans and later in some cases involving Roman citizens, eventually came to be regarded as law common to all peoples. The early writers of international law, relying heavily on a natural law concept, drew upon the *jus gentium* for the content of natural law.

After the breakdown of Roman authority in the fourth century A.D., followed by a chaotic period of semibarbarism, a system of feudalism gradually developed to fill the vacuum. In theory feudalism was a hierarchical system extending from the serf at the bottom through lords, vassals, and kings to the emperor at the peak. In reality it was a complex and confusing system of personal arrangements. Authority, the economy, and life in general were decentralized. Nevertheless, the ideal of Christian unity persisted, and men thought of themselves as Christians rather than as Frenchmen, Italians, or Englishmen. This ideal expressed itself in the Roman Catholic Church, and in the Holy Roman Empire which came into being in A.D. 962 when the Pope crowned Otto the Great as emperor. With the authority of the emperor largely confined to southern Germany and northern Italy, it was the church with its strong hold on the minds of men that provided the principal unifying force.

Although feudalism performed a useful function by introducing a degree of order and stability, by the fourteenth century it began to yield to the pressure of new forces calling for new forms. An emerging middle class interested in commerce and security over a wider area than was possible under feudalism supported certain strong figures against the feudal nobility. This combination of forces proved too strong for the unadaptive feudal elite within the emerging states, and eventually too strong as well for the Papacy and the Emperor that challenged from without.

European State System to 1914

From the fourteenth through the nineteenth century, and to a lesser degree even down to World War II, Europe was the central stage of world events. The leading powers were located there, and they had a major interest and role in most of the important happenings elsewhere. It was in Italy, however, that we find the precursor of the modern state system. There by the twelfth century a number of city-states—Venice, Pisa, Florence, Naples, Genoa, Milan—had effectively asserted their independence. Relationships among them were similar to those among the ancient Greek city-states, and among the parts of the early Roman Empire.

Meanwhile, by 1500, several states similar in name and roughly similar in area to those of the twentieth century (such as England, Spain, France, and Portugal) had emerged on the broader European scene. Until 1815, these powers engaged in bitter clashes both in Europe and in the new world overseas. Vast empires were won, lost, and passed from one power to another. Meanwhile the commercial revolution shattered the localized feudal economy, the Protestant revolt broke the unity of Christendom, gunpowder and printing came into more extensive use, and a new scientific attitude toward matter and the universe paved the way for the development of modern science and technology. Although complicated by religion, economics, personal ambition, and location, the pattern was clear. Usually a powerful aggressor state threatening to disturb the distribution of power and to engulf the other states evoked coalitions which eventually led to its defeat.

Modern Period Through the Napoleonic Wars. As the sixteenth century opened, Spain was the dominant European power and the leading empire-builder. When in 1519 the dominions of the Austrian Hapsburgs were added to those of Spain, the stage was set for a series of struggles which ended with the Thirty Years' War (1618-1648). France constituted the principal power in the several anti-Hapsburg coalitions. The Peace of Westphalia (1648) ending the conflict is a landmark in the development of the Western state system. It reduced the power of the Holy Roman Empire to a position no higher than that of the dynasties of France, Sweden, England, and Spain. More important, from the negotiations and treaties emerged the principle of the essential equality of independent sovereign states. Whatever had persisted of the medieval unity ideal was now replaced by

the era of absolutist states, jealous of their territorial sovereignty to a point where the idea of an international community became an almost empty phrase and where international law came to depend upon the will of states more concerned with the preservation and expansion of their power than with the establishment of a rule of law.[2]

From 1648 to 1815, France replaced the Hapsburgs as the chief threat to the other states and the multistate system itself. Louis XIV, ambitious to humble the Spanish and Austrian Hapsburgs, to extend France to her "natural boundaries," and to build up an empire, embarked in 1668 on a series of wars which were not to end until 1713 with her exhaustion and defeat. Following the established pattern, most of the states of Europe, including England after 1688, rallied against the Grand Monarch. The Treaty of Utrecht (1714) established the framework of European states for the next half-century. Although France lost some of her empire to England, her recovery was rapid, and by the middle of the century she was again a strong continental power.

In the next major series of wars, two additional powers, Prussia and Russia, played important roles. There was no dominant aggressor at the beginning of the period as there had been in the previous conflicts, although France filled this role during the final years. Opening in 1740, the War of the Austrian Succession saw Prussia allied with France and Spain against Austria, England, and the Netherlands. The results were inconclusive. Renewed in 1756 as the Seven Years' War, a changed lineup—frequently called a "diplomatic revolution" and cited as a classic demonstration of the principle of the "balance of power"—now saw England and Prussia opposing France, Austria, Russia, and Sweden. Only the military genius of Frederick the Great averted disaster for Prussia. With the restoration of peace in 1763, Great Britain emerged victorious over France in the colonial contest and Prussia was recognized as a great power.

Between 1763 and the Napoleonic Wars the American Revolution created a weak new state and the partition of Poland destroyed an old one. France, smarting from defeat in the Seven Years' War, played a major role in the success of the American cause.

Meanwhile, pressure was building up in France which was soon to be released in the truly cataclysmic forces of the French Revolution. This paved the way for the eventual overthrow of the "Old Regime," heralded the triumph of the middle class and of capitalism, and stimulated the development of nationalism and democracy. As an immediate consequence, the Revolution engulfed Europe in a series of wars which threatened to extinguish the state system and leave France master of the world. Threatened by the intervention of Prussia and Austria, France declared war in 1792, thus beginning a struggle which raged with interruptions for twenty-three years. In the end, however, Napoleon's invasion of Russia,

---

[2] Leo Gross, "The Peace of Westphalia 1618-1948," *American Journal of International Law*, XLII, (Jan. 1948), 38.

his defeat there, and British mastery of the seas, contributed to his downfall.

The Congress of Vienna (1814) and the treaties which ensued therefrom established the European status quo which with some modifications lasted until 1914. That France was to emerge virtually unpunished is attributed to the brilliant diplomacy of her representative, Talleyrand, to mutual jealousies among the victors, and to the attempt of the archconservative Austrian statesman Metternich at restoring the general status quo of 1792.

Only passing references have been made to the overseas empires established by several of the European powers from the sixteenth century onward. Known as the "Old Imperialism" in contradistinction to the new outbursts of colonial expansion toward the end of the last century, it had about spent its force by the time of the American Revolution. The early success of the independence movements in most of Spain's American colonies and the later loss of Brazil by Portugal were virtually assured by the successful revolution to the north.

In Asia, however, Britain and the Netherlands claimed vast areas, and Spain and Portugal held on to the remnants the British allowed them to retain. France had lost virtually all of her empire by 1763. The carving up of most of Africa and additional parts of Asia, in which France was again to join the colonial parade alongside Belgium, Germany, and the United States, was to await the "New Imperialism" of the later nineteenth and early twentieth centuries.

Nineteenth Century and Pax Britannica. The period between the Congress of Vienna and 1914, despite its revolutions and limited wars, was the most peaceful of modern centuries. Democracy, liberalism, capitalism, and nationalism spread and flourished. In comparison with previous centuries and the years since 1914, international trade flowed freely, and national currencies were stable and readily convertible. While a unified Italy and Germany replaced a multitude of smaller states, many new states were born in the Americas and in the Balkans. Italy, Germany, Japan, and the United States joined the ranks of the great powers. But Great Britain was the dominant power of the century, the lone world power. This, combined with the relative peace to which she made a major contribution, has led some to label the period *Pax Britannica.* Her nineteenth-century power was based upon an unusual combination of geographic, economic, military, and political circumstances. Her lead in the industrial revolution; her navy, far-flung bases and overseas empire; her strategic location at the small end of a geographic funnel within which her major competitors were located; all were the chief elements of her strength. The spread of the industrial revolution, the rise of the United States and Japan as major powers, and the development of the submarine

—which almost succeeded in severing Britain's lifeline in World War I—marked the end of her dominance.

At the conclusion of the Napoleonic Wars, the victorious powers with a series of treaties pledged themselves to preserve the status quo in Europe. The Holy Alliance, as this loose organization was often called, was composed of Great Britain, Russia, Austria, Prussia, and after 1818 France. It bore a certain resemblance to the League of Nations and the UN. Britain at first played the most important role in the system, but when, under the leadership of Metternich, armed intervention was used to preserve the status quo within a number of states, and plans were made to restore the Spanish colonies in America, Britain broke away and supported the U.S. Monroe Doctrine. Although the Holy Alliance collapsed by 1825, the practice of Great Power consultation—the "Concert of Europe"—continued, with a few interruptions, until 1914. The Greeks, supported by France, Great Britain, and Russia, but opposed by Metternich, gained their freedom from the Ottoman Empire in the decade 1825-1835. Thereafter, Great Britain supported Turkey and followed a policy of containment against Russia in the Balkan area. The rivalry between the two great powers largely ceased by 1907, however, in the face of a combined German-Austrian threat to both Russia and Great Britain.

Germany, after its unification in 1871 under the leadership of Bismark until his dismissal in 1890, played the role of a satisfied state. Concerned with the French desire for revenge following her defeat in the Franco-Prussian War (1870-1871), Bismark surrounded her by a series of alliances, including the Triple Alliance of 1882 (Germany, Austria-Hungary, and Italy), and a neutrality treaty with Russia in 1887. After 1890, Germany's policy became aggressive. She built a navy, pushed toward the Middle East, and began to carve an overseas empire out of the unclaimed "backward" areas. The reaction of the other powers ran true to form. France and Russia formed the Dual Alliance in 1904, and France and Great Britain composed their differences, entering the Entente Cordial, which was expanded into the Triple Alliance by the addition of Russia in 1907. The Anglo-Japanese Alliance of 1902 and the "silent alliance" between the United States and Great Britain after 1900 were indicative of Britain's response to the new situation. From 1890 to 1914, clashes between the members of the opposing alliances inevitably involved the others. It seems that after 1890 the road of European politics led almost steadily to World War I.

The new race for colonial empires, which set in after 1870, saw most of the remainder of the "backward" areas divided among the great and some of the lesser powers, either as formal colonies or as "spheres of influence." By conquering large sections of Africa and Indo-China, France became the second largest imperial power. The U.S. joined the parade at the turn of the century. Of the non-Western powers, only Japan embarked on imperial adventures.

Inter-War Period—1919-1939

In World War I Great Britain, France, Italy, Russia, Japan, and—after 1917—the United States were the chief members of the Allied and Associated States which by 1918 emerged victorious over Germany, Austria, Turkey, and their allies. When the representatives of the thirty-two victorious powers assembled in Paris in January, 1919, the world eagerly awaited the arrangements resulting from the "war to end war." It was generally understood that peace would be based upon the "Wilsonian Code," which promised that moral principles, democracy, and the self-determination of peoples would constitute the basis for peace. Hard reality soon conflicted with high idealism. Still, Wilson believed that the League of Nations more than compensated for the faults and shortcomings in the other provisions of the peace treaties, and provided a means by which these might be remedied. Many of the treaty provisions soon came in for bitter criticism. In the light of subsequent history, we might argue that they should have been either far more generous or far more severe. Instead they created a desire for revenge without seriously impairing the power to take revenge.

The history of the interwar years of frequently interrupted peace falls into two rather equal periods. The first, from 1919 to 1931, was a period of reconstruction, return to normalcy, and attempts to strengthen the structure of peace in order to prepare the way for disarmament. The second, which opened with the Japanese conquest of Manchuria in 1931, witnessed the repudiation of the peace treaties, the defiance of the League, and the beginning of World War II.

First Phase—1919-1931. Much of the international history in the first period revolved around the problems of security and disarmament. France from 1919 on sought security by almost all possible means. Denied security through the partial dismemberment of Germany, she sought in vain an alliance with the United States and Great Britain. Thwarted in this, and lacking confidence in the League collective security system, she turned to alliances with Belgium, Poland, and later the states of the Little Entente—Czechoslovakia, Romania, and Yugoslavia.

Her other approach, more clearly related to the League, was to find a basis for disarmament. France insisted that security must precede disarmament, whereas Great Britain and the United States, who after 1945 adopted the French position, contended that disarmament would bring security. A number of agreements, all of which failed to go into effect, were drafted prior to 1925 to meet the demands of France and her allies.

The Locarno Pact, concluded in late 1925, and subsequently ratified, constituted a regional agreement whereby Great Britain and Italy promised to come to the aid of Germany or France in case one was attacked by the other. The "Locarno Spirit" was hailed as the dawn of a new era, one marking a *rapprochement* between France and Germany and the acceptance in principle of the latter's equal status in the family of nations. The United States, where, in refusing to join the League, the ideology of isolation had prevailed over the reality of interdependence, was one of sixty-three members of the 1928 Kellogg-Briand Pact. War as an instrument of national policy was condemned and renounced; the settlement of disputes should "never be sought except by pacific means." The Pact was hailed by some because it "outlawed" war, thus prohibiting certain wars which the League Covenant had permitted; but the more practical minded argued that the U.S. could now hardly insist on its neutral rights if League sanctions were applied against aggressors.

Disarmament negotiations were resumed when a Preparatory Commission first met in 1926, with both Germany and the United States represented. A year later the Soviet Union was also included. So minimal was the agreement reached over the next few years that when the representatives of sixty-odd states met at the 1932 Geneva Disarmament Conference, the prospects for disarmament were dim. These prospects had been darkened by the Japanese invasion of Manchuria the previous year; they were virtually extinguished when Hitler came to power in Germany in January, 1933. Moderate proposals by the United States and Great Britain, a call for general and complete disarmament by the Soviet Union, and France's demands for an international police force were all rejected.

It should be noted that the Washington Naval Conference of 1921-1922 and the London conference of 1930 did result in a limitation of naval armaments and certain related agreements concerning Pacific defenses and China. The ability but reluctance of the United States to outbuild Great Britain and Japan, and the willingness of the British to terminate the Anglo-Japanese alliance, were important factors underlying the agreements, which were terminated in the deteriorating situation of the thirties.

Second Phase—1931-1939. From the Japanese invasion of Manchuria in September, 1931, to September 1, 1939—when the German invasion of Poland marked the beginning of World War II—the "war of nerves" and limited hot wars created tension at least as high, if not so dangerous, as those of the cold war. The League condemned Japan, but sanctions were never seriously considered. Henceforth the prestige of the League declined, despite its half-hearted application of sanctions against Italy after she invaded Ethiopia in 1935.

The course of diplomacy and war pursued by Hitler's Germany was the central factor in bringing the Soviet Union into the mainstream of world events. The Communist government was recognized by the United States in 1933; the Soviet Union was admitted to the League in 1934; a military alliance with France followed a year later. Henceforth until the Soviet-German Pact of August, 1939, the Soviet Union was the League's most ardent advocate of collective security and of opposition to German expansion. Both France and Great Britain, concerned with the German threat, were perfectly willing to forget their League obligations in their wooing of Mussolini; and France was willing to forego her treaty promises to Czechoslovakia in the hope of appeasing Hitler. Although Italy vacillated for a time and was fearful of an Austrian-German union, by 1936 Hitler and Mussolini had composed their differences and the Rome-Berlin Axis was born. They united in their support of Fascist Franco and his civil war in Spain, while only Communist Russia gave other than lip-service support to Spain's democratic forces.

By 1937 two rival groups, with Germany, Italy, and Japan as the major partners of one, France and the Soviet Union of the other, were lining up for war. Great Britain was sympathetic to the latter group, but was unwilling to make a firm commitment.

Flushed with a series of successes—absorbing Austria in 1938, re-uniting the Rhineland to Germany, and rearming his country—Hitler now demanded the "return to Germany" of the territory and the German-speaking people of Czechoslovakia's Sudetenland. The sacrifice of Czechoslovakia followed; Hitler solemnly pronounced his last territorial aspirations in Europe fulfilled; and Britain's Chamberlain promised "peace in our time." Russia had been excluded from the negotiations, as had Czechoslovakia. When, in 1939, Hitler demanded Polish territory and Great Britain and France finally guaranteed Polish independence, German aggression meant war. An unsuccessful attempt on the part of the Western powers to form an alliance with the Soviet Union was a prelude to the German-Soviet "non-aggression" pact of August 23, 1939. War followed in short order. During the next five years millions were killed by force of arms and millions more by disease and starvation. In addition to the destruction of material things, the social fabric of much of the world was torn apart.

Just as World War I saw the advent of communism in Russia, World War II paved the way for its triumph in China. Two powers, the United States and the Union of Soviet Socialist Republics, emerged supreme from the war, with Great Britain occupying a rank between these and the lesser states whose prestige and strength had declined. During the concluding stages of hostilities the UN Charter was drafted at San Francisco. Based on the assumption of continued unity among the victorious powers, it was to be an instrument to preserve the peace and to usher in an era of prosperity and progress.

These high hopes were to be short-lived. By 1947 many of the states of the world had joined one of two opposing blocs, each led by the two superpowers. The tensions of the cold war mounted. In place of disarmament, atomic and hydrogen bombs were added to the arsenals of destruction; as the years passed, peace was widely held to rest on mutual fear and terror.

In the preceding pages we have sketched some 2,000 years of development of the modern state system, with emphasis on the more recent period. Whatever else may be concluded from this survey, it should be plain that change—at times so slow as to be almost indiscernible, at others so rapid as to seem cataclysmic—has been continuous. We are now living in one of the historical periods of rapid change which holds vast potentialities—for good or for evil. Whether the second half of the twentieth century of the Christian era will see these potentialities harnessed and used for the good life or unleashed for terrorism and death is at best uncertain.

STRUCTURE OF INTERNATIONAL SOCIETY

Man is naturally a social animal because no one is really human who is completely isolated from others. In its broadest sense, human society means a system of interaction of any sort, or people being held together in a network of mutual stimulus and response. To fulfill their social needs, men form various groups. Some are organized and joined quite consciously; others arise spontaneously, and one ordinarily does not "join" these but rather is "born" into them. Examples of the former are labor unions and service clubs; the family, some churches, and nations exemplify the latter. Most individuals belong to several different social groups; and all but stateless persons are members of at least one—or two in the case of "dual nationality"—major group known as a state.

A social group is a system of social interaction. It is usually held that such a group involves a "sense of belonging" and some degree of cooperation in the attainment of common goals. This does not preclude antagonism among its members; but if it is too great, cooperation will be at a minimum, conflict will be severe, and the group may break up. Antagonism within families leads to conflict and sometimes to divorce; within territorial groups such as states and dependent areas it may lead to civil war, and possibly to the division of a territory and its people into separate states, as in the cases of the partition of India in 1947 and the division of Vietnam in 1954.

The nation is the largest social group toward which most men feel intense loyalty and a sense of belonging. This feeling we call nationalism. From the standpoint of the national group with its inclusive membership, smaller groupings may be regarded as subgroups. Although most groups presumably perform functions valued by their members and command some display of loyalty, in the twentieth century it is the nation to which most men give their primary allegiance.

Nevertheless, since mankind has developed a high degree of interdependence and a system of interaction, it is correct to speak of *world society*. Moreover, the entire human race possesses some of the psychological characteristics of a group. If mankind is viewed as a group, then most international organizations, nations, and dependent peoples may in turn be regarded as subgroups within the larger whole. The UN constitutes the closest approximation to a political institution serving the group constituted by mankind. It is granted that this concept of all mankind as a group is more an ideal than a description of the present situation. The sense of belonging to the human group, except in a biological sense, hardly exists as far as most men are concerned. Moreover, the UN does not command the loyalty, nor is it endowed with the resources necessary to enable it to play a major role in serving the needs or controlling the international behavior of states. Perhaps it is more accurate to say that whereas there is a world society, it is decentralized, disintegrated, and quite defective in those features of community feeling and political institutions characteristic of the group. It is this characteristic of the international milieu that was largely responsible for and justified the development of the discipline of International Relations.

The study of intergroup relations constitutes a large segment of the subject matter of the social sciences. Although all intergroup relations involve people, we may distinguish two kinds of intergroup relations: those which take place between individuals of different groups acting in their personal capacities, and transactions between two or more representatives of these groups. As a student of a certain college or university you may have personal relations with individuals of other institutions. On the other hand, you may represent your institution and enter into relationships with like representatives of other colleges and universities. In the latter role you would have the right and the obligation to act for your group—probably to commit it to an agreement—and otherwise to look after certain of its interests. Since International Relations, as defined herein, is concerned with interactions between the representatives of three kinds of entities—states, dependent people, and public international organizations—it is a form of intergroup relations of the second type. Hence we are concerned with the components of human behavior which assist us in understanding both the how and the why of the interactions or relations between their officials or leaders.

"Structure" implies the existence of parts, relationships, and some degree of stability among them. Since the dawn and spread of the modern state system, states have been the principal parts (entities) of international society and interactions among them, or their foreign relations, the primary concern of the student of International Relations. Although we have chosen to include dependent peoples and areas as well as international organizations among the parts, it is granted that, in comparison with the sovereign states, they are minor entities, and their actors exert relatively little power and influence.

The number of states, their internal political, economic, and social systems; their ideologies; their international objectives; their capacity and will to exert power and influence on the international scene; and their foreign policies—all have varied from period to period. After the consolidation of Germany and Italy in the eighteen seventies, the number of states remained relatively stable for half a century. Several were then born, or reborn, after 1918, with the collapse of the Russian, Austro-Hungarian, and Turkish empires. Since 1945, the outburst of nationalism in non-Western areas, coupled with changes in the Western world had by the nineteen sixties increased the number more than a third, to slightly over one hundred. With the virtual disappearance of colonial dependencies, future increase or decrease in numbers would depend largely on the breakup or consolidation of existing sovereign states.

It is readily apparent that although these states may all be "equally sovereign," as well as similar in some other ways, no two are identical with respect to the components of human action: the personalities of their actors, their objectives, their resources, and their internal and external situations. Identical international behavior, therefore, is not to be expected. On the other hand, to the extent that states are similar in the above respects they can be expected to behave in a similar way. Our present knowledge, however, does not enable us to be sufficiently sure of the factors we need to examine; and we are even less certain of how a single factor, much less several in combination, is related to a given course of behavior on the part of state actors. Hence we are not able to make highly reliable predictive or scientific statements.

Nevertheless, there are several broad criteria of varying degrees of usefulness and validity for explaining international behavior whereby we may classify states. We assume on the basis of logic and empirical evidence—*other things being equal*—that states with plentiful resources behave differently from those whose resources are limited. The well-established categories of super, world, big, middle, and small powers grow out of this assumption. A more useful classification in future years may well be between the atomic-missile powers and the non-atomic-missile powers. Ideology is also frequently employed as a basis for classification on the assumption, for example, that an authoritarian state will behave differently from a democratic one under similar circumstances. Whether a state is insular or continental, more or less underdeveloped or developed, recently colonial or long independent, landlocked or maritime, economically self-sustaining or dependent, will influence its behavior on the international scene. These are among the important factors which will receive attention in subsequent chapters.

Several key concepts, forces, institutions, and procedures need brief discussion in order to round out our preliminary picture of the structure of international society. These are nationalism, sovereignty, international law, methods of peaceful intercourse and adjustment, and international organization.

Nationalism

Briefly defined, nationalism is the feeling or sentiment of a people which distinguishes them as a nation, and expresses itself politically in a demand for an independent state. Although the European states of the early modern period antedated the development of nationalism, since 1800 it has been the primary force behind the disruption of empires and the creation of new states. It is the bulwark of sovereignty; it largely determines the character of international organizations. In short, it is nationalism which principally sustains the states and the state system, and is the major force shaping behavior within the system. Its role in determining the general international atmosphere or milieu is of particular importance here.

We have indicated the influence of basic consensus upon the character of intra- and intergroup relations. It is the absence of that consensus, or positively put, the existence of nationalism, which constitutes the denial of the physical fact of world interdependence. Our basic modern dilemma is the existence of a world society without a commensurate community.

A community ordinarily means a body of people, occupying a definite territory, who have common interests, attitudes, sentiments, traditions, customs, and modes of behavior. Unity, cohesion, a feeling of "we" and a "common consciousness" are the essential characteristics of a community. Although an ideal community is a group with common and identical values, beliefs, and attitudes, such a condition is rare; but individuals among which there is a degree of community may be able to work together despite their differences. A community feeling is necessary for concession and compromise in the adjustment of conflicting interests and views of justice. Within a perfect community, behavior would be in accordance with the principle of "all for one and one for all" and cooperation would characterize all relations. In contrast, in a society without community the principle of conduct would be "each for himself"; all interaction would be political, with force and violence its principal form.

What is the status of community in international society? Do men feel themselves to be members of the human group or of national groups? Are national loyalties being replaced by more inclusive, but still limited, allegiances? Specifically, is the term "Atlantic community" mere rhetoric, or does it express a growing sense of solidarity? Are the citizens of the Benelux nations (Belgium, the Netherlands, and Luxembourg), France, Italy, and West Germany beginning to feel they are "Little Europeans"? A number of distinguished scholars maintain that the countries of the North Atlantic region have some but not all of the requirements of what they call a Security Community, i.e., one in which there is real assurance that its members will not fight each other physically, but will settle their disputes in some other way.[3]

Although among some men and in some areas nationalism may be diminishing or changing, nowhere is its force spent; and in most parts of the world it is growing. Under these circumstances, international society will remain disintegrated, cooperation will be more difficult to achieve, and conflict will be more prevalent than within national societies that have a more highly developed sense of community.

Legal Framework: International
Law and Sovereignty

The term law, as used in this context, means a system of coercive norms setting forth standards of human behavior. It is what we mean when we say that one is subject to fine or punishment by authorized persons if he behaves, or fails to behave, in a certain way. The persons or subjects of a legal system are those human beings to whose behavior the law applies, or whose rights and obligations it defines. Corporations such as General Motors are said to be subjects of United States domestic law, just as the United States is a subject of international law. This is only a convenient way of saying that the laws apply to persons acting as official representatives of General Motors or of the United States. Although the traditional concept was that states were the sole persons of international law, that view is gradually giving way; the UN, dependent peoples, and even private individuals are also regarded by an increasing number of writers as subject to its jurisdiction.

The essential and distinguishing characteristic of international law is that it is decentralized. A decentralized legal system is one without government organs which have authority to change, interpret, and enforce its rules or norms. Under the international legal system these functions remain with the individual states who perform them, according to legal theory, on behalf of the international legal community. A few exceptions exist, where centralization has been vested in international organs such as the UN Security Council, the International Court of

---

[3] See Karl W. Deutsch, *et al.*, *Political Community and the North Atlantic Area* (Princeton, N.J.: Princeton University Press, 1957).

Justice, and certain other organizations entrusted with essentially non-political responsibilities.

Sovereignty is a legal term. To be a sovereign entity, and thus a state, means to possess certain rights under international law. Sovereignty consists of those legal rights which constitute the "domestic jurisdiction" of a state, as determined by international law. A state has legal obligations as well as rights, i.e., it is bound, or limited, by international law. But it is not limited by the legal authority of another state or, to any significant extent, by that of supranational agencies such as a world government. If such a government were established, both states and international law would disappear. For the former would no longer be sovereign, and hence no longer states; and international law would be transformed into, or discarded in favor of, a centralized system.

The root of sovereignty is nationalism, which is also responsible for the primitive nature of the international legal system. As long as people and their leaders insist on maintaining their national sovereignty, an effective government for international society will be impossible.

The interrelationships among nationalism, a government for serving and regulating the world society, and the nature of international relations is set forth in the following statement by Werner Levi:

> Sovereign nations indulge in international cooperation, let alone altruism, only if such luxury does not weaken them. This situation is due to the absence of any supranational agency capable of guaranteeing the life of nations and of social controls normally assuring the life of members in a community. As long as the citizen regards the preservation of his own nation in absolute freedom from restraint by a higher authority as paramount, even at the sacrifice of other nations, this state of affairs will continue. Under such conditions the "national interest," which is in the final analysis the citizens' interest that their states as such, not they as human beings, should survive absolutely free and unbound, permeates every national act and dominates foreign policy.[4]

Methods of Peaceful Adjustment

The members of all state systems have maintained channels of communication. Diplomats assigned by each state to the capitals of other states have been the conventional agents of *bilateral* diplomacy in the modern period. *Multilateral* diplomacy, or negotiation among the representatives of several states—particularly in international organizations—has been a rapidly growing feature of the past hundred years as the complex problems of the modern world have proved intractable to the bilateral approach.

Diplomacy, or negotiation, as well as certain other methods, are the peaceful procedures by which international actors may adjust their

---

[4] *Fundamentals of World Organization* (Minneapolis: The University of Minnesota Press, 1950), p. 11. Copyright 1950 by the University of Minnesota.

differences. Mediation, conciliation, arbitration, and adjudication, all involve "third parties" in addition to the disputants. The growth of international organizations has stimulated the involvement of third parties, but negotiation remains the dominant form of peaceful intercourse in international relations.

International disputes can be resolved either by peaceful means, or by force. The adequacy of peaceful means, therefore, is of crucial significance for the maintenance of peace. But as long as sovereignty is regarded as a precious possession, the use in international society of authoritative methods characteristic of governments is bound to be at a minimum. Under general international law, parties to disputes are under no legal obligation even to submit their differences to peaceful settlement. Although the charters of international organizations increasingly obligate their members to utilize peaceful means, except when they submit to arbitration and adjudication they are under no obligation to accept the final settlement. Even when states agree in advance to submit their *legal* disputes to courts or arbitral bodies whose decisions are legally binding, they frequently weaken the agreement by ingenious reservations. International organizations may improve upon these procedures, and make their use more likely, but they cannot change them basically as long as the members are sovereign states.

International Organization

States have traditionally carried on their relations and adjusted their disputes by the use of peaceful methods, or have engaged in forms of conflict ranging from propaganda to physical combat. The frequent occurrence of wars and the inadequacy of the traditional international institutions to cope with all the problems of an interdependent world stimulated the development of international organizations. The ill-fated League of Nations and the UN are the prime examples of this process.

Aside from the Holy Alliance, the first permanent and effective international organizations dealt with common economic and social problems. There were approximately thirty of these organizations prior to 1914, most of them established after 1860. With increasing interdependence resulting from scientific and industrial progress, problems of transportation, communication, crime, trade, and commerce could no longer be satisfactorily handled on a national basis. The older practices of bilateral diplomacy or temporary multilateral conferences were also inadequate to deal with problems of permanent concern to many nations. Undoubtedly the growth of a humanitarian conscience which transcended national boundaries had some effect on international efforts to cope with the evils of the slave trade and opium traffic, and with problems of health.

It has been the urge for international peace and national security, however, that has given the impetus to the establishment of most of the *general*—general in terms of membership and functions—organizations such as the UN, as well as many of the regional ones. So compelling and persuasive is the peace and security argument that the organization of international social and economic activities is commonly justified by this appeal. Hence the *nonpolitical* functions of the United Nations are usually justified by their presumed contributions to removing underlying causes of conflict. The UN and the Organization of American States, as well as some other regional groups, also approach peace and security by more direct and immediate routes. These range from multilateral diplomacy to collective military sanctions. Even the organizations which have developed out of contemporary military alliances, such as NATO, the Southeast Asia Treaty Organization (SEATO), and the Warsaw Pact, are justified by their supporters primarily in terms of their contributions to peace. All of them profess to be concerned with economic and social matters, even if there be little action in these fields. On the other hand, a growing number of international or supranational regional organizations, such as the European Coal and Steel Community, the European Common Market, and the Inter-American Development Bank, although not without important political and security purposes, are primarily economically motivated.

Only a few of these organizations—and these to a very limited extent—really deprive the states of their decision-making powers. Nevertheless, the obligations which states assume by joining them, and even more the cooperative relationships that develop, to some extent do circumscribe the independence of the state actors. These organizations are compromises between the desire for independence and the facts of interdependence. Their growth represents the pressure of circumstance far more than it does the diminution of nationalism. Essentially they are attempts to reform rather than to transform the multi-state system. Some people, of course, view them as seeds from which government may or is destined to grow; but ardent nationalists view this possibility as a danger to be curbed rather than as a hope to be nurtured.

NEW FORCES AND OLD FORMS

The world has become so interdependent that there is now a world society; all mankind constitutes one group, at least in a physical sense. But most men, while dimly conscious that this is so, have failed to adjust their attitudes, and have thwarted the development of institutions adequate to meet the demands of the rapidly changing situation. Instead, the loyalties and practices of the primitive tribe have been transferred to the larger group constituting the nation, which insists upon its sovereign independence in the state. In the modern state system, with its decentralized law, its forms of peaceful intercourse, and its useful, although inadequate, means of settling disputes, states have traditionally resorted to force, and superior power has eventually triumphed. Nevertheless, mankind has not only demonstrated a remarkable capacity for surviving, but has multiplied at an ever increasing rate. It is an anomaly of the second half of the twentieth century that the population explosion carries the threat of producing too many people while the atomic explosion threatens to destroy them all.

In a rapidly changing world, today's adjustments to yesterday's demands are soon rendered obsolete by the needs of tomorrow. It may well be that the statesmen assembled in Paris in 1919 and at San Francisco in 1945 were thinking in terms of the conflicts from which they had just emerged, rather than trying to envisage the demands of the future. No matter how adequate or inadequate the traditional state structure has been in the past, even when reformed by international organization it may be obsolete for accommodating the present and future. An increasing number of men everywhere doubt that the state system can survive. One discerning scholar, John H. Herz, writes as follows:

Students and practitioners of international politics are at present in a strange predicament. . . . We are no longer sure about the functions of war and peace, nor do we know how to define the national interest and what its defense requires under present conditions. As a matter of fact, the meaning and function of the basic protective unit, the "sovereign" nation-state itself, have become doubtful. On what, then, can policy and planning be built?[5]

Herz contends that the "peculiar unity, compactness, coherence of the modern nation-state" was due to the fact that it was "an expanse of territory encircled for its identification and its defense by a 'hard shell' of fortifications," which "rendered it to some extent secure from foreign penetration, and thus made it an ultimate unit of protection for those within its boundaries." The former impenetrability is giving way to a "permeability which tends to obliterate the very meaning of unit and unity, power and power relations, sovereignty and independence." The present possibility of "hydrogenization" is only the culmination of a process, beginning with the nineteenth century, which has "rendered the traditional defense structure of nations obsolete through the power to by-pass the shell protecting two-dimensional territory and thus to destroy —vertically, as it were—even the powerful ones. Paradoxically, *utmost strength now coincides in the same unit with utmost vulnerability, absolute power with utter impotence.*" [Italics mine—CPS][6]

---

[5] "Rise and Demise of the Territorial State," World Politics, IX (July 1957), 473. For a more comprehensive treatment of this thesis, see John H. Herz, *International Politics in the Atomic Age* (New York: Columbia University Press, 1959).
[6] *Ibid.*

Attempts of states to perform their basic protective function by the traditional methods now threaten the destruction of man "in every one of his most intimate, personal interests." There is also a universal interest in the solution of world problems such as poverty. Given this situation, "it is not entirely utopian to expect the ultimate spread of an attitude of 'universalism' through which a rational approach to world problems would at last become possible. . . ."[7] Herz points out that, historically, the unit which could protect people within its boundaries "has tended to become the basic political unit; people, in the long run, will recognize that authority, any authority, which possesses the power of protection."[8]

In short, the capacity of the state to retain its cohesion and to perform its historic protective function has been brought into question by its vulnerability in the modern age. Its economic interdependence has made it susceptible to economic blockade. Physical devices of unprecedented and potentially unlimited destructiveness, which have made it possible to leap over terrestial boundaries, have transformed war into contests for the destruction of civilization. Ideological forces and propaganda through new means of communication have facilitated the possibility of undermining the morale of the enemy population and opened the way for the penetration of "fifth column" forces and the subversion of traditional loyalties. Under the impact of new forces and conditions, men seek both to hold to the old and adjust to the new.

TABLE 1

DATA ON STATES AND DEPENDENT AREAS

Country	Area in Sq. Miles[1]	Population[1] (Est. 1-1-60)	Annual Pop. Inc. (%)[2] (53-58)	Density Per Sq. Mile[1] (Est. 1-1-60)	Real GNP Per Head[3] Est. 1961 ($US)[a]
United States	3,675,633	179,323,175	1.7	50.0	2790.0
Canada	3,851,809	17,678,000	2.8	4.6	2048.0

(a) The Gross National Product (GNP) per head is an estimate of purchasing power in terms of United States dollars at United States 1961 prices.

[1] *Rand McNally Commercial Atlas and Marketing Guide,* 92nd ed. (Chicago: Rand McNally and Co., 1961), pp. 4-5.

[2] *Statistical Yearbook, 1959* (New York: United Nations, 1959), Chart 1, pp. 21-28.

[3] Rosenstein-Rodan, P. N., "International Aid for Underdeveloped Countries," *The Review of Economics and Statistics,* Vol. XLIII, No. 2, May, 1961. Table 1-A World Gross National Product and Population, 1961, p. 118. Table 2-C Gross National Product Per Head ($US), pp. 126-27. Table 6 Sharing the Burden of Aid, p. 138.

[7] *Ibid.,* p. 493.

[8] *Ibid.,* p. 474.

GREAT BRITAIN AND WESTERN EUROPE

Country	Area in Sq. Miles	Population (Est. 1-1-60)	Annual Pop. Inc. (%) (53-58)	Density Per Sq. Mile (Est. 1-1-60)	Real GNP Per Head Est. 1961 ($US)
Austria	32,365	7,082,000	0.2	218	
Belgium	11,775	9,117,000	0.6	774	1658.0 (a)
Denmark	16,614	4,580,000	0.7	276	1587.3 (a)
Finland	130,085	4,435,000	1.1	34	1286.3 (a)
France	212,766	44,927,000	0.9	211	1444.5 (a)
Ger. Fed. Rep.	95,885	55,746,000	1.2	581	1591.5 (a)
Greece	51,169	8,319,000	0.9	163	613.1
Iceland	39,750	171,000	2.3	4	
Ireland	27,137	2,893,000	−0.7	107	
Italy	116,273	49,363,000	0.5	425	896.8 (a)
Luxembourg	998	320,000	1.1	320	1870.8 (a)
Monaco	0.6	22,500	−	37,500	
Netherlands	12,526	11,389,000	1.3	909	1478.2 (a)
Norway	125,032	3,574,000	1.0	29	1578.8 (a)
Portugal	35,589	9,108,000	0.8	256	383.4
San Marino	23.5	15,100	−	643	
Spain	194,345	30,090,000	0.8	155	513.6
Sweden	173,577	7,468,000	0.7	43	2024.0 (a)
Switzerland	15,937	5,246,000	1.2	329	1944.5 (a)
United Kingdom	94,194	58,591,000	0.4	555	1749.5 (a)
Yugoslavia	98,742	18,796,000	1.3	190	489.1
Liechtenstein	60.6	16,000	−	264	
Andorra	175	6,500	−	37	
Vatican State	0.2	1,050	−	5,250	

(a) Derived by dividing average family income by 4: Based on Table 6.

SOVIET BLOC

Country	Area in Sq. Miles	Population (Est. 1-1-60)	Annual Pop. Inc. (%) (53-58)	Density Per Sq. Mile (Est. 1-1-60)	Real GNP Per Head Est. 1961 ($US)
Albania	11,097	1,562,000	3.0	141	825.0 (a)
Bulgaria	43,036	7,859,000	1.0	183	825.0 (a)
Latvia	24,600	2,134,000	−	87	825.0 (a)
No. Vietnam	61,516	14,788,000	−	240	199.0
Czechoslovakia	49,353	13,639,000	1.0	276	825.0 (a)
Hungary	35,909	9,943,000	0.6	277	825.0 (a)
No. Korea	47,811	8,083,000	−	169	211.0
U.S.S.R.	8,650,140	212,801,000	−	25	986.0
Poland	120,327	29,550,000	1.9	246	825.0 (a)
Rumania	91,675	18,398,000	1.4	201	825.0 (a)
E. Germany	41,634	16,403,000	−0.9	394	825.0 (a)
Comm. China	3,767,751	699,966,000	2.8	186	167.0
Tibet	469,194	1,699,000	−	3.6	
Outer Mongolia	625,950	1,056,000	1.1	1.7	

(a) Average for Eastern Europe.

Country	Area in Sq. Miles	Population (Est. 1-1-60)	Annual Pop. Inc. (%) (53-58)	Density Per Sq. Mile (Est. 1-1-60)	Real GNP Per Head Est. 1961 ($US)
Afghanistan	250,900	13,310,000	—	53	117.0
Australia	2,974,581	10,050,000	2.2	3	1513.0 (a)
Burma	261,689	20,303,000	1.0	78	121.2
Cambodia	67,550	5,056,000	—	75	154.8
Ceylon	25,332	9,643,000	2.5	380	214.5
China (Taiwan)	13,885	10,323,000	3.6	743	202.8
India	1,269,506	404,330,000	1.3	318	139.8
Indonesia	575,893	87,802,000	1.9	152	147.9
Japan	142,773	93,031,000	1.1	651	613.0
Rep. of Korea	37,414	22,834,000	1.0	610	158.4
Laos	91,482	1,754,000	3.2	19	104.0
Nepal	54,362	8,978,000	1.5	165	94.4
New Zealand	103,736	2,332,000	2.2	22	1513.0 (a)
Pakistan	364,702	86,733,000	1.4	238	124.8
Philippines	115,600	23,721,000	2.5	205	282.3
Thailand	198,404	22,003,000	1.9	111	202.4
Viet Nam, Rep. of	65,709	12,988,000	—	198	210.3
Fed. of Malaya	50,677	6,809,000	2.7	134	552.4
Maldive Islands	115	83,500	—1.2	726	161.8
Bhutan	19,300	670,000	1.6	35	92.4

(a) Average for all of Oceania.

THE MIDDLE EAST AND NORTH AFRICA

Country	Area in Sq. Miles	Population (Est. 1-1-60)	Annual Pop. Inc. (%) (53-58)	Density Per Sq. Mile (Est. 1-1-60)	Real GNP Per Head Est. 1961 ($US)
Egypt	386,100	25,319,000	2.4	66	225.0
Syria	71,209	4,556,000	3.9	64	259.9
Iran	620,180	20,577,000	2.4	33	180.4
Iraq	171,554	6,784,000	—	40	225.3
Israel	7,990	2,111,000	3.9	264	1,026.8
Jordan	37,291	1,702,000	3.0	45	189.4
Lebanon	4,014	1,719,000	2.8	428	479.2
Libya	679,358	1,200,000	1.4	1.8	101.0
Saudi Arabia	617,600	6,159,000	—	10	254.7
Tunisia	48,319	3,987,000	1.2	83	240.0
Turkey	296,108	26,494,000	2.7	89	333.7
Yemen	75,270	4,900,000	—	65	160.4
Cypress	3,572	559,000	1.7	156	683.8
Morocco	170,382	10,165,000	1.8	60	210.0
Bahrein	231	129,000	3.8	558	286.6
Oman and Muscat	81,979	623,000	—	7.6	126.4
Qatar	8,497	41,800	—	4.9	
Trucial Coast	32,269	91,000	1.5	2.8	629.8
Kuwait	5,998	219,000	2.0	37	2,988.9

Country	Area in Sq. Miles	Population (Est. 1-1-60)	Annual Pop. Inc. (%) (53-58)	Density Per Sq. Mile (Est. 1-1-60)	Real GNP Per Head Est. 1961 ($US)
Cameroun	166,752	3,303,000	0.7(a)	20	166.0 (a)
Central Afr. Rep.	227,118	1,224,00	1.2	5.4	160.0 (d)
Chad	466,640	2,612,000	2.0	5.6	160.0 (d)
Congo Rep.	125,890	816,000	2.2	6.5	160.0 (d)
Rep. of Congo	905,329	13,732,000	2.2	15	154.0
Dahomey	44,713	1,750,000	1.8	39	150.0 (c)
Ethiopia	457,147	21,351,000	—	47	129.0
Gabon	98,283	434,000	0.3	4.4	160.0 (d)
Ghana	91,819	4,847,000	1.6	53	210.0
Guinea	94,945	2,667,000	—	28	160.0 (d)
Ivory Coast	124,550	3,145,000	5.3	25	150.0 (c)
Liberia	42,989	1,350,000	—	31	136.0
Malagasy Rep.	228,510	5,225,000	2.7	23	
Mali	465,050	3,748,000		8.1	
Mauretania	419,390	685,000	3.5	1.6	150.0 (c)
Niger	459,180	2,515,000	2.8	5.5	150.0 (c)
Nigeria	350,291	33,441,000	1.9	95	134.0
Senegal	76,153	2,337,000	1.8	31	150.0 (c)
Sierra Leone	27,925	2,185,000	2.3	78	
Somalia	246,137	2,047,000	0.3-0.9(b)	8.3	102.0 (e)
Sudan	967,248	11,549,000	2.0	12	120.0
Tanganyika	362,688	9,052,000	1.8	25	127.0
Togo	22,002	1,136,000	1.1	52	99.0
Union of So. Af.	472,550	14,435,000	1.8	31	598.0
Voltaic Rep.	105,879	3,516,000	4.0	33	150.0 (c)

(a) Figure for French Camerouns.
(b) Figure for British Somaliland and Ital. Somaliland.
(c) Average for former Fr. West Africa.
(d) Average for former Fr. Equatorial Africa.
(e) Figure for Ital. Somaliland.

LATIN AMERICA

Country	Area in Sq. Miles	Population (Est. 1-1-60)	Annual Pop. Inc. (%) (53-58)	Density Per Sq. Mile (Est. 1-1-60)	Real GNP Per Head Est. 1961 ($US)
Argentina	1,072,467	20,737,000	1.9	19	799.0
Bolivia	424,052	3,366,000	1.4	8	122.3
Brazil	3,286,344	64,837,000	2.4	20	374.6
Chile	286,322	7,560,000	2.5	26	452.9
Colombia	439,405	14,105,000	2.2	32	373.4
Costa Rica	19,647	1,194,000	4.0	61	361.6
Cuba	44,217	6,627,000	1.9	150	516.0
Dom. Rep.	18,811	2,929,000	3.5	156	313.2
Ecuador	104,479	4,191,000	2.9	40	222.7
El Salvador	8,260	2,556,000	3.5	309	267.5
Guatemala	42,031	2,584,000	3.0	61	257.7
Haiti	10,711	3,492,000	1.2	326	149.2
Honduras	43,266	1,915,000	3.3	44	251.7
Mexico	758,061	33,954,000	2.9	45	415.4
Nicaragua	48,636	1,489,000	3.4	31	288.4
Panama	28,745	1,040,000	2.9	36	371.0
Paraguay	157,006	1,736,000	2.3	11	193.2
Peru	482,133	10,640,000	2.5	22	268.5
Uruguay	72,153	2,709,000	1.3	38	560.9
Venezuela	352,051	6,622,000	3.0	19	644.5
The West Indies	8,005	3,279,000	2.2	410	(a)

(a) Jamaica 464.7, Trinidad and Tobago $556.7, rest $334.6.

TERRITORIES AND DEPENDENCIES

Country	Area in Sq. Miles	Population (Est. 1-1-60)	Annual Pop. Inc. (%) (53-58)	Density Per Sq. Mile (Est. 1-1-60)	Real GNP Per Head Est. 1961 ($US)
Belgium					
Ruanda-Urundi	20,916	4,941,000	2.5	236	117.0
British					
(Europe)					
Channel Is.	75.2	101,000	−0.7	1,343	
Isle of Man	227	57,300	−0.5	252	
Gibraltar	2.3	26,000	−	11,304	
Malta	122	325,000	0.3	2,663	
(Africa)					
Kenya	224,960	6,444,000	1.7	28	150.0
Basutoland	11,716	742,000	1.2	63	114.0 (a)
Bechuanaland	274,928	368,000	1.0	1.3	114.0 (a)
Gambia	3,978	307,000	−0.7	77	99.0
Mauritius	809	650,000	3.2	803	337.0
Camerouns	34,080	1,613,000	1.8	47	112.0
St. Helena	119	5,900	−	50	114.0 (a)
Seychelles	156	47,500	−	304	114.0 (a)
Swaziland	6,705	277,000	4.4	41	114.0 (a)
Uganda	93,981	5,892,000	1.6	63	115.0
Rhodesia and					
Nyasaland	487,639	7,805,000	2.7	16	225.0
(America)					
Bahamas	4,404	136,000	9.4	30	
Bermuda	22	46,000	−	2,091	
British Guiana	82,978	558,000	2.9	6.7	354.0
Br. Honduras	8,864	91,000	2.7	10	213.1
Falkland Is.	4,618	2,000	−	0.4	150.0
Virgin Islands	67.2	8,300		124	
(Asia)					
Aden Colony	80	147,000	−	1,837	
Aden Protect.	111,971	671,000	−	6	
Borneo	78,681	1,178,000	2.0 2.8 (b)	15	189.2 223.4 (b)
Hong Kong	391	2,877,000	4.1	7,358	306.0
Singapore	224.5	1,595,000	4.9	7,105	552.3
(Oceania)					
Fiji	7,055	385,000	2.9	55	
Gilbert and					
Ellice Is.	369	41,000	−	111	
New Hebrides	5,700	60,000	2.2	10.5	
Solomon Is.	11,500	106,500	1.1	9	
Tonga	269	62,000	3.7	230	

(a) Average for this group.
(b) Figures for No. Borneo and Sarawak.

Country	Area in Sq. Miles	Population (Est. 1-1-60)	Annual Pop. Inc. (%) (53-58)	Density Per Sq. Mile (Est. 1-1-60)	Real GNP Per Head Est. 1961 ($US)
Australia					
Papua	90,540	516,000	4.2	5.7	
New Guinea	93,000	1,409,000	3.3	15	
Norfolk	13	1,150	–	88	
Solomon Is.	4,100	58,000		14	
Nauru	8	4,300	–	537	
New Zealand					
Western Samoa	1,133	106,000	2.5	94	
Denmark					
Faeroe Is. (Self govern.)	540	36,000		66	
Greenland (Integral)	839,782	28,900	–	0.03	174.1
Ethiopia					
Eritrea (Self)	46,000	1,587,000		34	129.0
France (Africa)					
Comoro	834	183,000		219	
Fr. Somaliland	8,492	69,300	1.1	8.2	
(Americas)					
Fr. Guiana	35,126	31,000	–	0.9	246.7 (a)
Guadeloupe	687	268,000	2.9	390	246.7 (a)
Martinique	425	275,000	2.4	647	246.7 (a)
St. Pierre and Miquelon	92.6	5,100	–	55	246.7 (a)
(Oceania)					
Fr. Oceania	1,544	144,000	3.7	93	
New Caledonia	7,202	81,000	1.9	11	
New Hebrides	5,700	60,000	2.2	10.5	
Netherlands					
Netherlands Antilles	371	202,000	1.5	544	232.2
Surinam	55,198	254,000	3.6	4.6	282.4
Neth. New Guinea	159,375	754,000	–	4.7	90.0
Portugal (Africa)					
Angola	481,226	4,496,000	1.1	9	
Cape Verde	1,557	193,000	3.6	124	114.0 (b)
Mozambique	297,654	6,253,000	1.1	21	114.0 (b)
Portugese Guinea	13,944	563,000	1.1	40	114.0 (b)
Sao Tome and Principe	372	65,000	2.4	175	
(Asia)					
Macao	6.2	228,000	1.0	36,774	272.5
Portugese India	1,618	647,000	0.2	400	270.0
Timor	7,332	491,000	1.4	67	280.9

(a) Average for this group.
(b) Average for this group.

Country	Area in Sq. Miles	Population (Est. 1-1-60)	Annual Pop. Inc. (%) (53-58)	Density Per Sq. Mile (Est. 1-1-60)	Real GNP Per Head Est. 1961 ($US)
Spain					
Sp. Morocco	579	65,000		112	114.0 (a)
Sp. Sahara	102,676	13,000	—	0.1	114.0 (a)
Sp. Guinea	10,828	216,000	1.0	20	114.0 (a)
United States*					
(Non Self-					
Governing)					
Am. Samoa	76	23,000	—	302	—
Baker, Howland					
and Jarvis					
Canal Zone	553	60,000	—	108	549.9
Canton and					
Enderbury	27	300		11	
Guam	206	42,000	—	204	
Johnston Is.					
Kingman Reef					
Midway	2	600		300	
Virgin Is.	133	32,000	—	240	158.5
Wake	3	600	—	200	—
(U.S. Trusteeship)					
Mariana Is.	154	10,000	4.1 (b)	65	
Caroline Is.	461	48,000	4.1 (b)	104	
Marshall Is.	70	16,200	4.1 (b)	231	
Puerto Rico	3,435	2,403,000	1.0	700	771.6
Union of S. Africa					
So. West Afr.	317,725	608,000	3.1	2	180.0

* Islands under Provisional U.S. Adm.—Inch., Okinawa, Iwo Jima, etc.

(a) Average for this group.
(b) Average for this group.

SUGGESTED READINGS

Aron, Raymond and August Heckscher, *Diversity of Worlds: France and the United States Look at their Common Problems.* New York: Reynal & Company, Inc., 1957.

Birdsall, Paul, *Versailles Twenty Years After.* New York: Reynal & Company, Inc., 1941.

Boulding, K. E., "National Images and International Systems," *Journal of Conflict Resolution,* III (June 1959), 120-31.

Brinton, Crane Clarence, *From Many, One: The Process of Political Integration,*

The Problem of World Government. Cambridge: Harvard University Press, 1948.

Brookings Institution, Washington, D.C., The Changing Environment of International Relations: Brookings Lectures, 1956, by Grayson Kirk and others. Washington, D.C.: 1956.

————, International Studies Group, The Search for Peace Settlements, by Redners Opie and others. Washington, D.C.: 1951.

Brown, Harrison and others, The Next Hundred Years: Man's Natural and Technological Resources. New York: The Viking Press Inc., 1957.

Callis, Helmut, "The Sociology of International Relations," American Sociological Review, XII (June 1947), 323-34.

Carr, Edward Hallett, International Relations Between the Two World Wars. London: Macmillan & Co., Ltd., 1947.

Choate, Joseph Hodges, The Two Hague Conferences. Princeton, N.J.: Princeton University Press, 1913.

Churchill, W. S., The Second World War: Vol. I, The Gathering Storm; Vol. II, Their Finest Hour; Vol. III, The Grand Alliance; Vol. IV, The Hinge of Fate; Vol. V, Closing the Ring; Vol VI, Triumph and Tragedy. New York: Houghton Mifflin Company, 1948-1953.

Coudert, Frederic René, A Half Century of International Problems: A Lawyer's Views, ed. Allan Nevins. New York: Columbia University Press, 1954.

Deutsch, Karl W., "The Growth of Nations: Some Recurrent Patterns of Political and Social Integration," World Politics, V (1953), 168-95.

————, Political Community at the International Level: Problems of Definition and Measurement. Garden City, N.Y.: Doubleday & Company, Inc., 1954.

Fay, Sidney B., The Origins of the World War, 2nd rev. ed. New York: The Macmillan Co., 1938.

Feis, Herbert, Between War and Peace: The Potsdam Conference. Princeton: Princeton University Press, 1960.

————, Churchill, Roosevelt, Stalin: The War They Waged and the Peace They Sought. Princeton, N.J.: Princeton University Press, 1957.

Freund, Gerald, Unholy Alliance: Russian-German Relations from the Treaty of Brest-Litovsk to the Treaty of Berlin. London: Chatto and Windus, Ltd., 1957.

Gathorne-Hardy, Geoffrey M., A Short History of International Affairs, 1920-1939, 4th ed. London, New York: Oxford University Press, Inc., 1950.

Gross, Leo, "The Peace of Westphalia, 1648-1948," American Journal of International Law, XLII (Jan. 1948), 20-41.

Harrison, J. B., The Age of Global Strife. Philadelphia: J. B. Lippincott Co., Inc., 1952.

Herz, John H., International Politics in the Atomic Age. New York: Columbia University Press, 1959.

————, "Rise and Demise of the Territorial State," World Politics, IX (July 1957), 473-93.

Kelman, Herbert C., "Societal, Attitudinal and Structural Factors in International Relations," Journal of Social Issues, XI (1955), 42-56.

Kertesz, Stephen D. and Matthew A. Fitzsimmons, eds., Diplomacy in a Changing World. Notre Dame, Ind.: University of Notre Dame Press, 1959.

Lederer, I. J., ed., The Versailles Settlement—Was It Foredoomed to Failure? Boston: D.C. Heath & Company, 1960.

Lee, Dwight E., Ten Years: The World on the Way to War, 1930-40. Boston: Houghton Mifflin Company, 1942.

LuKacs, John A., *A History of the Cold War*. Garden City, N.Y.: Doubleday & Company, Inc., 1961.

Mattingly, Garrett, *Renaissance Diplomacy*. London: Jonathan Cape, Ltd., 1955.

Schenk, Hans, G., *The Aftermath of the Napoleonic Years: The Concert of Europe, an Experiment*. New York: Oxford University Press, Inc., 1947.

Schroeder, Paul W., *The Axis Alliance and Japanese-American Relations, 1941*. Ithaca, New York: Cornell University Press, 1958, for the American Historical Association.

Seaman, Lewis Charles Bernard, *From Vienna to Versailles*. London: Methuen, 1955.

Toynbee, Arnold J., *Civilization on Trial*. New York: Oxford University Press, Inc., 1948.

————, *The World and the West*. New York: Oxford University Press, Inc., 1953.

Warth, Robert D., *The Allies and the Russian Revolution, from the Fall of the Monarchy to the Peace of Brest-Litovsk*. Durham, N.C.: Duke University Press, 1954.

Welles, Sumner, *Seven Decisions that Shaped History*. New York: Harper & Brothers, 1951.

Wright, Quincy, *Problems of Stability and Progress in International Relations*. Berkeley, California: University of California Press, 1954.

II

DYNAMIC FORCES
AND OBJECTIVES

INTRODUCTION

With our conceptual framework established, and having traced the evolution and explained the general nature of international society, we proceed in Part II to consider the principal dynamic forces and objectives which influence behavior on the international scene. These include both objectives that men consciously pursue and conditions to which they react, often not fully aware of why they do so. Although all states are motivated by nationalism and the desire for national security, even these operate differently from state to state, and from time to time in a particular state. The influence of ideology and economic factors is even more variable. These are some of the reasons one must be careful about making broad generalizations. The force of a particular goal depends on the value men place on it, especially in comparison with other goals, and the conditions under which it is pursued.

As you consider each of these factors you should attempt to evaluate its significance, especially in relation to other factors. Above all, avoid overrating or underrating the relevance of any particular force or objective, and keep in mind that these are only a part of the components of human behavior on the international scene, as in other types of relationships.

3

Nationalism

Of all the dynamic forces in international society, nationalism is the most important. Its understanding is a master key to many of the rooms of international relations. We have previously noted the antithetical nature of nationalism and international community, and the major consequences which flow from an almost total absence of community at the international level. Nationalism is both the foundation of the sovereign state system and a powerful determinant of behavior within the system. What is nationalism? What are its manifestations? How should we judge it?

NATURE AND ORIGIN
OF MODERN NATIONALISM

It is quite difficult to arrive at a satisfactory definition of nationalism. Some writers maintain that it is not capable of scientific definition.[1] Nation is derived from the Latin word *natio*, which means birth, "hence a creature's entire offspring at one time, hence a clan's offspring, hence a people's, hence that people itself. . . ."[2] A nation is a group of people with a feeling of solidarity among themselves and a sense of distinctness from others. Nationalism is a modern phenomenon of consciousness, feeling, or corporate sentiment among a group of people that is conducive to a process of identifying the fortune and destiny of the individual with that of a nation-state, desired or achieved. The other side of the coin is a sense of separation from other peoples, the "foreigners." From foreigner

---

[1] H. L. Featherstone, *A Century of Nationalism* (New York: Thomas Nelson & Sons, 1939), p. 10.

[2] Patridge, Eric, *Origins: A Short Etymological Dictionary of Modern English,* 2nd ed. (New York: The Macmillan Co., 1959), p. 428.

to enemy is but a short step. Nehru has written that "nationalism is essentially an anti-feeling."

Nations and states have become so identified in the modern mind that they are often used interchangeably—thus the League of Nations and the UN. This was not always so. The state is actually much older than the nation. No one in the sixteenth century would have thought of using the two terms interchangeably or have spoken of the nation-state. Nor until relatively recently was the idea generally accepted that the existence of a nation carried with it the moral, and perhaps even the legal right of "self-determination," i.e., the right to organize politically as an independent state. A nation may or may not be so organized. The old Austro-Hungarian Empire was a multi-nation state. If Arab nationalism is taken to mean the feeling of Arabs that they should be united in one state, whereas they are divided into several, the situation may be termed a multi-state nation.

Crane Brinton maintains that "nationalism is at bottom no more than the important form that the sense of belonging to an in-group has taken in our modern western culture."[3] While this statement emphasizes an important aspect of nationalism, it does not indicate how the "sense of belonging" to the nation differs from a somewhat similar attitude which people take toward other groups of which they are members. The members of a family, a church, a political party, a trade-union, an educational institution, a certain business, may feel a "oneness," and be concerned with the existence and welfare of the group as such. A person may demand and be willing to make sacrifices in the interest of the group, and rejoice or suffer with its fortunes regardless of how these affect his own immediate self. These attitudes are also manifested toward the nation-group. *But it is the nation to which is supposedly due his highest and final loyalty.* Hans Kohn, generally recognized as a leading authority on nationalism, writes on this point as follows:

> The modern period of history, which started with the French revolution, is characterized by the fact that in this period, and in this period alone, the nation demands the supreme loyalty of man, that all men, not only certain individuals or classes, are drawn into this common loyalty, and that all civilizations which up to this modern period have followed their own, and frequently widely different, ways are now dominated more and more by this one supreme group-consciousness, nationalism.[4]

This group-consciousness manifests itself not only in requiring supreme loyalty to the nation, but also, and this is its most distinguishing characteristic, it *demands political independence.* There is, therefore, both truth

---

[3] Brinton, *Ideas and Men: The Story of Western Thought* (Englewood Cliffs, N.J.: Prentice-Hall, Inc., 1950), p. 416.

[4] Kohn, "The Nature of Nationalism," *American Political Science Review*, XXXIII (Dec. 1939), 1009-10.

and wit in the anonymous statement that "a nation is a people which has or wishes to have a foreign office of its own so it may behave as though it alone constitutes humanity."

Thus Professor Kohn says:

Nationality is therefore not only a group held together and animated by common consciousness; it also seeks to find its expression in what it regards as the highest form of organized activity, a sovereign state. As long as nationality is not able to attain this consummation, it satisfies itself with some form of autonomy or prestate organization, which, however, always tends at a given moment, the moment of "liberation," to develop into a sovereign state. Nationalism demands the nation-state; the creation of the nation-state strengthens nationalism; here, as elsewhere in history, we find a continuous interdependence and interaction.[5]

We shall characterize as nations or nationalities groups which desire to organize or maintain an independent state for themselves. It is quite true that within nations there may be cultural groups with certain separatist tendencies, such as many within the Soviet Union, or the Welsh, Scottish, and English within Great Britain. Perhaps these should be called subnationalities. Over a period of time they may merge within the larger nation. On the other hand, the separatist tendencies may increase to the point where they can be satisfied only by complete political independence. Only if and when they seek independence, however, as may now be the case with respect to some groups in South India, and within some of the newly emerged African states, are they, according to our definition, really nations.

Manifestations

Nationalism manifests itself in many ways, some of which we have noted. A nationalist tends to be exclusive, inward-looking, and indifferent or hostile to "out" groups. He usually regards his own nation as superior to all others. Frequently, although not necessarily, he has a kind of missionary zeal. Florian Znaniecki, a leading sociologist, notes that conflicts between nationalities originate "when a particular nationality purposely tends to expand at the cost of another or when two nationalities continue to expand in a way that makes the expansion of one interfere with the expansion of another."[6] He discusses four types of "aggressive" expansion which lead to conflict: geographic, economic, assimilative, and ideological.

A nation expands *geographically* when some of its members move into other occupied areas but maintain their social connections with the group of their origin. Conflicts are intensified if the nation to which the

---

[5] *Ibid.*, p. 1016.

[6] *Modern Nationalities: A Sociological Study* (Urbana, Ill.: The University of Illinois Press, 1952), p. 115.

immigrants belong raises claims to the lands in which they have settled and the previous occupants also claim the area. Many conflicts within Eastern Europe, as well as the continuing struggle over Palestine, originated in this way. *Economic* expansion is defined as "increasing utilization for its own benefit of the material products and the technical actions of members of another group."[7] This is frequently called economic imperialism or dollar diplomacy.

Assimilative expansion "consists in the cultural assimilation and incorporation into a nationality of people who by ethnic standards are not supposed to belong to it."[8] If the people being assimilated belong to another distinct nationality, expansion results in resistance and social conflict. Austrian, German, and Russian attempts to assimilate the Poles are prime examples of this type of expansion. *Ideological* expansion results when "nationalistic leaders develop certain ideals of social order and cultural progress and assume that it is their task or 'mission' to have these ideals accepted and applied by leaders of other nationalities. . . ."[9] This century's German, Japanese, and Russian attempts to spread their "superior" cultures or ideologies all are examples. Professor Znaniecki also considers the "present American effort to spread the ideal of democratic freedom as the only way to universal progress" to be within this category.[10]

Origin and Development

Nations usually evolve over long periods of time. The first modern states developed in the late medieval period of European history, but they were dynastic rather than nation-states. Undoubtedly certain small groups were imbued with a feeling of nationalism long before this sentiment permeated the masses. Professor Znaniecki notes "we find that at a certain stage in the evolution of every national culture society it includes only a relatively small number of intellectuals, who are united by the belief that they belong to a collectivity with a common culture different from other cultures and who cooperate in perpetuating and developing this culture."[11] The masses are at this stage unconscious of such common bonds. Gradually nationalism spreads, by propaganda and education, first in the urban and later in the rural sections. Professor Kohn contends that nationalism originated in Western Europe in the seventeenth and eigtheenth centuries, but that it did not become a general European movement until the nineteenth.[12] In any case, the ideas of the Enlighten-

---

[7] *Ibid.*, p. 122.
[8] *Ibid.*, p. 126.
[9] *Ibid.*, p. 132.
[10] *Ibid.*, p. 134.
[11] *Ibid.*, p. 81.
[12] Hans Kohn, *Prophets and People* (New York: The Macmillan Co., 1944), p. 15.

ment interacted with the forces of the French Revolution to give certain emerging trends increased impetus. Early in the nineteenth century Englishmen, Frenchmen, Irishmen, Danes, Swedes, Russians, Poles, Greeks, Hungarians, and to a lesser extent Germans and Italians, were each united by common bonds of nationalism. Nationalism later spread to the Americas and Asia; and after World War II, to Africa. Generally it is on the ascent.

Whether it is decreasing anywhere is a debatable question. Arnold Toynbee believes that it has sufficiently abated in Western Europe to permit the establishment of common political institutions in that area. Barbara Ward, although contending that nationalism is "still the strongest, most persuasive force of our day," also argues:

There are, however, a few signs that it is beginning to spend itself a little and beginning to give ground to other concepts. And it is significant that these changes are to be remarked in Western Europe, first home of modern, industrialized, democratic nationalism and also the arena where the worst consequences of this type of nationalism have been worked out.

Europe's ghastly feuds, which we might well call the tribal wars of modern man, have led to disgust with the extreme forms of nationalism. A new and absorbing struggle is in progress between the old concept of France, of Germany, of Italy, of Holland, and of Belgium as separate, sovereign, absolutely autonomous states and a new concept of supranational communities; a new sense that they must work together if they are to survive. Behind the talk of political and economic union in Europe today there is in many hearts a sense of disillusion, a revulsion from the consequences of perfervid nationalism. The chance that this is the sign of a new trend, of a new seminal idea, is made all the more plausible by the place of its emergence—Western Europe, where national communities have been longest in being and have worked the longest havoc with each other.[13]

THE ROOTS OF NATIONALISM

What accounts for the origin, growth, and persistence of nationalism? We may obtain some answers to these questions through a twofold approach. First, in this section we shall examine the basic factors, or roots—in human nature, geography, race, religion, and so forth—which retard or promote its growth. In the following section, "Making Patriots," we shall consider the more conscious efforts—watering and cultivating the roots—which sustain it and cause it to grow.

Human Nature

Man has certain biological needs which express themselves in drives or urges to action. His needs for food, shelter, and self-preservation lead to

---

[13] Barbara Ward, *Five Ideas That Change the World* (New York: W. W. Norton & Company, Inc., 1959), pp. 27-28.

various activities through which they may be satisfied. But man also develops a multitude of other desires and action-patterns over and above those necessary to his physical existence. There is something in the make-up of most men which makes them more provincial than cosmopolitan, more inclined to like the familiar and the similar rather than the unknown and the unlike. We have already observed the tendency to associate in groups with common interests and objectives, and to develop group loyalties. Attachment to a territorial group, love of country, or patriotism, is very ancient, common, and in this sense, "natural." Although these manifestations are necessary to nationalism, they do not in themselves constitute it. In short, nationalism is neither a biological nor a psychological necessity, but there are certain human characteristics which, under the proper conditions, are conducive to, or at least do not prevent its development.

Geography

Geographical features promote the development of nationalism as they unite a particular group and isolate it from other groups. Ramsay Muir writes: "Undoubtedly the most clearly marked nations have enjoyed a geographical unity, and have owed their nationhood in part to this fact." The Pyrenees which separate the Iberian Peninsula from the remainder of Western Europe certainly contributed to the development of the Spanish nation, as did the Alps to the Italian. The mountainous nature of the Balkan area, on the other hand, played a divisive role in the development of its several nations.

"Natural boundaries" have been important in the defense of states, and the lack of internal barriers facilitates the mobilization and use of power. The boundaries of most states are, in part, determined by geographical features. A glance at a physical-political map demonstrates this point. Undoubtedly the English Channel and the Atlantic Ocean were important in determining that there would be British and American nations, just as similar factors were influential in creating Japanese and Indonesian nationalism.

If an area is geographically homogeneous it tends to promote a similarity of interests and outlook among the people who occupy it. The geography of the southern part of the United States played a major role in creating the "southern way of life," which, had the Confederacy won the "war between the states," might well have provided the foundation for a separate nation below the Mason-Dixon line.

It should be noted, however, that there are many cases where nationalism has developed with little reference to geographical influences. The nations in the great plains of central and eastern Europe which sweep from the Rhine to the Urals cannot be explained on geographical grounds. On the other hand, in spite of the geographical extent and variety of continental United States, Californians and Vermonters are members of one nation. One totally ignorant of anything other than the topography of the North American continent might well guess that the present areas of Canada and the United States constitute at least three nations, one along the eastern seaboard, another in the middle plains, and a third west of the continental divide. That his guess would be wrong is determined by other than geographical influences. Yet on the South American continent we find ten nation-states, and three colonies, partly because of geography, but in considerable part the result of boundaries devised for the purposes of Spanish colonial administration. The grouping of peoples within the boundaries of many of the states of the Middle East, Southeast Asia, and Africa was also the result of the "chance pattern of imperial conquest."[14] Thus several nations may exist within one homogeneous geographical unit, while one nation may extend over wide and varied areas.

Geographical factors largely influence nationalism through their effect on transportation—and communication—of goods, people, armies, and ideas. It may be argued, therefore, that modern inventions—the radio, television, telegraph, airplane, etc.—reduce the significance of physical barriers, and will eventually serve to unite a divided world. Undoubtedly they have affected and will continue to affect nationalism. But there are several facts which must be borne in mind in this connection. Nationalism arose in many countries before these means of communication became important, and is deeply rooted. Secondly, it has increased over the past hundred years along with the growing physical interdependence of the world. Thirdly, these instruments are being used to promote nationalism in all countries far more than they are to develop an international community.

Race

Anthropologists and other students of race agree almost unanimously that: (1) no national group constitutes a race, for through time and immigration there has been an intermingling and intermixture of many races in all nations; (2) there are no important, if any, psychological characteristics of men explainable on racial grounds alone. Moreover, criteria for determining race, such as cephalic index, hair texture, and pigmentation, are no more valid than are height or length of nose. But it does not follow, therefore, that "race" has no significance for nationalism.

If a group of people has certain distinct physical features, especially skin pigmentation, which differentiate it from other groups, these differences may constitute the basis for social groups, and for discrimination

---

[14] *Ibid.*, p. 39.

by the dominant group. The United States and South Africa, with their large colored populations, afford well-known examples. On the other hand, in Latin America and certain European nations, coloration is less important. The difficulty in the way of full assimilation of Asians to the American nation is largely a matter of physical features. Wherever physical differences lead to segregation and discrimination, the integration of peoples is impeded.

Racial myths which many people accept as truth have also been used to fortify the claim of nationhood. The most extreme case in point is "Aryanism," which arose in Europe in the nineteenth century and flowered in the creed of Nazism. The idea of a pure superrace was accepted by many, perhaps the vast majority of the German people, itself a mixture of many races. Carleton J. H. Hayes says: "Nationality actually cuts through and across race, though it must be confessed, in deference to racial propaganda, that an imaginary belief in blood relationship, that is, in race, has been an effective force in building and cementing nationalities."[15]

Religion

Catholicism impeded the development of nationalism in medieval Europe, and it is not wholly accidental that the Protestant revolt which split the Catholic church came at a time when the roots of nationalism were sprouting. By breaking the unity of the Church, Protestantism in turn helped pave the way for the growth of separate churches which generally supported the growth of nations and independent states.

The basic incompatibility of the ideals of religions such as the Christian and Islamic, which aspire to universality, and the exclusiveness of the faith of nationalism, is quite clear. Some writers maintain that nationalism has become a religion which has replaced supranatural faiths.

Nevertheless, the role of religion in nationalism must not be discounted. An important case in point is that of the division of the Indian subcontinent into states of Pakistan and India. The importance of religion in this split can be understood only if it is realized that the Hindu and Islamic faiths mean basically different cultures and ways of life. The importance of religion is again attested by its role in political Zionism, and its expression in the creation of the state of Israel. But the common bond of Islam has not prevented the development of separate nations based on nonreligious factors, any more than Christianity has prevented the development of many "Christian" nations.

The unity of a nation is weakened or strengthened by the religious similarities or differences among its peoples. Undoubtedly the development of religious freedom and tolerance has reduced the dividing force

---

[15] Hayes, *Essays on Nationalism* (New York: The Macmillan Co., 1926), p. 8.

of religion, but it may well be that this development was in part made
possible by a decline in religious faith. There are those who believe that
only a universal religion to which men are fervently committed, one
which unites them in devotion to a single God and in a common brotherhood, will serve to overcome divisions among men and the worship of
the secular nation-state.

Language

Writers are more nearly in agreement on the importance of language to
nationalism than on any other single feature. Ramsay Muir maintains that
"there is indeed nothing that will so readily give unity to divergent races
as the use of a common tongue, and in very many cases unity of language
and the community of ideas which it brings, have proved the main binding force in a nation."[16] Carleton Hayes regards it as the most important
factor. He even goes so far as to contend that "the use of the English
language in the United States tends to link American thought and action
with that of England and at the same time to obstruct the growth of an
absolutely separate American nationality. . . ."[17] On similar grounds,
he denies that there is a Swiss nation.

A common language is an important unifying factor because it facilitates the dissemination of ideas and feelings, and promotes the development of a national literature, traditions, and customs. With increased use
of printing and new means of communication a common language becomes an even more effective means of unifying a people. The significant
role of language in maintaining a sense of nationality is indicated by a
variety of state policies and practices. "Russification" under the Czars
took the form, in part, of wiping out the languages of minority groups
and replacing them with Russian. Various national minorities have
maintained national-language schools in the United States, partly to keep
the sense of the nation alive. The struggle of the several nations in the
Austro-Hungarian empire to maintain their separate languages grew out
of a sense of pride in, and a determination to maintain, their national
identity.

There is no doubt that language differences, usually combined with
cultural and religious factors, reduce the intensity of cohesion among a
people, as evidenced by the divisions within Canada, with its large
French-Canadian population and in India, with its fourteen major
languages and hundreds of dialects. Yet nations can and do arise and
exist despite linguistic divisions. Modern India, Indonesia, China, (with a
common written language but a diversity of spoken tongues), and even

---

[16] Muir, *Nationalism and Internationalism* (London: Constable & Co., Ltd., 1917),
p. 43.
[17] Hayes, *Essays on Nationalism*, p. 15.

Great Britain demonstrate this fact, as do Switzerland, Belgium, and the Soviet Union. A common language is an important but nonessential element in building a nation. Moreover, one language does not necessarily mean only one nation.

History and Tradition

John Stuart Mill rates common historical traditions of prime importance, and Hayes considers them to be second only to language in their effect upon nationalism. Every nation has its common heroes, often military figures—William Tell, Marlborough, Wellington, Napoleon, William the Silent—who become symbols of the heroic past and unifying forces of the present. The wars of the past, frequently perpetuated in myth and history as gloriously and justly waged, with one's own nation gallant in victory and courageous in defeat, serve to sustain the national soul.

Economics

The effect of nationalism on economics is clearer than the effect of economics on nationalism. Nevertheless, in certain rather subtle ways, economic factors contributed to the origin of nationalism. We have noted the importance of the union of the middle class and royal forces in the consolidation of the first European states. This consolidation preceded widespread nationalism, but it provided the political framework within which many nations were developed.

Nationalism grew and flourished along with the economic and political ascendancy of the middle class in the eighteenth and nineteenth centuries. It was this class which was most imbued with the nationalistic spirit, and which furnished most of the national leaders. According to the Marxian analysis, the middle class deliberately encouraged the development of nationalism in order to maintain and extend its power and to cloak its economic motives in the garb of patriotism.

In those areas of the world with a very small middle class, but where nationalism is growing, this pattern is repeated. An American student who made a study of Iranian nationalism wrote as follows:

My study of nationalism in Iran leads me to believe that it is definitely a middle-class movement. There is a growing support of the nationalist cause among the urban masses in Teheran—and much less so in the provincial cities. But it is not orthodox nationalism they [the masses] believe in. They are stimulated by religious leaders who favor a reaction away from secularism, and secularism and nationalism have too much in common for either to live by itself.[18]

---

[18] Richard W. Cottam in personal correspondence to the author.

Socialism, like Christianity, professes to know only humanity as a whole; but despite its condemnation of war in general as a capitalistic inevitability or conspiracy, in both world wars socialists, with few exceptions, found little difficulty in supporting their respective nations. In the Western world, nationalism has permeated with little regard to class every people, with the possible exception of some communists outside of the Soviet Union.

Democracy

Democracy, nationalism, and capitalism all flourished during the nineteenth century. What influence, if any, did democracy have on the development of nationalism? Prior to the late eighteenth century, individual men gave their loyalty to the monarch rather than to the collective nation; but with the growth of democracy, it was transferred to the group itself. The king could no longer say, "I am the state"; henceforth the truth was, "We are the state." The growth of the doctrine of popular sovereignty, with its influence on the identification of the people with the state, thus served to promote nationalism.

The great leaders of nineteenth-century nationalism, such as the Italian patriot Mazzini, were liberals and democrats. They believed, as did Wilson, that the failure to allow self-determination of peoples was a principal cause of war. Mazzini regarded the full expression of nationalism as a necessary development along the road to universal brotherhood. Just as there was no basic incompatibility—perhaps there was common reinforcement—among love of family, of province, of region, and of nation, so there need be none between nation and humanity.

During the nineteenth and early twentieth centuries nationalism was generally regarded as a part of, or at least necessary to democracy. It was embodied in the "self-determination" of Wilson, and thus played a major role in World War I and its aftermath. The reasoning went something like this. Does not democracy demand that the question of government be determined by the governed? Unless a nation establishes its own independent government it cannot be democratically governed. There is some truth and a great fallacy in this reasoning.

The element of truth has a great appeal for people held in colonial subjection. To the Czech, Slav, and other subject nations in the Austro-Hungarian Empire, to the Polish subjects of Russia and Germany before 1918, to the Indonesians under Dutch rule, to the people of Indochina under French domination, independence appeared to be and probably was a necessary requisite to democratic government. But independence does not necessarily mean that democracy will follow, as evidenced by most of the governments of Eastern Europe following the first world war, and by many of the newly independent states of Asia and Africa.

Basically, the demand for national independence is a demand for international anarchy, since it calls for sovereign states. Carried to its logical conclusion, it would require independence for every group which feels it is a nation. If this be the requirement of democracy, the South, during the American Civil War was fighting for a realization of democratic principles. The self-determination argument is fallacious because democracy implies shared power, compromise, and deference, rather than sovereign states and anarchy. An interdependent world in which peace, at least one other than a Roman peace, is to prevail, requires that it be organized on a democratic basis rather than on an anarchistic one.

The tenets of democracy and liberalism tend to part company with those of nationalism. However, it should be recognized that, much in the pattern and under some of the conditions of the nineteenth century, the leaders and people of subjugated or recently emancipated countries combine nationalistic and democratic principles as did Mazzini and Wilson. Nevertheless, many of the nationalists of today are conservatives or reactionaries (the fascists, for example), whereas

those statesmen and intellectuals who carry on the liberal rather than the nationalist tradition of the nineteenth century are now the champions of the United Nations [and of regional and world federation], of peaceful international collaboration and the recognition of the unity of mankind above races and nations. But those—and it is a large number—who absorbed the aggressive nationalism rather than the enlightened liberalism of the national movements of the nineteenth century, have become the champions of the absolute State.[19]

A chief ingredient of fascism is "integral" nationalism, a mass movement devoid of the humanizing qualities of liberal democracy, with the state itself the great god for which all must be sacrificed. Writing in 1940, Sharp and Kirk contended that

a superficial view of the situation might easily lead to the assumption that fascist nationalism has little or nothing in common with the national state of mind now prevalent under democracy. But a more thorough examination of the factors that have produced fascism . . . suggests that the seeds of fascist nationalism are inherent in a state system which has made of national sovereignty a political fetish.[20]

Social Disintegration
and Individual Insecurity

Hans J. Morgenthau regards this factor as the basic explanation of modern nationalism. The nineteenth and twentieth centuries saw the

---

[19] W. Friedman, *An Introduction to World Politics* (London: Macmillan & Co., Ltd., 1951), p. 42.

[20] Walter R. Sharp and Grayson Kirk, *Contemporary International Politics* (New York: Holt, Rinehart & Winston, Inc., 1941), p. 143.

emancipation of the individual from the ties of tradition, especially in the form of religion, of the increased rationalization of life and work, and of cyclical economic crises. The insecurity of the groups affected by these factors found an emotional outlet in fixed and emotionally accentuated nationalistic identifications.[21]

German fascism is the most important example of the outcome of these forces.

There is little doubt that discontent, insecurity, and frustration are likely to seek outlets in extreme forms—nationalism, war, and revolution. Writing on Germany in 1933, shortly after Hitler came to power, Calvin B. Hoover expressed the opinion that Germany was ripe for revolution. He further stated:

> The Treaty of Versailles was no doubt responsible for the fact that radicalism in Germany took a nationalistic turn. . . . Inflamed nationalism determined the form which the revolution was to take, and it hastened the triumph of revolution. But it was the hostility of the people based on economic grounds which gave the mass weight to the movement against the system and insured its overthrow.[22]

Extreme nationalism is a form of group hysteria. Men identify themselves with the state and thereby receive a kind of vicarious satisfaction. Pent-up desires, suppressed in normal society, become acts of patriotism when released in action performed in the name of the state. Norman Thomas once said that Englishmen who did not own a three by six space in which to be buried nevertheless were thrilled by the thought that the sun never sets on the British Empire.

Common Government
and International Conflict

Many states—France, Great Britain, Spain, and the United States—are older than their respective nations. Many of the roots of nationalism—language, tradition and culture, and the territory of the state itself—were, in part, creations of the state. The vernacular languages which had developed in Western Europe by A.D. 1300 did not correspond to the newly unified states; a language coextensive with state boundaries followed rather than preceded the creation of many of them. The state itself played a major part in breaking down the barriers of feudalism, and in introducing law common throughout the realm.

If a single government had been established over wide areas of Latin America, perhaps half a dozen rather than twenty nations would have resulted. Certainly these nations, with the exception of Brazil and some in the Caribbean areas, such at Haiti, correspond to no definite cultural

---

[21] *Politics Among Nations*, 3rd. ed., p. 106.
[22] Hoover, *Germany Enters the Third Reich* (New York: The Macmillan Co., 1933), pp. 30-31.

groups. On the other hand, had the Confederacy won in the Civil War, one or more nations would have developed in what is now the southern part of the United States. The preservation of the Union determined that there would be one nation rather than several. Had the Indian Hindus and Muslims been able to agree upon a common government, it might in time time have provided the basis for the development of one nation. Their failure to do so itself gives impetus to greater diversity rather than to homogeneity in an area containing a sixth of the human race, with all that it portends for future conflict. The problem of Jammu and Kashmir, for example, would not have arisen in an undivided India.

One of the primary reasons for nationalism and state loyalty is that national governments today are increasingly the source of satisfaction for men's economic and psychological needs. Why should men not give support and supreme loyalty to their benefactors? They cannot look to international authority, weak and inadequate as it is today, for anything approaching what they expect and normally receive from their own governments.

Finally, a common government is a vital and important factor in creating and sustaining nationalism because of the role of conflict in the development of group solidarity and of animosities toward "out" groups. Once several areas and diverse peoples are joined in a single state, conflicts among them are more or less suppressed, while they share common experiences against a common foreign foe. Thus the temperature of nationalism rises with international tensions and wars. Undoubtedly the American Revolutionary War helped to create the American nation, which was developed more fully by the international conflict culminating in the War of 1812. In colonial areas the dominating power constitutes a force and symbol against which the subject peoples are able to rally. The struggle for national independence and its traditions of sacrifice and heroism are a part of the stuff of which nationalists are made.

The part played by a common government in the development of a sense of community among a people is of great significance for a student of International Relations. The kind of social solidarity so badly needed in international society today develops slowly, if at all, since there are no international institutional arrangements comparable to the governments of existing states. Yet if a common government could somehow be established for the present nations of the world, it would help to eradicate nationalism and to create and sustain the common values and loyalties necessary for its own successful existence.

MAKING PATRIOTS

With these sturdy roots, nationalism would flourish with little care. But in almost every country it is promoted by the combined resources of society; of these the schools are among the most important. The display of the flag, repetition of national creeds, the curricula and reading matter, especially books dealing with history, are all devices for indoctrinating pliable minds with the sentiments of nationalism. An international group which conducted a study of international cultural relations reported:

The rise of nationalism has been accompanied by the development of national educational systems, an ordinary function of which is education in the national culture and for the national interest. Cultural bodies have been established under national charters; each nation cherishes its own literature and art and industry and political outlook. In self-protection and self-conscious growth many nations regulate in some measure, wisely or unwisely, the flow of cultural as well as commercial materials across their boundaries. The very degree of intensity of nationalism which has arisen leads toward forms of censorship and control or toward public assistance to movements regarded as in the national interest. Many such movements are governmental, others private and voluntary, but all are within national patterns.[23]

The media of mass communication—the newspapers, radio, television, the screen, and music—all play their role in developing nationalism, as do the home and the church. These facts are too well known to require further elaboration. There is no doubt that mass media could be used, on the other hand, to lower nationalistic barriers. Many persons have great faith—indeed, more than is warranted—that this will be done. They tend to disregard or to underestimate the strong influence of nationalism on the human mind, and in particular to disregard its more basic roots. Moreover, as long as nationalism has so strong a hold on the minds of men there will always be certain individuals and groups willing to use the sentiments of nationalism for their own purposes. They will endeavor to prevent an effective utilization of these instruments to build up a world community. Liberal forces will thus work under a great handicap in using mass media for molding attitudes that conform to the one world of fact. Movements such as those represented by UNESCO, are important and deserve support by those who believe in the UNESCO philosophy, but they are insufficient to overcome forces working in opposite directions.

In particular, it must be realized that nationalism is a potent force in mobilizing the power of states; until some substitute for state power is found, therefore, states will not and dare not undergo a process of psychological demobilization by diluting the force of nationalism. The dilemma should be faced: nationalism makes for world anarchy; international conflict and war itself are products of anarchy; these in turn usually augment the force of nationalism.

COMMUNISM AND NATIONALISM

Communism, in practice, is a combination of economic socialism and political authoritarianism. One of the most important and difficult ques-

---

[23] "National Programs of International Cultural Relations," *International Conciliation*, No. 462 (June 1950), 304-5.

tions of the mid-century concerned the relative importance of communism and nationalism as motivating forces of Soviet imperialism. Znaniecki writing in 1952, contends that

during the last twenty years the expansion of communism and that of the Russian national society have been so closely connected that it is difficult to decide which is now the main goal of the Russian communists. Of course, to those who consider that it is the "mission" of the Russian people to spread communism over the world, the two are inseparable.[24]

Is Soviet foreign policy motivated by nationalism, using communist ideology and foreign communist movements as instruments? Or is the spread of communism the basic objective toward the realization of which all the instruments of Soviet foreign policy are devoted? Despite the basic incompatibility between Marxian theory, which is international in character, and nationalism, the Soviets may be motivated by both, and by additional, goals. While this question cannot be answered with any degree of confidence, it seems that the latter possibility is the more probable, and that nationalism has become increasingly important with the passage of time.

Immediately after the 1917 Revolution the Bolshevik leaders reversed the Czarist policy of "Russification," and encouraged the cultural and linguistic autonomy of the various Russian "subnationalities." Independence was even permitted. This strategy lessened opposition to Bolshevik rule. In addition, since world-wide communist revolutions were expected, it would facilitate the entrance of various nations into a world union of Soviet Republics. But despite the theoretical possibility of independence for the Union Republics, which is authorized still by the written Soviet constitution, any attempt to exercise the right is regarded as "nationalist bourgeoisie deviation," and promptly suppressed.

After Stalin came to power in 1924, and as World War II approached, there was an increased use of nationalistic symbols and appeals to patriotism. The practice continued after the war. "Glory to the Russian people—people of heroes, people of builders," who originated every worthwhile theory and invented every scientific gadget from the telephone to the atomic bomb. Is all this simply a recognition of the great force of nationalism which exists among the Russian people, which the men of the Kremlin tap to sustain national morale in the battle of production and in the cold war, while they themselves remain completely above it, deeply devoted to the ideal of world communism, with never a thought of Russia except as it is useful for realizing the great goal? Or could it be, as some maintain, that power for themselves is the real objective, with both communism and Russian patriotism but useful tools to that end?

---

[24] Znaniecki, *Modern Nationalities*, pp. 135-6.

NATIONALISM—CURSE OR BLESSING

Is nationalism good or bad? The answer which one gives to this question depends upon the basic values which he holds, and his judgment of the relationship of these values to nationalism under conditions both as they now prevail and as they are likely to develop throughout the second half of the twentieth century. It is assumed that most readers will be concerned with the basic tenets and ideals of the democratic faith rooted in the background of Judeo-Christian ethics—in short, the essential dignity and equal worth of the personality of all men, and the belief that these values can best be realized in a society in which men have an opportunity to make basic social decisions by the process of compromise and majority rule.

A democratic society requires basic agreement on fundamental social issues among most of its members. Nationalism tends to promote unity among the members of a state. Democracy also requires compromise and sacrifice. There is little doubt that nationalism contributes to this kind of behavior, just as does any kind of group loyalty.

Nationalism often supplies the dynamic force for cultural and economic creativity. Kohn holds that the nationalist sees nationality as "the source of all the creative energy and economic well-being."[25] The economic resurgence of Communist China probably owes as much to nationalism as it does to communism. The response of Japan to Western contacts in the late nineteenth and early twentieth century was due in part to the sense of Japanese national identity. Among the newly awakened people in Asia and Africa, nationalism retains the same liberating and exhilarating spirit which it possessed in the North Atlantic area in the late eighteenth and nineteenth century. "Contemporary nationalist movements seek to channel popular feelings and discontents to forge new nations from the ruins of the colonial empires."[26] It is a part of the consciousness which for the first time gives the masses of men in those areas a feeling of strength and of the coming of a new and better future.

Nationalism also contributes to the faith and strength of subject nations struggling to throw off alien rule. Its role in the Balkan struggle for independence in the nineteenth century, as well as in the twentieth, attests to this. After World War I it contributed to the independence of many nations—of Poland, Finland, the Baltic states, and Czechoslovakia, for example—just as it did to the independence of several Asian and African nations after 1945. That this has not all been clear gain is fully

[25] Hans Kohn, *Nationalism: Its Meaning and History* (Princeton, N.J.: D. Van Nostrand Co., Inc., 1955), p. 10.
[26] "Ideology and Foreign Affairs," A Study by the Center for International Affairs, Harvard University, for the Committee on Foreign Relations, United States Senate, No. 10 (Washington, D.C.: Government Printing Office, Jan. 17, 1960), p. 6.

recognized. Lastly, nationalism contributes to the mobilization of national power. If power is necessary, as it is in the modern state system, then nationalism must be listed as a national asset in this respect.

Most of what must be said here with respect to the negative side is implicit in what has been said. Nationalism is the main bulwark of independent sovereign states, and thus of international anarchy. It has been responsible for the failures of attempts to organize the world for peace, plenty, and human freedom, as indicated by the experience of the League of Nations, the UN, and a multitude of less ambitious plans. It has been a major obstacle not only to world government but also to European and Atlantic Federation. While it has facilitated the breakup of empires, it remains an obstacle to the participation of these new nation-states in democratic union. If and when a regional or world government is formed nationalists will attempt to keep it weak, just as the proponents of states' rights have weakened all existing federal systems.

The present hope for world peace, and for solving major international political, economic, and social problems, lies in the possibility of cooperation, accommodation, and "peaceful" struggle among nation-states. Nationalism as it exists at present is a great handicap to the realization of these goals. So far it has retarded inter-European trade, acted as a brake on British cooperation with the continental states, handicapped the functioning of the Marshall Plan, and made it difficult for the relatively prosperous countries to undertake a sustained program of raising levels of living in the underdeveloped countries except on the basis of self-interest, rationalized in terms of anti-communism. If it is correct, as many believe, that Russian nationalism flourishes under the cloak of communism, nationalism is a major factor behind Russian imperialism.

Many writers regard nationalism as the chief force behind war. That it has provoked wars of national liberation is quite clear. It is also probable that nationalism has been a factor behind wars growing out of the extension of colonial imperialism. Hayes contends that "nationalist warfare, beginning as a struggle for human freedom, may soon lead on to a struggle for conquest and domination of dissident nationalities."[27] George Kennan, after a study of the many explanations for the United States' acquisition of the Philippine Islands in 1898, offers the following hypothesis:

. . . when one notes the variety of arguments put up by the expansionists for the territorial acquisitions of 1898, one has the impression that none of them was the real one—that at the bottom [of] it all lay something deeper, something less easy to express, probably the fact that the American people of that day, or at least many of their more influential spokesmen, simply liked the smell of empire and felt an urge to range themselves among the colonial powers of the time, to see our flag flying on distant tropical isles, to feel the thrill of foreign adventure

---

[27] Hayes, *Essays on Nationalism*, p. 140.

and authority, to bask in the sunshine of recognition as one of the great imperial powers of the world.[28]

Nationalism is often a cause of, or at least an excuse for, wars to incorporate into the nation minorities living under foreign rule. Such, for example, was the reason given by Hitler for the "liberation" of the Sudeten Germans of Czechoslovakia, and the Germans in the Polish Corridor. Moreover, the pride and egoism of the nationalist tolerates no slight to the national honor. Both major wars of the present century are regarded by many writers as growing out of nationalism. It should not be overlooked that nationalism may not only provoke wars among sovereign states, but, more basically, it is the sustaining pillar of the international system of anarchy, itself a major cause of modern wars.

These are the principal consequences of nationalism, but not the only ones. Individual freedom and individuality live uneasily in an ideological climate which glorifies the nation-state, as the Italians and Germans learned too well under fascist rule. Lord Acton holds that nationalism "overrules the rights and wishes of the inhabitants, absorbing their divergent interests in a fictitious unity; sacrifices their several inclinations and duties to the higher claims of nationality; and crushes all natural rights and all established liberties for the purpose of vindicating itself."[29]

SUMMARY

Nationalism is the result of complex factors which vary from time to time and from state to state. Its chief characteristics are the elevation of the nation above all other values, and a demand for political expression in a sovereign state. It is thus the bulwark of international anarchy.

It is rooted in and produced by a number of factors of which a common government and conflict with other nation-states, language, tradition and culture, social disintegration and individual insecurity, and geography, are usually the most important. However, these vary in importance with time and for each nation.

These roots are nurtured through indoctrination by the combined influence of many of society's institutions, of which the school is one of the most important. While it is conceivable that these instruments could be important in creating supranational loyalties, they are not now, and probably will not become so in the near future.

Nationalism has played a positive role in the realization of democratic goals. It is a unifying force in a democratic society, although not an indis-

---

[28] *American Diplomacy, 1900-1950* (Chicago: University of Chicago Press, 1951), p. 17.

[29] *The History of Freedom and Other Essays* (London: Macmillan & Co., Ltd., 1907), p. 288. He held that this was true of the French, but not of the English system at that time.

pensable one. It has disrupted colonial empires. And it is an important ingredient of national power.

On the other hand, it is probably the major cause of modern wars both through its insistence on the maintenance of the sovereign-anarchistic state system, and through its direct influence on the foreign policies of statesmen within such a system. In addition, it impedes, if it does not prevent, peace-time collaboration. And finally, it is doubtful whether, in the modern age, free states are compatible with free men. It is the essence of the democratic faith that the state exists for man rather than man for the state.

SUGGESTED READINGS

Barghoorn, Frederick C., *Soviet Russian Nationalism.* New York: Oxford University Press, Inc., 1956.

Carr, Edward H., *Nationalism and After.* New York: The Macmillan Co., 1945.

Deutsch, Karl W., *Nationalism and Social Communication: an Inquiry into the Foundations of Nationality.* Cambridge: Published jointly by the Technology Press of the Massachusetts Institute of Technology and John Wiley & Sons, Inc., New York: 1953.

Eagleton, Clyde, "Excesses of Self Determination," *Foreign Affairs,* XXXI (July 1953), 592-604.

Emerson, Rupert, *From Empire to Nation: The Rise to Self-Assertion of Asian and African Peoples.* Cambridge: Harvard University Press, 1960.

————, "Nationalism and Political Development," *Journal of Politics,* XXII (Feb. 1960), 3-28.

Guetzkow, Harold Steere, *Multiple Loyalties: Theoretical Approach to a Problem in International Organization.* Princeton, N.J.: Center for Research on World Political Institutions, 1955.

Hayes, Carleton J. H., *Essays on Nationalism.* New York: The Macmillan Co., 1926.

————, *The Historical Evolution of Modern Nationalism.* New York: R. R. Smith, Inc., 1931.

Hodgkin, Thomas L., *Nationalism in Colonial Africa.* London: Frederick Muller, Ltd., 1956.

Kedourie, Elie, *Nationalism.* London: Hutchinson & Co., Ltd., 1961.

Kohn, Hans, *American Nationalism: An Interpretive Essay.* New York: The Macmillan Co., 1957.

————, *Nationalism: Its Meaning and History.* Princeton: D. Van Nostrand Co., Inc., 1955.

————, The United Nations and National Self-determination," *Review of Politics*, XX (Oct. 1958), 526-45.

Lacqueur, Walter Z., *Communism and Nationalism in the Middle East*, 2d ed. London: Routledge & Paul, 1957.

Preston, R. A., "Nationalism in the Atomic Age," *International Journal*, XI (Summer 1956), 177-84.

Shafer, Boyd C., *Nationalism: Myth and Reality*. New York: Harcourt, Brace & World, Inc., 1955.

Shaheen, Samad, *The Communist (Bolshevik) Theory of National Self-determination: Its Historical Evolution up to the October Revolution*. The Hague: W. van Hoeve, 1956.

Snyder, Louis L., *The Meaning of Nationalism*. New Brunswick, New Jersey: Rutgers University Press, 1954.

Whitaker, Urban G., Jr., comp. and ed., *Nationalism and International Progress*. San Francisco: Chandler Publishing Co., 1960.

A World on the Move: A History of Colonialism and Nationalism in Asia and North Africa from the Turn of the Century to the Bandung Conference. Amsterdam, Djambatan; New York: Institute of Pacific Relations, 1956.

Znaniecki, Florjan, *Modern Nationalities, A Sociological Study*. Urbana, Illinois: University of Illinois Press, 1952.

4

Ideology and
International Relations

The influence of ideology on human behavior is subject to widely divergent interpretations. Some discount it entirely, whereas others see it as the major, if not the sole, determinant. F. S. C. Northrup writes that the problems growing out of conflicting ideologies must be faced and if possible resolved. "Otherwise, the social policies, moral ideals and religious aspirations of men, because of their incompatibility one with another, will continue to generate misunderstanding and war instead of mutual understanding and peace."[1] Jeremy Bentham held an opposite view. Ideologies are "fig leaves of the mind" used to justify behavior while concealing the real motives for it.

Among those who believe that ideology influences international relations there is disagreement on how it does so. For example, some contend that communist ideology sets a basic goal of world conquest for the Soviet Union. Others regard it as solely instrumental for serving traditional national goals pursued by both Czar and Commissar. Exponents of conflicting ideologies disagree vehemently in interpreting their own and that of their opponents. Communists argue that Marxism-Leninism is anti-imperialistic and democratic; Western democrats see it as inherently aggressive and authoritarian. On the other hand, communists have usually contended that "bourgeois capitalism" necessarily breeds war and imperialism, whereas the exponents of "democratic capitalism," as they term it, claim that it is essentially conducive to peace and international cooperation. Each side is inclined to attribute its own

---

[1] *The Meeting of East and West* (New York: The Macmillan Co., 1946), p. ix.

departure from the ideals called for by its ideology to the machinations of its ideological opponents. Thus Americans see their country engaged in power politics regretfully made necessary by international communism, whereas the Soviet Union cannot permit the state to "wither away," as called for by communist ideals, as long as it has to contend with "capitalistic aggression." Those outside the two power blocs are likely to apportion blame more equally, and even to see the conflict as the result of basically similar values and behavior. Many Indians hold that both Soviet and American society represent Western materialism, and that the conflict is between shades of gray rather than between black and white, bad and good. And it is decidedly *not* between East and West!

Objective observers concede the difficulty of arriving at satisfactory answers to such questions. They are generally agreed, however, that ideology makes a difference in behavior in the international arena, but not so great a difference as is commonly believed. Three factors are chiefly responsible for the difficulty: the nature of ideologies; the almost impossibly complex problem of measuring the relative weight of several influences, of which ideology is only one; and the extreme, impassioned, and divergent claims made for and against particular ideologies.

WHY INCREASED ATTENTION TO IDEOLOGY?

Students of international relations have given increased attention to ideology in the modern period mainly for two reasons. The first and most apparent is the development in a number of powerful states of ideologies and institutions which contrast sharply with those of liberal and democratic societies that carry on the traditions predominant in the nineteenth-century Western world. The communist revolution of 1917 in Russia, followed by fascism in Italy and National Socialism in Germany—and their subsequent spread to other countries—were major events in world history. These ideologies seemed to many observers to have had a significant influence on the foreign policies of the states in which they were established, and hence, on their relations with other countries. Professor Carleton writes that, although hitherto ideology other than nationalism has not played a dominant role in international relations, "this middle of the twentieth century may be witnessing the epoch-making shift in the foundation of international politics from the nationalistic balance of power to ideology, evidence of which we shall ignore at our peril."[2]

The second major reason is that ideology has become more important with the growing influence of the masses on decision-making, especially

---

[2] William G. Carleton, "Ideology or Balance of Power?" *Yale Review* (Summer, 1947), 590-602.

in the area of foreign affairs. Their concern is of relatively recent origin. A prominent student of international relations had said:

Prior to 1914, the conduct of international relations was the concern of persons professionally engaged in it. In democratic countries, foreign policy was traditionally regarded as outside the scope of party politics, and the representative organs did not feel themselves competent to exercise any close control over the mysterious operations of foreign offices.[3]

There are many aspects of foreign affairs, as of governmental affairs generally, which must be entrusted to the experts. Some of these attract little attention because the public is generally unaware of them, they do not affect the particular interests of organized groups, or they meet with general approval by those who are politically conscious and informed.

Increasingly, however, foreign affairs affect the citizens in most intimate ways. Even though the general public does not exert a continuous and positive influence over their direction, public opinion, nevertheless, limits the range of alternatives available to decision-makers. Although this is obviously true in a democracy, domestic public opinion is also of concern to leaders of totalitarian states. In contrast to the older dictatorships, which largely disregarded the opinion of their subjects, modern totalitarian movements attempt to shape opinion in support of their policies. They do so in two ways—by denying their people access to information which the leaders regard as detrimental to their interests, and by indoctrinating them with ideas favorable to the regime. Although democratic governments also engage in similar forms of "thought control," the degree of effectiveness with which they are able to do so is significantly different from that of the totalitarian dictatorships. In any case, the ideology of a people, despite its ambiguity, sets broad outside limits to foreign policy decisions, and serves as an instrument by which policy-makers mobilize public support for their decisions. In the latter instance ideology may either be a rationalization, i.e., a conscious or unconscious disguising of the real reason for policy, or policy may in varying degrees be actually motivated and guided by one or more of its aspects.

The new mass character of contemporary society requires statesmen to be concerned not only with their domestic audiences but those of other countries whose foreign policies they seek to influence. The remarkable growth of international "information" programs is a testimony to this new dimension of diplomacy. From educational projects in the true sense of the term, such as technical assistance training, these activities extend to short-range propaganda of the most blatant type, as evidenced in the propaganda of disarmament. The populace of the newly developing

---

[3] Edward Hallett Carr, *The Twenty Years Crisis, 1919-1939,* 2nd ed. (London: Macmillan & Co., Ltd. and New York: St. Martin's Press, Inc., 1946), p. 1.

countries provides especially fertile ground for influencing the minds of men. Here societies are in a process of transition, with its unsettling impact on traditional social and intellectual foundations. Nationalism provides the principal unifying intellectual force. Although it served to unite the people in the struggle for independence, and to some extent provides an *élan* for social and economic development, it is inadequate in three respects. It does not provide an adequate explanation of reality; it is insufficient as a satisfying philosophy of values; and it has almost nothing to say about the kinds of economic and political institutions needed—or how to attain them—to enable peoples to satisfy their changing and growing aspirations. Under these circumstances, proponents of competing ideologies attempt to fill the vacuums left by the passing of the old order. To be effective, ideologies must be adapted to local conditions. In particular they must not offend sensitive nationalistic feelings. Marxist-Leninist philosophy has in many respects fulfilled certain ideological needs, and its practitioners have often (although not always) been sufficiently elastic in their interpretation of dogma to make it fit particular circumstances. Lenin's explanation of imperialism provides a ready and often acceptable explanation of colonialism. Communist theory, which emphasizes the exploitive aspects of colonialism, also enables the newly emerged nations to attribute their present poverty to their former exploitation. The example of the Soviet Union, and increasingly of Communist China, where economic advance has been rapid under circumstances far more comparable to that of the underdeveloped than of the more advanced democratic ones, exerts a powerful appeal, especially among the dissatisfied intellectuals. Although the connection is not clear, their ideology is assumed to have had something to do with economic progress in the totalitarian states. Therefore, whereas many of the leaders of the non-communist underdeveloped countries have absorbed the basic tenets of Western liberal thought and prefer its values over those of totalitarian creeds, they may also believe that Western institutions are unsuited to their circumstances. They may, therefore, envy the United States but emulate the Soviet Union, either on the assumption that Western political values can still be retained, or that they must be sacrificed on the altar of economic progress.

THE NATURE OF
IDEOLOGY—A GENERAL ANALYSIS

Ideology: A Definition

An examination of a number of writings revealed the following to be listed as examples of ideologies: liberalism, conservatism, constitutional democracy, democracy, laissez-faire capitalism, democratic socialism, welfare liberalism, communism, fascism, authoritarianism, neo-fascism, nationalism, internationalism, neutralism, Christianity, Catholic action, Islam, Buddhism, Hinduism, Shintoism, and Gandhism. An exhaustive enumeration of comparable phenomena would extend the list almost indefinitely. Whether the authors whose writings were examined would agree on a definition of ideology that would encompass all of these is uncertain. Yet it is clear that they have certain elements in common. They are all ideas, or sets of ideas, that purport to explain some or all aspects of reality; they contain value preferences with respect to means and ends; they include certain action programs for the attainment of the ends; they are all similarly vague in varying degree; each contains widely varied or incompatible elements; and the adherents of none conform perfectly in either values or actions to the tenets of their creed. As used herein, *an ideology is a system of abstract ideas held by an individual which purports to explain reality, expresses value goals, and contains programs of action for the retention or attainment of the kind of social order in which its proponents believe the goals can best be realized.*

Probably no one ideology embraces all of life, although communism and fascism approach totalitarianism. It follows, therefore, that a particular individual may, and ordinarily does, adhere to several ideologies. And he may do so despite the fact that they contain elements of logical incompatibility. Thus the ideologies embraced by a single individual may be nationalism, liberalism, Christianity, socialism or capitalism, neutralism, and Gandhism. As incongruous as it may seem, the author has known persons (not Americans, of course!) who professed to be Christians, communists, and nationalists!

The definition of ideology as a system of abstract ideas held by an *individual* requires explanation. One may also speak of group ideology. The group may be a subgroup within the nation or it may include the entire nation—hence, a national ideology. It may be transnational, consisting of limited numbers of individuals in several nations. Catholics and communists are both transnational groups in this sense. Conceivably an ideology could be held by the entire population of two or more nations, or even by all humanity. The latter is the aim of communist ideology as well as of universal religions such as Islam and Christianity. Group ideology, however, is an abstraction. It is the sum total in similarities of the ideologies of individuals composing the group. It resembles public opinion, which represents the common ideas of many individuals on public matters.

The greater the number of individuals included, the more likely it is that group ideology will be abstract. This is necessarily the case if different individuals who profess to hold the same ideology differ in its interpretation, and adhere to certain of its tenets with different degrees of tenacity. The ambiguity of group ideology is further compounded by the fact that many individuals embrace more than one ideology. If a national ideology be taken to mean the common ideological elements of the entire citizenry, it will be vague indeed.

Ideology and Interest

Writers usually juxtapose ideologies and interests. What is the relationship between them? What is the respective influence of each on human action? In this context an interest means either something with which one is concerned, something that he regards as important to him, or the feeling which grows out of attachment to the object he considers to be important. Thus one may say either that his interest *is* food or that he has an interest *in* food. A group interest is something generally held to be important by all or most of its members, or the concern felt by them with respect to the object. The security of the state is almost universally regarded as one of the most important interests of the nation. Those who discount ideological factors tend to regard them as "mere verbal pseudo-rationalizations after the fact and at worst insignificant if not completely irrelevant."[4] The opposite view is that interests themselves, at least those above the elementary biological level, are the result of ideologies. For example, interest in the security and survival of the nation-state, which may be at the expense of the material interest and even the survival of particular individuals, is held to be derived from the ideology of nationalism.

There is ordinarily a close relationship between interest and ideology. Each seems to be affected by the other because the interest may both shape ideology and be shaped by it. They tend to converge, although they are not always entirely compatible. The relative influence of each, where they are not mutually reinforcing, seems to depend on the intensity of attachment to interest and ideology.

What is often regarded as a clash between interest and ideology may actually involve opposing ideological elements. The acquisition of the Philippine Islands by the United States is an illustration. Why were they annexed? The United States has traditionally been opposed to imperialism, at least of the "overseas" variety. Did interest in trade with the Philippines, and in using the Islands as an entry into the Chinese market, triumph over anti-imperialism? President McKinley found another reason (or justification) for annexation. It was our Christian duty to educate, civilize, and Christianize the Filipinos in the interest of Christian brotherhood! Annexation was thus made to harmonize with humanitarianism, which was as much a part of American ideology as was anti-imperialism.

---

[4] F. S. C. Northrup, "Ideological Man in His Relation to Scientifically Known Natural Man," in *Ideological Differences and World Order*, ed. F. S. C. Northrup (New Haven: Yale University Press, 1949), p. 407.

It is doubtful that either humanitarianism or profit was among the *causes of*, as opposed to *rationalizations for*, annexation. Probably, as Kennan maintains, the real reason was that the American people, or at least some of their official spokesmen, "simply liked the smell of empire." It is possible to argue that the "smell of empire" was an interest; it is equally plausible to contend that it was one of the values of the ideology of nationalism expressing itself once the continental boundaries were rounded out and new worlds to conquer beckoned across the Pacific.

Ideology and Rationalization

This case may also be used to illustrate additional characteristics and uses of ideology. First, a particular ideology may be used either to justify or to condemn a particular course of action. Annexation was obviously incompatible with anti-imperialism, and its opponents also argued that it was contrary to democracy and humanitarianism. On the other hand, McKinley used the humanitarian argument to justify annexation, which necessitated suppressing the anti-imperialistic aspects of the ideology. Secondly, it illustrates the use of ideology to justify a policy by advancing an acceptable but false explanation. This does not necessarily mean that McKinley was guilty of conscious deception. Mannheim has shown that there is a "whole series of possible types of ideological mentality."[5] At one extreme there is the type in which one is incapable of being aware of the "incongruence of his ideas with reality" because of the "whole body of axioms involved in his historically and socially determined thought." A second intermediate type, the "cant personality," is one which can understand the incongruences between ideas and conduct, "but instead conceals these insights in response to certain vital-emotional interests." Finally, there is the ideological mentality which engages in conscious deception, not of self but of others.

A SYSTEMATIC APPROACH

An examination of the role of ideology in international behavior requires systematic analysis if we are to avoid a dangerous pitfall—that of either exaggerating or underrating its importance. When concentrating on a particular factor the human mind has a remarkable capacity for distorting its significance. "Mythologies consist [in part] of the substitution of a single factor for the plurality of causes. . . ."[6] Ideology is clearly only one of the factors which influence international behavior.

---

[5] Karl Mannheim, *Ideology and Utopia*, trans. Louis Wirth and Edmund Shills (New York: Harcourt, Brace & World, Inc., 1936), p. 195.

[6] Raymond Aron, *The Century of Total War* (Garden City, N.Y.: Doubleday & Co., Inc., 1954), p. 97. Copyright 1954 by Raymond Aron. Reprinted by permission of Doubleday & Company, Inc., Garden City, N.Y.

In the following pages we shall employ quite systematically the conceptual framework set forth in Chapter 1. We are concerned with relations among states, their dependencies, and international organizations;
our task here is attempting to determine the influence of ideology over
their interactions.

Types of Interaction

Our focus, it should be recalled, is on official relations. It involves all
kinds of subject matter and includes both political and cooperative relationships. The concept of official relations presents no particular problems
when applied to democratic regimes where political parties have limited
international ties and influence the international behavior of the government actors rather than seek to supplant them. The situation is more
complicated, however, in totalitarian states, particularly where the
dominant ideology takes on a strong international orientation. There,
one party monopolizes the field. It is the instrument for interpreting and
proclaiming the ideological doctrine, which then becomes the only legitimate truth. But that is not all; ordinarily the major policy decisions are
made by the party, and it may even be an agent for their execution. The
party thus tends to become the real government. International relations
among two or more communist states may in fact be conducted even
formally by the respective party leaders, who may or may not at the
same time hold positions in their governments.

The parties of communist states, where they are the effective governments, also enter into relationships with their counterparts in countries
where the party is not in control—or even outlawed. Here is a case of
what is in effect the government of one country attempting to influence
the conduct of that of another by endeavoring to modify the internal
environment, or even to supplant the existing government by one more
favorable to the communist state. In principle, this type of activity is
similar to propaganda and economic activities directed by any government to the people of other countries. Whether one regards such govern-
ment-to-people relationships as moral or immoral will depend in part
upon his ideological outlook, as well as upon his interests.

Because of the structure of non-totalitarian societies and the nature of
their party and governmental systems—and perhaps because nationalism
militates against close transnational ties among similar national parties—
international political party relations among them are seldom of consequence. Certainly the bonds of international socialism have been too
fragile to confine the nationalism of its adherents. The Christian Democratic parties in the six nations of "little Europe" did cooperate more
effectively after 1950, and the common institutions developed in the area
owe their existence in some part to that fact. If one looks to the realities,

i.e., knows who in fact makes the foreign policy decisions, and even executes them in part, this deviation from the more traditional practice does not impair the concept of international relations as official relations among the interacting entities.

In totalitarian states almost all international relations, economic and cultural for example, are state monopolies. But in this respect the difference is only one of degree. Both democratic socialist and welfare capitalist societies increasingly operate or control vast areas of economic life. Cultural and other activities are also objects of concern to them, and are directed in the international area to promote foreign policy objectives. Interests, circumstances, and presumably ideology are all responsible for this trend, but in no two areas do they affect the situation in an identical manner. It would be presumptuous to be more definite, given our present state of knowledge.

Ideological affinity between individuals and groups is conducive to cooperative relationship. This is one of the several factors which explain the common purposes and courses of action of the rulers in the Soviet Union, Communist China, and other communist regimes. Yet it was not sufficiently strong to prevent the Yugoslav defection in 1948, or, to be more accurate, the rejection of Yugoslavia by the other members of the communist bloc. This factor appears to play a stronger role in Chinese-Soviet relations than it does in Soviet relations with the East European satellites. Chinese communism is much more of an indigenous movement than is that of Eastern Europe, and Soviet-Chinese power relationships are more nearly equal than are those between the Soviet Union and the East European regimes. Moreover, unlike the Chinese, the communist leaders of East Europe depend on Soviet support for their continuance in power.[7]

Presumably, common ideological elements are of some significance in undergirding cooperative relationships among certain non-communist states, especially those of the North Atlantic area and of Latin America. The worth of individual liberty, the rule of law, and democratic processes, are usually cited as among those prevalent in North America and most of Western Europe. Within the area, Catholicism, as we have noted, may be of some influence as a binding force among the Community of Six, just as it may be in Latin America. Ideologies which contain quite different, or like but incompatible elements, exercise an opposite influence. We have noted the divisive effects of nationalism. In the present era, and for the foreseeable future, relationships between the communist and democratic states will be a center of attention, and the effect that ideology has in determining their relationships will undoubtedly continue to be de-

---

[7] "Ideology and Foreign Affairs," A Study by the Center for International Affairs, Harvard University, for the Committee on Foreign Relations, United States Senate, No. 10 (Washington, D.C.: Government Printing Office, Jan. 17, 1960), pp. 29-33.

bated. Insofar as ideology is an influential factor in those relationships it will presumably be divisive. Yet, "the passage of time and changing conditions may reshape the content and priorities of the ideology."[8] Provided this reshaping results in their becoming more alike, or less unlike, its effects may be salutary.

Components of Human Behavior

We have noted that the personalities of the actors, the working objectives they pursue on behalf of their groups, their internal and external settings, and the resources available to them, determine the policies of the entities of international relations and the interactions among them.

Ideology and Personality. The influence of personality on human behavior is the central subject matter of psychology. One's personality is the result of his biological heritage, physical environment, and culture. Ideology is an aspect of the latter. As a part of culture it continues as an environmental factor, interacting with personality to influence action. The importance attached to indoctrination, especially of the young, indicates a strong belief that ideology can be used to shape personality, and through it human behavior. Evidence that many of the young people in the communist states of Eastern Europe continue to reject communism does not prove that indoctrination has had no affect on their personalities, but only that it has been counteracted by other forces. Who can deny that his personality is in part the result of ideological conditioning? Cultural differences, including ideological elements, account principally for personality differences between Russians, Americans, Frenchmen, Chinese, Iranians, and Congolese. Their biological differences are insignificant; variations in physical conditions are ordinarily of little importance as a direct influence on personality, although they may be more significant as long-run factors.

Personality influences one's objectives and the way he views a situation. Objective facts are variously interpreted even by people with similar personalities. The interpretations of a set of facts by a Russian Communist, an Indian nationalist, and an American liberal may be astonishingly divergent.

Since personality is shaped only in part by ideology, and personality is only one of the components of human behavior, ideology in this area does not seem to be of great significance. It seems reasonable to assume, however, that it is more important in shaping the personalities of some official actors than it is of others.

Objectives and Ideology. To what extent are working objectives influenced by ideology? Ultimate foreign policy goals are probably affected more than are those lower in the ends-means hierarchy. This is true be-

---

[8] *Ibid.,* p. 7.

cause the former are related more directly to ultimate ideological values goals, such as the preservation of the nation-state and the protection and expansion of "ways of life"—for example, democracy, communism, and fascism.

Both the ideologies of the leaders and those of the influential citizenry enter into the shaping of foreign policy ends, the latter as a part of the internal setting. Assume that the leaders of a dictatorial and a democratic group are each equally ideologically motivated, have available roughly similar resources, and are confronted with comparable conditions. The personal ideologies of the leaders in the dictatorial regime will, in this setting, be of greater importance in shaping objectives than will those of the leaders in a democracy. On the other hand, the ideology of the active public in a democracy will be more important in this respect and under these conditions than will that of the people in a non-democratic group. The qualifications are important, for otherwise these generalizations do not necessarily hold.

Ideology and the Setting. Ideology is probably most important in international affairs, as it determines and is a part of the setting within which decision-making takes place. We have made frequent references to this in previous contexts, especially in the discussion of nationalism. Nationalism has been referred to as the "justifying ideology of a nation-state," and as a system of "symbols of justification for the acts of a state," or symbols by which "the state-organized cohesiveness of a nation are advanced and justified."[9]

Ideologies other than nationalism affect the international milieu. Unlike nationalism, however, which is always divisive among nations, some ideologies may act as integrating forces. Ideology may therefore, as we have seen, be conducive to either cooperative or oppositional behavior. A common ideology such as liberalism or communism among a group of states tends to unite them. Contrariwise, communist and democratic regimes will find it more difficult to get along together because of their ideologies. In the Western Hemisphere traditional Latin-American and Anglo-Saxon ideals conflict. The cohesion of the Commonwealth of Nations is weakened by the inclusion of more and more states with widely different cultures. At the same time, certain elements in their ideologies work in an opposite direction. Even though the net effect of ideologies may be more conducive to conflict than to cooperation, this may be more than counterbalanced by common interests, which may be no more than mutual protection against common enemies. The opposite may also be true.

Resources and Ideology. The resources available to the decision-

---

[9] H. H. Gerth and C. Wright Mills, *Character and Social Structure* (New York: Harcourt, Brace & World, Inc., 1953), pp. 198-99.

makers in conducting external relations are affected by ideology in two ways. First, it may influence the proportion and the form in which resources of the group are made available to the decision-makers. An appeal to nationalism, because it places a high value upon the nation-state, will ordinarily result in a willingness to make sacrifices for security, especially to build up a state's own military strength. Military and economic aid to others may also gain approval if justified by nationalism and national selfishness —labeled "national interest." More often than not, however, appeals of this kind are reinforced by references to altruistic principles of religious brotherhood, humanitarianism, or proletarian solidarity. Various groups will respond differently, depending upon their attitudes, to the rather heterogeneous justifications for a given foreign policy. Legionnaires and Quakers, by and large, are differently motivated. Russian and Chinese communists appear to be willing, perhaps in part—but only in part—because of the nature of their ideology to make greater relative contributions to fulfill foreign policy objectives than do democratic Americans and Frenchmen.

Secondly, ideology may affect, either favorably or adversely, the total resources of a state. A society which values material wealth, other things being equal, will be more productive in goods and service than will one which values leisure or spiritual qualities. Calvinism with its emphasis on hard work and its view of wealth as a symbol that one was among the elect has been acclaimed as an important factor in American industriousness. Nationalism in the newly developing countries has been noted as a principal source of "dynamics and political activism." Communist ideology, perhaps largely in the same manner, but also because it is used to justify sacrifices in the name of the future classless society—and possibly because of state planning and ownership under political autocracy which it permits—is certainly a factor in the rapid economic development of the Soviet Union and Communist China. It seems to be more doubtful that such is the case in other communist areas such as East Germany and Czechoslovakia, where conditions are considerably different.[10]

DEMOCRATIC AND COMMUNIST IDEOLOGIES: EFFECTS ON INTERNATIONAL BEHAVIOR

Although almost any ideology may affect international behavior, those backed by organized movements or embodied in political institutions are the most effective in this respect. Ideologies which attempt to explain and which express values directly relevant to international relations, while in addition providing more or less specific guides for international behavior, are likely to have a greater impact on international behavior than are

---

[10] See below, pp. 243-45, for a discussion of the relevance of political and social institutions to national power.

those more remotely related. Nationalism, by and large, fulfills these two requirements in greater degree than does any other single ideology. Furthermore, it is the most nearly universal ideology. For nationalism is a part of the ideological make-up of most communists, democrats, and fascists, as well as of those who may think of themselves as adherents of other ideologies. Within communist nations, those who do not embrace the ideology of communism nevertheless appear to take pride in the achievements of communist institutions because they serve the cause of the state.

Aside from nationalism, communism by almost universal agreement among friend, foe and neutralist, is one of the most influential ideologies of the present era. Almost one-third of the human race is included within the communist orbit, and communists are influential in varying degrees in almost all national societies elsewhere. To say that people—indeed, one-third of the human race—live under communism is very different, however, from saying that they embrace communism as an ideology. We simply do not know how many of them do so; it may be a relatively small percentage, especially outside the Soviet Union. Since communist leaders cannot entirely disregard public opinion, non-communist ideologies presumably are not without significance even within communist areas. Yet the leaders of totalitarian societies are relatively free to control or disregard public opinion in their own domains.

During the interwar interval, and especially after the National Socialists came to power in Germany in January, 1933, fascism vied with communism for prominence. With the defeat of the Axis powers in World War II, it was largely destroyed as an effectively organized force, despite its persistence in fascist Spain, in semi-fascist Portugal, and in varying degrees elsewhere. Although fascism seems to be rather thoroughly discredited, there are small neo-fascist groups in a number of states, and fascist ideas, often unrecognized as such, are a part of the mental baggage of the extreme racist and nationalist everywhere.

Although communism and fascism are in many respects nebulous and shifting creeds, it is generally agreed that they are less so than the comparable ideology of the liberal and democratic societies. It is even difficult to suggest an acceptable term for the latter. Liberalism is acceptable only if it embraces, as a minimum, both conservatives and liberals. In the nineteenth century, when liberalism stressed economic laissez-faire, it stood in contrast to socialism. But in the contemporary period, with laissez-faire everywhere rejected and socialists ready to settle for half-way measures, a socialist is likely to claim that he is more liberal than a conservative, and at least as liberal as one who calls himself a liberal! Probably the term "democracy" is subject to fewer objections than is "liberalism," "capitalism," "welfare capitalism," or "democratic socialism," to designate common elements in the ideologies of free societies. Even in many states where democracy is in eclipse (at least temporarily) the democratic ideal seems to evoke favorable responses. That is certainly true in parts of Africa, Latin America, and non-communist Asia. Communists will object to the label, for it is their claim that only communist societies are and can be democratic! For the reasons indicated above, we shall limit the following description and analysis principally to democracy and communism, with occasional reference to other ideologies for purposes of comparison. Those aspects of the ideology which are pertinent to international behavior will be stressed, since that is our sole concern.

Democracy

Democracy may be defined as an ideology and a method of behavior; or as a system of values and a way of decision-making in a society. Thus defined, it refers to the nature of a society in general—to the values and behavior which characterize private-individual and group conduct, as well as that of public government, both domestic and international.

Democracy's central and basic value is the equal worth and dignity of every human being. Differences among men do not justify private or public conduct which violates this principle of the democratic creed. Classification of people according to certain criteria and the differential treatment of those in each group for certain purposes—but not for others—is harmonious with the principle. People may be grouped on the basis of age differentials, for example, but not according to race or color, for purposes of education, without violating a cardinal principle of democracy. Those with high incomes may be required to pay a higher rate of taxation than are persons with low incomes. But blonds and redheads may not be taxed more than dark-haired whites and Negroes. In short, certain types of different treatment are democratic, whereas others are deemed discriminatory and contrary to the premise of democratic equality. Equality of opportunity for each person is perhaps the basic corollary to the tenet of equal human worth. Gunnar Myrdal writes that:

Economic integration is the realization of the old western ideal of equality of opportunity. The essential element of this ideal, as we commonly understand it when it is related to social relations within one country, is the loosening of social rigidities which prevent individuals from choosing freely the conditions of their life and work. The economy is not integrated unless all avenues are open to everybody and the remunerations paid for productive services are equal, regardless of racial, social, and cultural differences.[11]

In recent decades most of the advanced industrial and democratic nations have moved internally to a relatively high degree of social and economic integration.

Does the democratic ideal of equality stop at the boundary of the na-

---

[11] An International Economy: Problems and Prospects (New York: Harper & Brothers, 1956), p. 11.

tion-state? Since it speaks of the equality of all men, and not of all Americans, Englishmen, and so forth, its consistent application calls for the integration of all peoples. Yet there are few who are willing to apply this principle beyond their national boundaries. Differential treatment, which would be regarded as discriminatory and repugnant if applied among Americans or Italians, is hailed as wise statesmanship when the government of the United States discriminates on behalf of Americans against Italians, and vice versa. For example, tariffs on the importation of Italian goods is regarded as normal, whereas impediments to the free movement of goods and people within the American market is condemned as both uneconomic and undemocratic. Myrdal believes the lag in international integration is due to three factors: lack of social cohesion and solidarity across national boundaries; the primitive and ineffective techniques of international political settlement; and the tendency for the process of national integration in each country, with the perfection of "national political machinery for its advancement tend, in the present stage of world development, to lower people's international allegiances. This results in increased international disintegration."[12] Whatever the reason, the democratic ideal, which is contrary to discrimination, is less likely to be applied, even by predominantly democratic governments and peoples, on the international than on the domestic scene.

Since the individual is regarded as the supreme end, the state is simply an instrument for furthering human welfare. Nationalism, which places supreme value on the state, is clearly inconsistent with the democratic emphasis on individual worth. Democracy also places a high value on personal freedom. A democratic individual, while jealous of his own rights, equally respects the rights of others. Yet complete freedom, however it may be idealized, is practically impossible. The freedom of some is likely to result in the subordination of others. This dilemma is reconciled by equating *legitimate* freedom with *liberty,* and *illegitimate* freedom with *license;* this interpretation is usually expressed as "liberty under law." Liberty is likely to flourish only when the established order is relatively secure from both within and without. In times of war and international crisis it is always in danger of curtailment in the name of order and group survival. Democracy is concerned with maximizing the liberty of man everywhere; it is, therefore, opposed to its violation from any source. Nationalism, however, subordinates the individual to the state. The nationalist is also jealous of national sovereignty and opposes "outside" intervention even to further the democratic ideal; it is condemned as encroachment on the freedom or sovereignty of the state to violate the liberty of the individual! A national society which purports to be democratic, and is at the same time jealous of its sovereignty and respects that

---

[12] *Ibid.,* pp. 13-14.

of its neighbors, labors under an extreme handicap. The only way out of the difficulty is to remove human rights from the domestic jurisdiction of states, and to make them of international concern. The recognition in the Nuremburg and Tokyo trials, following World War II, of an international law prohibiting crimes against humanity; the Universal Declaration of Human Rights; the Genocide Convention; and the development of Covenants on Human Rights by the UN; all indicate a trend in this direction. The failure of the United States to ratify the Genocide Convention and her opposition to the Human Rights Conventions, however, is an example of the triumph of the ideology of nationalism over that of democracy.

As a method of government, both in the private and public area, democracy means the right of each responsible individual to exercise an equal voice in the making of decisions, at least on matters of consequence to him. This is essentially the ideal of self-government. Democracy is thus contrary to imperialism where some men rule others without their joint and equal participation in decision-making. This practice can be reconciled with democracy only if dependent people are placed in the same category as citizens who are deprived of the right of participation because they are too young, mentally defective, criminals, or otherwise irresponsible.

Democracy is often defined as government based on consent. If this be taken to mean that no man is subject to a decision he opposes, it is obviously incorrect. It is more accurate to say that democratic government is based on the consent of a majority of responsible citizens, and that the minority, as long as they are permitted to participate freely and equally in decision-making, may be bound without their consent. The alternative is to permit the minority to rule, which is repugnant to the democratic belief. There is a basic dilemma involved here, for if democracy means majority rule, it is possible for the majority to infringe upon the liberty and rights of individuals—which is also undemocratic. For our purpose the matter need not be pursued further.[13] The essential point is that the democratic principles of "one man, one vote" and decision-making by majority rule are grossly violated in international affairs. That is quite evident in international organizations where states with unequal populations have equal votes. But if the representation and votes of states were in proportion to their populations, and even if so-called decisions were made by majority vote, there would still not be majority rule. That is so because, with a few exceptions, the so-called decisions are actually recommendations, which, regardless of their varying degrees of effectiveness, do not bind states in a legal sense.

All states, despite the democratic or non-democratic character of their

---

[13] Henry Steele Commager, *Majority Rule and Minority Rights* (New York: Oxford University Press, Inc., 1943), for a provocative discussion of this dilemma.

domestic societies, are alike in departing from certain democratic principles. But to recognize this is not necessarily to condemn it. The ideal of democracy is seldom if ever attained in practice. The equal representation of unequal states in the United States Senate is at least as undemocratic as is one vote for each member of the United Nations General Assembly. Nor is the veto in the Security Council essentially different in principle from the filibuster in the Senate of the United States, or dictation by the Rules Committee of the House of Representatives. A realistic comparison of domestic and international politics, while revealing some basic differences, indicates that both powerful individuals and groups, including states, nearly always exercise considerably more influence on actual decision-making than is called for by the democratic principle of the right of equal participation by each responsible individual. The fact that conduct falls considerably short of conforming to democratic standards and that this is widely accepted whether out of necessity or preference by those who think of themselves as democratic, indicates the influence of ideologies, interests, and circumstances which more than counterbalances the influence of democratic values and standards of conduct. If this be so even in cohesive and democratic national societies, it is quite understandable that it is even more so in the relatively disintegrated international milieu. It is, therefore, very difficult for the ideals of democracy to be realized internationally and even for predominantly democratic states to conduct their foreign relations in accordance with their creeds.

To the extent that democratic ideology is influential in international relations it should shape behavior, in several respects. First, it should be conducive to practices which further the welfare of all men regardless of their social, economic, racial, or national status. Specifically, it would mean that the welfare of the people in one national group would not be advanced by discrimination against others. The ideal would be the social and economic integration of world society. Secondly, the state would be evaluated wholly in terms of its contribution to individual dignity, not only of its own nationals but of people in general. Since the state would never be an end in itself, a decision to restrict the freedom of particular individuals and groups would be based on its contribution to the maximization of freedom and other human values. Thirdly, sovereignty would never be allowed to stand in the way of the protection of human rights, or of the protection and advancement of other democratic values. Fourthly, a democratic ideology would favor the development of international institutions whereby men would have equal rights to participate by peaceful means in the making of important decisions which affect their interests and values. It would seek to curtail the exercise of unequal power by equal men. Each group would be allowed representation and voting rights in proportion to the number of people it contains. Since the domination of some men by other men would be repugnant, democracy would oppose colonialism of any sort. Fifthly, the democratic creed would be conducive to the pacific settlement of disputes and of peaceful change in accordance with the will of the majority, but at the same time it would surround the process with procedural safeguards to insure the fullest possible freedom for individuals consistent with the welfare of the greatest possible number of people. I have attempted to indicate what certain basic tenets of democracy, if they were fully effective, would mean for international behavior. To do so is not necessarily to suggest that they can be made effective, or that an attempt should be made to apply them at the present juncture in human society. One needs to be reminded that some of the worst crimes in history have been committed in pursuit of various versions of ultimate truth and perfection. The democrat is tolerant of different views and practices, and is in a degree skeptical of all truths, including his own.

Communism

The ideology of communism differs from that of democracy in both form and substance. Although it may be somewhat more specific, or rather less ambiguous, than that of democracy, it is probably more variable over the course of time. Both characteristics are due primarily to the authoritarian nature of communism. Unlike communism, democracy has no founder who compares with Karl Marx and no bible like his *Das Kapital;* nor has it authoritative interpreters like Lenin, Stalin, Khrushchev, and Mao Tse-tung. The result for communists is that, although the "party line," and hence to them the absolute truth, may be fairly clear at a particular time, absolute truth at one moment may be absolute falsehood at another.

Even the possibility of knowing the absolute though temporary truth existed only as long as it was proclaimed from one center which went largely unchallenged, or if it were challenged, possessed the means of making its views prevail. Prior to 1948, the Kremlin's was the voice of authority. After the Titoist deviation in 1948, and, even more important, the seizure of the Chinese mainland by the communists in 1949, the Kremlin's voice no longer prevailed as before. This emergence of "polycentrism" led to strains within the communist orbit, and to controversies over the correct interpretation of Marxist-Leninism.[14] Under these circumstances it is fully as difficult to write with confidence of communist as it is of democratic ideology with respect to its meaning and significance for international behavior.

The continuous reinterpretations of communist ideology are explained as changes in tactics called for by changing circumstances. Stalin main-

---

[14] Vernon V. Aspaturian, "Soviet Foreign Policy," in *Foreign Policy in World Politics,* ed. Roy C. Macridis (Englewood Cliffs, N.J.: Prentice-Hall, Inc., 1958), pp. 201-07.

tained that Marxism was not "a collection of dogmas that 'never' change despite changes in the conditions of the development of society . . . Marxism as a science cannot stand still, it develops and improves. . . . Marxism does not recognize invariable conclusions and formulae obligatory for all epochs and periods."[15] Nevertheless, it is doubtful that the interpretations, frequently drastic, are simply logical deductions, resulting from the application of basic Marxian principles to different circumstances. It is more likely, as Ulam maintains, that "Soviet ideology . . . has been secreted in the interstices of the totalitarian system, which has now existed for over forty years, and that the early millenarian Communist faith has been modified by the experience of almost two generations' application of the original theories to the stubborn facts of life."[16] The fact that the ideology is used to justify different policies at the same time, as well as over a period of time, raises grave doubts about its role as a guide to conduct. Indeed, we may well ask whether the term "communist" ideology has real meaning. Perhaps it would be more accurate to speak of Soviet, Chinese, and Yugoslav ideology. But even Soviet ideology has meant rather different things under Lenin, Stalin, and Khrushchev. The situation resulting from divergent interpretations is quite comparable to that which arises when Christian fundamentalists draw different conclusions from a common infallible source. Since there can be only one "correct" interpretation, all others are obviously heretical and intolerable. Nevertheless, the leaders of communist regimes continually proclaim, even more than do those of the democracies, the primacy of ideology as the basis for both their foreign and domestic policies. Marxist-Leninist ideology is regarded by communists as a scientific, indeed as an infallible, tool for analyzing the social situation and for determining the proper course of action. Although men may err through improper use of the methodology, that does not impair its essential soundness.

The ways in which communist ideology influences the international behavior of communist states is thus difficult to determine. Yet despite its different meanings at different times and places, there are certain more or less abiding elements which may be of significance in this respect. The basic assumption of the philosophy seems to provide an outlook for viewing world events. The theory is that all history follows certain historical laws as determined by the material conditions—hence the term "materialistic determinism." Institutions and culture are but reflections of the material conditions prevailing at a particular stage of social development. Although man cannot alter the basic course of historical change, he can hamper or expedite the inevitable. All societies hitherto

---

15 J. V. Stalin, *Concerning Marxism in Linguistics* (London: *Soviet News*, Nov. 1950), pp. 39-40, as cited in *ibid.*, p. 146.

16 Adam B. Ulam, "Soviet Ideology and Soviet Foreign Policy," *World Politics*, XI (Jan., 1959), 1954.

have been class societies, in which slaveholders, feudal lords, and capitalists have held dictatorial power over slaves, serfs, and workers. This will continue to be so until the advent of the communist classless society. Communism does not appear with a communist seizure of power, according to the modern communist interpreters of Marx, but must first go through a socialistic stage in which the way is prepared for the perfect communist society. Conflict between reactionary and progressive forces is inevitable in a class society. Capitalism, at first progressive, struggled and won over reactionary feudalism. Now, having become reactionary itself, it struggles in vain against the workers (proletariat), represented by their vanguard, the Communist party. The communist seizure of power in Russia in 1917 meant that for the first time the communist movement was in possession of the paraphernalia of state power. Henceforth, the Soviet Union could serve as a base for furthering the inevitable downfall of capitalism and preparing for the advent of the communist millennium.

If the communist decision-makers take their ideology seriously, their world viewpoint is affected in the following ways: (1) conflict between communist and capitalist states is regarded as inevitable; (2) time is on the side of communism, for that is ordained by historical inevitability; (3) the Sino-Soviet bloc, as the leaders of the progressive forces, are struggling not on behalf of these nation-states, but for the proletariat everywhere. Although communist theory, especially as developed by Lenin, held that imperialism was the inevitable result of the monopoly stage of capitalism, and that wars among capitalist states developed inevitably out of imperialism, there is nothing in communist theory that says communist states must further their ends by war. Nevertheless, communists have spoken of "just" war—that undertaken to further "progressive" forces— and presumably would engage in it if the Marxist prism showed that it was called for by the existing balance of forces. Thus, though conflict is inevitable, war is not. There was considerable evidence, however, that on this point Mao Tse-tung and Khrushchev at times interpreted the prism differently, for the former regarded Khrushchev's "peaceful coexistence" with capitalism as a perversion of Leninism. If one believes himself to be riding the tide of inevitability, he will conclude that time is on his side. Although this may serve to sustain morale and to justify "strategic retreats" it does not necessarily mean that there is a time table for victory. The theory of "ebbs and flows" means that there is a time to stand still or retreat, and another to advance, but it depends on events and not the calendar. If the "capitalistic democracies" can prevent the "inevitable," they can, even according to communist theory, postpone their demise indefinitely. In accordance with the thesis that communism serves the purpose of the international proletariat—who are destined to inherit the future—it is natural, moral, and progressive for communists everywhere to give primary allegiance to international communism, and to further the ends of the Soviet Union and the other communist states rather than those of their capitalist masters. In doing so, according to communist theory, they are serving the cause of communism, for existing communist states are but instruments to that end. In short, communist theory is truly international, on a class basis; whatever concessions it may make to nationalism are wholly strategic and temporary.

We have said that democratic ideology is important primarily because of its moral implications, which influence both objectives and the means for their attainment. In particular, the individual is the center of value. Communist ideology also contains certain basic values. It promises a utopia in which every individual, once freed from the corrupting influences of private property and a class society, will receive an income in accordance with his needs, and will live in a blissful state of cooperative anarchy. Meanwhile, he must be willing to pay almost any cost, including liberty and the products of his labor, to advance the date of the bright future. To the extent that this vision influences the international behavior of communist leaders, it would justify the use of almost any means to hasten the day when all humanity could enjoy the blessing of communism. Although neither fascist nor nationalist ideology is concerned with individual freedom and human welfare as ultimate ends, they resemble communism in their disregard of the individual while pursuing their basic goals.

SUGGESTED READINGS

Almond, Gabriel A., *The Appeals of Communism*. Princeton, N.J.: Princeton University Press, 1954.

Aron, Raymond, "The Leninist Myth of Imperialism," *Partisan Review*, XVIII (Nov. 1951), 646-62.

Berding, Andrew H., "The Battlefield of Ideas," *Department of State Bulletin*, XXXVIII (June 23, 1958), 1043-48.

Berlin, Isaiah, "Political Ideas in the Twentieth Century," *Foreign Affairs*, XXVIII (Apr. 1950), 351-85.

Brogan, Denis W., "Who is the Enemy?" *Virginia Quarterly Review*, XXIX (1953), 339-50.

Brzezinski, Zbigniew, "Communist Ideology and Power: From Unity to Diversity," *Journal of Politics*, XIX (Nov. 1957), 549-590.

Burns, Edward McNall, *Ideas in Conflict: the Political Theories of the Contemporary World*. New York: W. W. Norton & Company, Inc., 1960.

Carleton, William G., "Ideology of Balance of Power?" *Yale Review*, XXXVI (June 1947), 590-602.

Carr, Edward Hallett, *The Soviet Impact on the Western World*. New York: The Macmillan Co., 1947.

Chadwick, H. Munro, *The Nationalities of Europe and the Growth of National Ideologies*. Cambridge: The Cambridge University Press, 1945.

Fiszman, Joseph R., "The Appeals of Maoism in Pre-industrial Semi-colonial Political Cultures," *Political Science Quarterly*, LXXIV (Mar. 1959), 71-88.

Footman, David, *International Communism*. London: Chatto & Windus, Ltd., 1960.

Hudson, G. F., "Russia and China," *Foreign Affairs*, XXXIX (Oct. 1960), 1-10.

Katona, Paul, "Soviet Propaganda to the Colonial World," *Year Book of World Affairs, 1955*, IX (1955), 149-73.

Kelsen, Hans, *The Political Theory of Bolshevism: A Critical Analysis*. Berkeley, Calif.: University of California Press, 1948.

Leites, Nathan, *A Study of Bolshevism*. Glencoe, Ill.: Free Press of Glencoe, Inc., 1953.

Lenin, Nikolai, *Imperialism, the Highest Stage of Capitalism*, new rev. trans. New York: International Publishers Co., Inc., 1939.

Lifton, Robert Jay, *Thought Reform and the Psychology of Totalism: A Study of Brainwashing in China*. New York: W. W. Norton & Company, Inc., 1961.

Mannheim, Karl, *Ideology and Utopia: An Introduction to the Sociology of Knowledge*. New York: Harcourt, Brace & World, Inc., 1936.

Marcuse, Herbert, "Dialectic and Logic Since the War," in *Continuity and Change in Russian and Soviet Thought*, ed. Ernest J. Simmons, Cambridge: Harvard University Press, 1955.

McVicker, Charles P., *Titoism; Pattern for International Communism*. New York: St. Martin's Press, Inc., 1957.

Meyer, Alfred G., *Leninism*. Cambridge: Harvard University Press, 1957.

Morris, Bernard, "Soviet Policy Toward National Communism: The Limits of Diversity," *The American Political Science Review*, LIII (Mar. 1959), 128-37.

Neumann, Sigmund, "The International Civil War," *World Politics*, I (Apr. 1949), 333-50.

Niebuhr, Reinhold, "Democracy as a Religion," *Christianity and Crisis*, VII (Aug. 4, 1947), 1-2.

Northrop, Filmer Stuart Cuckow, *Ideological Differences and World Order: Studies in the Philosophy of the World's Cultures*. New Haven: Yale University Press, 1949, for the Viking Fund.

Page, Stanley W., *Lenin and World Revolution*. New York: New York University Press, 1959.

Plamenatz, John, "Interests," *Political Studies*, II (Feb. 1954), 1-8.

Prothro, James W. and Charles M. Grigg, "Fundamental Principles of Democracy: Bases of Agreement and Disagreement," *Journal of Politics*, XXII (May 1960), 276-94.

Riefe, Robert H., "Moscow and the Changing Nature of Communist Ideology," *Journal of International Affairs*, XII (1958), 159-67.

Roucek, Joseph S., "A History of the Concept of Ideology," *Journal of the History of Ideas*, V (Oct. 1944), 479-88.

Steiner, H. Arthur, "Ideology and Politics in Communist China," *The Annals of the American Academy of Political and Social Science*, CCCXXI (Jan. 1959), 29-39.

U.S. Senate, Foreign Relations Committee, *United States Foreign Policy; Compilation of Studies Nos. 1-13*, 2 vols. No. 10. "Ideology and Foreign Affairs," by the Center for International Affairs, Harvard University. Committee Print, 86th Cong., 2d sess., 1960, pp. 991-1078. Washington, D.C.: Government Printing Office, 1960.

Ulam, Adam B., "Soviet Ideology and Soviet Foreign Policy," *World Politics*, XI (Jan. 1959), 153-72.

Van der Kroef, J. M., "The Appeals of Communism in Southeast Asia," *United Asia*, VII (Dec. 1955), 290-97.

5

Economic Factors

That economic goals and conditions are influential in society—international and domestic—is fairly obvious. The vast majority of the human race is still so close to the starvation level that food, clothing, and shelter are ever pressing concerns. Nor does the demand for material goods and services seem to abate as wealth increases. The human appetite seems insatiable. Governments have always responded to economic factors. Today they are generally given the responsibility of maintaining high levels of employment, assuring minimum standards of well-being, and increasing economic productivity, which makes it necessary for them to play a major role in the operation of the economy.

The world has become highly interdependent economically, as in other respects. Because economic conditions in a particular country affect people elsewhere, these matters frequently become the subject of intergovernmental relations. This was not always so, at least to the extent of the present period. During the nineteenth century governments allowed international imbalances, such as large excesses of imports over exports, to run their course, even though this meant temporary unemployment, idle factories, and depressed prices. Furthermore, international movements of capital were primarily the concern of private investors in search of profits, though they frequently sought and obtained the protection and support of their governments. Today, governments often adopt domestic economic policies, which are nevertheless of concern to other governments. These may be designed to promote high levels of domestic employment, to maintain high and stable prices for agricultural and other primary commodities, to stimulate industrial development, to protect monetary reserves, etc. Since these policies frequently involve the curtailing of imports, and sometimes the dumping of goods on foreign markets, they often lead to retaliation on the part of other governments. But they may also lead to international agreements in attempts to control the prices of such commodities as wheat, sugar, and coffee, or to undertakings such as the General Agreement on Tariffs and Trade (GATT), or the Organization for Economic Cooperation and Development (OECD). Among the purposes of these organizations is the regulation or prevention of practices harmful to other countries, and cooperation in dealing with common economic problems.

States also pursue their goals directly by international policies. They do so because they depend in varying degrees on the international interchange of goods and services, and many of them are interested in obtaining technical assistance and capital from other countries and international organizations. Some countries are also interested in exporting capital. Outside the communist countries, the bulk of these transactions is still in private hands, though governments increasingly regulate the interchange of goods and services and the movement of capital. Governments also engage directly in trade and in large-scale capital transactions with varied motives. The richer, and therefore the lender and donor states, have been concerned principally with political purposes such as security, prestige, the expansion of their influence, and to some extent with humanitarian ends. The recipient countries, although concerned with similar goals, are quite naturally more concerned with economic development than are the more economically advanced states. Contrary to the Marxist-Leninist thesis, there has often been a scarcity rather than a surplus of capital in advanced industrial countries. For this and other reasons capitalists have been reluctant to invest heavily in most of the newly developing countries. Among the other reasons are the unfavorable investment climate and the need for capital to develop what is known as social "overhead," or the infra-structural part of the economy—roads, dams, schools, hospitals. Many governments reserve the right to nationalize foreign property (usually but not always with compensation), control the repatriation of capital and earnings, and require that control over basic decisions rest in the hands of its nationals or the government itself. Private capitalists are simply not interested in investing in social overhead. Governments and international organizations are therefore the chief sources of capital for these purposes.

Our concern at this point is with the extent of the influence of economic factors on foreign policies and international relations. We begin, however, with a discussion of the influence of economic purposes and conditions on human behavior in general in order to provide background and suggest methods for a similar analysis in the international arena.

THE ROLE OF ECONOMIC FACTORS IN
HUMAN BEHAVIOR—A GENERAL ANALYSIS

Most men devote the major portion of their time and energy to tasks related, directly or indirectly, to the production of goods and services.

From that fact it is tempting to conclude, as many do, that economics is primarily, or even exclusively, at the root of all human behavior. Any type of activity, therefore—political and religious, for example, as well as that concerned with the production and distribution of goods and services—is thought to be directly or indirectly caused by economic factors.

Belief in Economic Causation Widespread

The belief that economics is the root of all human endeavor is held both tenaciously and extensively. It may have a Marxist coloration, but it is far from being confined to adherents of that ideology. Charles A. Beard—although he later modified his views somewhat—held that the United States Constitution was essentially an instrument of the dominant elite, formulated to protect and further their economic interests.[1] L. L. Bernard, a social psychologist, after considering a number of factors which he categorized as psychological, concluded that "back of them almost invarialby lie those economic causes which have conditioned them. Even the ideologies . . . have been clearly shown to rest in nearly all instances ultimately upon economic interest and processes."[2] The reverse of this contention can be argued with at least equal persuasiveness. Since all actions begin in the minds of men, almost invariably back of economic factors lie the psychological causes which have conditioned them. By a somewhat similar process of reasoning some scholars—geographers, theologians, political scientists, psychologists, anthropologists—conclude that phenomena with which they are especially concerned are the basic cause of human endeavor. "If specialists could realize how easily they fall into error merely because they know so much about one of the aspects of society, there would be a great gain in our understanding of society."[3]

Unless one attributes inordinate influence to a few economists, and to Marxists in general, the source of the widespread belief in the predominance or exclusiveness of economic causation must be sought elsewhere. The views advanced on this matter by non-Marxian economists are usually more reserved and qualified than are those held by the general public. Both Marxist and non-Marxist theories on economic causation are also subtle and complex. Moreover, there is no one theory held by either group, though Marxists are likely to be in basic agreement. Nevertheless,

---

[1] *An Economic Interpretation of the Constitution* (New York: The Macmillan Co., 1913); see also Beard, *The Idea of the National Interest* (New York: The Macmillan Co., Inc., 1934). In the latter work he argues that the national interest of the United States was identified essentially with the promotion of the interests of powerful economic groups.

[2] *War and Its Causes* (New York: Holt, Rinehart & Winston, Inc., 1944), p. 328.

[3] Willard Walter Waller (ed.), *War in the Twentieth Century* (New York: The Dryden Press, Inc., 1940), p. 11.

a combination of economic naïveté and the search for a single simple answer seems to be the most valid explanation for the easy acceptance of the economic interpretation of human behavior.

There is truth, but not the complete truth, in views such as these. For some men and some groups, economic motives and conditions predominate; but to argue that this is universally so regardless of time and circumstance is to deny that other factors of a non-economic nature, such as goals, personality, environment, and resources, are of consequence. In the international field there are many forces that must not be dismissed as unimportant in influence. Nationalism, ideologies such as communism or democracy, religion, demands for national security and survival must all be weighed, not discounted or viewed simply as reflections of basic economic phenomena. Even if men are primarily engaged in economic tasks, does it necessarily follow that they are principally motivated by, and that the products of their labor will be used for, economic purposes? The truth is that the products of land, labor, and capital serve many purposes, of which the satisfaction of economic demands is only one.

Economic Ends and
Purposeful Behavior

The role of economic influences may be approached from two different points of view. The first is concerned with ends or goals, and thus with conscious and purposeful behavior. It is assumed that man has certain objectives in mind and that his actions are consciously directed toward their realization. Since he has at least some degree of freedom in choosing his goals, his actions are not *determined*, in the fatalistic sense of that term. To what extent is man's behavior the result of basic motivations or drives directed toward the satisfaction of economic ends? An objective is economic in nature when it can be satisfied by the consumption of material goods or services. A minimum of food, clothing, and shelter is necessary to fulfill certain bodily needs. Most people also want and obtain satisfaction from the consumption of goods obviously unnecessary for the relief of hunger, or protection against the elements. These demands for comforts and luxuries (which soon become "necessities") are nevertheless economic in nature. But what if one wants goods and services, or money, for any one or more of the following reasons: to "keep up with the Joneses"; to contribute to humanitarian and religious causes; to buy physical protection; to be able to pay taxes for the support of programs designed to enhance national security; or to bring the blessings of democracy (or of communism) to the unenlightened or unfortunate? Surely it requires considerable sophistry to reduce these objectives to a common economic denominator. In these instances, as in similar ones, the apparent is more likely to be nearer the truth than is the devious and obscure.

Economic Conditions and Forces

The second approach to economic causation is through environment. In contrast to purposeful action to achieve his ends, man reacts to certain conditions which the economic determinist maintains are, at bottom, economic in nature. Often, responses to conditions are habitual and emotional; men do not realize why they respond as they do. That the setting or situation is, in many instances, the most important of the four components of human behavior is argued in this work. That its economic elements are important is obvious. But to contend that they are all-embracing is as fallacious as to argue that man's wants are all economic in nature.

ECONOMIC INFLUENCES
ON INTERNATIONAL BEHAVIOR

Our task is less inclusive, but not necessarily less difficult, than that of pursuing the elusive mainsprings of all human behavior. We are concerned with the official relations of states, international organizations, and dependent peoples—specifically with the influential role of economics on their policies and interactions. We are concerned with the latter for the light they may throw on economic causes. The conclusions drawn from observing behavior are likely to be at least as reliable as are the reasons which people, and especially national decision-makers, advance for their actions. We may or may not, however, be able to discover by such an examination that a particular policy, a tariff or trade agreement, or a war, for example, was the result of economic factors. We are also interested in private international economic transactions, but only because they too may contain clues to our query. For relations among public international entities are sometimes the result of these private international activities.[4]

It is necessary to keep in mind the distinction between ends and means if we are to avoid confusion. Economic means (policies) may be directed toward any number of ends, including economic ones. Many of the economic policies, both domestic and foreign, of both the Soviet Union and the United States are undertaken with only minor, if any, economic ends in mind. These countries may even pursue economic policies that entail an economic sacrifice. The latter is certainly true of the complete embargo imposed by the United States on the importation of goods from Communist China, as it is of the United States restrictions on the export of strategic goods to the Soviet bloc countries, or on the importation of sugar

---

[4] The latter are of direct concern to the student of international economics; they are among the multitude of matters in which the student of International Relations has an indirect interest and some aspects of which he must understand.

from Cuba. It is true, of course, that the confiscation of American-owned property in Cuba was one of the factors that led to a deterioration in United States-Cuban relations. The countries of Western Europe also restricted their trade with the Soviet bloc, often at considerable economic sacrifice, but only after considerable pressure by the United States. The latter in turn at least partially compensated for their losses by making them larger economic grants than would otherwise have been required. When in 1959 and 1960 the Soviet Union and Communist China agreed to purchase a major portion of Cuba's sugar, neither did so out of economic or humanitarian concerns. Likewise, the public grants and loans for both economic and military development made by many countries—especially the United States, the Soviet Union, and France—were primarily for political purposes. Although in the long-run some of these policies might rebound to their economic benefit, in most instances this purpose served as a rationalization rather than as a major influence.

The relationship between economics, imperialism, and war bulks large in writings on the role of economics in international behavior. In particular, Lenin's view of imperialism as the monopoly stage of capitalism, and war as the inevitable outcome of imperialism, has received a great deal of attention. One of the results of this concentration has been the neglect of the influence of economic factors on international relations in general, and especially on cooperative as opposed to oppositional behavior. Our endeavor is to present a balanced view, to discover the economic factors which lead to international cooperation, as well as conflict—both peaceful and forceful.

Impact of Economic Factors Differ From State to State

Two or more states may enter into economic or other relationships for different reasons. Whereas the motivation of the wealthier and stronger powers may be wholly or primarily political, the poorer countries are likely to be interested more in the economic welfare of some or all of their citizens. Yet as economically needy as they may be, they are often hesitant to accept economic aid for fear of limitations on their independence. They insist on "aid without strings." They are also interested in economic development for political ends. Prime Minister Nehru of India has frequently stressed the necessity for economic development to make India's voice really count in international affairs.

As previously noted, states pursue their own economic ends not only by international means—economic and otherwise—but also by domestic policies. Were they economically self-sufficient or willing to satisfy their wants without dependence on others, and were economic goals the sole consideration, their domestic economic policies would not lead to international negotiations. Since the facts are quite otherwise, so-called domestic policies frequently have wide international repercussions. For example, the United States government adopted an agricultural policy to attain what it regarded as a fair share of the national income for its farmers. High prices were then maintained by curtailment of production and by government price supports. In order to make the policy effective, tariffs and quotas on agricultural products were imposed to protect the artificially maintained domestic prices from foreign competition. Policies of this nature, pursued for essentially domestic purposes, have led almost inevitably to international policies. Since the domestic agricultural policy resulted in the accumulation of "surpluses" of wheat, rice, and other products, attempts have been made to dispose of them abroad, frequently at prices below those prevailing on the world market. This has often resulted in friction between the United States and countries interested in exporting similar products. In 1960, Thailand anticipated selling rice to India. Without consulting her Thai ally, the United States arranged to dispose of a quantity of her surplus rice to unaligned India on terms considerably better than those proposed by the Thai government. Although Thailand later disposed of her crop elsewhere, relations between Washington and Bangkok deteriorated, and the latter indicated an interest in overtures of economic assistance from the Soviet Ambassador. India, on the other hand, was the beneficiary of American surpluses. Purchased by Indian rupees, which would probably be returned eventually to India as gifts, the rice would enable her to relieve hunger without diverting her limited foreign exchange from the task of economic development. The United Nations, at the suggestion of President Eisenhower, was also developing a plan whereby agricultural surpluses could be utilized for worthwhile purposes without disrupting the world market and causing friction between competing producers.

Economic Influences More Important Domestically Than Internationally

Economic factors exert a greater influence on the domestic scene than they do internationally, principally because of the differences between the two environments. Some of the man's wants—especially security—are reasonably well provided for within many countries because of the degree of community feeling, a system of centralized law, and relatively effective political institutions. Where these conditions prevail, it is possible to relax and to concentrate on economic and other ends. Internationally, security and similar objectives are the principal goals of states; they therefore require continuous attention. This does not mean that domestic security, peace, and order are less desired or less necessary—only that in proportion to the extent they are attained, they demand less effort than where they are non-existent or precarious.

Individuals usually place greater value on the nation and its continued existence than on sub-groups, which is an additional reason for the greater importance of non-economic ends in international than in domestic society. This is due primarily to nationalism, which regards the nation as entitled to man's highest and final loyalty, to which all else must yield. Although the family, the tribe, sometimes a group such as the church, and —among communists—the party itself, may compete with and sometimes win out over loyalty to the nation-state, it is the latter which usually exerts the stronger pull. In contrast, most domestic groups—trade-unions, political parties, business associations—are regarded primarily as instrumental, and do not command the allegiance of their members except as they serve their purposes. Disloyalty to the state, but not to other groups, is almost universally regarded as treason.

In the following passage, Professor Quincy Wright indicates the relationships between the value placed on the nation-state, the international environment, and the importance of the security objective in international relations.

International politics has also differed from national politics in that its characteristic end has been the continued existence of the groups that participate in it. Because of the relative freedom of these groups to use all available means to forward political ends, the existence of each group is more threatened by others than is usual in domestic political situations. Consequently, other ends of these groups, such as the development of group prosperity and the maintenance and propagation of group values, have tended to be subordinated to the major end— the continuance of the existence of the group.[5]

Economic Impact Greater in Private Than in Governmental International Relations

Economic factors are more influential in private than in official international relations. The validity of this proposition is more apparent than is that of the one set forth in the previous section. Certainly the dominant motivation of private traders, lenders, and borrowers is to maximize their gains and to minimize their losses, and governments very frequently help them to do so. This aid may take many forms. Foreign representatives of governments gather information on trade and investment opportunities, and assist private groups in their negotiations with both governments and other private groups abroad. Commercial and trade agreements provide for the reduction of trade barriers, and the fair and equitable treatment of foreign investors and traders in their respective markets. They may also

---

[5] *The Study of International Relations* (New York: Appleton-Century-Crofts, Inc., 1955), p. 134.

prohibit nationalization of foreign property, or provide for fair compensation if it is nationalized. Governments also intervene to protect the economic interests of their nationals against unfair treatment, and in instances where there is a breakdown of local law and order. Although armed intervention for these purposes is no longer usual, this was not always so. American forces, prior to 1930, were often sent to countries (such as Nicaragua) in response to the demands of American business interests there. It does not necessarily follow, however, that the exclusive or even primary purpose of government intervention has been economic. The protection of the Panama Canal for security reasons was a more important motive for United States intervention in the Central and Caribbean area during the early part of the present century than was the protection of the trade and investment of American firms in the republics of that area. Prior to World War II, the United States government was only mildly interested in American oil investments in the Middle East. After 1945, however, the exploitation of these resources, their availability to the members of the Western Alliance or, as a minimum, their non-availability to the communist bloc countries, became a matter of prime importance. By 1960, when the Soviet Union had developed her own resources more fully, and additional oil and other sources of power outside the Middle East were available in greater quantities, "oil diplomacy" abated, at least temporarily. Although the countries of Western Europe were interested in Middle East oil for economic as well as strategic purposes, the government was concerned primarily with the latter. Even the European countries were probably interested far more in general economic welfare than in protection of particular private investors. Whatever aid, comfort, and profit American oil companies gained as a result of their government's support was principally the incidental result of its concern with security. Nevertheless, the persistence of the belief that economics is the root of all evil, and possibly of some good, led to charges during the 1956 Suez Canal crisis that the United States government was motivated principally by concern for the bank accounts of Standard of New Jersey, Socony-Vacuum, and Gulf Oil Corporation.[6]

Conditions and Demands
Determine Economic Influence

The significance of economic and political ends for international relations depends on both the relative premium placed on the ends and the circumstances under which they are pursued. Prior to 1914, or even 1939, the economic policies of the United States were usually undertaken for economic ends. The tariff, for example, was largely the result of economic

---

[6] M. S. Venkataramani, "Oil and U.S. Foreign Policy During the Suez Crisis 1956-7," *International Studies* II (New Delhi, Oct., 1960).

pressure groups operating in a political system more likely to serve particular interests than to promote the common welfare. Liberal immigration policies before World War I, and restrictive policies provided for by the Immigration Acts of 1921 and 1924, were also primarily economically motivated. After 1945, American trade and economic policies, both restrictive and expansive, although not without their economic causes, tended to be dominated by political considerations.

It is difficult to determine whether the British government was influenced more by economic factors before than after World War II. Unemployment was a serious problem from the nineteen-twenties down to 1939. The welfare state, however, was less-firmly established then than it was after the triumph of the Labour party in the 1945 election. From then on, a high level of employment and welfare was both maintained and demanded by almost all segments of the population. Economic factors apparently exerted an almost equal effect on British policy during both periods. With respect to national security, it appears to have been regarded as less threatened from 1919 to 1938 than it was in the years after 1945. On the other hand, powerful British groups contended, with only limited success, that Great Britain was incapable of defending herself by military means in an age of thermonuculear-missile weapons, and should therefore forego the attempt. With economic demands exercising an approximately equal influence from the nineteen-twenties onward, and with security provoking a greater response after 1938 than before, it appears, on balance, that the security objective, in comparison with the economic, was relatively more important in Britain after World War II. Yet it is clear that economic considerations continue to be more influential for Britain internationally than for the United States.

Two general conclusions may be drawn. First, the more dependent a country is on international trade and finance for its economic welfare, the greater will be the economic influence on its international behavior. Secondly, the greater the perceived threat to a nation's security, the more likely is it that political objectives will dominate economic ones.

Effects of Differential
Incomes Between Countries

What is the effect on international relations of major disparities in national income levels? If a nation cannot stand half-slave and half-free what is the prospect for a world one-third of whose people are over-stuffed and the other two-thirds half-starved? Is this situation primarily a cause of competition, conflict, and even war? Or does it lead to compromise and cooperation? There is no simple, nor single correct answer to these questions any more than there is to most others worth asking. We can be rather certain, however, that in an age of rapidly rising human aspirations the affect of poverty on international behavior is of greater consequence than it was in former times, when men were more prone to accept economic deprivation as part of the divine order, or in any case as necessary given the existing limitations on production. It is also evident that it may lead to either or both cooperation and conflict, depending on circumstances and the nature of the parties involved. There is no evidence, in the modern age at least, that countries with the lowest income have engaged in aggression against wealthier ones in order to gain at the latter's expense. On the contrary, many of the wealthier countries have conquered, or have attempted to conquer, peoples whose resources and levels of living were below theirs. The principal explanation is that wealth brings power, and thus makes aggression possible, rather than that it generates a frame of mind which calls for aggression for economic or other reasons. Yet there is some indication that a country which has developed economically to the point where it has considerable power, but in which the per capita income lags considerably behind rising demands, may be more inclined to pursue an energetic and possibly an aggressive foreign policy for economic reasons, than will either a much poorer or much wealthier country. Whether this inclination will result in conflict, and possibly war, depends on both international and domestic circumstances. A country highly dependent on foreign trade for its livelihood is likely to be tempted more in this respect than is one with a balanced economy. Economic forces in both Japan and Italy during the interwar period may have been influential, although not necessarily decisive, in causing them to become imperialistic.

In the light of history, the major programs of economic cooperation developed after 1945 may prove to have been more significant than the release of atomic power and the conquest of space. A host of motives and circumstances, never exactly the same for different countries, international organizations, and dependent peoples, are responsible for these programs. We have already suggested the major role that security, and possibly ideological goals, played in the economic policies of the major powers, and the comparatively greater economic interest of the poorer countries. In short, for the former there have been primarily economics of power and for the latter economics of welfare. The significant point to be made here is that despite these major programs, disparities in national income, which widened as the rich nations became richer and the poor countries only slightly less poor, did lead to major cooperative undertakings. Some of these were bilateral, some multilateral—especially those conducted through international organizations. That these programs were more the result of antagonisms between the major power blocs than the expression of an identity of interests or a feeling of community between the possessors and the dispossessed, does not change the fact. In this case cooperation can truly be said to have been partly the result of conflict.

THE INFLUENCE OF ECONOMIC GOALS

It has been demonstrated that different international entities, and the same entities over periods of time, are motivated in varying manner and degree by economic factors. It remains to consider some relatively specific situations and entities, and to deal with a general question: Is the pursuit of economic goals more likely to lead to international cooperation or conflict? We have defined goals as economic when they can be satisfied by the consumption of goods and services. The desire for wealth to impress one's neighbors is a psychological objective; the desire for wealth to contribute to national defense is a political goal.

United States-Russian Relations

The most critical relations in contemporary international society are those between the United States and the Soviet Union. What if anything, do the economic goals of either have to do with this relationship? Economic objectives are responsible for almost none of the policies of either which set them at odds. Trade between them is of minor importance. Nor does either state seek trade or investment opportunities abroad for economic ends which have a significantly adverse affect on the other. Nevertheless, the income of the people of both would benefit by freer economic interchange, and by cooperative rather than competitive policies directed to the improvement of economic conditions in the newly developing nations. Their military competition results in a net economic sacrifice, even if certain individuals should, in the short run, benefit thereby. The conclusion seems inescapable that neither has anything to gain economically and that both are the losers as a result of the nature of their relationships. It is probable that the few cooperative relationships which they do enjoy have some economic basis. For example, economic motives may influence, to a limited extent, their negotiations over disarmament, as well as their economic and cultural exchanges.

Western-European Relations

Relationships among the states of Western Europe, and especially the movement toward cooperation and integration among them, grew out of complex considerations. Nevertheless, the expectation of economic gain, for powerful groups if not necessarily for their general population, is one reason for their cooperation. Conversely, the fear of economic loss, real or imagined, simultaneously serves to slow down the progress of integration among both the "Six" and the "Seven," and even more to prevent or retard the integration of the economies of the two groups. The net effect, however, of the hope of economic gain and the fear of loss is greater integration among these countries.

Economic Motives and United States
Mutual Assistance Programs

What are the economic motives behind the American programs of mutual economic assistance—so-called foreign aid? Little needs to be added here to what has already been said. Certain individuals do stand to benefit. For example, American shipping has reaped a profit from the public treasury by receiving preferential treatment in carrying abroad goods purchased through United States government loans and grants to foreign countries. And some Americans may benefit economically by the disposal abroad of agricultural surpluses. Moreover, it is probable that an affluent America would be even more prosperous in a prosperous world. Notwithstanding all this, the desire for economic gain, or even the altruistic aim of gain for others, has not loomed large in the minds of those who approved and administered the programs of mutual economic aid.

Economic Goals and
International Organizations

International organizations are also affected by economic ends and forces. As with states, the economic impact varies. The purpose of NATO, the Warsaw Pact, and other military alliance organizations is primarily security through military means. The limited economic objectives grew out of their concern with military strength rather than with economic welfare. They are nevertheless affected by economic conditions, for military and economic demands compete for shares of national incomes. The "dollar gap in reverse," which the United States experienced in the late nineteen-fifties and early sixties, caused her to put pressure on her allies to pay a larger share of NATO costs, and also led her to consider reducing troops assigned to the Alliance. More butter has sometimes been preferred to more guns.

The motivating forces and purposes of organizations such as the United Nations Educational, Scientific, and Cultural Organization (UNESCO), and the World Health Organization (WHO) are more diverse. Although the activities of both are partly aimed at improving the economic welfare of the people in their member states, UNESCO is more concerned with changing and enriching the minds of men, and WHO with preventing disease and healing bodies to alleviate unnecessary suffering and to prolong life. The fundamental goal of each, according to its charter and many of its ardent supporters, is to eliminate the scourge of war. That the extent and nature of the actions of such organizations are affected by their budgets and the economic conditions of those whom they serve is obvious. But nationalism and politics are more important in determining the resources at the disposal of such organizations than is the economic capacity of their member states.

Cooperative and Oppositional Behavior

What effect has the pursuit of economic goals on international co-operative and oppositional behavior? Specifically, is the effect, on balance, more conducive to conflict or to cooperation? Although we have cited instances of economic causes for both types of behavior, the indication so far is that not only is more to be gained economically by cooperation but that there is a distinct tendency for economic ends to be sought through cooperation, or in any case to be settled by compromise and accommodation rather than by conflict.

As long as states and coalitions of states seek security and similar political objectives by relying principally on their own power, competition and conflict are almost inevitable. Systems of collective security have failed to change the situation appreciably. The contention that political objectives sought in a decentralized milieu lead to conflict is, however, subject to an important qualification. Conflict between certain parties may generate cooperation among others. The willingness of the United States to cooperate with authoritarian countries such as Spain, Poland, and Yugoslavia, just so long as they are opposed to, or not aligned too closely with, the Soviet Union, far from being extraordinary, is an exemplification of the ancient principle that enemies of my enemy are my friends. We have noted that both the Soviet Union and the United States, because of their mutual antagonism, were motivated to enter into cooperative economic relations with the underdeveloped countries. Prior to the outbreak of the cold war, American-Russian relations were characterized far more by mutual support than by antagonistic behavior, despite the fact that in political philosophy and governmental systems the two countries have always been poles apart. Common opposition to Great Britain, France, and Germany provides the principal explanation. Not only was there no danger of war between them; they were both members of the victorious coalition of both world wars.

It is contended here that as long as the objectives are economic in nature, their net effect is to generate cooperative behavior. The question arises as to whether there is something peculiar about economic as opposed to political ends, which naturally leads to this result. Professor Quincy Wright contends that theory, as well as practice, indicates that economics "centering attention on the problem of man against physical nature and assuming human rationality, concludes that men will in the long run co-operate with, rather than fight, one another whether this co-operation takes the form of fair competition or organized planning: War is generally uneconomic; peace is generally economic."[7] On the other hand, "Conflict . . . in the short run injures both parties to the conflict and may do so in the long run. Furthermore, the struggle for power in preparation for the conflict is very likely to reduce the prosperity of all participants."[8] He further points out that whereas competition for economic ends may lead to conflict, its normal effect is to promote economic progress and cooperation. Competition for power, however, differs radically in its effect from that of competition for economic ends. This is because power is relative, and one nation's gain is another's loss, whereas economic gain may be mutual, and one nation's prosperity may actually increase the prosperity of others. Competition over economic ends, therefore, tends to lead to cooperation; political objectives have the opposite effect.[9]

The relative success of international organizations in the non-political, as compared with the political field, affords substantiation for this hypothesis. Conflicting economic goals impede progress here, but it is the increasing politicization of all aspects of international life, i.e., the use of economic and other means to achieve political ends, that constitutes the principal obstacle to progress on the economic and social front.

EFFECTS OF NATIONAL ECONOMIC SYSTEMS ON INTERNATIONAL BEHAVIOR

Land, labor, and capital are the basic factors of production, regardless of a country's economic system. Any advanced economic system is essentially capitalistic in the sense that it uses vast aggregates of capital, i.e., "roundabout" methods of production. By an economic system, however, is meant the social arrangement for the ownership of land and capital, the distribution of goods and services, and the status of workers and managers. Land and capital may be owned primarily by the state or by private individuals and groups, and workers may be slaves, serfs, or free men.

[7] *The Study of International Relations*, p. 241.
[8] *Ibid.*
[9] *Ibid.*, pp. 241-42.

Capitalism and Socialism
as Economic Systems

Capitalism is a system of private ownership of land and capital, and ordinarily of free labor, wherein both owners and workers, in performing their economic roles, are principally motivated by the hope of maximizing gains and minimizing losses. Profits, wages, interest, and rents are determined through competition, subject to monopolistic restrictions and government regulation. Frequently referred to as free enterprise, or competitive systems, all capitalistic orders fall far short of this ideal model. Limitations on freedom are the result of both concentrations of private power and of government regulations. Governments, furthermore, own and operate economic enterprises even within essentially capitalistic systems. In short, the extent to which the economic system of a country is organized along capitalistic lines, as well as the extent to which capitalism is a free enterprise system, is a matter of degree. Thus, whereas the economic systems of both the United States and Great Britain are essentially capitalistic, there is more public ownership and probably less competition within the private sector in Great Britain.

In a socialistic economic system, land and capital are owned by the state, and production is supposed to be geared for use rather than for profit. In democratic socialistic systems workers are permitted to enter into contracts over wages and working conditions. However, since they also share in the public ownership of the other production factors, the theory is usually advanced that strikes and other means of exerting power are less justified than they are within a capitalistic system. Why, it is contended, should the workers strike against themselves? The practice is often quite different, for workers, along with other groups, are still concerned with maximizing their share of the national product. The socialistic ideal is that each should be paid according to his contribution. Communists and socialists would organize the economy in a similar manner, but the ideal of the former is to distribute production according to need rather than contribution. Although the economics of the communist-controlled states are essentially socialistic, some private ownership, especially outside the Soviet Union and Communist China, is still permitted.

Political authority may be vested in the few or the many in states with either capitalistic or socialistic systems. Germany under the Nazi regime was authoritarian politically, whereas economically there was a type of tightly controlled capitalism. The Soviet Union and Communist China are also politically authoritarian, but with socialistic economies. The United States represents a combination of democracy and capitalism, whereas certain states such as Denmark and Sweden are more socialistic from an economic standpoint; but at the same time their political decisions are subject to popular control.

Does the Economic System of a
Country Affect Its Foreign Policies?

Does it really matter, from the standpoint of its foreign relations, whether the economic system of a state is socialistic or capitalistic? It would be difficult to envisage a more peaceful state than capitalistic Switzerland, or Sweden. Nor can one discern any change in Sweden's foreign policy attributable to her swing toward socialism. On the other hand, a capitalistic Germany was aggressive under National Socialism, but it was certainly no more so other capitalistic states with the restoration of democratic institutions after 1949. Both the Soviet Union and Communist China, with socialistic systems, appear to be imperialistic. The United States has at various times been expansionist, isolationist, and imperialistic, but the fact that she has been capitalistic at all times indicates that factors other than the nature of her economic system have been responsible for the variation in her foreign policies. It is possible, of course, with the introduction of major social reforms after 1932, and the gradual acceptance of the principles of the welfare state, that there was less temptation to seek relief from domestic pressures by foreign adventures. Nevertheless, so overriding have been the other factors shaping foreign policy since the nineteen-thirties that it is very doubtful whether either the general nature of her economic system, or reforms therein, have really shaped her foreign policy in any important respect.

Some theorists disagree vehemently with the reasoning and conclusions advanced here. It was noted above that both Marxists and certain liberal economists—as well as others—have attributed imperialistic and warlike tendencies to countries with capitalistic systems. But a diametrically opposed viewpoint has been advanced by others, of whom the most prominent spokesman was the late economist-sociologist, Joseph A. Schumpeter. According to him, capitalism is essentially pacific; if countries with capitalistic systems nevertheless evince imperialistic tendencies, it is despite, rather than because of capitalism. Obviously one of these theses in incorrect; the point of view advanced here is that both are wide of the truth.

Capitalism Causes
War and Imperialism

Both Marxists and non-Marxists who regard capitalism as being conducive to war and imperialism would agree with the liberal or "revisionist" socialist, Norman Thomas, that "no one would deny the role of modern imperialism in producing war, or would contend that imperialism in large part is not based on strife for markets, sources of raw material, and places to invest surplus capital."[10]

Although orthodox Marxists (communists) on the one hand, and revisionists (socialists) and certain liberal economists on the other, concur with Thomas, they nevertheless differ with respect to how capitalism and economic factors in general affect international relations. The former hold that material conditions determine the economic system, which in turn largely controls human behavior. Despite the prominent role they attribute to ideology, both it and other non-material cultural factors are regarded as reflections of the conditions of production prevailing at a particular stage of economic development. Hence they are materialistic rather than economic determinists. The second group, and particularly the revisionists among them, without denying that material conditions are influential, and that the culture is affected by the economic system, reject the strictly deterministic approach, and contend that other factors also play a part. In particular, they regard conscious purpose as having a much larger and more independent role than do the orthodox Marxists, who are greatly influenced by Lenin. Thus the liberal economist, Hobson (and presumably Thomas), although they would agree with the Leninists that states with a capitalistic economy often engage in imperialism and war, do not agree that this is inevitable.[11] They hold that policies are purposefully chosen, rather than determined, to deal with problems resulting from depressions, surplus capital, and saturated markets. If different policies were adopted, especially social reforms leading to higher wages and generally more equitable distribution, the pressure for imperialistic expansion would be relieved. A capitalism thus reformed would be no more likely to lead to imperialism than would one structured along socialistic lines. Capitalism was not held to be the *basic* cause of imperialism. Although overproduction and underconsumption generated imperialism, the responsibility rested with those who chose to follow this course rather than to reform the system. Were Hobson writing today he would probably conclude that the reforms he saw as necessary have largely been adopted by non-communist industrialized states, and that economic pressures are at most a minor force in accounting for whatever imperialistic tendencies remain in their foreign policies. Likewise, although non-Marxists may believe that purposeful

---

[10] Norman Thomas, *Appeal to the Nations* (New York: Holt, Rinehart & Winston, Inc., 1947), p. 4.

[11] J. A. Hobson, *Imperialism*, 3rd ed. (London: G. Allen & Unwin, 1938). This work was first published in 1902.

behavior is directed principally to economic ends, they do not deny that it is possible for men to choose non-economic goals.[12]

Capitalism Leads to Peace

As noted above, the late Joseph A. Schumpeter concluded that instead of leading to war, capitalism was actually conducive to peace. He pointed out that capitalism could not be held responsible for the long history of war and imperialism that antedated it. His definition of imperialism, however, was a restricted one: "objectless disposition on the part of a state to unlimited forcible expansion."[13] Although the ordinary concept of imperialism—domination of one people by another, regardless of the causes—is preferable to Schumpeter's more limited one, it does seem true that "most nations furnish an example at some time or other—that seek expansion for the sake of expanding, war for the sake of fighting, victory for the sake of winning, dominion for the sake of ruling."[14] The essential point of Schumpeter's argument is that there are certain forces to which men rather unconsciously respond rather than ends which they purposefully seek. These he believes to be such forces as the existence of a war machine, militaristic attitudes, and social conditions which propel nations to expansion and war. Presumably wars were, at some period in history, fought for conscious purposes, for he says that *created by wars that required it, the machine now created the wars it required.*"[15] The conditions and vested interests—the results of past problems, circumstances and policies—persist as forces which lead men to respond as in the past, but for no real purpose. Hence the responses are "objectless."

Capitalism is not among these forces. Rather it is a recent phenomenon, coexisting rather uneasily along with the other and incompatible "atavistic" forces which are actually responsible for the policies often incorrectly attributed to capitalism. Under capitalism people tend to become individualistic, rational, democratic, and peace-loving. Thus peace movements, capitalistic opposition to war, anti-imperialism, and pacifism are characteristic of nations in which capitalism has developed. Although trade barriers and the monopolies which they made possible, competition for markets, etc., might contribute to war, these are the products of the pre-capitalistic milieu, and are destined to disappear as capitalistic attitudes become dominant.

Schumpeter's contention that many wars have been the result of

---

[12] See below, Chapter 13, for further discussion of this matter, and especially of Leninist views on capitalism, imperialism, and war.
[13] *Imperialism and Social Classes* (New York: Augustus M. Kelly, Inc., 1951), p. 7.
[14] *Ibid.*, p. 6.
[15] *Ibid.*, p. 33.

unconscious responses to conditions rather than undertaken to achieve definite goals, is quite plausible when we consider the multitude of varied and often contrary objectives for which particular wars, as well as wars in general, have supposedly been waged. His contention that capitalism can or does produce the benevolent and ameliorative attitudes he attributes to it is the weakest part of his argument. It certainly did not do so in Germany, Italy, or Japan before World War II. Nor does there seem to be convincing evidence that countries are more or less inclined to peace or war, or toward any other kind of international action, simply or principally because of the ways they have chosen to organize the means of production and distribution of goods and services. The influences he attributes to capitalism were probably the result of other factors, such as religion and humanitarianism. In short, both Lenin and Schumpeter seem to have been indulging in special pleading, and both seem to be equally wrong.

From this analysis we may conclude generally that the effect of economic goals and systems on international behavior has been exaggerated by many writers. Increasingly, as economic means are used to attain non-economic ends, the primacy of politics over economics is asserted. The explanation of this lies chiefly in the nature of the international environment and the high premium placed on group ends, such as the security and preservation of the nation-state. But the force of economic ends varies from entity to entity, depending on such factors as their economic situation and the threats to their political goals. The tendency is for economic ends to generate international cooperation in contrast to conflict which is so often the result of the pursuit of political goals. The evidence indicates that, despite vehement claims to the contrary, it makes very little difference, as far as its international behavior is concerned, whether the economy of a state is organized along capitalistic or socialistic lines.

SUGGESTED READINGS

Clark, Grover, *The Balance Sheets of Imperialism: Facts and Figures on Colonies.* New York: Columbia University Press, 1938.

Handman, Max, "War, Economic Motives, and Economic Symbols," *American Journal of Sociology*, XLIV (Mar. 1939), 629-48.

Hawtrey, Ralph G., *Economic Aspects of Sovereignty*, 2nd ed. New York: Longmans, Green & Co., Ltd., 1952.

Heimann, Edward, "Schumpeter and the Problems of Imperialism," *Social Research*, XIX (June 1952), 177-97.

Hobson, John A., *Imperialism: A Study*. Rev. and reset ed. London: George Allen and Unwin, Ltd., 1948.

Knorr, Klaus, "Theories of Imperialism," *World Politics*, IV (Apr. 1952), 402-31.

Kruger, Daniel H., "Hobson, Lenin and Schumpeter on Imperialism," *Journal of the History of Ideas*, XVI (Apr. 1955), 252-59.

Lasswell, Harold D., *World Politics Faces Economics: with Special Reference to the Future Relations of the United States and Russia*. New York: McGraw-Hill Book Co., Inc., 1945.

Lincoln, George A., *Economics in National Security: Managing America's Resources for Defense*, 2d ed. Englewood Cliffs, N.J.: Prentice-Hall, Inc., 1954.

Niesser, Hans, "Economic Imperialism Reconsidered," *Social Research*, XXVII (Apr. 1960), 63-82.

Robbins, Lionel C., *The Economic Causes of War*. New York: The Macmillan Co., 1940.

————, *The Economic Problem in Peace and War: Some Reflections on Objectives and Mechanisms*. London: Macmillan & Co., Ltd., 1947.

Robinson, E. A. G., *Economic Consequences of the Size of Nations*. New York: St. Martin's Press, Inc., 1960.

Schumpeter, Joseph A., *Imperialism and Social Classes*, trans. by Heinz Nordon; ed. with an introduction by Paul M. Sweezy. New York: Augustus M. Kelley, Inc., 1951.

Simons, Hans, "Accommodation between Nations," *American Journal of Economics*, XVI (Apr. 1957), 236.

Staley, Eugene, *Raw Materials in Peace and War*. New York: Council on Foreign Relations, Inc., 1937.

Thornton, Archibald P., *The Imperial Idea and Its Enemies: A Study in British Power*. London: Macmillan & Co., Ltd., and New York: St. Martin's Press, Inc., 1959.

U.S. Senate, Foreign Relations Committee, *United States Foreign Policy: Compilation of Studies, Nos. 1-13*, 2 vols. No. 1. "World-wide and Domestic Economic Problems and Their Impact on the Foreign Policy of the United States," by the Corporation for Economic and Industrial Research, Inc. Committee Print, 86th Cong., 2nd sess., 1960, pp. ix-92. Washington, D.C.: Government Printing Office, 1960.

Winslow, Earle M., *The Pattern of Imperialism: A Study in the Theories of Power*. New York: Columbia University Press, 1948.

6

National Security
and Survival

Everyone is in favor of security—at least for his own nation. No one ever admits that he wants other nations to be insecure. To many, national security means national defense, which they equate with military preparation. Others, however, see military means as the path to destruction rather than to national security and survival. They believe, therefore, that alternatives must be found to replace the traditional policies upon which nations have relied for their protection.

THE APPEAL OF THE
NATIONAL SECURITY SYMBOL

Varied and contradictory programs ranging from nuclear deterrence to complete disarmament, worldwide or unilateral; from isolation to world government; from non-alignment to involvement in a variety of military alliances; from economic self-sufficiency to free trade—all claim security and peace as their paramount aim. In the U.S., wool growers and oil producers, as well as manufacturers of watches and clothespins, are among those who demand import quotas or tariffs, just as advocates of missiles and space vehicles press for increased appropriations, all in the name of national security. However tenuous may be the connection between a particular policy proposal and greater security for the nation, the claim that they are related indicates that references to security are expected to evoke a sympathetic response. Moreover, national policies, both domestic and international, are sometimes affected by such claims, however specious they may be.

Notwithstanding the extravagant claims that almost everything is conducive to national security, it is true that an increasing number of matters are closely related to it. For example, the educational level of a people affects the productive capacity of a nation, which in turn affects its ability to protect itself. A people better able to understand the complexities of the modern world will also be more likely to support alternatives to the traditional military approaches to national security. The nature of human relationships within a particular country also bears on its capacity to win support abroad. The disparity between American ideals and the treatment of racial minorities within the nation is a handicap to the United States in dealing with the growing number of independent countries in Asia and Africa, which, if they are not entirely free of color discrimination themselves, are deeply resentful of white domination anywhere.

National security clearly has high priority, probably the highest, among the foreign policy objectives of most states. With the increasing realization that the ends which it serves would be jeopardized by war, especially if nuclear weapons were used, peace is seen as a means to or condition of national security. There is a tendency, therefore, to evaluate policies according to their contribution to the end of peace, which is the path to national security. The stress on the deterrent aspects of armaments is one evidence of this. We have seen that the primary purpose of most international organizations is proclaimed to be the preservation of international peace and security. This means, essentially, the prevention of war, and hence the promotion of national security. Thus both national states and international organizations have the safety of nations as an important or primary concern. Nevertheless, whether it be based on a realistic assessment of the contemporary world, or a mental legacy largely obsolescent, the belief persists that if security through peace fails, a nation must be in a position to counter an actual attack if it is to be secure.

WHY SECURITY IS AN IMPORTANT
OBJECTIVE IN INTERNATIONAL SOCIETY

Something is secure when it is safe. This we may refer to as *objective* security. A *feeling* of security, i.e., *subjective* security, may exist whether or not there is security in the objective sense. Security is essentially a negative term in that it is the absence of real or felt threats to certain values. Since action is based on feelings or beliefs, whether or not these reflect the actual situation, most nations take measures, within their capacity, to increase their security if they feel insecure, even though they may not be endangered. Nations will fail to act if a false sense of security prevails. Since it is difficult to measure the capacity and intentions of potential enemies and allies, and even its own capacities, states are not only likely to be insecure in varying degrees but to feel even more insecure than they really are. Sometimes, however, the opposite is true. An intelligent approach would appear to be an attempt to enhance security for all. That is the purpose of the UN. Unfortunately, most policies of the historical type such as armaments and alliances, designed to increase security for some at the expense of others, usually result in greater insecurity for all.

Why does national security loom so large among the objectives of decision-makers on the international scene, and why is its importance increasing? The explanation is two-fold. First, national security, although the objective of a wide variety of institutions and programs, is itself regarded as a means to preserve certain highly regarded values already acquired. Secondly, it is, or is thought to be, in frequent jeopardy, especially from outside sources.

The Protection of Highly Regarded Values

What are the values which are thought to depend on national security? They would seem to be those connoted by the term "national." But, as we noted in discussing "national" in an attempt to determine what it meant as a component of inter*national* relations, it is vague and rather meaningless. If national security does have a definite meaning for some, it has a different meaning for others. Statesmen frequently use but seldom define it. True, they seem to imply, by mellifluous references to freedom, peace, a way of life, justice, and honor, that these are the goals of security. Quite as often, however, freedom, peace, and well-being for others as well as for one's own nation are viewed as conditions of national security. Considerations such as these lead one author to refer to "'national security' as an ambiguous symbol." He suggests that when such terms are used they evoke such a favorable response they should be examined with particular care. "They may not mean the same thing to different people. They may not have any precise meaning at all. Thus, while appearing to offer guidance and a basis for broad consensus they may be permitting everyone to label whatever policy he favors with an attractive and possibly deceptive name."[1]

It should be obvious that although national security is an important ends-means value, we must inquire as to the ends it is supposed to serve if we are to understand why it is so highly desired. There are two different approaches to an understanding of foreign policy objectives, includ-

---

[1] Arnold Wolfers, "National Security as an Ambiguous Symbol," *Political Science Quarterly*, LXVII (Dec. 1952), 481.

ing that of national security. The first, and probably the dominant one among American analysts of international relations, as well as among politicians and statesmen, is the national interest approach. The objective of all foreign policy is, or ought to be, promotion of *the* national interest. Wolfers maintains that, whereas in the United States national interest has in the past tended to be equated with economic ends, today, under the threats of the cold war and external aggression "the formula of the national interest has come to be practically synonymous with the formula of national security. Unless explicitly denied, spokesmen for a policy which would take the national interest as its guide can be assumed to mean that priority should be given to measures of security. . . ."[2]

The second approach is, in one respect at least, the reverse of the first. Instead of utilizing a concept such as the national interest and attempting to deduce meaning from it, it begins by examining the basic goals or interests of a people, or of their decision-makers, and from these, to determine the foreign policy objectives most conducive to the protection or realization of the basic ends. The ends of foreign policy are thus seen as intermediate rather than ultimate ones. We shall now examine these two approaches in greater detail.

The National Interest and National Security. The national interest approach is characteristic of those who fall into the school usually known as the realists. They maintain that all national decision-makers should be, and all wise ones are, guided by *the* national interest in pursuing foreign policy.

One of the most brilliant and vigorous spokesmen for the American *Realpolitik* school is Professor Hans J. Morgenthau, who argues in his many writings that "it is not only a political necessity but also a moral duty for a nation to follow in its dealings with other nations but one guiding star, one standard for thought, one rule for action: THE NATIONAL INTEREST."[3] He contends that national interest has an essential minimum meaning "inherent in the concept itself," and in addition a "whole gamut of meanings which are logically compatible with it." Its essential meaning or content is national survival, which means the preservation of the "integrity of the nation's territory, of its political institutions, and of its culture."[4] National security is a means to the preservation of these values. It is not clear whether by "nation" Morgenthau means a group of people, a state, or a nation-state, but probably he means the latter since he sometimes uses that term.

---

[2] *Ibid.*, pp. 482-83.

[3] Hans J. Morgenthau, *In Defense of the National Interest* (New York: Alfred A. Knopf, Inc., 1951), p. 242.

[4] "Another 'Great Debate': The National Interest of the United States," *American Political Science Review,* XLVI (Dec. 1952), 973.

The contention that the concept "national interest" has an essential inherent meaning is not convincing. Words have uses rather than meaning; i.e., they are given content by men. True, some mean by national interest the values indicated by Professor Morgenthau. But not all do so. For example, some may hold that the destruction rather than the preservation of certain political and economic institutions is required by the national interest. Hitler and Mussolini seemed to have believed that the overthrow of democratic institutions in Germany and Italy furthered that end. Likewise, some of its territory and inhabitants may be lost, yet the nation-state may survive. Germany continued with the loss of territory and population after 1919, just as did France after the loss of Alsace-Lorraine in 1871, and Mexico after the annexation of vast areas of her territory by the United States. In none of these instances was the integrity of the nation's territory preserved.

Although national interest can have no inherent meaning, and does not have specific content in common usage, we can nevertheless distinguish, in a broad way, some of the things it ordinarily does *not* mean. Considered within the state, it implies, very much as does the public or general interest, that it is something different from the values and interest of particular individuals and subgroups; although these may or may not be contrary to the interests of the people in general, they are not the same as the general interest. It is a democratic principle that the welfare of the people as a whole, rather than that of lesser groups, should prevail where the two are in conflict. Communists hold that special interests will be eliminated with the advent of a classless society. Looking beyond the borders of a state, national interest implies something less inclusive than the interests of other states, or of mankind as a whole. It is also usually regarded by the realists as being different from moral ideals, especially those of a universal nature. Thus Professor Morgenthau writes of "The National Interest vs. Moral Abstractions."[5] An appeal to the national interest is usually effective when the purpose is to persuade the citizens of one's own country, as well as their representatives, but it is apt to arouse suspicion abroad. Imagine the response of de Gaulle to an appeal by an American president that he should agree to a policy because it would serve the national interest of the United States.

In an examination of statements by American presidents and secretaries of state made between 1945 and 1958 concerning the national interest, general and specific goals, and strategies of U.S. foreign policy, Brower concludes that they have not been "entirely comfortable" with the implication of "national interest" of the United States as something

---

[5] "The Mainsprings of American Foreign Policy: The National Interest vs. Moral Abstractions," *American Political Science Review*, XLIV (Dec. 1950), 833-44.

different from the interests of other nations. They have tended to empha-size that the United States must search for "common interests" with all or some other countries. He also found that the phrase "international interests" has found some currency.[6]

Certainly nations do have many interests, just as do individuals and groups within nations. These may coincide, they may be pursued har-moniously even though they do not, or they may lead to conflict either because they are basically incompatible or cannot be reconciled under existing conditions. The latter is usually the case when nations seek security by relying on their own power, especially military strength. The real problem in international society is to find means of adjustment and cooperation, and to confine the instruments of conflict to non-suicidal means.

The original purpose of the study cited above—to determine the definition and content of "the national interest" of the United States as expressed by its principal spokesmen—was abandoned because "the term was found to be unsuitable for these purposes, and, in the author's opinion, generally unsuitable for any sharply-defined analysis of con-temporary American foreign policy."[7] Nevertheless, considerable atten-tion was given to the "Uses of the National Interest Concept" by these leaders. In addition, the works of about twenty prominent authors who used the term in their writings were examined.[8]

As used by presidents and secretaries of state, Brower found that "the only common element in all the examples is that the speaker has been discussing some situation or policy which he believed to be of concern to the United States, and he usually has had in mind some direction, situation, or action which he felt would be to the benefit of the United States." More often than not, the plural *interests* was used, implying there was no such thing as *the* national interest. Quite as frequently they spoke not of an interest, but of "an interest *in*. . . . But it has almost never been given any specific content.[9]

Summarizing the writing of ten prominent authors including Morgen-thau, who used the term, as well as two who were quite critical of it, Brower tells us that:

---

[6] Michael J. Brower, *The U.S. National Interest—Assertions and Definitions* (Cam-bridge, Massachusetts: *Center for International Studies, Massachusetts Institute of Technology*, 1959) (Mimeographed), p. 220. For criticism of the term and its implica-tions, see also: Adolph A. Berle, Jr., *Tides of Crisis: A Primer of Foreign Relations* (New York: Regnal & Company, Inc., 1957); Thomas I. Cook and Malcolm Moss, "The American Idea of International Interest," *American Political Science Review*, XLVII (Mar. 1953), 28-44; C. B. Marshall, "National Interest and National Re-sponsibility," *Annals of the American Academy of Political and Social Science*, Vol. 282 (July 1952), 84-90.

[7] Brower, *The U.S. National Interest*, p. 1.

[8] *Ibid.*, pp. 307-33.

[9] *Ibid.*, pp. 218-22.

. . . among the scholars, some of those who have used . . . [national inter-
est] with the most authoritative ring in their writings have done the least in
clearly defining it.

The result has often been to hide questionable basic philosophical assumptions and inconsistencies beneath a barrage of invective on a policy level, and
to lead into unproductive argument which skims the surface rather than investigating [*sic*] the core of the questions involved.[10]

The conclusion is reached that " 'the national interest' is not susceptible
to a single acceptable definition, and that it is a highly subjective term,
the definition of which depends almost entirely upon the specific content given it by a particular person at a particular time."[11] He concludes
that "nothing but confusion is lost by dropping the term from an analytical scheme."[12]

The term "national interest," therefore, is at best a useless tool of
analysis for students of International Relations, and is likely to carry
connotations when used by statesmen that are inimical to the values they
seek. As Charles Burton Marshall puts it, somewhat paradoxically, in
suggesting that the principle of "responsibility" would be a better guide-
line than "national interest," ". . . we can serve our national interest in
these times only by a policy which transcends our national interest. This
is the meaning of responsibility."[13]

Goals, Objectives, and National Security. The second approach, as
suggested above, is to examine the actual interests and goals of a people
and their decision-makers and then attempt to see how these affect the
formulation of foreign policy objectives. Basic to all national goals is the
survival of the state. We have previously contended this does not mean
any particular economic, political, or cultural system, or even territorial
integrity, for nation-states can and do survive drastic changes in all
these respects. The continuity of the Russian state was not disrupted by
the Bolshevik revolution of November 1917, and the subsequent loss of
territory. The essential element in national survival is sovereignty or
independence. As long as a political entity is sovereign, it continues to
be a state, and therefore survives as such. The answer to the controversial and far from settled question as to whether the German state disappeared with unconditional surrender in May 1945 turns upon what is
believed to have happened to its sovereignty. Those who contend that
Germany disappeared, and that the political entity known as the West
German Republic, which became sovereign in 1955, was a new state,
maintain that with the unconditional surrender, the collapse of the
German government, and the assumption of "supreme authority" or
sovereignty, by the four occupying powers, the old Germany ceased to

10 *Ibid.,* p. 307.
11 *Ibid.*
12 *Ibid.,* p. 308.
13 "National Interest and National Responsibility," p. 89.

be sovereign, and hence was no longer a state. Some who deny that the German state ceased to exist, suggest that her sovereignty was only suspended.[14]

The reason for the high premium placed on the maintenance of national sovereignty lies in nationalism. The central manifestation of nationalism is the desire to have the nation organized as a state, i.e., as a sovereign entity. The highest loyalty of the nationalist is allegiance to the state, and sovereignty is the essence of statehood. This means, quite obviously, that not all territory and people may be lost, for the state would then disappear, and there would be nothing to which sovereignty could apply.

Although the survival of the state has sometimes been at stake in the past, other somewhat lesser values have usually been involved. More often than not a particular territory and its inhabitants, which were regarded as a part of the national self, have been threatened. India believes that Jammu-Kashmir rightly belongs to it, and is a part of its national self; Pakistan holds the same belief. France and Germany long contended for Alsace-Lorraine. One may compare the attitude of a nation toward parts of its territory and people with that of a person toward parts of his body: some parts are more vital than others. The loss of a leg is regrettable and painful but not necessarily fatal, whereas one could not exist with the literal loss of his heart or head. The vital part of a nation is its sovereignty, whereas a particular bit of territory may be likened to a less vital part of the human body. Obviously some territory and people are regarded as more valuable than others. France, for example, faced with the loss of Algeria, could endure that with somewhat less anguish than she could the severance of Britanny from her territorial body.

It is sometimes contended that there are additional values for which the preservation of the state is necessary. A particular political and economic system, or a culture, for example, are sometimes so regarded. This does not appear necessarily to be true. Sovereignty might be lost without any change in these respects, just as a nation might become a state without these being affected. When Scotland disappeared as a sovereign entity by the Act of Union (1707), and merged with England, there were no material changes in her culture or her economic and political institutions. Likewise, when former colonies gained their independence with the surge of nationalism in the post-World War II period, this did not automatically transform their economic and social orders, although it did quicken the pace of change.

Whether the disappearance of sovereignty, and hence the state, results

---

[14] See M. E. Bathurst and J. L. Simpson, *Germany and the Atlantic Community: A Legal Survey* (London: Stevens & Sons, Ltd., 1956), pp. 30-41.

in important changes in the nature of the values and institutions of a people depends in large part on the kind of authority with which national sovereignty is replaced. If, as some see as the likely outcome of the trend toward integration, the sovereignty of six states of Western Europe should be merged in a political federation, the result would probably be not only the preservation, but the augmentation of the basic values of the people in the former states. Some contend that only if the nations of the Atlantic Community, including the United States, agree to establish a new state based on federal principles, can they hope to preserve their basic values. Still others believe that world federation, although it would mean the loss of national sovereignty, is necessary to the preservation of values jeopardized by policies which most states necessarily follow in the name of national security in an anarchistic state system. On the other hand, if a non-communist nation were annexed or dominated by the Soviet Union or Communist China, its entire way of life would be materially changed. Such has been the result of Soviet annexation of Estonia, Latvia, and Lithuania, as well as her domination of the nominally sovereign Soviet satellite states of eastern Europe.

Although the disappearance of the state would not necessarily mean the loss of any value other than sovereignty, as long as states remain the dominant form of political organization in international society national security will be necessary to protect many values, including life itself. In particular, peace will constitute the basic requisite for national security, and indirectly the security of values held by a people. This does not mean that nations may not resort to war to obtain rather than to secure values, or even that they will not initiate a preventive or pre-emptive war if they feel their vital interests threatened.

Stress on Security a
Result of Growing Insecurity

Our second contention is that the quest for security is a dominant force in international behavior because insecurity is inherent in the multi-state system, and that insecurity is increasing. One of the greatest differences between the century before 1914 and the years since is the contrast between the relative peace and security of the former and the increasing fear and feeling of insecurity that has prevailed since. The frantic attempts to make nations secure is a rough measure of their failures rather than of their successes in achieving security. In a previous chapter we raised the question of whether a number of developments, particularly the revolution in military technology which has made it possible to "overleap" the territorial boundaries of states and to destroy life and its material base, have not made it impossible for the nation-state to perform its basic function—that of protecting its own existence and the other values of society.[15] If man is persuaded that this is so, then he must conclude that the multi-state system has outlived its usefulness. As long as the multi-state system exists, however, national security will remain a vital objective. Moreover, its influence will increase if, as is highly probable, the feeling of insecurity continues to grow.

Our discussion of the evolution and nature of international society has indicated that even in the less precarious past nations have frequently been destroyed, or, escaping that fate, have nevertheless been unable to protect many values against outside foes. The process of organizing the world society has had as its principal impetus concern with peace and the national security for which peace was deemed necessary. In particular, the League of Nations and its contemporary counterpart, the UN, were organized principally to realize these ends. Both attempted to do so by almost every conceivable device consistent with the existence of sovereign states. However successful either might have been in former ages, and however worse off the world would have been without them, it has nevertheless grown more insecure even with them. That political objectives, and especially national security, is a dominant concern for most nations was evident in our discussion of both ideological and economic forces and objectives. It was particularly clear that economics is more often a tool of politics than the reverse. In the following chapters we shall see the variety of means and policy patterns, almost every conceivable one in fact, either used or advocated, to further peace and security. In view of the wide variety of medicines tried or prescribed for the disease of national insecurity—while all the time the patient grows steadily worse—one may well wonder whether the difficulty has been correctly diagnosed, or indeed whether the malady is curable.

COSTS OF INSECURITY

Those of you who have read to this point may be under a strong impression that if only peace could be preserved all would be well. This does not necessarily follow, for national security measures are costly even if they succeed in preventing wars. Indeed one may well raise the question whether many of the values sought by national security policies may not be destroyed by these very means. The huge monetary outlays for military preparation, always and everywhere claimed to be necessary for national defense, may not be the most important of the sacrifices made upon the altar of national security.

Martin Wight, in warning us to guard against the notion that political morality is especially or exclusively an Anglo-Saxon product, points out that Gladstone's Britain and Roosevelt's America were "Dominant

---

[15] See above, pp. 36-38.

Powers." "This will remind us of the great truth that morality in international politics is not simply a matter of civilized tradition, but is equally the result of security. . . . Once security is destroyed, all the higher objects of politics are swallowed up in the struggle for self-preservation, a tendency seen in every war."[16]

A student of modern European history writes in a similar vein. Surveying the period after 1815, following the Napoleonic Wars, when Europe experienced her greatest security since the advent of the modern state system, he concludes that "it seems as though men became generous and tolerant toward their fellows as they felt themselves to be secure."[17]

The return of military insecurity to the European world [after 1914] enhanced the role of the state far beyond anything that the first democrats could possibly imagine. The state must tax as never before, it must employ more people, train more soldiers, build up defense industries, restrict the freedom of the individual, establish the loyalty of its subjects, and so on. Government presses us on every side. The situaton shows clearly that men cannot be free when dominated by the fear that they are threatened by the aggression of a Power capable of destroying them. Rarely has it appeared so self-evident as now that men who desire to retain their freedoms should not permit a situation to arise in which their choice is between freedom and security. It is inconceivable that men will place freedom ahead of fundamental security in our time. Security has become the concept before which men will bend their minds and wills today. [18]

The study of the history of the last three generations, Rudin holds, offers some principles of relevance for action:

1. The greatest insecurity is that arising from the threat of modern war. To place other considerations ahead of that threat will be to lose all.

. . .

3. No people's military . . . security can be successfully based on the insecurity of others, whether the latter be Russian, Asian, or African. . . .

4. Men must be warned against attaching their sense of security to existing . . . institutions in the belief that these institutions will serve in the future the security needs they serve at the present time. Men must learn that no institution is proof against the changes that time sooner or later produces in them. No matter how beneficial they may be in conferring a sense of security, they cannot be made permanent, however reverential the awe in which they are held, however great the sacrifices may be that are made for them. To bind one's security to what must change will be fatal to all hope. To blame adherents of other ideologies and practices for the changes wrought by passing time in our institutions and beliefs is a dangerous superstition that may lead to wars destructive of everything.[19]

---

[16] Martin Wight, *Power Politics* (London: *Royal Institute of International Affairs,* 1946), pp. 64, 65.

[17] Harry R. Rudin, "Diplomacy, Democracy, Security: Two Centuries in Contrast," *Political Science Quarterly,* LXXI (June 1956), 169.

[18] *Ibid.,* p. 179.

[19] *Ibid.,* pp. 180-81.

SUGGESTED READINGS

Almond, Gabriel A., "Public Opinion and National Security Policy," *Public Opinion Quarterly*, XX (Summer 1956), 371-78.

Beard, Charles A. and G. H. E. Smith, *The Idea of National Interest: An Analytical Study in American Foreign Policy.* New York: The Macmillan Co., 1934.

Brower, Michael J., *The U.S. National Interest: Assertions and Definitions.* Cambridge: Center for International Studies, Massachusetts Institute of Technology, 1951. (Mimeographed.)

Burns, Arthur, "International Consequences of Expecting Surprise," *World Politics*, X (July 1958), 512-36.

Butterfield, Herbert, "The Tragic Element in Modern International Conflict," *Review of Politics*, XII (1950), 147-64.

"The Idea of National Interest," Symposium, *American Perspective*, IV (Fall 1960), 335-401.

Kirk, Grayson, "In Search of the National Interest," *World Politics*, V (October 1952), 110-15.

Lincoln, George A., *Economics of National Security: Managing America's Resources for Defense*, 2d ed. Englewood Cliffs, N.J.: Prentice-Hall, Inc., 1954.

McNeil, Elton B., "Psychology and Aggression," *Journal of Conflict Resolution*, III (1959), 195-293.

Marchant, P. D., "Realism and Foreign Policy," *International Relations*, XI (Apr. 1959), 557-76.

Marshall, Charles B., "The National Interest and Current World Problems," *Department of State Bulletin*, XXVI (May 5, 1952), 698-702.

Morgenthau, Hans J., "Another 'Great Debate': The National Interest of the United States," *American Political Science Review*, XLVI (Dec. 1952), 961-88.

———, *In Defense of the National Interest: A Critical Examination of American Foreign Policy.* New York: Alfred A. Knopf, Inc., 1951.

"The National Interest: Alone or With Others," *Annals of the American Academy of Political and Social Science*, ed. Norman D. Palmer, CCLXXXII (July 1952), 1-118.

Padelford, Norman J., "The Insecurity of States," *Western Political Quarterly*, IV (Sept. 1951), 387-96.

Rockefeller Brothers Fund, *International Security: The Military Aspects; Report of Panel II of the Special Studies Project.* Garden City, New York: Doubleday & Company, 1958.

Rudin, Harry R., "Diplomacy, Democracy, Security: Two Centuries in Contrast," *Political Science Quarterly*, LXXI (June 1956), 161-81.

Schuman, Frederick L., "International Ideals and the National Interest," *Annals of the American Academy of Political and Social Science*, CCLXXX (Mar. 1952), 27-36.

Shelling, Warner R., "The Clarification of Ends, or, Which Interest is the National," *World Politics*, VIII (July 1956), 566-78.

Stanley, Timothy W., *American Defense and National Security*. Washington, D.C.: Public Affairs Press, 1956.

Thompson, Kenneth W., "National Security in a Nuclear Age," *Social Research*, XXV (1958), 439-48.

Tucker, R. W., "Professor Morgenthau's Theory of Political 'Realism,'" *American Political Science Review*, XLVI (Mar. 1952), 214-24.

Wolfers, Arnold, "National Security as an Ambiguous Symbol," *Political Science Quarterly*, LXVII (Dec. 1952), 481-502.

III

FORMS AND
PROCEDURES

INTRODUCTION

International decision-makers, in responding to dynamic forces and pursuing their goals, operate through a complex set of institutional forms and procedures. Each state has political and legal institutions and personnel responsible for performing the several tasks involved in its relationships with other states and international organizations. Some states must also deal with dependent peoples under their jurisdiction. International organizations, of which the United Nations is only the most prominent, are instruments through which states and dependent peoples carry on their relationships and at the same time entities which interact among themselves and with states and dependent peoples. There are also established methods for settling international disputes and changing international legal rights and obligations.

In Part III, we first examine the machinery and personnel established by governments for carrying on their relations. We then turn our attention to international organizations, some of which are world-wide while others have more limited membership. Either type may have a wide range of responsibilities or be concerned with but a narrow range of activities. A final chapter deals with the methods and institutions available to states and international organizations for settling differences by means short of force.

7

Government Structure and
the Conduct of Foreign Relations

The purpose of organization is to relate people, ideas, and things in ways that will maximize their effectiveness. The way a government is organized, however, influences not only the efficiency with which its foreign policy is administered, but its substance as well. The increasing concern of analysts and officials with organization reflects the growing recognition of its importance.[1]

Recent changes in the magnitude, character, and tempo of international relations have led to many changes in governmental machinery, especially on the administrative side. Although government structures vary from country to country, all governments must perform certain tasks in order to conduct their foreign relations. To enable them to do so, they have established organizations and procedures, alike in many respects, both in their own countries and abroad.

Foreign policy is variously defined. In its broadest sense, it includes the objectives, plans, and actions taken by a state relative to its external relationships. Some writers, however, prefer to speak of foreign *policies*, rather than policy. For example, a state is said to have economic, military, or cultural policies, or even several policies relating to each of these matters. The UN does not have a *foreign* policy; from its standpoint there is nothing foreign. One might, perhaps, refer to its policies

---

[1] For a review of the literature on the subject, see: Arthur W. Macmahon, "The Administration of Foreign Affairs," *American Political Science Review*, XLV (Sept. 1951), 836-66. Also see: Kurt London, *How Foreign Policy is Made* (New York: D. Van Nostrand Co., Inc., 1919); William J. Gore and Fred S. Silander, "A Bibliographical Essay on Decision Making," *Administrative Science Quarterly*, IV (June 1959), 97-122.

as being international. Nor does a dependent area have a foreign policy in the same sense as does a state, although its people and leaders may have a policy toward the governing power.

As used in this context, foreign policy is more narrowly defined: it refers to the *actions* (including words) *of government officials to influence human behavior beyond the jurisdiction of their own state.* It thus excludes objectives, especially the ultimate ones, as well as policy plans. Plans and policies do not necessarily correspond. The U.S., for example, stated in its early 1945 postwar plans that it intended to break up the German cartels, although its representatives in that country were not doing so. Plans were later changed to correspond with policy, rather than the other way around.

Foreign policy is not international relations, although it is one of its elements. A relationship is an interaction. International relations result from the action (policy) taken by officials of an international entity and the responses, or reactions, by those of one or more of the other entities. The network of these interactions constitutes international relations in the strict sense of that term. This chapter, therefore, is concerned with only one aspect of international relations. Its vantage point is that of states as entities or parts of the system, rather than the system itself.

THE FOREIGN AFFAIRS TASKS

The actions referred to herein as foreign policy necessitate a number of tasks or functions: (1) the formulation of objectives; (2) the development of plans; (3) their administration (foreign policy in the strict sense); and (4) co-ordination. Although it may appear that the first three tasks should take place in sequence, the reality is quite different. Rather, they proceed simultaneously as the objectives (especially subordinate ones) as well as the plans and policies are modified in response to changing circumstances and to insights gained through experience.[2]

Many subordinate functions, ranging from typing to fighting, are required to carry out these major tasks. One of the most important of these is "intelligence." This refers to the collection, classification, and evaluation of pertinent data about the internal and external situation. Since such data can seldom be evaluated by mathematical or other objective means, it is at this point that the personality characteristics of the actors are especially important. No two men are likely to see precisely the same significance in identical data. The different estimates made by responsi-

---

[2] For somewhat different classifications of these tasks or functions see: Richard C. Snyder and Edgar S. Furniss, Jr., *American Foreign Policy* (New York: Holt, Rinehart, & Winston, Inc., 1954), Chap. 3, "The Decision Making Process"; Charles O. Lerche, Jr., *Foreign Policy of the American People*, 2nd ed. (Englewood Cliffs, N.J.: Prentice-Hall, Inc., 1961), Chap. 1, "What is Foreign Policy?"

ble American decision-makers with respect to the intentions and policies of the Soviet Union, and of the capacity and actions required by the United States to meet the Soviet challenge, are evidence of this fact. Another function consists of explaining plans to others—colleagues in the government, political leaders, powerful public groups, even allies—and obtaining their agreement. This is necessary because seldom can one decision-maker or group act alone.

Determining Basic Objectives

Basic objectives refer to the actual ends of foreign policy pursued under the existing circumstances, rather than aspirations which might be sought in a different environment. A country might, for example, give far greater weight to the end of elevating the levels of living for others out of pure humanitarianism were it not confronted by the necessity of building military strength. "Working objectives" are the product of historical tradition, basic values or ideologies, particular interests and interest groups, the existing environment—internal and external—and the resources which a state may employ in their pursuit. The general public can seldom accept fully, at face value, the statements of its officials in this respect. For what the latter may call "objectives" are in reality a mixture of objectives and propaganda designed for both home and foreign consumption. While greater frankness is often desirable, under the prevailing state of public opinion, international tensions, and slanted news reporting, any considerable improvement is hardly to be expected.

Developing Policy Plans

Policy may be wholly improvised, or it may be planned in minute detail before its execution; but in practice, either extreme would be impossible, undesirable, or both. At best, the major outlines may be blueprinted and some of the more important details sketched in. This is so because the determinants of foreign policy undergo continuous change, because not all contingencies can be foreseen, and because the conduct of foreign relations, more art than science, of necessity requires experimentation and revision. For all these reasons, policies, more so than basic objectives, are continually readjusted.

Yet policy plans are necessary. Only through careful planning can their executors be expected to act with intelligence and dispatch; without it, indecision and conflicting policies are inevitable. It is generally agreed that in the years immediately after 1945 in particular, the United States Department of State—and indeed the entire central government—were inadequately organized to develop a coherent foreign policy. Policy was "made on the cables" it was often said. Top officials in the Department of State were so involved in day-to-day operations that they had little time to develop long-term plans, and there was no existing machinery to do so at a lower level. Although the situation was subsequently improved, it remained far from satisfactory.

Administering Policy Plans

Implementation constitutes the third of the major functions necessary for the conduct of foreign affairs. There was a time when foreign policy consisted primarily of negotiations over political matters and the threat or use of force; today, it also covers a wide range of economic and social affairs. Moreover, and of even greater importance, foreign policy increasingly involves operations *within* other countries which affect the lives of people in a direct and intimate way not characteristic of traditional diplomacy, where the contacts were primarily between government officials. There are many examples of this trend. One is the increasing use of propaganda employed by a government to influence the attitudes and actions of the peoples of another country, and through them their governments. Most governments are engaged in activities of this nature, some on a modest and others on an elaborate scale. The economic programs operated by wealthier countries and by international organizations in the lesser developed states and dependent areas are especially characteristic of the "new dimensions of diplomacy." This had been described as a

. . . shift of the arena of world politics from "arms-length diplomacy" and "strategy" to the "domestic affairs" (political institutions, economic development, internal security) of the less developed nations outside of Europe. . . .

It is not too much to say that, for an American in the 1960's "international affairs" will be predominantly concerned with the internal affairs of other countries. Most Americans in responsible overseas jobs already perceive that by their action—or, indeed, their inaction—they are deeply affecting foreign societies from the inside, rather than dealing with them from the outside.[3]

States vary considerably in the extent and manner in which they participate in these newer types of programs, depending on their resources and their needs. Those which are willing and able to contribute to the development of those less fortunately endowed are far more involved in the so-called internal affairs of the receivers than are the latter in theirs. The results of these changes are many. Their impact must be considered in formulating foreign policy objectives and plans. To effect long-term development, governmental structures must be expanded and

---

[3] "The Operational Aspects of United States Foreign Policy," A Study by the Maxwell Graduate School of Citizenship and Public Affairs, Syracuse University, for the Committee on Foreign Relations, United States Senate, No. 6 (Washington, D.C.: Government Printing Office, Nov. 11, 1959), p. 9.

modified, and personnel with qualifications considerably different from those required for performing traditional functions must be selected and trained.

Coordinating Policy

Coordination consists of actions aimed at harmonious adjustment. Since development and implementation of effective foreign policy plans depend on coordination, this function is singled out for the purpose of emphasis rather than because it is, strictly speaking, a distinct function. The process of determining objectives is one of selecting the possible, or most desirable, among a number of alternatives, and of keeping all in proper relation one to another. Policy formulation likewise consists of deciding on those methods likely to accomplish the determined objectives by the use of available resources under existing conditions. Most agencies of government are concerned, in varying degree, with some aspect of the foreign relations of a country. An important part of the coordinating function, therefore, consists of seeing that all of them work to common purposes. It is small wonder that, under these circumstances, a succesful foreign policy calls for a high degree of centralized control.

GOVERNMENT ORGANS AND
THE CONDUCT OF FOREIGN RELATIONS

For purposes of analysis a distinction may be made between the "home" and the "field" organizations. This section deals with the former—the domestic ones. The following section discusses the latter—the agencies which carry on the conventional diplomatic and consular functions, representation at international organizations, and other types of activities abroad ranging from technical assistance to military occupation.

The Executive Branch

Although detailed arrangements for performing foreign policy tasks differ from country to country, they have certain common features and problems. Executive branches have primary responsibility for the conduct of foreign relations, even more so than for domestic policy. The President (as in the United States) or the cabinet (as in parliamentary systems) coordinates and directs the administrative branch and provides policy leadership and guidance for the legislature. In every country it is the executive branch which represents the government in its foreign relations, and this alone gives it a strategic advantage over the other organs of government.

The Legislature

In general, the influence of legislatures on foreign affairs is increasing, except within the dictatorships where they presumably have no more power in foreign than they do in domestic policy. As the public is more and more affected by foreign relations, it is inevitable that its representatives should be increasingly concerned with them. Furthermore, since almost any policy has its domestic and foreign repercussions, any influence a legislature might have is felt both at home and abroad. If food for India involves foreign policy, then so does soil conservation and parity payments for the Kansas wheat farmer. Finally, most foreign policies cost money, and in all democratic countries legislatures control the size of the governmental purse. Whether it is a question of the size of the military establishment or support of a technical assistance program, the decisions are reflected in the burden of taxation.

Executive-Legislative Relationships

Although executive-legislative relationships present problems in all democratic countries, the nature of these problems depends in large part on constitutional systems and party structures. In a country like the United States, with a separation of powers and relatively undisciplined and irresponsible parties, there may be no way, or at least no satisfactory one, to resolve a conflict between the President and the Congress. The problem is especially severe when Congress and the presidency are controlled by different parties. Although "bipartisanship" may be proposed to overcome the difficulty, it seldom does so in practice.

In a parliamentary or responsible-cabinet system, such as Great Britain's, where a one-party cabinet supported by a disciplined parliamentary majority is normal, and disagreement may be resolved by dissolution of Parliament, ordinarily deadlocks cannot occur. Under these circumstances the executive branch can speak with a firmer voice than it can where there is a separation of powers. Yet in a country with a parliamentary government, but with a multi-party system, the cabinet may be of the coalition type and thus dependent on the support of several parties. Even if dissolution is resorted to, no clear majority is likely to emerge. Although a deadlock is rare under a system of this sort, cabinets may fall and interparty adjustments take place. Under the latter circumstances executive leadership may be less firm than under presidential systems. Such was the case in France prior to 1958.

The Foreign Ministry

The main responsibility for foreign relations in every country rests in a foreign ministry. Yet it should be stressed that though it is the principal agency involved in these relations it is not the only one. Though its duties are seldom defined by law in precise terms, it usually performs a number of important functions. First, it supplies the political executive, the other administrative agencies, and the legislature with information on which foreign policies may be based. Either on its own initiative or that of other agencies, it formulates, or participates in the formulation of objectives and policies. It supervises the diplomatic and consular service stationed abroad. It conducts negotiations with the representatives of other governments, and usually works closely with other agencies which share in this responsibility. Lastly, it may engage in "operations," such as economic and propaganda activities. More often than not, however, these operations are carried on by other agencies, such as the British Board of Trade and the United States Information Agency (USIA).

Since the beginning of World War II, the increase in the volume and variety of the work of foreign ministries has led to an expansion of their budgets and personnel, as well as to organizational changes. A comparative survey of fourteen countries revealed that between 1940 and 1950 budget increases for support of the foreign office, the foreign service, and contributions to international organizations, ranged from one-third to fourteen times the prewar figure. For certain of the larger states the staff of the foreign office and foreign service appeared to have increased by nearly 500 per cent. In particular, large numbers of specialized personnel had been added to handle economic and technical as well as "informational" matters.[4]

Other Administrative Agencies

The dividing line between foreign and domestic affairs, always a thin one, has been broken as more and more of what happens within any one nation affects others. Nearly all agencies of government are therefore, in one way or another, involved in foreign affairs. The post office, for example, may be primarily responsible for internal policies; yet the postal ministry also determines policy in regard to the Universal Postal Union. Others, of which the military establishment is the most typical, may be primarily instruments for the conduct of foreign policy. Some may be concerned with applying international standards, such as labor and aviation conventions, on the domestic scene. Frequently a ministry is assigned major responsibility for formulating policy, and even for conducting negotiations on particular topics. In India the Labour Ministry serves as the "operative" agency for the International Labor Or-

---

[4] *National Administration and International Organization: A Comparative Survey of Fourteen Countries,* Report of an Inquiry Conducted Jointly by the International Institute of Administrative Sciences and UNESCO (Brussels: 1951).

ganization, the Finance Ministry for the International Bank and Fund, and the Agricultural Ministry for the Food and Agriculture Organization. In most countries, responsibilities for relations with the United Nations Economic and Social Council and its commissions, and with the specialized agencies of the UN are allocated in this fashion.

Coordinating Machinery

Since many administrative agencies participate in various aspects of foreign affairs, and relations are maintained with a large number of countries both bilaterally and multilaterally through international organizations, it is as important as it is difficult to act consistently.

The problem of interdepartmental coordination is attacked in many ways. Informal means such as telephone calls, memoranda, discussions over the luncheon table, and *ad hoc* meetings help to resolve differences and to arrive at common understandings. Useful as these devices are, more formal and permanent arrangements are also required. The final responsibility for coordination lies at the presidential or cabinet level. But men in those positions are exceedingly busy and only the most important matters should be brought to their attention.

Many countries have established interdepartmental committees. At the highest level are the subcommittees of the cabinet, such as the National Security Council in the United States. If these organs are to work effectively they must be provided with a permanent secretariat which gathers information, drafts proposals, prepares the agenda, and sees that the decisions are carried out. But even the most efficient "top" committees cannot possibly handle the entire burden of coordination among agencies. Lower-level committees are therefore established by most governments. Here issues may be resolved which are then reviewed only perfunctorily, if at all, by the high officials; and many papers are prepared for higher consideration which contain essential background facts, and present the advantages and disadvantages of policy alternatives. Through these various formal and informal devices governments attempt to work out consistent foreign policies and to make certain that their representatives work to common purposes in the different national capitals and in the many international organizations.[5]

FOREIGN REPRESENTATION

Traditionally, most of the official business between countries at peace has been transacted between diplomats and officials of the governments

---

[5] For an excellent description of how fourteen countries have organized to meet the problems of dealing with the UN and its affiliated organs, see the study cited in Note 4. In addition to its primary purpose, this study also throws considerable light on the broader problem of governmental organization for handling foreign affairs.

to which they have been accredited. Moreover, their relations have been confined largely to political matters. The impact of contemporary international relations has been as great on the "field" as it has on the "home" organization. Bilateral diplomacy continues to be important, but with the proliferation of international organization, especially since World War II, foreign relations are channeled more and more through multilateral international bodies. Furthermore, although the professional diplomat still plays an important role in conducting political negotiations, if he is to be effective he must be informed about and concerned with a broad range of subjects. An increasing number of specialists in economics, finance, culture and propaganda, education, agriculture, health, public welfare, military matters, and the like, are also required to carry on the modern business of foreign relations.

In many instances those who work abroad have little or nothing to do with the conventional type of diplomacy; they may work more closely with the people of a country than with the government. A Point Four technician is likely to find a knowledge of native customs and rice culture more valuable than drawing-room manners and an acquaintance with international law.

The Diplomatic Service

The exchange of diplomatic agents on a temporary basis is as old as recorded history. It became a regular practice with the Greeks, who recognized the exchange of ambassadors as among the rights and duties of sovereign states. The Italian city-states exchanged diplomatic agents in the late Middle Ages, and, about 1450, Milan established a permanent embassy in Florence. The practice of permanent representation spread rapidly throughout Europe.

Prior to 1815 rank and precedence among representatives stationed at foreign courts were frequent sources of difficulty. Since an envoy represented his sovereign, the way he was treated indicated the power and prestige of that sovereign and of his state. These matters were therefore taken quite seriously. The absence of standard rules of protocol often obstructed the conduct of diplomatic relations, led to threats of, and sometimes prolonged, war. The Peace of Westphalia (1648) was delayed for several years for this reason. At the Congress of Vienna in 1814, diplomatic agents were divided into four classes: ambassadors, envoys extraordinary and ministers plenipotentiary, ministers resident, and chargés d'affaires. Representatives of each class, in the order indicated, took precedence over those of lower rank. Within each class, seniority, that is time in residence at a particular capital, determined precedence.

Although ambassadors were once generally exchanged only among the most important powers, if any rule applies today in determining the rank of the head of a mission it is that of the importance attached to the relation between particular countries. Prestige, therefore, has led to the elevation of most heads of missions to ambassadorial rank. The practice has also developed of appointing representatives to international bodies and as members of special missions with the personal rank of ambassador or minister, even though they do not head missions or legations. In some instances a high-ranking staff member in an embassy may be given the title of minister if it is necessary for him to substitute frequently for an ambassador.

The members of diplomatic missions are, by customary international law, accorded certain rights and privileges. The establishment itself is regarded as a part of the territory of the state represented, and members of the diplomatic corps are exempt from the criminal and civil processes of the receiving country. These rules are among the best observed of all international law.

It is debatable whether the functions of diplomats are more or less important than they were when communication with the home office was a matter of weeks rather than minutes. Although they make fewer decisions on their own today, they are not less important; and they may be more so than formerly, in view of their manifold duties.

What are the chief functions of the diplomatic service? In the first place, the chief of mission, and to a lesser extent other members of his staff, represents the home government in ceremonial and social affairs. These extend not only to the receiving government, but to the other diplomatic services represented in the capital. In addition, he is expected to appear before many non-official groups. Among the most time-consuming and often vexing of duties is that of helping the nationals of his home country. This may range from performing marriages and issuing passports to getting fellow citizens out of jail.

One of the most important functions of the diplomatic service is that of an intelligence agency, reporting its findings to the home government. Only on the basis of facts will the latter be able to formulate wise and consistent policy. So wide and varied is the range of information needed that even the largest and ablest foreign service establishment is still quite inadequate. The home government will of course be interested in political developments, both internal and international. It will also want to know about the personalities of key figures in government, politics, labor, and industry. Industrial production, the size and morale of the military establishment, the state of public opinion, especially its attitude and reaction to the policy of his government, are indicative of the information useful to the home office.

An enumeration of facts will not be sufficient; an analysis and evaluation from persons on the spot is most important for the policy-makers at home. Implicitly, if not explicitly, these reports contain recommendations which may influence a country's policy. In any case, a diplomat is likely to shape policy more at this stage than in the actual negotiating process, where he may be allowed little discretion. Only a well-trained and courageous foreign service, and one that is protected from vindictive retaliation, can be expected to report the situation abroad in an objective fashion. If reports contain unpleasant, and sometimes even mistaken but honest judgments, they are less likely to lead to bad consequences than are those shaped to please the home government.

In the strict sense of the term, diplomacy means negotiation. This is the oldest, and in previous ages the most important function of diplomats. Although many writers on diplomacy tend to overrate the importance of the skill and other personal qualities of diplomats, and to underrate that of well-conceived policy plans and the power with which a negotiator can back up his demands and proposals, the former is still of some importance. Equally, if not more important than skill at the conference table is the ability of a diplomat to establish proper relationships with the government to which he is assigned. The care with which he prepared the ground may be quite important for the growth and ultimate fruition of negotiations over specific matters. Diplomacy is not entirely a cold and mechanical affair; personal qualities do enter in. It is, therefore, the diplomat's duty to attempt to establish friendly personal relationships with those with whom he transacts the business of state.

The importance of the conventional bilateral diplomatic services in conducting negotiations is diminished by three developments. The first is the tendency of foreign offices to supply detailed instructions, not only prior to the opening of negotiations but as they progress from day to day. The representatives of the Soviet Union appear at times to be little more than phonograph records for relaying instructions from the Kremlin; the old record is played until a new one is received. The British and French representatives are less circumscribed, and those of India appear to have considerable freedom.

In the second place, many of the negotiations are taken out of the regular channels of bilateral diplomacy as foreign policy is increasingly channeled through international organizations. If policy relates to technical and non-political matters, such as health, labor, and aviation, the home ministries primarily concerned ordinarily participate in the negotiations just as they do in policy formation.

Thirdly, if major political considerations are involved, negotiations may be conducted by "top level" officials. Roosevelt, Stalin, and Churchill personally conducted some of the most important diplomacy of World War II, not only at Cairo, Teheran, and Yalta, but through correspondence and over the telephone. After World War II, foreign ministers participated directly in the most important of the negotiations. Several attended the United Nations Conference at San Francisco, as well as subsequent meetings of that organization. In a series of sessions, the Council of Foreign Ministers hammered out the European peace treaties and dealt with problems relating to Germany and Austria. Both the foreign and the prime ministers have taken an active role in the negotiations relating to the integration of Western Europe. The most important decisions of NATO are made when its Council meetings are attended by the foreign ministers.

In 1955, and for a period thereafter, "summitry" was again in vogue as the heads of state met, or planned to meet, to solve problems apparently thought too important or too refractory to be handled at lower levels. Students of international relations tend to be skeptical of this diplomacy. Although they grant that it may have a place, their view is that only when agreements are first negotiated by experts at lower levels should higher level officials sometimes assemble to dramatize the meeting of minds. Conventional diplomats may have an important role in negotiations of this type. The American ambassadors in London and Paris will sound out the foreign offices there, inform them of the views of the United States Department of State, and attempt to reconcile divergent positions prior to a conference of high officials.

Though these are the major functions of the diplomatic service, they are by no means all of them. Nearly all diplomatic missions are responsible for certain aspects of information and propaganda programs, such as that of the United States Information Agency. Countries which operate overseas economic programs—technical and economic assistance, for example—may assign at least supervisory responsibility to the diplomatic mission. Whatever the relative importance of diplomatic services today and a hundred years ago, one may certainly conclude that they perform indispensable functions in the conduct of foreign relations.

The Consular Service

Permanent consulates were established several hundred years before the first permanent embassies. Their primary purpose has always been the protection and promotion of trade and commerce. But they also perform an almost infinite variety of other functions, of which the following are illustrative rather than inclusive. Services to nationals are among their prime duties. While these may at times require intercession with local authorities, they more often take the form of advice on local laws and customs. Persons stranded for lack of funds frequently turn to consulates. The care of the effects and estates of nationals who die abroad is another important consular function. Nationals living abroad may be required to register at the nearest consulate. The issuance of visas is frequently a time-consuming and trying function, especially for consulates of countries such as the United States which receive considerable numbers of immigrants. Consulates may also issue and renew passports. They work closely with the diplomatic missions, and to some extent their work overlaps. Normally, however, consulates do not conduct negotiations with the central governments, for that is the distinct function of the diplomatic service.

Consular officials usually enjoy privileges and immunities necessary to the performance of their functions, but these are less extensive than those accorded diplomats. Although the basis of their immunities is not entirely clear, they appear to rest upon treaties and conventions rather than customary international law. So extensive and inclusive is the network of bilateral agreements respecting these matters that the difference is without much significance.

Consular officers are usually divided into five classes: consuls general, consuls, vice-consuls, vice-consuls of career, and consular agents. The consul general is usually in charge of all of his government's consulates in a given country. If there is no consul general in a country, a consul may perform the general supervisory function. Otherwise consuls and vice-consuls head consulates in certain districts, or serve as subordinate officials.[6]

Informational, Cultural, and Economic Representation

An increasing number of those working abroad for their governments are not representatives in the traditional sense. Rather they serve as advisers to foreign governments or actually work in their administrations. As the British Empire is liquidated, members of Her Majesty's Overseas Civil Service often continue on to assist the governments of newly independent countries. Many American advisers and workers help governments abroad in the furtherance of the United States Mutual Assistance Program. Those who serve the UN and its affiliated agencies are similarly engaged.

Equally important is the fact that an increasing number of persons are sent abroad by their governments to work directly with the people of foreign countries rather than with their governments, although through government-to-government arrangements. Those who conduct "information" programs, both of a short-time propaganda and a long-term cultural and educational character, serve in this manner. So do many of those in technical assistance and economic programs.

Those in these newer types of activities may or may not be a part of

[6] See Graham Stuart, *American Diplomatic and Consular Practice*, 2nd ed. (New York: Appleton-Century-Crofts, Inc., 1952), Chap. XVII.

the regular foreign service. Great Britain has a unified Foreign Service, whose personnel are subject to assignment at home and abroad (outside the Commonwealth and Empire), and to diplomatic, consular, diplomatic-commercial, and informational activities. On the other hand, the United States, in addition to its regular Foreign Service, has a separate set of personnel for its overseas information activities and still another for its technical and economic assistance programs. In most countries, there were originally separate diplomatic and consular services, and another to staff the foreign ministries. The trend has been to combine all these into a unified service, subject to assignment at home and abroad, and to either diplomatic or consular work. The forces which account for this consolidation will probably result eventually in the inclusion of those engaged in these newer activities in a unified foreign service.

Diplomacy by Conference

Many governments have organized special agencies or committees to assist in the formulation of policy for and to coordinate the work of their delegations to international organizations.[7] Most states have found it advantageous to maintain permanent representation at UN headquarters, and to a lesser extent at those of its regional offices in Geneva. Others in addition assign permanent missions to the headquarters of several of the specialized agencies, such as UNESCO, and to the regional UN commissions.

The permanent missions to the UN maintain liaison with the Secretariat and with other missions, report to their home offices, and represent their governments in the many meetings held throughout the year, especially those of technical committees. At the more important meetings, especially of the main organs, they handle housekeeping arrangements for the national delegations and serve as their advisers.

The delegations to the major meetings of the UN, as well as to other important conferences, usually consist, in part at least, of persons selected for that particular purpose. Members of administrative agencies, parliaments, and in some cases private citizens, make up the delegations. When members of parties which oppose the government in power are included, it is sometimes difficult to get them to carry out governmental policy.[8]

Delegates to international organizations represent governments, just as do members of diplomatic and consular services. If people are represented it is only through their governments. Yet there may be certain subtle differences between the outlook of the older divisions of foreign offices and foreign services on the one hand, and government agencies

---

[7] See *National Administration and International Organization: A Comparative Study of Fourteen Countries*, pp. 26-38.

[8] For a discussion of these matters see *ibid.*

concerned with and delegations to international organizations on the other. The report of a Woodrow Wilson Study Group suggested that one difference is probably due to

. . . the importance attached in United Nations circles, American and foreign, to the United Nations as an institution, rather than just a forum of diplomacy. [The Group members believe that] . . . few people can be long associated with United Nations headquarters without being affected by the symbolism and spirit which tend to give it its own meaning and its own institutional existence. [Closely related to this] . . . there is a different sense of relationship to the American public and Congress on the part of people engaged in United Nations work than on the part of people in the more traditional phases of American diplomatic activity. There is a feeling in some quarters that those people who represent the United States in the United Nations have a different and closer bond with the American public, and a greater duty to speak for the public directly, than would normally be felt by the traditional apparatus of the Department of State and the Foreign Service.[9]

Although these attitudes have hardly developed sufficiently to be of immediate importance, if they should continue to grow, their eventual effect on traditional foreign policy, on the international organizations themselves, and hence on international relations in general, would be revolutionary.

SUGGESTED READINGS

Acheson, Dean G., *Meetings at the Summit: A Study of Diplomatic Method;
    An address at the University of New Hampshire, May 8, 1958*. Durham,
    New Hampshire: University of New Hampshire Press, 1958.
———, "The Responsibility for Decisions in Foreign Policy," *Yale Review*,
    XLIV (Sept. 1954), 1-12.
Beloff, Max, *Foreign Policy and the Democratic Process*. Baltimore: The Johns
    Hopkins Press, 1955.
Bishop, Donald G., *The Administration of British Foreign Relations*. Syracuse,
    New York: Syracuse University Press, 1961.
Bourbon-Busset, Jacques de, "How Decisions are Made in Foreign Politics:
    Psychology in International Relations," *Review of Politics*, XX (Oct. 1958),
    591-614.
Byrd, Elbert M., *Treaties and Executive Agreements in the United States:
    Their Separate Roles and Limitations*. The Hague: N. V. M. Nijhoff, 1960.
Claude, Inis L., Jr., "Multilateralism: Diplomatic and Otherwise," *International
    Organization*, XII (Winter 1958), 43-52.

---

[9] Reprinted from *United States Foreign Policy: Its Organization and Control*, The Report of a Study Group for the Woodrow Wilson Foundation, William Y. Elliott, Chairman (New York: Columbia University Press, 1952), p. 167.

Cleveland, Harlan and Gerald J. Mangone, eds., *The Art of Overseasmanship*. Syracuse, New York: Syracuse University Press, 1957.

Craig, Gordon A., and Felix Gilbert, eds., *The Diplomats: 1919-1939*. Princeton, N.J.: Princeton University Press, 1953.

Grégoire, Roger, *National Administration and International Organization: The Administrative Problems Arising in Newly Independent Countries as a Result of their Participation in the United Nations and the Specialized Agencies*. Paris: UNESCO, 1956.

Hilsman, Roger, "Intelligence and Policy-Making in Foreign Affairs," *World Politics*, V (Oct. 1952), 1-45.

——, *Strategic Intelligence and National Decisions*. Glencoe, Illinois: Free Press of Glencoe, Inc., 1956.

Hoffman, Stanley, "National Attitudes and International Order: The National Studies on International Organization," *International Organization*, XIII (Spring 1959), 189-203.

Holt, Robert T. and Robert W. van de Velde, *Strategic Psychological Operations and American Foreign Policy*. Chicago: University of Chicago Press, 1960.

Kent, Sherman, *Strategic Intelligence for American World Policy*. Princeton, N.J.: Princeton University Press, 1949.

Macmahon, Arthur W., "Problems in the Administration of Foreign Affairs," *Indian Journal of Public Administration*, VI (Apr.-June 1960), 109-24.

Macridis, Roy C., ed., *Foreign Policy in World Politics*, 2nd ed. Englewood Cliffs, N.J.: Prentice-Hall, Inc., 1962.

Mayer, Arno J., *Political Origin of the New Diplomacy: 1917-18*. New Haven: Yale University Press, 1959.

Nicolson, Sir Harold George, *Diplomacy*, 2nd ed. London, New York: Oxford University Press, Inc., 1952.

——, *The Evolution of Diplomatic Method, being the Chichele Lectures delivered at the University of Oxford in November 1953*. London: Constable, 1954.

Ransom, Harry H., *Central Intelligence and National Security*. Cambridge: Harvard University Press, 1958.

Richardson, Channing B., "The United States Mission to the United Nations," *International Organization*, VII (Feb. 1953), 22-34.

U.S. Senate, Foreign Relations Committee, *United States Foreign Policy: Compilation of Studies, Nos. 1-13*, 2 vols. No. 9. "The Formulation and Administration of United States Foreign Policy," by the Brookings Institution. Committee Print, 86th Cong., 2nd sess., 1960, pp. 791-990. Washington, D.C.: Government Printing Office, 1960.

——, *United States Foreign Policy: Compilation of Studies, Nos. 1-13*, 2 vols. No. 6. "The Operational Aspects of United States Foreign Policy," by Maxwell Graduate School of Citizenship and Public Affairs, Syracuse University. Committee Print, 86th Cong., 2nd sess., 1960, pp. 555-634. Washington, D.C.: Government Printing Office, 1960.

Vagts, Alfred, *Defense and Diplomacy: The Soldier and the Conduct of Foreign Relations*. New York: King's Crown Press, 1956.

Westerfield, Bradford, *Foreign Policy and Party Politics: Pearl Harbor to Korea*. New Haven: Yale University Press, 1955.

Wriston, Henry Merritt, *Diplomacy in a Democracy*. New York: Harper & Brothers, 1956.

8

Organizing the World Society

International organizations exist because we live in an interdependent world, one in which many of the needs of man cannot be served adequately unless certain aspects of his life are organized on an international basis. Man's principal needs are security and welfare. To achieve these he needs peace and international cooperation. Two aims, therefore, the prevention of war and the improvement of the social and economic lot of man, are the principal drives behind the international organization process. The wealthier nations quite naturally stress peace and security, whereas the poorer ones emphasize improvement of the economic and social welfare of their citizens.

That nations should pursue additional, and often less noble aims, through these organizations should be quite understandable. Even within the more integrated domestic societies men also attempt to serve their personal goals and ambitions, often at the expense of the general welfare. It would, then, be little less than miraculous if international behavior were motivated by pure altruism. That individuals and nations are also expected to misbehave at times is evidenced by the fact that governments and many international organizations have responsibilities for dealing with certain kinds of misbehavior.

International organizations and governments are both alike and different. Their general purposes are similar, and they resemble each other in many of their functions and methods. Both promote cooperative behavior and perform a wide range of services. Both encourage and assist individuals and groups to settle their differences, as far as possible in accordance with standards of justice, and by means which do not endanger the peace and welfare of other members of society.

International organizations differ from governments principally in that they have very little authority to bind and coerce their members: they may assist in formulating policy plans but they do not enact law. There are no international law-enforcing executive agencies comparable to the executives of national states. Although international courts and arbitral tribunals do hand down binding decisions, there is no international hierarchy of courts; and, with some exceptions, jurisdiction is voluntary rather than compulsory. Thus, treaties are ordinarily not binding on states unless they have consented to them. International law depends for its interpretation, observance, and enforcement primarily upon individual states.

Yet it should not be assumed that governments, in any case democratic ones, behave very differently from international organizations when confronted with similar situations.

The truth is that all governments rely heavily—and that the most desirable governments rely predominantly—upon noncoercive methods for producing and maintaining social order. To say that international organization has distinguished itself most notably by creating a record of persistence, flexibility, and ingenuity in the development and exploitation of devices for inducing compliance by consent rather than compulsion is not to say that it has proved absolutely either the impossibility or the indispensability of creating a world government. Rather, it is to say that some of the basic means for governing the world have been evolved and are being utilized with increasing effectiveness by agencies which do not conform to theoretical models of governmental institutions. It is surprising how many estimable people, who would recoil with horror at the thought of a purely coercive government in the United States and insist with intelligent understanding that a decent political order in the nation must rest upon processes of inducement and adjustment rather than upon sheer force, seem to picture government solely in terms of a policeman beating criminals into submission when they shift their attention to the international scene. People are being governed at other times than when they cower before a policeman and languish in prison cells. Nations are being governed at other times than when they are being prohibited, restrained and compelled.[1]

The chief impediment to the development of effective international institutions is nationalism and its concomitant, the absence of a real world community. As long as people think of themselves as members of a national rather than of a world community, and insist upon sovereignty for their states, it will be difficult to create international institutions adequate to cope with the problems of an interdependent world and to realize the potential benefits of interdependence. The basic question, therefore, is the relationship between institutions and a feeling of community. Are institutions wholly dependent upon the pre-existence of a community

---

[1] Inis L. Claude, Jr., *Swords Into Plowshares: The Problems and Progress of International Organization* (New York: Random House, 1956), pp. 437-38.

feeling for their creation and effectiveness? Or do institutions play a role—and if so, how important a one—in the creation of loyalty and community, which in turn enhances the effectiveness of these very institutions?

Also, we must consider several related questions. Does the UN represent the greatest possible step forward at this time? Does it, and do other international organizations, tend to create mutual confidence, shared ideals, common loyalty, and habits of cooperation, which will pave the way toward world government? Would a bold advance along this road, one considerably beyond what national leaders seem to believe their peoples are now willing to accept, lead in a relatively short period of time to the development of sentiments and loyalties adequate to support these stronger institutions? These are the basic questions to keep in mind as one examines the structures and day-to-day tasks of the numerous international organizations men have established to serve their interests within the multi-state system.

TYPES OF INTERNATIONAL ORGANIZATIONS

Prior to the nineteenth century, there were many international conferences—such as the Congress of Paris (1856) held at the conclusion of the Crimean War—called for particular purposes, primarily the conclusion of peace treaties. Although "temporary" bodies of this sort continue to meet, the term "international organization" usually refers to those of a more formal and "permanent" nature, such as the Universal Postal Union and the UN. It is with these that we are concerned. International organizations may be classified on the basis of the following criteria: (1) scope of responsibility, (2) breadth of membership, (3) types of functions, and (4) authority.

Scope of Responsibility—General Purpose and Functional Organizations

A few international bodies, which we shall refer to as general-purpose organizations, have responsibilities almost as broad as those of national governments. The League of Nations and the UN are the prime examples. Others, such as the Organization of American States and NATO, may in practice perform less extensive functions, although their constitutions may permit them to undertake a wide range of activities.

The vast majority, however, act in restricted fields, usually economic, social, or cultural, rather than political in nature. These are known as functional or specialized agencies. The oldest still in existence is the Central Commission for Navigation of the Rhine, established in 1804.

The International Telegraphic Union (1865) and the General Postal Union (1874) were also of this type.[2] The specialized agencies of the UN all fall into this category, as do the several organizations among the six Western European states.[3]

Membership—Universal and Regional Organizations

The two most common classifications from the standpoint of membership are *regional* (or limited) on the one hand and *universal* (or general) on the other. The International Joint Committee for the United States and Canada, of which only these two states are members, and the Organization of American States, with its twenty-one American Republics, are both *regional* organizations; the Universal Postal Union claims almost every state in the world as a member. Although few organizations have achieved the success of the UPU in this respect, the League of Nations drew its members from a wide geographical area, and aspired to universality, as does the UN.

Functions—Policy-Making, Administration, etc.

International organizations may also be classified on the basis of the type of functions they perform. Ordinarily much more limited in authority than are state governments with respect to making policy, enforcing law, administering services, and settling disputes, they nevertheless perform roughly analagous functions—although some organizations may emphasize one more than another. The UN performs all these functions, as does the UPU, though the main concern of the latter is with administration, or the performance of service. The International Labor Organization, on the other hand, has been concerned primarily with policy-making, which assumes the form of conventions drawn up for ratification by member states, or of recommendations for the adoption of national legislation. International courts and arbitral tribunals perform judicial functions very much as do national courts.

Authority—Legal and Political

International organizations may also be classified according to the type of authority which they exercise. The terms *legal* or *decisional* designate actions which are legally binding on states or individuals, while *political* or *nondecisional* refer to those which promote and facilitate, but do not

---

[2] Now called the International Telecommunication Union (ITU) and the Universal Postal Union (UPU), both are specialized agencies of the UN.

[3] These states are: Belgium, Netherlands, Luxembourg (the Benelux nations), France, Italy, and West Germany.

create legal obligations. Recommendations are examples of the latter type. Most international agencies have political rather than legal authority, except with respect to certain internal matters, such as determining their own membership and officers. Among the principal organs of the UN, only the International Court of Justice and the Security Council have authority to take legally binding action with respect to states, and that of the latter is quite limited and so obstructed as to be almost nonexistent. All courts and arbitration tribunals, of course, exercise legal authority. Some of the administrative bodies, which function in narrow and nonpolitical fields, may make "administrative" decisions binding on states, although most of their limited legal authority applies only to private parties.

Proposals for disarmament usually envisage a central organization, to be related to the UN, with authority to make decisions necessary to carry out inspection and other responsibilities. The organizations among the six states of Western Europe—The European Coal and Steel Community, the European Economic Community, and the European Atomic Community—are endowed with a degree of legal authority. They are, therefore, frequently referred to as supranational rather than international organizations. One fact worth noting is that states became much more concerned about voting arrangements in organs which can take binding action. The veto in the UN Security Council and the vetoless General Assembly are cases in point. The voting arrangements in the Western European organizations are such that the larger states can usually prevent action on important matters which they oppose.[4]

THE LEAGUE OF
NATIONS AND ITS FORERUNNERS

It was not for want of ideas that the development of general-purpose organizations was so long delayed, for many proposals to create organizations of this type were made prior to 1914.[5] Whether these "utopian" schemes ever exerted any influence on those who held power is debatable; certainly their adoption was never seriously considered. Yet most of them grew out of concrete rather than fancied needs; war and its sufferings provided the stimulus to search for alternative means of settling differences among states. Internationalism flowers when bombs fall. Not only did proposals grow out of wars and their aftermaths; so also did three "grand" attempts to organize the world for peace after the Napo-

---

[4] See pp. 208-11.
[5] For a comprehensive list of proposals, with brief descriptions of each, see Edith Wynner and Georgia Lloyd, *Searchlight on Peace Plans* (New York: E. P. Dutton & Co., Inc., 1944).

leonic and the two world wars. These were: the Holy Alliance, the League of Nations, and the UN.

International Organizations Before 1919

The Holy Alliance and the "Concert of Europe." The loose arrangement made by the major victorious powers at the conclusion of the Napoleonic wars was the first systematic attempt to maintain international peace. These arrangements we shall call the Holy Alliance, although, strictly speaking, the Holy Alliance was provided for in the last and least important of three treaties. The Quadruple Alliance of November 20, 1815, confirmed the provisions of a previous treaty in which Austria, Prussia, Russia, and Great Britain agreed to maintain the international status quo, and provided for periodic meetings to consider measures relating to the prosperity and peace of Europe. After 1818 France also became a member.

These agreements constituted the only "charter" of the Holy Alliance. While several conferences were held under the system, no permanent agencies similar to those of the League or of the UN developed. Nevertheless, the Holy Alliance bears a striking resemblance to the international security provisions of the UN, at least as these were planned at Dumbarton Oaks and agreed to at San Francisco. In both instances international security measures depended upon agreement and concerted action among the great powers.

When Great Britain refused to support the Holy Alliance in its efforts to preserve the internal status quo in Europe and to restore Spain's American colonies, and later when Russia and Great Britain were in opposition over Eastern Europe and Turkey, the Holy Alliance ceased to function. (Similarly, after 1946, with the collapse of the World War II coalition and the outbreak of the cold war, reliance could no longer be placed on the collective security provisions of the UN.)

The "Concert of Europe," or the practice of big-power consultation, continued to 1914. But the Concert rested on no formal agreement: the members were not obliged to meet, and when they did so there was no permanent secretariat to serve them and no agreed formal procedure. The two Hague Conferences (1899 and 1907) were continuations of this practice of consultation. But with more states represented—twenty-six at the first, and forty-four at the second, including small powers and many outside Europe—something closely akin to the League and the UN assemblies had come into existence. The Hague Conference also resembled these bodies in that, unlike most of the previous international conferences which dealt with specific crises, they were concerned with long-run problems such as disarmament, the codification of international law, and the pacific settlement of international disputes. World War I prevented the holding of a third conference scheduled for 1915.

Functional Agencies.   As previously noted, it was in the so-called non-political area that international organization had its healthiest growth prior to 1914. Just as rugged individualism within domestic societies yielded to cooperative and governmental action, so on the broader scene the pressure of cirumstances led states to establish international bodies known as public international unions to serve their common purposes. Problems of transportation, communication, health, crime, commerce, and resources, to mention only a few, could no longer be dealt with effectively on a national basis. Nor were the older practices of bilateral diplomacy or temporary conferences suited to deal with the problems of concern to many nations. An additional factor, the development of a humanitarian conscience which transcended national boundaries, had some effect on international efforts to eradicate evils such as the international slave trade, and traffic in women and children for immoral purposes.

The first international steps to cope with these problems were usually taken by two states through established diplomatic channels. Conferences of several states might follow, out of which would come a multilateral convention, with its enforcement and administration left to the individual states. In fields such as communication and health, international conventions drawn up by temporary conferences provided for some type of permanent organization. Some, of which the river commissions were typical, were of a regional nature, whereas the postal organization, usually regarded as the most successful of all the older organizations, had a wide membership.

Although there was considerable variation in the form and structure of the several unions, all of them had certain common features. The constitution of each consisted of a convention drafted by a special conference and referred back to the states for ratification. Subsequent changes in the constitutions were considered at deliberative conferences provided for in the original conventions. The day-to-day administrative functions were carried on by a permanent and continuous body usually called a bureau or an office. In some instances there was an intermediate body, known as a council, board, or commission, which was empowered to supervise the work of the bureau and to revise the administrative regulations.

The League of Nations

Before 1914 men had generally persuaded themselves that henceforth war, if it could not be avoided entirely, would be limited in scale and area. War would not pay, and anyway civilized man would not revert to such barbarism. World War I thus came as a rude shock and a great surprise to most men in western society. Why had it occurred? There were many short-range and often superficial explanations, varying from the murder of an Austrian archduke at Sarajevo in June, 1914, to the failure of Great Britain to align herself firmly with France and Russia against an imperialistic Germany. World War I, as well as war in general, was regarded as largely accidental. How could war be prevented? It was thought that there was nothing fundamentally wrong with the multi-state system; war within it was abnormal rather than to be expected. It was also held that had there been regular procedures and machinery to call the representatives of the nations into conference World War I could have been prevented. These were basic assumptions of many of the delegates assembled in Paris in 1919 to draft the Covenant for the League of Nations. Since the state system was fundamentally sound, a little dose of reform would put it in good order. The reform was the League.

The League Covenant.   During the course of the war, the governments of the United States, Great Britain, and France, partly in response to public pressure, committed themselves to a postwar association of nations. They also formulated plans, prior to 1919, for what became the League of Nations. The British and American proposals, especially as embodied in a joint draft by the principal legal advisers of the two delegations, and known as the Hurst-Miller Draft, became the basis for discussion in the League Commission of the Versailles Conference, and its essential provisions were incorporated in the Covenant.

In comparison with the UN Charter, the League Covenant was a short, concise, and lucid document. In form it was a multilateral treaty which established certain obligations for its members and provided for a number of organs and procedures for the conduct of interstate relations. It established a general-purpose international organization which aimed at but never quite achieved universality of membership; it was entrusted with functions ranging from policy-making to adjudicating, though it had very limited authority except of a political or nondecisional nature. The preamble declared its purposes to be "to promote international coopera-tion and to achieve international peace and security."

The League not only left the state system intact; it drew largely upon past principles and practices. The Council, in which the big powers were dominant, was similar to the Holy Alliance and the Concert of Powers. The Assembly, with its periodic meetings in which all League members were represented, was a successor to the Hague conferences. The Permanent Court of International Justice was the realization of a project considered at the 1907 Hague Conference. The International Labor Office had its prototype in the pre-1914 public unions, whose bureaus were also the forerunners of the League Secretariat. The various methods of pacific settlement, some ancient and some dating from the Hague conferences, were adapted to League purposes. The principle of collective security dates back to the Holy Alliance, and even further; for the medieval and early modern concepts of unjust and just war were similar to those of illegal and legal wars under the Covenant. Furthermore, under the early doctrine, any state had the right to come to the aid of the victim of an unjust war, and a nonbelligerent must not hinder a state whose cause was just or help one whose cause was unjust. Although the League was supposed to transform the *right* to help a victim of an illegal war into an *obligation* to do so, the Covenant was so weakened by interpretation that the situation was basically similar to that of the earlier period.

The Secretariat was the first truly international civil service, just as the Permanent Court of International Justice was the first world-wide international judicial body. The Mandate system, although not without precedent, was also a notable forward step. *The really novel quality of the League, however, was its attempt to combine systematically many approaches to peace and to the solution of common economic and social problems in one permanent international organization aspiring to universal membership.*

Structure and Organization. There were four principal groups of League organs: First, there were three main bodies—the Assembly, Council, and Secretariat. Secondly, two closely associated but "autonomous" organs, the Permanent Court of International Justice and the International Labor Organization, functioned as a part of the system. Thirdly, over a period of time a dozen or more auxiliary agencies with a wide variety of structures and functions were established. Of these the Economic and Financial Organization, the Organization of Communications and Transit, and the Permanent Mandates Commission were probably the most important and best organized. The fourth group consisted of a number of special institutes or organizations supervised by the League. The International Institute of Intellectual Cooperation located at Paris—the predecessor of UNESCO—is the most prominent example.

Membership. Membership in a general international organization with responsibility for world peace is an important and often controversial matter. It is contended that if major states remain outside, the organization will not ordinarily be able to command their support, and they are likely to be more inclined to obstruct its operations than if they are included. On the other hand, it is argued that unless a state (such as Communist China today) meets certain basic qualifications and accepts its obligations in good faith, it will be more disruptive in than outside the organization. The League Covenant provided that the signatories of the peace treaties and thirteen other states should be eligible for original membership. Other states, dominions, and colonies could be admitted by a two-thirds vote of the Assembly. Members could withdraw under certain conditions, or they could be expelled by a unanimous vote of the Council. Although sixty-three states were members of the League at one time or another, its greatest membership at any one time (1937-38) was fifty-eight. More significant than total members was the fact that the United States never joined and that one or more of the other big powers was a nonmember throughout the League's history. Germany became a member only in 1926, and the Soviet Union in 1934. Japan, Italy, and Germany all withdrew in the thirties, and the Soviet Union was expelled in 1939.

The Council and Assembly. The Council of the League, on which the more powerful members had permanent representation (although eventually they held only four of the fifteen seats), was originally designed to be the center of the League's activities. The Assembly might meet on occasion—some suggested once every four years—presumably to engage in a general review of the League's work. The Covenant, however, bestowed general jurisdiction on the two organs in identical terms: any matter "within the sphere of action of the League or affecting the peace of the world." (Arts. 3 and 4.) In addition, each was entrusted with certain specific functions, but it was never clear in such instances, whether the other organ was supposed to be excluded from acting, despite its general jurisdiction. The Council felt free to deal with any matter within the League's sphere of action. It gave particular attention to peace and security matters, and to the mandate system, which responsibility was specifically assigned to it. The Assembly early established its right to discuss any problem, whereas the Council usually refrained from considering those few matters specifically referred to as Assembly responsibilities. The Assembly did not, however, unlike its counterpart in the UN, play an important role in attempting to settle disputes. Over the course or years the Assembly's prestige and influence increased in comparison to that of the Council. The primary reasons for this were the demands of the smaller powers, and the feeling that recommendations were more likely to be heeded if backed by the more representative Assembly. Since any member of the Council or Assembly could veto a recommendation or decision on any important matter, voting procedure in the Council did not cause matters to be transferred to the Assembly.

The Secretariat. The Paris Conference was in general agreement that the League should have a permanent Secretariat. The Covenant so specified, but its composition and organization were left for future determination. One of the first and most important questions was whether to continue the familiar practice used in public unions of having states assign their own nationals to the Secretariat, or to create a genuine international civil service owing loyalty to the League. Sir Eric Drummond, who was named in the Covenant as the first secretary-general, proposed and obtained approval for the latter arrangement. Thus the League Secretariat was the first truly international civil service.

Its personnel, consisting at its height of almost 750 persons drawn from fifty states, including a number from the United States, was required to take an oath pledging loyalty to the League and neither to seek nor to receive instructions from any outside source. On the whole, the group of men and women at Geneva developed a spirit, unique in history to that time, of loyalty to the League and to supranational interests, although they did not cut their national ties.

The principal functions of the Secretariat consisted of: (1) coordinating the widespread activities of the League carried on by its many organs; (2) providing a source of continuity and follow-up for League work; (3) furnishing information and analyses to organs and delegates; (4) keeping the records of the League agencies; and (5) sometimes directly, but more often indirectly, influencing in a limited manner the settlement of disputes and the formulation of League policy.

Since there was no such body as the Economic and Social Council (ECOSOC) of the UN to co-ordinate and promote activities of this nature, the work of the League Secretariat was especially important for this purpose. In a sense the Council, to which organs concerned with economic and social matters were generally responsible, played a role similar to that of the later ECOSOC.

Other Organs. The autonomous organs—the Court and the International Labor Organization—although a part of the League system, functioned with a considerable degree of independence. Their budgets were determined by the Assembly, which, along with the Council, elected the judges of the Court. Membership in the Court was independent of the League proper; although League members were automatically members of the ILO, nonmembers could also belong to it.

Auxiliary organs of the League were basically similar in purpose and function to the ILO and to other public unions previously described. However, they were more closely related to the League than were the autonomous organs. The framers of the Covenant conceived of the League as a coordinating center for the various international efforts and organs concerned with nonpolitical questions. Although it did not attain its original goal, owing chiefly to the refusal of the United States government to agree to place under League supervision bureaus of which it was a member, the League's achievements were nevertheless considerable. It initiated action and established organs on problems of trade and finance, communication, health, dependent peoples under mandate, opium and dangerous drugs, and general social questions; and it supervised special institutes on intellectual cooperation, unification of private international law, and cinematographic matters.

Evaluation of the League

It is debatable whether the League of Nations was a success or a failure. The answer depends in part on the criteria used. To those who would judge in terms of creating a Utopia, or even of achieving its purposes, the verdict is clearly adverse. However, if one is satisfied with the more modest test of better or worse, the evidence calls for a more favorable judgment. It was probably more successful in the social, economic, and humanitarian fields than in the political, although the approbation sometimes bestowed upon it in the former areas is exaggerated. It is impossible to determine the total effect which it exercised on international politics. The evidence however, is that the world was somewhat better off as a result of the League.

Whether or not the League failed, it certainly fell short of realizing its principal purpose of providing a sense of security for its members and of preventing war. Did the fault rest with its members? Or with its constitution? These questions raise the basic issue of the role of institutions.

Implicit in the view that the members were responsible is the assumption that there was in the nature of the League constitution no basic fault which accounts for its failure. It is argued that if the members had lived up to their obligations the League would have succeeded. To this contention it may be retorted that if the Ten Commandments were obeyed there would be no need for government.

The depression of the thirties, which disrupted the world economy, contributed to the rise of German Nazism and generally weakened the fabric of social order everywhere, created international problems and tensions which a far stronger institution than the League would have had difficulty in solving. Though unproved, perhaps it is true that the nature of the problems then existing and the deep-seated attitudes, habits, and values among statesmen and the mass of people alike, made it impossibly difficult to devise a more effective system. It would have led to the failure of the most ideal institution. Despite its inability to prevent World War II, the League was a great experiment; whether the builders of the UN have constructed a more enduring structure only the future will determine.

THE UNITED NATIONS

The United Nations was not inevitable. The failure of the League to avert World War II might have led to the assumption that it was useless to try to prevent physical conflict among sovereign states by programs of cooperation and collective security. Either of two extreme positions might have then been taken. One would have been that nothing could be done. Each nation would have to continue to fend for itself as best it could. Or it might have been concluded, as was the case in the American Constitutional Convention of 1787, that only radical measures would suffice. Had the latter view prevailed, some type of world federation would have been attempted. Neither of these extreme positions was taken by those responsible for postwar world organization. War stimulated a determination "to save succeeding generations from the scourge of war," but the means was to be an improved League of Nations. Since the UN came into official existence on October 24, 1945, an extensive and complex organization has evolved to deal with a vast range of undertakings.

Background

Although private groups had some part in preparing the ground for the UN Charter—probably because the British and United States governments took the initiative—they were less active than in the case of the League Covenant. Official preparation began in the United States even before Pearl Harbor, and continued through the war. Congress and the major parties during the course of the war endorsed United States membership in an international organization to maintain the peace. In early 1944, the United States sent its "Tentative Proposals for General International Organization" to the British, Soviet, and Chinese governments, who soon responded with less comprehensive suggestions.

A number of international agreements and declarations—the Atlantic Charter of August 14, 1941, and the Moscow Declaration of four nations, October 1943, were the most important—relating to a permanent organization to replace the League were made during the course of the war. The Moscow Declaration set the tone. The signatories "recognize the necessity of establishing at the earliest practical date a general international organization, based on the principle of sovereign equality of all peace-loving states, and open to membership by all such states, large and small, for the maintenance of international peace and security."

At the Dumbarton Oaks Conference (August 21-October 7, 1944) representatives of the Soviet Union, the United Kingdom, and the United States, using the latter's suggestion as the basis for discussion, drew up the Dumbarton Oaks Proposals. These were later endorsed by China. Stated in the form of general principles, these were dispatched to the other wartime "United Nations" for their consideration. Some of the matters on which agreement had not been reached at Dumbarton Oaks were again considered at the Yalta Conference (February 4-11, 1945). The Inter-American Conference, which met at Mexico City ten days later (February 21-March 8) discussed the Proposals, and also agreed to draw up plans for a regional organization of American States. These plans, which conflicted at some points with the Dumbarton Oaks Proposals, were reflected in the final UN Charter.

Delegates of fifty nations developed the Charter at the United Nations Conference on International Organization (UNCIO) held at San Francisco between April 24 and May 26, 1945. Although serious disagreements relating to the organization arose among the major powers, these were all finally solved by pressure and compromise; the real cleavage was between the large and the smaller powers. The debate over certain aspects of Security Council voting was especially acute. However, on all major issues, the large states presented a common front and their will ultimately prevailed, for it was generally recognized that without their membership there would have been no organization. V-E Day arrived in the midst of the Conference, and thereafter the delegates became increasingly concerned with events at home.

The Charter

The UN Charter, like the League Covenant, is a multilateral treaty. It is a lengthy document, consisting not only of the Charter proper— nineteen chapters, divided into III consecutively numbered articles—but also of the Statute of the International Court of Justice with its five chapters and 70 articles.

Preamble, Purposes and Principles.   Chapter I outlines the main objectives of the organization, its functions, and limitations (principles) on the organization and its members.

Membership.   Chapter II defines original membership, and sets forth the qualifications for additional members, as well as procedures for suspension and explusion.

Organs.   Seven chapters (III, IV, V, X, XIII, XIV, XV) provide for the organization, jurisdiction, powers and procedures of the six principal organs: the General Assembly; the Security Council; the Economic and Social Council; the Trusteeship Council; the International Court of Justice; and the Secretariat.

Pacific Settlement.   Chapter VI covers the obligations of the members with respect to the peaceful settlement of disputes, and procedures for the guidance of the Security Council in effecting such settlements. Although the General Assembly is referred to in this chapter, Chapter IV is a more important source of its authority.

Collective Security.   Chapter VII defines types of sanctions, and the responsibility of the Security Council for their application. The final article permits self-defense in case of armed attack, until the Security Council has taken effective action.

Regional Arrangements. Chapter VIII permits these arrangements as long as they are consistent with the principles and purposes of the organization.

Economic and Social Cooperation. Chapter IX treats the economic and social responsibilities of the United Nations.

Non-Self-Governing Territories and Trusteeship. Chapters XI and XII provide for the trusteeship system and set forth members' responsibilities for their dependent peoples.

Miscellaneous Provisions. Chapters XVI-XIX deal with treaties and their registration, privileges and immunities of the organization and of delegates, transitional security arrangements, amendment, and ratification of the Charter.

Amendments

Amendments are proposed by a two-thirds vote of the Assembly's members, or by a like vote of a general conference. A similar Assembly vote, and a favorable procedural vote in the Security Council, is necessary to convene the latter. They must then be ratified by two-thirds of the members, including all the permanent members of the Security Council. Thus any state other than one of the "big five" may be bound by amendments to which it is opposed. The only alternative would be for it to withdraw, and on this the Charter is silent. Although it is usually assumed that a member is free to withdraw, it has been argued that it may not do so without the consent of all members, in the absence of a Charter provision to the contrary.[6]

Interpretation

The Charter is silent with respect to its interpretation. As it true of treaties and international law in general, each organ of the UN and each of its members is free to interpret the Charter, and one interpretation is as legally binding as another. An advisory opinion of the International Court of Justice is simply advice which may be accepted or rejected. Even if it should interpret the Charter in a dispute between two or more states, it would bind only the parties to the case. Since many parts of the Charter are general and ambiguous, and several different ones referring to the same matter may be interpreted so as to conflict, the absence of a single body to hand down a uniformly binding interpretation is conducive to conflict and confusion. The majority of the members of the General Assembly, for example, has rejected the contention of South Africa that its treatment of its non-European population is within

---

[6] For a persuasive argument that unilateral withdrawal is not permissible, see Hans Kelsen, "Withdrawal from the United Nations," *Western Political Quarterly*, I (Mar. 1948), 29-43.

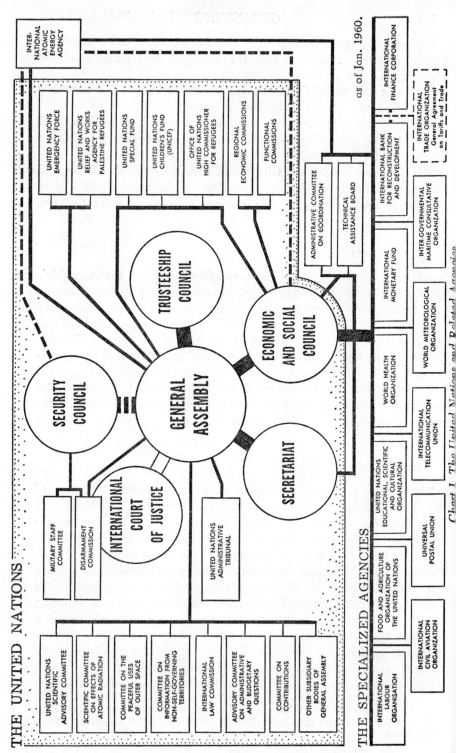

THE UNITED NATIONS

as of Jan. 1960.

THE SPECIALIZED AGENCIES

SECURITY COUNCIL

GENERAL ASSEMBLY

TRUSTEESHIP COUNCIL

ECONOMIC AND SOCIAL COUNCIL

SECRETARIAT

INTERNATIONAL COURT OF JUSTICE

INTER-NATIONAL ATOMIC ENERGY AGENCY

UNITED NATIONS EMERGENCY FORCE

UNITED NATIONS RELIEF AND WORKS AGENCY FOR PALESTINE REFUGEES

UNITED NATIONS SPECIAL FUND

UNITED NATIONS CHILDREN'S FUND (UNICEF)

OFFICE OF UNITED NATIONS HIGH COMMISSIONER FOR REFUGEES

REGIONAL ECONOMIC COMMISSIONS

FUNCTIONAL COMMISSIONS

ADMINISTRATIVE COMMITTEE ON COORDINATION

TECHNICAL ASSISTANCE BOARD

INTERNATIONAL FINANCE CORPORATION

INTERNATIONAL TRADE ORGANIZATION General Agreement on Tariffs and Trade

INTERNATIONAL BANK FOR RECONSTRUCTION AND DEVELOPMENT

INTER-GOVERNMENTAL MARITIME CONSULTATIVE ORGANIZATION

INTERNATIONAL MONETARY FUND

WORLD METEOROLOGICAL ORGANIZATION

WORLD HEALTH ORGANIZATION

INTERNATIONAL TELECOMMUNICATION UNION

UNITED NATIONS EDUCATIONAL, SCIENTIFIC AND CULTURAL ORGANIZATION

UNIVERSAL POSTAL UNION

FOOD AND AGRICULTURE ORGANIZATION OF THE UNITED NATIONS

INTERNATIONAL CIVIL AVIATION ORGANIZATION

INTERNATIONAL LABOUR ORGANISATION

MILITARY STAFF COMMITTEE

DISARMAMENT COMMISSION

UNITED NATIONS ADMINISTRATIVE TRIBUNAL

UNITED NATIONS SCIENTIFIC ADVISORY COMMITTEE

SCIENTIFIC COMMITTEE ON EFFECTS OF ATOMIC RADIATION

COMMITTEE ON THE PEACEFUL USES OF OUTER SPACE

COMMITTEE ON INFORMATION FROM NON-SELF-GOVERNING TERRITORIES

INTERNATIONAL LAW COMMISSION

ADVISORY COMMITTEE ON ADMINISTRATIVE AND BUDGETARY QUESTIONS

COMMITTEE ON CONTRIBUTIONS

OTHER SUBSIDIARY BODIES OF GENERAL ASSEMBLY

Chart 1. The United Nations and Related Agencies

its domestic jurisdiction, and therefore outside the legitimate concern of the UN. However, South Africa's interpretation is as valid legally as is that of the Assembly. As a consequence of the nature of the Charter and its decentralized interpretation, it is impossible to say what many provisions of the Charter really mean.[7]

Purposes and Principles

Chapter I (Arts. 1 and 2) on Purposes and Principles contains three elements—the *ends or objectives* of the organization, the general *functions* which it is to perform in pursuit of these ends, and *limiting principles* on both the UN and its members, as well as obligations of the latter.

Objectives and Functions. The objectives are to maintain international peace and national security, and to promote the economic and social welfare of the people of member states. To achieve the end of of peace and security the organization is: (1) to take "collective measures" to prevent and remove threats to the peace and to suppress acts of aggression or other breaches of the peace; and (2) to bring about the settlement by peaceful means of international disputes or situations which might lead to a breach of the peace.

Limiting Principles and Obligations. Most of the limiting principles and obligations are found in Article 2: "The Organization and its Members, in pursuit of the Purposes . . ., shall act in accordance with the following principles." Despite this statement, principles 1 and 7 limit only the organization, and 2-5 limit or obligate only the members. Principle 6 applies to nonmembers.

LIMITATIONS ON THE ORGANIZATION. Principle 1 states that the organization is based on the principle of the sovereign equality of all its members." In view of the ambiguity of sovereignty, the principle simply connotes in a general way that the organization is to have little power and authority. In practice, the sovereignty principle is used by states to resist action to which they are opposed, and is disregarded or interpreted in a different way when it is in their interest to do so. Principle 7 is a specific limitation on the organization in the interest of sovereignty. It provides that the UN may not "intervene in matters which are essentially within the domestic jurisdiction of any state" and that the members are not required to submit such matters to settlement by the organization. The one exception is that it "shall not prejudice the application of enforcement measures under Chapter VII."

Principle 7 is almost as ambiguous as the one referring directly to

---

[7] The outstanding work on the law of the Charter is Hans Kelsen, *The Law of the United Nations* (New York: Frederick A. Praeger, Inc., 1950), and his *Supplement, Recent Trends* (. . . , 1951).

sovereignty, and its interpretation has been quite controversial. Whether matters are *essentially within the domestic jurisdiction* of a state depends on some standard. "Essentially" is a nebulous term. Domestic jurisdiction cannot mean simply that which under *international law* a state is "essentially" free to do with as it pleases, for the Conference deliberately rejected that criterion as being too restrictive. Another possible interpretation is that a matter is no longer within the domestic jurisdiction of a state if it concerns two or more states. So interpreted, the principle is meaningless, for these are the only matters the organization would be likely to deal with in any case. Thus, according to international law the United States is essentially free to regulate immigration as it sees fit; yet the matter is of importance to other states. "Intervene" is equally nebulous. The UN is deeply involved, with the consent and endorsement of their governments, in the internal affairs of many states. Intervention has been variously interpreted in the UN to mean anything from discussion to armed interference. Like the sovereignty principle, this provision is interpreted according to the political preference of states. The organization has not, however, been restrained in taking action on matters despite frequent protests that to do so would be to intervene in a member's domestic affairs.

OBLIGATIONS OF MEMBERS.   Principle 3 obligates members to settle their disputes by peaceful means in a manner which does not endanger international peace, security, and justice. Principle 4 provides that members shall refrain in their international relations from the threat or use of force against the territorial integrity or political independence of any state, "or in any other manner inconsistent with the Purposes of the United Nations." Obviously if members obey principle 3 and settle their disputes by peaceful means they can hardly violate the fourth principle. The latter resembles Article 10 of the League Covenant in its concern with territorial integrity and political independence. But by its inclusive prohibition against the use of force it does not leave any "gaps" in the Charter, as there was in the League Covenant. Presumably "a manner inconsistent with the Purposes of the United Nations" precludes the use of armed force other than when taken under the authority of the organization or in the case of an armed attack (Art. 51). It should be noted that members of NATO are obligated to come to each other's defense only under the latter circumstances. Principle 5 seems to mean that when enforcement action is taken by the Security Council under Chapter VII, the members are obligated to assist the organization and to refrain from assisting the offending state.

Membership

The fifty-one original members of the United Nations were the states represented at the San Francisco Conference, plus Poland. Additional members may be admitted by a two-thirds vote of the General Assembly following a favorable recommendation by the Security Council in which, as a matter of practice, no permanent member votes in opposition.

The problem of membership has been one of the most controversial issues faced by the UN. By 1951, nine new members had gained admittance, and almost twenty applications were pending. No additional members were admitted until December 1955, when sixteen applicants were approved. By the end of 1961, a number of additional states, mostly from Africa, gained membership as the European powers withdrew from that continent in the face of exploding nationalism. Aside from divided Germany, Vietnam, and Korea, and Switzerland, all states were then members of the UN, giving it a total membership of one hundred and four.

The legal controversy over admitting states has revolved around two constitutional questions—voting requirements in the Security Council and the meaning of Article 4 concerning qualifications for membership. On each question the International Court of Justice has given an opinion. With respect to Security Council voting, it was of the opinion that it was a matter requiring a favorable recommendation, including the approval of the five permanent members. The problem of qualifications is more complicated. According to the Charter members must: (1) be states; (2) be peace-loving; (3) accept their Charter obligations; and (4) in the judgment of the organization be able and willing to carry them out. If a member believes an applicant possesses these qualifications, is it legally obliged to vote in favor of its admission? Or can it make its decision on additional grounds? By a 9-6 vote the International Court of Justice advised in 1948 that the Charter stated the *maximum* qualifications, and that a state could not "legally lay down as a condition that it would vote for admission of a state if other states were admitted to membership." However, even if this conclusion is accepted by all states, they still have to judge whether the rather intangible qualifications are fulfilled.

The controversy has really been a political one, though at times cloaked in legal dress. Two conflicting points of view have been advanced. One is that each applicant for membership should be examined to determine whether it meets the Charter's admission standards; the other, that all should be admitted without close scrutiny of their qualifications. In 1946, the Soviet Union took the first point of view and the United States the second. Positions were then reversed: when the United States accepted the Soviet position, the latter shifted. The real reason for the shift was that each state hoped to gain additional support for its position among the newly admitted states. With the exception of Indonesia, no new members were admitted from 1949 to 1955. In the eyes of the United States, applicants favored by her met the Charter qualifications, whereas those sponsored by the Soviet Union did not. Although the Soviet Union vetoed some applicants on other grounds, she generally favored a "package deal" whereby she would vote in favor of those favored by the United States, provided the latter would cease opposing those sponsored by the Soviet Union. Yielding to considerable General Assembly pressure in 1955, the United States finally reverted to her original position. This cleared the way for the "package deal" of December 1955.

The problem of determining the representation of a state which is already a member of the UN is distinct from that of membership. Assume two different groups claim they are entitled to represent Texas in the Democratic presidential nominating convention. The problem, to be decided by the convention itself, is which set of "credentials" to accept. That is analogous to the problem of Chinese representation. The problem of Chinese membership has not arisen in the UN, for China was an original member. There is no guide in the Charter as to how the representation problem should be decided. Moreover, since each organ has the right to determine the question for itself, it would be possible for the Chinese Communist representatives to be seated in the General Assembly and the Nationalists in the Security Council. Whether the decision of the Security Council would be subject to a veto of a permanent member is also uncertain.

The Principal Organs of the United Nations

The Charter states (Art. 7) that the General Assembly, the Security Council, the Economic and Social Council, the Trusteeship Council, the International Court of Justice, and the Secretariat shall constitute the "principal" organs of the UN. Only the General Assembly, the Security Council, and the Court, however, are principal organs in the sense of being more or less independent; the other three are subordinate to the General Assembly.

The General Assembly. COMPOSITION AND ORGANIZATION. The General Assembly consists of representatives of all members; each member may have a maximum of five representatives, but it has only one vote.

Its organization is quite similar to that of its League predecessor. Its president is selected for one session from among the representatives of the smaller powers. The General Committee is composed of the president and seven vice-presidents, among whom all the "big five" are represented, and of the chairmen of the six main committees. The latter, on which each member is entitled to representation, are as follows:

First Committee—Political and Security (including armaments)
Second Committee—Economic and Financial

Third Committee—Social, Humanitarian, and Cultural
Fourth Committee—Trusteeship (including non-self-governing terri-
    tories not under trusteeship)
Fifth Committee—Administrative and Budgetary
Sixth Committee—Legal

The First Committee has been so burdened that an *Ad Hoc* Political
Committee has been created to share its work. There is also a Credentials
Committee, and standing committees on Administration and Budget. In
addition there are many subsidiary and *ad hoc* bodies which deal with a
wide range of questions.

JURISDICTION AND AUTHORITY.   The jurisdiction and authority of the
General Assembly are set forth in Articles 10-17. Of these, Article 10 is
the most important; the others (except 12), while more specific, probably
neither add to nor subtract from it. "The General Assembly may discuss
any questions or any matters within the scope of the Charter or relating
to the powers and functions of any organ provided for . . . and except
as provided in Article 12, may make recommendations to the Members of
the United Nations or to the Security Council or to both on any such
questions or matters" (Art. 10). Except as restricted by principles 1 and 7,
and by Article 12, the range of the General Assembly's permitted activities is commensurate with international relations.

The purpose of Article 12 is to prevent overlapping and conflict
between the Assembly and the Security Council. When the latter is considering a dispute or situation, the General Assembly may discuss but
may not recommend with respect to it, unless the Security Council so
requests. Several questions, such as those of the Balkans and of Korea,
have been removed from the agenda of the Security Council to permit
the Assembly to deal with them. The votes of any seven members are
sufficient to take an item off the Security Council agenda. As long as a
matter is on the agenda, however, the General Assembly is supposed to
be limited. Nevertheless, in the Palestine and Korean cases, as well as in
some others, both really considered and made recommendations, presumably on the supposition that each was dealing with different aspects
of the problem. Although the General Assembly may deal with this
broad range of matters, including peace and security, the jurisdiction of
the Security Council is, with a few exceptions, restricted to the latter.
Thus their jurisdiction is in part overlapping.

The General Assembly has both legal and political authority. Like the
League Assembly, its binding authority is confined almost entirely to internal or organizational matters. In some instances it has exclusive authority, while the joint approval of the General Assembly and of the
Security Council is required in others. It alone has the authority to elect

nonpermanent members of the Security Council, to determine the organization and rules of the Secretariat, to approve agreements on behalf of the organization (such as the assumption of the assets of the League of Nations), to determine its own organization, to elect the members and supervise the work of the Trusteeship and of the Economic and Social Councils, to approve trusteeship agreements (except strategic), and to vote and apportion the budget. It acts jointly with the Security Council in selecting the secretary-general (although it alone determines the term of his appointment), in electing the judges of the Court, and in expelling members.

VOTING. The General Assembly voting procedure has attracted very little attention, although it is a marked departure from the unanimity requirement of the League Assembly. On important questions, several of which are specified in the Charter (Art. 18), approval of two-thirds of the members present and voting is required, while for other questions a simple majority is sufficient. Whether a question is "important" is determined by a simple majority. It has sometimes been difficult, but not impossible, to attain two-thirds agreement on organizational questions, such as the election of members of the Security Council and Court judges. A higher voting requirement might hamper the work of the organization on matters of this nature. On matters of substance, however, where effectiveness depends on political pressure rather than legal obligation a higher majority requirement would not be without merit.

The General Assembly was from the beginning intended to play a more important role than that originally envisaged for the League Assembly. Its prestige has been on the increase, partly because, unlike the Security Council, it includes representatives of *all* the members. A more important influence has been the inability of the Security Council to function effectively because of the split among its permanent members,

GENERAL ASSEMBLY AND SECURITY COUNCIL JURISDICTION*

Matters Essentially Within Domestic Jurisdiction of States	International Peace and Security, as well as Economic and Social Questions	
No U.N. organ may intervene, except in the case of a threat to the peace, breach of the peace, or act of aggression.	Matters other than peace and security—economic, social, trusteeship, human rights questions, etc. General Assembly alone may act. The Security Council can deal with strategic trusteeships.	Peace and Security Matters—pacific settlement of disputes, regulation of armaments, threats to and breaches of peace and acts of aggression. General Assembly and Security Council have concurrent jurisdiction. General Assembly is limited by Article 12.

* Exclusive of internal or organizational matters.

and the consequent use of the veto. In dealing with many matters, such as disarmament, the settlement of disputes, and even collective security, where it was expected that the Security Council would play the primary if not the sole role, the General Assembly has become increasingly important.

If, as some believe, the General Assembly should be given authority to pass laws binding on members, certain important changes would surely have to be made. Any move to convert the UN into a government would call for a drastic restriction in its jurisdiction. Despite the domestic jurisdiction clause, the UN is concerned with a far more extensive range of matters than even the most ardent world federalists would entrust to a world government. To be able to recommend on these matters is one thing; to legislate with respect to them is quite different. There would also be a strong demand for, and equal resistance to, a change in the present system of "one nation—one vote."

The Security Council. COMPOSITION AND ORGANIZATION. The size of the Security Council is fixed in the Charter at eleven, and the permanent members (China, France, Union of Soviet Socialist Republics, the United Kingdom, and the United States) are named therein. A change would require a Charter amendment which could be blocked by the refusal of a permanent Security Council member to ratify it. Nonpermanent members are elected for a two-year period, three of the six being replaced each year, and are ineligible for immediate re-election. Although "freezing" these matters in the Charter may obviate disputes similar to those which arose in the League, their inflexible character may give rise to others no less difficult. Time may bring the rise of certain nations and the fall of others. What justification is there for denying India or Japan a permanent seat, especially with Nationalist China (Formosa) holding that privilege?

Some states are "middle" powers, e.g., India and Canada, whose disparity of strength in relation to that of the great powers is less than it is in relation to that of many small ones. It was the demand of these states which led to the provision that in selecting the members of the Security Council due regard would be paid to the contribution of members to the maintenance of peace and security. Equitable geographical distribution is another criterion. The last consideration, at least, is regularly followed.

The Security Council was kept small to enable it to act promptly. On the theory that it could not perform its duties without them, the "Big Five" were given permanent seats. The Security Council is "so organized as to be able to function continuously," and for this reason each member is required to be represented permanently. The Council selects its own president for a one-month period, using the English alphabetical order of its members' names.

Because of its limited size the Council has only a few committees, such as the Committee of Experts on Rules and Procedures, and on the Admission of New Members. The Military Staff Committee, created by the Charter, consists of the chiefs of staff (or their representatives) of the five permanent members. In addition, *ad hoc* or special committees (or commissions) were established to deal with such matters as Palestine, the Jammu-Kashmir dispute, and the Balkan question.

JURISDICTION AND AUTHORITY.   As its name implies, the Security Council has jurisdiction over questions which involve peace and security. It has "primary," although not exclusive, responsibility in this realm (Art. 24). Presumably (and this has been the "working interpretation") if it does not assume responsibility, or does so unsuccessfully, the General Assembly is not precluded from acting. The Council may administer "strategic trusteeships," and incidentally thereto deal with economic and social matters in those areas. Chapters VI and VII, relating to peaceful settlement and enforcement actions, are more specific in setting forth the responsibility of the Security Council than is Chapter V, which deals with its jurisdiction only in a general way.

The Council has legally binding powers with respect to the few organizational matters over which it has jurisdiction, such as the admission of members, the selection of the secretary-general and the members of the International Court of Justice. In all of these it acts jointly with the General Assembly. It alone regulates its own internal business, although the General Assembly may discuss and recommend with respect to this. If a dispute or situation is not sufficiently serious to be likely to endanger international peace and security, the Council is not supposed to deal with it (Arts. 33, 34, 35); but in practice this limitation has been interpreted so liberally as to be of no practical consequence. If a matter is a serious one, yet there is no threat to or breach of the peace, and no aggression has taken place, the Security Council can recommend only. But if there is a threat to the peace, the Security Council has authority to make certain decisions of a legal nature. Having decided that the peace is threatened or breached, or that an act of aggression has taken place (Art. 39), it may decide to apply diplomatic, economic, and military sanctions (Arts. 41, 42), and the member states are legally obligated "to accept and carry out the decisions of the Security Council in accordance with the . . . Charter" (Art. 25).[8]

VOTING.   No problem relating to the UN has attracted more attention,

---

[8] Sanctions are treated more fully in Chapter 15. It may be argued that the Security Council may make binding decisions on any matters of peace and security whether or not the peace is threatened or broken. Moreover, the decision may require a settle-

provoked more controversy, and probably been less understood, than Security Council voting. The controversy began at Dumbarton Oaks and has continued ever since.

As finally set forth in the Charter (Art. 27), the procedure is as follows: (1) each member has one vote; (2) decisions on procedural matters are made by any seven members; (3) on substantive matters an affirmative vote of seven members must include the concurrence of the five permanent ones except that; (4) in matters of pacific settlement under Chapter VI and Article 52, a party to a dispute abstains from voting.

Why should these voting arrangements provoke so much controversy? It is evident that the four states represented at Dumbarton Oaks wanted to protect themselves against Security Council action to which they were opposed. To do this and at the same time to enable the Council to function effectively, was probably an impossible task, not unlike eating one's cake and having it.

Although the other powers at San Francisco were generally opposed to the special privileges of the permanent members of the Security Council, they eventually became reconciled to the veto on enforcement measures. In the realm of pacific settlement, however, they were in vigorous and resolute opposition.

The great powers were opposed to enforcement action against themselves. If such action became necessary, it was argued, it would mean a general war and the destruction of the UN. Nor should enforcement be taken against other states without big-power unanimity. It would have been possible to devise a formula whereby a great power would not have been obliged to use its own forces in such cases, but at the same time it would not have been able to prevent action by the organization. Against this it could be argued that it would provoke disagreement among the big powers, and that without their general cooperation the application of sanctions would be difficult or impossible.

The smaller powers contended at San Francisco that although all this might be true with respect to sanctions, peaceful settlement presented a different problem. Since no coercion, or even legally binding decisions could be made in this realm, the unanimity of the permanent members was unnecessary. It was undesirable because it would impede the settlement of disputes in a peaceful manner and thus lead to a situation in which sanctions might be necessary. The big powers argued that beyond

---

ment opposed by a state, but it is bound to accept it and the members are equally bound to enforce the settlement if the Security Council so decides. The argument is based on a liberal interpretation of Articles 24 and 25. While the meaning of these articles is far from clear and the practice contradictory, it seems improbable that the states which ratified the Charter intended to bestow the authority of a world government on the Security Council. See Kelsen, *The Law of the United Nations*, pp. 279-93, for a discussion of this point.

procedural matters, Security Council action might introduce "a chain of events" or be a first step on "a course of action from which it could withdraw only at the risk of failing to discharge its responsibilities." In short, it would be dangerous to start something which they might not be able to finish. The test came on an Australian amendment which would have permitted any seven Security Council members to make decisions on pacific settlement matters. The Commiteee vote on the matter was ten affirmative, twenty negative, and fifteen abstentions. Only the "take it or leave it" attitude of the "Big Five" enabled them to obtain the adoption of the original proposal for the veto. One important modification has taken place in the original plan: by common consent an abstention is not regarded as a veto, despite the Charter reference to concurring votes.

It is difficult to determine to what extent the veto has adversely affected the functioning of the UN. During the first fifteen years, it was used over ninety times, principally by the Soviet Union. Over half of the vetoes occurred on membership applications, and most of the remainder when the Council was attempting to bring about the pacific settlement of disputes. Several vetoes have applied to the same question. It is possible, though not at all certain, that the pacific settlement of some disputes might have been expedited had it not been for the veto. Yet, in this latter realm, it must be remembered that the Security Council can only recommend. Some disputes, including those of the Balkans and Korea, were taken off the agenda of the Security Council so that the General Assembly could deal with them, but that body was unable to do so successfully. In many other instances the "vetoless" General Assembly has been unable to obtain compliance with its recommendations. No proposal for sanctions has been vetoed in the Security Council. There can be little doubt, however, that the possibility of a veto of resolutions proposing sanctions was the most important influence behind the "Uniting for Peace" resolution, which has led to a far-reaching change in the original plans for the application of collective security.[9]

The real test of the UN lies in its ability to influence the action of states. If states are unwilling to accept its recommendations, or even its legal decisions, changing the voting procedure will have little or no effect. The veto is a symptom of disagreement rather than its cause; its abolition would accomplish little. However, there are several types of questions to which the veto applies, and it might be possible and desirable to modify it with respect to some and not others. A procedural vote on membership and pacific settlement questions would probably be a step forward. It might be desirable to allow the Council to determine the existence of a threat to or a breach of the peace, or an act of aggres-

---

[9] See pp. 325-26.

sion, by a similar vote, although the effects would be mainly psychological if sanctions could still be vetoed. Whether it would be advisable to permit the Security Council to decide upon sanctions without the concurrence of all permanent members is more debatable.[10]

The Secretariat. The Secretariat's role, as envisaged in the Charter, is much more important than that played by the Secretariat of the League. Under the dynamic leadership of its first secretary-general, Trygve Lie of Norway, and his successor, Dag Hammarskjöld, it developed into an agency which exercised initiative and leadership in addition to performing essential functions of a service and administrative nature. It is the organ which, more than any other, "transforms the United Nations from a series of periodic meetings of Assembly and Councils into a permanent and cohesive organization."[11] It is the most international, or supranational, of the principal UN organs, with the possible exception of the Court.

PERSONNEL AND ORGANIZATION. The Secretariat consists of the secretary-general and "such staff as the Organization may require." Since it is the secretary-general, however, in whom the authority and responsibility is centered, his office, rather than the Secretariat as a whole, is really the principal organ to which the Charter refers. The secretary-general is appointed by the General Assembly upon the recommendation of the Security Council. The decision of the former body is by simple majority, but in the Security Council it may be vetoed.

The Secretariat is organized on a functional basis. This means that any of its departments serve the other organs of the UN according to the type of work they are performing. There are five major departments, each with an under-secretary, as follows: Political and Security Affairs; Economic and Social Affairs; Trusteeship and Information from non-self-governing Territories; Public Information; and Conference Services. In addition, there are five offices concerned with staff and administrative functions. The eleventh major division is the Technical Assistance Administration.

The Secretariat staff is composed of over 3000 persons in New York, and about an additional 1000 in Geneva and several other centers. The Charter states that in selecting the staff the paramount consideration shall be efficiency, competence, and integrity, but that due regard shall be given to as wide a geographic basis as possible. As a matter of practice only the higher headquarters positions—about a thousand—are "internationally recruited"; no effort is made to maintain geographic balance for the remainder. American citizens hold the great majority of the lower

---

[10] See pp. 327.

[11] *The United Nations Secretariat* (New York: Carnegie Endowment, 1950), pp. 8-9.

positions and almost one-third of the "international" ones. Only a few are held by nationals of the Soviet Union, although not because of discrimination on the part of the Secretariat. Member states are obliged to respect the "exclusively international character" of the Secretariat, and staff members must affirm their loyalty to the UN.

FUNCTIONS AND AUTHORITY. As previously indicated, the Charter vests the power of the Secretariat in the secretary-general. Although he cannot perform all the varied and burdensome tasks, he is nevertheless responsible for them and possesses commensurate authority over the Secretariat. According to the Charter, he is the chief administrative officer of the UN (Art. 97), acts in the capacity of secretary-general for all principal organs except the International Court of Justice, and performs all other functions entrusted to him by those organs (Art. 97). Under Article 99 he may bring to the attention of the Security Council any matter which, in his opinion, may threaten international peace and security. Although a proposal to give him the same right with respect to the General Assembly was rejected at San Francisco in 1945, on the grounds that it might impinge upon the Security Council's primary responsibility for the maintenance of international peace and security, he may and does bring problems of this nature to the attention of the General Assembly through his annual report to it on the work of the organization. In actual practice, the secretary-general has carried out his duties without meticulous reference to the rather general, if not ambiguous, Charter provisions, on the general assumption that he has adequate authority.

The functions of the Secretariat fall under six headings: administrative and executive; technical; financial; organization and administration of the Secretariat; representational; and political. Among its more important *administrative* and *executive* functions are those of providing a channel of communication between the members and the organization, coordinating UN activities, and carrying out its decisions. The coordinating work of the Secretariat is especially important, for it is the only body which commands a continuous and comprehensive view of the entire organization's work. The administration of the technical assistance program, which requires the combined efforts of several of the main organs and specialized agencies, is a splendid example of this type of Secretariat activity. The so-called *technical* functions range from routine matters, such as the providing of space, to rendering legal advice, preparing statistical studies, and analyzing problems on which decisions are to be made. On the *financial* side the Secretariat formulates and defends the annual budget adopted by the General Assembly, allocates money, controls expenditures, and collects and disburses funds. It also consults with the specialized agencies in attempts to coordinate their budgets and to assure high standards of administration. As the head of the Secretariat, the secretary-general is responsible for its *organization, staffing,* and *management.* He is the only official in a position to *represent* the organization as a whole. In this capacity he signs agreements on its behalf, such as the Headquarters Agreements, and presents documents to and sometimes even pleads before the International Court of Justice.

It is in the so-called political realm (that is, in the exercise of discretion in influencing the substance of policy) that the UN Secretariat differs the most from its League predecessor.[12] For the first two years the secretary-general proceeded rather cautiously; after 1947 he took a vigorous stand more frequently; and with the advent of the North Korean aggression he threw his whole influence behind the application of collective security measures.

There are many different channels available to the secretary-general through which he may influence policy. In the Korean case he specifically invoked his power under Article 99. His implied powers under that Article, however, are much wider than simply calling the attention of the Security Council to a matter. He has asserted without contradiction his right to make a full and impartial investigation of a matter to determine whether he should bring it to the attention of the Security Council. In his annual report to the General Assembly, in the work of preparing the agenda of the several UN bodies, and by participating in actual discussions on many matters, the secretary-general makes his influence felt. Many of the resolutions of the organs, although perhaps not the most important ones, are actually drafted by the Secretariat. Some of these resolutions gave the secretary-general considerable discretionary authority both in appointing officials to carry them out and in their actual administration. In authorizing the technical assistance program the General Assembly prescribed that "the amount of services and the financial conditions under which they shall be furnished . . . shall be decided by the Secretary-General."

The Secretariat has frequently taken the initiative in interpreting the Charter. Although legal in form, such activity has distinct political overtones. In the Iranian case of 1946, a Secretariat memorandum stated that when a party (Iran) dropped its complaint and requested that an item be removed from the Security Council agenda, this should be done. In the Palestine controversy, the Secretariat held that the Security Council could enforce a resolution of the General Assembly even if a threat to the peace were not involved.

In 1960, the UN—in effect the Secretariat—was charged with a novel responsibility, when on July 31 of that year the former Belgian Congo received its independence and law and order collapsed. Acting with

---

[12] For an excellent account of the political powers and practice of the Secretariat, see Stephen M. Schwebel, *The Secretary-General of the United Nations* (Cambridge: Harvard University Press, 1952).

great dispatch in accordance with a Security Council resolution, the secretary-general took over virtual responsibility for governing the country on behalf of the UN.

Economic and Social, and Trusteeship Councils. The Economic and Social Council and the Trusteeship Council function under the direct supervision of the General Assembly, and are served by the Secretariat. The former (ECOSOC) consists of the representatives of eighteen members of the UN elected by the General Assembly, six of which are elected each year for a three-year term. The composition of the Trusteeship Council is more complicated. Those members who are administering trust territories, and all permanent members of the Security Council are automatically entitled to be represented. The General Assembly elects an additional number of states for three-year terms, in order that the Council may be equally divided between representatives of administering and non-administering states.

As several former trusteeship areas became independent in the late nineteen-fifties and early sixties, it became impossible to adhere to the Charter provisions concerning the organization of the Council. There was supposed to be a balance between administering and non-administering states, but the five permanent members of the Security Council were also guaranteed representation. If, as appeared probable, France, the United Kingdom, and Belgium granted independence to their trusteeship areas, the United States would be the only administering power remaining. In that case, there would be four non-administering powers with their permanent seats, but only the United States to offset them. Balance would therefore be impossible. Perhaps it would be possible to amend the Charter to meet this unforeseen development.

The International Court of Justice. The framers of the Charter were confronted with the problem of either continuing the Permanent Court of International Justice or starting anew. The Court had functioned efficiently; with one or two exceptions its decisions were regarded as free from partisan bias; and several treaties contained provisions for referring cases to it for settlement. On the other hand, since the Statute of the Court was silent concerning its amendment, the consent of all signatories would be required, and sixteen of them were not represented at San Francisco. Moreover, there was a feeling that the Court had been a part of the League which had failed, and that there should be a new start. For these and other reasons the Committee of Jurists which had been agreed to at Yalta drafted a statute for a new court, but in doing so followed the existing pattern closely, even to the extent of numbering articles identically. The principal difference between the two organs is that membership in the old Court was independent of League membership, whereas all members of the UN are automatically parties to the new

Court Statute. However, under conditions laid down by the Security Council and General Assembly, states may adhere to the Statute alone, and Switzerland, Liechtenstein, and San Marino have done so.

STRUCTURE, COMPOSITION, AND PROCEDURE.   A court requires impartial judges rather than partisan nationals. Nevertheless, the establishment of a court was impossible at both Hague Conferences principally because each state insisted that one of its nationals "represent" it on the judicial body. The system devised for the election of judges of both courts is a compromise between judicial impartiality and national prestige. Though the Court is composed "of independent judges elected regardless of their nationality from among persons of high moral character, who possess the qualifications required in their respective countries for appointment to the highest judicial offices, or are jurisconsults of recognized competence in international law" (Statute, Art. 2), no two may be nationals of the same state, and the principal legal systems and forms of civilization are supposed to be represented. Judges are nominated by the national groups of the Permanent Court of Arbitration, and are elected by the Security Council and General Assembly by an absolute majority vote in each organ.[13] The fifteen judges are elected for nine-year terms, and are eligible for re-election, five being chosen every three years. A state which is a party to a dispute before the Court may select one of its nationals to serve, in addition to others, if it is not otherwise represented.

The Court makes its own rules except as set forth in the Statute. It elects its president and vice-president, and appoints the Court registrar. It remains in session continuously except during official vacations. Nine judges constitute a quorum; decisions and opinions are by majority vote. The president votes only in case of a tie. Parties present their cases both in writing and orally.

JURISDICTION.   Only states, not individuals, may be parties to disputes before the Court. Membership in no way obligates a state to submit to its jurisdiction. Cases come to the Court in three ways: (1) by agreement of the parties concerned in a particular case; (2) on the application of one party alone if the disputing states have agreed by treaty, in advance, to submit certain types of cases to it; (3) in like manner if both parties have accepted the "optional clause."

The third method is the result of a compromise between the advocates of compulsory jurisdiction over all "justiciable" questions and those who would leave the submission of cases entirely voluntary in each instance. States may or may not adhere to Article 36, par. 5 (the optional clause) of the statute; if they do so they are henceforth bound to submit certain types of cases to the Court. The clause provides that states may at any time recognize the submission of all *legal* disputes to the Court as com-

---

[13] An absolute majority is more than 50 per cent of the entire membership.

pulsory without special agreement if the other state involved has also accepted the clause.[14] Thirty-six states had accepted the clause as of 1958, but many had done so with reservations.

Members of the Commonwealth exclude disputes between themselves. The United States Senate, in consenting to adherence, made three reservations, the most important of which excluded "disputes with regard to matters which are essentially within the domestic jurisdiction of the United States . . . *as determined by the United States. . . .*" [Italics mine—CPS.] Since the Court could not consider such a case anyway, or if it did it would have to rule in the interest of the United States, the significance of the reservations resides in the final clause which makes the United States the judge of what matters it will submit. What was given with one hand would appear to have been withdrawn by the other.

In addition to the disputes between states in which the Court hands down decisions or binding judgments, it is also authorized to give advisory opinions requested by the Security Council or the General Assembly, or by other organs and specialized agencies authorized by the General Assembly to make such requests. In this respect it follows continental European rather than Anglo-Saxon practice. However, no state or organ is obliged to follow an advisory opinion, and many states have refused to do so. So far, in its advisory role the new Court has been far less effective than was the old.

BASES OF COURT JUDGMENT.   As long as the Court functions as a judicial body it can decide cases only on the basis of law. According to the Statute (Art. 38), "The Court, whose function is to decide in accordance with international law," applies international conventions or treaties, international customary law, and the general principles of law recognized by civilized nations. However, if the parties agree, it may decide a case *ex aequo et bono,* that is, on the basis of right and justice rather than law. In such an instance, however, it is legislating rather than adjudicating.

APPROACHES TO
INTERNATIONAL PEACE AND WELFARE
THROUGH INTERNATIONAL ORGANIZATION

In the preceding pages we have discussed the essential features of general and universal type international organizations and referred to their approaches to the twin objectives of international peace and human welfare. These approaches will now be summarized: the more important ones will be treated in greater detail in subsequent chapters.

---

14 The clause covers all legal disputes concerning the interpretation of a treaty, any question of international law, the existence of a fact, which if established, would constitute a breach of an international obligation, and reparations for such a breach. Since there are probably no other types of legal disputes the itemization appears to be superfluous.

We have noted the dual purpose claimed for the economic and social functions of international organizations. Whether it be the relief of hunger, the interchange of ideas, peoples, and commodities, the development of standards for civil aviation, or the promotion of self-government and independence for colonial peoples, it is contended that the cause of peace is served simultaneously as peoples are fed, knowledge and goods are shared, air passage is expedited, and dependent peoples educated and led to freedom.[15]

The proponents of international organization, however, have approached the problem of maintaining peace by more direct routes, five in particular. First, they have sought to improve the international legal framework. In particular, members of international organizations have assumed obligations to settle their disputes peaceably, to limit their rights to resort to force, and to come to the aid of victims of aggression. Although it was widely assumed, especially during the interwar years and in the United States, that peace could be bought by simply "outlawing war," both the League and the UN went considerably beyond that point. Law is necessary, but insufficient by itself, to achieve peace.

Secondly, it has been assumed that disarmament is conducive or necessary to national security and to a peaceful world. Both the League and the UN have, therefore, devoted a great deal of effort—so far without tangible results—to reduce the burdens and dangers of the arms race.

Thirdly, it has been thought better to talk than to fight—that somehow words are a substitute for bullets. This "grand debate" approach to peace finds clearcut expression in the discussions held in the assemblies of the world organizations, although it is not confined to them. Frequently referred to as "open multilateral diplomacy," it bears little resemblance to diplomacy proper, i.e., negotiation in which representatives engage in the exchange of ideas in an attempt to arrive at a solution of relatively specific problems. A more apt comparison is with debates conducted in legislatures and parliaments, in which words are directed as much towards constituents as they are towards the other members of these bodies. In short, all that is open and multilateral is not diplomacy.

Fourthly, general international organizations not only obligate members to settle their disputes in peaceful ways; they also establish procedures and organs to assist, to induce, and, indirectly, to coerce them to do so.

Finally, the League and the UN provided for a system of collective security. In the event war broke out despite the other means to prevent it, sanctions of a diplomatic, economic, and military nature might be applied. The possibility of sanctions is also some assurance that they will not be necessary.

---

[15] See pp. 185-87 for a fuller treatment of this thesis.

TABLE 2

LIST OF PUBLIC INTERNATIONAL ORGANIZATIONS

Organizations under categories I through VI include all the important ones and most of the others, whereas VII (Miscellaneous) includes only typical organizations. See Union of International Association, *Yearbook of International Organizations,* 7th ed., 1958-59 (Brussels, Belgium) for a list of 149 governmental organizations.

I.–*United Nations System* (universal)
    A.–General Purpose
        1.–The United Nations (UN)
    B.–Specialized Agencies of the UN–(Functional-Universal)
        2.–International Labour Organization (ILO)
        3.–Food and Agriculture Organization of the UN (FAO)
        4.–UN Educational, Scientific and Cultural Organization (UNESCO)
        5.–World Health Organization (WHO)
        6.–International Bank for Reconstruction and Development (IBRD)
        7.–International Finance Corporation (IFC)
        8.–International Monetary Fund (IMF)
        9.–International Civil Aviation Organization (ICAO)
      10.–Universal Postal Union (UPU)
      11.–International Telecommunication Union (ITU)
      12.–World Meteorological Organization (WMO)
      13.–Inter-Governmental Maritime Consultative Organization (IMCO)
      14.–International Atomic Energy Agency (Autonomous International Organization Under the Aegis of the UN) (IAEA)
    C.–UN Affiliated Organizations (Functional-Universal)
      15.–Technical Assistance Board (TAB)
      16.–Permanent Central Opium Board (PCOB) and Drug Supervisory Body (DSB)
      17.–UN Children's Fund (UNICEF)
      18.–Office of the UN High Commissioner for Refugees (UNHCR)

II.–*The European "Community of Six"* (*Regional-Functional*)
      19.–European Coal and Steel Community (ECSC)
      20.–European Economic Community (EEC)
      21.–Euratom
      22.–European Parliamentary Assembly
      23.–Court of Justice (of the European Community)
      24.–Economic and Social Committee
      25.–European Investments Bank

III.–*Other European Regional-Functional Organizations*
      26.–Administrative Centre of Social Security for Rhine Boatmen
      27.–Bank for International Settlements (BIS)
      28.–Central Commission for the Navigation of the Rhine
      29.–Council of Europe (CE) (General advisory)
      30.–Danube Commission
      31.–European and Mediterranean Plant Protection Organization (EPPO)
      32.–European Commission for the Control of Foot-and-Mouth Disease
      33.–European Company for the Financing of Railway Rolling Stock (EUROFIMA)
      34.–European Conference of Ministers of Transport (ECMT)
      35.–European Forestry Commission (EFC)
      36.–European Organization for Nuclear Research
      37.–European Productivity Agency (EPA)
      38.–General Fisheries Council for the Mediterranean (GFCM)
      39.–Inter-Parliamentary Consultative Council of Benelux
      40.–Nordic Council (General Consultative)
      41.–Scandinavian Patent Committee

IV.–*Military Alliances* (Regional)
    42.–Australia-New Zealand-United States (ANZUS)
    43.–Balkan Alliance
    44.–Central Treaty Organization (CENTO)
    45.–North Atlantic Treaty Organization (NATO)
    46.–Southeast Asia Treaty Organization (SEATO)
    47.–Warsaw Treaty Organization
    48.–Western European Union (WEU)

V.–*Western Hemisphere (Regional)*
  A.–General Purpose
    49.–Organization of American States (OAS)
    50.–Organization of Central American States
  B.–Miscellaneous
    51.–Central American Research Institute for Industry
    52.–Institute of Nutrition of Central America and Panama (INCAP)
    53.–Inter-American Commission of Women
    54.–Inter-American Conference on Social Security
    55.–Inter-American Council of Jurists (OAS)
    56.–Inter-American Defense Board (IADB) (OAS)
    57.–Inter-American Indian Institute (III)
    58.–Inter-American Institute of Agricultural Sciences
    59.–Inter-American Peace Committee (OAS)
    60.–Inter-American Radio Office

VI.–*African (Regional)*
    61.–African Postal and Telecommunications Union (APTU)
    62.–Commission for Technical Co-operation in Africa South of the Sahara (CCTA)
    63.–Conference of Independent African States
    64.–Inter-African Bureau for Epizootic Disease (IBED)
    65.–Inter-African Bureau for Soils and Rural Economy (BIS)
    66.–Inter-African Committee on Statistics
    67.–Inter-African Labour Institute (ILI)
    68.–Inter-African Pedological Service
    69.–Inter-African Phytosanitary Commission (IPC)

VII.–*Miscellaneous*
    70.–Asian Legal Consultative Committee
    71.–Asia-Pacific Forestry Commission (APFC)
    72.–Colombo Plan Council for Technical Co-operation in South and South-East Asia
    73.–Commonwealth Telecommunications Board
    74.–Council for Mutual Economic Aid (COMECON)
    75.–Diplomatic Conference of International Maritime Law
    76.–The Hague Conference on Private International Law
    77.–Indo-Pacific Fisheries Council (IPFC)
    78.–Intergovernmental Committee for European Migration (ICEM)
    79.–Intergovernmental Copyright Committee (IGC)
    80.–International Bureau of Education (IBE)
    81.–International Bureau of Weights and Measures
    82.–International Coffee Organization
    83.–International Commission for the Northwest Atlantic Fisheries (ICNAF)
    84.–International Commission of the Cape Spartel Light in Tangier
    85.–International Committee of Military Medicine and Pharmacy (ICMMP)
    86.–International Cotton Advisory Committee (ICAC)
    87.–International Council for the Exploration of the Seas (ICES)
    88.–International Institute for the Unification of Private Law (UNIDROIT)
    89.–International North Pacific Fisheries Commission
    90.–International Patent Institute
    91.–International Rice Commission (IRC)

92.–International Sugar Council
93.–International Tea Committee
94.–International Tin Council
95.–International Union for the Protection of Literary and Artistic Works
96.–International Union for the Publication of Customs Tariffs
97.–International Whaling Commission (IWC)
98.–International Wheat Council
99.–International Wool Study Group (IWSG)
100.–Joint Institute for Nuclear Research
101.–League of Arab States
102.–Permanent Court of Arbitration
103.–Postal Union of the Americas and Spain (PUAS)
104.–South Pacific Commission (SPC)

SUGGESTED READINGS

Ahman, Sven, "Mr. Hammarskjöld's Not-So-Quiet Diplomacy," *Reporter*, XIX (Sept. 4, 1958), 9-13.

Alger, Chadwick F., "Non-Resolution Consequences of the United Nations and Their Effect on International Conflict," *Journal of Conflict Resolution*, V (June 1961), 128-45.

Bailey, Sydney D., "The Future Composition of the Trusteeship Council," *International Organization*, XIII (Summer 1959), 412-21.

————, *The General Assembly of the United Nations: A Study of Procedure and Practice.* New York: Frederick A. Praeger, Inc., 1960.

Ball, M. Margaret, "Bloc Voting in the General Assembly," *International Organization*, V (Feb. 1951), 3-31.

Brierly, James L., *The Covenant and the Charter.* Cambridge: The Cambridge University Press, 1947.

Cheever, Daniel S. and H. Field Haviland, Jr., *Organizing for Peace: International Organization in World Affairs.* Boston: Houghton Mifflin Company, 1954.

Clark, William, "New Forces in the United Nations," *International Affairs*, XXXVI (July 1960), 322-29.

Claude, Inis L., Jr., *Swords Into Ploughshares: The Problems and Progress of International Organization.* New York: Random House, 1956.

Cohen, Maxwell, "The United Nations Secretariat: Some Constitutional and Administrative Developments," *American Journal of International Law*, XLIX (July 1955), 295-319.

Commission to study the Organization of Peace, *Strengthening the United Nations*, Arthur N. Holcombe, Chairman. New York: Harper & Brothers, 1957.

De Russet, Alan, "Large and Small States in International Organization—II," *International Affairs*, XXXI (Apr. 1955), 192-202.

Goodrich, Lelan l M. and Edward Hambro, *Charter of the United Nations: Commentary and Documents*, 2nd and rev. ed. Boston: World Peace Foundation, 1949.

———, "The U.N. Security Council," *International Organization*, XII (Summer 1958), 273-87.

——— and Anne. P. Simons, *The United Nations and the Maintenance of International Peace and Security*. Washington D.C.: The Brookings Institution, 1955.

Goodspeed, Stephen S., *Nature and Function of International Organization*. New York: Oxford University Press, Inc., 1959.

Gordenker, Leon, "Policy-Making and Secretariat Influence in the U.N. General Assembly: The Case of Public Information," *American Political Science Review*, LIV (June 1960), 359-73.

Hadwen, John G. and Johan Kaufmann, *How United Nations Decisions are Made*. Leyden, Netherlands: A. W. Sijthoff, 1960

Hammarskjöld, Dag, "The Developing Role of the United Nations," *United Nations Review*, VI (Sept. 1959), 8-18.

———, "The Development of a Constitutional Framework for International Cooperation," *United Nations Review*, VI (June 1960), 26-32.

Haviland, H. Field, *The Political Role of the General Assembly*. New York: Carnegie Endowment for International Peace, 1951.

Hemleben, Sylvester, Jr., *Plans for World Peace through Six Centuries*. Chicago: University of Chicago Press, 1943.

Hovet, Thomas, *Bloc Politics in the United Nations*. Cambridge: Harvard University Press, 1960.

Howard-Ellis, Charles, *The Origin, Structure and Working of the League of Nations*, 2 vols. Boston: Houghton Mifflin Company, 1929.

Jiménez de Arechaga, Eduardo, *Voting and the Handling of Disputes in the Security Council*. New York: Carnegie Endowment for International Peace, 1950.

Johnson, D. H. N., "The Effect of Resolutions of the General Assembly of the United Nations," *British Year Book of International Law*, 1955-56, XXXII (1956), 97-122.

Jordon, William M., "Concepts and Realities in International Political Organization," *International Organization*, XI (Autumn 1957), 587-96.

Joyce, James Avery, *Revolution on East River: The Twilight of National Sovereignty*. New York: Abelard-Schuman Limited, 1956.

Lie, Trygve, *In the Cause of Peace: Seven Years with the United Nations*. New York: The Macmillan Co., 1954.

Lissetzyn, Oliver James, *The International Court of Justice: Its Role in the Maintenance of International Peace and Security*. New York: Carnegie Endowment for International Peace, 1951.

Levi, Werner, *Fundamentals of World Organization*. Minneapolis, Minnesota: University of Minnesota Press, 1950.

Loveday, Alexander, *Reflections on International Administration*. Oxford: The Clarendon Press, 1956.

MacIver, Robert M., *The Nations and the United Nations*. Prepared for the Carnegie Endowment for International Peace. New York: Manhattan Publishing Co., 1959.

Mangone, Gerard J., *A Short History of International Organization*. New York: McGraw-Hill Book Co., Inc., 1954.

Nicholas, Herbert G., *The United Nations as a Political Institution*. London, New York: Oxford University Press, Inc., 1959.

Niemeyer, Gerhart, "The Balance-Sheet of the League Experiment," *International Organization*, VI (Nov. 1952), 537-58.

Riches, Cromwell A., *Majority Rule in International Organization: A Study of the Trend from Unanimity to Majority Decision*. Baltimore: The Johns Hopkins Press, 1940.

Riggs, Robert E., *Politics in the United Nations: A Study of United States Influence in the General Assembly*. Urbana, Illinois: University of Illinois Press, 1958.

Russell, Ruth B., *A History of the United Nations Charter: The Role of the United States, 1940-1945*. Washington, D.C.: Brookings Institution, 1958.

Schwebel, Stephen M., *The Secretary-General of the United Nations: His Political Powers and Practice*. Cambridge: Harvard University Press, 1952.

Scott, F. R., "The World's Civil Service," *International Conciliation*, No. 496 (Jan. 1954).

Sharp, Walter, *Field Administration in the United Nations System*. New York: Frederick A. Praeger, Inc., 1961.

Sohn, Louis B., ed., *Basic Documents of the United Nations*. Brooklyn, New York: The Foundation Press, Inc., 1956.

Swift, Richard N., "The United Nations and Its Public," *International Organization*, XIV (Winter 1960), 60-61.

Triska, Jan and Howard E. Koch, Jr., "The Asian-African Nations and International Organization: Third Force or Collective Impotence?" *Review of Politics*, XXI (Apr. 1959), 417-55.

The United Nations Conference on International Organization; San Francisco, California, April 25 to June 26 1945; Selected Documents. Department of State Publication 2490, Conference Series 83, Washington, D.C.: Government Printing Office, 1946.

U.S. Senate, Committee on Foreign Relations, Subcommittee on United Nations Charter, *How United Nations Charter Has Developed, Staff Study No. 2*. Committee Print, 83d Cong., 2nd sess., May 18, 1954. Washington, D.C.: Government Printing Office, 1954.

————, *Problem of Membership in United Nations, Staff Study No. 3*. Committee Print, 83d Cong., 2nd sess., May 21, 1954. Washington, D.C.: Government Printing Office, 1954.

————, *Problem of Veto in United Nations Security Council, Staff Study No. 1*. Committee Print, 83d Cong., 2nd sess., 1954. Washington, D.C.: Government Printing Office, 1954.

Walters, Francis P., *A History of the League of Nations*, 2 vols. London, New York: Oxford University Press, Inc., 1952.

Wright, Quincy, "International Conflict and the United Nations," *World Politics*, X (Oct. 1957), 24-48.

9

Regionalism and Functionalism

Regional and functional organizations numbering into the hundreds exist alongside the universal general-purpose UN. The majority, like the European Coal and Steel Community (ECSC) and the World Health Organization (WHO), are concerned with problems in a particular field. The Organization of American States (OAS), however, is a regional arrangement with purposes and functions nearly as varied as those of the UN. Although most of these organizations deal with social and economic problems, some of the most important ones are concerned with military matters. Of the latter, NATO and its Soviet-bloc counterpart, the Warsaw Collective Security Pact, are the principal examples. Both functional and regional organizations may be a part of, related to, or separate from the UN. The Economic Commission for Europe (ECE) is a functional agency of the Economic and Social Council (ECOSOC); the United Nations Educational, Scientific and Cultural Organization (UNESCO), a specialized agency with its own constitution and staff, is related to the UN through ECOSOC; NATO is completely apart, although according to its constitution its actions must not violate the UN Charter.

The situation resulting from the co-existence of the UN and a multitude of regional and functional organizations is the despair of all who prefer simplicity and order. Membership and jurisdiction overlap; purpose and methods not only vary, but in some cases raise grave questions of compatibility. More than half of the members of the UN are also members of one or more of the military alliances; nearly all participate in regional or functional arrangements within or without the United Nations. The Economic Commission for Latin America (ECLA) under ECOSOC has a responsibility almost identical to that of the Inter-American Economic and Social Council of OAS. Given good will and intelligent planning, it is usually possible to minimize conflict and confusion among agencies concerned primarily with socio-economic problems. It is doubt-ful, however, that this is possible in the case of regional and universal peace and security arrangements. Universalists and regionalists argue bitterly on this point; functionalists also disagree with advocates of the general-purpose approach. The argument between the latter two is more over the efficacy of each approach than over their compatibility.

REGIONALISM

Regionalism is the concept of organizing states and dependent areas on a regional basis. But what is a region? Does the area of NATO, ex-tending from Hawaii eastward through Turkey, constitute a region? And does that of the far-flung Commonwealth of Nations, with London as its symbolic capital? Although a region is a *part* of the globe's surface, if NATO and the Commonwealth constitute regions, the *part* is not neces-sarily territorially contiguous. To add to the complexity, a state may be-long to several regional organizations, each with different areas. Among the many such organizations of which the United States is a member, five are regional security organizations, each encompassing different regions.[1] Furthermore, in no instance are *all* the states within the area indicated by the name of the organization included in its membership: but on the other hand, some states geographically distant *are* included. SEATO is an extreme case in point. Of the eight states located in Southeast Asia, only two—Thailand and the Philippines—are members of SEATO. Six[2] of its eight members, including the more powerful ones, are located on four different continents and two islands. Confronted with problems of this nature, one can only conclude with Alejandro Alvarez, Chilean Judge of the International Court of Justice, that "there is no rule to determine regions. Their existence must be shown by circumstances, and, in par-ticular, by the agreements made by the states who constitute them. . . . Regions are constituted by certain countries having affinities of race, in-stitutions, or, above all, political interests."[3]

In brief, an international region consists of the area of a number of countries with certain common interests which for at least one purpose distinguish it from other areas. Professor Hill suggests that "the term 'limited international' organization instead of regional . . . might be

---

[1] NATO, SEATO, OAS, Central Treaty Organization (CENTO), Australian, New Zealand, United States Security Treaty (ANZUS). The United States is associated with, but is not a member of CENTO.

[2] The United States, United Kingdom, France, New Zealand, Australia, and Paki-stan.

[3] Alejandro Alvarez, "La Reforme du Pacte de la Société des Nations sur des bases continental et régionales," a report to the fifth session of the Union Juridique Interna-tionale, 1926, p. 99, as quoted in Norman Hill, *International Organization* (New York: Harper & Brothers, 1952), p. 87.

more precise and less confusing."[4] That is quite true, but it is difficult to change accepted usage, however ambiguous.

Those who argue for regionalism usually regard themselves as "realists." A limited number of countries or dependencies may have a similarity of interest and a sense of community sufficient to enable them to work together effectively; extending the area to the world is courting failure. Arrangements such as NATO or the Organization of American States may work, it is contended, although world-wide collective security arrangements will not.

Proponents of the universal approach stress the fact of world interdependence in the economic, social, and political realms. Peace and prosperity are indivisible; what concerns anyone, anywhere, is the concern of all people everywhere. Regions are no more isolated than states. Regional arrangements, especially for purposes of "collective defense," divide rather than unite the world, and replace interstate with interregional conflict.

There are merits in the arguments of both regionalists and universalists. Certainly there may be advantages to regional cooperation in social and economic fields, especially if the alternative is not universal cooperation but none at all. It may be, as some contend, that regionalism is a step on the way to universalism. In any case, the real questions relate to which matters may be dealt with most effectively on a regional basis, which require the universal approach, the balance between them, and the relationship between limited and universal organizations. Even the UN has found it desirable to deal with certain economic and social problems regionally, and the Charter specifically permits the formation of "regional arrangements or agencies" for dealing with peace and security matters. The United States, concerned with the Western Hemisphere, has been an avid champion of regionalism, although aware at the same time of its possible conflict with a global approach.

THE FUNCTIONAL APPROACH

Functionalism originated in the public international unions of the nineteenth century; it continued to flourish under the auspices of the League and the UN. The specialized agencies and the functional commissions of ECOSOC are present examples. Although the direct concern of functional agencies is welfare rather than peace and security, it is argued that they contribute to peace by removing some of the causes of war, and by developing habits of cooperation which may rub off on those who deal with political matters. Some go even further by contending that they are

---

[4] *Ibid.*, p. 88.

a "peace by piece" approach to the elimination of international war through world government.

Functionalists believe that progress in organizing the world society is most likely to succeed when nations tackle concrete problems they have a mutual interest in solving, rather than when they deal with political matters over which conflict is inevitable. The godfather of functionalism, David Mitrany, writes that "the problem of our time is not how to keep the nations peacefully apart but how to bring them actively together."[5] He is skeptical about concern with covenants and charters, and organizations which attempt to do too much. Rather he prefers meeting each special situation as circumstances permit and the problem demands. Because international problems, by definition, transcend national boundaries, he holds that the tendency of efforts to organize around them will be to "break away from the traditional link between authority and a definite territory."[6] "[Functionalism] stresses the question of what contributions are essential to the creative work of solving common problems rather than of what sacrifices are required for the negative task of reconciling conflicting interests."[7]

Some of the advocates of functionalism contend that it is world "federation by installments." By emphasizing needs which cannot be met by nations in isolation, by proceeding gradually and empirically, and by integrating nations economically and socially, political boundaries will become meaningless. Eventually, finding that most important segments of life are organized horizontally across national boundaries, and having developed experience and cooperative habits and attitudes, it will be relatively easy to gather these functions under one governmental umbrella. When that occurs, a world federation will have been born.

The continuity and increased tempo of functionalism regionally and on a near-world scale, within and without the UN and other organizations with comprehensive purposes and functions, demonstrates its usefulness for cooperation on a wide range of problems that refuse to be confined within national boundaries. Yet some claims advanced by its most ardent advocates do not seem valid. It has never been proved that nations fight either because they are poor, or because of the other economic and social problems which functionalism would help solve. Nor is there evidence, at least so far, that functional organizations have in any substantial way changed the provincial and nationalistic attitudes of men. Moreover, it is an illusion that social, cultural, and economic affairs can be separated from politics. For politics is a type of interaction involving

---

[5] *A Working Peace System* (London and New York: Royal Institute of International Affairs, 1946), p. 7.

[6] *Ibid.*, p. 6.

[7] Claude, *Swords Into Plowshares*, p. 375, Chapter 16, "The Functional Approach to Peace," is one of the best in this excellent work,

conflict, very often with material goods, social mores, and cultural values the stakes in the struggle. The primary need is for institutions through which national power can be limited and directed, international conflicts solved, and security made less precarious. Non-political problems await progress in the political realm; once substantial advance is made here, economic and social problems will be more tractable. Until we are more certain of how and where to proceed, however, the wiser course seems to be to work on all fronts simultaneously in the hope that advance at one point will further progress elsewhere along the line.

The remainder of this chapter is devoted to a consideration of regionalism and the UN; the Organization of American States, a regional general-purpose organization; NATO, a military alliance organization; the Universal Postal Union as an example of a well-established functional organization with near-universal membership; and integration within the European "Community of Six."

REGIONALISM AND THE UNITED NATIONS

The relationship of regional organizations to the UN is one of the most controversial issues which confronted the framers of the UN Charter. Although the problem arose early and was considered at length, it is doubtful that it was resolved satisfactorily.

Regionalism in Postwar Planning and the Dumbarton Oaks Proposals

At one stage in the planning for a postwar organization it was suggested that it be based on three regional councils: one for Europe, a second for the Western Hemisphere, and a third for Asia. A world council would be composed of the United States, the United Kingdom, the Soviet Union, and possibly China, as well as "certain other powers" selected from the regional councils. The four big powers would also sit on the regional councils in which they were directly interested. Originally proposed by Prime Minister Churchill in 1943, and supported by President Roosevelt and Under Secretary of State Sumner Wells, it was strongly opposed by Secretary of State Cordell Hull. After an extensive study, the Department of State concluded that regional organizations might substitute interregional for national conflicts and wars, place the United States, as a member of several regional councils, in the unenviable position of mediator, and encourage isolationists who might favor participation in Western Hemisphere cooperation but oppose it elsewhere. Furthermore, European participation in the Western Hemisphere organization would be embarrassing to the United States.[8]

Thereafter, the regional basis for the world organization was dropped. Although there might also be regional peace and security agreements, Hull was determined that they should be kept subordinated to the general arrangement. The Dumbarton Oaks Proposals reflected this point of view. Neither they nor the Charter refer to regional arrangements pertaining to economic and social matters, nor is the following discussion concerned with them.

The Charter and
Regional Arrangements

Although it is usually contended that the Charter, as it developed subsequently to Dumbarton Oaks, retained the basic principle of subordinating regional arrangements to the UN, the changes and exceptions adopted at the San Francisco Conference, and later interpretations of and developments under these modifications, raise considerable doubt that this is the case. An understanding of this point requires a somewhat involved analysis of pertinent provisions of the Charter. Chapter VIII ("Regional Arrangements") contains the essentials of the Dumbarton Oaks proposals on that subject, and along with Articles 51, 53, and 107, the modifications. Nothing in the Charter "precludes the existence of regional arrangements or agencies for dealing with such matters relating to the maintenance of international peace and security as are appropriate for regional action, provided that such arrangements or agencies and their activities are consistent with the Purposes and Principles of the United Nations" (Art. 52). Terms are not defined. An amendment, submitted by the Egyptian delegate at San Francisco, defining regional arrangements was rejected as being too narrow. Article 53 implicitly refers to such bilateral arrangements as the treaty of alliance between the Soviet Union and the United Kingdom of May 26, 1942, as regional ones. The states interested in these arrangements were quite as much concerned with *inter-* as they were with *intra-*regional problems. This was true not only of those powers especially concerned with "alliances" against the enemy states, but also of the states of the Western Hemisphere among whom the principle of continental solidarity against outside aggression was well developed. *If such arrangements had been definitely limited to dealing with peace and security within regions they might have developed into genuine collective-action organizations.* Since they were not so limited, there was nothing to prevent their becoming, in part, alliances, or "collective defense" arrangements as some prefer to designate them.

---

[8] Cordell Hull, *The Memoirs of Cordell Hull* (New York: The Macmillan Co., 1948), II, pp. 1643-46.

Pacific Settlement. The pacific settlement of disputes under regional arrangements posed no particular problems at the San Francisco Conference. Members of the UN are obligated to submit disputes likely to endanger international peace to one of the conventional methods of peaceful settlement, or to "resort to regional arrangements" (Article 33). Members entering into regional arrangements are to "make every effort to achieve pacific settlement of local disputes through such arrangements before referring them to the Security Council," which is to encourage pacific settlement of such disputes through regional arrangements or by regional agencies (Art. 52).

The Problem of Enforcement and Article 51. The difficult problems arose over application of enforcement measures, and it was in this connection that two far-reaching exceptions were made at San Francisco to the provision that "no enforcement action shall be taken under regional arrangements or by regional agencies without the authorization of the Security Council . . ." (Art. 53). One of these exceptions concerned measures against an enemy state, defined as "any state which during the Second World War has been an enemy of any signatory of the . . . Charter" (Art. 53). Measures could be taken against these states (1) pursuant to Article 107, or (2) in regional arrangements directed against a renewal of aggressive policy on the part of such states (Art. 53). The latter provision was to apply only until the organization, "on request of the Government concerned," was charged with the responsibility of preventing further aggression. Article 107, a part of Chapter XVII, "Transitional Security Arrangements," states that the Charter does not invalidate or preclude action against an enemy state by a Charter signatory taken or authorized as a result of World War II. Although under Article 107 action was permitted under any circumstances, under regional arrangements it was limited to instances of "renewal of aggressive policy." The provisions of these two articles (53 and 107) were to be temporary, presumably to end not later than the admission of a former enemy state to membership in the organization. It was contended by the Soviet delegation, in both the Berlin blockade and the Korean questions, that Article 107 not only permits action without Security Council permission, but also bars consideration of such questions by the UN. The majority of members, however, have acted on a contrary assumption.

Several states, including France, Belgium, and the Soviet Union, made proposals at San Francisco to permit action against the former enemy states. The United States delegation agreed to these changes, and they were accepted during the first days of the Conference. It was under Article 53 that the Soviet Union negotiated her network of mutual defense treaties with the Eastern European states and China.

The second condition under which enforcement action is permitted without the authorization of the Security Council is stated in Article 51: "Nothing in the present Charter shall impair the inherent right of individual or collective self-defense if an armed attack occurs against a member of the United Nations. . . ." The history of this article, and the developments which have taken place under it, are as interesting as they are important. To understand its history several strands must be brought together. Principle 4 of the Charter obligates members to refrain in their international relations from the threat or use of force against the territorial integrity or independence of any state, *or in any other manner inconsistent with the purposes of the United Nations.* Does this mean that a member may not defend itself in the case of an armed attack or other threat to its security? If a "Purpose" of the UN is to substitute collective security by the organization for individual measures of self-defense by the members, this would seem to be reasonable interpretation. On the other hand it may be, and actually was assumed, that the right of self-defense is "inherent" and was not impaired by principle 4. The danger of the latter position is that if it is left up to an individual state to determine when it is authorized to employ force in self-defense, principle 4 becomes a mockery. Both Japan and Germany contended that they acted in self-defense in World War II! Article 51 may be interpreted either as an explicit statement of an existing inherent right, or as an exception to the obligation in principle 4 to refrain from the threat or use of force. Since states do not have inherent rights (in the sense that they may not be abrogated by treaty), but only legal rights, the latter interpretation is the only logical one; it is also the only interpretation compatible with an effective system of law.

Why was Article 51 adopted? The initial and most important reason was the demand of the Latin-American states for a regional peace and security system with a considerable degree of autonomy from the UN. The United States and the Latin-American countries had agreed, in the Act of Chapultepec, to meet in the near future to form such an organization. It appears that the United States delegates did not realize the probability of a conflict between the Act and what had been agreed upon at Dumbarton Oaks and Yalta. It was originally assumed at San Francisco that only the Security Council could authorize enforcement action under regional arrangements. Moreover, since it could do so only by a substantive vote, a permanent member could veto a proposal to permit a regional organization to engage in enforcement action. The Latin-American states threatened to walk out of the Conference unless a way out could be found. The big powers resisted any tampering with the veto. Vyacheslav M. Molotov of the Soviet Union had attained his ends by the changes in Articles 53 and 107. Moreover, the American delegation was split, some of its members opposing opening the door any further to enforcement action by regional agreements for fear they would result in dividing the world into armed camps and thus destroy the effectiveness of the UN. The matter was finally referred to President Truman who sided with the "realists." The result was Article 51. But the chief Soviet delegate, Andrei Gromyko (Molotov had returned to Moscow) refused to accept it until Secretary of State Stettinius issued a press statement publicly committing the United States to the principles contained in Article 51. Gromyko finally gave in.[9]

Other states also were interested in Article 51, particularly the members of the Arab League; and France felt that her treaties of mutual assistance required similar recognition beyond that given by Articles 53 and 107, which were supposedly temporary in nature. Thus states became interested in what was to become Article 51 beyond its application to strictly regional arrangements. As Georg Schwarzenberger stated:

At this stage, the connection between the original proviso and the regional agreements had worn so thin that a Soviet proposal for [transfer to Chapter 7] . . . appeared to be merely logical. . . . Whoever might have happened to realize the significance of this shift, thought it wise to keep his own counsel. In the British Commentary on the Charter, however, the implications . . . are stated with engaging simplicity: "In the event of the Security Council failing to take any action, or if such action as it does take is clearly inadequate, the right of self-defense could be invoked by any member or group of members as justifying any action they thought fit to take."[10]

The Charter does attempt to prevent the abuse of the right. Measures taken under Article 51 are to be reported immediately to the Security Council, and its authority to take action is not to be impaired by the article in any way. When it has taken measures necessary to maintain international peace and security the right of the members to do so ceases. One may well question whether, measures once having been taken by individual members, the Security Council would find itself in a position to intervene. Would the United States, in the event of an act of aggression within the Western Hemisphere, be likely to approve a proposal for action by the Security Council, especially if Soviet troops were to be sent to Latin America?

Was Article 51 in part an expression of want of confidence in the UN? Though the right of *individual* self-defense is subject to abuse unless surrounded by proper safeguards, no state can be expected to permit invasion of its territory without resistance. A good case can also be made for permitting regional collective security systems. But both Chapter

---

[9] For an account of this see John Foster Dulles, *War or Peace* (New York: The Macmillan Co., 1950), pp. 89-92.

[10] *Power Politics*, A Study of International Society, 2nd rev. ed.; (New York: Frederick A. Praeger, Inc., 1951), p. 512.

VIII and Article 51 also permit "collective self-defense," and in practice at least, advance plans for such defense. If the UN afforded states an assurance of security there would be no need for these military alliances. If the men assembled at San Francisco in 1945 had believed the UN could be fully relied upon would they have been so concerned with alternative security arrangements? In any case, the historical system of alliances, by whatever name we may call them, has developed under the Charter.

THE ORGANIZATION OF AMERICAN STATES— THE REGIONAL GENERAL-PURPOSE APPROACH

The Inter-American system has been in the process of development since 1826, when Simon Bolivar called a conference of American States at Panama. The United States became active in the movement only in 1889-90, when the first Inter-American Conference was held in Washington, D.C. Until the nineteen-thirties, Latin Americans were too fearful of the "Colossus of the North" for Pan-Americanism to become a reality. Prior to that time, cooperation had been confined largely to the non-political field. With the development of the "Good Neighbor Policy" in the late twenties and early thirties, and the threat of World War II, there was considerable collaboration on political matters. A feeling developed that the rather loosely-knit system should be reorganized and established on a more formal basis. The Mexico City Conference on War and Peace held in 1945 resulted in an agreement (Act of Chapultepec) to that end. The success of the struggle at San Francisco to modify the Dumbarton Oaks Proposals opened the way for the subsequent development of the Inter-American system.

The Organization of American States, as it was officially designated at the Ninth International Conference of American States at Bogotá, Colombia, in March-April 1948, is provided for principally in three main instruments (the first two drawn up at this conference)—the Charter of the Organization of American States, the American Treaty of Pacific Settlement (Pact of Bogotá), and the Inter-American Treaty of Reciprocal Assistance (Rio treaty of 1947). The Pact of Bogotá consolidated and systematized existing instruments for the pacific settlement of international disputes. It has not been ratified by the required number of states to make it operative, but the existing agreements remain in effect unless superseded by the Pact.

The OAS Charter drawn up at Bogotá resulted in considerable "clarification, simplification, and centralization," and for the first time specified the system's powers and scope of action. Innovations, however, were

ORGANIZATION OF AMERICAN STATES

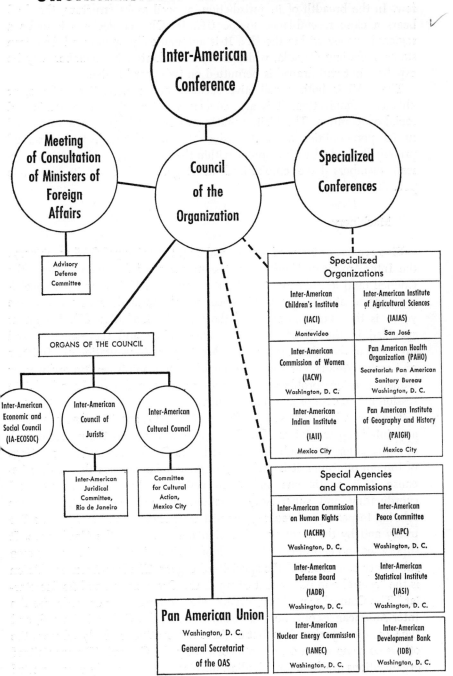

Inter-American Conference

Meeting of Consultation of Ministers of Foreign Affairs

Council of the Organization

Specialized Conferences

Advisory Defense Committee

ORGANS OF THE COUNCIL

Inter-American Economic and Social Council (IA-ECOSOC)

Inter-American Council of Jurists

Inter-American Cultural Council

Inter-American Juridical Committee, Rio de Janeiro

Committee for Cultural Action, Mexico City

Pan American Union
Washington, D. C.
General Secretariat
of the OAS

Specialized Organizations

Inter-American Children's Institute (IACI) Montevideo	Inter-American Institute of Agricultural Sciences (IAIAS) San José
Inter-American Commission of Women (IACW) Washington, D. C.	Pan American Health Organization (PAHO) Secretariat: Pan American Sanitary Bureau Washington, D. C.
Inter-American Indian Institute (IAII) Mexico City	Pan American Institute of Geography and History (PAIGH) Mexico City

Special Agencies and Commissions

Inter-American Commission on Human Rights (IACHR) Washington, D. C.	Inter-American Peace Committee (IAPC) Washington, D. C.
Inter-American Defense Board (IADB) Washington, D. C.	Inter-American Statistical Institute (IASI) Washington, D. C.
Inter-American Nuclear Energy Commission (IANEC) Washington, D. C.	Inter-American Development Bank (IDB) Washington, D. C.

Chart 2.

few. In the breadth of its jurisdiction, as well as its structure, the OAS bears a close resemblance to the UN. Its Charter declares it to be a regional agency within the UN. It is automatically open to all American states, including Canada, which ratify the Charter. No member may be expelled, but withdrawal is permitted on two years' notice.

The OAS is both a collective security and a collective defense, or alliance, organization. It is also concerned with regional economic and social cooperation. The United States was originally primarily interested in its potentialities as a defensive alliance, although it has served principally to deal with disputes within the hemisphere. The Latin-American members have emphasized at Bogotá and since its economic potentialities.

Machinery

Five organs, or types of organs, make up the principal OAS machinery: the Inter-American Conference, the meetings of foreign ministers, the Council (and its subcouncils), the Pan-American Union, and the specialized organizations. The Conference, which normally meets every five years, is the "supreme organ of the Organization" (Art. 33). Except as specified in the Charter, it determines policy and the structure and functions of the other organs. The "Meetings of Consultation of Ministers of Foreign Affairs," as the meetings of foreign ministers are awkwardly named, consider problems of an urgent nature, and must be called into session in the case of an armed attack.

The Council, with its seat in Washington, D.C., consists of an especially appointed representative of each member who carries the personal rank of ambassador. Although subordinate to the Conference and the meetings of foreign ministers, it is probably of greater importance than either because it is continuous and more active. It has extensive political coordinating and supervisory functions. Its political functions (those relating to peace and security) consist of those assigned to it in the Rio treaty and by the meetings of foreign ministers and the Conference. It supervises and coordinates the work of the Pan-American Union, its own subsidiary councils, and the specialized organs. The Pan-American Union is the "central and permanent organ of the Organization and its Secretariat." The Council's subsidiary organs, also designated as councils, are the Inter-American Economic and Social Council, the Cultural Council, and the Council of Jurists. The first of these is a continuous body whereas the others convene when called into session by the Council. The specialized organizations are functional bodies, developed haphazardly over a period of time. Since 1948 many have been eliminated and others brought into relationship with the OAS or one of its councils.

The Inter-American Treaty

The Inter-American Treaty of Reciprocal Assistance, although ante-dating the Charter, assumes its existence and is in turn referred to in the Charter.

The Rio treaty provides for joint action in the event of an armed attack within a specified area, or other threat to the peace of the Western Hemisphere. First, it defines a security zone running from pole to pole around the American continents and Greenland. Secondly, an armed attack from within or from outside the zone is declared to be an attack against all, and each member is obliged to assist in meeting it until the organization takes over. The OAS Council may meet provisionally, but it must immediately convoke a meeting of the ministers of foreign affairs. This group is empowered to decide, by a two-thirds vote, on measures to be taken, and all members are bound to comply, except that no state may be required to employ its armed forces. But no member may prevent such action by the organization. Thirdly, reciprocal assistance is stipu-lated in the case of aggression, or the threat of aggression, that is not an armed attack. The procedures are essentially the same as in the case of an armed attack, except that no provision is made for mutual assistance as an emergency measure. An organ of consultation, either the Council or a session of the ministers of foreign affairs, must be called into session immediately, and binding action is decided by two-thirds vote. Urgent matters are supposed to be referred to the meetings of ministers of foreign affairs. The Council, however, may constitute itself a provisional organ of consultation, and, since there is no time limit, and it may deter-mine what is urgent, it may in fact continue to function as long as it chooses to do so. Although the use of armed force is not specifically prohibited by the treaty in situations where no armed attack has taken place, it would appear to be so by the UN Charter. If this interpretation is correct, the United States is prohibited from using force to prevent a violation of the Monroe Doctrine if that violation does not involve an armed attack. Fourthly, in less serious situations, and in the case of an armed attack on an American state outside of the defense zone, such as on its military forces in Europe, or Asia, only consultation is called for.

The OAS and the United Nations

If words can make it so, the OAS is subordinate to the UN. Not only is it declared to be a regional organization under Chapter VIII of the UN Charter, but other articles are designed to prevent conflicts between them. For example, the third section of the OAS Charter begins: "None of the provisions of this Charter shall be construed as impairing the rights and obligations of the Member States under the Charter of the

United Nations." Provisions are also made, and have to some extent been implemented, for cooperative relationships between the specialized agencies and their UN counterparts.

Several controversies have been handled by the OAS with considerable success and without any serious threat to the impairment of the wider system of collective action. Most of these have involved the Caribbean area. Charges have been made that governments, or groups within certain countries abetted by their governments, have engaged in aggression against or interfered in the internal affairs of rival states. The OAS Council has considered the charges, appointed investigating committees, and on the basis of their reports has made recommendations which usually have been accepted by the parties directly concerned.

Two situations, however, have involved serious questions of conflict between the OAS and the UN. The first arose on June 26, 1954, when the Security Council met to consider Guatemalan charges that Honduras and Nicaragua, at the instigation of foreign monopolies (the United Fruit Company in particular), had engaged in armed aggression against Guatemala. The essential background fact is that the left-wing Arbenz government of Guatemala was probably Communist-inspired, and the United States was fearful that its continuation in power would enable the Soviet Union to gain a foothold in the Americas. The United States was therefore determined to overthrow the government of Guatemala. She supported, as did Honduras and Nicaragua, a Security Council resolution referring the controversy to the OAS and calling upon all parties to cease hostilities. The Soviet Union supported Guatemala, charging that the OAS was dominated by the United States. Although the resolution received ten favorable votes, it was killed by a Soviet veto. Another resolution was then passed simply calling for the cessation of hostilities. On June 28, the United States' representative on the OAS Council requested that a meeting of an organ of consultation be convened to consider an insurrection which had broken out in Guatemala. Since the Arbenz government was overthrown on July 1, with considerable assistance from the United States, the meeting was never held.[11]

The second case of a similar nature arose in 1960, when Cuba charged before the Security Council that the United States had engaged in economic aggression. The Soviet Union supported Cuba as she had the Arbenz government in Guatemala. After mutual recrimination between the Soviet and the United States representatives, a resolution was passed, with Cuban support, to refer the case to the OAS. The Cuban delegate maintained, however, that the matter was still under the jurisdiction of the UN. The OAS Council later voted to refer the controversy to the foreign ministers at a meeting in San José, Costa Rica, in August 1960.

---

[11] Philip B. Taylor, Jr., "The Guatemalan Affair: A Critique of United States Foreign Policy," *American Political Science Review*, L (Sept. 1956), 787-806.

The United States favored a resolution condemning the Soviet Union for interfering in the Western Hemisphere, and Cuba for being willing to accept Soviet assistance in the case of United States aggression, as well as for allowing her territory to be used as a beachhead for extending the influence of Communist countries in the area. Although the Latin-American countries were willing to condemn the Soviet Union, they were reluctant to censure Cuba directly, for the social and economic revolution in that country was viewed favorably by large segments of the Latin-American public. The Declaration of San José, which largely reflected the Latin-American point of view, was approved by nineteen of the twenty-one American Republics.[12] Its two main provisions were as follows:

The Seventh Meeting of Consultation of Ministers of Foreign Affairs
1. Condemns emphatically intervention or the threat of intervention, even when conditional, from an extra-continental power in the affairs of the American republics and declares that the acceptance of a threat of extra-continental intervention by any American state jeopardizes American solidarity and security, wherefore the Organization of American States is under obligation to disapprove it and reject it with equal vigor.
2. Rejects, also emphatically the attempt of the Sino-Soviet powers to make use of the political, economic or social situation of any American state, inasmuch as that attempt is capable of destroying hemispheric unity and jeopardizing the peace and the security of the hemisphere.[13]

Although a sound legal case can be made for the United States' position, her attitude in both of these instances was hardly consonant with her insistence that matters involving relations between the Soviet Union and her satellites are proper subjects for the UN. Moreover, if this precedent were generally followed in cases involving disputes among members of regional groupings, the jurisdiction of the UN would be seriously impaired.

THE NORTH ATLANTIC
TREATY ORGANIZATION—MILITARY ALLIANCE

Military alliances have been prominent features of all state systems. What distinguishes some of those which sprang up after 1945—and especially NATO—from their predecessors, is the permanent organization and advance planning that accompanies them. For this two factors are mainly responsible. The first is the premium on time resulting from the impact of the new military technology on warfare and strategy. It is no longer enough to develop plans and mobilize joint military resources

---

[12] All except Cuba and the Dominican Republic. Cuba withdrew shortly before the vote was taken. The Dominican Republic had withdrawn previously when diplomatic sanctions and an arms embargo were voted against her for aggression against Venezuela.
[13] New York Times, Aug. 29, 1960, p. 3.

NATO CIVIL AND MILITARY ORGANIZATION
MARCH, 1961

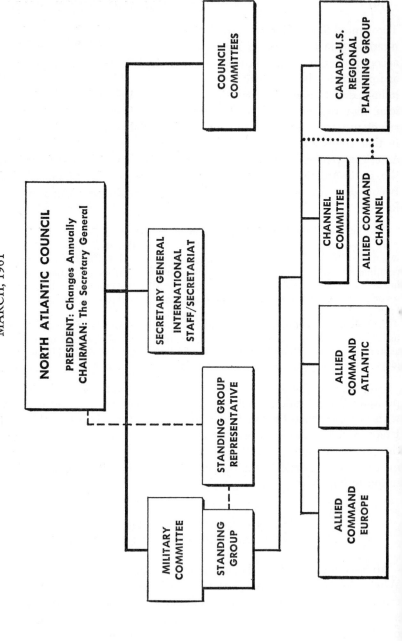

after the beginning of a war, the outcome of which might be decided in a few hours. Secondly, if, as widely claimed, the primary purpose of armaments is "deterrence," i.e., to make war less probable by making it more destructive, the combined strength of allies during peace time is a necessary element in the strategy. This necessitates common political and economic planning. It is also felt that closer integration in the non-military realm serves as a cohesive force among the members of the alliance when the need for military strength temporarily slackens. Some proponents contend that regional military pacts "serve as stepping stones to larger political communities." This can take place only if the central organs are entrusted with ever broadening functions and powers.

NATO is the central element in the network of multilateral and bilateral alliances of the noncommunist world. The United States is the strongest, and the pivotal power in the system. Two factors, fear of Soviet imperialism and serious doubt that the UN would be adequate to protect its members against Soviet expansion, were primarily responsible for the formation of NATO.

The Brussels Treaty of March 17, 1948, limited to France, Great Britain, and Benelux, grew out of similar fear and doubt. President Truman declared, on the day the latter treaty was signed, that the "determination of the free countries of Europe to protect themselves will be matched by an equal determination on our part to help them to do so." The Vandenberg Resolution, passed on June 11, 1948, put the United States Senate on record as favoring the "progressive development of regional and other collective arrangements for individual and collective self-defense . . ." and the "association of the United States . . . with such . . . as are based on continuous self-help and mutual aid and as affect its national security." The North Atlantic Treaty, signed on April 4, 1949, was the logical sequence. Consisting originally of twelve states, in 1952 the organization was expanded, by unanimous consent, to include Greece and Turkey, and in 1955 West Germany.[14]

Although the treaty sets forth mutual obligations, and calls for the establishment of basic machinery, its greater significance lies in subsequent developments within its framework. While the latter—the establishment of joint military commands, military aid by the U.S., and so forth—were quite consistent with its purposes, they were not legally required by the treaty.[15] Senator Arthur Vandenberg reasoned that "a

---

[14] The members are France, Great Britain, Belgium, The Netherlands, Luxembourg, Denmark, Norway, Italy, Portugal, Iceland, United States, Canada, Greece, Turkey, and West Germany.

[15] This matter was discussed at considerable length in the Senate hearings. Secretary of State Acheson contended that while members would be obligated to accept the principle of mutual assistance, each senator, in voting on the military assistance program, "must use his own best judgment within the confines of that principle to

Senator could logically say that he accepts this obligation when it arises under Article 51 without accepting an obligation to prepare in advance to implement Article 51.[16]

The heart of the treaty is Article V. Members agree that an *armed attack* against one or more of them in Europe or North America shall be considered an attack against all. Secondly, each agrees in the case of an armed attack to take, individually or in concert with the other members, *such action as it deems necessary* to restore and maintain the security of the North Atlantic area. Other articles call for the elimination of conflict among the signatories, for collaboration in economic relations (Art. II), and for self-help and mutual aid to develop their capacity to resist armed attack (Art. III). The ambiguity of the obligations, plus the fact that each state determines for itself what constitutes an armed attack—as well as the form and extent of assistance required in that event —leaves each state essentially as free to act as it would be in the absence of the treaty.

The treaty alone was regarded primarily of threefold psychological significance: (1) it served to warn the Soviet Union that the United States would come immediately to the aid of any member in the event of a Soviet attack; (2) it originally provided an umbrella of security under which the European countries might proceed with their programs of economic and military development; and (3) by making the notification and promise matters of formal record, it enhanced the probability that the people of the United States will be better prepared psychologically to go to war immediately in the event of Soviet armed aggression. As the Senate Foreign Relations Committee put it, "since the course of action envisaged in treaty is substantially that which the United States would follow without the treaty, there is a great advantage to the United States and the entire world in making clear our intentions in advance." In short, the treaty supposedly recognized that the United States would enter a war immediately rather than attempt to "wait it out," as it did in both world wars.

The treaty did not establish an elaborate organizational structure, and what machinery there is has been adjusted as dictated by experience and the changing nature of the problems with which it has had to cope. At the apex of the structure is the North Atlantic Council, on which each member is represented, and which is empowered to set up subsidiary bodies. The Council consists of top ministers—of foreign affairs, defense, and finance in particular—and permanent representatives from each of

---

determine whether or not we can and we should, so far as the world situation is concerned, approve the military-assistance program as a means of mutual assistance." *The North Atlantic Treaty, Hearings before the Committee on Foreign Relations,* U.S. Senate, 81st Cong., 1st Sess., Part I, 1949, p. 16.

[16] *Ibid.,* pp. 23-24.

the member states. The permanent members are in continuous session in Paris, the Council's permanent headquarters, while the cabinet members meet two or three times each year. A permanent international staff, headed by a secretary-general, was established in 1952.

The higher military organization consists of the Military Committee, the Standing Group, the Commands, and a Regional Planning Group. The Military Committee, composed of the chiefs of staff of the NATO countries (Iceland, having no military organization, may be represented by a civilian), advises the Council and supplies guidance on military questions to subordinate authorities. Permanent military representatives of the chiefs of staff carry on the business of the Military Committee between sessions of the chiefs. The Committee is located in Washington, D.C. The Standing Group, also located in Washington, D.C., is a permanent full-time agency consisting of representatives of the chiefs of staff of the United States, the United Kingdom, and France. As the executive agent of the Military Committee, it is responsible for the strategic guidance of the NATO military commands and the Canada-United States Regional Planning Group.

Three commands (and subordinate commands) and the Regional Planning Group are responsible for developing defense plans in their areas and for the supervision of NATO forces. As of the early nineteen-sixties, these were the European, the Atlantic Ocean, and the Channel commands, in addition to the Regional Planning Group.

What is the relationship of NATO to the UN? The agreement for assistance in the case of armed attack is declared to be "in exercise of the right of individual or collective self-defense recognized by Article 51 of the Charter of the United Nations. . . ." It is a moot point, however, whether arrangements such as NATO are permissible under Article 51.[17] The Charter is silent on this point. It is quite possible that had the question been raised at San Francisco the answer would have been negative. The Soviet Union has argued not only that such arrangements are not authorized by Article 51, but that NATO is aimed at aggression against the Soviet Union and is therefore specifically contrary to the Charter. The Western powers have denied this, pointing out that it is aimed at aggression from any source.

Is NATO a regional arrangement? Although it has been officially justified under Article 51 of the Charter rather than under Chapter VIII, there would appear, in view of the ambiguity of the term "regional," to be no reason why it does not so qualify. Perhaps the explanation of why it is not advanced as such lies partly in the uncertainty of the meaning of "regional," but more in the requirement of Article 54 that the Security

---

[17] See F. B. Schick, "Peace on Trial—A Study of Defense in International Organization," *Western Political Quarterly*, II (Mar. 1949), 1-44.

Council shall at all times be kept fully informed of activities undertaken *or in contemplation* under regional arrangements or agencies. Under Article 51 only "measures taken" must be reported. In the event of war between the Soviet Union and the members of NATO it is difficult to believe that full details would be revealed to the Security Council, especially if the representative of the Soviet Union were present!

As previously noted, the chief reason for NATO was the belief that the UN would not provide adequate security against the Soviet Union. It is true that NATO was established before the "Uniting for Peace" resolution, which made collective security a responsibility of the General Assembly.[18] But after the resolution was passed, there was no indication that it had restored sufficient confidence among the members of the UN to induce them to forego the old system of alliances. Moreover, it is questionable whether the formation of such arrangements would not in any case undermine or prevent the development of the mutual confidence essential to an effective general collective security system. If, however, collective security is unsound in its basic principles, or in any case unworkable under present or foreseeable circumstances, alliances are likely to be regarded as necessary. They seem to be practically inevitable consequences of "balance-of-power" politics.

Another basic question concerning NATO is whether it is but a half-way bridge. Can the planning, coordination, and execution necessary to build adequate strength be carried through when the decisions are made in fifteen different capitals? Or, as many believe, will it be necessary, to achieve the goal, to organize an Atlantic Federation on the NATO foundation?

THE UNIVERSAL POSTAL UNION— UNIVERSAL FUNCTIONALISM

Prior to the establishment of the UPU, international correspondence was complicated, costly, and inefficient. The rates were determined by adding the postage rates of the countries of dispatch, the sea rates, the transit rates imposed by each country through which the letters passed, and finally, the domestic rates of the countries of destination. If, as was frequently the case, there was more than one route, each with different rates, the sender had to choose one in advance. A one-half ounce letter to Austria might cost fifteen, thirty, or forty-two cents, depending on whether it went via Hamburg direct, via England, or via France. After a route had been chosen, the letter would have to go that way even if it had to wait a month for a ship, although one by another route was departing the next morning. From a public administration standpoint, this

---

[18] See pp. 325-26 for a discussion of the Resolution.

situation was as unsatisfactory as it was to the individual correspondent. Each state had to maintain a set of accounts for each country with which it had postal relations, including a record of each piece of mail.

After attempts to cope with the problem by bilateral treaty proved unsatisfactory, states resorted to the multilateral approach. A proposal by Postmaster General Blair of the United States resulted in a meeting in Paris in 1863 to discuss mutual problems. Not until 1874, however, was action taken. In that year, representatives of twenty-two states assembled at Bern, Switzerland, for the first International Postal Congress, signed an International Postal Convention, and formally established the General Postal Union. The second Postal Congress, convened at Paris in 1878, changed the name to Universal Postal Union.

The Postal Convention of 1874 has been revised and improved by later Congresses. The twelfth Congress, which met in Paris in 1947, changed it to make the UPU a specialized agency of the UN.

Under the original Convention and until 1947, the UPU's organs consisted of the Congress and the International Bureau. The Congress, the "legislative" organ of the UPU, was supposed to meet every five years (actually only fourteen Congresses assembled between 1874 and 1957; there were several intervals greater than five years, the longest being from 1906 to 1920). Each member may be represented at the Congress, and has one vote. The Bureau, located at Bern and supervised by the Swiss government, is the permanent secretariat. Although it is supposed to be international in character, its members are all Swiss nationals appointed by the Swiss government. Its functions, in general, are collecting, coordinating, and disseminating information, serving as a clearing house, examining requests for amendments to the Convention, and giving notice of ones adopted. As revised in 1947, the Convention established a permanent Executive and Liaison Committee. Also located at Bern, it consists of twenty members elected by the Congress. The Committee meets once a year, elects its president and four vice-presidents and appoints, on the recommendation of the Swiss Supervisory Authority, the director and other high ranking personnel of the Bureau. It maintains close relations with members of the UPU in order to improve the international postal service, studies technical questions, establishes working relations with the UN, specialized agencies, and other international organizations, and controls the activities of the Bureau.

The Fourteenth Congress (1957) established a new permanent body, the Consultative Commission on Postal Studies, to carry out studies and issue advice on technical, operational, and economic questions of concern to postal services. All UPU members are full members of this Commission. It elects a Steering Committee consisting of twenty members who choose a chairman and three vice-chairmen from among themselves. The Steering Committee reports annually to the UPU's Executive and Liaison Committee.

Some changes in the Convention must be approved by a two-thirds majority vote of the Congress, whereas minor modifications need only a simple majority. Although decisions must be ratified by states before they become binding on them, in reality an individual state has little choice in the matter, since the decisions are put into effect at a given date, without even waiting for formal notice of ratification. Should a state refuse to accept the changes its only alternative is to withdraw and face the consequences. None has chosen to do so.

The Convention also provides for the arbitration of certain disputes by two impartial members of the UPU, one selected by each of the disputing parties. In case of disagreement between the two, they select a third. Awards are by majority vote and are binding on the disputants.

The territories of the members constitute "a single postal territory for the reciprocal exchange of correspondence." Each member guarantees freedom of transit of foreign mail through its territory by the fastest available means. Uniform rates are fixed on the basis of weight and distance. Questions of routes and boundaries no longer perplex the individual correspondent. The collection of postage is simplified, and the Bureau serves as a clearing house for the settlement of international accounts. All in all, the UPU is one of the most useful, necessary, and tightly organized of the existing international organizations.

What Professor Vinacke says of the international arrangements to overcome postal difficulties is true in most other areas:

The International Postal Convention was not the result of the development of an international outlook so much as that of a more realistic conception of the national interest. This is significant because it reveals the fact that international organization of international interests may be the only satisfactory way of conserving the national interest.[19]

THE EUROPEAN "COMMUNITY OF SIX"

Long-term trends, accelerated by two world wars, changed Europe from the main center of world power into a temporary power vacuum. After World War II, confronted by the problems of her own economic and political weakness and disunity, menaced by a strong and expansionist Soviet Union, and uncertain about but dependent upon the U.S. she began stumbling spasmodically toward integration.

European unification has been a goal of many private groups as well as of governments. The United States Mutual Security Act of 1951 au-

---

[19] Harold M. Vinacke, *International Organization* (New York: F. S. Crofts & Co., 1934), p. 405.

thorized the use of funds "to further encourage the economic and political federation of Europe," and on January 22, 1952, General Eisenhower called for a European constitutional convention "to examine and actually cope with the problems of greater economic and political unity." When the Republican administration came to power a year later, one of its first and major items of business was to encourage and cajole the Western European powers to continue their efforts toward this end.

European unity has long been a goal of certain nongovernmental groups within Europe. In 1946, Winston Churchill dramatically took the initiative in bringing several of these together. The result was the European Movement, formally organized in October 1948, following the "Congress of Europe" held at the Hague in May of that year. An Action Committee for a United States of Europe, with M. Jean Monnet, the "Architect of Europe," as President, pressed for greater integration in the early nineteen-sixties.

The postwar history of European unification has been one of success and failure, blueprints and improvisation. At times when the outlook has seemed gloomy, new ideas have been put forward and further advances made. On the whole, the movement has been one of extraordinary endurance and resilience. Integration within the "Community of Six"—France, German Federal Republic, Italy, and Benelux—as well as in Western Europe as a whole, has been pragmatic rather than doctrinal. According to M. Monnet: "The feature of the progress made so far [1960] in uniting Europe has been the step-by-step advance by means of concrete measures bringing solutions to problems as and when they have arisen."[20] Secretary-General Dag Hammarskjöld spoke in similar vein with respect to evolution within Europe and of international organization generally:

> . . . I think it is wise to avoid talking of this or that kind of ultimate political target and to realize that the development is still in the early stage of institutional evolution, although a few vanguard penetrations into the constitutional [governmental] area have taken place. What seems imperative is to push forward institutionally and, eventually, constitutionally all along the line, guided by current needs and experiences, without preconceived ideas of the ultimate form.[21]

Prior to 1950, the principal center of pressure for general European integration, including political federation, was within the Consultative Assembly of the Council of Europe. The Council, established in 1949, consists of a loose cooperative grouping of fourteen European countries, including Iceland. The Committee of Ministers of the Council generally

---

[20] "Economic and Political Unity in Europe," *Bulletin from the European Community,* No. 40 (July 1960), p. 6.

[21] "The Development of a Constitutional Framework for International Cooperation," *United Nations Review,* VI (June 1960), 27.

refused to pass the Assembly's recommendation on to their governments. The United Kingdom in particular, but the Scandinavian states also were reluctant to proceed other than on a strictly cooperative basis. Britain was also opposed to any association which might interfere with her Commonwealth commercial and trade relations.

The proposal for the establishment of the European Coal and Steel Community (ECSC), first made by the French Foreign Minister, Robert Schuman, in May 1950, was in response to United States pressure for the end of Allied occupation of Germany, to be followed by her rearmament and admittance into NATO. A month later, and for essentially similar reasons, the French National Defense Minister, René Pleven, proposed a European Defense Community (EDC) among the six countries. After reaching a peak in 1950-52, the movement decreased in momentum, reaching a low point when the French Assembly rejected EDC in the summer of 1954. However, M. Monnet and his small band of determined followers continued to press hard for a resumption of integration.

In June 1955, the foreign ministers of the "Six" adopted the Messina Resolution which eventually led to the Economic Community, as well as the Atomic Community for the development of atomic energy (Euratom). From the winter of 1955-56 onward, progress was rapid. The Rome treaties were signed in the spring of 1957, and the two organizations came into existence in January 1958.[22] The movement promises to continue, although its shape and dimensions are uncertain. Writing in 1958, Ernst B. Haas concluded:

> . . . Once governments have committed themselves—for whatever reasons—to certain common measures of fundamental importance to the daily lives of their entire citizenry, they can resolve future problems of implementing the agreement only by means of further delegation of power to the center. This "administrative spill over" is an essential consequence of initial acts of integration in a crucial policy sector. Withdrawal from its implications is not possible—as in the case of NATO—when the external stimulant changes. Since the range of issues which gave rise to the initial step is woven completely into the contemporary preoccupation with welfare, withdrawal would imply a sacrifice of economic advantage—a step not taken lightly by elected politicians.[23]

In 1960, the process of creating the common market was speeded up; steps were underway to fuse the executives of the three organizations, and to provide for the direct election of the already fused European Parliament.

These two organizations, and Euratom, are based on separate treaties

---

[22] For an account of the background and the early history see Miriam Camps, *The First Year of the European Economic Community*, Policy Memorandum No. 17, Center of International Studies (Princeton University, Nov. 10, 1959).

[23] "The Challenge of Regionalism," *International Organization*, XII (Autumn 1958), 454; for a fuller treatment of European integration to 1958, see Ernst B. Haas, *The Uniting of Europe* (Stanford: Stanford University Press, 1958).

which define the purpose, functions, and the basic structure of each. The principal organs are an assembly, a court, an executive authority, and a council of ministers. The European Parliamentary Assembly and the Court of Justice, however, are common to all three agencies, although their functions and powers differ with respect to each community, according to its constitution.

The European Parliamentary Assembly

When the Economic Community and Euratom were established, the ECSC Assembly was enlarged (78 to 142 members) and made the joint organ of all three communities. As originally constituted, the new Assembly was composed of members selected by the six national parliaments in proportion to party strength in each parliament. In 1960, in accordance with Article 13 of the Common Market Treaty, the Assembly drew up proposals for election by direct universal suffrage in each state. The Assembly would also be tripled in size—from 142 to 426 members—each state being affected as follows:

Members	Present	Proposed
Belgium	14	42
France	36	108
Germany	36	108
Italy	36	108
Luxembourg	6	18
Netherlands	14	42

The Assembly elects its own president and other officers. It has established commissions to cope with the principal functions of the communities—on the internal market, commercial policy, agriculture, and so forth. Although the Assembly has no legislative authority, the executive organ of each community is collectively responsible to it and must resign if a motion of lack of confidence is passed by two-thirds vote. The Assembly so far has no permanent seat, and has alternated its meetings among several European cities.

The international and parliamentary character of the Assembly, which would probably become more pronounced if its members were directly elected, is indicated by the organization of the members in three political groups—Christian Democrats, Liberals, and Socialists—rather than in six national delegations. Debates are along party lines, although national viewpoints are sometimes stressed, somewhat as sectional points of view are asserted in the United States Congress.

The Court of Justice

The common court of the three communities is also, in effect, a continuation of that of ECSC. It consists of seven judges, appointed by agreement of the member governments for six-year terms. Its authority is outlined in the respective treaties. Unlike most international courts, in which only states can be contestants, the European Court also has jurisdiction over private parties. Between 1952 and the middle of 1960, it had received 144 appeals and requests for stay of execution concerning ECSC High Authority decisions. Of these, twenty-four were withdrawn, judgments were made in sixty-seven cases, and fifty-three were in process by 1960.

European Coal and Steel Community

The objectives of ECSC are both economic and political. It was hailed as a means of integrating the economies of France and Germany so that "any war between them is not only unthinkable, but in actual fact impossible." With its inauguration on August 10, 1953, for the first time in modern history there was a "partial fusion of sovereignty" among the six nations of Western Europe to create a weak supranational government in an important though limited area. The plan was to come into operation in three stages. The first, of six months, was a preparatory phase. Then followed a five-year transitional stage, after which it came into full operation for the remaining fifty-year period of the treaty's duration.

The general purpose of ECSC is to establish a "single market" in coal and steel and eliminate trade barriers as well as obstacles to the free movement of workers. Monopolistic and discriminatory prices are forbidden, and minimum and maximum prices are set only after investigation by the High Authority.

The High Authority. The High Authority of ECSC, with its headquarters in Luxembourg, consists of nine persons, no more than two of whom may be nationals of any one country. Eight of these are selected by the Council of Ministers, on the basis of competence, for six-year terms, three retiring each biennium. The eight in turn select the ninth member by majority vote. The governments, by unanimous consent, and after consultation with the High Authority, choose its president and vice-president. The Authority's decisions are all made by majority vote. It functions on the basis of collective responsibility to the other organs of the community. It has been said to resemble, especially with respect to its powers, independence, and voting procedure, the United States Federal Trade Commission rather than an executive.[24] In some instances,

---

[24] Haas, *The Uniting of Europe,* p. 43.

such as making general rules to insure competition, it has binding legislative authority; on other matters it reviews and recommends. This latter function is quite important, for normally the other organs, principally the Council of Ministers, approve or disapprove policy which the High Authority initiates. Although it has a legal right to make certain binding decisions of a legislative and administrative nature, and sometimes does so, it has been circumspect with respect to the wishes of the other organs, and especially of the Council.

The Council of Ministers. The Council is composed of national ministers selected by their respective governments. Its principal purpose is declared to be that of "harmonizing the actions of the High Authority with those of the governments." It also has responsibilities for carrying out a number of obligations, not entrusted to the High Authority, but assumed by the member states in the ECSC treaty. Although its members represent their governments, the Council nevertheless can be said to possess supranational authority to the extent that it can make binding decisions, especially by less than a unanimous vote. Its voting procedure is complicated. Depending on the matter under consideration, it decides by a simple, two-thirds, or five-sixths majority, or by unanimity. A simple majority suffices to request the Court to annul a decision of the High Authority; decisions to admit new states and to decide many other important matters require unanimity. A so-called simple majority ordinarily consists of four states, including either France or Germany. The High Authority must consult and obtain the consent of the Council in many instances.

The European Economic Community (EEC)

The European Economic Community differs from ECSC in several important respects. It is concerned with the creation of a general common market rather than being limited to particular commodities such as coal and steel. It would have been possible to combine the two organizations had it not been for French opposition to an impairment of its sovereignty to the extent that ECSC was held to have done. The organs of the Economic Community, therefore, have fewer supranational powers than does the Coal and Steel Community. The purpose of EEC is to create a common market for the almost 170 million citizens of "little Europe." A common market is more than a customs union and less than an economic union. It aspires to eventual freedom of trade within the area as would a customs union, but it also extends to the free movement of people and capital. It is less than an economic union in that there is no common currency or monetary and fiscal policy. In order to achieve its goal, the Treaty provides that the member states "shall consider their policy relating to economic trends as a matter of common interest. They shall consult with each other and with the Commission on measures to be taken in response to current circumstances" (Article 103). Since approval of these measures requires the unanimous consent of the Council of Ministers, each state has in effect a veto over them. Nevertheless, some progress has been made on these matters, although considerably more will be necessary as the barriers to the movement of goods, people, and capital are lowered.

The Commission. The EEC Commission corresponds to the High Authority of ECSC. It also consists of nine nationals of the member states selected for four-year terms by common agreement of the governments on the basis of their "general competence" and "indisputable independence" (Article 157). Decisions of the Commission are by simple majority vote. It is responsible to the European Parliamentary Assembly, to which it submits annual reports, and replies to questions. Its general responsibility is to carry out the Treaty and measures adopted by the other organs. In addition to formulating recommendations for the consideration of these organs and members of the community, it may make binding decisions with respect to matters specifically required by the Treaty and it may authorize measures to be taken by member states in an emergency, such as a crisis on balance of payments. The latter action, however, may be overridden by the Council. On the whole, power rests with the Council of Ministers rather than with the Commission.

The Council of Ministers. The EEC Council, like that of ECSC, is composed of one member from each government. Ordinarily it acts on recommendations of the Commission, which it may not amend except by unanimous vote. Nevertheless it is the principal policy-making body, for nearly all important decisions require its approval. Unanimity is required for most of the Council's decisions during the twelve to fifteen years prior to the full effectiveness of the Treaty, and even after that for most important ones. For certain decisions requiring less than unanimous agreement, a system of weighted voting is used. In this instance the six states have a total of seventeen votes—the three larger states four each, Belgium and The Netherlands two each, and Luxembourg one. Twelve votes are required for passing a measure, but except when acting on a proposal from the Commission, these twelve must include the votes of at least four states. Despite the fact that the Commission has considerably less power than the High Authority, and the voting procedures of the Council of EEC are less liberal than is that of the ECSC, during the first year and a half of the common market progress was at least as rapid as had been that of the Coal and Steel Community during a comparable period.[25]

---

[25] See Serge Hurtig, "The European Common Market," *International Conciliation,* Carnegie Endowment, No. 517 (Mar. 1958); also see Camps, *The First Year of the European Economic Community.*

In the summer of 1960 it was decided to accelerate the implementation of the Treaty beyond that originally contemplated. Quota restrictions would be completely removed by December 31, 1961, in contrast with the previous plan for doing so by 1969 at the earliest. By the end of 1960, tariffs would be reduced by thirty per cent instead of twenty per cent as originally planned. The new plan called for the first move to bring existing national tariffs into line with the common external tariff by December 31, 1960, a year ahead of schedule. The removal of internal trade barriers on agricultural products, which will lag behind those for industry, was also speeded up, as were plans for a common agricultural policy.

Barring the unforeseen, integration within the "Community of Six" promised to continue at an accelerated tempo. Perhaps the gravest question is whether this integration will leave Europe as a whole more divided than before, as Great Britain and other European countries, constituting the group of "Seven," has developed the European Free Trade Association.[26] Unless some way could be found to reconcile the divergent views of the two groups, not only would economic relations between them disintegrate, but their political relations would probably also be undermined.[27] In 1961, Great Britain decided to apply for admission to the common market, but it was uncertain whether her conditions of membership would be agreed to, especially by France.

SUGGESTED READINGS

Ball, M. Margaret, *NATO and the European Union Movement*. London: Stevens & Sons, Ltd., 1959.

Baumann, Carol Edler, "Britain Faces Europe," *Political Science Quarterly*, LXXIV (Sept. 1959), 351-71.

Bebr, Gerhard, "Regional Organizations: A United Nations Problem," *American Journal of International Law*, XLIX (Apr. 1955), 166-84.

Camps, Miriam, "Britain, the Six and American Policy," *Foreign Affairs*, XXXIX (Oct. 1960), 112-22.

---

[26] In addition to Great Britain, the members were: Denmark, Norway, Sweden, Portugal, Switzerland, and Austria. Although the goal was to eliminate trade barriers among the Seven, each would maintain its separate tariffs, etc., against other countries, in contrast to the common tariff for the Six.

[27] See Agostino Soldate, "Economic Disintegration in Europe," *Foreign Affairs*, XXVIII (Oct. 1959), 75-83.

————, *The First Year of the European Economic Community.* Princeton, N.J.: Center of International Studies, Princeton University, 1958.

Casteñada, Jorge, "Pan Americanism and Regionalism: A Mexican View," *International Organization,* X (Aug. 1956), 373-89.

Connell-Smith, Gordon, "The Organization of American States," *The World Today,* XVI (Oct. 1960), 447-56.

Council of Europe, Information Department, *The Council of Europe, 1949-1959.* Strasbourg, 1959.

Diebold, William, *The Schuman Plan: A Study in Economic Cooperation, 1950-59.* New York: Frederick A. Praeger, Inc., for the Council on Foreign Relations, 1959.

Fenwick, Charles G., "The Inter-American Regional System: Fifty Years of Progress," *American Journal of International Law,* L (Jan. 1956), 18-31.

Frank, Isaiah, *The European Common Market.* New York: Frederick A. Praeger, Inc., 1961.

Freeman, Harrop A. and Theodore Paullin, *Road to Peace: A Study in Functional International Organization.* Ithaca, New York: The Pacifist Research Bureau, 1947.

Friedmann, W., "Limits of Functionalism in International Organization," *Year Book of World Affairs, 1956,* X (1956), 256-69.

Furniss, Edgar S., Jr., "Re-examination of Regional Arrangements," *Journal of International Affairs,* IX (1955), 79-89.

Gordon, Lincoln, "NATO and European Integration," *World Politics,* X (Jan. 1958), 219-31.

Haas, Ernest B., "The Challenge of Regionalism," *International Organization,* XII (Autumn 1958), 440-58.

————, "Regionalism, Functionalism and Universal International Organization," *World Politics,* VIII (Jan. 1956), 238-63.

————, *The Uniting of Europe: Political, Social, and Economic Forces, 1950-1957.* Stanford, California: Stanford University Press, 1958.

Hitchner, D. G., "Supranational Organization and Democracy in Western Europe," *Parliamentary Affairs,* XI (Summer 1958), 273-86.

Hoffman, Stanley, "The Role of International Organization: Limits and Possibilities," *International Organization,* X (Aug. 1956), 357-72.

Kitzinger, U. W., "Europe: The Six and Seven," *International Organization,* XIV (Winter 1960), 20-36.

Lindsay, Kenneth, *Toward a European Parliament.* Strasbourg: Secretariat of the Council of Europe, 1958.

Mitrany, David, "The Functional Approach to World Government," *International Affairs,* XXIV (July 1948), 350-63.

————, *A Working Peace System: An Argument for the Functional Development of International Organization.* London: Royal Institute of International Affairs, 1946.

Moore, Ben T., *NATO and the Future of Europe.* New York: Harper & Brothers for the Council on Foreign Relations, 1958.

Ovin, Marc, *The O.E.E.C. and the Common Market: Why Europe Needs an Economic Union of Seventeen Countries.* Paris: Organization for European Economic Co-operation, 1958.

Padelford, Norman J., "Regional Organization and the United Nations," *International Organization,* VIII (May 1954), 203-16.

Pan American Union, General Legal Division, *Applications of the Inter-American Treaty of Reciprocal Assistance, 1948-1956: with a Discussion of the*

Inter-American System of Peace and Security and Its Operation within the World System. Washington, D.C.: Pan American Union, 1957.

Pan American Union, Division of Law and Treaties, *The Organization of American States and the United Nations*, 5th ed., by Manuel Conyes. Washington, D.C.: Pan American Union, 1956.

Patterson, Gardner and Edgar S. Furniss, Jr., *NATO: A Critical Appraisal.* Princeton: Princeton University Conference on NATO, 1957.

Pike, Frederick B., "Guatemala, the United States, and Communism in the Americas," *Review of Politics*, XVII (Apr. 1955), 232-61.

"Regional Organizations: Their Role in the World Community," *Columbia Journal of International Affairs*, III (Spring 1949).

Sanderson, Fred H., "The Five-Year Experience of the European Coal and Steel Community," *International Organization*, XII (Spring 1958), 193-200.

Sannwald, Rolf and Jacques Stohler, *Economic Integration: Theoretical Assumptions and Consequences of European Unification.* Princeton, N.J.: Princeton University Press, 1959.

Strauss, Emil, *Common Sense about the Common Market: Germany and Britain in Post-War Europe.* London: George Allen and Unwin, Ltd., 1958.

"The Treaty for a European Economic Community: A Critical Analysis," *World Today*, XIV (July 1958), 304-15.

Valentine, Donald Graham, *The Court of Justice of the European Coal and Steel Community.* The Hague: N.V.M. Nijhoff, 1955.

Wandycz, Piotr S., "Regionalism and European Integration," *World Affairs Quarterly*, XXVIII (Oct. 1957), 229-59.

Zurcher, Arnold J., *The Struggle to Unite Europe: 1940-1958; an Historical Account of the Development of the Contemporary European Movement from Its Origin in the Pan-European Union to the Drafting of the Treaties for Euratom and the European Common Market.* New York: New York University Press, 1958.

10

Peaceful Settlement and
Change in International Society

All societies have developed institutions to settle differences that arise among individuals and groups. Broadly speaking, there are only two methods—peaceful ones and those that involve the use of force. The successful adjustment of international differences by peaceful means depends in part, therefore, upon the adequacy of available procedures and organs. In domestic societies legislative, executive, and judicial bodies and processes are of paramount importance in preserving peace by settling disputes and facilitating peaceful change. Their inadequacy in international society makes an examination of other methods of especial importance.

Often the sources of disagreement are deep-seated and obscure. In these instances serious quarrels arise over matters which would otherwise seem trivial. Settlement of the immediate problem is often difficult; or, if settlement is reached, the underlying tensions may lead to other disputes. Similar problems, given a general harmony of interests, may cause little or no difficulty, and may be capable of generally satisfactory adjustment.

The existing methods of peaceful settlement and change are inherently incapable of dealing with tensions, and are of limited use in settling controversies which grow out of them. It is necessary to keep these factors in mind in considering peaceful adjustment in international society. In this chapter we shall be concerned only with disputes, which, it should be noted, are less important than other kinds of international problems. *An international dispute is a disagreement among states, etc., over something more or less tangible, to which the parties have formulated claims and counterclaims sufficiently definite to permit an inquiry into the facts and the formulation of proposals or decisions for its settlement.*

THE NATURE OF PACIFIC SETTLEMENT

Pacific settlement in international society means all methods, other than those employing force, for dealing with controversies among states and other international entities. The settlement may be on the basis of law, or may result in changes in the law. Peaceful change refers to the latter: to change in the international legal status quo. It is one aspect of pacific settlement.

Although methods of pacific settlement include all those which do not involve the use of force, the term is often used in a technical way to mean certain procedures such as negotiation and judicial settlement. The United States' attempt to induce Cuba to refrain from nationalizing property of Americans in that country by reducing Cuba's sugar quota in the American market was a peaceful method in the general sense; negotiation over the matter within the UN and the OAS exemplifies its technical meaning. More often than not, pressures of various kinds accompany the formal types of pacific settlement. The words of a representative of a strong power, therefore, are more persuasive than are those of one representing a weak state. Salvador de Madariaga makes the point forcibly:

The fact is that armaments are more useful in time of peace than in time of war. The normal wielders of armaments are not the soldiers, but the diplomats. . . . The diplomacy of the big powers is carried out not exclusively, not always openly, not always consciously, but always nevertheless on such a principle. The foreign secretary of this or that nation may be the most conciliatory man on earth; yet the minimum which will be granted him by his adversaries will be considerably higher for the fact of his armaments.[1]

Not only are both formal and informal pacific methods frequently used simultaneously—they may be accompanied by the use of force as well. This was obviously true in the Jammu-Kashmir, Korean, Dutch-Indonesian, Suez, Hungarian, and Palestine cases, all of which came before the UN. The cases indicate that methods separable for purposes of analysis are likely to be intermingled in a real situation.

Categories of Pacific Settlement[2]

Pacific settlement may be divided into two main categories—*nondecisional* and *decisional*. The former consists of procedures which do not result in a final action the parties are legally obligated to accept. They

---

[1] *Disarmament* (New York: Coward-McCann, Inc., 1929), pp. 57-58.

[2] The chief result of the First Hague Conference (1899) was a comprehensive "Convention for the Pacific Settlement of International Disputes." As revised by the Second Conference (1907), almost fifty states, including the United States, had adhered to it before 1939. Although methods of pacific settlement are much older, the phrase owes its prominence to the Convention. References in this chapter are to the Convention as revised.

may accept or reject proposals or recommendations resulting from negotiation, good offices, mediation, inquiry, and conciliation. The contrary is true of arbitration and adjudication, the two types of decisional settlement. Although a state has no obligation under customary international law to submit a dispute to arbitration or to judicial settlement (or to the nondecisional methods for that matter), once it is submitted the decision or award is legally binding on the contesting states. For example, the Alabama Claims were submitted to arbitration at Geneva after the Civil War by Great Britain and the United States, with the result that the former was obligated to pay the United States $15,500,000 in gold for the depredations of three ships built in British shipyards and illegally sold to the Confederate states.

Legal and Political Disputes

During the nineteenth and twentieth centuries there has been a growing demand that all states legally obligate themselves to submit certain kinds of disputes to decisional procedures. The question arose as to what kinds of disputes should be submitted to binding settlements if there were to be compulsory jurisdiction. The usual answer was, since arbitration and adjudication are judicial procedures, only legal disputes are appropriate for settlement by these methods. The Hague Convention provided (Art. 38):

In questions of a legal nature, and especially in the interpretation or application of International Conventions, arbitration is recognized by the contracting Powers as the most effective, and, at the same time, the most equitable means of settling disputes which diplomacy has failed to settle.

Treaties and conventions, including the statutes of the two "world courts," providing for decisional procedures, have usually followed this principle.

Unfortunately, the question immediately arose in another form. What are legal disputes? Which are justiciable and which non-justiciable? To these questions three different answers have been given.[3] It has been contended by some that disputes are nonlegal, or political, if they are not covered by existing rules of international law. This contention is specious, and is refuted by the fact that judges are able to find a legal rule for all questions, and have not refused to adjudicate on the grounds that none is available. Nevertheless, there is uncertainty about international law in many areas. This is obviously true of the law of the upper atmosphere and outer space. In such situations, a court must really legislate under the guise of adjudication. It may be argued, therefore, that the dispute is

---

[3] See L. Oppenheim, *International Law*, ed. H. Lauterpacht, 6th ed. (London: Longmans, Green & Co., Ltd., 1940), Vol. II, 3-6.

essentially a political one according to this conception. Although there is truth in this, the problem is not peculiar to international society. The chief responsibility of the United States Supreme Court, for example, is to act as a superlegislature.

The second view is that disputes which affect the vital interests of a state—its territory, sovereignty, or perhaps its national honor—are political in nature. All that this can possibly mean is that only *unimportant* disputes are judicial ones, and that states are unwilling to submit all others to impartial settlement according to law.

Modern writers generally reject these two tests in preference for a third. According to this prevailing view, a legal dispute is one in which the contending parties are in disagreement over the meaning of existing law. It is political if one or more of the disputing parties wants the law changed. It is quite obvious that if a state desires a change rather than an interpretation of the law, it will not be satisfied with a process which usually results in confirming the status quo. In all probability the International Court of Justice would have upheld the right of Great Britain to occupy the Suez Canal Zone under the 1936 Anglo-Egyptian treaty. Egypt wanted the British out of the Zone; so Great Britain, but not Egypt, was willing to submit the dispute to the International Court.

Although the third distinction is logically satisfying, practically it presents a difficulty. States that adhere to the optional clause (Art. 36) of the Statute of the International Court of Justice agree to submit their *legal* disputes to adjudication by the Court. If the Court could hear only those disputes that parties were willing to have settled according to existing law, a state could, by demanding a change in the law, free itself from its jurisdiction. On the other hand, if the Court accepted the view that all disputes are legal because international law provides an answer, all disputes would have to be submitted to it, and the only changes possible would be those made by the Court under the guise of adjudication. Neither the Permanent Court of International Justice nor the International Court of Justice has given an answer to this basic question. While the former assumed jurisdiction in fifteen cases on unilateral applications, no state against which a judgment was asked refused to appear before it or to accept its decision on the grounds that the dispute was political.

NON-DECISIONAL PACIFIC SETTLEMENT

Since non-decisional types of pacific settlement do not result in binding action, their effectiveness depends on their contribution to a meeting of minds. Any dispute may be settled by non-decisional methods. Moreover, the settlement may be on the basis of law, or existing legal rights may be changed. Even if a dispute is settled on the basis of law, the process remains non-decisional, for the parties are not obliged to accept the settlement.

Negotiation

Unless there is a specific agreement to the contrary, a state is not obligated to utilize any of the methods of pacific settlement. However, negotiation has been an established practice for so long that it is sometimes contended states are obliged to use it, at least prior to an appeal to force.[4] Treaties and conventions frequently provide that disputes "which diplomacy [negotiation] has failed to settle" shall be settled by other pacific means, thereby assuming a certain primacy for negotiations. Most interstate disputes are solved by negotiation, or left unsolved. It is extremely flexible, and may be used to deal with disputes ranging from minor claims of a citizen to the unification of Germany. Moreover, agreement to use other pacific means is usually reached through negotiation.

Negotiation is an essential element in all types of non-decisional pacific settlement. For example, in good offices and mediation, the purpose is to facilitate agreement of the parties through negotiation. Finally, and not wholly peculiar to negotiation,

. . . whether arguments are based on grounds of expediency, law, or morality, there is always at the back of any diplomatic discussion mutual awareness of the scale of increasing pressure that negotiating parties may bring into operation against each other.[5]

Good Offices and Mediation

In all methods of pacific settlement except negotiation, a third party, or parties, is always involved. Good offices is a process by which contending states may be brought together by other states or individuals; the third parties may not suggest a solution or participate in the negotiations. Good offices, once accepted, have usually led to mediation. Such was the case in 1905 when President Theodore Roosevelt proffered good offices to the belligerents in the Russo-Japanese War. Although he did not act as a formal mediator, he worked behind the scenes. For this he was awarded the Nobel peace prize.

The Hague Convention (Art. 4) defines the functions of mediators as "reconciling the opposing claims and appeasing the feelings of resentment which may have arisen between the States at variance." Article 3 provides that an offer of mediation or good offices "can never be regarded . . . as an unfriendly act." Mediation is used frequently, and

---

[4] Charles Fenwick, *International Law*, 3rd ed. (New York: Appleton-Century-Crofts, Inc., 1948), p. 508.

[5] Georg Schwarzenberger, *Power Politics*, p. 197.

may be performed by one or several parties. France acted as mediator between Spain and the United States after the Spanish-American War. Argentina, Brazil, and Chile mediated between the United States and Mexico in 1914. In 1916 President Wilson offered to mediate between the European belligerents. After the German seizure of Czechoslovakia in March 1939, Franklin D. Roosevelt, in a message to Hitler and Mussolini, offered to mediate for a settlement of European difficulties. After World War II, Frank Graham of the United States served as mediator on behalf of the UN Security Council in an attempt to settle the India-Pakistan dispute over Jammu-Kashmir.

Inquiry and Conciliation

The Hague Convention provided for an "International Commission of Inquiry" (Art. 9), to be selected by the parties for each dispute, "to facilitate a solution of those disputes [arising from disagreement over facts] by elucidating the facts by means of an impartial and conscientious investigation." Disputes involving "honour" and "vital interest" were excluded. Apparently state honor could not stand close examination! Only a few disputes were dealt with through inquiry; its chief importance was its contribution to the conciliation process.

Conciliation is really a combination of inquiry and mediation, plus formal recommendations. Oppenheim defines it as

. . . the process of settling a dispute by referring it to a commission of persons whose task it is to elucidate the facts and (usually after hearing the parties and endeavoring to bring them to an agreement) to make a report containing proposals for a settlement, but not having the binding character of an award or judgment.[6]

Both the League and the UN have utilized the conciliation process. The Lytton Commission of Inquiry, which investigated the Manchurian episode of 1931 on behalf of the League, not only reported the facts but made recommendations. The UN General Assembly appointed a Conciliation Commission for Palestine which endeavored to arrange for a permanent peace between Israel and the Arab states.

In the interwar years hundreds of treaties provided for conciliation, and over one hundred permanent commissions were set up. However, "there was no recorded instances of actual recourse to the machinery established by the treaties."[7]

The Interim Committee of the General Assembly gave considerable attention to conciliation, and four resolutions adopted by the General Assembly, in April 1949, all relate to it in some respect.[8] One resolution

---

[6] Oppenheim, *International Law*, Vol. II, p. 12.

[7] *Ibid.*, p. 18.

[8] *United Nations Yearbook*, 1948-49 (New York: Columbia University Press in Cooperation with the United Nations, 1950), pp. 415-16.

called for the appointment of a permanent panel of inquiry and conciliation from which members of commissions could be selected *ad hoc* when
states desired to use the process. Each member of the UN was invited to
designate from one to five "persons who, by reason of their training, experience, character, and standing, are deemed to be well-fitted to serve
. . ." and who would be disposed to do so.

Mediation and negotiation, especially the latter, are by far the most
frequently used methods of non-decisional pacific settlement. Since their
effectiveness depends on agreement, they are likely to succeed only if
the contending states are not too far apart at the outset. Furthermore,
the final result may well reflect the relative power of the disputants.
While this may be true more frequently of negotiation than of procedures
which utilize the services of more or less impartial third parties, it is
often the case when these methods are employed.

DECISIONAL PACIFIC SETTLEMENT

To overcome the weakness of settlement procedures which depend, in
the final analysis, on the agreement of states to agree, considerable
thought and effort have been devoted to improving the methods that
result in legally binding decisions that do not require agreement by the
disputants. These methods are arbitration and adjudication. Of the two,
the former is by far the older, dating back at least to the classical Greek
era. It was used in the medieval period, but there were very few arbitrations from 1500 to 1794. Under the Jay Treaty of 1794 several disputes
between Great Britain and the United States were arbitrated. Between
1872 and 1899 Great Britain was a party in thirty arbitrations, other
European states in sixty, Latin-American states in fifty, and the United
States in twenty.[9]

The Central American Court of Justice (1907-17) was the first real
international court or adjudicating body. Although the establishment of
a world court was considered by both Hague Conferences, not until the
Versailles Conference in 1919 was there agreement to establish a court
with wide membership. The result was the Permanent Court of International Justice, which was succeeded in 1945 by the International Court
of Justice.

Arbitration and Adjudication Distinguished

Although arbitration and adjudication differ in some important respects, they are basically similar. Their common features are: (1) settle-

---

[9] See Manley O. Hudson, *International Tribunals* (Washington, D.C.: Carnegie
Endowment and Brookings Institution, 1944).

ment by an impartial outside agency on the basis of principles and rules of law;[10] (2) the awards (arbitration) and decisions (adjudication) are binding on the parties; (3) submission is voluntary in each case unless by previous agreement states have obligated themselves to settle certain disputes in this manner. Both processes are judicial in nature. Though it is sometimes said that arbitrators may be influenced by extra-legal considerations, and may sometimes attempt to compromise in order to reach a satisfactory settlement, this is the exception rather than the rule.[11] Moreover, unless an arbitration tribunal is authorized to compromise by the states which have agreed to the arbitration, the award may be rejected on the grounds that the tribunal has exceeded its powers.

The essential differences between these methods are: (1) arbitration is performed by persons or states designated by the parties for each particular dispute, whereas in adjudication the agency is a permanent body existing in advance, ordinarily selected by a process in which a number of states have participated; (2) an arbitration body will be guided by whatever rules the contending states agree on, whereas a court (unless it is asked to apply justice in a case in which application of the law would result in injustice) will refuse to be limited or guided by the contending parties with respect to the law it applies. The main advantage of a permanent agency is the continuity which enables it to build up a body of case law. In addition, it obviates the necessity of selecting a judicial body for each dispute. It is possible also to allow the permanent body to decide whether it has jurisdiction in a particular case even though one state may deny it, a difficult arrangement if contending states must agree to establish an agency for handling a dispute which one of them denies it is obligated to submit to arbitration.

Arbitration

Prior to the first Hague Conference there was no designated group of persons from which arbitrators could readily be selected. One of its chief accomplishments was the establishment of the Permanent Court of Arbitration, which, commentators delight in pointing out, was neither permanent nor a court. It consisted of a panel: for its membership each contracting power selected "four persons at the most, of known competency in questions of international law, of the highest moral reputation, and disposed to accept the duties of arbitrator," to serve for a six-year term

---

[10] If the parties agree, a case may be settled according to the principles of equity and justice, but in this instance the process is legislative rather than judicial. Several treaties have provided for settlement of disputes on this basis, and a few have been so decided.
States by Judges of their own choice on the basis of respect for law." (Hague Convention, Art. 37).

[11] "International arbitration has for its object the settlement of disputes between

(Art. 44). Parties wishing to use the "Court," but unable to agree upon the arbitrators, appointed two persons each from the panel, only one of whom could be its own national or a person originally selected by it. These four then chose a fifth member, called an Umpire.

On the vital question of obligation to arbitrate, the leading powers were unwilling to commit themselves in advance. Having agreed to establish the panel, they agreed to use it in a particular controversy only if and when they wished to do so. The furthest they went was to declare that, in legal disputes, *it would be desirable, if the case arose, insofar as circumstances permit,* to resort to arbitration!

Adjudication

Although arbitration continued to be used, after 1922 many disputes which otherwise would have been arbitrated were submitted to the Permanent Court of International Justice. International adjudication came to mean settlement by this Court, while binding processes by other bodies were usually referred to as arbitration.

The International Court of Justice, like its predecessor, consists of fifteen eminent jurists selected by the Security Council and the General Assembly. Its judgments are based on international law, or if all parties consent, a case may be decided *ex aequo et bono,* which means on the basis of equity and justice rather than law. No cases, however, have been decided on the latter basis.

On the problem of obligation to submit to the jurisdiction of the Court, little progress has been made. Although the Committee of Jurists which drew up the original Court Statute recommended that states be required to submit cases, the League Council and Assembly rejected the proposal. No further progress was made at the UN Charter conference in 1946. Membership in either court did not impose compulsory jurisdiction. However, both courts had in a sense a measure of compulsory jurisdiction which could be conferred in either of two ways. First, separate treaties might confer it specifically or generally. The peace treaties after World War I specified that certain questions involving mandates, labor, minorities, and transit must be referred to the Court. The Japanese peace treaty of 1951 likewise contained a clause providing that disputes over its interpretation would be so decided. Other treaties conferred more general jurisdiction.[12] The Statutes also contained an "optional clause" (Art. 36) which states could accept if they wished, as many did. Adherence obligated them, under certain conditions, and exclusive of reservations made in accepting it, to submit their legal disputes to the courts.

---

[12] Clyde Eagleton, *International Government* (rev. ed.; New York: The Ronald Press Company, 1948), pp. 227-37.

What James Headlam-Morley said in his *Studies in Diplomatic History* (1930) about arbitration characterizes adjudication as well:

Arbitration has generally been used in matters of secondary importance and even where it has been most successful, investigation seems to show that first of all a definite decision has been made by two States in controversy that it is for their common advantage that a peaceful settlement should be arrived at.[13]

THE UNITED NATIONS
AND PEACEFUL SETTLEMENT

Among their several direct approaches to the problem of war and peace, both the League and the UN emphasized pacific settlement. In contrast to collective security measures, which were taken by the League only in the Italo-Ethiopian dispute of 1935-36, and only in the Korean conflict of 1950-53 by the UN, resort to pacific settlement has been the usual course in interstate controversies—even those in which the disputing parties have resorted to force.

The Role of the Security Council

Although Chapter VI of the UN Charter is concerned with pacific settlement in general, and is therefore of some importance for an understanding of the General Assembly's role therein, references are mostly to the Security Council, presumably on the assumption that most of the disputes would come before it, since it had "primary responsibility" in that field. The essential features of Chapter VI are:

1. The first responsibility is placed on the disputing states for seeking a solution of their international disputes, which disputes if continued would be *likely to endanger international peace and security* (Art. 33). Inasmuch as no time limit is imposed, and members may be unable to agree on the type of settlement to be used, the requirement is not of much significance. However, even if disputes are not settled peacefully, members are prohibited from resorting to force (Art. 2). The Security Council may also call upon the parties to settle these disputes by peaceful means.

2. If such disputes are not so settled, the parties are obligated to refer them to the Security Council (Art. 37). Again this means little, for there is no time limit, and it is up to the parties themselves to decide when they have failed.

3. Any member of the UN may bring a serious dispute or situation before either the Council or Assembly, as may a non-member if it accepts the Charter obligations of pacific settlement for that dispute (Art. 35). So far, most cases have been brought to the Security Council under this Article.

---

13 Quoted in Schwarzenberger, *Power Politics,* pp. 238-39.

4. The Security Council may investigate to determine whether a dispute or situation is sufficiently serious to warrant its intervention (Art. 34). On its face this Article appears clear and innocuous, but it has been the source of bitter controversy. The majority has taken the view that it bestows a general power of investigation on the Security Council, and that it is a procedural matter, not subject to the veto. The Soviet Union has taken a contrary view, and exercised its veto to prevent an investigation of the Czech coup d'état of February 1948. It has also contended that since the Council has only political authority under Chapter VI, an investigation cannot be conducted on the territory of a state without its consent. However unfortunate the consequences of these interpretations may be, a strong legal argument can be made in support of the position of the Soviet Union.

5. If the Security Council concludes that the situation is sufficiently serious to justify its intervention, it may endeavor to bring about a satisfactory settlement (Arts. 35, 37, 38). As a matter of practice it seldom makes a formal finding as to its right to intervene, usually simply proceeding on the assumption that it has jurisdiction. The Security Council may at any time recommend *procedures* or *methods* of settlement (Art. 36), but according to the Charter wording, it may recommend *terms* of settlement only if the dispute is referred to it by one or both of the parties concerned. Again as a matter of practice, the Council has paid little attention to this provision, and has made recommendations concerning actual terms as well as methods as it has deemed appropriate. Finally, if *all the disputing parties* request the Council to do so, it may make recommendations concerning the settlement of *any* dispute, presumably international. The purpose of this provision is to allow it to deal with less serious disputes than those included in Articles 33 and 34.

The Role of the General Assembly

The only reference to the General Assembly in Chapter VI provides that a dispute of the indicated nature may be referred to it, and if brought before it under Article 35, it is subject in its proceedings to Articles 11 and 12. It has been noted that Article 10 is an ample grant of jurisdiction to the General Assembly. Nevertheless, subsequent articles refer to its specific jurisdiction and authority. It may discuss and recommend on questions relating to international peace and security brought before it by a member, a nonmember, or the Security Council, except that on matters before the Security Council it is limited to discussion. Article 11, paragraph 2, also provides that "any such question in which action is necessary shall be referred to the Security Council by the General Assembly either before or after discussion."

THE PROBLEM OF PEACEFUL CHANGE

Changing conditions and goals lead to demands for changes in the international legal status quo. The problems arising from these demands are therefore political, requiring changes of existing law, rather than legal problems calling for settlement on the basis of law. In contrast to legal problems, political ones are usually more controversial and more dangerous. In disputes over the former, in which the parties are agreed in principle with respect to the justice of the legal situation, differences dividing them are not likely to be great. On the other hand, demands for changes in the law may involve widely divergent views over what each disputant regards as morally right, or essential to its interests.

There has probably never been a legal dispute which would have resulted in war if it had not been solved by one of the existing methods of pacific settlement, or even if it had been left unsolved. On the other hand, insofar as wars arise out of disputes, at least one party wants a change in the existing legal rights and obligations. Hitler was not at all concerned with preserving German legal rights but with drastic changes in those rights. Disputes over the Suez Canal, Jammu-Kashmir, Palestine, and Berlin were all over what the law ought to be rather than what it actually was.

There are disputes that, on the surface, are legal in nature, in that the parties claim or deny a violation of international law, but for which a judicial decision would be of little significance. In 1960, the Soviet Union shot down an American plane which the United States claimed was thirty miles outside the Soviet border. The Soviets, however, charged a violation of their territory. Had the case been submitted to the International Court of Justice a decision based on international law would have been readily forthcoming. But the tensions, of which the incident was but a reflection, would have been unaffected.

The nations favoring the maintenance of the status quo usually try to equate the existing scheme of things with justice, and to brand the revisionist states as would-be lawbreakers. Since the latter frequently stand to gain at the expense of the status quo nations, the latter naturally resist. They regard the use of force to uphold their rights as moral, and its use by their opponents to change the situation as immoral. Both often appeal to the "right" of self-determination. It would appear to be a reasonable assumption that the use of force to change an unjust situation is more moral, or less immoral, than is the use of force to uphold an unjust one. Unfortunately, in most conflicts of this nature the struggle is not between right and wrong, but between parties with equally strong convictions of the justice of their cause. With respect to a state trying to change a situation it found unsatisfactory, John Stuart Mill wrote, "it does not entitle those who imposed the conditions to consider the lawlessness only and to dismiss the more important situation, whether, even if it was wrong to throw off the obligation, it would not still be more wrong to persist in enforcing it. If though not fit to be perpetual, it has been imposed in perpetuity, the question when it becomes right to throw it off is but a question of time."[14]

Peaceful change in domestic society depends on a number of factors: a sense of community uniting people in spite of their differences; public opinion to bring pressure on contending parties; overlapping membership in various groups which induce individuals to moderate their claims as a member of any one; legislative bodies to change the existing status quo, even against the desires of some whose interests are involved; and a police force to prevent changes in the legally established order by illegal means. Domestic disturbances and even civil war occur within states deficient in a number of these qualities. That force should have been the major instrument of change in an international society largely devoid of most of them should be quite understandable.

Despite all this, there are innumerable instances of relatively peaceful changes in international society. In many more, although force has been used, it has been but one contributing factor. Yet what was said in general about the intermingling of force and formal and informal methods of pacific settlement holds true equally of peaceful change. The liquidation of empires after World War II is a recent demonstration of this contention. Although Indians take great pride in their peaceful liberation from the British Raj, this view overlooks the long history of not-so-peaceful conflict and concentrates instead on the final months of negotiation preceding the granting of independence in August 1947. Whenever treaties are ratified, or international law evolves through custom, change occurs. The development of the UN and other international organizations through the treaty process are examples of peaceful change.

Nevertheless, international society is basically defective in providing methods for peaceful change universally recognized as essential within states. The non-decisional methods of pacific settlement are the only formal ones available. They ordinarily work effectively only when parties can be persuaded, or frightened, into agreeing to change. Yet more adequate methods and the sovereign state system are incompatible. For a really adequate method there must be established a *bona fide* international legislature. States may agree to international enforcement to preserve the status quo, and to submit certain of their minor disputes to judicial procedures for settlement, on the basis of existing law, but they usually draw the line when it comes to agreeing to a legislative body in

---

[14] John Stuart Mill, "Treaty Obligations," *Fortnightly*, XIV (1870) 715-20, as cited in Werner Levi, *Fundamentals of World Organization* (Minneapolis: University of Minnesota Press, 1950), p. 55.

which they do not possess a veto. The few limited exceptions to this rule are some of the nonpolitical international organizations such as the International Civil Aviation Organization (ICAO), and the supranational organizations of the European "Community of Six."

In formulating the League Covenant and the UN Charter, the importance of peaceful change was neither overlooked nor solved. Article 19 of the Covenant provided that "the Assembly may from time to time advise the reconsideration by Members of the League of Treaties which have become inapplicable and the consideration of international conditions whose continuation might endanger the peace of the world." Its counterpart in the Charter, Article 14, is more general: "the General Assembly may recommend measures for the peaceful adjustment of any situation, regardless of origin, which it deems likely to impair the general welfare or friendly relations among nations. . . ." All that either article does is to allow discussion and recommendation. Whether the matter ends there depends on the various political factors which determine whether there will be change, and if so whether it will be brought about by means short of force.

From this brief analysis of peaceful change it should be clear that it is a basic problem in international society. Change is inevitable; the alternative is between peaceful and forceful change. If forceful change is intolerable under present conditions, but existing methods of peaceful change are basically inadequate, the task is to find more suitable ones. But if the only really adequate method is the legislative one, and it is incompatible with sovereignty, it follows that the alternatives are the sovereign state system and war or world government and peace. One may of course challenge the validity of one or more of the "ifs" in this analysis. Is forceful change really intolerable? Are existing methods of peaceful change basically inadequate? Is "legislative" change the only adequate method? Would world government really assure peace? Is it probable that the growing destructiveness of war will deter nations from resorting to force, and at the same time cause them to turn more to the use of formal and informal methods of peaceful change?

SUGGESTED READINGS

Bloomfield, Lincoln P., *Evolution or Revolution? The United Nations and the Problem of Peaceful Territorial Change.* Cambridge: Harvard University Press, 1957.
———, "Law, Politics and International Disputes," *International Conciliation,* No. 516 (Jan. 1958), 257-316.

Borchard, E. M., *Distinction Between Legal and Political Questions*. Sen. doc. 118, 68th Cong., 1st sess., 1924. Washington, D.C.: Government Printing Office, 1924.

Carlston, Kenneth S., *The Process of International Arbitration*. New York: Columbia University Press, 1946.

Chase, Stuart, *Roads to Agreement: Successful Methods in the Science of Human Relations*. New York: Harper & Brothers, 1951.

Claude, Inis L., Jr., "Multilaterialism: Diplomatic and Otherwise," *International Organization*, XII (Winter, 1958), 43-52.

Corbett, Percy E., *Law in Diplomacy*. Princeton, N.J.: Princeton University Press, 1959.

Cruttwell, Charles R. M. F., *A History of Peaceful Change in the Modern World*. London, New York: Oxford University Press, Inc., 1937.

Dunn, Frederick Sherwood, *Peaceful Change: A Study of International Procedures*. New York: Council on Foreign Relations, Inc., 1937.

Fenwick, Charles G., "Inter-American Regional Procedures for the Settlement of Disputes," *International Organization*, X (Feb. 1956), 12-21.

Fox, William T. R., "The Varieties of Diplomacy: They Provide a Means of Adjusting Disputes Among Nations," *Worldview*, II (Aug. 1959), 3-6.

Goodrich, Leland M., "The Peaceful Settlement of Disputes," *Journal of International Affairs*, IX (1955), 12-20.

Gordenker, Leon, *The United Nations and the Peaceful Unification of Korea: The Politics of Field Operations, 1947-1950*. The Hague: N.V.M. Nijhoff, 1959.

Hambro, Edward I., "The International Court of Justice," *International Affairs*, XXX (Jan. 1954), 31-39.

Jackson, Elmore, *Meetings of Minds: A Way to Peace through Mediation*. New York: McGraw-Hill Book Co., Inc., 1952.

Kertesz, Stephen D. and Matthew A. Fitzsimons, eds., *Diplomacy in a Changing World*. Notre Dame, Indiana: University of Notre Dame Press, 1959.

Kunz, Joseph L., "The Problem of Revision in International Law: Peaceful Change," *American Journal of International Law*, XXXIII (Jan. 1939), 33-55.

Lawson, Ruth C., "The Problem of the Compulsory Jurisdiction of the World Court," *American Journal of International Law*, XLVI (Apr. 1952), 219-38.

Lissitzyn, Oliver J., *The International Court of Justice: Its Role in the Maintenance of International Peace and Security*. New York: Carnegie Endowment for International Peace, 1951.

Mayer, Arno J., *Political Origins of the New Diplomacy, 1917-18*. New Haven: Yale University Press, 1959.

Morse, Oliver, "Methods of Pacific Settlement of International Disputes: Difficulties and Revision," *Brooklyn Law Review*, XXV (Dec. 1958), 21-32.

Osborne, John, "The Importance of Ambassadors," *Fortune*, LV (Apr. 1957), 146-51ff.

Pearson, Lester B., *Diplomacy in the Nuclear Age*. Cambridge: Harvard University Press, 1959.

Plischke, Elmer, "A More Open Diplomacy vs. Greater Secrecy," *Foreign Service Journal*, XXXIV (Apr. 1957), 31-32, 34.

Price, Peter, *Power and the Law: A Study in Peaceful Change, with Special Reference to the British Commonwealth and the United Nations*. Geneva: Librairie E. Droz, 1954.

Rolin, Henri, "The International Court of Justice and Domestic Jurisdiction," *International Organization*, VIII (Feb. 1954), 36-44.

Rusk, Dean, "Parliamentary Diplomacy: Debate *vs.* Negotiation," *World Affairs Interpreter*, XXVI (Summer 1955), 121-38.

Simpson, John L. and Hazel Fox, *International Arbitration: Law and Practice.* New York: Frederick A. Praeger, Inc., 1959.

"Techniques of Mediation and Conciliation," *International Social Science Bulletin*, X (1958), entire issue.

Thayer, Charles W., *Diplomat.* New York: Harper & Brothers, 1959.

U.S. Senate, Committee on Foreign Relations, Subcommittee on United Nations Charter, *Pacific Settlement of Disputes in United Nations, Staff Study No. 5.* Committee Print, 83d Cong., 2d sess., Oct. 17, 1954. Washington, D.C.: Government Printing Office, 1954.

Verzijl, J. H. W., "The System of the Optional Clause," *International Relations,* I (Oct. 1959), 585-610.

Williams, Sir John Fischer, "Justiciable and Other Disputes," *American Journal of International Law*, XXVI (Jan. 1932), 31-36.

IV

RESOURCES AND
INTERNATIONAL POLICIES

INTRODUCTION

Resources are the tools which statesmen or diplomats use to accomplish their tasks. Logically, then, we begin with an examination of these resources. We have stated that most behavior falls into two broad categories—oppositional and cooperative. Resources may be used by a party to makes others do something; in this case the relationship is political. But if two or more parties choose to work together without exerting power on one another, their relationship is cooperative.

In Chapter 12 through 16 we discuss these relationships. Chapter 12 deals with the general nature of politics in international society, the following chapter with the use of force, and the next two with broad policy patterns. The final chapter treats international cooperation in a general way, and explores four case studies in international cooperation involving: narcotics control; trusteeships and dependent people; education, culture, science; and technical assistance.

11

Resources and Capacity

The resources at the disposal of a state, an international organization, or a dependent area, are among the factors which influence the manner and extent of its involvement in international affairs. The international role of a state such as Iceland will be relatively insignificant, whereas the United States, with its great agricultural and industrial capacity, and an abundance of extractive resources such as forests, minerals, and petroleum, can hardly escape exercising a major influence. All international organizations are quite limited in their resources, dependent as they are on their members for men, money, and matériel.

THE CONCEPT OF CAPACITY

It is conventional to deal with the subject matter to be discussed in the following pages under some such title as "Elements of Power," or "Why Some States are Weak and Others Strong." A somewhat different viewpoint is set forth here, necessitating both explanation and justification. In essence, this view is that resources constitute important factors, but by no means all of them, which determine the capability of a state or other international entity. Capability is the capacity to attain an end. Capability is relative, and depends on a number of factors, including resources, the consent of other states, and the conditions which prevail. The United States, for example, had the ability to get Canada to join her in a military alliance, but she certainly cannot, at the present time, get Communist China to do so, and possibly not India or Indonesia. Now it is obvious that the power of the United States, i.e., her ability to exercise restraining or directing control to make a state do what it would otherwise not do, is one, but only one, of the factors that determines her capacity. Did the members of NATO join with the United States because the latter made them do so? Power may have been used in some instances, but for the most part they joined of their own consent, out of fear of the Soviet Union, rather than because the United States coerced, bribed, or frightened them into joining. The Soviet Union, from the standpoint of the United States, is an external condition which affects the capacity of the latter. India, unlike the countries which allied with the United States, preferred to follow a policy of independence or non-alignment. Whether the United States had the capacity to make India join SEATO is debatable. It is conceivable that the United States, with the help of her allies, could have applied sufficient pressure to make India give up her non-alignment policy; but the fear that this might cause her to swing to the side of the Soviet Union, and the probable adverse effects of pursuing such a course upon the attitudes of other countries that preferred to stay out of the cold war, were among the considerations which caused the United States to limit the pressure she put upon India. Had the United States chosen to exert her full power, her total capacity to accomplish other objectives might have suffered. Because of such considerations, decision-makers may choose in a particular instance not to exercise their capacity to the full.

The resources of a state enable it to cooperate as well as to exercise power. The great capacity of the United States enables her to join in extensive international military, economic, and cultural programs on a cooperative basis, both bilaterally and through a large number of international organizations. The capability of a state, in short, is a function of its resources (which it may use to cooperate as well as to exercise power); the consent of other states, international organizations, and dependent peoples; and the circumstances under which action takes place.

These factors are of significance for international behavior quite apart from the way they affect a state's capacity for conflict and cooperation. Three examples illustrate this point. First, Japan lacks many raw materials and is consequently less capable; but this fact also causes her to pursue certain trade and other economic policies in order to maintain standards of living demanded by the Japanese people. She acts not because of her weakness but in order to feed and to clothe her citizens. Secondly, different geographical locations may influence states to pursue different foreign policies. The proximity of Sweden to the Soviet Union, and of India to both Communist China and the Soviet Union, has been a factor in their non-alignment policy. It is contended by both that, given their locations, they would be in greater danger were they aligned with the West than if they remained aloof; for, unaligned, their bargaining capacity would thus remain greater and their relations with either or both Communist China and the Soviet Union more likely to be amicable. Thirdly, the United States, presumably in part because of her democratic society, reacted somewhat differently to the Cuban situation of the nine-

teen-sixties than did the Soviet Union, under a totalitarian regime, confronted with a somewhat comparable situation by the Hungarian revolution of 1956.

It would be possible, therefore, to examine each of the resource factors
solely from the standpoint of how they affect international relations, irrespective of whether they contribute to the power available to decision-
makers. Some of them have been so examined—economic systems, for
example—in the preceding pages. In subsequent chapters we shall examine the way resources are used in conducting various types of international policies. The remainder of this chapter deals chiefly with the principal factors which determine the resources available to decision-makers
to pursue their objectives in international society.

Anyone who attempts to think realistically about international relations
must be concerned with power. Statesmen attempting to formulate and
to execute foreign policy must act in part on the basis of facts and guesses
about relative national strength. At best, power can be estimated rather
than measured with a high degree of accuracy. Factors such as morale,
in particular, are intangible and likely to be highly fluid. Strength according to any absolute standard is meaningless; what matters is the relative
power of any one state, or combination of states, as compared with that
of any other, or possible combination of states. A statesman must be
concerned not only with the resources of his own state, but with those
of others as well.

Because power is as important internationally as it is domestically, the
significance for power of each of the resource factors will be emphasized.
We should always bear in mind, however, that too great an emphasis of
this kind can distort reality. The exercise of power is only one—however
important it may be—of the uses of resources.

RESOURCES AND TYPES OF CAPABILITY

The resources of a state depend principally upon the following elements: geography, natural resources, population (numbers and quality),
productive capacity, economic and political institutions, and military
preparedness. The several elements vary in their degree of stability and
in their ability to be measured. Thus geography and natural resources
are both more stable and measurable than are institutions and the quality
of the population. These elements constitute the ingredients of the three
types of resource capability—economic, psychological, and physical. Industrial potential, for example, is important both economically and
physically. National resources capability thus represents a merging of
many components.

The ingredients of economic, psychological, and military capability change, as does their relative significance. These changes serve as a constant reminder of the danger of overrating the value of any one element, or of assuming that a particular element is equally significant regardless of time or circumstance. A hundred years ago, population and territory were relatively more important than they are today. Uranium deposits were until recently only unrealized potentials. The location of Great Britain, close to the European continent but separated from it by the Channel, has been an important British asset in the game of international politics. But in an age of guided missiles, space satellites, and superbombs, the advantages of insular position may be more than offset by proximity to continental airfields and missile-launching sites.

Geography

Geography is the most permanent, although not necessarily the most important, of the elements of capacity. The width of the oceans and land configuration have varied but little through the centuries. It is true that men have tunneled through mountains, and have dug interoceanic canals. The future may see the reversal of ocean currents, the removal of mountain barriers, and the redirection of vast rivers. Despite the changes of the past and those foreseeable in the future, most geographical factors must be accepted as stable conditions, rather than as factors to be removed or modified. There are four interrelated geographical factors—size, contour, topography, and location.

Size and Contour. Size and contour have important effects on the strength of a state; but like the other geographical factors, their significance varies considerably with changes in the other elements of national power. Other things being equal, the larger a state the greater is its power of defense. Between 1937 and 1945 Japan could have conquered all China had the Chinese armies not been able to retreat into the vast western region. Similarly, the military advantage afforded by the "strength in depth" of Russia was a major factor in the defeat of the Nazi hordes just as it had been in repelling Napoleon. Size limits the possibilities of dispersing industries. With the new military technology, small, compact Great Britain, in comparison with China, the Soviet Union, Canada, or the United States, is clearly at a disadvantage. However, sheer size may in some respects contribute to weakness. Transportation and communication are more costly and difficult with a more extensive area. Moreover, the political unity of a people may be affected adversely if they are widely dispersed.

Contour—that is, the shape of the boundaries of a state—also affects its strength. The more compact a state the shorter are its boundaries. A compact state has fewer transportation difficulties and less extensive boundaries to defend than does one with equal but more extended territory. From this standpoint Germany, France, and Switzerland are more fortunate than are states such as Norway and Chile.

Topography. Topography is the configuration of the surface of land, the location and direction of flow of river systems—in short, the general ensemble of physical features. Topography affects capacity in varied and diverse ways. Along with location, it determines the climate of a region. Climate in turn conditions the productiveness of the soil. The citrus groves of the Mediterranean, situated on a parallel with the New England states, are accounted for in considerable part by the climatic influences of the Alps. Climate may have an influence on the vigor of people. If it does, certainly the productive capacity of a state, as well as its ability to wage war, may be affected by the temperature, humidity, and seasonal changes as they influence mental and physical activity. It should be noted that this latter point has never been demonstrated conclusively.

Topography also affects economic development. Western Europe and parts of the eastern United States have "sinking" coasts and "drowned" river valleys which provide excellent harbors and easy access to the interior. The western coasts of Africa, and of North and South America, with rather even shore lines and high mountains a short distance inland, stand out in contrast. Both communication and rainfall are adversely affected by these physical features. The land and ice barriers of the Soviet Union have been and remain vital factors in influencing its foreign policy. While they serve as barriers to Russian aggression, they are at the same time a cause of that aggression. They also add to Russian strength by serving as defensive barriers. In contrast, the open plains which stretch from Germany to the Urals have been broad avenues for attacking Russia and for Russian aggression against the West. The Alpine barrier which separates Italy from northern Europe has been a source of defensive strength for Italy, but because of its precipitous southern slopes it has been an even greater barrier to Italian aggression against northern Europe.

Mountain barriers which divide a country may serve as an impediment to the unification of a people. Thus physical divisions have caused disunity in Italy, Spain, and the Balkan states.

Location. Location may be considered from both a world and a regional standpoint. The former means position with respect to such things as land masses, bodies of water, climatic zones, and raw materials; whereas regional location refers to the situation of a state with respect to other states.

Certain areas, and the states located therein, are especially fortunate from the standpoint of world location. Western Europe and the United States have generally adequate rainfall, temperate climate, and access to abundant raw material. Because the most advanced industrial states are located in proximity to each other, they are able to carry on interstate trade without excessive transportation costs. For this reason, plus the fact that much of the land surface is located in the Northern Hemisphere, it is not surprising that much of the world's recorded history has been made between 25 and 60 degrees north latitude.

The effect of regional location on national capacity, and foreign policy generally, is more direct. Up to 1914 at least, the three thousand miles of ocean between the United States and Europe, combined with the European distribution of power and weak neighbors in the Western Hemisphere, enabled the United States to pursue a course of economic development with little attention given to the maintenance of large land and naval forces. Its military power potential in both world wars was greater than it would have been had the United States been forced during times of peace to devote a larger proportion of its energies and resources to the maintenance of standing armies and a large navy.

Regional location has been of considerable importance from the standpoint of military strategy. Great Britain has been able to exercise influence upon Europe as a result of her location at the western outlet of Eurasia. By controlling certain strategic points, Britain in particular, as well as other powers, has been able to influence the course of world politics. The Rock of Gibraltar, located almost anywhere else in the world, would be but another rock; the Falkland Islands would be of little importance if they were a thousand miles to the south of their actual location; the Cape of Good Hope would be of little significance as a projection out of the Antarctic ice mass. Certain important narrow sea passages—Suez, the Panama Canal, the Sea of Marmora, the Straits of Malacca, the Skagerrak-Kattegat—illustrate the importance of strategic location, an importance reduced, but not eliminated, by improved techniques of land and air transport. Other areas have become of great strategic significance in an air-space age, as exemplified by the postwar policy of the United States in establishing a number of bases outside her continental boundaries, especially in the Arctic region.[1]

Although geography is important and relatively permanent, its significance as an element of power undergoes modification as the other elements change. The affects of rapid communication illustrate this point, although it is not clear whether the geographical element in national power is now of greater or lesser importance than it was formerly. A noted geographer has contended that "size and distance as elements of defense have acquired even greater significance since men have flown through the air instead of walking on the ground."[2] On the whole, modern means

---

[1] See Hanson Baldwin, *The Price of Power* (New York: Harper & Brothers, 1947), Chap. VII.

[2] Nicholas J. Spykman, "Geography and Foreign Policy," *American Political Science Review*, XXXII (Feb. 1938), 32.

of communication, combined with the new military technology, have probably tended to reduce the significance of distance.

Natural Resources

To the American Indian before the coming of the white man, coal was not important as a natural resource. The early eastern seaboard settlers looked upon the vast timber stand as more of an obstacle than a useful material. Raw material becomes of value only when its products are desired by man, and can be procured and utilized. Whether they can be obtained and used depends on the stage of technological and industrial development, which illustrates again the interdependent nature of the elements of resource capacity.

Types of Natural Resources. A great variety and vast quantities of natural resources are required to feed the industrial machine, to maintain or raise levels of living, and to sustain and augment the capacity of states. These resources may be classified as: (1) food; (2) construction materials; and (3) energy producers. Perhaps to the saying that "armies travel on their stomachs" it should be added that they do not travel far on empty ones. Land and climate are the basic factors conditioning the amount of food which an area can produce. Only a few areas are self-sufficient in the basic foods necessary for life and sustained effort. Among the greater powers only the United States, the Soviet Union, and France fall into that category. Before 1914, Great Britain relied on imports for two-thirds of her food; after 1945 imports supplied about fifty per cent of her food consumption. Certain countries are, of course, net food exporters—the United States, Canada, Argentina, New Zealand, and Australia being the major ones.

The basic construction materials are iron and the ferro alloy materials such as manganese, chromium, nickel, and tungsten, and the non-ferrous metals—aluminum, magesium, copper, zinc, lead, and tin. Many other metals, and nonmetallic materials, such as timber and rubber, are also important. Certain areas are more fortunate than others in containing varied and plentiful construction materials—the United States, the Soviet Union, and the Commonwealth being the best supplied—but not even these are self-sufficient.

Resource capacity can perhaps be measured most accurately in terms of horsepower. Production increases in general ratio to the substitution of nonhuman for human energy. Coal, petroleum, gas, water power, and potentially uranium are the chief sources of energy. These are necessary for efficient production of food, for transportation, and for turning the wheels of industry. Coal, still the most extensively used of all these materials, is costly to transport because of its bulk. Oil is a particularly strategic material because modern military machines run chiefly on petroleum and its products. It is little wonder, with over two-fifths of the world's known oil reserves located in the Middle East, that that area should be a crucial one in world politics. To be powerful a state must have access to these materials. This does not necessarily mean, however, that they must be located within its political boundaries.

The Problems of Accessibility. If all international exchange of commodities should cease for any considerable period the result would be drastic in terms of starvation and deprivation, adjustment of living levels and habits, and reduction of the productivity of every state. Since states vary so greatly in respect to their self-sufficiency, the results would be very uneven; changes in terms of power would be among the more revolutionary.

Why does the degree of self-sufficiency matter in terms of capacity? Two contrasting cases provide an answer to the question. France, deficient in coal, normally imports this fuel from the Ruhr area of West Germany. Since she does not have political control over the Ruhr, she must rely almost wholly on her ability to purchase coal from German producers. If economic (profit) considerations alone controlled the decisions of German coal producers, it would not ordinarily matter materially who exercised sovereignty over the Ruhr. But political considerations do matter. At war with Germany, France would be cut off from this source of supply, with the result that her power would be lessened. Even if she were able to obtain coal from other sources it would be more costly; consequently, less of her productive capacity could be devoted to the production of other commodities. One of the purposes of the economic integration of Western Europe is to make the states concerned more interdependent, so that war between them will be "unnecessary and impossible."

A contrasting example is the United States. After 1945, with the near exhaustion of the high-grade iron ore of the Mesabi Range, it turned to foreign sources—Venezuela and Labrador. United States-Canadian difficulties which might interfere with this exchange can be discounted almost completely. Nor is a wartime enemy of the United States likely to interfere seriously with transportation, although submarines might be a difficult problem in the case of Venezuelan imports. Aside from the possibility of greater costs of production and transportation, it does not matter greatly whether Mesabi or Labrador ore is used in the United States.

In times of peace, power considerations may also dictate the course of trade. As the cold war tension increased between the United States and the Soviet Union, the former attempted to cut off certain exports to the Soviet Union, despite the economic disadvantage of such a course.

Short of conquest to assume political control over resources, how do states often react to situations of this kind? First, they stockpile goods.

Only nonperishable commodities lend themselves to this kind of treatment. "Critical" and "strategic" materials which are not of great bulk, are the kind usually stockpiled—tin, tungsten, vanadium, and chromite, for example, in the case of the United States. Secondly, they attempt to become self-sufficient. Such efforts take the form of curtailing imports and then making up for them by increased internal production. Thirdly, they promote increased scientific research in an effort to develop substitute products.

The nature of modern warfare casts doubt upon the military wisdom of stockpiling and policies of economic self-sufficiency. If the outcome of a war is to be decided in the course of a few hours, or even minutes, military power-in-being, rather than potential power, is all that matters. In that event, a policy of self-sufficiency is likely to reduce the quantity and quality of usable resources. On the other hand, in a war which is limited in terms of arms and weapons employed, the traditional considerations remain valid. Since the wise policy seems to be to prepare for both eventualities, nations must strike a balance between these courses.

The problem is complicated still further by the necessity of conducting international relations both of a cooperative and a cold war nature. Although a nation may increase its power by a policy of self-sufficiency, it may thereby decrease its capacity to attain its objectives. Military alliances will be weakened, if not destroyed, if each member insists on going it alone. Economic interchange helps weld together the military links. The suspicion that members of an alliance are preparing to protect only themselves leads to loss of confidence and tends to destroy the very foundation of the coalition. Cooperative economic relations among countries are also impaired by trade barriers. Whether this cooperation be visualized in terms of short-term security, altruism, mutual economic gain, or the long-range goal of building a world order based upon community, none can be advanced by a policy of economic isolationism.

Despite the fact that national power may be increased by a policy of autarky (national economic self-sufficiency), such a policy is at best a necessary evil, and not to be undertaken lightly. It is almost always uneconomical; the cost in terms of labor, capital, and land is greater than it would be if many commodities were obtained through international trade. The additional effort and resources needed to procure these goods subtract from those available to produce other commodities.

Population: Number and Quality

As long as men are necessary for production and fighting, other elements being equal, the state with the largest number of men and women to perform such tasks will be the most capable. It is because other factors are not equal that the most populous states—China and India—are less powerful than are several others. Nevertheless, there is still some truth in Voltaire's statement that "God is always on the side of the biggest battalions," and in Clemenceau's exclamation that "France's tragedy is that there are twenty million Germans too many." In World War I American military manpower tipped the scales in favor of the allied powers. In World War II, China and the Soviet Union were able to trade both men and space for time.

Manpower is necessary for the armed forces; to perform direct services, such as supply, for the forces in training and in the field; to produce food, clothing, weapons and munitions; and to perform necessary civilian duties. It may be contended that modern warfare requires fewer fighting men than did war in former periods, yet the United States in the nineteen-sixties maintained a military force of about two and one-half million men, and the U.S.S.R. perhaps three million. It is estimated that during World War II, for every American man in uniform, from one and a half to two and a half were engaged in war industries. But manpower is also necessary to maintain production in times of peace. After 1945 United States foreign policy required goods and services, valued in the billions of dollars, to carry out foreign relief, rehabilitation, reconstruction, economic improvement, and containment of the Soviet Union, in addition to the normal production of consumer goods.

When economists refer to "optimum population," they usually mean the proper number of people to maintain the highest possible per capita production. But optimum for power may require more, or conceivably even fewer people, than does optimum for economic welfare. India and China are probably "overpopulated" for both power and economic welfare. Fewer people in these countries would probably result in greater power, for there would be fewer mouths to feed. Many of the present population do not produce a surplus, nor are they necessary for the armed forces. This is a cold-blooded way to look at the situation, but it does not at all follow that other values should be sacrificed for power considerations. Moreover, it is probably impossible to determine in any specific case the optimum in terms of either power or economic welfare.

Although quantity of population is important in war and peace, quality is even more desirable. Modern industrial technology requires skilled workers. Age distribution is also important. A state with a large proportion of people between the ages of eighteen and forty-five can mobilize greater manpower than can one with a larger number of younger or older people. Moreover, its potential population increase is greater. Lastly, the percentage of literacy and the level of health among a population are also important for resource capacity.

Far more difficult to assess, but no less important, is the intangible state of mind called morale. High or low morale influences the application of one's power to the task at hand. Among the factors which seem to influence morale are belief in the worth of the task, and judgment concerning the possibility of its accomplishment. National character, if there be such, consists of distinct attitudes and behavior patterns which characterize the vast majority of the individuals in a state. Thus it is sometimes said that Germans are submissive in their individual but aggressive in their group behavior; Americans are energetic, materialistic, and at the same time, highly idealistic!

Industrial Capacity

Technology and the quality and size of the industrial machine, provided the other necessary elements are present, determine the productivity of a state. Since industrial goods are an important source of both economic and military power, no state deficient in these respects can rate as a great power. Only a few places in the world are favored by a unique combination of circumstances which permit the maintenance of a large heavy industry. The United States, Western Europe, parts of the Soviet Union, India, Japan, and China, are the principal existing centers. In part because of its strategic location, the control of the iron-coal complex of the Ruhr, France, Luxembourg, and Belgium—the Lorraine Triangle—has been the coveted goal of states which have aspired to European or world hegemony. The ECSC and the Soviet attempt to prevent its formation attests to the productive capacity of this region.

The United States is the world's most capable state in terms of economic productivity and potential military power, largely because of its highly developed industrial plant. The Soviet Union's production, at the beginning of the 1960's, was probably about forty per cent of that of the United States.

Industrial capacity depends in part upon technology. Technical knowledge in turn depends upon basic scientific research. The National Science Foundation authorized by the United States Congress after World War II is an indication of the realization of the importance of scientific knowledge and technology to national capacity, as is the Soviet stress on scientific and technological education. The release of nuclear energy is made possible by national resources, scientists and technologists, and a large and efficient industrial plant.

Political and Economic Institutions

The relationship of political and economic institutions to capacity is far from clear to even the most objective mind. Moreover, pride and prejudice tend to obscure the real issues. For this reason, it is indeed difficult to examine with dispassion the relative merits of capitalism, socialism, communism, fascism, and democracy, as they contribute to the resource capacity of a state. It is much easier to believe in the absolute superiority in all respects of the particular institutions to which one is emotionally attached.

There are many facets to this question, only a few of which will be discussed here. The first relates to human response. Do men work and fight better under an authoritarian political system, such as fascism or communism, or under a democratic society such as that in the United States or Great Britain? World War II does not appear to afford an answer. Whatever differences there may have been to the responses of Germans under fascism, Russians under communism, and Americans and British under democratic institutions, they cannot, with any degree of certainty, be traced to their different political institutions.

Nor do peacetime conditions provide a clearer answer. In the nineteen-thirties when much of the world was in the throes of a depression, Russian production continued to increase, and after Hitler came to power in Germany in January 1933, unemployed men were put to work and the wheels of industry began to turn again. Production in both countries made greater headway than in the democratic states, with a resulting greater increase in the power of Germany and Russia. How account for this? It appear that the leaders, often by ruthless steps which democracies hesitated to take, so organized the economic system that opportunities to work and to produce were opened up. Undoubtedly morale, especially in Nazi Germany, improved as a result. But this does not prove that had the opportunities been provided in the democracies, the responses of free men would not have been as great or greater. Is the production of the Soviet Union today greater under the authoritarian system of that country than it would be were the government responsive to a free public will?

Was the abolition of the cruder forms of the police state in the Soviet Union after 1953 based upon the assumption that greater security and freedom were necessary for the realization of the success of the ambitious economic plans? But if so, how does one account for the fact that productivity was greater in a somewhat more democratic postwar Japan than under a semi-authoritarian prewar regime? In any case, we cannot deny the tremendous increase, at a frightful cost in human lives and other values, in production under Soviet totalitarianism. Can one be sure that if the same methods were used in the United States its production would be greater than it is? What if these methods had been used in the past? What would have been the long-range results?

So far our discussion has dealt with certain aspects of how men respond under democratic or authoritarian political systems. We now turn to a second problem, an equally difficult one: *the relative merits, from the standpoint of productivity, of economic systems.* Under any sophisticated, economy—whether the basically capitalistic, socialistic, or mixed (as most are)—production and distribution are exceedingly involved and complex.

The production task is essentially one of organizing land, labor, and capital so that the desired goods and services may be produced in the most efficient manner.

Government plays a major role in the functioning of a socialistic system, just as it does in a capitalistic one. Varying degrees of state control today characterize every capitalistic system. Whatever be the fiction, actually socialism and capitalism differ only in degree with respect to the amount of government control over the economy. From 1933 on, increasing governmental control and direction of Germany's capitalistic economy was primarily for the purpose of preparing for war; but the depression saw governments broadening their control of the economic systems in other countries as well, though primarily for economic reasons. With the coming of war, the degree of governmental control and direction of the economy became increasingly similar among all states. After 1945, economic and social disruption prevented the return to the prewar status in any country, although considerable headway was made toward that goal in the United States. Then, as the Western states began again to prepare for possible war, it was deemed necessary almost everywhere— including the United States—for government to tighten its control over the economy. Restrictions on international trade, international exchange rates, prices, credit, and raw materials were introduced. One can reasonably conclude that all governments saw fit, in varying degrees, to control their economies in the interest of state power. It was thus almost impossible to determine the respective contributions of the "socialistic" and "capitalistic" parts of the economy.

If it is at all possible to arrive at any objective conclusions concerning the relationships between power and political-economic institutions, all one may infer is that that which is best for power in one country is not necessarily so for another. These institutions function in a total social fabric of historical, material, and psychological threads. For Great Britain and the Scandinavian countries an interwoven economy of capitalism, consumers' cooperatives, and socialism, under democratic political institutions, may be superior; whereas in Russia, authoritarian political and socialistic economic practices may be necessary for the maximum creation and mobilization of national power. In the U.S. it may be possible and desirable to meet the problem with a larger proportion of private capitalism, a minor consumer-cooperative movement, and less governmental control.

Military Power-in-Being

The use of force in international society, and military preparation therefore, will be considered in greater detail in a subsequent chapter.[3]

---

[3] Chapter 13, "Armed Force as an Instrument of National Policy."

At this point we shall confine our attention to some general propositions.

As has been true in the past, the capacity to use force continues to be of great importance in international society. Even many disarmament proposals visualize not a disarmed world, but only disarmed states; that is, they would centralize the use of force in an international police of some sort. Collective security systems are all based in part on the principle of the use of force by most to protect some. Few are so sanguine as to believe that men can live in peace without some kind of coercion available to back the voice of legal authority.

Short of genuine and controlled disarmament, or an effective universal collective security system, states will be vitally concerned with their own military power. Their military potential depends on how well or how poorly they are endowed with many of the ingredients of force already considered. A few, such as Iceland, or Denmark in the interwar years, are so lacking in this respect that they do not even enter the military race. Nevertheless, Iceland chose to be a disarmed member of NATO.

An increasing number of people, especially in the weaker states but even many in the stronger ones, seriously question whether an effort to build military strength is worthwhile. This attitude has nothing to do with pacifism, although it is sometimes called "nuclear pacifism." It is essentially a problem of whether they can compete at all with the giants; a feeling that the arms race inevitably leads to destruction anyway; or that they are less likely to be destroyed, or defeated, if their country is disarmed. The new and rapidly evolving military technology of unprecedented power, destructiveness, and cost, not only imperils all mankind; it puts meaningful competition beyond the capacity of most countries. This statement runs contrary to a popular assumption, namely, that if a country manages to produce, or otherwise come into the possession of an atom or nuclear bomb, its power status will be transformed; it will become the equal of the other members in the "nuclear club" overnight. There is no doubt that the speed of atomic weapons, and equally important, missile delivery systems, will be upsetting, and will probably make an already dangerously unstable military situation more precarious. Nevertheless, it seems doubtful that very many countries have, or will have in the foreseeable future, the capacity to produce and maintain the costly and complicated instruments of war to compete with the nuclear missile giants. A recent study concludes that:

It may well be true that "nearly all the world's nations have scientists who can eventually succeed in designing and making their own atom bombs," and that a handful of technologically advanced nations may succeed in creating and maintaining one or two modern weapons systems. But only the United States and the Soviet Union can proceed with that variety of highly specialized and expensive weapons projects requisite to the maintenance of strategic military power in an age of rapid technological development and obsolescence.

And even between these two great powers, one or the other must be granted the ability to achieve significant technological leads in given areas of priority.[4]

THE TASKS OF STATESMEN

A state favored by geography, national resources, population, technological skills, industrial capacity, and efficient economic and political institutions, has potential psychological, economic, and military capability. The several factors which enter into the formulation and conduct of foreign policy will determine the proportion of a state's resources which it devotes to its international relations; the relative emphasis on each of the three forms of capability; and whether they will be used in oppositional or cooperative behavior. In time of war or its imminence a larger proportion will normally be devoted to foreign policy, and of that amount the military will receive a major share.

Conditions such as the distribution of power, the nature of the implements of war, and geographical characteristics are among the factors which will influence proportion and emphasis. Thus, before 1939, the United States found it possible to expend a small amount of energy and resources on foreign relations. Behind its ocean barriers, with weak and generally friendly states to the north and south; with the distribution of power among other states apparently such as to prevent a rapid victory of any one or probable combination of powers; and in a day when the range of planes was relatively limited, with atomic bombs and missiles but wild dreams, it could at least expect a margin of time in which to mobilize its vast potential military strength. After 1945 many of these conditions, and others, had changed; the impact on the entire foreign policy of the United States was revolutionary. It was quite certain that these drastically changed conditions which confronted the world made a "return to normalcy" impossible. What proportion of their resources should states devote to foreign policy? How much should be expended for economic development and the assistance to allies? What proportion of the wealth of the richer states should go to the development of areas in which two-thirds of the world's population lived in poverty?

How much of their resources should states devote to building up military strength, without undermining their economies and thus destroying the very basis of their military power? If, as many authorities seemed to agree, the Soviet Union did not intend to use its own forces in any all-out aggression, might not overemphasis on building up the military force of the non-communist world really provoke what it was intended to

---

[4] "Developments in Military Technology and their Impact on United States Strategy and Foreign Policy," A Study by the Washington Center of Foreign Policy Research, The Johns Hopkins University, for the Committee on Foreign Relations, United States Senate, No. 8 (Washington, D.C.: Government Printing Office, Dec. 6, 1959), p. 82.

prevent? Lastly, might not the building up of military might really weaken the Western powers in waging the "cold war," which was essentially economic and psychological? Different answers to these and other questions led to internal divisions within each of the Western-bloc countries, seriously impeded agreement among them, and generally taxed the ability and patience of both the decision-makers and people in general. In the early nineteen-sixties, after a decade and a half of cold war, with the threat of Soviet and Chinese expansion growing, the "grand alliance" was still uncertain of the answers to certain questions, and in many instances unwilling to make the necessary responses even when the correct answers were fairly clear.

SUGGESTED READINGS

Ash, Maurice A., "An Analysis of Power, with Special References to International Politics," World Politics, III (Jan. 1951), 218-37.

Baldwin, Hanson, The Price of Power. New York: Harper & Brothers for the Council on Foreign Relations, 1947.

Bidwell, Percy W., Raw Materials: A Study of American Policy. New York: Harper & Brothers for the Council on Foreign Relations, 1958.

Cook, Thomas I. and Malcolm Moos, "Foreign Policy: The Realism of Idealism," American Political Science Review, LXVI (June 1952), 343-56.

——, Power through Purpose: The Realism of Idealism as a Basis for Foreign Policy. Baltimore: The Johns Hopkins Press, 1954.

Cressey, George B., The Basis of Soviet Strength. New York: McGraw-Hill Book Co., Inc., 1945.

Davis, Kingsley, "The Political Impact of New Population Trends," Foreign Affairs, XXXVI (Jan. 1958), 293-301.

Fox, Annette, The Power of Small States: Diplomacy in World War II. Chicago: The University of Chicago Press, 1959.

Gregg, Richard B., The Power of Non-Violence. Philadelphia: J. B. Lippincott Co., 1934.

Gross, Ernest A., "Moral Power in International Relations," Journal of International Affairs, XII (1958), 132-37.

Halle, Louis J., Jr., Civilization and Foreign Policy: An Inquiry for Americans. New York: Harper & Brothers, 1955.

——, "Force and Consent in International Affairs," Department of State Bulletin, XXIX (Sept. 21, 1953), 376-80.

Huszar, George B. de, Soviet Power and Policy. New York: Thomas Y. Crowell Company, 1955.

International Economic Association, *Economic Consequences of the Size of Nations: Proceedings of a Conference Held by the International Economic Association,* ed. by E. A. G. Robinson. London: Macmillan & Co., Ltd., and New York: St. Martin's Press Inc., 1960.

Jones, S. B., "The Power Inventory and National Strategy," *World Politics,* VI (July 1954), 421-52.

Kitagawa, Daisuke, "The West and the Afro-Asian World," *Political Quarterly,* XXX (Apr. 1959), 157-70.

Knorr, Klaus, *The War Potential of Nations.* Princeton, N.J.: Princeton University Press, 1956.

Lasswell, Harold D. and A. Kaplan, *Power and Society: A Framework for Political Inquiry.* New Haven: Yale University Press, 1950.

Lindsay, Franklin A., *The Growth of Soviet Economic Power and Its Consequences for Canada and the United States.* Washington, D.C.: Canadian-American Committee, 1959.

Marshall, Charles Burton, *The Limits of Foreign Policy.* New York: Holt, Rinehart & Winston, Inc., 1954.

Mende, Tibor, *World Power in the Balance.* New York: The Noonday Press, 1953.

"The Military Strength of the U.S.S.R. and the NATO Powers," *Political Quarterly,* XXXI (Jan.-Mar. 1960), 71-88.

Mouzon, Olin T., *International Resources and National Policy.* New York: Harper & Brothers, 1959.

Russell, Bertrand, *Power: A New Social Analysis.* New York: W. W. Norton & Company, Inc., 1938.

Schilling, Warner R., "Science, Technology, and Foreign Policy," *Journal of International Affairs,* XIII (1959), 7-18.

Smith, T. V., "Power: Its Ubiquity and Legitimacy," *American Political Science Review,* XLV (Sept. 1951), 693-702.

Sprout, Harold and Margaret, eds., *Foundations of National Power: Readings on World Politics and American Security,* 2nd ed. New York: D. Van Nostrand Co., Inc., 1951.

Strauz-Hupé, Robert, *The Balance of Tomorrow: Power and Foreign Policy in the United States.* New York: G. Putnam's Sons, 1945.

Wallace, Lillian Parker and William C. Askew, eds., *Power, Public Opinion and Diplomacy: Essays in Honor of Eber Malcolm Carrol by his Former Students.* Durham, North Carolina: Duke University Press, 1959.

Wright, Arthur F., "Struggle *vs.* Harmony: Symbols of Competing Values in Modern China," *World Politics,* VI (Oct. 1953), 31-44.

12

International Politics

We have suggested throughout this study that most human interactions may be viewed as either cooperative or oppositional. Cooperation includes all those relationships in which human beings interact without controlling, or attempting to control, each other's behavior. Cooperation, however, does not exclude influence. Obviously, the behavior of individuals or groups may be influenced by their associates. One party may persuade another to adopt a course of action. Or the behavior of one or more of the interacting parties may change because of the removal of misunderstanding or the growth of mutual confidence. These are instances of modification of behavior through influence, but not control; in short, the interaction is cooperative.

An attempt to control the action of others is an exercise of power, and the relationship is oppositional. Only if the subject of control does not resist, either because he lacks the resources, or the will to do so, is conflict avoided. Thus children may sometimes submit to the exercise of power by parents, somewhat in the same sense that Denmark, with only a minimum of resistance, came under German domination in 1940.

The very fact that international society affords so few examples of nonresistance to the exercise of power, and that power plays such an important role in that society, indicates that oppositional tends to predominate over cooperative international behavior. Oppositional behavior, conflict, and politics, are used interchangeably in this context. Yet, since politics does not entirely crowd cooperation off the international stage, international relations and international politics are not synonymous. Hence the former rather than the latter term was chosen as the title of this book.

THE NATURE OF POLITICS

The term politics is used in various ways. In a popular sense, it often denotes party activity, as when it is said that one engages in politics by participating in a political campaign on behalf of a political party. Service in an appointed civil service position, or even simply voting for party candidates, may not be regarded by some as political in nature. A somewhat broader and different conception is that politics is the formulation of policy plans, or decision-making, as opposed to the carrying out or administering of these plans. Sometimes party activity and the policy-making process are thought of as applying only to public government, although their extention to mean school, business, or even church politics, is not unusual. In academic circles, politics may mean a discipline—hence a Department of Politics—in which instance politics means political science.

It is obvious that one has to choose among a large number of possibilities, of which those indicated above are far from exhaustive. Most conceptions of politics, either explicitly or by inference, conceive of it as involving, or consisting of, "struggle," "strife," or "conflict," which in turn implies the use of power. Some students of international relations say quite succinctly that "politics is a struggle for power." Others object to both components of this definition. Although they do not usually deny that politics often includes struggle, they contend that it includes cooperation as well. They are likely to define politics as the making of "authoritative," or governmental decisions, or the formulation of governmental policy, which usually includes conflict. Although the making of governmental decisions is a workable definition when applied to the national scene, as in the making of foreign-policy decisions, it has grave defects when applied to international relations. This is so because, whereas by definition states possess governments to render such decisions, international society is gravely deficient in this respect. Only a few international organizations are authorized to make decisions; for the most part they may only recommend. Even in those instances in which they can make decisions, either unanimity or near unanimity of the membership is required. For example, the convention on the Organization for Economic Cooperation and Development provides: "Unless the Organization otherwise agrees unanimously for special cases, decisions shall be made by mutual agreement of all the members." (Art. 6/1).

To say that politics is a struggle *for power* is to conceive of it in terms not only of action but also of purpose. It is similar to saying that imperialism is the expansion of a state for monetary gain or profit. Hence expansion for power, adventure, security, or any other reason, is by definition non-imperialistic. Quincy Wright says that "the ends of politics may be anything."[1] Certainly an examination of the foreign policy goals indicates that this is true. It is simply not correct, therefore, to say that politics is a struggle for power, or at least for power alone.

---

[1] Wright, *The Study of International Relations*, p. 132.

But the contention that power is the purpose of politics may not be dismissed so easily. It is sometimes contended that whatever may be the ultimate end of politics, power is the immediate end. Certainly this is sometimes true, for power is one means, and an important one, to obtain goals. This is the essential meaning of the enigmatic statement that "the principal cause of war is war itself," for the author explains that he means the aim for which both war and diplomacy are conducted is often something which will enhance a state's power.[2] Political activity is only one way of gaining power; goods are produced and armed forces maintained for that purpose also. The basic defect in the statement that politics is a struggle for power is that it simply is not always true, even in an immediate sense. A nation struggling to maintain its independence, or its security, may exercise power without in any way trying to increase it. The "struggle for power" definition of politics, even if it is, in an immediate sense, sometimes a correct description of political activity, may be interpreted to mean that power is the ultimate end of foreign policy. Ordinarily, however, it is only one objective, along with national security, economic welfare, or altruism. Where power is a goal of political behavior, it usually occupies a lower rank in the means-ends hierarchy than do national security and like purposes. In short, it is more a means than an objective.

When considering international relations, it seems preferable to define politics in terms of action rather than of purpose. As used here, *politics means directing or restraining, i.e., controlling, the actions of others. Power is the ability to exercise such control—to make others do what they otherwise would not do by rewarding or promising to reward them, or by depriving or threatening to deprive them of something they value.* To influence, in contrast, is to change the behavior of others through gaining their consent by persuasion or example, rather than through the exercise of power.

This is a workable concept of politics for international relations because (1) it does not presuppose the existence of governmental institutions to make decisions for the whole of a society, and (2) it does not narrow political action to the pursuit of any particular purpose. It is in this sense a broad definition because it encompasses struggle between individuals and groups, and between groups. It does not, however, include relations between individuals unless they be representatives of groups. Boxing contests and family quarrels are simply not regarded as political. The groups or entities with which we are concerned, as students of International Relations, are states, international organizations, and dependent peoples. International politics consists, therefore, of all conflict relationships among these entities.

Although this definition of politics is broad in one way, it is somewhat

---

[2] R. G. Hawtrey, *Economic Aspects of Sovereignty*, 2nd ed. (London: Longmans, Green and Co., Inc., 1952), p. 72.

restrictive in another. This follows from the definition of politics as an exercise of power, and the distinction between power and influence. The reader should be aware that the majority of writers include capacity to influence as a part of power. There is, however, a real difference between control through power and influence through consent, so great a difference that it seems misleading to call them by the same name. The United States, as well as many other countries, prefers to achieve its ends by gaining consent rather than by controlling the actions of others. Yet in the general relations of any two or more countries, as well as in any specific aspect of those relations, there is likely to be an admixture of cooperation and oppositional behavior.

In addition to the cleavage between those who identify politics with power and those who prefer more inclusive definitions, there is a somewhat similarly confusing argument between those who speak of politics and power politics. Confusion on this point is unnecessary. Defined as any relationship in which power is used, logically all politics is power politics, and other relationships are non-political. In that case it is as redundant to speak of power politics as it is to speak of cold ice or female women. But if politics sometimes refers to other matters, or to activities in addition to power conflicts, then it is logical to refer to non-power politics, to "power plus" politics, and to power politics. For even if it is agreed that all politics involve the use of power, power politics may refer to a particular type of power struggle. In popular terminology, power politics connotes the iniquitous use of a particular kind of power. It is a translation of the German term *Machtpolitik*, which means the conduct of relations, especially among states, by the use or the threat of force, with no consideration given to right and justice. Since views of justice and righteousness so often differ, what is to one nation a legitimate use of force often seems to another to be power politics. For this reason it is frequently used as a term of disapprobation in the international name-calling game.

Because in its physical form power is so obvious, it is all too frequently assumed to be the only form of power. The distinction is sometimes made between the use of physical and other types of power, with only the latter designated as political in nature. Thus viewed, an armed clash is nonpolitical. It was thus said that the UN military objective in Korea was confined to repelling aggression, unification being a subsequent political objective. What was meant was that unification would be pursued by other than military means. According to the definition used here, a relationship is a political one irrespective of the type of power used.

TYPES OF POWER

The several resource elements considered in the previous chapter are the ingredients of three types of power: psychological, economic, and physical. On the international scene, physical and military power are synonymous terms. Military power was previously considered briefly; it will be dealt with more fully in the following chapter on the use of armed force as an instrument of national policy. In the remainder of this chapter we discuss psychological and economic power, and compare domestic and international politics.

Psychological Power

Psychological power consists of symbolic devices which appeal to the minds and emotions of men. Often it is synonymous with propaganda, or the use of verbal or pictorial symbols to influence actions in a manner conducive to the realization of purposes the propagandist has in mind. Like other forms of power, it may be used for good or evil. Propaganda differs from education in that the latter is designed to enlighten, and to enable a person to make his own decisions. However, the line between education or information on the one hand, and propaganda on the other, is frequently anything but clear.

Propaganda is not a new phenomenon in the field of international relations, but its relative importance as a form of international power has increased with improved instruments of communication, with growing mass influence on foreign affairs, with the growth of total diplomacy and of total war, and with the development, among certain groups, of loyalties conflicting with the main loyalty to the state. Not until after World War II did the United States pursue an organized program of international "information." Prior to 1945 she resorted to so-called psychological warfare mainly during actual military conflict.

Psychological power is employed in various ways. The maintenance of armed forces as distinguished from their employment in combat is essentially psychological in its effect on the action of other states. This is true because there is always the implication that under some circumstances these forces will be used in action. When the diplomatic representatives and military attachés of foreign countries are invited to view the parade of tanks and planes passing through and over Moscow, it is hardly for the purposes of revealing advances in military technology for the advantage of the "backward capitalist nations." Likewise, a United States or British fleet is maintained in the Mediterranean or the Straits of Formosa not only for the eventuality of combat, but also for its psychological effects. The building up of the armed might of the Western world, insofar as it is designed to deter Russian aggression, is essentially the employment of psychological power. President Theodore Roosevelt had this in mind when he advised speaking softly and carrying a big stick.

These illustrations demonstrate another point of propaganda technique. From the standpoint of psychological power, influence on thoughts and attitudes is the important factor. American propaganda disseminated abroad, painting a picture of American society as one of equal opportunity and treatment, *may* influence the action of foreign peoples, whether or not it be true. But the lynching of a Negro, or racial discrimination of any kind, receives international publicity which far outweighs the effect of contrary propaganda. The propaganda of the deed is needed to reinforce the propaganda of the word. This conclusion refers particularly to a free society, for it cannot deny access to information about itself to the outside world and still remain free.

Many people in the United States are perplexed by the apparent effectiveness of communist propaganda, especially in view of its totalitarian nature. Does the iron curtain prevent the people of the underdeveloped areas, for example, from gaining a true picture of life in the Soviet Union, while at the same time, through clever propaganda techniques, these people are given a false but attractive impression of Soviet communism? Both factors account in part for the propaganda appeal of the Soviet Union. The combination of poverty among two-thirds of the people of the world and the example of real economic progress in the Soviet Union and Communist China (which, though gained at tremendous human costs, nevertheless appeals to people who have known neither plenty nor liberty) are additional contributing factors. The international character of communism as opposed to the essentially nationalistic orientation of non-communist countries and people also contributes to the success of communist propaganda. It may well be that the Soviet and Chinese leaders and people are as nationalistic as are those of the West. Outside of the Communist bloc, however, there is an international communist movement which looks to Moscow, and perhaps to Peking, as the source of wisdom, leadership, and strategy. The voice of a French or Indian communist is often far more convincing to a Frenchman or an Indian than is any "Voice of America." There is no arm of the Democratic or Republican party of the United States working in France or India for Washington as there is an arm—or at any rate an ally—of the Communist party of the Soviet Union or Communist China propagandizing in these countries for Moscow and Peking.

Communism, however, is limited in its internationalism, for it promotes the objectives of communist countries through the use of agents in foreign areas, without at the same time affording a reciprocal opportunity for noncommunists within the communist domain. In Soviet satellite countries, such as Poland and Czechoslovakia, where the communists are in political control, the party and the government are practically identical. In other countries, with the exception of Yugoslavia, the party provides the main instrument of action and channel of communication for the dissemination of propaganda. These disciplined communist parties are able to employ all the arts designed to influence the minds and actions of men.

The nationalistic basis of society and of democratic political parties in the non-communist countries handicaps them in uniting for the employment of similar techniques behind the iron and bamboo curtains. They are also impeded in doing so by the very nature of a totalitarian regime, which attempts to maintain a monopoly of propaganda. If democratic societies employ totalitarian techniques at home, they are likely to become totalitarian themselves; they must, if they are to remain democratic, therefore rely mainly on other methods to combat internal subversion.

The democratic countries are severely limited in presenting a united front because of their nationalistic orientations. As noted above, there are no effective international groups and parties bringing the peoples of the democratic nations together. Among their noncommunist political parties the social-democrats sometimes make a pretense of uniting their forces—the Christian Socialist parties of France, Belgium, Western Germany, and Italy also have a kind of "silent coalition"—but their results do not compare well with those of the communists.

Economic Power

Economic power consists of the ability to control behavior by affording or denying access to economic goods and services. Great Britain's early lead in the industrial revolution, her nineteenth-century role as the world's financial center, and her prominence in international trade, combined with other favorable circumstances to make her the leading world power. As the industrial revolution spread, first to the continent and then beyond, Britain's position was slowly undermined. By 1945, partly because of the liquidation of her overseas assets during World War II, she was in dire economic straits. Although she has made a remarkable recovery, she is in no position to compete effectively with the United States in terms of economic strength.

The purpose of the postwar economic policy of the United States has been mainly political, in that it has utilized economic power to control the foreign policies of other states in order to enhance its own security. Even the Reciprocal Trade Agreement program, the purpose of which is to reduce obstructions to international trade, is essentially a use of economic inducements to further political as well as economic ends. The Marshall Plan and economic assistance to underdeveloped countries, while conducive to long-range American prosperity, were approved by the Congress almost wholly in terms of building up the strength of the non-communist world as a bulwark against the advance of Soviet power. It is necessary to stress, however, that the criterion of the form of power is the means employed rather than the ends sought. While any particular type of power, or combination of types can be used to promote single or multiple ends, that does not modify the form of the power itself.

The economic resources of the United States have been used mainly to induce rather than to coerce. Most of the economic arrangements have been freely entered into and cooperatively executed, and hence are not political in the sense of power relations. Nevertheless, only if the recipient countries agreed to use the funds for certain purposes and to comply with certain other conditions were they made available. The attempts to prevent the shipment of goods of strategic value to the Soviet bloc has been a more obvious form of the use of economic power. The partial economic embargo on Communist China approved by the UN General Assembly in 1951 is another example.

Not until after 1953 did the Soviet Union turn to the use of economic instruments on any broad scale. Prior to that, her economic relations were largely confined to the countries within the communist bloc. Although she has exploited her Eastern European satellites extensively, it was her military superiority and the dependence of the communist leaders of those countries on the Soviet Union, rather than her economic strength, which enabled her to do so. The situation with respect to Communist China, however, was different. From 1950 onward, the more advanced economy of the Soviet Union has enabled her to influence, and probably to exert power, over the Chinese leaders. Although most commentators on Sino-Soviet relations in the early nineteen-sixties believed that there were real conflicts between these two countries, they also concluded that Chinese economic dependence on the Soviet Union was one of the factors which made a break between them unlikely, and enabled the latter to remain the dominant power within the bloc.

The economic weakness of the Soviet Union in the early postwar period, vis à vis Western Europe and the United States, meant that the former relied primarily on psychological and military weapons to conduct her cold war strategy. By 1953, with the rebuilding of the Soviet war-devastated economy largely accomplished, she was in a position to embark upon a program of trade and economic aid outside the communist orbit. A somewhat changed view of the international situation by those who succeeded Stalin upon his death in 1953, as well as economic conditions within the Soviet Union, were responsible for the new trade-and-aid offensive. The program continued apace with the rapid economic growth of the Soviet economy in subsequent years. It was estimated that between 1953 and 1960 the Soviet Union and the other countries within the bloc, including Communist China, had given or promised aid, mainly in the form of low-interest rate loans (2.5 per cent), to the extent of approximately three billion dollars. Of this amount the Soviet share was $2,470,000,000; Czechoslovakia's, $225,000,000; Communist China's, $143,-

700,000; Poland's, $81,600,000; and East Germany's, $31,500,000. Unlike the aid furnished by the United States, which was widely dispersed, that of the Soviet bloc was concentrated in seven countries, all of which followed a policy of non-alignment. These countries, and the amounts of credit extended to each, were: India, $810,500,000; United Arab Republic (UAR), $547,100,000; Indonesia, $484,500,000; Afghanistan, $210,000,000; the Syrian Province of the UAR, $170,300,000; Iraq, $167,500,000; and Ethiopia, $111,500,000.[3]

For the most part the aid was free of political "strings," and was therefore more an example of cooperation than of the exercise of power. Among the considerations which probably motivated the Soviet Union, as it certainly did the United States and the Western powers, was the hope that the recipients of economic aid would at least remain out of the enemy camp. In the long run, they might be induced or coerced into joining the Communist bloc, especially if they became economically dependent on it. It would be a mistake, however, to assume that the motivations of the Soviet Union's new economic policies were solely political. A leading authority on Soviet "economic warfare" writes as follows:

> Present Soviet foreign economic activities are not simply another weapon in the "cold war" and a political venture which when exploited to the full will be abandoned. Rather, they reflect a permanent change in the Soviet economic position, to be reckoned with henceforth on both political and economic grounds. Soviet foreign policy should not be viewed from the standpoint of either economic *or* political considerations alone. Both are operative. Whereas there is little doubt that political considerations currently appear to have the predominant influence, Soviet foreign trade has always been and will always be used to better its economic position. It is fortunate for the Soviet Union that the present position of its economy is such that economic and political interests coincide in its foreign economic undertakings. Sufficient evidence is available to give credence to the tentative conclusion that the Soviet Union now occupies a new economic position which adds greater flexibility to its foreign policy, magnifies the potency and duration of its economic efforts abroad, and orients the Soviet Union toward expanded economic relations with primary producing countries.[4]

DOMESTIC AND
INTERNATIONAL POLITICS—A COMPARISON

Domestic and international politics are in many respects similar. They both involve the use of power, frequently for similar ends; they employ the same forms of power and many of the same techniques. Nevertheless, there are significant differences. There are many people who assert that the chief need of international politics is to assume more of the character-

---

[3] *New York Times*, Mar. 5, 1961, Section I, p. 3.

[4] Robert Loring Allen, *Soviet Economic Warfare* (Washington, D.C.: Public Affairs Press, 1960), p. 61.

istics of domestic politics, especially those of a democratic society. The chief differences between domestic and international politics lie in the *direct and indirect use of power, and in the relative use of its different categories.*

Direct Use of Power

When steel workers strike against the steel management, this is a direct use of economic and psychological power to gain the ends their union wants to achieve. The management resists the demands hoping that its economic staying-power and manipulation of public opinion will in the end prove superior to the strength of the union. A lockout would differ only with respect to the party that initiated the struggle. Although frequently not regarded as such, activity of this kind is political according to the terminology employed here. It remains political activity, whether either or both of the parties resort to the use of physical force. In the latter instance, it is the duty of government to intervene, for most forms of physical conflict within national societies are prohibited by law. Nor is either party entirely free in its use of nonviolent forms of power. For example, a secondary boycott may be illegal as may be certain kinds of propaganda. Nevertheless, the right to use economic and psychological power, *within the bounds of law,* is an essential feature of a free society. In a totalitarian society the right to exercise power is largely monopolized by one party, which in reality constitutes the government. In a free society, the government monopolizes principally the right to use coercive violence.

In international society the clash of arms is only the most obvious and dramatic use of the direct approach. Examples given in the discussion of psychological and economic power were all of the direct variety. As a matter of fact, there are few instances of the indirect use of power in international society.

Indirect Use of Power

Indirect use of power means working through government to accomplish objectives. Although management and labor within states may employ direct methods, they may, and increasingly do resort to government. Thus labor brings pressure on government for the enactment of laws requiring the observance of standards of wages and working conditions, and of collective bargaining; management in turn secures the passage of legislation regulating the right to strike.

Why do states not resort in like manner to international government for the protection of rights and the pursuit of interests? The reason is that effective international government does not exist. As long as there are sovereign states, no change affecting their legal rights can be made by any supranational authority. If it were otherwise, they would no longer be sovereign, according to most concepts of that term. The regulation of tariffs, the right to regulate immigration, to maintain armed forces at whatever level a state desires and is able and willing to support, are all "internal" affairs subject to the legal control of that state alone. Its a general rule, the legal rights and obligations of a state can be changed only with its consent. Under these circumstances it is quite understandable why states employ direct power, including force, to make other states "consent." Only in a completely static society, or one in which politics is in some mysterious manner eliminated, would states no longer resort to the use of power among themselves. Only if effective government replaces international anarchy will states be able to relinquish the possession and probably the direct employment, of physical power.

The contrast between domestic and international politics may be summarized briefly. Direct action is common to both. Indirect action is of great importance in national society, while in international relations it is necessary to rely almost wholly on the direct use of power. In a national society, government usually possesses preponderant physical power and has a legal monopoly of the right to use it. In international society, while most states have renounced the right to employ force except in the case of armed attack, they retain a monopoly of the instruments of violence, on which they rely for "protection" at least. Physical force, therefore, is more frequently applied in international than in national group relations.

SUMMARY

International politics, although of paramount importance in international society, is only one phase of international relations. Politics is a type of interaction in which opposing parties resort to the use of power. Power is the ability to control the actions of others. Since all politics is "power politics," taken literally, the term is redundant. Power and its use —politics—is neither moral nor immoral. The problem is to control those who possess power so that it will be directed to constructive ends.

The resources of a nation may be used in competition and cooperation as well as in conflict. When devoted to power, resources may be used to create psychological, economic, or military strength. Psychological power is of ever-increasing importance in international relations. Economic power is used to provide or to deny goods and services. It was a major source of British strength in the nineteenth century just as it has been a principal instrument of the U.S. in the cold war. Military power, when used as a deterrent, is psychological in nature.

International and domestic politics are essentially similar in that conflicting parties use all three forms of power, both directly and indirectly. Their dissimilarities are due to the differences between the conditions of domestic and international society, especially to the lack of effective political institutions on the international scene. Lacking supranational governmental institutions to which to turn, states of necessity exert power directly. Possessing physical power, again with no government over them, they are more apt to use it than are conflicting parties within states.

One, perhaps the principal, reason for the international struggle for power is that power is essential to security in an anarchistic world—one without world government. Since power is relative, the equal enhancement of the strength of two antagonists, through military means, increases the security of neither and the insecurity of both.

SUGGESTED READINGS

Acheson, Dean G., *Power and Diplomacy*. Cambridge: Harvard University Press, 1958.

Arnold, G. L., *The Pattern of World Conflict*. New York: The Dial Press, Inc., 1955.

Barrett, Edward W., *Truth is Our Weapon*. New York: Funk & Wagnalls, Co., 1953.

Brassert, James E., "Power Politics *versus* Political Ecology," *Political Science Quarterly*, LXXI (Dec. 1956), 553-68.

Burns, Arthur Lee, *Power Politics and the Growing Nuclear Club*. Princeton: Center of International Studies, Princeton University, 1959.

Carleton, William G., "Wanted: Wiser Power Politics," *Yale Review*, XLI (Dec. 1951), 194-206.

Coleman, James S., *Community Conflict*. Glencoe, Illinois: Free Press of Glencoe, Inc., 1957.

Daugherty, William E. and Morris Janowitz, *A Psychological Warfare Casebook*. Baltimore: The Johns Hopkins Press for Operations Research Office, Johns Hopkins University, 1958.

Davison, W. Phillips, *The Berlin Blockade: A Study of Cold War Politics*. Princeton, N.J.: Princeton University Press, 1958.

Dyer, Murray, *The Weapons on the Wall: Rethinking Psychological Warfare*. Baltimore: The Johns Hopkins Press, 1959.

Esposito, Vincent J., "War as a Continuation of Politics," *Military Affairs*, XVIII (Spring 1954), 19-26.

Feis, Herbert, *The Diplomacy of the Dollar: First Era, 1919-1932*. Baltimore: The Johns Hopkins Press, 1950.

Gilbert, Rodney Y., *Competitive Coexistence: The New Soviet Challenge*. New York: Distributed by the Bookmailer, 1956.

Grob, Fritz, *The Relativity of War and Peace: A Study in Law, History, and Politics.* New Haven: Yale University Press, 1949.

Halle, Louis J., *Choice for Survival.* New York: Harper & Brothers, 1958.

Hart, H. Liddell, *Strategy: The Indirect Approach.* New York: Frederick A. Praeger, Inc., 1954.

Herz, John H., *International Politics in the Atomic Age.* New York: Columbia University Press, 1959.

The International Sociological Association, *The Nature of Conflict: Studies on the Sociological Aspects of International Tensions.* Paris: UNESCO, 1957.

Kaplan, Morton A., "An Introduction to the Strategy of Statecraft," *World Politics,* IV (July 1952), 548-76.

Kautsky, J. H., "New Strategy of International Communism," *American Political Science Review,* XLIX (June 1955), 478-86.

Kintner, William R., "Organizing for Conflict: A Proposal," *Orbis,* II (Summer 1958), 155-74.

Kisker, George W., ed., *World Tension: The Psychopathology of International Relations.* Englewood Cliffs, N.J.: Prentice-Hall, Inc. 1951.

Mack, Raymond W. and Richard C. Snyder, "The Analysis of Social Conflict: Toward an Overview and Synthesis," *Journal of Conflict Resolution,* I (1957), 212-40.

Martin, Leslie J., *International Propaganda: Its Legal and Diplomatic Control.* Minneapolis, Minnesota: University of Minnesota Press, 1958.

McDonald, John Dennis, *Strategy in Poker, Business and War.* New York: W. W. Norton & Company, Inc., 1950.

Morgenthau, Hans J., *Dilemmas of Politics.* Chicago: University of Chicago Press, 1958.

Niebuhr, Reinhold, "Is Social Conflict Inevitable," *Scribner's Magazine,* XCVIII (1935), 166-69.

Northedge, F. S., "Law and Politics between Nations," *International Relations,* I (Apr. 1957), 291-302.

Possony, Stephen T., *A Century of Conflict: Communist Techniques of World Revolution.* Chicago: Henry Regnery Co., 1953.

Sargent, William, *Battle for the Mind.* Garden City, N.Y.: Doubleday & Company, 1957.

Schelling, Thomas C., "Bargaining, Communication and Limited War," *Journal of Conflict Resolution,* I (1957), 19-36.

———, *The Strategy of Conflict.* Cambridge: Harvard University Press, 1960.

Seton-Watson, Hugh, *Neither War Nor Peace: The Struggle for Power in the Postwar World.* New York: Frederick A. Praeger, Inc., 1960.

Strausz-Hupé, Robert and others, *Protracted Conflict.* New York: Harper & Brothers, 1959.

Wallace, Lillian Parker and William C. Askew, eds., *Power, Public Opinion, and Diplomacy: Essays in Honor of Eber Malcolm Carrol by his Former Students.* Durham, North Carolina: Duke University Press, 1959.

Wasserman, Benno, "The Scientific Pretensions of Professor Morgenthau's Theory of Power Politics," *Australian Outlook,* XIII (Mar. 1959), 55-70.

Wight, Martin, *Power Politics.* London, New York: Royal Institute of International Affairs, 1949.

Wolfers, Arnold, "The Pole of Power and the Pole of Indifference," *World Politics,* IV (Oct. 1951), 39-63.

Wright, Quincy, "International Conflict and the United Nations," *World Politics,* X (Oct. 1957), 24-48.

13

Armed Force as an
Instrument of National Policy

War as an "instrument of national policy" was "condemned and re-nounced" by some sixty-three states in the Kellogg-Briand Pact of 1928. The members of the UN are obligated by the Charter to refrain in their international relations from the "threat or use of force against the terri-torial integrity or political independence of any state, or in any way incon-sistent with the Purposes of the United Nations" (Chap. I, Art. I). Three principal ideas with respect to force are set forth or implied in one or both of these passages: (1) it is a means used by states to further their foreign policy objectives; (2) its use for these purposes should be severely restricted; (3) it may be used legitimately to accomplish certain interna-tional purposes. The last of these concepts is a logical corollary of the fact that both the League and the UN provided for a system of collec-tive security in which national forces were to be concerted to protect members of these organizations under conditions stipulated in their con-stitutions.[1]

WHY NATIONS WANT MILITARY POWER

Nations want military power for several reasons. Armed forces are use-ful, and in a sense used, as instruments of foreign policy whether or not they are actually employed in physical combat. If they are not so em-ployed, they are useful essentially as a threat that they will be under cer-tain conditions. Were they not useful instruments of foreign policy, most

[1] For a discussion of collective security, see Chapter 15.

states would reduce their armaments drastically. They would not disarm completely because they would still need military forces for domestic purposes, and perhaps as instruments of international policy.

Despite the condemnations and renunciations of war, the obligation to refrain from the use or threat of force as an instrument of foreign policy, and collective security organizations whereby a state is supposed to be able to rely principally on the aid of other members for its protection, there has been no diminution in the reliance of states on military power. On the contrary, the period after 1950 witnessed the greatest armament race in history. In the early nineteen-sixties the direct monetary cost of the world's armaments was about $120 billion annually. It was emphasized, as the destructive potential of weapons mounted, that their principal use was deterrence, i.e., the reduction of the likelihood that they would be employed.

Domestic Purposes

Military power has several uses within domestic societies. It is especially important to preserve order in countries lacking in consensus and stable political institutions. In countries such as Pakistan, Indonesia, Burma, Laos, and South Vietnam, as well as in the newer African states, national armies have played a major role in this respect. They have also been used to prevent the seizure of power by organized minorities. The Indonesian Army has played a role of this nature against non-communist groups, whereas the armies of Burma, South Vietnam, and Malaya have been used against well-organized and armed communist minorities. After 1947, the strong communist movements in Italy and France were held in check partly by the armed forces of these countries. Even in the United States, federal forces have been used to preserve law and order, as evidenced by their use in Little Rock, Arkansas, in 1958, to prevent interference with court orders to integrate certain public schools in that city. In Burma and Pakistan the military forces seized power when civilian leaders were too divided or inept to preserve order and to promote economic progress. Military forces may, of course, get out of hand, and threaten the civilian authorities, as they did in France on several occasions between 1958 and 1961. Military *coups* have been frequent in Latin America.

A military establishment may also be desired by certain elements of a country to satisfy desire for personal prestige and careers, as was certainly the case in Germany, especially in the period before 1914. They may also satisfy demands for parades, for national prestige, and for power for its own sake. Although armaments are usually regarded as wasteful in that their maintenance requires resources which would otherwise be available to satisfy economic wants, expenditures for military purposes may be made to reduce unemployment and to bolster national economies. Yet, except for internal security purposes in some countries, most of these purposes are seldom decisive in causing states to maintain military forces, at least on a large scale. Were there not more compelling reasons for doing so, it seems likely that other means would be found for performing many of these functions.

International Purposes

National military forces are used for certain international purposes. We have noted that collective security systems are based upon military contributions from the member states. Even if there should be substantial disarmament, military force would be necessary as an international sanction. Only if an international police force were organized to perform this function would it be possible to dispense with national military power as an instrument of collective security. National military forces have been used for preserving order in the Middle East, and for a period after 1960 they were utilized to restore order in the former Belgian Congo. But in none of these instances have national military forces been maintained for these purposes. Rather their possession for other reasons has made it possible to use them in these situations.

To Further Foreign Policy Goals

Nations want national military power principally because it is regarded as necessary to realize certain foreign policy objectives.

As an Arm of Diplomacy. First, power, including physical power, is as useful to the diplomat as it is to the general, for it influences his ability to advance the claims of his state and to resist the claims of others. The oft-repeated contention that a nation can negotiate effectively only from strength is an indication of this point of view. When the United States embarked on a program of rearmament after 1947, it was contended that this would make the Soviet Union more amenable to reason at the bargaining table. Likewise the West German government, although not without wide debate and considerable opposition from within Germany, contended that the reunion of the country through negotiations would be facilitated once Germany was rearmed. Even if the subject matter of negotiations is disarmament, it sometimes is contended that one must "arm to parley." Not infrequently nations fear to negotiate when they are militarily weak, but feel that compromise, the essential of successful negotiation, is unnecessary when they are strong. One might conclude that equality of strength is the situation most conducive to effective diplomacy. Between 1925 and 1932, the one period of the interwar years when France and Germany appeared to be of approximately equal strength, these countries were able to agree on a number of measures, including the Locarno treaties. Nevertheless, with power relationships inherently unstable, and accurate measure of power so uncertain, even with an appearance of relative equality of power among them, antagonistic states find agreement elusive. On the other hand, given a larger area of mutual interests, satisfactory negotiations are usually possible in spite of power disparities. As a rule, the United States and its allies have been able to reconcile their differences through compromise and accommodation even though the power of the United States in the period after World War II has overshadowed theirs.

For National Security. Secondly, all states are concerned with their national security, and armaments and military alliances have been the traditional methods relied upon to achieve this end. So far, neither collective security nor disarmament has changed the situation materially. States that are satisfied with the international status quo, or that, despite dissatisfaction, do not intend to try to change it by force, arm primarily to preserve the existing situation. But even militarily aggressive states rely on arms for their security. Although Americans have difficulty, given their peaceful intentions, of believing that the leaders of the Soviet Union or of Communist China have any reason to feel insecure because of external dangers, and especially of an attack by the United States or its allies, it is understandable that they should have such fears, whether or not they are well grounded. Even if a state plans an armed attack it will have to be concerned with its security against retaliation, especially in an age of long-range delivery systems which can "leap over" traditional defense barriers and against which there are at present no effective means of defense. Aggressive nations also have to take precautions against a "pre-emptive" war, i.e., one started by a defensive power in order to forestall an attack believed to be imminent. There is also the possibility of a so-called preventive war, which differs from a pre-emptive one only in that the danger of attack is thought to be more distant in time. Thus most states, regardless of other purposes for which armed forces are deemed useful, want them for defense. There is truth then, but not the whole truth, in the claim made by all states that their armed forces are for national defense. All such forces are administered by "defense departments," never by departments of offense!

As defensive instruments, military forces may play two roles. They may act as deterrents, to discourage an aggressor from attacking because the attainment of his goals would be too costly, or even impossible. And, if they fail to deter, it is argued that they are then necessary to enable the intended victim to resist the attack.

To Change the International Status Quo. Thirdly, armed forces may be wanted to obtain goals which can be realized only through the use of force to change the status quo; in short, for use in an aggressive manner. We have noted that peaceful change in international society is very difficult, in many instances virtually impossible, and that this is one of the factors which seem to account for the use of force for purposes which, in domestic societies, are ordinarily achieved by peaceful means. Whether Britain, France, and Israel used their armed forces in 1956 against Egypt to protect their legal rights or to change the international status quo is debatable. If the former, we have an example of the use of force for defensive purposes, or, if the latter, to change the status quo by aggression. Both were illegal under the UN Charter, unless Egypt had attacked one or more of the other three nations. Certainly Israel had a good case against Egypt, for she had been the victim of many Egyptian raids within her territory. Whether illegal or not, all four countries used armed force as instruments of national policy.

Covert Warfare. Fourthly, armed forces may be used to promote the objectives of one country by aiding the governments or rebel forces of another, without the aiding government becoming officially involved, or formally at war. German and Italian aid to the Franco rebels, and Russian assistance to the legal democratic government during the Spanish Civil War which began in 1936 were of this nature. The fiction that Chinese Communist "volunteers" assisted the North Korean forces during the period from 1950 to 1953 is another example. Aid to "national liberation" forces, a publicly approved policy of the communist states, and the Truman Doctrine, "to support free people who are resisting attempted subjugation by armed minorities or by outside pressures," are additional cases in point, as was American and communist aid to rival forces in Laos. There is no acceptable terminology to characterize warfare of this type, although the communist powers called it capitalistic imperialism and the non-communist powers subversion, or "war by proxy." Covert war is perhaps as good a term, and as neutral a one, as any other.

MILITARY POLICIES

Nations have military policies just as they do economic and psychological ones. They therefore formulate plans or strategy for the use of military force to accomplish their objectives. During the course of a war military power, however, ordinarily does not replace, but rather supplements, the use of economic and psychological power. This is the essential meaning of the following passage by Karl von Clausewitz, the great German military theorist.

We maintain . . . that War is nothing but a continuation of political intercourse, with a mixture of other means . . . in order thereby to maintain at the same time that this political intercourse does not cease by the war itself, is not changed into something quite different, but that, in its essence it continues to exist . . . , and that the chief lines [of the war] are only the general features of policy which run all through the War until peace takes place.[2]

American Attitudes Towards War

Relatively secure behind two great oceans during most of their history, and by tradition if not always in action a peaceful people, Americans have difficulty in conceiving of military force, especially its actual use in war, as one of the arms of foreign policy. War is regarded as an abnormal and basically immoral act. However, if it regretfully becomes unavoidable they are likely to forget the general foreign policy aims and to proclaim that the "purpose of war is victory," and that nothing short of unconditional surrender will suffice. Shortly before the United States entered World War I in 1917, Americans regarded it as an imperialistic war which they were "too proud to fight"; with their entry in 1917, it was suddenly transformed into a holy war "to make the world safe for democracy." Attitudes of this nature were the chief sources of the controversy that divided the American people during the Korean War which began in 1950. On one side were those who appeared to advocate victory at any price, even the price of a general and unlimited war. On the other side, and the one which prevailed, were those who would limit the war in terms of terrain, types of weapons, and objectives. A wise military policy is one which regards force as but one of several instruments for the promotion of national goals.

Military Plans and Preparation

Military plans for the accomplishment of specified objectives, and the development of military capacity to accomplish them, are obviously necessary. The obtainable objectives, and the forces required to realize them, depend upon the circumstances under which force may have to be employed. Only if military planners know the kind of war they are going to fight, the objectives, and the conditions under which it will be conducted, can their plans be at all precise. The more imminent the outbreak of war, the more certain, or less uncertain they are likely to be of its conditions and requirements.

A nation planning an offensive war has certain advantages in this respect—it can at least choose the time and place for the initial strike, as well as the weapons it will employ. But on the other hand the defender must ordinarily attempt to gear his planning to the possibility of different kinds of war at any moment. The great destructiveness of nuclear weapons, the rapidity of modern delivery system, such as missiles and possibly

---

[2] Carl von Clausewitz, *On War*, trans. by Colonel J. J. Graham, new and rev. ed. (London: Kegan Paul, Trench, Trübner & Co., Ltd., 1911) Vol. III, Bk. VIII, p. 121.

space vehicles, and the difficulty of defense against them, are especially advantageous to the initiator of a thermonuclear-missile war. Considerations such as these explain in large part the emphasis placed upon deterrent capacity.

Since no nation can be prepared at all times to fight all kinds of wars in all places and under all conditions, basic assumptions, of varying degrees of reliability, must be made, and plans and preparations shaped accordingly. Because it is impossible, probably unnecessary, and certainly unwise to prepare against all states, top priority must be given to assumptions about prospective enemies, allies, and neutrals. Could Britain and France rationally assume, in 1914 or in 1939, that the United States would eventually come to their aid? Or, in the latter year, that the Soviet Union would become an ally? Or could Germany assume that the United States would not enter the conflict, or in any event in time to turn the tide? Could European states have full confidence that the United States would come to their assistance in the event they were attacked by the Soviet Union? Would the United States do so if this meant almost certain suicide? Similar questions illustrate the kinds of estimates and assumptions that must be made in developing military policies. Would the theatre of war be in the jungles of Laos, the deserts of the Middle East, and North Africa, the densely populated terrain of Korea or Western Europe, or the United States? Or would it be waged everywhere? What weapons would the probable enemy have, and which would be used? Would there be time to convert potential into actual military power, or would only that in existence at the outset matter? How long would the struggle last? At what future time would hostilities begin? What would be the state of military technology at that time? Would it be wise to concentrate on certain kinds of weapons which may be obsolete five years hence, especially if this would mean delay in the production of those more likely to be used at that time? Would a military buildup by state A cause B (and its allies) to increase its military strength, with the result that war might be more likely than before, and either A or B, or both, would be less secure? Would disarmament—and if so under what conditions—be more likely to maximize foreign policy goals, including national security and personal survival, than would armaments? Assumptions covering such questions are always hazardous. Once made, they require continuous re-examination and adjustment in the light of new developments, additional knowledge, and further insights.

Impact of New Military Technology. The revolutionary changes in military technology since 1945 have vastly complicated the problem of military strategy. Weapons have become outdated, replaced by costly new ones, only in turn to be discarded and again replaced. The great battleship is a symbol rather than a useful instrument of war. The blockbuster of World War II, with an explosive power of twenty tons of TNT, is a mild conventional weapon compared with modern hydrogen bombs with an equivalent of millions of tons. And we are told there is no theoretical upper limit! The equipment of United States ground forces changed very little between the two world wars. The B-17 "Flying Fortress," on the other hand, was operationally useful for eight years; the B-36 inter-continental bomber was obsolescent in less than five; and the B-52 jet bomber was outdated before the Strategic Air Command (SAC) was completely equipped with it.[3] It is certainly not beyond the realm of possibility that intercontinental ballistic missiles may soon be old-fashioned, to be replaced by satellites loaded with cobalt "earth-busters" encircling the globe.

The development of military alliances has meant additional problems, for they have necessitated the development of joint and coordinated strategies, and attempts to have each nation prepare to fulfill its par-ticular military mission. One writer contends that the problems of military strategy are so novel and complex that "the ablest students of the subject are either in complete contradiction or in a state of frank bewilderment."[4]

Schools of Military Strategy. Nevertheless, military planners have to act on the basis of certain assumptions. Since it is not possible, practicable, or wise to prepare to fight war in general, they have to prepare to fight particular wars, or in any case particular kinds of wars. An almost new vocabulary has been developed by contemporary writers on military strategy. Gordon B. Turner notes that "more than a dozen different kinds of war are mentioned as possibilities for the future, and the number of names given to the strategies by which those wars may be conducted is steadily mounting."[5] He contends, however, that most military strategists may be classified as falling into the one of two schools of thought—the un-limited or total, and the limited. The first think in such terms as massive retaliation, deterrence, and continental strategy, all of which "are inter-changeable since they all depend upon the swift and awful striking power of nuclear air weapons either to prevent war or to win it quickly."[6] This school also insists that if war comes, it will be total. The limited-war group, on the other hand, stresses graduated deterrence, and war limited in terrain, weapons, and objectives.[7] Because of the fear of universal

---

[3] *International Security: The Military Aspect,* Special Studies, Report II of Rocke-feller Brothers Fund (Garden City, New York: Doubleday & Company, Inc., 1958), pp. 8 and 13.

[4] Walter Millis, *Arms and Men* (New York: G. P. Putnam's Sons, 1956), p. 345.

[5] "Classic and Modern Strategic Concepts," in Gordon B. Turner and Richard D. Challenger, eds., *National Security in the Nuclear Age* (New York: Frederick A. Praeger, Inc., 1960), Part I, Ch. I, p. 5.

[6] *Ibid.,* p. 7.

[7] A strategy of graduated deterrence is one in which it would be made clear to a prospective or actual enemy that as, but only if, he applied greater force, or intro-duced more powerful weapons, these measures would be matched step by step.

destruction if wars are not kept limited, they hold that limited war is more likely than total war.

Different Tasks Require Different Strategies. We have noted that armed forces are used internationally as instruments of foreign policy to support diplomacy, to make the nation secure, to wage aggressive war, either limited or total, and to support contending groups within other nations. A given military strategy and forces adequate for one of these tasks, however, may be inappropriate or useless for another. For example, when the Korean War broke out it was said that the United States was prepared to fight the wrong enemy, at the wrong place, and with the wrong weapons. The enemy envisaged had been the Soviet Union, which, it was feared, would invade Western Europe, probably some time after 1950; the United States would retaliate by using SAC to drop atomic bombs on Soviet soil. The Korean War, on the other hand, was fought by ground forces, with air and naval support, using conventional weapons within the confines of Korea. For this kind of war the United States was ill prepared.

Despite the fact that the limited-war school in the United States commanded more attention and support after the Korean War, it was clear that the total-war strategists continued to dominate the scene. As long as the United States possessed a monopoly, or a clear superiority in atomic weapons and delivery systems, a threat of massive retaliation against the Soviet Union or Communist China, for example, might have carried with it a degree of credibility. But when this strategy was proclaimed by the then Secretary of State, John Foster Dulles, in 1954, it was, or rapidly became outdated.[8] For the Soviet Union had, or soon acquired, a "second-strike"—i.e., retaliatory—capacity against the United States. It was, therefore, very unlikely that the latter would be willing to use nuclear weapons against the Soviet Union, or even Communist China, short of a direct attack on the United States, and probably on its European allies. It was far from certain, however, in the event of a Soviet attack on Western Europe, especially by conventional weapons, that the United States would be willing to retaliate by a nuclear attack against the Soviet homeland. For in that event it seemed inevitable that the Soviet Union would strike a devastating blow against the United States.

Although it was denied in high official circles, and by military strategists, especially those in the Air Force, there was widespread belief that the United States was inadequately prepared to fight either conventional or covert type wars. That the Democratic Administration, which took office in January of 1961, subscribed to this belief is indicated by the fact that one of its first military decisions was to step up the airlift

---

[8] John Foster Dulles, "Policy for Security and Peace," *Foreign Affairs,* XXXII (Apr. 1954), 353-64.

capacity for conventional forces and to train additional military units for guerrilla warfare.

CAPACITY AND STRATEGY FOR UNLIMITED WAR

A nation prepared to wage unlimited war must possess weapons system capable of wholesale destruction. In the present stage of military technology it must have an arsenal of nuclear weapons, as well as rapid delivery systems such as long-range jet bombers and missiles. Only the United States and the Soviet Union were major nuclear powers by the early nineteen-sixties, although Great Britain had both atomic and hydrogen weapons, and France exploded her first small atomic bomb in 1960. Only the first two, however, had made rapid strides in developing intercontinental ballistic missiles, with the Soviet Union estimated by some authorities as having a lead of from one to three years. The "missile gap," if it existed, referred to the period during which the United States would lag behind the Soviet Union in the possession of operational long-range missiles. Until this gap was closed, it was feared that the Soviet Union, by striking first, would be capable of destroying a large proportion of the retaliatory capacity of the United States.[9] It was the officially proclaimed policy of the United States that it would never strike first, which, if taken literally, would rule out even a pre-emptive war. But even were she willing to do so, it appeared quite improbable that she had the capacity to destroy enough of the Soviet's retaliatory capacity to prevent the latter from severely damaging, if not destroying, the industrial and heavily populated centers of the United States.

Experts on military technology have claimed that "nearly all of the world's nations have scientists who can eventually succeed in designing and making their own atomic bombs," and that a few technologically advanced ones may be able to create and maintain one or two modern weapons systems.[10] Nevertheless, some also maintain that it is highly improbable that nations other than the United States and the Soviet Union "can proceed with that variety of highly specialized and expensive weapons projects requisite to the maintenance of strategic military power in an age of rapid technological development and obsolescence."[11]

---

[9] Brig. Gen. Thomas R. Phillips, "The Growing Missile Gap," *The Reporter*, XV (Jan. 8, 1958), 10-16.

[10] Howard A. Wilcox, "Weapons, Science, and Civilization," *Astronautics*, IV (May 1959), 81.

[11] "Developments in Military Technology and their Impact on United States Strategy and Foreign Policy," A Study by the Washington Center of Foreign Policy Research, The Johns Hopkins University, for the Committee on Foreign Relations, United States Senate, No. 8 (Washington, D.C.: Government Printing Office, Dec. 6, 1959), p. 82.

Strategy of Mutual Nuclear Deterrence

Arms are wanted to deter war and to wage war if the deterrent fails. Although the use of the term deterrence has been especially prominent in the nuclear-missile age, the concept is an old one. In essence, it means that a state which could otherwise attack is restrained from doing so because it believes the gains would not be worth the cost. The Swiss have long relied upon a deterrent military policy. As a matter of fact, deterrence is to some extent inherent in any military force.[12]

The stress on deterrence was the direct outgrowth of the potential destructiveness of modern armaments. It is often referred to as nuclear or strategic deterrence. During the short-lived atomic monopoly of the United States, this, coupled with her long-range bomber force, and advanced bases on foreign soil, was one of unilateral deterrence. But when the Soviet Union accumulated a stockpile of nuclear weapons, and developed intercontinental ballistic missiles and probably submarines capable of carrying missiles equipped with nuclear warheads, the term "mutual deterrence" came into vogue. This referred to a situation in which neither power could rationally expect to be able to destroy the other's capacity to strike back "with a blow of unacceptable proportions." As long as the United States and the Soviet Union retained this duopoly they would be the only powers capable of playing the nuclear deterrent game. Although each was capable of destroying the other, there was serious doubt that a situation of mutual deterrence as defined really existed. The fear of a "missile gap" was an indication of this concern. Even though there might be periods of stability, i.e., situations in which changes would not favor one power or another in such a way as to lead either to believe that it could launch a first strike without suffering greater damage in return than it was willing to accept, it was quite possible or probable that there would be future gaps as dangerous as the possible missile gap of the early nineteen-sixties. It seemed quite possible—there were those who maintained it was a certainty—that total war meant total destruction. If that were true, deterrence was the only kind of rational military defense policy. Some, however, denied that the destruction would be so drastic as to imperil individual and national survival. A defensive war, therefore, was a rational alternative if deterrence failed, and a meaningful victory, or at least the termination of war without victory or complete destruction of either one or all antagonists, was still a possibility.

Requirements for Reliable Deterrence. What are the requirements for effective mutual deterrence against a total nuclear war? The first is

---

[12] Charles M. Ferguson, Jr., "Military Forces and National Objectives," *Military Review*, XXXV (Oct. 1955), 12-29.

sufficient retaliatory capacity, i.e., "ability to strike back with a retaliatory blow of unacceptable proportions."[13] Secondly, the power relying upon deterrence must be willing to employ its forces to the extent necessary to convince the potential aggressor that war will not be worth the cost. Thirdly the aggressor must believe that the defender has both the capacity and the will to strike with the necessary force; otherwise he will not be deterred. Contrary to the conventional military doctrine of extreme secrecy, deterrence seems to require that a potential attacker be aware of the capacity and intentions of the defender nation. This conclusion is based on the assumption that knowledge of the facts is necessary to convince. Since it is assumed that the best way to convince the potential aggressor, or to make the deterrence credible, is to convince him by facts, a reliable deterrent policy requires a well-planned strategy, as well as a capacity and a willingness to fight.

But there is certainly no tenet of international morality which forbids lying about one's will and capacity to use force. If lies were as convincing as knowledge of the facts, they would be equally effective in deterring aggression. It is not unreasonable to believe that lies, or propaganda without basis in fact, if one prefers the latter expression, are used as deterrents. It follows, therefore, that neither capacity nor will would be necessary for deterrence, if by other means the potential aggressor could be convinced that they do exist. Since it is the belief that counts, deterrence is essentially the exercise of psychological power. In this respect military force plays the same role that it does as an arm of diplomacy. It is the basis of the statement that bombs are used even though they are not dropped.

There are several important corollaries to the three major requirements. In the first place, the potential aggressor should be convinced that the defender state will not strike first, just as he should be that initiative on his part will surely lead to a retaliatory blow. Otherwise, the danger of a preventive or pre-emptive war is enhanced. There are several ways of attempting to assure the aggressor power that it need not fear a first strike. Official statements to this effect are desirable, but hardly enough. If a defensive state feels that its retaliatory forces can absorb the impact of an attack and still be able to retaliate in a way unacceptable to the enemy, the latter will be more confident that his potential enemy will not be tempted to strike first, and he in turn will be less likely to do so. It is argued, therefore, that invulnerable retaliatory capacity by one state is really an assurance to another that the capacity will not be used in a first strike. Hardening of bases, concealment, dispersal, mobile launching platforms on land, missile-carrying submarines, as well as solid-fuel missiles that can be fired without a lengthy warm-up, are among the

---

[13] "Developments in Military Technology and their Impact on United States Strategy and Foreign Policy," p. 2.

methods suggested for reducing vulnerability to a sudden attack. Unfortunately, most of these measures also increase the capacity of a state to strike a devastating surprise first blow. It seems to be widely assumed, however, correctly or not, that their net effect would be greater stability than instability.

The second and third of the principal requirements of effective deterrence—the willingness of a state to retaliate and the belief on the part of other states that it will do so—can also be made credible by certain types of unilateral action. Active and passive defense systems to protect retaliatory capacity and to protect centers of population and industry serve this purpose. Active defense refers to warning systems and means of destroying attacking planes and missiles. Anti-missile missiles, if they prove feasible, would be the most effective active defense weapons. Passive (or civilian) defense seeks to reduce the damage to non-military targets. Shelters, dispersal of population and industries, and the stockpiling of critical supplies, are the principal passive defense measures. They are of course desirable in their own right, for if carried out they would reduce the death and destruction if active deterrence failed to deter. The point made here, however, is that they are also deterrence measures. It is assumed that the first strike would aim to destroy the military capacity of the enemy. Third and subsequent attacks, however, would certainly be directed toward industrial centers and large cities. Defense measures would have a deterrent effect, because by reducing damage to civilian lives and property as well as to military capacity they would increase willingness and ability to retaliate. Defensive measures would also require greater expenditures on offensive efforts without adding to their effectiveness. Although this argument is sometimes advanced as a reason for better defense, it is difficult to see how it would have any other effect than to increase the cost of mutual deterrence. In general, one may conclude that "the task of strategy is to decide on the relative emphasis to be given to offensive capabilities and to active and passive defense and on the 'mix' which will provide the greatest degree of deterrence."[14]

In addition to these so-called unilateral actions, there are several kinds of international measures, which, if they could be agreed upon, would make mutual deterrence more reliable. Inspection to prevent surprise attack has been proposed in most of the postwar so-called disarmament negotiations. Inspection is a means of armament control rather than disarmament, although it is necessary to the latter. It has also been suggested that an agreement to limit the number of nuclear bombs each power possesses would increase stability and therefore the reliability of mutual deterrence.

---

[14] *International Security: The Military Aspect,* p. 22.

Weaknesses in Deterrent Strategy. Our purpose has been to examine the concept of a policy of mutual nuclear deterrence, and to suggest how it could be made more stable and reliable. It has not been to suggest that there are no possible alternative policies, or that it is a safe means of defense. A possible alternative would be substantial disarmament, to be examined subsequently.[15] Even if one had confidence that mutual deterrent policies would prevent total war, the direct monetary costs constantly become more formidable. Moreover, living in a world with a sword hanging over the head of mankind is not a very pleasant prospect.

What are the chances of peace through mutual terror? To put it another way, to what extent will strategic or nuclear deterrence mutually deter? It has several grave weaknesses. First, even if a stable situation prevailed, it would depend on cold and calculated decisions among decision-makers for its effectiveness. A madman, or anyone else who is in a position to do so, could wreck the world. This is one of the reasons for concern with the extention of nuclear capacity to more and more nations. There is also the danger in a policy of "nuclear brinkmanship," or attempting to go only to the edge of war, but at the critical moment falling into the abyss. Futhermore, one party might decide, even at the risk of suffering grave damage to itself, that war was imminent, and that it must initiate a pre-emptive war.

Secondly, there is the danger of "war by accident." Will a radar screen enable observers to distinguish between a flock of geese, or meteors and other celestial phenomena, and a flight of bombers or missiles? The premium on "fast reaction" enhances the dangers of an accidental war. This second difficulty is closely related to the first, because it makes a rational decision of highly reasonable men difficult if not impossible. Types of measures described above to make a nation less vulnerable would also permit it to take time to think, and thus less likely to go to war as a result of mistaken judgments.

Thirdly, the possibility of achieving stability is far from certain. Unless nations act wisely and with great restraint, probably unless they can agree upon international control measures, one nation may achieve an offensive or defensive "breakthrough." For example, an effective anti-missile missile in the possession of one nation would constitute a shield behind which it would be safe to use the thermonuclear-missile sword either to blackmail or destroy the potential enemy. The temptation to take advantage of this fleeting moment of safety might be overwhelming.

Fourthly, since local wars fought with conventional, or possibly tactical nuclear weapons, will probably occur, there is the grave possibility that they will expand into unlimited nuclear war. Fifthly, will a nation have the foresight and will to make sacrifices for effective deterrence over an

---

[15] See Chapter 20.

indefinite period of time? If deterrence prevents war, that very fact may seem to many to make preparation for war unnecessary. On the other hand, there may be a desperate bid to end the terror rather than to endure terror without end. Finally, the threat of retaliation may not be credible. Let us suppose that state A delivers a surprise attack which severely damages state B's capacity to retaliate, but otherwise leaves it substantially intact. Let us further assume that B can still retaliate with "city busting" bombs, and perhaps can even destroy some of A's military capacity, but only at the almost certain cost of wholesale destruction to itself. The dilemma is this: if deterrence fails, retaliation on the part of B is irrational, unless death be preferred to surrender. Only if A believes B will act irrationally, or rationally prefers destruction, will it be deterred. Yet mutual deterrence assumes rationality.

THE CAUSES OF WAR
AND THE CONDITIONS OF PEACE

Two world wars since 1914, plus innumerable lesser ones, and now the growing fear of a third world war which would make all previous ones look like mild skirmishes, have destroyed the easy optimism of the Victorian Era. Then men asked whether war was possible. It was regarded as an "absurdity," an anachronism in civilized age.[16] Today one asks not whether war is possible but whether and how it can be prevented, or if that is thought impossible, whether it can be limited and controlled so that it will not destroy mankind. To many it seems a paradox that with people everywhere wanting peace, and in wide agreement that in any general war victory would be impossible, or meaningless in any case, that nations continue to prepare for war. Although one may have some hope that deterrence will really deter, surely there must be less dangerous and costly means of keeping the peace. In the concluding pages of this chapter we shall examine three questions. What is war? What are its causes? What are the conditions of peace?

What is War?

As Quincy Wright points out in his comprehensive and scholarly work, there are many ways to view war:

To different people war may have very different meanings. To some it is a plague which ought to be eliminated; to some, a mistake which should be avoided; to others, a crime which ought to be punished; and, to still others, it is an anachronism which no longer serves any purpose. On the other hand, there are some who take a more receptive attitude toward war and regard it as an adventure which may be interesting, an instrument which may be useful, a

---

[16] See Hugh R. Wilson, *The Education of a Diplomat* (London: Longmans, Green & Co., Inc., 1958), p. 3.

procedure which may be legitimate and appropriate, or a condition of existence for which one must be prepared.[17]

Although there are both civil and international wars, we shall confine our attention to the latter. War will be examined as a legal status and as a type of relationship among states.

War as a Legal Status. From the point of view of traditional international law, war is a *"legal condition* which *equally* permits two or more hostile groups [states] to carry on a conflict by armed force."[18] War, however, is not, from this viewpoint, synonymous with physical conflict. The use of force "short of war," as in a "pacific" blockade, or armed intervention of one state in the internal affairs of another, is not regarded as war. Moreover, states are at war even if they are not engaged in actual fighting, as during lulls in warfare or a complete cessation of hostilities. It is quite usual for a period of time to intervene between an armistice and the formal conclusion of a war. After 1948, several of the Arab states continued to proclaim that they were in a state of war with Israel.

According to the traditional view, war as a legal status depends upon intentions. If there is a formal declaration, there can be no doubt of the intention, but large-scale hostilities may take place without war being declared. In 1931, and again in 1937, Japan and China were not at war in the legal sense, for there was no formal declaration, and neither party preferred that a legal state of war should exist. China did, however, declare war upon Japan in December 1941. Although there were several declarations, or recognitions, of a state of war immediately prior to and during the course of World War II, war fought since then have taken place without formal declarations.

During the Middle Ages and well into the eighteenth century, jurists attempted to distinguish between just and unjust wars, only the former being regarded as legal. Afterward the distinction broke down, and until the League of Nations, international law simply recognized war as an instrument of state policy, which could be undertaken quite legally at any time and for any purpose. Attention was then given to developing rules for its conduct, including ones to regulate relations between belligerents and neutrals.

The contemporary legal status of war, as well as that of the historical laws of welfare, is confused and uncertain. The League Covenant made war for its members illegal under certain conditions; the Kellogg-Briand Pact attempted to "close the gaps"; the UN Charter prohibits the use of force except in the case of an armed attack. What is the legal status of a situation in which a member of the UN legally counters an illegal armed attack? Actually both warring states may act contrary to the UN Charter

---

[17] *A Study of War* (Chicago: University of Chicago Press, 1942), I, p. 3. Copyright 1942 by the University of Chicago.

[18] *Ibid.,* p. 8.

or presumably the right to resist an armed attack ceases if and when the Security Council has taken the measures necessary to maintain international peace and security. (Art. 51). As long as one party is legally permitted to use force, perhaps it is correctly regarded as in a legal state of war. If so, there is a severe restriction of the traditional legal definition of war which *"equally* permits" all parties to employ force. A more logical view is that the defending state is acting on behalf of the international community pending the application of the collective security measures of the UN, but it acts illegally if it does not cease its unilateral action once the UN takes over. In the latter, the armed conflict between the parties is legally similar to a gang war within a domestic society. According to this concept, war has been abolished as a legal status for all members of the UN, just as has civil war within nations. Henceforth, there is only the illegal use of force by one or more states, and the legal enforcement of law by others, or by the UN.

What about the traditional rules of warfare? It is argued that neutrality is incompatible with a system of collective security, for the violator of the law against the illegal use of force has no rights, and the victim is entitled to the aid of all members of a collective security system. What about the other rules of warfare? Is the state which resorts to war illegally nevertheless obliged to fight it by legal means? Certainly municipal law does not say you are prohibited from committing murder, but if you nevertheless do so you may not kill your victim with a gun larger than a .22 caliber! Are states which legally employ force, acting for the UN, limited by the rules of warfare while the lawbreaker is not? The general supposition seems to be that traditional rules of warfare remain applicable in all these circumstances. Although illogical, the purpose remains commendable, but one may wonder whether the result will differ regardless of the legal status. In the modern age the rules of warfare seem to be largely of historical interest.

War as Armed Conflict. Whatever be its legal status, international war is a type of group conflict in which hostile states employ armed might against one another. Nevertheless, not all armed clashes between states are so viewed, even from this standpoint. Border skirmishes and occasional clashes between armed planes, for example, are not commonly so regarded. Only if the forces are relatively large and the conflict of some duration, do we ordinarily call the situation war. Nor are so-called 'covert wars" conventionally called wars, although there is an increasing tendency to regard them as such. As for cold war, and economic and psychological warfare, it can only be observed that these are rather loose usages of words.

The use of force as an instrument of national policy, both as a threat and in a physical way, has been and continues to be an established institution in international society. In this sense it is normal. It is correctly envisioned as only one of the instruments of policy, and in a sense as the ultimate resort of states in an ascending degree of conflict among them. A one extreme we may visualize "perfect peace." Although such a condition has in all probability never existed, it might conceivably exist if there were no differences, no misunderstandings, and no fear among states Even if sources of conflict existed, it might be that states would prefer to endure the status quo rather than to change it by the use of power. Or perhaps some of the difficulties could be solved by cooperation and compromise, and the others endured.

Between *perfect peace* at the one extreme, and *total* or *absolute war* at the other, we may envisage a realm closer to reality. At certain time in international society, accommodation and cooperation may be at a maximum, with political behavior (that is, conflict, or the use of power to direct or restrain the action of others states) being kept to a minimum. In any case, short of war, only economic and psychological power is used Eventually relations deteriorate, fear increases, alliance begets alliance military forces and armaments increase, economic and psychological power are increasingly applied between the potentially warring states Finally, force is threatened or used by one side or the other, and eventually there are large-scale hostilities. The greater the number of states involved, the larger the percentage of population and resources employed in the prosecution of war, the more the belligerents attempt to destroy the industries and population of the enemy, apply all-out propaganda, deny each other access to trade from other areas, and fight for complete victory, the more nearly is there an approach to *total* war. Despite the loose use of the term, we have never had total war; however, the tendency has been and is in that direction. Professor Wright describes the historic trend as follows:

War has during the last four centuries tended to involve a larger proportion of the belligerent states' population and resources and, while less frequent, to be more intense, more extended, and more costly. It has tended to become less functional, less intentional, less directable, and less legal. In the most recent period the despotic states have attempted a more efficient utilization of war as an instrument of policy and have led the nations to a more complete organization of the states' resources, economy, opinion and government for war even in time of peace. States have become militaristic and war has become totalitarian to an unparalleled extent.[19]

The Causes of War

Cause is that which produces or contributes to a result. The difficulty lies in discovering, among a great number and variety of factors, those which are really responsible for the occurrence of an event such as war. It is altogether too easy to mistake one's particular obsession for the correct

---

[19] *Ibid.*, p. 248.

explanation of why something takes place. To select one or more factors to the exclusion of others that are also significant is to oversimplify.

The problem of cause in the social sciences is similar to that in the natural sciences. A simple example illustrates the point. A spark applied to a mixture of hydrogen and oxygen results in an explosion. Hydrogen "applied" to oxygen and a spark would have a like result. What caused the explosion—spark, hydrogen, oxygen, or the person who combined them? Professor Wright maintains:

> There is no single cause for war. Peace is an equilibrium among many forces. Change in any particular force, trend, movement, or policy may at one time make for war, but under other conditions a similar change may make for peace. A state may at one time promote peace by armament, at another time by disarmament; at one time by insistence on its rights, at another time by a spirit of conciliation.[20]

The elimination of war is not the same as the prevention of conflict, i.e., the use of power, or even of force. The problem is to prevent states from using physical force against one another. Peace is a condition in which individuals and groups within a society carry on their relationships, including oppositional ones, without using force. Viewed in these terms, the problem of the prevention of war is more manageable than the abolition of political behavior. In short, *the causes of war are those factors which account for the use of force by states against one another.*

There are several ways of classifying these factors. Historians often distinguish between the immediate cause, or precipitant, such as the attack on Pearl Harbor on December 7, 1941, and the more remote, or underlying factors, such as the American opposition to Japanese conquest of the Asian mainland. Kenneth M. Waltz finds that the views of political theorists concerning the causes of war divide into three schools. One attributes war predominantly to "human nature," another to the nature of national societies, and the third to the influences of the international system.[21]

The method employed here may be called the analytical, with the causes of war classified under four main categories: psychological, cultural, economic, and the international system. The first and fourth correspond roughly to the first and third of Waltz' categories, and the second and third to his second, the nature of national societies.

Most of what has been said in previous chapters—all in fact that has been said about conflict—has a direct bearing upon the "causes of war." To re-emphasize, we are inquiring as to why conflict is carried on by forceful means. Most of the so-called causes of war, are, therefore, similar or identical to the causes of conflict in general.

---

20 *Ibid.*, II, 1284.
21 Kenneth N. Waltz, *Man, the State, and War: A Theoretical Analysis* (New York: Columbia University Press, 1959).

Psychological Causes.   In this category we shall consider the innate na
ture of man as well as certain learned psychological traits which may
have a bearing on warlike behavior. Few would maintain that man has a
fighting instinct, but it is sometimes held that he is endowed with an in
nate urge or instinct to dominate. The following passage indicates thi
point of view:

> Man is born a wild animal and civilized nurture can only partially tame
> him. His instinctive urge to dominate others is coupled with a willingness to
> yield obedience to the strong when circumstances require it: not merely sub
> mission but also allegiance and support; and when these divergent trend
> reach their peak man may become the most cruel of tyrants, or he may become
> the most long-suffering of beasts of burden. . . . The strife that develop
> the strong leaders engenders in the others the willingness to be led; it is per
> ceived by them that fighting a common enemy is better than fighting each
> other.[22]

While man probably possesses urges, it is by no means a proven fac
that domination is among them. Even if it were, it would not necessarily
lead to war. Domination can be achieved by instruments of power other
than physical force; men can dominate their wives, children, and
neighbors rather than gain vicarious satisfaction by identification with a
nation-state which attempts to dominate other states by forceful means
A group of eminent social scientists agreed: "To the best of our knowl
edge, there is no evidence that wars are necessary and inevitable con
sequences of human nature as such."[23]

Some psychologists claim people have unlimited natural capacity for
friendship and affiliative living, and that expectations determine behavior
Hate springs from interference with love. Aggressive nationalism repre
sents a case in point; it is contrary to man's basic capacity for love and
loyalty. Whether the behavior of man is channeled into war or peace
depends on leaders. "The greatest menace to the world today are leaders
in office who regard war as inevitable, and thus prepare their people for
armed conflict. For by regarding war as inevitable it becomes inevitable.
Expectations determine behavior."[24]

Other psychologists emphasize individuals and personality structure.
The failure of people to learn to live together leads to tensions and to

---

[22] J. G. Needham, "Wars Caused by One's Instincts," *Science Digest*, II (Mar.
1942), pp. 3-4.

[23] Hadley Cantril, ed., *Tensions That Cause Wars* (Urbana, Ill.: University of Illinois Press, 1950), p. 17. This work contains an account of the discussion which took
place in Paris in the summer of 1948 as a part of a UNESCO tensions project. Eight
persons, in addition to Professor Cantril as chairman, considered "the causes of nationalistic aggression and the conditions necessary for international understanding."
See also Otto Klineberg, *Tensions Affecting International Understanding: A Survey of
Research* (New York: Social Science Research Council, 1950), Bulletin No. 62.

[24] Cantril, p. 71.

anxiety; actions which avoid or relieve tensions result in enhanced self-respect or self-esteem. These tensions and anxieties interfere with harmonious relationships. There is a tendency to stereotype strangers in terms of individuals who are disliked. False images of the stranger tend to create international tensions. While it is true that better international understanding might tend to reduce tensions, basically the solution lies in better adjusted personalities. The late Harry Stack Sullivan, a psychiatrist, holds that

it is the inadequacies of the people in politically significant states, and in their leaders, which now imperil world peace and universal social progress. I do not believe that there are enough mature people anywhere in the world, today, to hold out great hope of dissipating international tensions by mere virtue of information about the common humanity of man.[25]

Studies of this kind are needed to bring the knowledge of psychology and psychiatry to bear on the problems of international society. All too often, however, they result in "selective inattention"—overemphasis on particular factors to the neglect of others of equal or greater importance. What is needed is a synthesis which takes into account, and indicates the relative significance of, a great number of factors. It is because political scientists have usually approached the study of war in this way that their writings on the subject have been the most fruitful.

Cultural and Ideological Causes. It is frequently held that cultural and ideological differences cause wars. Certainly a divergence of views and values among the members of a society constitutes an actual or potential source of conflict, and increases the difficulty of settling disputes peacefully. Yet within national societies cultural differences exist without leading to war. Although there are certain common cultural characteristics which correspond with national boundaries, for the most part nations do not represent distinct cultural entities. The cultural similarities among the people of Latin America; among those of Western Europe, the United States, and some of the members of the Commonwealth of Nations; and among some nations of Asia, are greater than are the cultural differences among the people who inhabit the territories of most of the separate states in each of these areas. Perhaps the *belief* that cultural differences among nations are far greater than they actually are is more responsible for conflict than are the differences themselves.

Certain wars have been designated as ideological in character. Undoubtedly basic differences in values have provoked conflict, but there have been many other contributing causes which may have had as great or greater influence. The so-called Muslim-Christian, Protestant-Catholic,

---

[25] *Ibid.*, pp. 107-08.

and the Hindu-Muslim wars were certainly influenced by opposing value systems. Yet the fact that "religious" wars have been few in number during the past three hundred years, even though differences among religions have not diminished, indicates that such differences need not lead to war. The wars growing out of the French Revolution were in part contests between the forces representing the ideals of "liberty, equality, and fraternity" and those supporting the conservative-feudalistic institutions of the old regime. World War II saw on one side an alignment of fascist powers, and on the other a conglomerate group, including the United States, China, and the Soviet Union. It is almost impossible to measure the influence of ideology among the many causes of these conflicts.

It is frequently assumed that the basic, if not the sole cause of the cold war (and potential "hot war") which followed World War II was the existence of two incompatible ideologies in one world. But they existed in the same world from 1917 to 1945 and did not produce war among the powers by which they were represented, nor prevent their more or less uneasy collaboration during World War II. The different systems of values prevailing in the United States and the Soviet Union constitute but one factor which influence their respective foreign policies. What relative weight they have among the many causes of existing tensions is a matter of acute differences of opinion among equally intelligent men. We have previously noted that at one extreme are those who regard ideology as a rationalization of policies undertaken for entirely different reasons, and on the other are those who believe it is the sole cause of foreign policy and of war.

Perhaps the dispute is in part, but only in part, concerned with *which* ideologies play a determining role. Certainly nationalism is a potent force in international politics. National unification, colonial imperialism, and demands for independence have been important elements in many wars. More important, however, it is the force behind sovereignty, and the chief impediment to the growth of political institutions which have been found to be necessary, although not in themselves sufficient, to preserve peace within states. It also impedes the growth of an international community. The discussion in Chapter 3 of the "causes" of nationalism has indicated the many facets which must be pursued to explain any one of the particular elements singled out for discussion here as being among the causes of war.

Economic Causes. We have contended in Chapter 5 that in general economic factors tend to be overrated as influences in international behavior, and in particular with respect to causing conflict and war. There is, of course, no one theory with respect to how economic factors contribute to war, but rather several. These are not only different but to some extent contradictory. Some versions of economic causes are briefly examined here: economic welfare; trade barriers; the economic devil theory; and capitalism.

One of the simplest explanations and probably the one most widespread in the U.S., is that states go to war to raise the standards of living of their people. Were not Japan, Germany, and Italy "have-not" states, that is, did they not need more territory and additional resources so that their people could enjoy more material goods? And was not the drive to extend their sovereign control over wider areas rooted in this economic motivation? Colonial imperialism, as well as much of foreign policy in general, is also frequently explained in this simple manner. It is quite correct that maintaining and raising living standards is usually a foreign policy objective. But that does not prove that states go to war for those purposes. Policy may take many forms such as attempts to remove barriers to international trade. Exponents of this view seldom offer proof of its validity; it all seems so obvious that they are surprised that it is questioned. And it must be confessed that proof to the contrary is complex.

Sir Norman Angell has advanced a persuasive argument that "wars do not pay." He meant not only that the economic costs of war were greater than the gains, but also that there was little or nothing of an economic nature to be gained by war. He maintained in particular that there was no economic value in enlarging the territorial extent of a state. He granted that at one period in history a state might benefit by seizing the goods and treasures of another people, or that the conquered could be made slaves of the victors. But today wealth consists of a "flow of commodities" rather than a storehouse of goods, and the age of slavery is past. It follows, therefore, that standards of living depend upon the production and exchange of goods, and that it makes little or no difference whether exchange takes place within or across political boundaries. This argument is essentially valid; it is still a "Great Illusion" that wars pay.[26] Perhaps Sir Norman's views about slavery and human exploitation were influenced by the optimism of the age before the advent of modern authoritarian regimes. Of course it may be possible for a conquering state to enslave or otherwise exploit a defeated people, or to exact reparations. It is doubtful, however, that the long-run economic gains will equal the costs and even more improbable that the benefits would not have been greater had there been no war.

Sir Norman was often misinterpreted as having implied that, since wars would not pay, they would not be fought. Actually, his position was that they might be waged under the mistaken opinion that they would pay.[27]

---

[26] See Norman Angell, *The Great Illusion* (London: Heineman, 1911). This book went through several reprints and editions in many languages.

[27] See *The Great Illusion* (New York: G. P. Putnam's Sons, 1933), p. 267. "I have never said or implied in any book, anywhere, at any time, that war has become impossible. . . . I have . . . again and again stated . . . that war was extremely likely,

Yet the more inclusive belief that war is not only economically wasteful, but that it will bring general distruction, has not in the past prevented it.

Liberal economic doctrines and war. In general, liberal economic doctrine holds war to be unnecessary and economically wasteful, at least as far as the nation as a whole is concerned. Most people therefore have an economic interest in living at peace. Nineteenth- and early twentieth-century liberal economists believed tariffs and other trade barriers constituted important causes of war and obstacles to peace. Many wars were fought over trade, but all the possible benefits, without the economic and human costs, could have'been realized through increases in international trade if national economic barriers had been eliminated.

> With the exception of Malthus they . . . assert that they have found in free trade the best possible solution of the problem of war: some assume, implicitly or explicitly, that freedom of commerce will eliminate all or nearly all wars . . . ; others, more moderate, that it will substantially reduce the risk of war.[28]

Free trade, they argued, would strengthen peaceful ties among nations. The world would be closely knit economically; since war would sever these ties people would have a vested interest in maintaining peace. Furthermore economic intercourse among people would breed a friendly spirit in contrast to the hatred engendered by war.

These optimistic hopes are based on a weak foundation. Even if international trade were free to follow its natural economic course, this would not prevent war. Moreover, fear is one factor which leads states to erect such barriers so that they may be more nearly self-sufficient in time of war. If free trade would have this power internationally, why is it not sufficient to preserve order within states?

The effects of trade barriers and the benefits of unrestricted international trade may influence war and peace in more subtle ways. If some nations become powerful while others are impoverished by the adverse effects of such barriers, peoples may become discontented, and may manifest this attitude in extreme nationalism and militarism. But the relationship between economic discontent and international war is far from clear. Most wars are fought by states relatively well off economically; by and large the poor nations have been the most "peace-loving."

The economic "Devil" theory of war means that in a satanic thirst for economic gain, munitions makers ("merchants of death"), international bankers, and "Wall Street" capitalists, provoke wars in order to profit by the blood of men's sons, including their own. This view gained consider-

---

indeed inevitable, so long as the political ideas which this book attacks were dominant in international affairs."

[28] Edmund Silberner, *The Problem of War in Nineteenth Century Economic Thought*, trans. Alexander H. Krappe (Princeton, N.J.: Princeton University Press, 1946), p. 282.

able headway in the U.S. in the interwar years. President Wilson, presumably, took the U.S. into the war to save the British loans of the House of Morgan! There is no real evidence to support this view, but even if it did contain a modicum of truth it is absurd to think that it was of any great importance. Taking advantage of a war situation to profit, which was widespread in the U.S. in both world wars, and starting wars in order to be able to do so, are quite different things.

Little need be added here to what was said in Chapter 5 about the relationship between capitalism and war. The orthodox Marxist view is that imperialism and war are inevitable consequences of capitalism; others hold that these are policies that countries with a capitalistic economy may or may not choose to follow.

Is this picture realistic? United States capitalists generally opposed the Mexican War of 1848, and there is no evidence that either a virile or decadent capitalism had anything to do with the Spanish-American War. It may be true that the desire for economic gain was an important factor in the British-China Opium War of 1842 and in the Boer War of 1899-1902. But this does not prove either that these wars were inevitable or that capitalism was responsible. They may have in part been caused by greed of individuals who happened also to be capitalists. While economic factors may have had something to do with both world wars, their role is far from clear, and the other factors combined appear to have been far more important.

Winslow[29] has written one of the best general analyses of this complex subject. He states that the economic interpreters of history made an advance over more naïve and surface explanations, but they forgot that the pursuit of power by states can arise from a number of factors in which economics has no part. Fear, love of adventure, prestige, strategy, civilizing missions, political and ideological clashes have certainly been important causes of imperialism and war. Nor is there any conceivable economic cause in the vicious circle wherein war itself engenders more war.

These powerful, yet uncomplex, motives and vicious circles, simple as they are, seem somehow to elude most of the modern interpreters of history. Their place has been so largely taken by the economic—essentially capitalistic—interpretation of modern imperialism and war, that one can only conclude that the scientific mind feels obliged to foreswear obvious causes and seek the underlying and mysterious, the hidden and complex forces. *This would be all right were it not for the danger that these forces, particularly the economic ones, may be imagined rather than real*—supplied by the interpreter rather than merely uncovered. [Italics mine—C.P.S.][30]

Though the theory may be false, it is nevertheless significant because it is so widely believed. On this point Winslow says:

---

[29] E. M. Winslow, *The Pattern of Imperialism* (New York: Columbia University Press, 1948).

[30] *Ibid.*, p. 68.

Through its doctrine of class warfare, based on the clash of economic rivalries between capitalist and worker, and its accompanying parading of economic "inevitables" flowing from the operation of the profit motive and the accumulation of capital, plus the grinding movement of its business cycle mechanism, which transmutes competition into monopoly, the economic interpretation of history, regardless of whether or not it describes and explains real events, has captivated the minds of untold millions and set them marching toward the socialist [communist] victory which from the first is promised as the inevitable end. The climax of this view of history, growing inevitably out of its doctrine of the class struggle, is the doctrine of the struggle between nations.[31]

The International System. Those who hold that the nature of the international system breeds conflict which erupts in the form of violent clashes see international society as anarchial, for it lacks effective governmental institutions. "Anarchy is the condition of those who try to live together without government." Though individual men find it impossible to live without government, states have managed to do so because they are more self-sufficient than are individuals. But they have seldom been able to live together in peace.

"Living together at war!" That strange and wonderful phrase tells the whole story of the tensions and frustrations which anarchy and sovereignty have bestowed upon man's corporate life. It also reveals anarchy—and with it sovereignty—to be the only causes of war among those who must try to live together.[32]

The implication of this rather extreme position, extreme in that it appears to regard anarchy as the only cause of war, is that the other factors which have been discussed play no part in influencing nations to resort to armed force. It is argued that these factors are always in operation even when nations are at peace. "That make it *seem* as if the so-called 'causes of war' were inoperative or held in abeyance." It is also contended that every one of these factors operates within states, yet individuals and groups do ordinarily manage to live together in peace.

None of these things [phenomena frequently listed as causes of war] is by itself or in itself a cause of war. Nor is war caused by a combination of all of them. Singly or together these factors and forces cause war *only when* their action is not restrained by the institutions and machinery of government. The *presence* of governmental controls prevents these factors from causing war within a single community. Hence we see that it is the *absence* of governmental controls which permits these things to cause war between communities.[33]

The statement that "these factors cause war only when their action is not restrained" is really an admission that they are among the factors which do cause war. What the writer apparently means is that singly or

---

[31] *Ibid.,* p. 69.

[32] Mortimer J. Adler, *How to Think About War and Peace* (New York: Simon & Schuster, Inc., 1944), p. 70.

[33] *Ibid.,* pp. 73-74.

in combination they are not alone sufficient to cause war, but when they are combined with the forces which operate in a state of international anarchy they will do so. Moreover, it is unduly optimistic to think that these other factors can be eliminated or controlled without government so that peace will be possible under anarchy.

What we are primarily concerned with examining here are those characteristic manifestations of international behavior conducive to war which are generated by a sovereign multi-state system. National security is a prime concern of all states, whatever be their other foreign policy objectives. In the absence of supranational institutions to guarantee this security they rely in considerable part upon their own power, the ultimate test of which is their capacity to wage war. States with similar or at least not incompatible interests frequently enter alliances when they feel that their own power is insufficient to guarantee their security against other powers. The other states in turn feel insecure, and therefore take countermeasures to augment their strength. Since power is relative, no state or group of states can possibly feel secure unless it in reality has preponderant power. At best only one state, or group of states can, therefore, really achieve security through reliance on power. Even an aggressor state may be motivated primarily by security objectives. Fear, hatred, insecurity, and ultimately war result from this vain attempt to achieve security. Collective security systems, arrangements in which the members guarantee each other against changes in the international status quo within the system by means of force, have so far been unsuccessful. Either it has been impossible, or an insufficient number of states have been willing, to mobilize a preponderance of power against states bent upon a change by force.

National armaments and armament races are a part of the politics of anarchy. It is usually argued by disarmament advocates that national armaments are a cause of war. On the other hand, it is contended that states have arms because they fight rather than that they fight because they possess arms. Whatever the relative merits of these divergent points of view, the history of the attempts at disarmament demonstrates that unless states have an assurance of security they will refuse to beat their swords into plowshares.[34]

International law in itself does not and cannot act as an effective restraint on the use of force among states. Legal rules in themselves contain no magic; the sanctions of community pressures as well as the organized force of government necessary to make law effective do not exist in international society. Moreover, international law is more a guarantee of sovereignty, and hence, anarchy, than it is a limitation on state power. The processes of pacific settlement and peaceful change are also inadequate,

---

[34] See Chapter 20.

and will remain so, as long as nationalism insists on the retention of state sovereignty, most versions of which are synonymous with international anarchy. In a dynamic world, change will take place either peacefully or through war.

According to this thesis, it is impossible, without adequate institutions of government (which are proscribed by the existence of sovereign states), to eliminate or control the forces which lead to war. Certainly it is highly improbable that we can have peace within states without government, and it is equally improbable that it can be attained in international society under anarchy. But anarchy itself is a cause of war independently of the psychological, sociological, and economic factors which have been discussed. This would be the case even if all states were concerned only with their own security, for the methods by which security is obtained by some states preclude security for others. Though government may be essential, it is not necessarily sufficient for peace, for, as civil war demonstrates, even the best of governments cannot guarantee peace if there is a fundamental divergence of interests among large and powerful groups.

The Conditions of Peace

The possibility of eliminating all of the forces conducive to international war is remote. To insure peace, however, it is necessary to control only some of them so that the remainder will not be sufficient to cause war. *Thus the prevention of war is a practical matter, requiring, first of all, a determination of conditions under which peace is possible, rather than of all the theoretically possible conditions under which war would be abolished.* For example, the danger of war would be greatly reduced if the United States were to join the Soviet Union, or *vice versa.* This is hardly a practical proposition. Practically, then, we should ask: *Which are the factors in the total situation that may be controlled, or which offer the most feasible course for rational men to attempt?* The other factors in the total situation we may regard as circumstances which we accept and to which we attempt to adjust.

There are four possible conditions under which peace might be possible. *The first is a degree of community feeling and harmony of interests sufficiently great that states will not resort to war even though they remain sovereign, with all that sovereignty implies.* This would require a greater degree of harmony in international society than that which exists within states. The institutions of international law, of peaceful settlement and change, and the organs of cooperation spawned by the UN, would remain available to ameliorate differences and to carry on common projects of an economic and social nature. It should be possible under these conditions to reduce the scale of national armaments materially and to increase international trade. Those who believe that such a condition is possible are optimistic souls whose future expectations find little or no support in the history of the past. Yet this seems to be the vision of a future peaceful order held by most of the people of the world.

The second possibility is that the states of the world will join in a common government in which their sovereignty is drastically limited or abolished. In this situation peace would require less community and harmony of interests than would be necessary under the international anarchy envisaged in the first condition. Government itself would serve to ameliorate the sources of conflict and to control the use of force. An increasing number of people believe that peace, at least a peace that is tolerable, can be assured only under government and effective law.

Those who hold this point of view fall roughly into two groups, those who believe that a sufficient community of interests now exists to make peace possible if adequate political institutions are established, and those who believe that a greater degree of world community is required. At best, the latter hold that only the people of certain states, such as those of Western Europe, are ready for a common government.

Thirdly, it might be possible to preserve "peace through preponderant power." This would require the concentration of considerable power among peaceful states. They would not only have to possess sufficient strength to deter any potential aggressor state from resorting to war, but also to convince it that they were able and willing to use force to prevent a change by force. This was the initial aim of the U.S. and its allies in NATO and other alliances, as well as the purpose of collective security systems such as the UN. A course of this nature requires the possession of whatever military force may be necessary to deter an aggressor. As in the first condition, such a policy does not preclude the simultaneous use of other types of power.

The fourth condition of future peace lies in the possibility that fear of mutual destruction will intimidate states into remaining at peace, i.e., the policy of mutual deterrence. Possibly the belief that the newer "instruments of mass destruction" would really mean the end of civilized existence will act as a deterrent to war. If there is truth in this point of view, or if it is the inevitable outcome of the present struggle for power, as many believe, the logic of the situation would seem to call for mutual cooperation among all states to produce and widely distribute among all willing "keepers of the peace" the greatest possible number of the most destructive weapons. Otherwise the existence of non-nuclear powers will remain at the mercy of the nuclear-missile giants.

SUGGESTED READINGS

Adler, Mortimer J., *How to Think About War and Peace*. New York: Simon and Schuster, Inc., 1944.

Angell, Sir Norman, *The Great Illusion: A Study of the Relation of Military Power to National Advantage*, 4th rev. and enl. ed. New York, London: G. P. Putnam's Sons, 1913.

Aron, Raymond, *On War*, trans. by Terence Kilmartin. Garden City, New York: Doubleday & Company, Inc., 1959.

Blackett, Patrick M. S., "Nuclear Weapons and Defense: Comments on Kissinger, Kennan, and King-Hall," *International Affairs*, XXXIV (Oct. 1958), 421-34.

Bondurant, Joan V., *Conquest of Violence: The Gandhian Philosophy of Conflict*. Princeton, N.J.: Princeton University Press, 1958.

Brodie, Bernard, *Strategy in the Missile Age*. Princeton, N.J.: Princeton University Press, 1959.

Burns, Arthur Lee, *The Rationale of Catalytic War*. Princeton, N.J.: Center of International Studies, Princeton University, 1959.

Cantril, Hadley, ed., *Tensions that Cause Wars: Common Statements and Individual Papers by a Group of Social Scientists, brought together by UNESCO*. Urbana, Illinois: University of Illinois Press, 1950.

Clarkson, Jesse and Thomas C. Cochran, eds., *War as a Social Institution: The Historian's Perspective*. New York: Columbia University Press, 1941.

Dinerstein, Herbert S., *War and the Soviet Union: Nuclear Weapons and the Revolution in Soviet Military and Political Thinking*. New York: Frederick A. Praeger, Inc., 1959.

Dollard, John and others, *Frustration and Aggression*. New Haven: Yale University Press for the Institute of Human Relations, 1939.

Gavin, James M., *War and Peace in the Space Age*. New York: Harper & Brothers, 1958.

Gollanez, Victor, *The Devil's Repertoire: or, Nuclear Bombing and the Life of Man*. London: Victor Gollanez, Ltd., 1958.

Kahn, Herman, *On Thermonuclear War*. Princeton, N.J.: Princeton University Press, 1960.

Kaplan, Morton A., *The Strategy of Limited Retaliation*. Princeton, N.J.: Center of International Affairs, Princeton University, 1959.

Kaufmann, William W., ed., *Military Policy and National Security*. Princeton, N.J.: Princeton University Press, 1956.

Kissinger, Henry A., *Nuclear Weapons and Foreign Policy*. New York: Harper for the Council on Foreign Relations, 1957.

Kotzsch, Lothar, *The Concept of War in Contemporary History and International Law.* Geneva: Librairie E. Droz, 1956.

Lasswell, Harold D., " 'Inevitable' War: A Problem in the Control of Long Range Expectations," *World Politics,* II (Oct. 1949), 1-39.

May, Mark A., *A Social Psychology of War and Peace.* New Haven: Yale University Press for the Institute of Human Relations, 1943.

McClelland, Charles A., *Nuclear Weapons, Missiles and Future War: Problem for the Sixties.* San Francisco: Chandler Publishing Co., 1960.

Miksche, F. O., *The Failure of Atomic Strategy and a New Proposal for the Defense of the West.* New York: Frederick A. Praeger, Inc., 1959.

Morgenstern, Oskar, *The Question of National Defense.* New York: Random House, 1959.

Osgood, Robert E., *Limited War: The Challenge to American Strategy.* Chicago: University of Chicago Press, 1957.

Pear, Tom H., ed., *Psychological Factors of Peace and War.* New York: Philosophical Library, Inc., 1950.

Peeters, Paul, *Massive Retaliation: The Policy and Its Critics.* Chicago: Henry Regnery Co., 1959.

Preston, Richard A., *Men in Arms: A History of Warfare and Its Interrelationships with Western Society.* New York: Frederick A. Praeger, Inc., 1956.

Schweitzer, Albert, *Peace or Atomic War?* New York: Holt, Rinehart, & Winston, Inc., 1958.

Silberner, Edmund, *The Problem of War in Nineteenth Century Economic Thought,* trans, by Alexander H. Krappe. Princeton, N.J.: Princeton University Press, 1946.

Snyder, Glenn H., *Deterrence and Defense.* Princeton, N.J.: Princeton University Press, 1961.

Strachey, Alix, *The Unconscious Motives of War, A Psycho-Analytical Contribution.* New York: International Universities Press, Inc., 1957.

Tucker, Robert W., "Force and Foreign Policy," *Yale Review,* XLVII (Mar. 1958), 374-92.

U.S. Senate, Foreign Relations Committee, *United States Foreign Policy: Compilation of Studies,* Nos. 1-13, 2 vols. No. 8. "Developments in Military Technology and Their Impact on United States Strategy and Foreign Policy," by the Washington Center of Foreign Policy Research, the Johns Hopkins University. Committee Print, 86th Cong., 2nd sess., 1960, pp. 665-790. Washington, D.C.: Government Printing Office, 1960.

Wallace, Victor H., ed., *Paths to Peace: A Study of War, Its Causes and Prevention.* Carlton, Victoria: Melbourne University Press, 1957.

Waltz, Kenneth N., *Man, the State and War: A Theoretical Analysis.* New York: Columbia University Press, 1959.

Wohlsletter, Albert, "The Delicate Balance of Terror," *Foreign Affairs,* XXXVII (Jan. 1959), 211-34.

Wright, Quincy, *A Study of War,* 2 vols. Chicago: University of Chicago Press, 1942.

14

Policy Patterns:
Isolation and Non-Alignment

Four broad patterns of foreign policy are considered in this and the following chapter: isolation, non-alignment, alliances, and collective security. The latter three are readily apparent on the current scene. Although isolationist policies may be thought to be of only historical interest, we shall see that this is not entirely so.

Any one, or certain combinations, of these policies may be followed by states concerned with preserving the international status quo, especially against changes which would have adverse effects on their power position. Collective security is essentially a system to prevent changes by means of violence. A state which is somewhat isolated may want to maintain the existing situation. Non-aligned states also may oppose change, and alliances may be wholly for defensive purposes. Nevertheless, with the exception of collective security, any of these policies may be used to change the status quo. It is quite obvious that alliances may be for aggressive as well as for defensive purposes; and when a country does not align itself with a power bloc, it does not necessarily mean that it is not aggressive. It depends upon what we mean by a policy of isolation as to whether it may call for a change in the existing status.

ISOLATION—CONDITION AND POLICY

Isolation may mean a condition as well as a policy. In the former sense, it means independence in contrast to interdependence, i.e., *insulation* from other states. A completely isolated state would neither affect nor be affected by what went on outside its borders. No state, of course, has ever been completely isolated, although some have been and continue to be more so than others. In the past there was more isolation than at present, just as it will diminish as the world becomes ever more interdependent. Geographical barriers have been the chief isolating factor, but as technology has revolutionized communication and transportation these barriers have been lowered or, as in the case of the air and sea, they have become avenues of communication.

There are kinds as well as degrees of isolation; thus we may speak of economic, cultural, or political isolation. Historically, the United States has been concerned primarily with the latter. With respect to both economic and cultural isolation, her policy has been ambiguous. For example, she has at times attempted to expand her exports and thus become more interdependent, while simultaneously seeking to cut off imports. She has asserted her own cultural uniqueness while drawing heavily on the cultural tradition of Europe. To be isolated politically, a state must neither influence nor be influenced by power considerations. The factors which have diminished or ended other kinds of isolation have had a similar effect on political isolation. But cultural and economic isolation are easier to achieve and maintain than is political. For example, as the Soviet and Western blocs drew apart economically and culturally with the outbreak of the cold war, their political impact on each other continued to mount. Political relationships may in a certain sense be closer between countries warring against one another than when they are at peace.

It is considerably easier to describe a condition of isolation than it is to define isolation as a policy. A state completely isolated does not need—in fact, it could not have—a foreign policy, for it would not be affected by—nor could it attempt to control—human behavior beyond its jurisdiction. If it is not so isolated it may attempt to become so. A genuine isolationist policy consists of courses of action to insulate a state against foreign influences. As incongruous as it seems to be, about the only way a state could achieve perfect isolation in the modern age would be to incorporate all other nations within its boundaries, i.e., to establish a world state or empire. If it moves in the opposite direction it will be necessary to sever economic and cultural ties with other countries, and to discover some miraculous way of living serenely behind its borders unconcerned with politics beyond them. The dim prospect of being able to attain such a condition indicates that genuine isolationist policies are hardly realistic reponses.

Does this mean that isolationist policies and impulses are of interest only to students of history? This does not necessarily follow. As long as there are isolationist attitudes they will shape the reaction of a country to other countries, even in a situation of interdependence.

Louis J. Halle, in his *Dream and Reality*, maintains that "one constant theme runs throughout" the history of American foreign policy, and that a similar theme is common in the history of nations generally.[1] China, Japan, and Russia have in particular been caught between tendencies toward isolationism and participation. The theme takes the form of a tension "between participation in world politics and withdrawal or aloofness or abstinence; between involvement and isolation, between alignment and neutrality."[2]

Isolation always connotes non-participation in international affairs, yet it is usually impossible, except in some degree and in some areas, for a state to remain aloof.

Typically, the non-participation is so limited that the term "isolation" is inappropriate and misleading. It means, merely, abstinence from involvement—or from permanent, inextricable involvement—in the political or military conflicts of other nations. It does not ordinarily mean, as it did in China and Japan, commercial and cultural isolation. It does not exclude trade or immigration. *What it does exclude, typically, is peacetime alliance, any obligation to take sides in the quarrels of other nations.* This is basic. Beyond this there may be other forms of non-participation practiced by particular nations, but the freedom from peacetime alliances or alignment is common to all the nations that practice this policy.[3] [Italics mine—C.P.S.]

The roots of isolationist inclinations are found in the historical background of a country, and are never exactly the same in any two instances. In the case of the U.S. there was the desire on the part of those who had migrated from Europe to be free from the hardships and turmoil from which they had escaped. Equally important was the challenge of the new continent upon which they wished to realize their dreams without being distracted by the quarrels of the lands from which they had departed. They wanted to keep out of trouble while they worked out their own destiny. Personal freedom and national independence were necessary to that end. As Halle notes, every international agreement entered into by a state, "abridges its effective sovereignty by giving the other country rights over it or claims upon it. Every agreement is a promissory note that reduces the independence of the nation that issues it."[4]

Aside from the roots of isolationism which are to some extent unique in each country, nationalism is a force common to all. Each nation, therefore, seeks to minimize the curtailment of its independence. Arthur K. Weinberg writes that the isolationists' ideal of independence "is the non-juridical counterpart of sovereignty and, as regards its parentage, a blood-brother of sovereignty."[5] The parentage is nationalism.

---

[1] *Dream and Reality: Aspects of American Foreign Policy* (New York: Harper & Brothers, 1959). See in particular Chapters 1-5.

[2] *Ibid.*, p. 1.

[3] *Ibid.*, pp. 5-6.

[4] *Ibid.*, p. 6.

[5] "The Historical Meaning of the American Doctrine of Isolation," *American Political Science Review*, XXXIV (June 1940), 540.

A country may dream of isolation but be confronted with the reality of interdependence. The degree and form of its non-involvement is likely to be a matter of circumstances. Even though it is not isolated, it may be able to avoid certain kinds of participation if circumstances are favorable. The most important circumstance is likely to be a relative balance of power among other states. Great Britain's "splendid isolation" of the nineteenth century was actually an attempt to avoid permanent commitments on the European continent, while at the same time maintaining freedom to intervene to prevent any one power or group of powers from becoming too strong. It was the European balance of power, with Great Britain as its holder, rather than the isolation of the United States, that enabled the latter to pursue her so-called isolation policy. Both in 1917 and again in 1941 the American dream of isolationism was shattered by the reality of interdependence. Hence she exercised her freedom to intervene when, in both instances, Britain proved unable to prevent a European power from establishing hegemony over the continent.

NON-ALIGNMENT

No country today professes to follow a policy of isolationism. There is, nevertheless, a quarrel over words. Actually the distinction between what used to be called isolationism, and what struggles for a new name, is a thin one, if indeed there are any differences at all. Neutrality, positive neutrality, independence, and non-alignment have all competed to become the title of the policies followed by about half the world's states, with approximately one-third of its inhabitants. In every instance these policies are characterized by the typical—actually the essential—characteristic of so-called isolationist policies—freedom from peacetime alliances, at least with one or the other of the great power blocs.

The quarrel over terminology does not date from the postwar period. Senator William Borah, generally regarded as a prototype of American isolationism, in defending United States policy in the nineteen-thirties contended as follows:

This, it will be said, is isolation. It is not isolation, it is freedom of action. It is independence of judgment. It is not isolation, it is free government—there can be no such thing as free government if the people thereof are not free to remain aloof or to take part in foreign wars. People who have bartered away or surrendered their right to remain neutral in war have surrendered their right to govern.[6]

Borah was correct in his characterization of the purpose of historical American policy, but he was wrong if he meant to imply that he was ad-

---

[6] "American Foreign Policy in a Nationalistic World," *Foreign Affairs,* Special Supplement to Vol. XII (Jan. 1934), xi.

vocating something different from what had been called isolation throughout most of American history. He struck the correct key when he wrote of "freedom of action" and "independence of judgment," for independence is a principal object of states which follow what are designated here as policies of non-alignment.

None of the newer terms is wholly satisfactory, although from a descriptive standpoint all are at least equally as appropriate as isolation. Neutrality, strictly speaking, means a legal status of remaining at peace during a war among other states, observing certain obligations and enjoying certain rights. From a political standpoint it is to a condition of war as non-participation in military alliances is to a condition of peace. Because participation in a universal collective security arrangement is incompatible with neutrality, it may be contended that all members of the UN have abandoned legal neutrality. Uncommitted is equally unsatisfactory, for these nations are committed in many ways, other than to one of the big power blocs. An "independent" foreign policy has, from some standpoints, an appealing connotation, but it is as much a myth as isolationism. No country is independent really. It cannot act independently. Nor is the term consonant with deep involvement in international affairs other than through military alliances. Non-alignment, therefore, from a descriptive standpoint, is probably the least inaccurate of these terms, although it implies aloofness only from military pacts.

The Basic Sources of Non-Alignment Policies

Most, but not all, of the newly emerged states are non-aligned; only a few of the older ones are not: the principal exceptions in both categories are accounted for by special circumstances. Most of the older non-aligned states are in Europe—Sweden, Switzerland, Austria, Yugoslavia, Ireland, and possibly Spain. The first two have remained non-aligned in peace and neutral in war for well over a hundred years. Their very success has encouraged their continuation of non-alignment. Although deserted in a sense by her Scandinavian partners who joined NATO, Sweden's proximity to the Soviet Union reinforced her inclination to remain aloof. Switzerland's military power would not have contributed materially to the Western Allies had she been inclined to join NATO. Austria's "neutrality" was the price for the restoration of her sovereignty and military evacuation after World War II. Ejected from the Soviet bloc in 1948, Yugoslavia has been disinclined to join the West even if, despite ideological objections, she had been welcomed into the fold. Ireland still prefers to be "independent" from Great Britain. Informally, through her military base agreements, Spain is allied to the United States, although the European countries have so far been hesitant about adding a fascist country to the "free world" alliance.

Among the states which have received their independence since World War II, only the Philippines, Pakistan, and North and South Korea are formally allied with either of the great military blocs. In the case of the first, the fact that the United States had, prior to World War II, promised independence, the ensuing common struggle against Japan, and its military and economic dependence on the United States, accounts for its willingness to join SEATO and to enter into a bilateral military agreement with the United States. The principal factors which account for Pakistan's membership in CENTO and SEATO are her enmity with India, the expectation of more economic aid should she join the Western powers, and her desire for recognition and prestige, which she felt were lacking even in the eyes of other Muslim nations. The two Koreas have been major battlefields. Two other new states, South Viet Nam and Malaya, are informally tied to the Western bloc. The former, like Austria, was committed to non-alignment as a price for independence and the cessation of the civil war, whereas Malaya, although dependent on Great Britain for military protection, has been reluctant to become too closely committed to the West. South Vietnam, however, is largely dependent on the United States for economic assistance and military protection, and is in a sense a willing ward of SEATO.

The bulk of the countries which today avoid alignment have just emerged from colonial status, as had the United States when Jefferson warned against "entangling alliances." What are the reasons and rationalizations which account for their attempts to pursue policies of non-alignment? Just as special circumstances account in part for the historical policy of the United States, so in the case of these countries there are special cultural, religious, and historical factors which partly account for their policies. Nevertheless, there are basic similarities among most of these countries, in many respects resembling those responsible for American "isolationism," which are the roots of their non-alignment policies. The reasons and rationalizations have a familiar ring to those acquainted with American history.[7]

First, there is the urge for independence, sharpened all the more by their recent emergence from bondage, their sensitive nationalisms, and the realization that they are lacking in the power necessary to bargain and compete with the older and stronger nations. Washington's advice in his farewell address, directed to a United States then in a similar position, strikes them as wise. "Such an attachment [permanent alliance] of a small and weak toward a great and powerful nation dooms the former to be a satellite of the other." By remaining out of military alliances, so it is

---

[7] See Robert A. Scalapino, "Neutralism in Asia," *American Political Science Review*, XLVIII (Mar. 1954), 49-62.

argued, they remain free to pursue an independent foreign policy on each issue as it arises, especially in the UN, rather than being bound or obligated to subordinate their interests in order to conform to the policies of their military allies.

Secondly, there is the desire to escape involvement in "foreign wars." No single factor was more important in accounting for the isolationist myth in the United States than the feeling that her commitment to alliances would drag her into wars with which she had only a remote concern. Every general European war from 1689 to 1815 had its counterpart in the Americas; to some extent the American Revolution was motivated by a desire to free the colonies from involvement in European wars. After the termination of the Franco-American "entangling alliance" of 1778, to which the colonies were materially indebted for their freedom, all alliances were carefully avoided until the period after World War II. Meanwhile, despite her policy of non-alignment, the United States found herself involved in both of the general wars which occurred during that period. Although the unaligned nations may believe that by remaining out of power blocs they are less likely to be drawn into limited wars, they are quite aware that they could not escape the effects of, and probably could not escape direct involvement in, a general war.

The third reason advanced, therefore, for their non-alignment policies, is that this is the course best designed to prevent war. It is contended that throughout history alliances and arms races have eventually resulted in armed conflict. An American in India is likely to be faced with the question: Why does the United States want war? An inquiry as to why anyone should believe that the United States is not seeking peace is likely to evoke the following reply. "It is quite obvious that your reliance on military force and alliances means war, just as it has throughout the course of history." He is unlikely to be convinced that the contemporary pursuit of a similar course will have a different outcome. At best he may concede worthy motives but mistaken means. More positively, however, it is contended that non-aligned nations are able to mediate between the power blocs, as they did in the Korean, Indochinese, and Congo conflicts. And they may be able to supply impartial policemen and observers, as they did in all these instances. They also provided manpower for the UN Emergency Force in the Middle East, and again in the former Belgian Congo. In general, it is argued that the more the cold war can be confined, and the larger the group of "neutralists," the less likely it is that World War III will begin.

A fourth factor is the need of these countries to get on with the task of social and economic development at home, a counterpart of the American desire to be left alone to exploit a continent. They do not wish to divert their limited resources from economic development to armaments, which they feel would result from their involvement in military alliances. Furthermore, since non-alignment is regarded as the best means of ameliorating the cold war and insuring peace, it is the course most likely to reduce military expenditures by the presently aligned states and to result in more economic assistance for the underdeveloped nations.

In the fifth place, non-alignment is held to be consistent with morality, whereas alliances are a part of the sordid game of power politics, bad in itself even if it should not result in war. The unaligned nations regard themselves as morally superior, even if, or perhaps because, they are weaker and lack material wealth. For example, in India, where the philosophy of Gandhi is greatly admired, and practiced to about the same extent as are Christian principles in the Western world, it is believed that "power politics" is contrary to Indian ideals. Likewise in Indonesia, alliances and power politics are regarded as contrary to a distinctively Indonesian form of democracy, known as *musjawarak,* which stresses decision-making through agreement, in the Quaker sense, rather than by majority rule. Historically, Americans have been sure it was their greater moral responsibility, rather than the Atlantic Ocean and the balance of power, which caused them to remain aloof from "power politics." Moreover, all moral nations have a duty to influence by example rather than to control through power.

Sixthly, the unaligned nations hold that theirs is a necessary policy to enable the UN to function successfully. They are able, by remaining independent, to judge each issue on its merits rather than in terms of its importance to the antagonists in the cold war. Furthermore, alliances are believed to be incompatible not only with the general spirit and perhaps the letter of the UN Charter, but specifically with the successful application of the system of collective security.[8]

Lastly, the unaligned states reap certain concrete advantages by attempting to remain on friendly terms with all powers. They are more likely to receive economic and technical assistance from both blocs. They also feel that they are less likely to be subjected to armed attack from either, and that if they do become involved in controversies or are attacked by a member or members of the communist or non-communist bloc, they can rely on the support of the other. In India's controversy with Communist China over contested areas on her northern borders, the Soviet Union at least remained neutral; and she supported India against Pakistan in the Jammu-Kashmir dispute. Aligned with the West, the Soviet Union would have taken a position less favorable to India. This "playing of one side against the other," may be regarded by some as immoral, but it is in the classical tradition of politics generally, and international politics in particular.

Whatever be the merits of these attitudes, so-called "neutralism" is a

---

[8] See below, pp. 328-29, for a discussion of this point.

powerful force in the world, and will probably grow in strength provided the world manages to escape general war. Its meaning and the forces behind it are almost identical with isolationism, in the United States and elsewhere. The fact that the isolationist dream expresses itself almost solely in the avoidance of military alignment with either of the major cold war blocs, and that the non-aligned nations participate in the UN, seems to be more a response to changed circumstances than it is to the fading of the dream.

SUGGESTED READINGS

Adler, Selig, *The Isolationist Impulse: Its Twentieth Century Reaction.* London, New York: Abelard-Schuman Limited, 1957.

Armstrong, Hamilton F., "Neutrality: Varying Tunes," *Foreign Affairs,* XXXV (Oct. 1956), 57-71.

Bowles, Chester, *Ambassador's Report.* New York: Harper & Brothers, 1954.

De Conde, Alexander, ed., *Isolation and Security: Ideas and Interests in Twentieth-Century American Foreign Policy.* Durham, North Carolina: Duke University Press, 1957.

De Russett, A., "On Understanding Indian Foreign Policy," *International Relations,* I (Apr. 1959), 543-56.

Fenwick, Charles G., "Legal Aspects of 'Neutralism,'" *American Journal of International Law,* LI (Jan. 1957), 71-74.

Froham, Herman, "An Analysis of Neutrality and Modern Neutralism," *Journal of International Affairs,* XII (1958), 187-93.

Graebner, Norman A., *The New Isolationism: A Study in Politics and Foreign Policy Since 1950.* New York: The Ronald Press Company, 1956.

Guetzkow, Harold, "Isolation and Collaboration: A Partial Theory of Internation Relations," *Journal of Conflict Resolution,* I (1957), 48-68.

Halle, Louis J., *Dream and Reality: Aspects of American Foreign Policy.* New York: Harper & Brothers, 1959.

Henderson, William, "The Roots of Neutralism in Southern Asia," *International Journal,* XIII (Winter 1957-58), 30-40.

Kahin, George McTurnan, *The Asian-African Conference, Bandung, Indonesia, April, 1955.* Ithaca, New York: Cornell University Press, 1956.

Kaplan, Lawrence S., "NATO and the Language of Isolationism," *South Atlantic Quarterly,* LVII (Spring 1958), 204-15.

Kripalani, J. B., "For Principled Neutrality: A New Appraisal of Indian Foreign Policy," *Foreign Affairs,* XXXVIII (Oct. 1959), 46-60.

Mayes, Stanley, " 'Neutralism' in South-East Asia," *Listener*, LXI (June 25, 1959), 1093-94.

Northrop, F. S. C., "Neutralism and United States Foreign Policy," *Annals of the American Academy of Political and Social Science*, CCCXII (July 1957), 42-68.

Scalapino, Robert A., "Neutralism in Asia," *American Political Science Review*, XLVIII (Mar. 1954), 49-62.

Weinberg, Albert K., "The Historical Meaning of the American Doctrine of Isolation," *American Political Science Review*, XXXIV (June 1940), 539-47.

15

Policy Patterns:
Alliances and Collective Security

Alliances, among the most ancient of state practices, continue to flourish on the world scene. One may well wonder whether they are inherent in a multi-state system. Although the United States condemned alliances for a century and a half after she extricated herself from the "entanglements" of the Franco-American treaty of 1778, to which she owed in part the success of her struggle for independence, she entangled herself with over two scores of states after 1947. In contrast with alliances, collective security is a relatively recent device by which sovereign states attempt to keep the peace and further their security by each promising to protect the other members of the system as it would itself. Embodied in both the League of Nations and the UN as a central, if not the central, feature, collective security has failed to fulfill even the minimum hopes of its advocates. Intended to replace alliances, one may wonder whether collective security has not instead been replaced by them.

Isolationism is obviously inconsistent with participation in alliances or collective security systems. Non-alignment and alliance policies are also antithetical. Both of these latter, however, appear to be consonant with the collective security system of the UN. In any case, nearly all the un-aligned states are members of the UN; and more than half of its members have joined one or more alliances. Whether this really means that the obligations assumed by members of a universal collective security system are consistent with the commitments and requirements of alliances requires an analysis of both.

ALLIANCE POLICIES

What is an alliance? Typically it involves a commitment among two or more states, formalized by a legally binding international agreement, to

304

come to one another's aid in the event of certain specified action by an outside state or states. The *casus foederis,* i.e., the action or event which calls for allies to fulfill their commitments, always includes military action, as does the commitment. Thus while it is literally permissible, it is somewhat unusual—in the context of international relations—to speak of non-military alliances.

Legal limitations on the use of force, even for defensive purposes, in the League Covenant, the Kellogg-Briand Pact, and especially in the UN Charter, are reflected in several contemporary alliance treaties. The Charter obligates its members to refrain from the threat or use of force other than in the event of an *armed attack against a member* of the UN. The one exception to this is the use of force against "ex-enemy states."[1] Since the bilateral alliances of the Soviet Union are directed against Germany or Japan, or other states allied directly or indirectly with either, they are not required to limit the *casus foederis* to an armed attack, nor do they do so. Most of the other postwar alliances, however, including the "Conference of European Powers for the Assurance of Peace and Security in Europe," better known as the Warsaw Pact, provide for military assistance to one of its members only in the event it is the victim of an armed attack. Article V of the North Atlantic Alliance is typical.[2] Both the Rio Pact and the Southeast Asia Treaty, however, are ambiguous on this point.

The Sources of Alignment

Nations ordinarily join alliances only if they are unable or unwilling to develop sufficient military power of their own to accomplish objectives for which they judge military means to be necessary. By alliances, they endeavor to add the military power of other nations to theirs. Strictly speaking, no nation becomes stronger simply by allying itself with others. Nevertheless, if in addition to the alliance the stronger nations bolster the military power of the weaker ones, the latter will be strengthened. An alliance is not necessary to accomplish this result, as both Soviet and United States aid to friendly but unaligned nations attests. Despite the fact that an alliance does not necessarily enhance the military power of

---

[1] See p. 189 above.

[2] "The Parties agree that an armed attack against one or more of them in Europe shall be considered an armed attack against them all, and consequently agree that if such an armed attack occurs each of them . . . will assist the Party or Parties attacked by taking . . . such action as it deems necessary, including the use of armed force."

It should be noted that it is illegal for members of the UN to protect a nonmember by resorting to force even in the event of an armed attack on the nonmember. The inclusion of Italy in NATO, prior to her admission to the UN in 1953, was therefore illegal.

its individual members, its over-all strength may be greater than the sum of the strength of its parts. This will certainly be the case if instead of each attempting to maintain competency in all aspects of military power, each member specializes in order to maximize over-all strength. But various factors interfere with the full application of this ideal principle in military matters just as it does in international economics. While it would probably be economical for the United States to supply the whole of NATO's nuclear strength, neither France nor Great Britain, partly out of pride and partly to maintain a degree of independence, has been willing to accept that arrangement.

Although a country with the power to go it alone (if there any longer be such) does not usually join a military alliance, it does not necessarily follow that weak nations will do so. In fact, weakness is one of the reasons for non-alignment policies. This does not necessarily mean that a weak non-aligned nation is indifferent to power considerations. Circumstances may endow it with considerable capacity despite its weakness. The United States during the nineteenth and early twentieth centuries is a case in point. Military power was centered in Europe. No single European power could realistically aspire to conquer the continent and from there dominate the world. Great Britain, in firm control of the seas, checked ambitious land powers, but she could not herself dominate the continent. Moreover, if she became too involved elsewhere, she could not play her balancing role in Europe. The Prussian Army and the British Navy were parts of a check-and-balance system. But after 1914 and again in 1939, Germany threatened to overthrow the European balance. Among the factors, perhaps operating more unconsciously than consciously, that took the United States into World War I was the fear that Germany would conquer Europe, perhaps much of Asia and Africa, and even Latin America. In that event the security of the United States would be in jeopardy. Similar considerations, this time far more clearly perceived, operated again after 1939 to draw the United States into a contest to preserve the European balance of power.

Immediately after World War II there was little inclination in the United States to attempt to withdraw from the world. Involvement, however, was not initially interpreted to mean joining military alliances. On the contrary, the purpose was to build the kind of world in which such evil practices of "power politics" would be unnecessary. Was not this the purpose of the UN, to which the United States gave its support and confidence? President Roosevelt expressed this hope upon his return from the Yalta Conference in the late winter of 1945. The Conference

. . . ought to spell the end of the system of unilateral action, the exclusive alliances, the spheres of influence, the balances of power, and all the other expedients that have been tried for centuries—and have always failed.

We purpose to substitute for all these, a universal organization in which all peace-loving Nations will finally have a chance to join.[3]

Why did the United States, beginning in 1947, change her policy of entanglement with none so diligently pursued for over 150 years, to one of entanglement with as many as possible? It was now feared that the Soviet Union, unless the United States stepped in to fill the "power vacuum," would be able to succeed where Germany had failed. Unlike the crises of 1914 and 1939, after 1945 there was no European power, or combination of powers, capable of checking the Soviet Union, even temporarily. The result was the North Atlantic Treaty, signed in April, 1949.[4]

There were additional contributing factors to this revolutionary departure from the traditional policy of non-alignment. The United States was now not only a world power, but one of the two "super powers." Hence it was virtually inevitable that she should play a major role in peace as she had in war. Nor would the effort necessarily be costly. The temporary atomic monopoly of the United States—expected to be considerably less temporary than was to be the case—combined with her strategic air force, would enable her to deter the Soviet Union without too much effort. At the time there was almost no fear of a direct Soviet attack on the United States. The situation was to change soon, and drastically, for the Soviet Union exploded an atom bomb in the fall of 1949, shortly after the North Atlantic Treaty went into effect. This was but the beginning of a series of events which were to have a profound influence upon alliances and military strategy.

Do the presently unaligned nations take advantage of the circumstances to remain aloof from both of the major power blocs? Specifically, does the nuclear balance of terror in a sense cancel out the power of the United States and the Soviet Union, and leave these states relatively secure despite their weakness? There seems to be little doubt that this situation, although seldom set forth by these states as a factor influencing their positions, nevertheless does so.

The Cohesiveness of Alliances

The vicissitudes of international politics produce many strange bedfellows. This is particularly evident when one observes the combinations of states which have constituted the alliances of the past. Historically, states have aligned essentially on the basis of power considerations; ideologies, types of political regimes, and economic systems have played

---

[3] "Address to Congress on Yalta Conference," *The Public Papers and Addresses of Franklin D. Roosevelt,* Samuel I. Rosenman, comp. (New York: Harper & Brothers, 1950), "1944-45 Volume, *Victory and the Threshold of Peace,*" p. 586.

[4] The Rio Pact of 1947 had preceded NATO, but it was more of a regional collective security arrangement than an alliance. Moreover, it was an outgrowth of a long history of inter-American relations.

almost no part. When the purpose of the alliance has been fulfilled, or the threat which brought it about initially has disappeared, it has usually fallen apart. This has been the case at the conclusion of almost every war; once the common enemy has been defeated, the victorious coalition has broken up, frequently in quarrels over the division of spoils. Although Germany, Italy, and Japan, the principal allies of World War II, were all totalitarian states, the wartime UN was composed of states of almost every hue, including such extremes as the United States and the Soviet Union. Although many hoped and some expected that the grand coalition of World War II would remain intact to win the peace, within a few years the historical pattern repeated itself.

The alliances which sprang up after World War II are both similar and different from previous ones. With the exception of the Warsaw Pact and the bilateral Soviet Alliances with her eastern European satellites, they have been responses to the necessity of augmenting the power of individual states. The post-1945 commitments to come to each other's aid by military means, despite the usual provision concerning an armed attack, are basically similar to those of previous alliances. Nevertheless, in three respects some of the postwar alliances, and the alliance systems in general, contain at least degrees of uniqueness. In the first place, as noted previously, the alliance organizations, the advanced planning, and the military sharing, especially in NATO and to some extent in the Warsaw Pact, are relatively novel.[5] Secondly, because of the greater degree of power bipolarity, the opposing alliance systems tend to revolve around two powers more than has been the case historically. Thirdly, in response to the subtle methods of contemporary politics, some alliance treaties recognize the need for action in instances other than an armed attack. Thus SEATO, the only one to do so explicitly, recognizes threats "in any way other than by armed attack or . . . any fact or situation which might endanger the peace of the area," and provides that the parties will immediately consult in such cases "in order to agree on measures which should be taken for common defense."

Despite the frequent assertions that alliances are based on unbreakable ties of common interests, ideals, and ideologies, such contentions cannot be accepted at their face value. There is almost no evidence that the bonds of a highly developed sense of community have replaced or transcended the separate nationalisms. Yet there are, despite the tensions and "contradictions" which exist in the communist camp, strong ties of interests and ideologies which might continue to hold it together even if it were not united by fears, hatred, and enmity of the "imperialist camp," as well as by visions of the communist utopia. The noncommunist alliance system, of which the United States is the hub, is a far more heterogeneous

---

[5] See above, pp. 197, 199.

grouping. It is an alliance of free nations only in the sense of being free from communism, consisting as it does of members ranging from advanced, industrially developed, and affluent democracies, through all gradations to medieval dictatorships of the Portuguese variety. Yet the more powerful, influential, and populous members, despite their differences, have a common heritage of freedom and respect for the personality of individuals. Whether their bonds were as strong as the factors which divided them, whether their unity would survive the disappearance of common foes, and in particular whether they could maintain a unity at all comparable to that of the members of the communist bloc, were among the questions to which no reliable answers were possible in the early years of the nineteen-sixties.

Contemporary Alliances

There are in existence two principal alliance systems, one among the communist bloc countries, headed by the Soviet Union, and another led by the United States. Roughly one-third of the world's population is included within each bloc, with the remainder living in the unaligned nations.

The Non-Communist System. The United States is the head of a system of bilateral and multilateral alliances embracing some forty-three countries. These fall into three subgroups: (a) the North Atlantic Alliance; (b) the American Alliance, as formalized in the Rio Pact and the Organization of American States; and (c) the alliances with countries outside Europe and the Western Hemisphere. The first two subgroups have been described as examples of regional international organizations. Their formation prior to 1950 completed the first phase of a process of bipolarization.

The second phase, beginning in 1951, resulted in a number of bilateral and multilateral alliances with Asian and Pacific countries. The United States decided to sponsor a peace treaty with Japan, signed in San Francisco on September 8, 1951. On the same date the United States-Japan Security Treaty was consummated. The latter in particular aroused fear among several nations that the remilitarization of Japan constituted a threat to their security. As a result the United States formalized its informal commitments to their defense in the Philippines-American Defense Pact and the ANZUS treaty with Australia and New Zealand, both signed in 1953. A treaty with the Republic of Korea, similar to that with Japan, followed in October, 1953. Whereas the first and last of these treaties were extensions of the line of containment, the others were designed to assure their adherents against a resurgence of Japanese imperialism and to obtain adherence to the Japanese Peace Treaty.

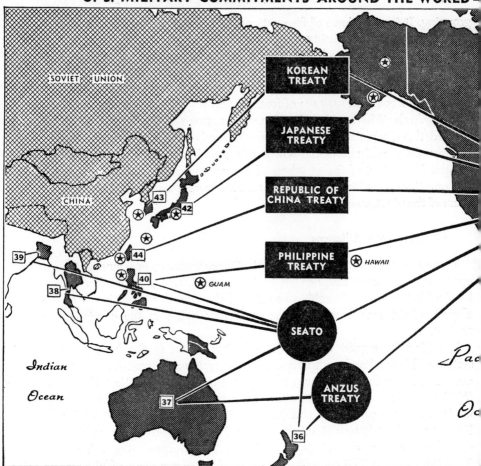

RIO TREATY

A treaty signed in August, 1947, under which the signatory nations pledge themselves, in the event of aggression against any one of them, to provide assistance to that nation on request. Members are:

1 UNITED STATES	**8** HAITI	**15** PERU
2 CUBA	**9** DOMINICAN REP.	**16** BOLIVIA
3 HONDURAS	**10** COSTA RICA	**17** PARAGUAY
4 MEXICO	**11** PANAMA	**18** BRAZIL
5 GUATEMALA	**12** VENEZUELA	**19** CHILE
6 EL SALVADOR	**13** ECUADOR	**20** ARGENTINA
7 NICARAGUA	**14** COLOMBIA	**21** URUGUAY

NATO

A treaty signed in April, 1949, set up the North Atlantic Treaty Organization under which the members agree to regard an attack on one as an attack on all. Members are:

1 UNITED STATES	**29** BELGIUM
22 CANADA	**30** LUXEMBOURG
23 ICELAND	**31** ITALY
24 NORWAY	**32** PORTUGAL
25 UNITED KINGDOM	**33** FRANCE
26 NETHERLANDS	**34** GREECE
27 DENMARK	**35** TURKEY
28 W. GERMANY	

ANZUS TRE

A treaty sign September, under which me attack in the P against any w volve all, and to "act to me common da Members

1 UNITED ST	
36 NEW ZEAL	
37 AUSTRALIA	

DEFENSE TIES THAT HAVE DEVELOPED SINCE WORLD WAR II

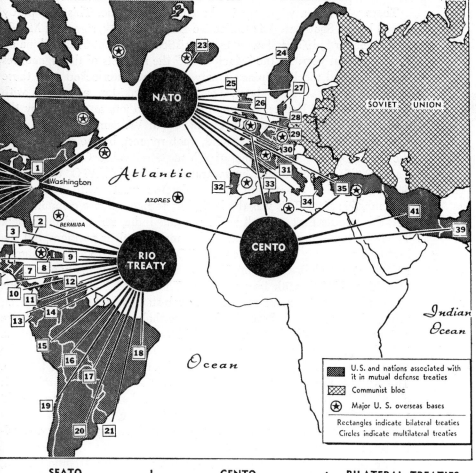

U.S. and nations associated with it in mutual defense treaties

Communist bloc

Major U. S. overseas bases

Rectangles indicate bilateral treaties
Circles indicate multilateral treaties

SEATO

treaty signed at Manila in Septem-
, 1954, that set up the Southeast
a Treaty Organization covering
"general area of Southeast Asia"
the western Pacific. In case of
ression its members are to "con-
immediately in order to agree
measures which should be taken
common defense." Members are:

UNITED STATES	37 AUSTRALIA
UNITED KINGDOM	38 THAILAND
FRANCE	39 PAKISTAN
NEW ZEALAND	40 PHILIPPINES

CENTO

The Central Treaty Organization is an
outgrowth of the Baghdad Pact which
set up the Middle East Treaty Organization. CENTO was formed in August,
1959, after Iraq, one of the five original
members of METO, withdrew. The
U. S. is not directly a member of
CENTO but has pledged to cooperate
in mutual defense. Members are:

25 UNITED KINGDOM

35 TURKEY   39 PAKISTAN

41 IRAN

BILATERAL TREATIES

These are treaties signed
by the United States with
individual nations. They
provide for mutual assistance in case of an attack.

PHILIPPINE TREATY
1 UNITED STATES 40 PHILIPPINES
JAPANESE TREATY
1 UNITED STATES   42 JAPAN
KOREAN TREATY
1 UNITED STATES   43 S. KOREA
REP. OF CHINA TREATY
1 UNITED STATES 44 TAIWAN

Courtesy of The New York Times

311

There was still a wide gap in the containment line. This was partly closed by the Southeast Asia Collective Defense Treaty, signed at Manila on September 8, 1954, following the Armistice agreement in Indochina on July 20 of that year. By the "Manila Pact" the interests of the signatories of ANZUS and the Philippines Treaty were now interlocked with those of two continental Asian states, Thailand and Pakistan, as well as with Great Britain and France. Although forbidden to join an alliance by the terms of the 1954 Armistice Agreement, South Vietnam, Cambodia, and Laos were nevertheless promised aid, upon request, by the signatories of the Pact. Since the Republic of China (Nationalist Government on Taiwan) was not welcomed by several members of SEATO, the United States concluded a separate mutual defense treaty with Taiwan on December 1, 1954. This was the last of its formal defense commitments. Yet, the Middle East, as well as Burma and India, remained unaligned. The latter two states were determined to maintain their positions, but the Middle East Treaty Organization (METO), or Baghdad Pact, was signed in 1955. It linked Great Britain, Turkey, and Pakistan, already aligned in SEATO or NATO, with Iraq and Iran. The United States, hoping thus to incur less enmity among most of the Arab states who opposed the Pact, refrained from joining formally, but nevertheless participated in three of its committees—the Economic and Military, as well as the Committee to Fight Subversion. With the withdrawal of Iraq in 1958, the name of the organization was changed to the Central Treaty Organization (CENTO). The Middle East Resolution, or Eisenhower Doctrine of March 1957, constituted a promise, if not a guarantee, that the United States would use armed force to assist any Middle East nation or group of nations requesting assistance against armed aggression from any country controlled by international communism.[6]

In contrast to the commitments in the Rio and North Atlantic treaties, those in the third group (except that with Japan) are somewhat indefinite. Each party simply recognized that an armed attack in the area defined "would be dangerous to its own peace and safety and declares that it would meet the common danger in accordance with its constitutional processes." Since Japan had no armed forces in 1951, the treaty with that country was actually a unilateral guarantee to Japan. The treaty was revised in 1960 to give Japan a less unequal status.

But whatever the treaty wording, the power of the United States was so much greater than was that of the Pacific and Asian states that the arrangements were in reality treaties of guarantee far more than they were assurances of mutual assistance. To some extent this was true of all alliances in which the United States was a member. Nevertheless, NATO was much less one-sided in this respect. The voice of Great Britain, of

---

6 See Chapter 15 for a further discussion of this subject.

West Germany, and of France, and to a lesser extent that of Italy, also counted materially in the concert of power.

What is the essence of the United States contribution to collective defense?

It is not military aid and advice, not the sale or gifts of arms, not the supply of military training missions . . . ; it is not even the stationing of United States troops, the location of a S.A.C. base on the allied territory, or the Seventh Fleet just over the horizon. The essence is the *commitment*. It is the extension to an ally of the magic concession that an attack upon *his* territory is an attack upon *ours*, or at least that it will be regarded as endangering our peace and security. For this concession spreads over his weakness the mantle of our strength. It sanctions the risks he must take when he combines his fortunes with those of his neighbor and thereby shares their vulnerability. In unity there is strength.[7]

The Soviet Alliance Network. The Soviet Union has a network of formal alliances with ten other communist states. These consist of eight bilateral treaties and the Warsaw Pact (1955), the latter including five of the seven European states also allied with her bilaterally, plus East Germany and Albania.[8] Those with the European satellite states contain mutual commitments to come to each other's assistance by military and other aid in the event of threatened aggression by Germany, or states allied with her. The treaty with China names Japan and her allies as the sources of danger. The main *casus foederis* of the latter is "involvement in military measures" to attack either the Soviet Union or China.

The Warsaw Pact in its essential features is a carbon copy of the North Atlantic Treaty. There are, however, two major differences. First, the Pact is open to any state, whereas unanimity is required to extend NATO's membership. Secondly, the Warsaw Pact is provisional in that, according to its terms, it is to remain in effect only until a European "collective security group" comes into existence. This is in keeping with its expressed purpose: to preserve world peace threatened by West Germany's admission to NATO.

These are, of course, matters of forms rather than of substance. In theory, all members of the communist bloc are on an equal basis. Actually they vary greatly in this respect, from what seems to approach equality in the instance of China, through various degrees to satellite status—with

---

[7] James E. King, Jr., "Collective Defense: The Military Commitment," in Arnold Wolfers, *Alliance Policy in the Cold War.* (Baltimore: The Johns Hopkins Press, 1959), p. 113.

[8] The Soviet bilateral treaties are with Outer Mongolia (1936); Czechoslovakia (1943); Poland (1945); Rumania (1948); Hungary (1948); Bulgaria (1948); China (1950), and North Korea (1961). All but the first and last two of these eight states are also members of the Warsaw Pact. In addition, there is the Soviet-Finnish treaty (1948) in which the Soviet Union is committed to guarantee Finland's territory against aggression by Germany or any country allied with her. Finland, however, is not committed to defend the Soviet Union.

Poland the least subordinated—to almost complete subjugation in the case of Bulgaria, Rumania, and Outer Mongolia. Perhaps to keep the Warsaw Pact truly regional, China did not become a member. But a Chinese "observer," present in Moscow when the Pact was signed, promised that China "would give its full support to the efforts of the eight signatories to implement the terms of the treaty. Chinese observers continue in regular attendance at its meetings.[9] Despite the dominant position of the United States in NATO, it does not overbalance the others nearly so overwhelmingly, nor is "equality" merely a formality, as in the case of the Soviet Union in relation to the other members of the Warsaw Pact. Nor does the military significance of the Pact compare with that of NATO. Very little, if anything, of importance is added by the Pact that is not included in the bilateral treaties between the Soviet Union and five of its members; similar treaties could be concluded with East Germany and Albania. But even in the absence of the Pact, as well as the other treaties, relations between the Soviet Union and these states would probably not be modified in any important degree. Still, they probably do provide a mantle of legality for Soviet intervention, as in the case of Hungary in 1956, and for the maintenance of Soviet troops in some of these countries. Moreover, propaganda statements can also be issued in the name of the organization which may help preserve the fiction of agreement.

The Sino-Soviet Pact is another matter. It possesses none of the organization features of the multilateral alliances, nor do there appear to be plans for the integration of the armed forces of the two countries. Nevertheless, the military capacity of either would be materially weakened without the support of the other. Unless and until the world situation changes materially, this bond alone will be a strong one between the two giants of the communist bloc.

Although there are differences between contemporary and historical alliances, they are both responses to basically similar needs and play the same kind of role. There is room for differences of opinion as to whether alliances have caused or prevented war. That wars have occurred because of or despite alliances is evident. Whether war is more or less likely to result from the competing alliance systems of the present era is debatable. But unless and until there are some drastic transformations in international society, groups of states will continue to seek security and other ends through commitments to concert their military force against other states, who will respond in a similar manner.

COLLECTIVE SECURITY

Collective security has at times been viewed as the supporting pillar of the edifice of peace. Reporting to the President in 1945, Secretary of

---

[9] "Warsaw Collective Security Pact," *International Organization*, IX (August, 1955), p. 446.

State Stettinius wrote of the collective security feature of the UN Charter (Chapter VII) that it "provides the teeth of the United Nations," and "upon the confidence which member states repose in the efficacy of the measures designed to halt aggression . . . the survival of the entire Organization and of world peace itself must ultimately depend."[10] Not on the other activities of the UN, not on alliances, not on a balance of terror, but on collective security rested the hopes of world peace. Surely there must be something great and magical in a system which might work such miracles if only members reposed sufficient confidence in its efficacy.

Collective security carries a technical meaning, but one debased by incorrect usage, all to frequently by those from whom one has a right to expect more care with words. The tendency to equate military alliances, or collective defense agreements, with collective security has been the principal abuse. One may suspect the confusion has not always been unintentional. Collective security is good; military alliances mean power politics, obviously an evil to be avoided. Hence the American people would be more willing to join an alliance, provided it was called collective security rather than by its correct name. They are not only different; according to Wilson, Hull, and Roosevelt, collective security was to make alliances and balances of power unnecessary. In fact peace depended on their replacement by a concert of power—the new collective security principle.

In essence, collective security is an arrangement among states in which all promise, in the event any member of the system engages in certain prohibited acts against another member, to come to the latter's assistance. It may, in addition, aim to prevent or punish attacks by nonmembers on one another, members on nonmembers, and nonmembers on one of its own members. In the latter instance the system functions as a defense alliance rather than as a collective security system. Although regional collective arrangements such as the OAS may be concerned with threats from without, a truly universal collective security system can obviously deal only with peace among its members. A collective security system which aspires to universality will emphasize peace within the system. The essential difference between an alliance and a collective security system is that the former is directed *against* a certain state—or states—*outside* the system, whereas collective security is primarily concerned with peace *among* its own members, all of whom are regarded as innocent until and unless any one of them is found guilty. Collective security, in keeping with the spirit and intent of the League and the UN (of which it was supposed to be a prime feature) is designed to reform the behavior of states within the multistate system rather than to replace it by a super-state.

---

[10] *Report to the President on the Results of the San Francisco Conference,* Department of State Publication No. 2349 (June, 1945), (Washington, D.C.: Government Printing Office), p. 88.

The basic purpose of collective security is to prevent the outbreak of war, or failing that, to protect the intended victim. The temptation, or yielding to temptation, to employ force as an instrument of national policy will be deterred or frustrated by the overwhelming power of the "peace-loving" members acting on behalf of the security community to protect the innocent. This is not war, but police action, similar to law enforcement within an orderly domestic society. International war, in contrast, is like civil war, where large groups of men engage in physical combat. Despite the basic similarity of collective security and domestic police action, there is one basic difference. The latter is ordinarily directed against individuals; the former is collective not only in the sense that sanctions are applied *by* a collectivity, but that they are also applied *to* a collectivity. The framers of the United States Constitution faced the issue in the Convention of 1787. James Madison observed that:

. . . the more he reflected on the use of force, the more he doubted the practicability, the justice and the efficacy of it when applied to people collectively and not individually. A union of states . . . [which used that method] seemed to provide for its own destruction. The use of force agst. [sic] a State, would look more like a declaration of war, than an infliction of punishment, and would probably be considered by the party attacked as a dissolution of all previous compacts by which it might be bound.[11]

It is sometimes contended that collective security makes no presumptions about the causes of war, nor does it attempt to remove them. Rather it deters or suppresses their overt manifestation, just as does a domestic police force. This point of view assumes that war and crime are not, in part at least, caused by the insecurity which almost inevitably prevails in the absence of institutions to protect the law-abiding citizen and the state against the law-breakers. We have contended throughout that insecurity is inherent in an ungoverned world, and that the above assumption is invalid. If this be so, collective security (provided it really "secured") would remove this cause of war. The argument that it would do away with power politics—alliances, arms races, aggression to enhance security, and so forth—supposes that an insecure world is a seedbed of conflict.

Conditions for Success

The relative success or failure of institutions depends not only upon their quality but also upon the conditions with which they are confronted in the fulfilment of their tasks. The best-devised institutions will not be able to carry too heavy a burden. How well, if at all, an ideal collective security arrangement works depends largely upon three cardinal factors:

---

[11] *The Records of the Federal Convention of 1787,* ed. Max Ferrand (New Haven: Yale University Press, 1923), p. 54.

(1) the attitudes among its members towards the fulfilment of their obligations; (2) the confidence which they repose in each other; and (3) the distribution of power among them. The first two are subjective, the third is objective, although difficult to measure.

Ideally, the first condition requires an attitude ably described by the representative of Haiti on October 10, 1935, in the League debate concerning the Italian attack on Ethiopia: "Great or small, strong or weak, near or far, white or colored, let us never forget that one day we may be somebody's Ethiopia."[12] This attitude rejects the notions of *foreign* wars, neutrality, and pacificism. A war anywhere, against anyone, and by anyone, is a war against everyone, everywhere. Each nation must respond as though it were the intended victim, with all the attendant risks and costs involved. The ideal posed here falls little short, if at all, of a highly developed sense of community realized within few, if any, existing domestic societies. Were it realized internationally, would people be willing to go beyond collective security for sovereign states and be willing to support a centralized system of law characteristic of government? Collective security may work without the full realization of the ideal attitude but it will surely fail if the real situation departs too far from it. For in the latter case it may be impossible to mobilize the preponderant power required to deter or repress aggression. Collective security neither assumes —nor is it practically necessary—that all nations will refrain from aggression, nor that all who do so will fulfill their obligation of aiding the victim. But it does require that the power of those who threaten or break the peace be relatively slight compared with that of others who are willing to mobilize power against them. Otherwise, the action will be war, waged in the name of collective security.

The second condition, that of confidence, is equally important. Ideally, every member should have confidence that the others will come to its aid just as they would protect their own territory were it threatened or invaded. Otherwise, those with little faith will resort to the traditional power game. Armaments, alliances, the playing off of rival against rival— in short, power politics—rather than collective security will characterize their policies. The spirit and the possibility of collective security will be destroyed as the disease spreads. All this will be proclaimed as within the spirit and letter of collective security. The proponents may even preempt the name for the historical practices. Collective security may of course work and satisfy the non-perfectionist, even though these conditions depart—but not too far—from the ideal.

The third condition depends not on attitudes, but on a favorable distribution of power. It must be physically possible to mobilize preponderant power against any member of the system that engages in practices

---

[12] W. P. Walters, *A History of the League of Nations,* Vol. II (New York: Oxford University Press, Inc., 1952), p. 653.

calling for the collective application of sanctions. The ideal is an equal distribution of power among a large number of states, the larger the number the better. This situation is called a complex balance of power. Two hypothetical examples will illustrate the principle. Fifty states of approximately equal strength form a collective security organization. Certainly forty-nine will be sufficient to deter or stay the aggression of the fiftieth. Perhaps even the strength of twenty would be sufficient if only one, two, or even three members were counted among the aggressors. But here we begin to reach the critical limits. In our second hypothetical example only two states form a collective security arrangement. One says to the other: "I'll come to your aid if I attack you!" The absurdity of this situation is readily apparent. A favorable distribution of power is necessary quite apart from the existence of the two subjective conditions. Yet the three are closely interrelated. Willingness to fulfill one's obligations and confidence that they will be fulfilled depend partly upon whether the power distribution is favorable. For there will be no confidence in what is impossible.

Subordinate and corollary to these three cardinal conditions are three others—breadth of membership, the state of armaments, and the possibility of peaceful change. Universality of membership in a collective security agreement will favor its successful application because the burden on each member will be lessened, willingness to act increased, and confidence in the system enhanced. Surely, if peace be the purpose of collective security, it is better to have a potential aggressor within the organization where he is subject to legal obligations, can be watched, and subjected to combined pressures, than to treat him as beyond the law, too much of a renegade to be permitted to associate with the "peace-loving" states, and less subject to collective restraints than a member of the arrangement.

Substantial, but less than complete disarmament is also favorable, and probably essential, to the effectiveness of collective security. Unless states have some arms they will be unable to mobilize military force against aggressors. But beyond a certain minimum, national armaments will be obstacles to rather than implements of collective security. The greater the military power in the hands of an aggressor the greater will be that necessary to counter it, and the more the action will resemble war rather than police action. Nations will be less and less likely to fulfill their obligations the greater the costs and dangers become, and their confidence in the system will sink lower and lower. The fact that most disarmament schemes propose that they be implemented by collective security arrangements, or an international police force only *after* substantial disarmament, is a recognition of the validity of this proposition. A former United States Secretary of State asked, following the 1959 demand of the Soviet Union for "general and complete" disarmament:

Then what, if any, force will there be, other than moral force, with which to maintain the peace as between nations insisting on going to war with each other, even with knives?

Are we going to come to a point where we are going to develop some form of international police force of sufficient strength and subject to a controlled direction on which the nations of the world can agree which can be effective in maintaining peace for all the world?[13]

The relationship between the status quo, peaceful change, and collective security is more complex. In the abstract, collective security does not favor any particular status quo; it is equally neutral toward peaceful change. But it does stand in opposition to changes by certain methods, usually those involving the threat or use of force. Force may, of course, be used to prevent a change by force. Collective security and peaceful change are interrelated in two ways. First, the efficacy of the institutions of peaceful change will determine the load carried by those of collective security. If peaceful change is impossible or extremely difficult, in practice collective security can only attempt to preserve the existing order. If powerful forces demand change by forceful means, since peaceful ones are unavailable the collective security system will probably fail. On the other hand an effective system of peaceful change would lighten the burden of preventing forceful change, and thus increase the chances of the success of collective security. The hypothesis is advanced here that weaknesses in the institutions of peaceful change have been as responsible for the failure of collective security systems as have been institutional arrangements for those systems. Secondly, an effective collective security system may itself facilitate the process of peaceful change. States would be more willing to use peaceful methods if forceful ones were made too costly. They would also be more willing to agree to changes, especially those which might have adverse effects on their own power, since they could rely on the world community for their protection; for similar reasons they would be less likely to demand change to increase their own power. It must be recognized, however, that collective security may at the same time work against peaceful change, for a weak state in particular will be less inclined to agree to a change demanded by a strong state if the former can rely on the combined force of the collective security community to protect it against forceful change.

The Institutionalization of Collective Security

An understanding of the essential nature of collective security and minimum conditions for its successful application is only the first step; the second is to institutionalize the principles; the third is to apply them.

---

[13] Secretary Herter before the United Nations Correspondent Association, September 22, 1959, *New York Times*, September 23, 1959, p. 26.

The institutionalization of collective security requires an answer to six principal questions: (1) Under what conditions or in what situations may sanctions be applied? (2) Who makes an authoritive finding of fact that this situation exists? (3) Who makes decisions concerning the application of sanctions? (4) What kind of sanctions shall be used and to what extent? (5) What arrangements or plans, if any, shall be made for their use? (6) For what purposes shall they be applied?

The answers given to these questions by the formulators of the League Covenant and the UN Charter, and the working interpretations which evolved, determined the nature of these two bodies as collective security organizations.

It was especially in the area of collective security that the UN was commonly supposed to be a marked improvement over its predecessor. Had the UN worked as intended there would be some validity to this claim, although in some major respects the League scheme was the more ambitious one. As previously noted, the UN Security Council was originally intended to be the primary, if not the sole organ for the application of collective sanctions. Although the League Covenant did not differentiate between the jurisdiction of the Council and Assembly in this respect, the former was also initially expected to handle such matters.

Conditions for Application of Sanctions. In the UN, the Security Council is supposed to limit its actions to peaceful settlement if disputes or situations are only *likely* to endanger peace and security. But if they become more serious, specifically if they constitute a threat to international peace, lead to its breach, or result in aggression, the Security Council is empowered to *decide* on the application of sanctions (Art. 39). Nevertheless it is not required to do so; instead it may continue to attempt a settlement by an application of peaceful methods. Under the League of Nations, sanctions were applicable only in the event of violations of specific undertakings set forth in Articles 12, 13, or 15. These were a "resort to war" (1) before submission of a dispute to pacific settlement; (2) before the expiration of a set time limit; (3) against a state which complied with an award or decision, or report by the Council or Assembly, provided the latter was approved by the required number of votes. War under other circumstances—for example if the Council found that a dispute was over a matter essentially within the domestic jurisdiction of a state—was legal, and League sanctions were not in order. "Gaps in the Covenant" meant that not all wars were prohibited by it.

Findings of Fact. "The Security Council shall determine . . ." the existence of the conditions under which sanctions may be applied (Art. 39), and the agreement of all the permanent members is necessary to make this determination. Since the conditions are defined in such general terms the Security Council has a broad realm of discretion. At San Francisco many of the smaller powers insisted, unsuccessfully, on incorporating a definition of aggression in the Charter. The delegates of the big powers, and especially those of the United States, argued that no definition could cover all possible forms of aggression; and that, if all presently conceivable forms were listed, the Security Council might later consider those not listed of lesser importance. It was also contended that the Security Council would be bound to automatic action under the instances listed, with the result that enforcement measures might be applied prematurely. For these reasons the conditions were stated in general terms. In the case of the League, the finding of fact was left to each member, whereas under the Charter it was originally intended to be centralized in the Security Council. Moreover, UN members are bound by the decision, since they agree "to accept and carry out the decisions of the Security Council" (Art. 25).

Whether these conditions existed has been the subject of bitter controversy in the UN. In several disputes some members have contended that the conflict was a civil war within the domestic jurisdiction of states, and that it did not constitute a threat to international peace. In only two instances has the Security Council made an explicit finding that sanctions were in order. After a long delay it determined, on July 15, 1948, "that the situation in Palestine constituted a threat to the peace within the meaning of Article 39 of the Charter." Sanctions, however, did not follow. Again, on June 27, 1950, the Security Council, in the absence of the Soviet representative, found that the armed attack on the Republic of Korea by the forces of North Korea constituted a breach of the peace. It is difficult to see how there could have been a breach of international peace, since North Korea was not recognized as a state, although the civil war could have been a *threat* to international peace.

With the return of the Soviet Union to the Security Council the scene shifted to the General Assembly. Yet only once has the General Assembly explicitly found conditions to exist which warranted sanctions. In February 1951, it resolved that the Peoples Republic of China (Red China) had committed aggression in Korea. Although ambiguous, no such unequivocal finding was made against Great Britain, France, and Israel after their attack on Egypt during the Suez Crisis of 1956; nevertheless this was implied in the Assembly resolution of November 2, 1956. In the same year the General Assembly also indirectly indicted the Soviet Union for aggression against Hungary.

Decisions on Application of Sanctions. The answer to the third question—where authority is to be lodged on the application of sanctions—is a crucial one. For it indicates whether the members are willing to give assurance that preponderant power will be forthcoming in case of need. Equally important, members will have little confidence in a system that will only provoke debate when action is imperative.

Any of three different answers may be given: sanctions will be voluntary, automatic, or decisional. Under the first, the decision to apply sanctions is left to each state. This simply *permits* their employment; and since their use was permitted under traditional international law, optional sanctions also mean very little. The *automatic* principle *obligates* states to employ sanctions under certain conditions. Whether these conditions exist may be determined by each state or by a central agency as indicated above. Under a third, or *decisional* arrangement, a designated agency of the organization decides upon the employment of sanctions. These three principles are analogous to a situation within a local community in which there is no centralized police force. Under the *optional* principle a central council might recommend that local citizens join together to apprehend and punish a criminal, but they would be free to accept or reject the recommendation. If the *automatic* approach were used they, or certain designated individuals, would be legally obligated to perform their duties under certain specified conditions. Under the last, or *decisional* system, the council could decide when the situation warranted action and the citizens would be obligated to carry out its decisions.

Under the League Covenant, economic sanctions were originally supposed to be automatic; each state was to sever *all* financial, economic, and personal intercourse with the offender. Each member was also to endeavor to prevent all communication between the nationals of the Covenant-breaking state and the nationals of members and nonmembers. It was generally assumed that no state would go to war, or if it did so, the war would not long continue. President Wilson explained that these economic sanctions would be more tremendous than war: "An absolute isolation, a boycott! . . . No goods can be shipped in or out, no telegraphic messages can be exchanged. It is the most complete boycott ever conceived in a public document . . . there will be no more fighting after that. There is not a nation that can stand that for six months."[14]

The history of this provision of the Covenant is long, controversial, and discouraging. Without formal amendment of the Covenant, it soon became understood that each member would decide for itself whether sanctions were applicable, and in effect whether or not to apply them. Nor would they be applied immediately and completely; instead they would be put into effect gradually and partially as recommended by the Council. With this development the automatic provision was converted into one wholly voluntary. Only once in the League's history were sanctions applied—against Italy in 1935 when she attacked Ethiopia. They were voluntary, gradual, partial, and ineffective.

Military sanctions were voluntary from the beginning. The wording of Article 16, paragraph 2, was ambiguous. "It shall be the duty of the Council to recommend [what forces] . . . the members . . . shall contribute

---

[14] Quoted in Hamilton Foley, *Woodrow Wilson's Case for the League of Nations* (Princeton, N.J.: Princeton University Press, 1923), p. 69.

to the armed forces to be used to protect the Covenants of the League." The Council would recommend, and thus attempt to insure planned and coordinated action; but the phrase "shall contribute" was probably not intended to constitute an obligation. In no case was an attempt made to apply military sanctions. The UN, by concentrating authority in the Security Council to decide when and what sanctions would be applied, and by obligating members to follow its decisions in the matter, departed most sharply from the automatic economic and the voluntary military sanctions scheme of the League. The "big five" plus two others, if they could agree, would be a limited world government for maintaining the peace.

The collective security structure of the UN was not completed at San Francisco. Article 43 provided that special agreements were to be worked out, under the auspices of the Security Council, whereby members would earmark certain of their armed forces and agree to the assistance and facilities to be made available upon call by the Security Council. Until these agreements were made, there would be no military forces for the use of the UN; meanwhile the permanent members of the Security Council would consult on how they might take joint action to maintain international peace and security (Art. 106).

By 1947 it was plain that the big powers could not agree on the composition of these "contingent" forces. Thus the original plan for centralizing decisions concerning the application of military sanctions under the Security Council has remained a dead letter. The Council does have the authority to apply diplomatic and economic sanctions, but the split which prevented agreement upon the earmarking of armed forces equally precluded the use of nonmilitary sanctions.

The sole action of this nature taken by the Security Council, that of June 27, 1950, in connection with the North Korean invasion, only *"recommends* that the members of the UN furnish such assistance to the Republic of Korea as may be necessary to repel the armed attack and to restore international peace and security in the area [Italics mine—C.P.S.]."[15] While it was probably intended by the Charter framers that the Security Council would *decide* on sanctions, and not recommend that they be taken, it is not impossible to interpret the Charter as permitting the *recommendation* of the use of armed force. However, since a recommendation has no legal effect, the application of it is voluntary or optional in such cases, and thus the situation is similar with respect to military sanctions to that under the League of Nations.

Nature and Extent of Sanctions. The Charter provides (Art. 39) that the Security Council shall either make recommendations or "decide what measures shall be taken in accordance with Articles 41 and 42, to maintain international peace and security." The enforcement means are thus set forth in, and limited to those specified by Articles 41 and 42. The first

---

15 United Nations, Doc. S/1508/Rev. 1.

includes any type of measure "not involving the use of armed force." The second is more specific, referring to action by air, sea, or land forces, including demonstrations, blockades, and other military operations. There is no limit placed on the extent to which the Security Council can obligate members to apply nonmilitary sanctions, but it was clearly stated in San Francisco that they could *not* be obligated to provide armed forces or military facilities in excess of those specified in the contemplated special agreements. In the absence of the latter the Article is inoperative. The nature and extent of military sanctions possible under the Covenant and Charter were identical, but the League statement concerning nonmilitary actions appears to have been somewhat less inclusive.

Advance Planning. The League Covenant contained no provision concerning planning in advance for the application of sanctions, French proposals to this effect having been rejected. Therefore, economic sanctions against Italy had to be improvised. The Charter makes no direct reference to economic plans, but it does contemplate that military plans would be worked out in advance, both contingent forces and facilities to be provided for as a part of the plan. It specifically provides that members shall "hold immediately available national air force contingents for combined international enforcement action" (Art. 45).[16] In addition, Article 47 provides for a Military Staff Committee consisting of the chiefs of staff, or their representatives, of the permanent members. Among its duties is that of assisting the Security Council with plans for military action, and the strategic direction of forces placed at its disposal. The sole concern of the Military Staff Committee has been the special agreements providing for contingent forces. A deadlock having been reached on the problem by 1947, the Committee has since confined its activities to token meetings.

Although the Charter obviously provides for more advance planning than did the Covenant, it does not call for a standing international army or police force under an international command. Such an arrangement is not prohibited, however, and it may well be that the United Nations Field Service, authorized by the General Assembly in November 1949, constitutes a precedent upon which a real international police force can be built. The Field Service, not to exceed three hundred persons, is under the control of the secretary-general and provides technical and protective services for UN field missions. The United Nations Emergency Force (UNEF), and that organized in 1960 for the Congo operation, may also be precursors of a real international force.

Purposes of Sanctions. The Security Council is limited in its authority by Chapter VII of the Charter to taking enforcement action. It would be possible, however, for it to recommend terms of settlement which would involve a change in international legal rights, and to regard a failure to

---

[16] The application of this article is also contingent upon the conclusion of the special agreements.

comply with the recommendation as a threat to the peace. If this were done, the Security Council would become a sort of "Holy Alliance" for the governing of the smaller powers, and the principle of "sovereign equality" would become even more of a mockery than it is now.

The general purpose for applying sanctions is clear—to protect the members of the organization and to prevent the conflict from spreading. Beyond this, the Korean episode raised the question of whether the UN was authorized to use force to unite Korea as opposed to repelling the aggression and restoring the territorial status quo as it existed prior to the outbreak of hostilities. The UN does not in all probability have authority to legislate a change, and then use force to bring it about. If this be true, it seems reasonable to conclude that it does not have the right to take advantage of a situation in which it can use sanctions to effect an otherwise unauthorized change.

"Uniting for Peace"—
the "New" Approach
to Collective Security

Prior to the outbreak of the Korean War, the General Assembly had increasingly concerned itself with matters relating to peace and security.[17] It had not, however, contemplated a drastic revision of the original approach to collective security such as that embodied in the "Uniting for Peace" resolution, or "Acheson Plan," adopted by the General Assembly on November 3, 1950. The plan does not preclude the revival of the original approach, but its passage by a vote of 52-5-2 indicated that the vast majority of the members regarded that approach as at least a weak reed on which to lean.

The purpose of the plan was to enable the General Assembly to consider an urgent matter which might require the application of sanctions, but on which a veto in the Security Council prevented action. In such a case the Assembly meets (if not already in session) within twenty-four hours if requested to do so by the Security Council, or by a majority of UN members. The decision in the Security Council is made by a procedural vote. The Assembly is then free to make recommendations to the members that they take collective action, including the use of armed force when necessary, to maintain or restore international peace and security. Sanctions under this plan are voluntary, unlike that originally contemplated under the Charter, for the General Assembly has recommendatory rather than decisional authority.

Although other changes, such as the earmarking of contingent forces, were contemplated under the "Uniting for Peace" resolution, none of

---

[17] See "The United Nations General Assembly," *International Conciliation,* No. 433 (April 1947).

these has materialized. It was under this resolution that the General Assembly condemned the Peoples Republic of China, called upon all states to continue to assist the UN forces in Korea, and on May 18, 1951, recommended an embargo on the shipment of arms to Communist China and North Korea. Action in the Suez and Hungarian cases was also taken under the banner of "Uniting for Peace," but no sanctions were recommended.

Collective Security in Operation—the Realities of the United Nations Experience

It requires no proof that collective security either in the League or the UN did not fulfill the hopes of its proponents. Indeed, by almost any criterion of success it has been a dismal failure. Why? One may search for the reason in the conditions confronting those organizations, in the institutionalization of the system, or in the basic principles of collective security itself. One might conclude that only if conditions are far more ideal than they have been since 1919, will a system of collective security succeed. Or one might contend that whereas a League of Nations might have prevented World War I, and the UN World War II, since 1945 neither could prevent World War III. Implicit in this assumption is the belief that the defect was partly in the nature of the institutions. On the other hand, the defect may not be in the particular means of implementing principles, but in the very principles themselves.

An examination of the record in the innumerable instances since 1919 where sanctions were certainly in order, but where they were not applied, is at least as important in seeking answers to these questions as is an examination of the two attempts to put collective security into operation. There is probably not a single instance in the history of the League or the UN in which, had the will to do so been present, the Covenant or Charter would have imposed serious obstacles to the application of sanctions. If this conclusion is valid, the difficulties must be found in either the conditions or the basic principles of collective security, or in both. Surely if the conditions were favorable—no members too powerful, enough of them willing to fulfil their obligations, and the vast majority reliant upon the organization rather than their own power, alliances, and the other devices of "power politics"—collective security would be successful. But if the conditions were such that it would be supported, would they not be such that nations would be willing to go beyond "the halfway house" of collective security—halfway between traditional anarchy and world government? Would they not then be willing to erect and live within the full house of government? It may be argued, of course, that the conditions necessary to support collective security are even more exacting than those to enable governments to work, in which case conditions would be ripe for erecting the house of the world government even before the halfway house of collective security.

We have sometimes referred to the League and the UN as, or aspiring to be, universal collective security systems. Yet a discerning author writes: "Indeed, the proposition that the Charter purports to create a collective security system, and that the founding fathers of the United Nations expected and intended the Organization to provide universal collective security against aggression, is one of the most persistent clichés of our time."[18]

Both the League and the UN did aspire to universality of membership, but that is something different from saying that their collective security provisions were universal. The League Covenant did not deliberately preclude the possibility of applying collective security against any member; it simply failed to provide for a strong system, and even this was further weakened as it was watered down through interpretation.

The UN declined to try to establish a universal system. The teeth which Secretary Stettinius spoke of were never intended to bite any of the permanent members of the Security Council. Quite in contrast to his statement quoted earlier in this chapter, in testifying before the Senate (when that body was considering the Charter), Stettinius noted that a permanent member of the Security Council could veto action against itself, and that "if one of these nations ever embarked upon a course of aggression, a major war would result."[19] The "Uniting for Peace" resolution of 1950, by providing for General Assembly action, was supposed to circumvent the veto. But as we noted above, only once, against Communist China in 1951, has the General Assembly recommended sanctions.

The original decision to permit a great power to veto action against itself was based upon the realistic assumption that any such action would mean war, rather than bringing preponderant power against an aggressor. It was not assumed that the permanent members of the Security Council would always be "peace-loving"—hence no sanctions against them would be necessary—but rather that if they chose to resort to force on a major scale there would be war, and the UN would collapse. The fact that the vetoless General Assembly could recommend sanctions against a big power did not change the power reality upon which the veto is based. The veto is a correct register of this reality. To abolish it with respect to the employment of sanctions against a great power would therefore be meaningless.

The great powers were intended to be the principle producers of sanc-

---

[18] Inis L. Claude, "The United Nations and the Use of Force," *International Conciliation*, No. 532 (Mar. 1961), p. 328.

[19] The Charter of the United Nations, Hearings Before the Committee on Foreign Relations, U.S. Senate, 79th Congress, 1st session, (Washington, D.C., 1945), p. 215.

tions, while the lesser members were to be the sole consumers. It was for this purpose that contingent forces were to be earmarked. The outbreak of the cold war led to the failure of the great powers to agree upon the size and composition of their forces, just as it would have prevented their use even had they been agreed upon. Although it is not impossible that the Security Council or the General Assembly might in the future recommend a program of voluntary sanctions against small states, it is clear that collective security, even on a limited scale, is at best temporarily dormant.

Nothing said here should be taken to imply that the UN has not and will not play an important role in the maintenance of world peace, nor that its use of force, or at least armed forces, could not play a constructive role in that respect. Both UNEF in the Middle East and the armed forces which in 1960 began to operate under the UN flag in the Congo so indicate. Both were drawn from the smaller and mostly unaligned states rather than from the larger powers, contrary to the original assumption. But in neither the Middle East nor the Congo were their forces used to defeat an aggressor, but to prevent a conflict or to preserve an uneasy peace in the hope of eventual pacific settlement. The role of UNEF was not to fight; it could not in fact stand against the military power of either contestant. The immediate purpose of the Congo forces was to preserve peace within a country. In the larger world picture, however, they were in both instances correctly seen as intended to keep the big powers out by getting the small ones in, and thus to neutralize both areas against the cold war struggle.[20]

Some concluding words about the relationships between alliances and collective security are in order. If the latter could be relied upon, states interested essentially in security and in preventing forceful change would not feel it necessary to form alliances. An alliance is a vote of lack of confidence in collective security. An aggressive state would obviously oppose the application of collective security measures against itself, although it might hope to have its cake and eat it too. It would also be likely to be interested in an alliance for aggression. Are alliances basically incompatible with collective security? As long as an alliance is for defensive purposes, and none of its own members themselves is guilty of aggression, breach of, or threat to international peace, it does not interfere directly with a more inclusive collective security system. It might even be that these concerted efforts on behalf of collective sanctions would add to the strength of the world organization. But as Suez plainly indicated, the

---

[20] For a stimulating discussion of the use of force, see: Claude, *The United Nations and the Use of Force*; also see Lincoln P. Bloomfield, *The United Nations and U.S. Foreign Policy* (Boston: Little, Brown & Co., 1960), especially Chaps. III–VI; and William R. Frye, *A United Nations Peace Force* (New York: Oceana Publications, Inc., for the Carnegie Endowment for International Peace, 1957).

members of NATO were more interested in preserving the alliance than
they were in applying sanctions against each other. The United States was
horrified when the Soviets suggested that the two powers join in repelling
British, French, and Israeli aggression against Egypt. Even her relatively
mild opposition to her NATO allies caused groans of agony in the United
States and despair in France and Great Britain. For a number of reasons,
none of her allies proposed sanctions against the United States when she
engaged in "indirect aggression" against Cuba in April of 1961. The indirect effects of an alliance, such as the generating of other alliances, and
the subsequent division of the world into power blocs, can have no other
than an adverse effect upon a collective security system. To argue, however, that the alliance systems were responsible for states' lack of ability
and faith in the UN to apply sanctions against the Soviet Union, or the
United States, is to overlook the fact that, for perfectly understandable
and valid reasons, it was never intended to do so. Nevertheless, to argue
that since collective security is unreliable, the only moral and realistic
alternative is for all states to join alliances overlooks the equally plausible
point of view that non-alignment for all would be a less dangerous course.
Both positions fail to consider that, depending on circumstances, either
alignment or non-alignment may be the more rational policy—rational in
the sense of furthering both national interests and those of the world
society.

SUGGESTED READINGS

Andrassy, J., "Uniting for Peace," *American Journal of International Law,* L
    (July 1956), 563-82.
Bloomfield, Lincoln P., "The U.N. and National Security," *Foreign Affairs,*
    XXXVI (July 1958), 597-610.
Bowett, D. W., *Self-Defense in International Law.* Manchester: Manchester
    University Press, 1958.
Buchan, Alastair, *NATO in the 1960's: The Implications of Interdependence.*
    New York: Frederick A. Praeger, Inc., 1960.
Claude, Inis L., "The United Nations and the Use of Force," *International Con-
    ciliation,* No. 532 (Mar. 1961).
Fleming, D. F., "Woodrow Wilson and Collective Security Today," *Journal of
    Politics,* XVIII (Nov. 1956), 611-24.
Frye, William B., *A United Nations Peace Force,* prepared under the auspices
    of the Carnegie Endowment for International Peace. New York: Oceana
    Publications, Inc., 1957.
Goodrich, Leland M., "Korea: Collective Measures Against Aggression," *Inter-
    national Conciliation,* No. 494 (Oct. 1953), 131-92.
Haas, Ernst B., "Types of Collective Security: An Examination of Operational
    Concepts," *American Political Science Review,* XLIX (Mar. 1955), 40-62.

Halle, Louis J., "The Western Alliance: Its Cultural Foundation," *Journal of International Affairs,* XII (1958), 9-16.

Hogan, Willard N., *International Conflict and Collective Security: The Principle of Concern in International Organization.* Lexington, Kentucky: University of Kentucky Press, 1955.

Hula, Erich, "Fundamentals of Collective Security," *Social Research,* XXIV (Spring 1957), 1-36.

"Improvement of the Organization for Collective Security: Alternatives to the Veto Power," *Proceedings of the American Society of International Law, 1957.* (1958), pp. 116-40.

Johnson, Howard C., Jr. and Gerhart Niemeyer, "Collective Security: The Validity of an Ideal," *International Organization,* VIII (Feb. 1954), 19-35.

Killen, E. D., "The Anzus Pact and Pacific Security," *Far Eastern Survey,* XXI (Oct. 8, 1952), 137-41.

Knorr, Klaus, *NATO and American Security.* Princeton, N.J.: Princeton University Press, 1959.

Kulski, W. W., "The Soviet System of Collective Security Compared with the Western System," *American Journal of International Law,* XLIV (July 1950), 453-76.

Kunz, Joseph L., "The Idea of 'Collective Security' in Pan-American Developments," *Western Political Quarterly,* VI (Dec. 1953), 658-79.

———, "Individual and Collective Self-Defense in Article 51 of the Charter of the United Nations," *American Journal of International Law,* XLI (Oct. 1947), 872-79.

Lauterpacht, E., *The United Nations Emergency Force: Basic Documents.* London: Stevens; New York: Frederick A. Praeger, Inc., 1960.

Martin, Andrew, *Collective Security: A Progress Report.* Paris: UNESCO, 1952.

Morgenthau, Hans J., "Alliances," *Confluence,* VI (Winter, 1958), 311-34.

Munro, Sir Leslie, "Can the United Nations Enforce Peace?" *Foreign Affairs,* XXXVIII (Jan. 1960), 209-18.

Padelford, Norman J., "SEATO and Peace in Southeast Asia," *Current History,* XXXVIII (Feb. 1960), 95-101.

Sohn, Louis B., "The Definition of 'Aggression,'" *Virginia Law Review,* XLV (June 1959), 697-701.

Stone, Julius, *Aggression and World Order: A Critique of United Nations Theories of Aggression.* Berkeley, Calif.: University of California Press, 1958.

Thompson, Kenneth W., "Collective Security Reexamined," *American Political Science Review,* XLVII (Sept. 1953), 753-72.

"Treaty of Friendship, Cooperation, and Mutual Assistance [Warsaw Pact]," *American Journal of International Law,* XLIX (Supplement) (Oct. 1955), 194-99.

U.S. Senate, Committee on Foreign Relations, *Favoring Establishment of Permanent United Nations Force Similar in Character to United Nations Emergency Force in Middle East.* Report No. 613, 85th Cong., Ist sess., 1957. Washington, D.C.: Government Printing Office, 1957.

"Warsaw Collective Security Pact," *International Organization,* IX (Aug. 1955), 445-46; XIII (Summer 1959), 485; XIV (Spring 1960), 362.

Wolfers, Arnold, "Collective Security and the War in Korea," *The Yale Review,* XLIII (June 1954), 481-96.

———, ed., *Alliance Policy in the Cold War.* Baltimore: The Johns Hopkins Press, 1959.

16

International Cooperation

Cooperation characterizes and reflects the consensus of a community. Conflict, on the other hand, unless it is repressed by dictatorial methods, predominates in a society deficient in the ameliorative community attitudes conducive to mutual respect, deference, and compromise. Though the degree of community varies from nation to nation, on the whole it is more highly developed within than among them. Cooperation, therefore, tends to characterize relations within nations in contrast to the predominately oppositional (political) nature of relations among them.

Community attitudes, however, are not the sole cause of cooperation. Just as two quarreling individuals may forget their differences and turn against an intruder who interferes with or threatens both, so may nations be "forced" into cooperation by common enemies, fancied or real. In the previous chapter we noted that alliances owe their existence far more to the fact that nations are afraid to live apart rather than that they prefer to live together. Antagonisms between some nations may lead them to cooperate with others on economic and cultural matters. Nations may also cooperate on the assumption that this is a necessary alternative to conflict, including war, among themselves. This made made explicit in the instance of the European Coal and Steel Community, and was implicit in the other cooperative ventures within Europe. It was also one of the motivating beliefs behind many other international organizations, such as the Arab League, the Organization of American States, and the UN. Finally, cooperation is an expression of humanitarianism, and the ethic inherent in most of the great religions. Perhaps it is not so much that the quality of mercy is growing as that modern communication techniques now bring suffering humanity more vividly to the attention of the more fortunate members of the human race.

The initial impetus to most integrative movements among nations is fear—of third parties or of each other. Once set in motion, however, the mutual benefits, the opportunities which open up, and the community feeling generated by the experience of harmonious association, may enable the process to continue even though the original stimulus is removed. An optimistic view of the European Community of Six, and perhaps of the "Atlantic Community," might lead one to believe that cooperation and further integration would continue if their members were convinced that the Soviet Union and Communist China no longer presented a menace to their existence.

COOPERATION AND CONFLICT

Conflict captures the headlines; the relatively unexciting and long-term cooperative process is interpersed, if indeed it receives notice at all, among the advertising in the inner pages of all but the best newspapers. To put it another way, nations make history by trying to destroy each other rather than by working harmoniously to advance their mutual welfare. Dean Rusk, Secretary of State, at the height of the multiplicity of recurring crises of early 1961, after noting the widespread prevalence of conflict, remarked that "foreign policy is also concerned with cooperation, with the recognition and nourishment of common interests which bind people together across national frontiers."[1] We are likely to exaggerate the time and energy nations spend in quarreling and to underestimate the quantity and the constructive nature of the undramatic and routine.

It is well, however, to guard against another fallacy—a tendency characteristic of many hopeful souls who see the world's salvation as wholly dependent on the cooperative aspects of the UN system. Disgusted with the perennial strife and seeming futility which mark the political arena, they often contend that it is futile to attack these problems directly. On the other hand, there are areas in the social, cultural, and economic realm which are tractable to the cooperative approach. If nations would concentrate on these, they would be able not only to solve some of the world's immediate problems, but in the long run, this, and only this, would transform the nature of world society. Both the League and the UN began with high hopes that through their political efforts, ranging from "grand debates" through collective security, peace would prevail. As this early optimism faded, both organizations continued and expanded their cooperative efforts in the somewhat less controversial so-called nonpolitical field. Particularly in the case of the League, instead of correctly interpreting this development partly as a response to failure in other areas, it was too often seen wholly as a sign of healthy growth of the world community.[2]

---

[1] *Christian Science Monitor*, April 26, 1961, p. 16.

[2] See pp. 185-87 above, for a discussion of the strength and weakness of functionalism.

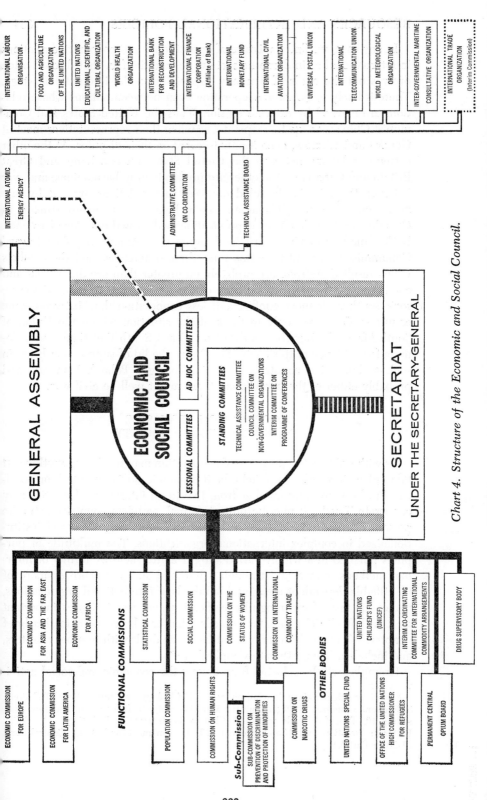

Chart 4. Structure of the Economic and Social Council.

GENERAL ASSEMBLY

ECONOMIC AND SOCIAL COUNCIL

SESSIONAL COMMITTEES

AD HOC COMMITTEES

STANDING COMMITTEES
TECHNICAL ASSISTANCE COMMITTEE
COUNCIL COMMITTEE ON NON-GOVERNMENTAL ORGANIZATIONS
INTERIM COMMITTEE ON PROGRAMME OF CONFERENCES

SECRETARIAT
UNDER THE SECRETARY-GENERAL

INTERNATIONAL ATOMIC ENERGY AGENCY

ADMINISTRATIVE COMMITTEE ON CO-ORDINATION

TECHNICAL ASSISTANCE BOARD

INTERNATIONAL LABOUR ORGANISATION

FOOD AND AGRICULTURE ORGANIZATION OF THE UNITED NATIONS

UNITED NATIONS EDUCATIONAL, SCIENTIFIC, AND CULTURAL ORGANIZATION

WORLD HEALTH ORGANIZATION

INTERNATIONAL BANK FOR RECONSTRUCTION AND DEVELOPMENT

INTERNATIONAL FINANCE CORPORATION (Affiliate of Bank)

INTERNATIONAL MONETARY FUND

INTERNATIONAL CIVIL AVIATION ORGANIZATION

UNIVERSAL POSTAL UNION

INTERNATIONAL TELECOMMUNICATION UNION

WORLD METEOROLOGICAL ORGANIZATION

INTER-GOVERNMENTAL MARITIME CONSULTATIVE ORGANIZATION

INTERNATIONAL TRADE ORGANIZATION (Interim Commission)

FUNCTIONAL COMMISSIONS

ECONOMIC COMMISSION FOR EUROPE

ECONOMIC COMMISSION FOR ASIA AND THE FAR EAST

ECONOMIC COMMISSION FOR LATIN AMERICA

ECONOMIC COMMISSION FOR AFRICA

STATISTICAL COMMISSION

POPULATION COMMISSION

SOCIAL COMMISSION

COMMISSION ON HUMAN RIGHTS

Sub-Commission
SUB-COMMISSION ON PREVENTION OF DISCRIMINATION AND PROTECTION OF MINORITIES

COMMISSION ON THE STATUS OF WOMEN

COMMISSION ON NARCOTIC DRUGS

COMMISSION ON INTERNATIONAL COMMODITY TRADE

OTHER BODIES

UNITED NATIONS SPECIAL FUND

UNITED NATIONS CHILDREN'S FUND (UNICEF)

OFFICE OF THE UNITED NATIONS HIGH COMMISSIONER FOR REFUGEES

INTERIM CO-ORDINATING COMMITTEE FOR INTERNATIONAL COMMODITY ARRANGEMENTS

PERMANENT CENTRAL OPIUM BOARD

DRUG SUPERVISORY BODY

In any case, we find a mixture of oppositional and cooperative relations in international as in domestic society, despite the fact that discord often drowns out the cords of harmony, especially on the international stage. There is likely to be some cooperation even between nations whose relations are marked by extreme tension. Thus the United States and Communist China manage to cooperate, as when their representatives meet at Geneva and Warsaw, even if only to carry on their disputes. At the other extreme, relations between the United States on one hand and Great Britain and Canada on the other are predominantly harmonious, and war between them is simply ruled out. Yet their relations are not by any means entirely serene. Canadians resent heavy American investments in Canada, and fear that Yankee publications will crowd out Canadian ones. Both Canada and Great Britain disagree with American policy toward Communist China. At the same time, these differences, and the conflicts which result therefrom, are probably no greater than are differences and conflict among groups *within* each of these countries. In many domestic societies there is more conflict and less cooperation than between some countries. One need only to think of the situation within the Union of South Africa, the Republic of the Congo, Laos, South Viet Nam, and Indonesia for evidence of this contention. Were the lid of suppression lifted in such authoritarian countries as Spain, Portugal, Poland, Hungary, and probably either of the two Chinas, there might well be civil war.

COOPERATION PERVASIVE
IN INTERNATIONAL SOCIETY

As with politics, the purposes of cooperation may be almost anything. It takes place in nearly every field, be it economic, social, cultural, or political. Furthermore, any number from two to all international entities may cooperate. Lastly, it may be quite informal, as when countries extradite persons charged with crimes, or it may be highly organized and institutionalized in complex international organizations. The multitude of purposes pursued in a widely varied subject matter field by formal or informal methods among and through a hundred states, a score or more of identifiable dependent areas, and hundreds of international organizations, makes the task of meaningful classification and description as important as it is difficult. The task far exceeds what can be covered in this brief chapter. We can only refer to what has been dealt with in other chapters, and include a few pertinent examples here.[3]

Examples will be selected from among the economic and social activi-

---

[3] See in particular the following chapters: 4, Ideology and International Relations; 5, Economic Factors; 8, Organizing the World Society; 9, Regionalism and Functionalism; 10, Peaceful Settlement and Change in International Society; 14, Policy Patterns: Isolation and Non-Alignment; 20, Disarmament and Arms Control; and 21-28 in Part VI.

ties of the UN system because: (1) of these only the Universal Postal Union has been treated in any detail elsewhere in this volume; (2) cooperation tends to be characteristic of non-political relationships; and (3) the UN is world-wide, depends primarily upon and is essentially devoted to prompting cooperative behavior.[4] The problem of selection from among the wide range of choice remaining is a difficult one.[5] It will be resolved somewhat arbitrarily by choosing: (1) narcotics control, a little-known activity, jointly performed by the UN and national governments; (2) the concern of the UN with dependent peoples; (3) educational, cultural, and scientific activities carried on by UNESCO, although these are far from being its exclusive preserve; and (4) technical assistance, a generally if not well-known function in which several organs of the UN, as well as the specialized agencies associated with it engage.

CONTROL OF NARCOTIC DRUGS

The international control of narcotic drugs is one of several duties of the United Nations Economic and Social Council (ECOSOC). Whereas most of its functions consist of making studies and reports, coordination, and drafting international conventions for submission to the General Assembly and the members of the UN, that of narcotics control is primarily regulatory, resembling in this respect the U. S. Food and Drug Administration.

International measures to control narcotic drugs antedates the UN. In 1909 the United States, primarily interested in controlling widespread drug addiction in the Philippines, met in Shanghai with twelve other states concerned with the prevalence of opium smoking in China. A number of resolutions passed by the conference indicated the future direction and stimulated the first world-wide International Opium Conference, held at the Hague in 1911. The Hague Opium Convention, adopted in the following year, awaited the end of World War I before being generally applied. Changes in the original convention, as well as the adoption of seven additional ones, improved the system over the years. One writer notes that "in no other area of social concern has there been such advanced development of organs and procedures of international control."[6]

---

[4] The chapter sets forth as a purpose of the UN "to promote social progress and better standards of life in larger freedom" (Preamble) and "to achieve international cooperation in solving international problems of an economic, social, cultural, or humanitarian character, and in promoting and encouraging respect for human rights and for fundamental freedom for all. . . ." (Art. I)

[5] See Robert E. Asher and Associates, *The United Nations and Promotion of General Welfare* (Washington, D.C.: The Brookings Institution, 1957), for a comprehensive treatment.

[6] Leland M. Goodrich, "New Trends in Narcotic Control," *International Conciliation*, No. 530 (Nov. 1960), p. 181.

Nevertheless, nations have not always been willing to agree to effective control measures. These have lagged behind scientific developments and knowledge, which, if applied, would aid in combating drug addiction.[7] The problem remains a serious one. The Commission on Narcotic Drugs reported at its 1960 session that in twenty-nine countries there was an addiction rate of at least one per thousand persons and in twenty-one at least one per five thousand. Some of the worst forms of addiction, especially heroin, were increasing in both developed and underdeveloped countries. Aside from the human losses, the economic ones are great. United States officials estimated the annual cost within that country to be about half a billion dollars.[8]

The League was entrusted with "the general supervision over the execution of agreements with regard to . . . the traffic in opium and other dangerous drugs" (Art. 23). Actually, it concerned itself with the entire problem, and in 1946 the UN took over this, as it did several other League responsibilities.

The eight existing conventions establish guiding principles for national governments, bind them to take certain legislative and administrative measures, and provide for the organization and functions of the international bodies. It is widely recognized that the conventions are inadequate in their coverage, are not all ratified by the same states, and are in need of revision and simplification.

Three organs, the Commission on Narcotic Drugs, the Permanent Central Opium Board (PCOB), and the Drug Supervisory Body (DSB), all under or closely associated with ECOSOC, in addition to the World Health Organization (WHO), administer the program. The first, consisting of fifteen members, is one of the nine functional commissions of ECOSOC. Although concerned primarily with drafting conventions and agreements, it also exercises a supervisory function by reviewing the annual reports submitted to the secretary-general by the governments. The Board consists of eight persons serving in their individual capacities, appointed by ECOSOC for five-year terms. Its primary responsibility is to observe international trade in narcotics in order to obtain national compliance with international agreements. The Supervisory Body consists of four members, two appointed by WHO, and one each by the Commission and the Permanent Board. On the basis of estimated needs which governments submit, or on its own estimates for those which do not, the Board determines world requirements for narcotics.

Governments are under certain international obligations to control the production and consumption of these drugs, whereas the international bodies have been primarily concerned with trade. Limiting production,

---

[7] *Ibid.*, p. 185.
[8] *Ibid.*, p. 227.

difficult in the past, has become increasingly so with the introduction of synthetic drugs. With respect to these, the secretary-general reported in 1952 that "it seems well-nigh impossible to devise measures which could effectually control the materials used for the manufacture of synthetic drugs and yet would not be far too expensive and burdensome." The World Health Organization, however, decides what new drugs should be brought under international control.

On March 30, 1961, a new multilateral treaty, the Single Convention on Narcotic Drugs 1961, was opened for signature at UN Headquarters. Drafted in response to a 1947 resolution of the General Assembly, it represented over ten years of preparatory effort on the part of several UN organs. The Single Convention, considered and approved by a UN Conference, would go into effect, replacing the previous conventions, thirty days after the fortieth ratification.

In addition to eliminating the overlapping and inconsistencies of the existing treaties, the Single Convention would simplify the control machinery and bring the system into line with technical, social, and political developments. The Commission would continue to act as the principal legislative and political body of the control machinery, subject to the supervision of ECOSOC or the General Assembly. An International Narcotics Control Board would replace and take over the functions of the Central Opium Board and the Drug Supervisory Body. The new Board would consist of eleven members who, like those of its predecessors, would serve as experts in their personal capacities.

The following are among the principal provisions of the Single Convention: (1) ratifying states would be obliged to limit the area of cultivation of the opium poppy, license cultivators, and purchase and take physical possession of the crops as soon as possible; (2) import certificates and export authorization would be required for international trade in poppy straw as in drugs; (3) wild coca bushes and illegally cultivated plants would be destroyed, and whenever feasible countries would prohibit cultivation of the opium poppy, coca bush, and cannabis plant; (4) states would be obliged to license and control persons and enterprises engaged in manufacturing drugs; (5) parties would give special attention to medical treatment and rehabilitation of drug addicts; (6) states would have a duty to assist each other and to cooperate with competent international organs in the fight against international traffickers in narcotic drugs.[9]

Existing agreements are based upon the principle of "indirect" control, i.e., the responsibility for dealing with private individuals is placed upon national governments, with the power of the international organs limited to supervising and controlling only the latter. Although direct control was

---

[9] "Single Convention on Narcotic Drugs Adopted," *United Nations Review,* VIII (May 1961), 28-29.

considered in some of the early deliberations on the Single Convention, the matter was quickly dropped, presumably on the basis, not that it would be less effective than indirect control, but rather that any possible loss of state sovereignty would not be risked even to protect citizens from the ravages of drug addiction. All told, the record of international cooperation in controlling drugs compares well, not only with similar international efforts in other fields, but also with that of governments generally operating within their domestic jurisdictions.

DEPENDENT PEOPLES

In 1945, one human being out of three lived in a colonial or politically dependent status; by the early nineteen-sixties, once mighty empires had shrunk to almost insignificant size. Only Great Britain and Portugal held extensive areas, all in Africa, and these were surely destined to be liberated, the first peacefully, the latter possibly only after considerable bloodshed. After that only a few scattered areas, too weak to stand alone or too important for military strategy to be freed, would remain as symbols of the former "white man's burden." This would be true, of course, only if new empires did not arise in the name of communism's program of "national liberation."

Along with the shrinking of empires there has been a growing sense of international responsibility for dependent peoples. Even during the nineteenth century at least lip service was given to the principle that they were governed as a "trust"; in a few instances this was expressed in formal international agreements whereby the governing powers assumed legal obligations to care for the well-being of the "natives." The League mandate system imposed additional obligations on the mandatory powers, and for the first time provided for international supervision of the administration of the "trusts." Only former German and Turkish colonies were placed under mandate, however, thus leaving out most of the colonial peoples. The UN trusteeship system in 1946 had responsibilities geographically less extensive than those of its predecessor. The former mandate areas of Transjordan, Syria, the Lebanon, and Palestine had become independent, and South Africa attempted to absorb the mandate of South-West Africa, rather than transform it into a trust territory. Only one new area, Somaliland, entrusted to Italy in 1951 and freed ten years later, was brought under trusteeship. Of the eleven trust areas once administered by seven different powers, by 1962 six had become independent, leaving only five relatively small areas: the Cameroons (U.K.); Nauru (Australia); New Guinea (Australia); Pacific Islands (U.S.); and Ruanda-Urundi (Belgium), with a combined population of approximately eight million inhabitants, in contrast to the original eighteen million.

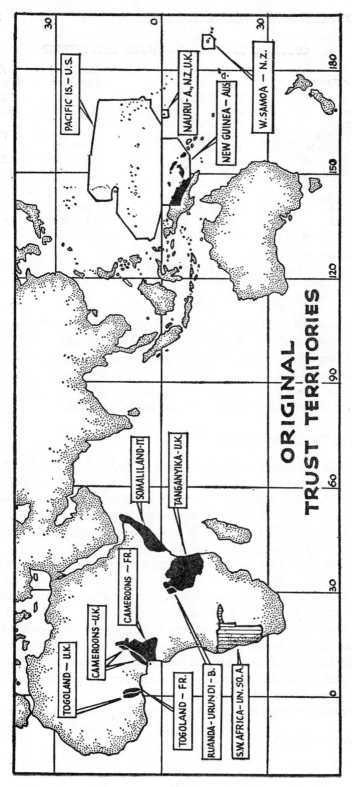

ORIGINAL TRUST TERRITORIES

PACIFIC IS. – U.S.

NAURU – A., N.Z., U.K.

NEW GUINEA – AUS.

W. SAMOA – N.Z.

SOMALILAND – IT.

TANGANYIKA – U.K.

TOGOLAND – U.K.

CAMEROONS – U.K.

CAMEROONS – FR.

TOGOLAND – FR.

RUANDA – URUNDI – B.

S.W. AFRICA – UN. SO. A.

ORIGINAL TERRITORIES UNDER TRUSTEESHIP

Trust Territory	Administering Authority	(1960 Est.) Population	Area (Sq. Miles)
*Cameroons	United Kingdom	1,613,000	34,080
Cameroons	France	3,303,000	166,752
*Nauru	Australia**	4,300	8
*New Guinea	Australia	1,409,000	93,000
*Pacific Islands	United States	77,000	685
*Ruanda-Urundi	Belgium	4,941,000	20,916
Somaliland	Italy	1,358,000‡	194,000
South West Africa†	Union of South Africa	608,000	317,725
Tanganyika	United Kingdom	9,052,000	362,688
Togoland	United Kingdom	426,000	13,041
Togoland	France	1,136,000	22,002
Western Samoa	New Zealand	106,000	1,133

* Trust territories as of 1962.
** On behalf of Australia, New Zealand, and United Kingdom.
† Remains obligated by the mandate agreement, but not under trusteeship.
‡ Estimate 1961.

The mandate and trusteeship systems were compromises between conflicting forces and interests, both within and among states. On one hand were those who preferred outright annexation, and on the other some who worked for stronger international controls or even complete independence. The desires of the dependent peoples, even if these could have been ascertained, played almost no part in the decisions.

The Trusteeship System

The UN trusteeship system is provided for in Article XII of the Charter, which sets forth general principles, and Article XIII which establishes the Trusteeship Council, corresponding to the Permanent Mandates Commission of the League. The Council, a principal organ of the UN whose composition has already been described, has functions more extensive than those of the Commission.[10]

The purposes of the trusteeship system are declared to be international peace and security; the promotion of general advancement, including progressive development toward self-government or independence; encouragement of respect for human rights and freedoms; and equal treatment in social, economic, and commercial rights for all members of the UN and their nationals. The latter provision for the "open door" was not to prejudice the attainment of the other objectives, nor was it to modify any rights included in the existing mandate for instruments pending the drawing up of trusteeship agreements.

In accordance with the Yalta Agreement, the particular territories to be

---

[10] See above, p. 174.

placed under trusteeship were left to future determination. Three types of areas were declared eligible for inclusion—existing mandates, territories detached from the enemy powers, and other dependent areas.

The functions of the trusteeship system, except for "strategic areas," are exercised by the General Assembly, assisted by the Trusteeship Council, and by the Secretariat. The Assembly approves the terms of the agreements and their alteration and amendment, reviews the work of the Trusteeship Council, and considers other problems brought before it. For areas designated as "strategic" the Security Council is responsible. The Security Council may, however, avail itself of the assistance of the Trusteeship Council.

Chapter XII declares it to be the duty of the "administering authority to ensure that the trust territory shall play its part in the maintenance of international peace and security." To this end it may use volunteer forces, facilities, and assistance from the trust area in carrying out obligations decided upon by the Security Council.

The United States was interested in a strategic trusteeship for certain Pacific territories formerly under Japanese mandate. Several other powers, including the United Kingdom, Australia, and New Zealand, were interested in the security features pertaining to all trusteeships. The compromise was to include the strategic area concept along with the functional approach which authorized military activities in all trust territories, an approach directly opposed to that of the mandate system, although the mandate principle was violated in several instances by both Japan and France.

Although the Charter does not automatically bring any area under trusteeship, it does set forth the procedures by which this may be done. Areas may be entrusted to one or more states, or to the organization. The terms upon which territories are brought into the system, and their alteration or amendment, are supposed to be first agreed upon by the states *directly concerned,* and then approved by the General Assembly, or by the Security Council in the case of strategic areas. Except for specific reference to those holding mandates, *states directly concerned* are not defined, and it has been impossible to reach agreement upon the meaning of the term. The result has been that the state holding an area has submitted a proposal to the General Assembly or Security Council, and the agreement has gone into effect after being approved by one of those organs.

The General Assembly's committee on Trusteeships and Non-self-governing Territories is the scene of important and controversial debates, frequently repeated in the Assembly. As well might be expected, that body, with its large number of ex-colonial members, does not always see eye-to-eye with the Trusteeship Council. Moreover, rather than confining its attention to matters passed on to it by the Council, it has in practice felt free to exercise any of the functions concerning dependent peoples entrusted to the UN.

The functions and authority of the Trusteeship Council are more extensive than were those of the Mandates Commission. As did the latter, it prepares a questionnaire and receives annual reports from the administrating authorities. It also receives petitions in oral as well as in written form, without their having to be submitted to the administering authorities as was required under the mandate system. One of the most important changes and improvements over the mandate system is the use of visiting missions. These, composed of representatives of designated Council members, visit each trustee area every three years. Another important difference between the Mandates Commission and the Trusteeship Council is that the latter may and does make recommendations directly to the administering authorities. It also makes an annual report, containing recommendations, to the General Assembly, or, for the Pacific Trust Territory, to the Security Council.

Other Non-Self-Governing Peoples

Although the trusteeship system was limited to areas formerly placed under it, the UN is concerned with other dependent peoples as well. Chapter XI of the Charter, "Declaration Regarding Non-Self-Governing Territories," expresses this concern. Members recognize the permanent interests of their dependent peoples, and accept, as a sacred trust, responsibility for promoting their well-being. To this end they declare their intentions to be general advancement and just treatment, development of self-government, promotion of international peace and security, and collaboration with each other and the UN. They also agree to transmit to the secretary-general statistical and technical information relating to "economic, social, and educational conditions," but not political ones.

Literally interpreted and conservatively applied, these provisions would mean little more than did a paragraph in Article 23 of the League Covenant by which members undertook "to secure just treatment of the native inhabitants of territories under their control." However, as interpreted and applied by the Assembly under continuous and bitter opposition from several of the administering powers, Chapter XI has gradually acquired far greater significance than had been contemplated at San Francisco in 1945. It has been referred to as an international charter of colonial administration.

Although hardly the cause of the divergent views with respect to its meaning, the ambiguity of the Chapter does not contribute to the achievement of agreement. Most of the members take positions somewhere between two extremes, with the colonial powers favoring a conservative or strict, and the Asian, African and Soviet members a more liberal or elastic interpretation. By the conservative extreme Chapter XI is viewed solely as a unilateral declaration of principles already accepted by the colonial powers. At the most, members are internationally obligated to observe these principles, and to furnish the secretary-general the kind of information, and no other, that is specified in Article 73e. In particular they are not obligated to submit information on political development. The determination of what are non-self-governing areas is the sole responsibility of each member. Chapter XI, unlike the chapters on trusteeship, neither provides for nor authorizes the establishment of supervisory organs. The government of dependent peoples remains within the domestic jurisdiction of the administering power, and even a recommendation on those matters is "intervention," and therefore prohibited by the Charter. Information transmitted is for information only, presumably for the personal enlightenment of the secretary-general, or at best to be placed on the shelves of the UN library.

The other extreme, exemplified by states such as India and the Soviet Union, views Chapter XI as imposing international obligations on the colonial powers for the observance of which the UN is responsible. Since these are "questions or matters within the scope of the . . . Charter," the General Assembly is free to discuss and recommend with respect to them as it is on other similar matters. Though Article 73e does not specifically call for information on self-government and other political matters, administrating states are obliged to develop self-government and the UN cannot perform its functions properly unless it has access to appropriate political information. As for special supervising organs, the General Assembly is free to establish committees and commissions for fulfiling its responsibilities for dependent areas as it is for other affairs. This liberal view has tended to prevail, at least in practice. The colonial powers, however, continue to object.

The major problems which have arisen in attempts to implement the Declaration have centered around definitions of non-self-governing areas, the kind of information to be supplied to the UN, the organization and functions of the Special Committee on Information from Self-Governing Territories, and the functions and responsibilities of the UN with respect to all dependent peoples.

How is one to evaluate international collaboration in the governing of dependent peoples? The UN has attacked these problems with considerably more vigor than did the League, and the administering authorities do not relish the resulting criticisms and recommendations made by the supervising organs. It is probable that the authorities attempt to solve problems so that they will not be subject to criticism; it is certain that they have made modifications in their policies after, and probably because of, discussions and recommendations by the UN. It may well be that the trusteeship standards and achievements have had a favorable effect on colonial administration generally. Furthermore, the UN has certainly speeded up the liquidation of the trusteeship system and the process of independence of colonial areas generally, although not always with desirable results.

The relatively few remaining colonial authorities are under continuous scrutiny and attack by the majority of UN members. Where the criticisms have been constructive and practical they have had a beneficial effect. But as they have become a part of cold war propaganda, they have tended to solidify the opposition of the administering powers. Despite strong pressure from the Trusteeship Council and the General Assembly, the Union of South Africa has refused to place South-West Africa under trusteeship, and the prospects after fifteen years of efforts to induce her to do so were dim indeed. So it becomes clear that the record of international cooperation in dealing with dependent peoples is a mixed one, and substantiates our observation that most types of relationships are an admixture of cooperation and conflict.

CULTURAL COOPERATION THROUGH UNESCO

The efforts of the League in the cultural and intellectual field were quite limited. It worked principally through the Institute of Intellectual Cooperation, a semi-independent organization located in Paris.

The United Nations Educational, Scientific and Cultural Organization (UNESCO), with its headquarters in Paris, is separate from the UN proper, but is affiliated with it through ECOSOC. It developed out of the wartime meetings of Allied Ministers of Education. On the basis of this plan, as modified by French suggestions which emphasized cultural aspects, UNESCO's constitution was drafted in November 1945, at a London conference called by the British and French governments. A Preparatory Commission carried on until November 1946, when the constitution was ratified. By the end of 1960, 100 countries were members. The Soviet Union joined in 1954. That that action signified a changed attitude toward international cultural cooperation was doubtful. To many it appeared to be temporary tactical move in the cold war.

According to Article I of its constitution, the purpose of UNESCO "is to contribute to peace and security." The preamble "recognizes" that "since war begins in the minds of men, it is in the minds of men that the defenses of peace must be constructed." The general task of UNESCO, therefore, is to change the minds of men so that wars will be less likely. If it is granted that the statement is at least partly true, the means by which "the defenses of peace" may be constructed in the minds of men remain very difficult to determine and more difficult to apply. And herein lies one of the sources of UNESCO's difficulty; it is little wonder that it has been called " an organization in search of a purpose." Certainly UNESCO cannot attain its goal by programs to eliminate illiteracy, for most wars have been fought among the most literate, the best "educated" people. Furthermore, since UNESCO is concerned with ideas, and an important part of the cold war is a "war of ideas," UNESCO can hardly escape involvement in international politics. Perhaps this is at least a partial explanation of the fact that its budget of approximately $32 million for 1961-62 is paltry compared with the hundreds of millions spent annually by governments for their international "information" programs. The violent attacks in the United States by certain "patriotic" groups on UNESCO's rather mild suggestions for teaching to develop world-minded attitudes also indicate the obstacles which it would encounter were it to develop a really effective program.

UNESCO has faced difficulties in developing unified and generally acceptable policies. The nebulous nature of its purpose, and the numerous functions which it is authorized to perform, have encouraged the submission of a large and varied number of projects by delegates of the members and by the Secretariat, each arguing, perhaps each seriously believing, that its projects were the most worthy ones. Limited funds have forced the elimination of many projects and the establishment of priorities.

Over the course of years of considerable controversy, confusion, and compromise, UNESCO has developed a program of real merit, despite the fact that on the whole it is related no more closely to peace and security than are most of the other social activities of the UN system. Yet when UNESCO engages in programs of mass education, relief assistance to supply pencils, paper, and books to those who do not have them, and technical assistance activities, its work is valuable regardless of whether it contributes directly, or at all, to international peace and security.

UNESCO's program falls under eight broad headings: education, natural sciences, social sciences, cultural activities, exchange of persons, mass communication, relief assistance services, and technical assistance. An example or two of each will suffice to indicate the nature of the activities.

The educational work consists of exchanges of information, extension of education, and education for international understanding. Missions are sent to states on request to give general advice, and experts are frequently dispatched to assist in implementing the recommendations. Mass education is one of the most promising programs. In 1951 the first of six planned projects, the Fundamental Education Training and Production Center, opened at Patzcuaro, Mexico. The purpose of the centers is to train specialists in techniques of fundamental education and to produce educational materials appropriate for the area. Less ambitious than the centers is the system of "Associated Projects," over one hundred and fifty in various countries that are tied together and assisted by UNESCO.

In the natural science field UNESCO has promoted organizations and meetings of scientists; subsidized scientific organizations; established a number of Field Science Cooperation Offices; stimulated research and its publication, and the improvement of teaching. In the social sciences it has promoted and subsidized the formation of international associations, conducted seminars, and published works on international tensions and other subjects. It also publishes the quarterly *International Social Science Bulletin*. Its cultural work, conceived as that relating to the arts and philosophy, is similar to that in the natural and social sciences.

The exchange of persons program consists of making information available, arranging international meetings of groups, and sponsoring a number of exchange fellowships. Its work in the field of mass communication ranges from attempting to unify Braille type to developing conventions to facilitate the flow of educational materials across national boundaries. UNESCO performed a valuable service by taking over certain relief and rehabilitation responsibilities from UNRRA, especially by raising funds and gathering supplies through voluntary agencies in such countries as the United States and Canada and sending them to needy areas. It cooperates with the other agencies in Palestine and Korea in providing educational services and in reconstructing and developing educational facilities. Along with several of the specialized agencies, it participates in the Expanded Technical Assistance Program. In Ceylon, for example, it has provided specialists at a demonstration center in fundamental and adult education in a newly reclaimed agricultural area.

Even a slight movement forward on the long, arduous, and perhaps impassable road which UNESCO seeks to travel is commendable if not satisfactory progress. Charges made against it by irresponsible ultranationalists are more an indication of the magnitude and difficulty of the task than they are an indication of either the intentions or performance of UNESCO. Wars may not have their deeper sources in the minds of men, but ideas are nevertheless potent for good and evil.

TECHNICAL ASSISTANCE

No people are so wise and none so ignorant, that each cannot learn something from the other. International technical assistance programs are aimed at the sharing of skills. It is essentially a program of education and training through advice and demonstration—a "cooperative pooling of wits, wisdom and skills . . . in which all countries are able to participate, that all may give as well as receive." Though usually regarded as aimed at economic development, it has been wisely if somewhat enigmatically said that the problem of economic development is not economic development. Rather it is development in general, or the building of social institutions. Political stability, efficient and socially responsible public administration, a healthy and literate citizenry, are prerequisites for economic development.

This does not mean that there are not many immediate and practical results to be achieved by the adoption of relatively simple changes in materials and techniques. Horace Holmes, "Point Four Pioneer," introduced a new kind of wheat (Punjab 541) to Indian farmers; the result was a 43 per cent yield over the native variety. The eradication of mosquitoes through the systematic application of DDT has saved millions of lives in India, and improved the health of millions more. The long-run significance of technical assistance, however, is its contribution to industrialization and major improvements in agricultural production. Economic development of the poor and underdeveloped countries also requires capital, in increasingly large amounts as technical assistance prepares them to use it effectively. Although the major part of this capital has come, and will undoubtedly continue to be derived mainly from domestic savings—more or less voluntarily or forced—it will be necessary to obtain large sums from outside sources, especially if the worst forms of authoritarianism are to be avoided and democratic development to remain a realistic choice. Various institutions of the UN system help supply the capital to the needy countries—the International Bank for Reconstruction and Development (IBRD) and its affiliate, the International Finance Corporation, being the principal ones.

Technical assistance, on a modest scale, was carried on by the UN from the beginning, especially in the areas of advisory social welfare services. By 1959 more than two million dollars were expended from the regular budget for technical assistance. Inspired by President Truman's proposal in his inaugural address of January 20, 1949, for "a bold new program for making the benefits of our scientific advances and industrial program available for the improvement and growth of underdeveloped areas," the General Assembly, in its autumn session, approved the "Expanded Program of Technical Assistance for Economic Development of the Underdeveloped Countries." The needy countries soon began pressing for a new organization to make grants or long-term, low-interest loans. Known as the Special United Nations Fund for Economic Development (SUNFED), it was successfully opposed by the wealthier states. The outcome was a compromise, the creation of the Special Projects Fund, established in late 1958, in accordance with an Assembly resolution. Its purpose is to enlarge the Expanded Program, although the two are to be kept separate. In the words of the resolution, it was to provide "systematic and sustained assistance in the fields essential to the integrated technical, economic, and social development of the less developed countries." The Special Fund has concentrated on important special projects in certain basic fields, such as research, training, and surveys.

As of January 1961, 115 projects were in various stages of implementation in fifty countries and dependent areas, involving a probable outlay of $227 million. Of this amount the Special Fund allocated $96 million, the remainder to be paid by the assisted countries. Among these projects was a survey of the electric power requirements and potentialities of Argentina, and research and training institutes in India and Israel. Like the Expanded Program, the Special Fund is financed by voluntary contributions from UN members, as well as from other states. The regular program, on the other hand, is financed by the UN budget, payment to which is obligatory.

Eight of the specialized agencies, as well as the UN, participate directly in the technical assistance programs. In fact, technical assistance is the principal function of several of the former, in particular WHO and the Food and Agriculture Organization (FAO). The administration of the program requires coordination among these agencies. The General Assembly, which has the basic responsibility, is assisted in its tasks by ECOSOC. Under the latter is the Technical Assistance Committee (TAC) composed of representatives of all ECOSOC members. Its principal duties are to evaluate the administration of the program. The chief body is the Technical Assistance Board (TAB), consisting of representatives of all the participating organs. TAB is responsible for screening requests, coordinating the program, and for reviewing its actual administration. It has its own secretariat, as well as forty-six TAB offices (1960), with additional ones planned, to supervise the program in the field.

In 1960 the Expanded Program was in operation in some sixty countries and dependent areas, and plans were under way to extend it to twenty-eight additional ones. Some 2,375 experts were at work in these areas, and more than two thousand fellows were training abroad, bringing the total fellowships awarded since 1950 to over eighteen thousand. Between 1950 and 1961 eighty-six governments had contributed or pledged more than $310 million for the work, and the annual expenditure as of 1961 was about $40 million.

The UN has engaged in activities which do not fall within the provinces of the Specialized Agencies, such as training in public administration. The Food and Agriculture Organization (FAO), carries on a wide range of activities involving research, demonstrations, training, and other techniques of bringing science and technology to bear upon agriculture and rural welfare problems. The technical assistance activities of UNESCO are noted above. One of the interesting and significant developments has been the rendering of technical assistance in the area of narcotic drugs. It was previously noted that national governments have the primary responsibility for implementing the narcotic conventions. Often they fail to do so, not out of opposition but because of incapacity. In 1956, ECOSOC invited governments to apply for technical assistance in narcotic control both under the regular and the Expanded Program. As a result, a number of governments have requested and are receiving help on such matters as administration, police, customs, the treatment of addicts, and the development of crops to replace opium poppy and cannabis plants. In addition, a number of regional conferences have been called by the secretary-general to consider problems common to several countries.[11]

SUMMARY AND CONCLUSION

Societal relationships require some degree of cooperation. The growth of civilization is indicated by the recognition of the rights of others and a willingness to work together for both separate and common ends. Most men agree that cooperation is preferable to conflict, although it is usually recognized that politics is virtually inevitable, and, if properly controlled, a degree of conflict is probably salutary. Internationally the chief need is to control men who exercise power, and to substitute cooperation for conflict in large areas of human relationships.

The basic cause of international cooperation is the growth of an interdependent world. Cooperation in any society is in rough proportion to the development of community attitudes, but common fear may also induce collaboration. The latter has usually supplied the initial impulse to cooperation, but it can be sustained on a healthy basis only if men come to think of "we" as embracing larger and larger proportions of mankind.

The four areas of international endeavor examined in this chapter bear out the above generalizations, as well as some lesser ones. In these relationships as in most, cooperation is intermingled with conflict. Even in the relatively noncontroversial area of narcotics control, limited vision and national sensitivity have impeded progress commensurate with need and knowledge. Yet the international record here stands comparison with governmental action within national societies. The levels of performance are somewhat lower in the three other areas. Nevertheless, the problems of trusteeship are rapidly disappearing as people become legally independent. All people, however, are dependent one on the other, in greater or lesser degree. Human development, to which technical

---

[11] For "Background notes on the activities of the UN family," see "The Expanded Program of Technical Assistance," *United Nations Review,* VIII (Feb. 1961), 46-48.

assistance is devoted, despite the less noble aims of many who participate therein, is an exemplification of the spirit of "trust" and the recognition of mutual dependency.

The need for a cooperative approach to the solution of international problems is indicated not only by their magnitude, but by the fact that in a world of sovereign states there are no significant international government institutions to deal with them, sometimes by forceful means, comparable to those within national societies. When one considers the kinds of problems dealt with by international institutions, primarily by inducement and influence rather than by the exercise of power and authority, in a world where men interpret "we" in provincial terms, their records, despite their shortcomings, are commendable.

What of the long-run significance of international cooperation? As the late Secretary-General of the UN, Dag Hammarskjöld, believed:

We are still in the transition between institutional systems of international coexistence and constitutional systems of international cooperation. . . .

[In this interdependent world, people] are forced to live together, fighting or in peace, as neighbors with limits put by nature to their possible self-sufficiency and for that reason with a need to develop forms for international intercourse, permitting more or less highly developed degrees of cooperation. . . .

[Although our basic institutional pattern is primitive], it carries within it seeds for the growth of higher social organisms, covering wider areas and groups of people. [As the system for coexistence develops, it passes, on single points or on a broad front] over into a constitutional system of cooperation. When that happens, we get in a first, necessarily rudimentary form, a form of society which, while preserving and protecting the lives of the nations, points towards an international constitutional system surmounting the nations, utilizing them to the extent that smaller units are more efficient instruments for evolution, but creating rules which limit the influence of the nations in fields where bigger units present greater possibilities for development and survival.[12]

SUGGESTED READINGS

Asher, Robert E., "Economic Cooperation under U.N. Auspices," *International Organization*, XII (Summer 1958), 288-302.
————, and others, *The United Nations and Promotion of the General Welfare*. Washington, D.C.: The Brookings Institution, 1957.
Beckel, Graham, *Workshops for the World: The Specialized Agencies of the United Nations*. New York: Abelard-Schuman Limited, 1954.

---

[12] "The Development of a Constitutional Framework of International Cooperation," *United Nations Review*, VI (June 1960), 26.

Berkov, Robert, *The World Health Organization: A Study in Decentralized International Administration*. Genève: E. Droz, 1957.

Blelloch, D., "Bold New Programme: A Review of U.N. Technical Assistance," *International Affairs*, XXXIII (Jan. 1957), 36-50.

Bonne, Alfred, "The Political Economy of Aid to Underdeveloped Countries," *Political Quarterly*, XXIX (July 1958), 289-300.

Chieh, Liu, "International Trusteeship System—Visiting Missions: Reports on Ruanda-Urundi and Tanganyika," *International Conciliation*, No. 448 (Feb. 1949), 97-184.

Cockcroft, John, "Peaceful Uses of Atomic Energy," *Science*, CXXIX (Jan. 30, 1959), 247-52.

Dulles, Foster R. and G. E. Ridinger, "Anti-Colonial Policies of F.D.R.," *Political Science Quarterly*, LXX (Mar. 1955), 1-18.

Freeman, Alwyn V., "The Development of International Cooperation in the Peaceful Use of Atomic Energy," *American Journal of International Law*, LIV (Apr. 1960), 383-92.

Glick, Philip M., *The Administration of Technical Assistance: Growth in the Americas*. Chicago: University of Chicago Press, 1957.

Haas, Ernst B., "The Attempt to Terminate Colonialism: Acceptance of the United Nations Trusteeship System," *International Organization*, VII (Feb. 1953), 1-21.

Hambidge, Gove, *The Story of FAO*. Princeton, N.J.: D. Van Nostrand Co., Inc., 1955.

Hester, Hugh B., "International Cooperation: The Challenge of our Times," *Virginia Quarterly Review*, XXXIII (Spring 1957), 189-208.

"International Responsibility for Colonial Peoples: The United Nations and Chapter XI of the Charter," *International Conciliation*, No. 458 (Feb. 1950), 49-112.

Laves, Walter H. C. and Charles A. Thompson, *UNESCO: Purpose, Progress, Prospects*. Bloomington, Indiana: Indiana University Press, 1957.

Loewenstein, K., "Sovereignty and International Cooperation," *American Journal of International Law*, XLVIII (Apr. 1954), 222-44.

May, Herbert L., "Narcotic Drug Control," *International Conciliation*, No. 485 (Nov. 1952), 491-99.

Murray, James N., Jr., *The United Nations Trusteeship System*. Urbana, Illinois: University of Illinois Press, 1957.

Myrdal, Gunnar, *An International Economy: Problems and Prospects*. New York: Harper & Brothers, 1956.

———, *Beyond the Welfare State: Economic Planning and Its International Implications*. New Haven: Yale University Press, 1960.

———, "Psychological Impediments to Effective International Cooperation," *American Journal of International Law*, XLVIII (Apr. 1954), 304-07.

"Partnership for Progress: International Technical Cooperation," *Annals of the American Academy of Political and Social Science*, CCCXXIII (May 1959), entire issue.

Rivlin, Benjamin, "Self-Determination and Dependent Areas," *International Conciliation*, No. 501 (Jan. 1955), 195-271.

Sady, Emil John, *The United Nations and Dependent Peoples*. Washington, D.C.: Brookings Institute, 1956.

Shy, J., "The Genesis of the Universal Postal Union," *International Conciliation*, No. 233 (Oct. 1927), 395-443.

Teaf, Howard M. and Peter G. Franck, eds., *Hands Across Frontiers: Case*

Studies in Technical Cooperation. Ithaca, New York: Cornell University Press, 1956.

Tinker, H., "The Name and Nature of Foreign Aid," *International Affairs,* XXXV (Jan. 1959), 43-52.

Trumbull, Robert, *Paradise in Trust: A Report on Americans in Micronesia, 1946-1958.* New York: William Morrow & Co., Inc., 1959.

United Nations, General Assembly, Report of the Secretariat, *Progress Achieved by the Non-Self-Governing Territories in Pursuance of Chapter XI of the Charter: Association of Non-Self-Governing Territories with The European Economic Community.* UN Doc. A/4197 (Sept. 3, 1959). New York: 1959.

V

LIMITING AND
CONTROLLING FACTORS

INTRODUCTION

All societies have means of controlling and regulating the behavior of their members. Otherwise there would be utter chaos and only brute force would matter. There is no more important problem concerning international relations than that of the imposition of restraints on the exercise of power. This is so for two principal reasons: the consequences of the abuse of power are very great; and the means for regulating it have hitherto been quite deficient.

We have previously considered collective security, primarily from the standpoint of a type of policy, but also incidentally as to its adequacy, or inadequacy, as an institution to preserve international peace and to enhance national security. In Part V, four additional topics, balance of power, international law, international morality, and disarmament and arms control, are analyzed to determine how and to what extent they may be relied upon to preserve order and to prevent the abuse of power in the international arena.

17

The Balance of Power

Power, and its distribution, is one of the major determinants of international behavior. "Balance of power" implies something about the relative strength of individuals and groups. A precise definition at the outset would allow us to proceed with dispatch to the central purpose of this chapter: to consider how the balance of power limits and controls the behavior of international decision-makers.

Unhappily, balance of power has no agreed definition. In fact, it has so many meanings that it is virtually meaningless. One is tempted to suggest that the phrase be abolished and other words used to designate each of the dissimilar phenomena to which it refers. The wiser course is to indicate how it is most commonly used, and to stipulate a working definition appropriate for our purpose. An awareness of the multiple meanings is necessary because it is often used without being defined, and writers, consciously or unconsciously, skip lightly from one meaning to another. Even if defined, it is quite common, even within the same treatment, for it to be applied to quite different phenomena, with no indication, or even realization, of inconsistent usage.

Several attempts have been made to sort out the principal meanings of balance of power, though even the categorizers do not entirely agree on their findings. In an illuminating article, Ernst B. Hass finds that it has eight fairly discrete meanings and four principal usages.[1] It means any distribution of power, a balance or equilibrium (as the words imply), hegemony or imbalance, stability and peace, instability and war, power politics generally, a universal law of history, and a system and guide to policy-makers. Depending on the intention of the users, it is employed simply to describe, as propaganda, to analyze, or to provide a guiding principle for those who make foreign policy decisions.

---

[1] Ernst B. Haas, "The Balance of Power: Prescription, Concept or Propaganda?" *World Politics*, V (July 1953), 442-77.

Not only is balance of power a bewildering phrase, it is also an emotional one. To some it is a sin and a danger to be avoided; to others it is a guide to be followed and a condition to be sought. In the traditional American view, it falls in the former category. William Graham Sumner believed that the founding fathers intended that "there was to be no grand diplomacy. . . . There was to be no balance of power and no 'reason of state' to cost the life and happiness of citizens."[2] Nevertheless, they attempted to establish a balance of power within the American government! Wilson, Hull, and Roosevelt were among those who regarded the balance of power as a cause of conflict and war, to be replaced by collective security arrangements. This was the typical nineteenth-century liberal view. Richard Cobden wrote that for a hundred years balance of power had been the burden of kings' speeches, the theme of statesmen, the subject of treaties, and the cause of wars, as it would no doubt continue to be the pretense for maintaining enormous standing armies. Nevertheless,

> . . . the balance of power is a chimera! It is not a fallacy, a mistake, an imposture—it is an undescribed, indescribable, incomprehensible nothing; mere words, conveying to the mind not ideas, but sounds like those equally barren syllables which our ancestors put together for the purpose of puzzling themselves about words. . . .[3]

On the other hand, Fénelon, an eighteenth-century moralist as well as practical statesman, took an opposite view. Action by a state to keep its neighbor from becoming too strong was

> . . . to guarantee one's self and one's neighbors from subjection; in a word it is to work for liberty, tranquility, and public safety; because the aggrandizement of one nation beyond a certain limit changes the general system of all nations connected with it. . . . The excessive aggrandizement of one may mean the ruin and subjection of all the other neighbors. . . . This attention to the maintenance of a kind of equality and equilibrium between neighboring states is what assures peace for all.[4]

Frequent references in literature to "the danger that the balance of power will be upset" imply that it is a condition that ought to be maintained. All this tells us principally that balance of power evokes a favorable response in some and is rejected by others. It is unlikely, however, that the term means the same thing in these several instances.

In the contemporary era the system of power relationships is worldwide. There have, however, been periods in history, as in ancient China

---

[2] "The Conquest of the United States by Spain," in *War and Other Essays* (New Haven: Yale University Press, 1911), p. 333.

[3] Richard Cobden, *Political Writings*, 2nd ed. (London: William Ridgeway, 1868), I, 259.

[4] Cited in Sidney B. Fay, "Balance of Power," *Encyclopedia of the Social Sciences* (New York: The Macmillan Co., 1930), II, 396.

and India, and among the Italian city states, when each of several regional systems operated in virtual independence of the other. But even today, and more so in recent centuries, there are regions within which power relationships are of importance irrespective of the larger world around. The Middle East, Central America, South Asia, and Southeast Asia are examples. At the same time, the distribution of power within each of these regions affects and is affected by the world system, and hence the regional systems may be regarded as sub-systems of the system as a whole. Much of what we shall have to say is pertinent to the functioning of these sub-systems, but our attention will be directed toward world-wide power relationships.

Is balance of power an illusion? This obviously depends on what it means. The majority of writers seem to conceive of it as either a status (or condition) or as a type of behavior, or both.

BALANCE OF POWER AS STATUS

Balance of power, in the sense of condition or status, refers to some distribution of power among the units of a system. In international society, the units may be either states or combinations of states. An examination of both historical and current usage reveals that balance of power, as condition, may mean: (1) any distribution of power; (2) a distribution in which some of the units are stronger than others, the balance being the margin of superiority; or (3) an equality or equilibrium of power among the units.

Balance as Any Power Distribution

Whenever the distribution of power, whether it be relatively in balance or greatly out of balance, is changed in either direction, it is frequently said that the balance of power is affected. Thus any change in contemporary power relationships between the United States and the Soviet Union, or between the former and Cuba (even though the effect is to strengthen the United States and to weaken Cuba) is regarded as a change in the balance of power. This is probably the most frequent, as well as one of the loosest usages. It is what most journalists seem to mean by the balance of power, although they seldom if ever attempt to make their meaning clear. Conceived in this manner, it covers such a wide range of situations, with the effects on state behavior varying greatly depending on the degree to which power is equally or disparately distributed. A loose definition of this kind is of little utility for either descriptive or analytical purposes.

Balance as Margin of Superiority

Balance of power is sometimes said to be the same as a bank balance, which is of course not a balance at all but a remainder. A balance must have at least two weights. A better analogy would be a teeter-totter with a small child on one end and an adult on the other. The balance refers to the difference between the two weights. When decision-makers say their aim is a balance of power, it usually means a favorable balance on their side. Whether such a balance in this sense is regarded as favorable or unfavorable depends on one's position on the teeter-totter.

Although the effects of an imbalance of power on international behavior may be analyzed, it will obviously be quite different from that of a real balance. As we shall note subsequently, when most analysts speak of the beneficial effects of a balance of power they usually have in mind a situation quite different from one which leaves weak states at the mercy of the powerful ones.

Balance as Equality

In the sense of equality or equilibrium, balance assumes its literal meaning. An analogy would be a scale which is brought into balance by adjusting the weights. Where there are several units in a system, the situation may be compared with a chandelier balanced by the proper spacing of candles or bulbs.

This more or less literal meaning seems to make the most sense. It is more precise than just any distribution of power, and it avoids the nonsense of saying balance when one means quite the opposite. Moreover, the more responsible writers, if their purpose is enlightenment rather than propaganda, mean that there is a balance of power to the extent that it is relatively equally distributed among the units of a system. It is always a matter of approximation, perhaps never a perfect balance. Finally, this is the only kind of situation which could possibly produce the benefits claimed for it.

Forms of the Balance

"Forms of the balance" signifies the number of units in the system. The usual classifications are the simple and complex balance. In the first, there are just two units or weights, as in the analogy of the scale. Where there are three or more, the form is said to be complex—the chandelier example. The more units there are, the more complex the balance. Since 1945, and especially after the outbreak of the cold war, the terms bipolar (or bisolar) came into use. Although the meaning was not always clear, it referred to the concentration of strength in the two super-powers, the United States and the Soviet Union. At the same time, many of the lesser states freely aligned with, or were coerced into becoming satellites of one or the other of the two power giants. Thus a bipolar system consists of (1) two large states constituting the poles which repel each other; and (2) a number of states clustered around each of the poles. Although from 1947 to about 1953 both the United States and the Soviet Union seemed to aim at complete bipolarization, many countries refused to be drawn into either camp. Subsequently, both super-powers tended to develop a three-world image, consisting of the communist bloc, the "free world alliance," and the "neutralists." As the power of both the Soviet Union and the United States decreased relative to that of other states, and as neutralism gained strength, even in some of the aligned countries, the world was said to be moving toward depolarization.

We have noted that the units in the balance may be either states or coalitions of states. The form of the balance is said to be simple if power is concentrated in two states or in two opposing groups. A bipolar world is actually an approach toward the simple balance of power, for it indicates both two powerful opposing states and two coalitions. A complex balance, on the other hand, refers to both a wide dispersal of power among several states and to a condition of general non-alignment. Thus from the perspective of states as units, there could be a complex balance, while simultaneously there would be a simple balance if there were two opposing alignments.

To use simple balance to mean two quite different situations—concentration of power in two states, as well as in two coalitions of states in which the members of one or both are of approximately equal strength—is open to certain objections. So far in modern history the winning coalitions in major wars have consisted of a number of states of relative power equality, no one state being so much stronger than the others that it could easily conquer them. Had Germany won either of the two great wars of the first half of the twentieth century the situation might have been quite different. One of the principal claims for the balance of power is that it has been the major factor in preventing a long succession of aspirants to world hegemony from realizing their ambitions. It is a basic assumption of balance of power theories that every state would expand its power unless checked by counter power. In any case, after World Wars I and II probably no country was in a position to dominate the world, and yet the two super-powers were able to deter each other.

Now that the power constellation has moved in the direction of bipolarization—or simple balance in both senses of the term—in the event of a general war in which at least one side survived there would be no balance of power to prevent either the Soviet Union or the United States from dominating the world. This does not prove that either of the two super-powers would attempt to conquer the world were they able to do so, for a basic assumption of the balance of power theory may be invalid. It only means that there would be no balance of power, in the correct sense of that term, to prevent it. This analysis indicates that the implication of the two quite different situations, although both are usually referred to as a simple balance of power, are quite different.

Either the simple or complex form of the balance may exist regardless of whether the balance of power means any distribution, an imbalance (margin of superiority) or an equilibrium. That should be quite clear if by balance one means the latter. If balance means imbalance, or preponderance, the simple form would exist if state or coalition A was twice as powerful as state or coalition B. There would also be a simple balance if a coalition of states of relatively equal strength (a complex balance among them) constituted one weight (either the heavier or the lighter one) and a single state the other.

BALANCE OF POWER AS BEHAVIOR

Although it is possible to sort out and clarify the different meanings of balance of power when it refers to status, it is very difficult—in fact almost impossible—to do so satisfactorily when it is used in other senses, and especially when it refers to behavior. We shall first consider how power is supposed to be balanced—or "methods of the balance" of power—and secondly, four types of behavior often referred to as policies or "laws" of the balance of power.

Methods of the Balance

This is a dynamic world in which the distribution of power is affected by changes which occur both within and among states. Changes in the resource capacity of a state will affect the distribution of power, unless counterbalanced by changes elsewhere. The dramatic developments in nuclear technology, missiles, and space vehicles have changed and will continue to change it. The industrialization of Communist China, and her acquisition of nuclear bombs in the near future, will surely have major impacts on world politics, although it is uncertain what many of them will be. The result could be a split with the Soviet Union; on the other hand, the alliance might be tightened and their joint quest for world domination intensified.

Most considerations of methods of the balance of power have concentrated on the external and neglected internal factors which affect it. More recently, however, greater attention has been given to internal changes. The reason for the past emphasis on external changes such as the loss and acquisition of territory and the shifting of alignments was that they were probably more important than in the contemporary era.

What are the types of action which are supposed to account for the balance of power, in the sense of a relatively equal distribution of power among the units of a system or sub-system?[5] If there is a balance of power, all actions which serve to maintain the power status quo also contribute to the preservation of the balance just as all others disturb it. If power is out of balance, it may be brought into equilibrium by decreasing the power of the stronger units, or by increasing that of the weaker ones, or by a combination of both. A state may affect the distribution of power by arming or disarming. Any of these changes are quite as likely to result in an imbalance as they are in a balance. By methods of the balance of power we shall mean various types of *international* behavior which, whether or not so intended, are frequently said to maintain a relatively equal power status among the units of the system.

Intervention and War. How may one state act to influence the distribution of power which results from developments within the internal jurisdiction of others? Armaments, industrial development, and political institutions are legally a state's own business. Practically, they are important concerns of others. We have already noted that trade and aid policies are major instruments in the cold war struggle, and that one of their purposes is to affect power distribution. Intervention and war are other means. Historically, states have intervened for a number of reasons, very frequently to change power relations, usually to create an imbalance. Intervention is a nebulous term, packed with emotions. In a realistic sense, foreign policies are interventions in the affairs of other states which the intervenors regard as their affairs also. Whatever other terms are used to disguise it, intervention continues to be an important method of foreign policy. After World War II, Great Britain intervened in Greece and Jordan, the United States in Guatemala, Cuba, Lebanon, and Laos, the Soviet Union in North Korea, Hungary, and Eastern Europe, to cite a few recent examples. In all instances, power motivations were dominant, although it is doubtful that any of these states was seeking a balance of power. It may nevertheless have been the unintentional result. The ultimate form of intervention is war. Whether any war has been initiated in which the aim was actually to balance power is debatable. Some wars may have brought about a more equal distribution than would have been the situation without them. In other instances, certainly in World War II, the outcome was to create a greater imbalance than existed at the outset, and in particular to change the form from the complex toward the simple.

---

[5] We shall use balance of power to mean equilibrium, or some degree of equality of power, unless we indicate that another meaning is intended.

Compensation and Partition. The practice of compensation, which means giving a state the equivalent of that which it is deprived, or the equal of that given other states, has tended to preserve an international equilibrium. Most peace treaties have resulted in territorial changes which reflected the concern of states for their relative power positions. The three partitions of Poland (1772, 1793, 1795) are familiar instances of compensation. During the nineteenth century, the great powers of Europe divided territory and agreed upon spheres of influence in the Balkans, the Middle East, Africa, and Asia, all in the name of compensation. The occupation by the United States of the Pacific mandates and several Japanese islands after 1945, and of the Kuriles and southern Sakhalin by Russia, are among the recent examples of the compensation principle as are the divisions of Korea, Viet Nam, and Germany.

Divide and Conquer. The British were accused, with some justification, of playing the Muslims and Hindus of India against one another, thus facilitating British control of both. The efforts of the Soviet Union to split the non-communist alliance, and of the United States to woo the Soviet satellite states, are current examples of attempts to alter the distribution of power. Both also attempt to influence the non-aligned countries, if not to win them over at least to keep them from falling into the camp of the enemy. In all such cases power may or may not be balanced.

Alliances. Alliance policies have been the central concern of writers on the balance of power. Indeed, alliances have been regarded as the principal method by which an uneasy equilibrium has been maintained. Sir Robert Walpole wrote in 1741:

> . . . it is by leagues well concerted, and strictly observed, that the weak are defended against the strong, that bounds are set to the turbulence of ambition, that the torrent of power is restrained, and empires preserved from those inundations of war that, in former times, laid the world in ruins. By alliances, Sir, the equipoise of power is maintained, and those alarms and apprehensions avoided, which must arise from vicissitudes of empire, and the fluctuations of perpetual contest.[6]

The theory is amazingly simple. States, naturally antagonistic, seek to expand and conquer one another. Confronted by an external danger and lacking sufficient strength to stand alone, a state is usually able to find others who share a similar fear. The two join to confront their common enemy with their combined strength. The enemy, now fearing that the strength of the combination endangers its own security, or can thwart its expansion, finds other states with similar fears and ambitions willing to enter into an alliance to counter the first combination of states. The latter seek additional allies to counter the coalition inspired by their original

---

[6] *Parliamentary History,* XII, 168-69.

act, thus continuing the chain reaction. Machiavelli set forth the cardinal guiding principle that a prince should always join the weaker side in order to counter the stronger. "The prince who contributes to the advancement of another power, ruins his own." Equally important, a state should be "flexible," ready to shift its weight from one ally to another should the first become too strong. Sentiment and economic benefits should never be allowed to interfere with realities: power considerations alone should determine one's allies. Churchill was willing to ally with the devil (Communist Russia) if necessary to ensure England's survival.

The idea of the balancer, which is said to "hold" the balance of power, has occupied a prominent place in the theory relating to the complex balance. To "hold" the balance, a state must be flexible and relatively powerful. Flexibility is necessary because it must always be ready to throw its weight to the lighter side. It must be strong in order to "tip the balance." Great Britain is the classic example of the "holder of the balance." "Splendid isolation" meant, as we have seen, non-alignment, or independence, so that Britain would be free to commit her power as her interests dictated. Among the numerous descriptions of this "guiding principle" of historic British policy, none is better than that set forth in 1907, in the classic Memorandum by Sir Eyre Crowe.

The first interest of all countries is the preservation of national independence. . . . History shows that the danger threatening the independence of this or that nation has generally risen, at least in part, out of the momentary predominance of a neighboring State at once militarily powerful, economically efficient, and ambitious to extend its frontier or spread its influence, the danger, being directly proportionate to the degree of its power and efficiency, and to the spontaneity or "inevitableness" of its ambitions. The only check on the abuse of political predominance derived from such a position has always consisted in the opposition of an equally formidable rival, or of a combination of several countries forming leagues of defense. The equilibrium established by such a grouping of forces is technically known as the balance of power, and it has become almost an historical truism to identify England's secular policy with the maintenance of this balance by throwing her weight now in this scale and now in that, but ever on the side opposed to the political dictatorship of the strongest single State or group at a given time.[7]

Such is the general theory. History certainly affords many examples of alliances in which power seems to have been the overriding consideration, although one may question whether the commitments have always been assumed and cast off so mechanically, lightly, and with such dispatch.

Did the alliances arise after World War II as indicated by the theory

---

[7] Memorandum by Sir Eyre Crowe on the Present State of British Relations with France and Germany, January 1, 1907, *British Documents on the Origin of the War 1898-1914*, ed. by G. P. Gooch and H. Temperly (London: His Majesty's Stationery Office, 1928), III, 403. See also Winston S. Churchill, *Second World War, The Gathering Storm* (Boston: Houghton Mifflin Company, 1948), III, 207-8.

and are states sufficiently flexible to be able to maintain an equilibrium? To fulfill the requirements of the theory, the United States must have been weaker than the Soviet Union after 1945; otherwise the European states would have joined the Soviet bloc in order to counter American power superiority. The fact is that at the time it was generally believed the United States was considerably stronger than the Soviet Union, although in mobilized ground forces she may have been temporarily inferior. The theory needs revision. The power of the United States, combined with the confidence that many other powers had in her forebearance, actually attracted rather than repelled allies. Yet it must be confessed that they felt at somewhat greater ease as they regained their strength and were able to deal with the United States on less unequal terms.

Whatever may be the degree of flexibility in past ages, it is not great today. Military plans and preparations have become so clearly integrated, economic dependence so great, in some instances ideological ties so strong, and, in the case of the Soviet bloc, controls so strict, that major defections appear unlikely, at least short of a total war. To the extent that this analysis is valid, the possibility that realignments will be a major factor in changing the distribution of power, much less in maintaining or bringing about a balance of power, can be largely discounted. The principal question appears to be the future position of the presently unaligned states.

Balance of Power as Policy and "Law"

Balance of power has been used to designate a varied and contradictory assortment of behavior. At one extreme it means almost any kind of international action, and at the other only those policies deliberately intended to maintain or establish an equilibrium—a real balance. We shall consider four of its several meanings: as international politics; as policies directed toward an imbalance; as policies whose purpose is to maintain or achieve a real balance; and as a "universal law," i.e., that a balance (equilibrium) is the natural, perhaps unintentional, but inevitable consequence of interaction among the members of the multi-state system.

International Politics. Two historians tell us that balance of power is "simply a convenient name for the way in which states act towards one another when there is no influence to persuade them to concord, nor force to coerce them, nor any court whose authority they are all prepared to recognize."[8] Thus stated, balance of power means action, presumably of the "power politics" variety. This may be "a convenient name" but it is certainly a loose, needless, and quite unwarranted abuse of words. We

---

[8] A. J. Grant and Harold Temperly, *Europe in the Nineteenth Century 1789-1914* (New York: Longmans, Green & Co., Inc., 1927), p. 3.

have previously discussed international politics; further consideration of this peculiar concept, therefore, need not detain us.

Policies Directed Towards an Imbalance. The purpose of NATO, the Warsaw Pact, the rearmament program of the United States as well as that of the Soviet Union, were all claimed by their proponents as being necessary to maintain the balance of power. The intent was quite otherwise. It was to gain a favorable margin of power, or "situation of strength" —preponderant if possible. To the extent that this action and reaction resulted in more of a balance of power it was incidental rather than intentional. States prefer a margin of power over their competitors, but what they prefer and what they are capable of may be quite different. A small state may despair of the competition and refuse to play the game. In the interwar period Denmark disarmed among heavily armed neighbors. Small states may attempt to accumulate strength, although they may not be able to bring their power up to that of others. Along with arming, they often enter into alliances, for only in combinations do they see any prospect of being effective.

Why states should pursue imbalance rather than balance of power policies is stated quite plainly in the following passage.

There are not many instances in history which show great and powerful states creating alliances and organizations to limit their own strength. States are always engaged in curbing the force of some other state. The truth of the matter is that states are interested only in a balance [imbalance] which is in their favor. Not an equilibrium, but a generous margin is their objective. There is no real security in being just as strong as a potential enemy; there is security only in being a little stronger. There is no possibility of action if one's strength is fully checked; there is a chance for a positive foreign policy only if there is a margin of force which can be freely used. Whatever the theory and the rationalization, the practical objective is the constant improvement of the state's own relative power position. The balance [imbalance] desired is the one which neutralizes other states, leaving the home state free to be the deciding force and the deciding voice.[9]

Policies as Equilibrium. The reader may at this point seriously wonder whether states ever pursue policies intended to maintain or restore a balance of power. The doubt is well founded. History does not seem to afford a single example of a state satisfied with an increase in its power just sufficient to attain an equilibrium. It would be equally difficult to discover an instance in which a superior power has deliberately weakened itself because it wanted a balance of power. This does not mean that the power ambitions of most states are unbounded. Nor does it mean that some states do not reduce their military power below what their resource capacities permit. They ordinarily do so, however, only if they believe the reduction leaves them in position to protect their "vital" interests.

---

[9] Nicholas John Spykman, *American Strategy in World Politics* (New York: Harcourt, Brace & World, Inc., 1942), pp. 21-22.

During most of the nineteenth century, Great Britain and the United States, as well as most other nations, failed to build their strength to full capacity, nor do they do so today. Most countries reduce their armaments after a war, and some fail to arm even though their potential enemies do so. Such was the case of Great Britain and the United States in the interwar period, even though Germany embarked on a major rearmament program soon after Hitler came into power in 1933. Policies of this sort may tend to bring about a more equal distribution of power, or they may even reverse the previous imbalance. But none of them are really deliberate balance of power policies.

The nearest approximation to a genuine balance of power is one pursued by a holder of the balance. Great Britain is said to have thrown her weight from one side to the other in order to prevent any one power from dominating the European continent. Even in a case of this nature the holder attempts to balance power among others, never its own power with that of its competitors. Since Great Britain was the dominant world power of the nineteenth century, it is just as accurate to say that her purpose was to preserve her own preponderance of power.

Balance of Power as "Law." We are told that "the aspiration for power on the part of several nations, each trying either to maintain or overthrow the status quo, leads of necessity to a configuration that is called the balance of power and to policies that aim at preserving it."[10] In short, men can do no other than to behave in certain ways which by a kind of "invisible hand," result in preserving an equilibrium. The assumption of "necessity" is hardly convincing. Even though one may believe certain policies to be absolutely necessary to realize his ends, he may or may not choose to pursue one or more of them.[11] Even the means necessary to preserve national sovereignty may be judged too costly in terms of other values.

The contention that a balance of power is the inevitable outcome of attempts to overthrow or maintain the status quo is equally open to doubt. Attempts to create an imbalance may be successful; or they may result in destroying the contending units, either literally in a nuclear holocaust or by the creation of a universal empire. Technological means of destruction as well as of domination now exist to make possible either of the latter results.

Even if states were interested in an equilibrium, there would be two insuperable obstacles in the way of its realization. One is the difficulty of measuring power, the other its instability. Power cannot be put on a scale

---

[10] Hans J. Morgenthau, *Politics Among Nations,* 3rd ed. (New York: Alfred A. Knopf, Inc., 1960), p. 167.

[11] For an illuminating discussion of this point, see Arnold Wolfers, "The Actors in International Politics," in William T. R. Fox, ed., *Theoretical Aspects of International Relations* (Notre Dame, Indiana: University of Notre Dame Press, 1959), pp. 83-106.

and weighed. Its constituents range from relatively concrete elements, such as the number of men and women in the military age-groups, and the number of missiles and bombs possessed by a country, to intangible factors such as the morale of the civilian and military forces. If leaders have great difficulty in weighing the importance of their own power resources, how can they with any degree of accuracy measure that of others? The inherent difficulty of measuring the weight of concrete elements is aggravated by incomplete information; with respect to the intangibles, the estimates are crude indeed.

An accidental equilibrium produced by these various forces would last but momentarily. We have noted the multitude of dynamic factors within states which are forever changing the distribution of the elements of power. The present form of the distribution of power also produces instability. This is so because the flexibility of states, which is supposed to have played an historically important role in maintaining the equilibrium, has all but disappeared in the contemporary era. Finally, it is even questionable whether one is justified in calling most previous power constellations balances of power. We have noted that Great Britain had a preponderance of power during the nineteenth century; and certainly the power of the United States in the Western Hemisphere has outweighed rather than been balanced with that of her neighbors. These various considerations raise grave questions about—indeed they seem to invalidate—the thesis of there being a law of the balance of power. The hypothesis that the rough balances which have existed have been accidental rather than inevitable is not entirely implausible. Nevertheless, it is true that so far no one powerful state has conquered the entire world. Furthermore the distribution of power has never been so out of balance that it did not have some part in acting as a limiting influence on state behavior.

EFFECTS OF THE BALANCE OF POWER

Three principal positive effects are usually held to result from an equilibrium of power. It serves to prevent or discourage the resort to force and war; it preserves the identity of the individual states; and it maintains the multi-state system. The theory that it acts as a deterrent to war is based on the assumption that a state cannot expect to win a war, and therefore will not begin one, if its power is in equilibrium with that of its potential victims. It is further assumed that under a complex balance an aggressor will realize that other states will follow Machiavelli's advice and come to the aid of the weaker state in order to prevent the stronger one from becoming still more powerful. If the balance of power does not prevent a war it will nevertheless prevent the destruction of any particular state, because, in their own interest, other states will not permit this to happen. By preserving the identity of the individual states, the mulistate system will also be preserved. So much for the theory. Why have events not actually worked out in this manner?

It is uncertain whether a balance of power has ever prevented war. It may well be true that no state initiates war without an expectation of victory. Yet many wars deliberately begun have ended in defeat for their instigators, apparently because they miscalculated the power situation. In any case, the attempt to further one's ends in a system in which power plays so important a role is a major factor in causing wars. Under these conditions, the distribution of power—balance or preponderance—has either failed to prevent some wars, or has served to bring them about.

It has been argued that peace is most in jeopardy when power is rather evenly balanced and war less likely when there is a preponderant power. Certainly both major world wars of the century came at a time when the sides appeared to be of nearly equal strength. Moreover, now that terror is balanced, there is more fear of war in the United States, and probably more in at least the noncommunist nations, than was the case when the power, mobilized and potential, of the United States seemed clearly to be superior to that of the Soviet Union. The argument that the nuclear stalemate has decreased the chance of war is unconvincing. On the other hand, the period of Roman dominance was also that of the *Pax Romana*. And the relative peace of the nineteenth century was accompanied by British ascendancy. Would peace in the Western Hemisphere be furthered by a balance of power? Or is it more likely to prevail if the power of the United States remains predominant? Certainly the United States has not been restrained from reducing the Latin-American states to colonial status because their individual or combined power matched that of the "Colossus of the North." It seems plausible that a balance of power in the Western Hemisphere would be conducive to greater strife, and war more likely than it is now. As long as the United States is predominant she does not fear attack from the Western Hemisphere; relatively secure from that source, she is unlikely to go to war against a Latin-American state. It is an entirely different matter, of course, if one or more of these states should constitute a base for an attack against the United States from a country outside the area. The principle of collective security is based partly on the assumption that balance of power politics lead to war, and that peace will be furthered by mobilizing a preponderance of power rather than by a balance.[12]

Several contemporary developments cast additional doubts on the stabilizing effects of interstate competition, and on the result supposed to flow from a balance of power. One is the blitzkrieg nature of modern warfare.

---

[12] It should be remembered, however, that the possibility of mobilizing overwhelming power against any member of the system—a basic prerequisite to a successful collective security system—depends on no one member being too strong. In short, there must not be too much inequality of power among the members of the system, and there must be a complex balance of power.

We have already noted that only certain types of mobilized military power would matter in a war conducted by nuclear-missile weapons. In the case of limited wars in which the stronger states are involved, none will be likely to employ its total power. If the battle should continue to be conducted primarily by nonmilitary means, it will not seriously tax the physical resources of the major contestants. In this event, will and wisdom will count far more than relative strength. Considerations such as these invalidate much of the conventional wisdom concerning the balance of power, as indeed of that about power in general.

The second and third functions of the balance of power—preservation of individual states and the state system itself—may be considered together, since the latter is dependent on the former. The process of birth and disappearance of states has gone on throughout history. War has been a major cause of both, although our concern is with the latter. Poland disappeared as a state when she was partitioned among Prussia, Austria, and Russia in the late eighteenth century. This was done under the principle of compensation, a method of the balance of power. The independent Italian and German states also disappeared during the latter part of the nineteenth century, as did the Baltic states during World War II. These are among the instances when the distribution of power—balanced or imbalanced—failed to preserve the identity of several of its members. Yet many states have survived and new ones have been born, thus preserving the multi-state system. But it is as impossible to speak with confidence of the responsibility of the balance of power for all this as it is of its role in preventing or causing war. It does seem clear, however, that many states owe their survival to strong protectors rather than to equal competitors.

SUMMARY AND CONCLUSIONS

After winnowing the wisdom of the balance of power, very little wheat remains. Only in the sense of equality or equilibrium is it a meaningful and useful concept. Although the contemporary era has seen the birth of more and more nations, it has simultaneously witnessed the concentration of power in fewer and fewer among them—a development toward a simple balance of power. There is some indication, however, that the present trend is toward a wider dispersal of power, and possibly toward nonalignment. Simple balance is used to refer to both a concentration of power in two states and in two opposing combinations of states, even though there is a complex balance within one or both of the groups. Nevertheless, the consequences of the two situations are quite different, despite the common nomenclature.

Because states want a large margin of superiority for themselves, they seldom if ever employ policies intended to balance their powers with that of others. A state may, however, endeavor to maintain a balance among other states. Yet very few have been both able and willing to play a balancing role. It follows, therefore, that to the extent there has been power equality among the units—either individual states or coalitions—of the state system, it is the incidental result of a whole complex of factors both within states and in the international system. Some have even argued that states must behave in certain ways which inevitably produce an equilibrium—hence balance of power as law. Since men may choose both ends and means, and imbalance has been at least as prevalent as balance, it is very doubtful that one is justified in contending that there is a law of the balance of power. The dynamic nature of contemporary society combines with the relative rigidity of the alignments among states to create instability in the international system.

The peace-preserving and the unit- and system-maintaining efforts of the balance of power are equally dubious. Wars have been frequent, and many states have disappeared, although the system has so far been maintained. But the evidence is conflicting as to whether a balance of power, and especially policies which are supposed to result in an equilibrium, have been more responsible for causing war or preserving peace, and in protecting rather than destroying states. Whether the state system will continue to exist is equally doubtful. The instability of the present balance of terror is a particular case in point. Certainly most serious students of international relations believe that there are better alternatives, if they could be realized, for assuring peace and human survival than by relying on a balance or imbalance of power in an anarchic and archaic state system.

SUGGESTED READINGS

Buehrig, Edward H., *Woodrow Wilson and the Balance of Power*. Bloomington, Indiana: Indiana University Press, 1955.

Carleton, William G., "Ideology or Balance of Power?" *Yale Review*, XXXVI (June 1947), 590-602.

Cobden, Richard, *Political Writings*, 2nd ed., 2 vols. London: W. Ridgway, 1868.

Friedrich, Carl L., *Foreign Policy in the Making: The Search for a New Balance of Power*. New York: W. W. Norton & Company, Inc., 1938.

Garthoff, Raymond L., "The Concept of the Balance of Power in Soviet Policy-Making," *World Politics*, IV (Oct. 1951), 85-111.

Gulick, Edward V., "Our Balance of Power System in Perspective," *Journal of International Affairs*, XIV (1960), 9-20.

———, *Europe's Classical Balance of Power: A Case History of the Theory and Practice of One of the Great Concepts of European Statecraft.* Ithaca, New York: Cornell University Press for the American Historical Association, 1955.

Haas, Ernst B., "The Balance of Power as a Guide to Policy-Making," *Journal of Politics*, XV, (Aug. 1953), 370-98.

———, "The Balance of Power: Prescription, Concept, or Propaganda?" *World Politics*, V (July 1953), 442-77.

Halle, Louis J., *Civilization and Foreign Policy: An Inquiry for Americans.* New York: Harper & Brothers, 1955.

Hume, David, "Of the Balance of Power," *Essays Moral, Political, and Literary*, eds. T. H. Green and T. H. Grose. London: Longmans, Green & Co., Inc., 1875.

Jordan, Amos A., Jr., "Basic Deterrence and the New Balance of Power," *Journal of International Affairs*, XIV (1960), 49-60.

Kaplan, Morton A., "Balance of Power, Bipolarity, and Other Models of International Systems," *American Political Science Review*, LI (Sept. 1957), 684-95.

——— and others, "Theoretical Analysis of the 'Balance of Power,'" *Behavioral Science*, V (July 1960), 240-52.

Mende, Tibor, *World Power in the Balance.* New York: The Noonday Press, 1953.

"New Balance of Power?" *Journal of International Affairs*, XIV (1960), entire issue.

Snyder, Glenn H., "Balance of Power in the Missile Age," *Journal of International Affairs*, XIV (1960), 21-34.

Strausz-Hupé, Robert, "U.S. Foreign Policy and the Balance of Power," *Review of Politics*, X (Jan. 1948), 76-83.

Tannenbaum, Frank, "The Balance of Power *versus* the Co-ordinate State," *Political Science Quarterly*, LXVII (June 1952), 173-97.

———, "The Balance of Power in Society," *Political Science Quarterly*, LXI (Dec. 1946), 481-504.

Thompson, Kenneth W., "The Limits of Principle in International Politics: Necessity and the New Balance of Power," *Journal of Politics*, XX (Aug. 1958), 437-67.

Vagts, Alfred, "The Balance of Power: Growth of an Idea," *World Politics*, I (Oct. 1948), 82-101.

———, "The United States and the Balance of Power," *Journal of Politics*, III (Nov. 1941), 401-49.

18

International Law

Rules for the regulation of human conduct are present in all societies. They are necessary for order and stability; without them man would not know how he should behave. It would be impossible, therefore, for one to predict the behavior of his fellow men, or to know how he should respond to their unpredictable actions. In short, in the absence of regulatory norms chaos would prevail, civilized existence would be impossible, and men would live as animals, if indeed they managed to survive at all.

These rules or norms tell men how they are expected to and how they "ought" to behave. Hence they are "ought" norms.[1] They fall into two classes, moral and jural. In the case of the violation of a moral norm one may be punished by a guilty conscience, by the more or less spontaneous disapproval of his fellow men, or by both. Although there may be certain moral norms common to all men, there are also variations from culture to culture. Sociologists usually refer to the expectations and demands concerning behavior as the mores of a cultural group. Truthfulness and dependability in one's personal relationships are valued in most societies, whereas lying and unreliability are frowned upon. Circumstances, however, may justify exceptions to the rules. By jural norms we mean standards or laws enforceable by organized governments. Just as in the case of moral norms, laws (as we shall henceforth refer to jural norms) vary from place to place, often within domestic societies and even more from country to country. One of the reasons for this variation is that laws usually reflect, at least to some extent, the mores of a community. Where there are major variations among the mores of different groups, the development, inter-

---

[1] In contrast to "ought" norms, these are statements with respect to uniform behavior, both in society and nature. These generalizations are also called laws, or scientific laws. Thus it is said that gas expands upon the application of heat and that states seek an optimum power situation. Because these laws purport to explain reality, they are "is" rather than "ought" norms.

pretation, and enforcement of a law common to all of them presents very difficult problems. This is a major factor in influencing the nature of international law.

Certain norms may be enforced by conscience, community sentiment, and by government organs. "Thou shalt not kill," except under certain circumstances, is a universal norm which is both moral and legal. Norms regarded as morally right, which are also enforceable as law, are likely to be effective in regulating human conduct. But where mores condone or require a practice, such as racial discrimination, and laws condemn it, the observance of law will suffer. This same principle is just as valid in international as it is within national societies.

THE NATURE OF INTERNATIONAL LAW

All law purports to regulate human behavior. It does so by specifying principles and rules, and providing for their interpretation and enforcement.

Subjects of International Law

The subjects of law are the persons who have rights and obligations as determined by its norms, i.e., the rules and regulations. Objects of law are the matters with respect to which human behavior is regulated. For example, a driver of an automobile—not the automobile—may be forbidden to travel over sixty miles per hour in certain areas. The driver is the subject, the speed of the automobile the object of the law. The subjects of *public* international law are therefore the persons to whom it applies.[2] The subjects and objects of international law are those provided by the law itself, and therefore change as the law evolves.

International law is traditionally defined as "the body of customary and conventional rules which are considered legally binding by civilized *states,* in their intercourse with each other."[3] [Italics mine—CPS] This concept is changing to bring it into harmony with the facts. Thus Philip C. Jessup, a leading American jurist elected to the International Court of Justice in 1960, defined it as law "applicable to states in their mutual rela-

---

[2] Private international law, sometimes referred to as conflict of laws, pertains to matters which fall within the jurisdiction of states, and ordinarily involves private parties. The problem is to determine whose law to apply. For example, it may be necessary to determine whether Mexican divorces and marriages will be regarded as valid in California. Basically, the same problem arises when California (or any of the other forty-nine states) must decide whether to recognize the validity within California of the laws of another state of the Union. In this chapter international law refers solely to public international law.

[3] L. Oppenheim, *International Law,* ed. H. Lauterpacht, 7th ed. (London: Longmans, Green & Co., Inc., 1948), II, 6-7.

tions and to individuals in their relations with states."[4] One author lists the following as subjects of international law: states, individuals, and "communities not having the characteristics of states."[5]

As we noted above, law applies only to human beings—hence only to individuals. The proper distinction is between individuals acting in their personal and in their official capacities. When it is said, therefore, that states are subjects of international law, this is but a shorthand way of referring to the individuals who act as official representatives of the group. They are the persons who are legally obligated to conform to the norms. They may or may not, however, be *responsible* for their conduct. To be responsible is to be punishable for wrong-doing. A child may act illegally but the parents may be held responsible for the child's misbehavior. Collective responsibility means that the entire group is held responsible for the misconduct of its individual members. Traditionally, the state, i.e., the collectivity, has been responsible for illegal actions of its foreign policy decision-makers. The war-crimes trials held after World War II marked a new departure in international law. Here German and Japanese leaders were held responsible and punished under international law for certain crimes.

Objects of International Law

Just as international law has been expanded to include private individuals and entities other than states among its subjects, so has it been enlarged to encompass more and more objects, both with respect to state-to-state and state-to-person relationships. We have already noted that since the days of the League of Nations the use of force has been severely restricted by law. Attempts to subject national armaments to the regulation of international law, although so far unsuccessfully, indicates a possible future object of regulation.

Private individuals have long been subjects of international law. Persons accused of piracy, of engaging in the slave trade, and violating laws of war are all examples. The present trend is to extend their rights and obligations—an expansion of the objects of international law. One of the results of the social and economic interdependence of nations has been the development of what is known as "international legislation." This simply means that by international treaties states have assumed legal obligations with respect to individuals, including their own nationals. Labor conventions sponsored by the International Labor Organization, and

---

[4] *A Modern Law of Nations* (New York: The Macmillan Co., 1949), p. 17, and chap. ii.

[5] Hans Kelsen, *Principles of International Law* (New York: Holt, Rinehart & Winston, Inc., 1952), pp. 96-188. Examples of the latter are: the Holy See, insurgents, protectorates, trust territories, and certain parts of states (Swiss cantons), and international organizations such as the League and the UN.

the Genocide Convention, are a few examples of hundreds of international agreements. The "crimes against humanity" for which individuals were tried and punished at Nuremburg and Tokyo after World War II, were based on the principle that individuals have rights under international law, even against their own states. The efforts of the UN to develop conventions on Human Rights would, if successful, be major extensions of this principle. Even though individuals may have rights under international law, it may be difficult or impossible for them to hale a state before court. A national of Great Britain may protest that his rights have been violated by the United Arab Republic, and that he cannot obtain justice in UAR courts. Because private individuals may not bring suits before the International Court of Justice, the British national could obtain redress there only if Great Britain were willing to argue his case as its own, and could get the UAR to agree to appear before the Court. States are most reluctant to permit their own nationals to take a case against them before an international court. Nevertheless, this has been done in a few instances. Individuals could take their cases to the Central American Court of Justice, established in 1907, and to the Arbitral Tribunal established by Germany and Poland in 1922 for dealing with the rights of persons in Upper Silesia. International courts also tried the major war criminals after World War II, but these were strictly *ad hoc* bodies. The most recent example is the European Court of Justice which serves the three communities established by the six states of Western Europe.

International Law Decentralized

International and municipal law are alike in many respects and different in some.[6] The principal difference is that municipal law is centralized whereas the international legal system is essentially decentralized. This simply means that whereas there are specialized agencies—legislative bodies, courts, and executive officials to perform certain kinds of functions —in a centralized system, in a decentralized one these are performed by the individual members of the legal community. This will become clear as we examine how international law is made, interpreted, and enforced. A decentralized legal system is characteristic of a relatively primitive community. International law compares in some respects with the common law as it developed in England during the Middle Ages. There were laws before there were legislative bodies, courts, and executive organs to enforce them. Law evolved through custom, and was interpreted and enforced by individuals and groups, much as is international law by states today. "Self-keep" was the customary recourse then, as it is now in the

---

6 Municipal law refers to all that law by which a state regulates behavior within its jurisdiction.

international society where specialized institutions are in a primitive stage.

A clear understanding of this point is necessary to avoid confusion. It also provides a clear answer to a question that nearly always arises in a discussion of international law. Is it really law? The dispute on this point is one over definitions. If it is contended that to have law there must be not only well-defined and adequate rules, but fully developed institutions, of course there is no such thing as international law. The correct view is that international law is really law, although imperfect. Institutions for its development, interpretation, and enforcement are inadequate, and this accounts for many of the shortcomings of the law itself, *i.e.*, the legal rules and principles.

Classifications of International Law

International law may be classified according to several different criteria. The broadest distinction is between *private* and *public* international law. Another is between procedural and substantive law. Methods of pacific settlement are examples of the former, whereas rights to territory are substantive rights. In the past, it was quite usual to draw a distinction between laws of peace and those of war, laws of neutrality being a part of the latter. With growing skepticism of the compatibility between law and war, increasing attention has been given to laws of peace and laws to prevent war.

A fourth classification is based on the number of states to which a particular international law applies. Depending on its extent, we may speak of *particular, general,* or *universal* international law. The Rush-Bagot Agreement of 1817, providing that neither Great Britain nor the United States should maintain armed naval forces on the Great Lakes, is an example of particular law, which applies to just two states. General international law extends to almost all states, including the principal powers. The Kellogg-Briand Pact of 1928, ratified by sixty-three states, and the UN Charter, would fall into this category. Sometimes a whole network of bilateral treaties may contain similar features which approximate general international law. Treaties relating to extradition of fugitives and consular rights are in this category. Universal international law is coextensive with the family of nations. Customary international law, such as that relating to diplomatic privileges and immunities, the marginal and the open seas, are usually considered to be of this nature.

A more penetrating and helpful classification is that made by Georg Schwarzenberger of the University of London.[7] He distinguishes between

---

[7] See his *Power Politics: A Study of International Society,* 2d ed. (New York: Frederick A. Praeger, Inc., 1951), chap. xiii.

the laws of *power, co-ordination,* and *reciprocity.* Master and slave relationships are regulated by the law of power. In a society marked by a low
degree of community feeling, and by weak political institutions, such as
international society of the past and present, the law of power is very
prominent. The law of co-ordination is sufficient, if law be necessary at all,
to regulate relations among the members of homogeneous groups such as
families and churches. Here law contributes "to the integration of the
community and is normally restricted to the enforcement in exceptional
cases of the minimum standards which are accepted unquestioningly by
the greater majority of the members of a community." He believes that
"in spheres remote from power politics, international law even shows
embryonic traces of a community law."[8] Among the best examples of the
laws of co-ordination are those which relate to the treatment of refugees,
the white-slave trade, opium traffic, and dependent peoples. There appears to be an emerging consensus with respect to fundamental human
rights and freedoms which may eventually bear fruit.

These types of law tend to be blurred in any society. The law of reciprocity is in reality an intermediate stage between the two. In certain relationships it is advantageous for a state to grant rights to other states in
return for reciprocal treatment. Laws relating to diplomatic privileges and
immunities, jurisdiction over territorial waters, extradition of criminals,
and others in the economic realm, all testify to the willingness of states to
limit their legal rights in return for reciprocal treatment.

The problems of international law are considerably different depending
on the degree of community feeling with respect to the particular matter
concerned. In those areas in which the law is one of co-ordination there is
considerable cooperation; competition and bargaining distinguish the area
of reciprocity; conflict characterizes those relations which are regulated
principally by the law of power.

WHY INTERNATIONAL LAW IS BINDING

The term "source" (or sources) of international law has two principal
meanings. First, it means *why* a norm takes on a legally binding character,
i.e., becomes law. Secondly, it means the methods by which laws are
made, as by legislative bodies. Our concern at this point is with source in
the first sense. This is a complex subject and a controversial one among
students of international law. Why is international law binding? Writers
are divided into several "schools" on this question. The main schools are
the naturalists and positivists. The latter in turn are divided into "dualists"
and "monists." The "eclectics" attempt to combine both natural and positive law.

---

[8] *Ibid.*, pp. 210-11.

Naturalists

Although the naturalists and the positivists developed side by side, the former were the more prominent in the early period. Francisco Vitoria (1480-1546), Professor of Theology at the University of Salamanca, was a representative of a group of thinkers who held that international law was based on the law of nature. As evidence of natural law he drew heavily on the *jus gentium,* which had been a part of the Roman law. To this school, *international law is binding because it is based on or is part of the law of nature.* Particular rules of international law are simply logical deductions from the basic principles of natural law, and are binding because they conform to these principles. International law, like all law, is discovered rather than made by men.

Undoubtedly these writers, like most theorists before and after them, were influenced by the conditions of the times in which they lived. They sought a rational basis for imposing legal restraints on abuses of power, and for providing order in the area of international relations. In the absence of more concrete laws, they utilized a widely accepted political theory upon which they attempted to build a legal framework. To those who regard law, with its rights and obligations, as simply the pronouncements of a definite legal superior, it can be pointed out that the American conception of natural rights of individuals assumes the existence of an order, or law of nature, as the basis of these rights.

Whether there is a phenomenon such as natural law is a question that need not concern us. If it does exist, it consists of moral rather than legal norms. There is no evidence to indicate that statesmen accept principles of natural law as legal obligations. Ideas of right and justice undoubtedly affect the nature of law, but law and justice do not necessarily correspond. Although men may agree that there is natural law, they may be in basic disagreement concerning its content. Natural law cannot be a guide to conduct insofar as men disagree on what it commands. For reasons such as these, most nineteenth and twentieth century writers on international law adopted a different theory to explain why it was binding.

Eclectics

Hugo Grotius (1583-1645), although perhaps with some exaggeration, is frequently called the Father of International Law. His greatest work, *On the Laws of War and Peace* (1625), was written in the midst of the chaos and suffering of the Thirty Years' War. He held that the sources of international law were both natural law and consent; hence he attempted to combine naturalism and positivism. Law arising from consent, which he called volitional law, was the same as that which later became known as positive law. To Grotius, natural law was the more basic, and if the two were in conflict it would prevail.

Most of the writers of the seventeenth and eighteenth centuries were influenced by Grotius. The most prominent of his followers, who continued to combine the positive and natural law views, but to give more weight to the former than did Grotius, were a German, Christian Wolf (1676-1756), and a Swiss, Emerick de Vattel (1714-1767). The latter's chief work, *The Law of Nations* (1758), was probably more widely read and cited during the eighteenth and nineteenth centuries that that of any other classical writer.

Positivists—the Dualist School

Positive law simply means man-made law. The dualists and monists are both positivists. The former, however, contend that municipal and international law have different sources, whereas the monists deny this. They insist that both have a single source. The dualists are the older group, and their view is the traditional one. As to municipal law, both groups agree that it has its source in a higher law, or legal authority such as a legislature, or a court in the case of customary law. But here they part company. The dualists assume that states were once unlimited by law—or *absolutely* sovereign. The source of international law is the *consent* of states to be legally bound by certain norms.

Richard Zouche (1590-1660), who taught civil law at Oxford, was the most prominent early writer to undertake a comprehensive and systematic treatment of international law, and to find its source in consent. In the introduction to his main work he defined international law (*jus inter gentes*) as that "which has been accepted by customs conforming to reason among most nations or which has been agreed upon by single nations" to be observed in peace and war.[9] In this passage we have the essential thesis of the positivist school. International law is binding upon states because, and only if, it has been "accepted," or "agreed upon," by them. "The rules rest partly on the assent of the states and partly on approved practice, assent to which is either presumed, or, in respect of a particular state declining adherence, immaterial."[10] Thus both customary and conventional international law have their source in consent.

There are many logical difficulties in the positivist position, only three of which are presented here. First, do new states coming into the family of nations really consent to international law? Did Indonesia, Pakistan, Israel, and Libya do so? If so, to what laws, and what is the evidence?

[9] As quoted in Author Nussbaum, *A Concise History of the Law of Nations* (New York: The Macmillan Co., 1947), p. 121.
[10] Edwin M. Borchard, *The Encyclopedia of the Social Sciences* (New York: The Macmillan Co., 1930), VIII, 167.

The usual answer is that by joining the family of nations, states give their consent, by implication, to all the customary, that is, the basic and universal rules of international law. They are, for example, deemed to have consented to the laws relating to diplomatic privileges and immunities, but not to those set forth in bilateral treaties, or in even such general conventions as the UN Charter. Brierly contends that such a state "does not in any intelligible sense *consent* to accept international law; it does not regard itself, and it is not regarded by others, as having any option in the matter. . . . The theory of implied consent is a fiction invented by the theorist. . . ."[11] But he admits that a *new* rule of law cannot be imposed upon states by the will of other states. Just why old, but not new ones can be so imposed he does not make clear.

Another criticism sometimes levied against the theory of consent is that states are forced to conclude treaties against their will. Germany in 1919, as well as the other defeated states, was given to understand that the cost of her refusal to sign the peace treaties would be either a resumption of war or indefinite occupation. Is it not a fiction to call acceptance under these conditions consent? The answer to this contention has been quite clear, at least until recently. Only *illegal* duress invalidates a treaty. Thus a treaty signed by persons under threat of physical harm would not be binding, but physical duress of a state, including war itself, has been quite legal. The situation in this respect is similar to that under municipal law. A contract to lease a dwelling signed under the threat of physical violence would not be binding, but there would be nothing illegal about a long-term lease which is signed because the alternative is higher rent.

The situation today is not so clear, especially with respect to states obligated by the UN Charter to refrain from the threat or use of force in any manner inconsistent with the purposes of the UN (Art. 2). Since aggression against another state is illegal, one might conclude that a peace treaty signed as a result of aggression would be invalid. However, a state resorting to self-defense when the victim of an armed attack (Art. 51), presumably could, if it emerged the victor, conclude a valid treaty with the defeated aggressor. Despite doubts which may be raised, international law does provide an answer. *Legal rights and obligations may be created by an illegal act.* For example, if long acquiesced in, and especially if recognized by a considerable number of states, Estonia, Latvia, and Lithuania would be held by an international court to be a part of the Soviet Union even though the latter probably acquired them by illegal means. If all illegally acquired possessions were invalid, the international situation would be more uncertain and unstable than it now is. Although this is largely the result of the decentralized nature of international law, it is not entirely unknown within centralized municipal systems. Thus a marriage

---

[11] J. L. Brierly, *The Law of Nations,* 4th ed. (Oxford: Clarendon Press, 1949), p. 53.

illegally consumated may remain valid, although the wrong-doers may be punished.

The most serious difficulty, and in the monists' view a fatal one which invalidates the entire dualist thesis, involves the question as to why consent itself is binding. The dualists, or at least most of them, do not really contend that a state may unilaterally free itself from an obligation based on a treaty or customary international law. Rather they accept the principle *pacta sunt servanda*, i.e., that pacts once consented to are henceforth binding, unless terminated or changed in accordance with principles of international law. Monists agree that treaties are binding because of *pacta sunt servanda*. But they ask, what is the source of that principle? Do states consent to be bound by these laws to which they consent? If so, the question is still not answered. To press the point to its logical absurdity, it may be asked: Why are states bound by the consent by which they consent to be bound? We shall return to this question in a discussion of monism.

Monists

The three most prominent representatives of this school, which is of relatively recent origin, are Krabbe (1859-1936), a Dutchman; Duguit (1859-1929), a Frenchman; and Kelsen (1883-   ), an Austrian. They focused attention on the fundamental question of how a sovereign state could be bound by international law.

Although monists arrive at their conclusions from different premises, they are in general agreement that all law has a common source. Krabbe maintains that it "springs from the sense of consciousness of right which is an innate psychological quality of man, like the moral sense, the religious sense, and so on."[12] Duguit sees law as flowing from the sentiment of social solidarity. Rules are followed because they are necessary for the group to exist. They become law when the vast majority of the members of the group feel that their violation justifies the use of force to induce compliance. Kelsen advances a "pure theory of law."[13]

In brief, and somewhat oversimplified form, the following is the monist position, essentially as represented by Kelsen. All law has its source in an axiom, *grundnorm,* or first legal principle that is outside the law. This is: *custom is a law creating fact. Pacta sunt servanda* was created through custom. Treaties once consented to are binding because of this basic legal principle of international law. It is fallacious to say that their source is consent. The latter is a method of creating international law, rather than the reason it is binding. A state is a legal entity with rights and

---

12 As quoted in Nussbaum, *A Concise History of the Law of Nations,* p. 283.
13 See his *Principles of International Law.*

obligations under international law. It gains membership in the international legal community through a legal process of recognition by existing members of that community, the sovereign states. Kelsen also contends that the admission of an entity to the UN constitutes recognition. Unlike the historical method of recognition of a new entity by the existing states —the decentralized method—the UN process is a centralized one, representing a progressive development of international law toward a centralized legal system.

Because a state is created by international law, the legal validity of municipal law—its source—is international law. In short, all law, except the first, has its source in a higher law. The basic source of all law is the first principle, or *grundnorm*. The dualists maintain that municipal law and international law are two different systems. According to this view, both are perfectly valid even though they may provide for conflicting rights. Monists, or course, reject this view. They hold that since international law is superior to municipal law, in the case of conflict between the two, international law prevails. For example, a provision of the U.S. Constitution would be illegal if it conflicted with international law, just as a clause of a state constitution would be superceded by the federal constitution.

The monist position is generally logical, and provides answers to certain basic questions that the dualists leave unanswered. In particular, the monists show quite convincingly that consent is not, and cannot be, the source of international law. All law has its source in a non-legal first proposition; and all subsequent law in a higher law. Municipal law is invalid if it conflicts with the higher, international law. It is illogical to maintain that an act can be simultaneously valid and invalid; it must be one or the other, as the monists contend.

The monist position also affords a guide to a clear meaning of the term sovereignty. It is simply the legal rights, or freedom, of a state as determined by international law. What international law does not specifically forbid, it permits. What it permits a state to do is national sovereignty. However, it should be borne clearly in mind that international law is decentralized. If government institutions were to be developed to make, interpret, and enforce international law, states would no longer be sovereign in the usual sense of the term. This follows from the concept of international law as a limitation on their freedom, but with the legislative, judicial, and enforcement processes retained in their hands. Of course international law is not entirely decentralized, as we previously noted. The UN Security Council and the International Court of Justice are both examples of limited centralization of the executive and judicial functions. But international law remains essentially decentralized and sovereignty, therefore, largely unimpaired.

HOW INTERNATIONAL LAW IS MADE

The *methods* by which international law develops is the second meaning of "sources." Since there is no supranational legislature, one method of development is through the gradual process of practice and usage; another, through the formulation and ratification of treaties. The product of the first process is customary and of the second, conventional international law.

Growth Through Usage

Until relatively recently the vast body of international law developed chiefly through usage and practice. At what time a usage becomes law is often difficult to determine. Moreover, the absence of a court system with compulsory jurisdiction to give a uniform interpretation of international law has been a severe handicap to its orderly development. The lack of precision and certainty in the law of territorial waters indicates the unsatisfactory results of the "decentralized" process by which customary international law develops. It is widely assumed that the international law of the "three mile limit" is clear and definite. Actually, there are many disputed points over this "maritime belt." Is a state sovereign owner of the belt or does it simply have certain rights in it. Does it begin at high or low tide, or at depths which cease to be navigable? Is it just three miles? Norway lays claim to four and Spain to six miles; certain states claim special rights over a "contiguous" zone beyond the three mile limit. Disagreement on such questions as these indicate that customs often assumed to be universal law are not really so.

Development Through Treaties

Because of difficulties such as these with respect to customary international law, especially its failure to keep up the dynamic pace of world events, states have turned increasingly, through bilateral negotiations and conferences, to the formulation of new rules. The process of treaty making is itself regulated by customary international law: the parties concerned must be states, only individuals properly endowed with authority may conclude treaties, and only states which ratify are usually subject to their provisions.

All types of international law to which we have previously referred are to be found among the thousands of international agreements. Some of them are examples of the cooperative efforts of states to meet common problems. Many relating to social, commercial, and economic matters fall into this category, as do some relating to peace and war. Numerous agreements exemplifying the law of reciprocity deal with commercial and trade matters. In addition, however, there are many treaties that exemplify the principle of power. Those concluded with the defeated states after World War I fall clearly into this category. The Anglo-Egyptian Treaty of 1936, concerning the Suez Canal Zone and the Anglo-Egyptian Sudan, although originated in a spirit of mutual agreement, soon came to rest upon the superiority of British power and was abrogated when that power was no longer adequate to enforce it.

Both the League Convenant and the UN Charter have attempted to make treaties readily available, with the primary purpose of preventing "secret diplomacy." The latter provides (Art. 102) that members shall register and the Secretariat shall publish every treaty and agreement. Those not so registered may not be invoked before any organ of the UN. The League Treaty Series consisted of 205 volumes containing 4,834 agreements of various kinds. By 1961 the United Nations Treaty Series, in 364 volumes, recorded 5,212 similar agreements.

Where is evidence of international law—proof of the existence of legal principles and rules—to be found? Obviously, properly ratified treaties are evidence of law for the adhering states. The meaning of treaties, however, as of law in general, is often a controversial matter. It is more difficult to find evidence of customary international law. Statements of national officials, including judges, and state papers of various kinds constitute the best evidence. Secondary evidence is found in decisions of international courts and arbitral bodies, and in the writings of qualified jurists.

ENFORCEMENT OF INTERNATIONAL LAW

There is a widespread, but probably erroneous notion, that the chief defect in international law is a lack of enforcement. Evidence of this is asserted to be frequent, flagrant, and unpunished disregard. As far as this writer is aware, no serious attempt has been made to compare the record with respect to the observance, or unpunished violation, of municipal law in a hundred or more countries, with that of international law. Certainly the international record would have to be a rather black one to exceed that within many domestic jurisdictions, including the United States. Actually most international laws are quite well observed; the few flagrant violations are largely responsible for the misapprehension. One of the reasons for what is probably the better international record is that many types of behavior prohibited by most municipal law systems have been permitted to states. For example, until relatively recent times a resort to war was a perfectly legal act, whereas similar behavior was prohibited within domestic societies. As international law has been "improved," i.e., the standards raised, its observance has probably fallen. A recording of violations of law under different circumstances, however, is hardly a criterion of its effectiveness in regulating human behavior.

Several factors account for the observance of legal norms, domestic and international. Habit, convenience, conscience, informal pressures, and self-interest are the principal ones. A state is free at any time to resort to various types of behavior, such as the employment of economic and psychological power against other states. Technically known as *retorsions*, actions of this nature are commonplace. But over and beyond these influences which operate in all legal systems, international law does have, again contrary to popular notion, formal methods of enforcement. These are known technically as *sanctions*. *A sanction (also called a reprisal) is an action, ordinarily illegal, permitted by a legal community against a law-breaker but not against one who observes the law.* For example, assume that only robbery and murder are subject to capital punishment. The taking of life by society would be legal for these acts but for no others. Historically reprisals range from mild actions such as the seizure of enemy property to the use of "force short of war." The UN Charter presumably outlaws reprisals which include the threat or use of force, although the issue is debatable.[14] Reprisals are legal sanctions taken under the authority of the legal community by its individual members. They are the only kind of law enforcement possible in a completely decentralized legal system. But they are enforcement measures, nevertheless, in principle identical to measures taken by executives and police in centralized systems.

Both the League and the UN represent limited moves in the direction of centralized law enforcement. Their law enforcement functions, however, have been incidental to the application of collective security. Under the UN, only if a violation of international law constitutes a threat to the peace, a breach of the peace, or an act of aggression (Art. 39) does the organization have the right to employ collective, or centralized sanctions.

Actually the UN Charter introduces considerable confusion into the international legal situation. It forbids states to use force or the threat of force (except in the instance of an armed attack), but it bestows only a limited amount of the authority on its organs which it prohibits to its members. If to be law a norm must be legally enforceable, as a last resort perhaps, by the application of physical force, it seems logical to conclude that the UN actually repealed international law insofar as it deprived states of, but did not itself assume, responsibility for its enforcement.

THE INTERNATIONAL JUDICIAL PROCESS

In one sense, the international judicial process is more highly centralized than are the legislative or executive processes. There are inter-

---

[14] See Evelyn Speyer Colbert, *Retaliation in International Law* (New York: Columbia University Press, 1948), pp. 199-208.

national courts, and *ad hoc* arbitral bodies are common. More significant is the fact that decisions and awards are legally binding for parties over which these bodies have jurisdiction. The latter is the fly in the ointment. Under customary international law states are free to submit or refuse to submit their *legal* disputes to judicial settlement, and only to a limited extent have they been willing to bind themselves by treaty, or the acceptance of the option clause of the UN, to compulsory jurisdiction. Thus the actual judicial process also remains essentially decentralized. This means that states ordinarily remain judges in disputes to which they are contesting parties, and that they are legally free to interpret the law for themselves. Even the UN Charter is interpreted by each member and by each UN organ. Disputing states may be perfectly sincere in their respective but conflicting interpretations of the law. International law is not peculiar in that it is often ambiguous and therefore lends itself to several interpretations, no one of which is necessarily the correct or true one. This situation is what makes a centralized organ with compulsory jurisdiction so desirable. Yet a centralization of adjudication would be far from the panacea often claimed for it. Only within narrow limits do courts change laws. And it must be borne in mind that most of the serious international disputes are not concerned with interpreting law but in changing it. Moreover, the really serious problems, such as those existing immediately before and after 1939, were not disputes over tangible things at all, but deep underlying tensions. Judicial organs are inherently incapable of contributing to the solution of such problems.

IMPROVEMENT AND EVALUATION OF INTERNATIONAL LAW

It is generally conceded that international law is quite inadequate to regulate human behavior in international society. Various proposals are therefore advanced for its improvement. One is to extend its sphere. We have noted developments along that line as both the persons of international law have grown and more and more objects have been included. National armaments, human rights, and outer space may be the principal objects of the next major extension.

Another proposal is to improve the enforcement processes. There are obviously inherent evils in a decentralized system in which only the strong can protect their rights. In most municipal systems ordinary injuries and breaches of contract (civil wrongs) are redressed by government organs only on the initiative of the injured parties. On the other hand, certain acts such as robbery and murder are regarded as everybody's business, for if they are not redressed all will be harmed. These acts are crimes, and the state rather than the individual directly concerned takes the responsibility for their prevention and for punishing the criminals.

It is proposed that this principle be applied in international society. All states would then make it their business to prevent and punish certain acts against individual states because all have a stake in the observance of the more basic obligations of international law. One way to accomplish this end would be to endow the UN with general law-enforcing authority, rather than to limit its sanctions to "flagrant wrongs" in which peace is directly and immediately endangered or broken.[15] Another would be to set up a strong international police force.

Codification has been suggested to overcome the ambiguity inherent in customary international law, especially in a system which operates without the benefit of a court with compulsory jurisdiction, to provide a uniform interpretation. Codification is a slow process, and may have raised as many problems as it has solved. Moreover, since codification is designed primarily to state rather than to change law, it does not provide an answer to the more basic problem of change. Nevertheless, if progress is made in this area, codification should be of some service in providing clarity and certainty; and by revealing disagreements and deficiencies, it may indirectly influence changes in the law itself. On the other hand, there is some evidence that attempts at codification have raised uncertainty where customary laws were seemingly accepted, or disagreement was latent.

We have commented on the proposal to enlarge the compulsory jurisdiction of the International Court of Justice. The creation of a hierarchal system of courts has also been suggested. Were this done, the problem of enforcement might be greater and necessitate improved enforcement measures if the decisions of the Court were not to be flouted. More far-reaching would be the establishment of courts with compulsory jurisdiction before which private individuals could call a state to account, including his own. Some go so far as to suggest that legislative bodies be established to change international as they do domestic law. A legislature empowered to impose "its fiat upon the dissenting State" has been proposed as the "only proper meaning of peaceful change as an effective legal institution of the international society."[16]

Undoubtedly there is merit in most of these proposals. Some of them would *improve* international law. But if the major ones were all adopted, including compulsory jurisdiction of international courts, the rights of individuals to appear as parties before them and to challenge states, and the creation of an international police force and a legislature, the result

---

[15] Philip C. Jessup, *A Modern Law of Nations.* This is one of the two main proposals made in this stimulating book.

[16] H. Lauterpacht, "The Legal Aspect," in *Peaceful Change: An International Problem,* ed. C. A. Manning (London: Macmillan & Company, Ltd., 1937), p. 141.

might be *improvement*, but it certainly would not be the improvement of *international law*. Rather it would be its transformation into a centralized system of municipal law for a world state. Even if all the proposals to *improve* international law were adopted, which means to leave it essentially decentralized, there would be very little effect in its efficacy as a regulator of human conduct. If it is now incapable of effectively limiting the behavior of international decision-makers, the shortcomings are not within the system, but inherent defects of a decentralized legal system. Certainly the so-called balance of power—even its nuclear mutual deterrent phase—international law, collective security, and all the other aspects of international society so far considered, are inadequate regulators of international behavior. We shall next consider whether international morality and the control and elimination of armaments hold out favorable prospects in this regard.

SUGGESTED READINGS

Bishop, William W., ed., *International Law: Cases and Materials*. Englewood Cliffs, N.J.: Prentice-Hall, Inc., 1953.

Borchard, E. M., *Distinction Between Legal and Political Questions*. U.S. Sen. Doc. 118, 68th Cong., 1st sess., 1924. Washington, D.C.: Government Printing Office, 1924.

Bowett, D. W., *Self Defense in International Law*. Manchester: Manchester University Press, 1958.

Brierly, James L., *The Basis of Obligation in International Law, and Other Papers*. Selected and edited by Hersch Lauterpacht and C. H. M. Waldock. Oxford: The Clarendon Press, 1958.

————, *The Law of Nations: An Introduction to the International Law of Peace*, 5th ed. Oxford: The Clarendon Press, 1955.

Clark, Grenville and Louis B. Sohn, *World Peace through World Law*. Cambridge: Harvard University Press, 1958.

Corbett, Percy E., *Law and Society in the Relations of States*. New York: Harcourt, Brace & World, Inc., 1951.

————, *The Study of International Law*. Garden City, New York: Doubleday & Company, Inc., 1955.

De Visscher, Charles, *Theory and Reality in Public International Law*. trans. by Percy E. Corbett. Princeton: Princeton University Press, 1957.

Fitzmaurice, Gerald G., "The Foundations of the Authority of International Law and the Problem of Enforcement," *Modern Law Review*, XIX (Jan. 1956), 1-13.

Goodhart, Arthur L., "The Rule of Law and Absolute Sovereignty," *University of Pennsylvania Law Review*, CVI (May 1958), 943-63.

Gould, Wesley L., *An Introduction to International Law*. New York: Harper & Brothers, 1957.

Honig, Friedrich, "Progress in the Codification of International Law," *International Affairs*, XXXVI (Jan. 1960), 62-72.

Jenks, C. W., "International Law and Activities in Space," *International and Comparative Law Quarterly*, V (Jan. 1956), 99-114.

Jessup, Phillip C., *A Modern Law of Nations: An Introduction*. New York: The Macmillan Co., 1948.

———, "The Subjects of a Modern Law of Nations," *Michigan Law Review*, XLV (Feb. 1947), 383-408.

———, *Transnational Law*. New Haven: Yale University Press, 1956.

Kaplan, Morton A. and Nicholas de B. Katzenback, *The Political Foundations of International Law*. New York: John Wiley & Sons, Inc., 1961.

Kelsen, Hans, *Principles of International Law*. New York: Holt, Rinehart & Winston, Inc., 1952.

Kunz, Josef L., "The Changing Law of Nations," *American Journal of International Law*, LI (Jan. 1957), 77-83.

Lauterpacht, Sir Hersh, *The Development of International Law by the International Court, being a revised edition of the Development of International Law by the Permanent Court of International Justice*. London: Stevens, 1958.

———, *International Law and Human Rights*. London: Stevens, 1950.

Lissitzyn, Oliver James, *The International Court of Justice: Its Role in the Maintenance of International Peace and Security*. New York: Carnegie Endowment for International Peace, 1951.

Northedge, F. S., "Law and Politics between Nations," *International Relations*, I (Apr. 1957), 291-302.

Nussbaum, Arthur, *A Concise History of the Law of Nations*, rev. ed. New York: The Macmillan Co., 1954.

Oppenheim, Lassa F. L., *International Law: A Treatise*, ed. H. Lauterpacht, 8th ed. Vol. I, *Peace*. London, New York: Longmans, Green & Co., Inc., 1955.

Rodrigues, Jayme A., "International Law and Sovereignty: Remarks on the Persistence of an Idea," *Proceedings of the American Society of International Law, 1953*. (1953), pp. 17-20.

Schachter, Oscar, "The Role of International Law in the United Nations," *New York Law Forum*, III (Jan. 1957), 28-49.

Schuschnigg, Kurt, *International Law: An Introduction to the Law of Peace*. Milwaukee, Wisconsin: The Bruce Publishing Co., 1959.

Sohn, Louis B., ed., *Cases on United Nations Law*. Brooklyn, New York: The Foundation Press, Inc., 1956.

Stone, Julius, *Legal Controls of International Conflict: A Treatise on the Dynamics of Disputes and War-Law*. New York: Holt, Rinehart & Winston, Inc., 1954.

Triska, Jan F. and R. M. Slusser, "Treaties and Other Sources of Order in International Relations: The Soviet View," *American Journal of International Law*, LII (Oct. 1958), 699-726.

Wilk, Kurt, "International Law and Global Ideological Conflict: Reflections on the Universality of International Law," *American Journal of International Law*, XLV (Oct. 1951), 648-70.

Wilson, Robert R., "International Law and Some Contemporary Problems," *Proceedings of the American Society of International Law, 1958*, (1958), pp. 26-33.
Wright, Quincy, *Contemporary International Law: A Balance Sheet*. Garden City, New York: Doubleday & Company, Inc., 1955.

19

Morality and
International Relations

Moral and legal norms regulate the behavior of men in both their individual and their group relationships. They are the basis of order: by imposing duties on each man to respect the rights of others they enlarge the freedom of all. If moral standards were fully effective, laws would be unnecessary. Moral codes ordinarily undergird a legal system; only a dictator with absolute power could rule by law alone.

A community is marked by a consensus on right and wrong, and by respect for the rights of others. In a society lacking common standards there is little agreement on moral attitudes. Each asserts his own rights with little regard for those of his neighbors. A true community is also characterized by the principle of equality of rights and duties. No man is a master or slave of any other man. Furthermore, the welfare of the few is subordinated to that of the many. It is because these elements are largely lacking in international society that the term "international community" expresses a hope more than it describes reality. And because this is so, there are those who deny that there is an international moral code. Nevertheless, most people insist that the behavior of officials who act on behalf of their states in dealing with other states is subject to moral judgments.

WHAT IS MORALITY?

International morality is probably the most difficult subject in the entire field of International Relations. Its understanding requires a preliminary consideration of the meaning of morality. All may agree that morality is "right conduct." But what is right conduct?

Universalist, Perfectionist, and Absolutist Concepts

One comprehensive answer is that there is a single or universal moral standard embodying true right and justice, and that moral action is conformity to this standard. It follows that the measure of immorality is the degree to which one's behavior departs from the requirements of the moral code. This is a universalist, perfectionist, and absolutist view of morality. It is a universal standard because man is obliged, in all his roles, to follow it. It is perfectionist in that regardless of circumstances the code stands as a moral obligation. It is absolutist rather than relativist because it exists over and above man, depending on truth rather than on man's view of truth. You may, however, logically accept some of the component elements of the conception but reject others. (For example, you may hold that although there is a moral code, circumstances may justify departures from it.)

Several major assumptions are implicit in this formulation. First, there is one and only one standard of morality. True, some may believe it requires that you love your enemies whereas to others it means you should eat them. But at least one of these codes is immoral, according to the universalist view. Secondly, it is possible for men to know what behavior the moral code calls for. Perhaps it is engraved in the law of nature, to be read by any reasonable man who, by searching his conscience, knows right from wrong. Or it may be a part of divine law set forth in sacred books or revealed to individual man either directly by God or through his intermediaries on earth.

Thirdly, this single code obligates men regardless of the roles they fulfill. This means that individuals in their interpersonal relationships, in their roles as leaders of groups interacting with other leaders, as well as with individuals of their own or of other groups, are morally obligated to guide their actions by a common moral code. To do otherwise is to be immoral. Fourthly, moral requirements are the same regardless of circumstances. If it is wrong to kill, it is simply wrong to kill. Murder, capital punishment, aggressive war, war in self-defense, and the collective use of force to counter aggressive war are all equally immoral. Although circumstances, particularly those with which international decision-makers are so frequently confronted, may explain why man acts immorally, they do not justify his doing so. If one accepts the proposition that the requirements of the moral code are identical for man in all his roles, *international* morality can refer only to right action on the international scene. It does not mean, for example, that a man acts morally when he lies to and spies upon the officials of other states any more than when he takes similar action toward his wife or neighbor.

Relativist, "Double Standard," and Non-Perfectionist Views

Probably very few people subscribe without reservation to the first answer, along with all its implications, as to the meaning of morality. A relativist, for example, unlike an absolutist, rejects the notion that there is only one true standard of morality—hence he will probably prefer the term *mores* to morals. He may or may not be a perfectionist. In either case, he believes that ideas of right and the call of conscience vary because of differences in historical experience and culture. He doubts that equally reasonable men, even if they accept the thesis of a natural or divine law, will be able to agree on its content, especially if their backgrounds differ. He may feel strongly that it is immoral to eat one's enemies, but he knows no way to prove that his values are superior to that of the cannibal.

The third assumption, that one is obliged to follow a similar moral code in all his roles, is also challenged. As a parent, one may spank his own child, but not his neighbor or his neighbor's child. In his role as group leader, especially as an official of a state in conducting relations with other states, he is expected to act differently than he does toward the citizens of his own state. And in both roles the moral codes differ from those which obligate him as parent and neighbor. It is argued in particular that there are different codes for intergroup and interpersonal relations. Those who contend that there is a single code, and that circumstances do not warrant departure from it, are likely to contend that intergroup behavior is simply more immoral than is interpersonal behavior.

The non-perfectionist challenges the perfectionist's assumption that circumstances may not justify actions which under other conditions would be immoral. He believes that a millionaire who does not steal is not necessarily more moral, and he may be less so, than a poor man who steals to feed his starving children. In the latter instance it may be even more moral to steal than to be "honest" and to allow one's family to suffer.

Conduct and Values

So far we have been discussing codes of conduct without reference to ends or values, although it seems to be implicit in the perfectionist position that action is itself a value. Yet no action is inherently good or bad—hence, the test of its moral quality is its consequences. Is it wrong to kill? Very few people in this anthropocentric world feel it is immoral to kill an earthworm; "cow-slaughter" however, is condemned by all good Hindus; and most people cringe at the thought of taking human life. It is often said that the "ends do not justify the means"; and the morals of those who hold otherwise are questioned. But how else is one to judge whether action is justified? "All decision sacrifices something. It sacrifices the course of action not chosen, and the approval of those who do not like the decision."[1] And it may sacrifice much more: self-respect, pride, security, wealth, and human life. The question to be answered in all cases is simply this: is the whistle worth the price? Gandhi argued that ends, no matter how worthy they may be, never justify bad means. They corrupt the actors and befoul the ends themselves. Nehru, confronted with Gandhi's perfectionist ethics, once wrote:

Ends and means: were they tied up inseparably, acting and reacting on each other, the wrong means distorting and sometimes even destroying the end in view? But the right means might well be beyond the capacity of infirm and selfish human nature. What then was one to do? Not to act was a complete confession of failure and a submission to evil; to act meant often enough a compromise with some form of that evil, with all the untoward consequences that such compromises result in.[2]

Nehru concluded that one could only act with courage and dignity and stick to the ideals that give meaning to life. This may be the best that mortal man can do, for it is very difficult to determine the consequences of one's decisions—the total price paid for the whistle. The more complicated the situation, the more unpredictable are the consequences of action. In the uncertain international scene no man can clearly foresee the future results of today's acts. But not to act also requires a decision with equally unpredictable consequences.

Undoubtedly agreement on common values would be conducive to the development of a common moral code. For example, if there were agreement that the promotion of human welfare, rather than that of the nation-state, or even that of the state's inhabitants, was the touchstone of moral conduct, it would facilitate agreement on an international moral code. But it would not insure cooperation rather than conflict. Communists and democrats profess to basically similar ends, but they divide sharply on the methods by which their Utopias are to be achieved. Identical objectives, such as security, may also be sources of conflict if they are pursued under conditions in which gain for some means loss for others. If aims are dissimilar and divergent, as in conflicts between proponents of different kinds of world order, or of different political and economic systems, it will be difficult indeed to attain agreement on either legal or moral norms.

---

[1] Dean Acheson, *Power and Diplomacy* (Cambridge: Harvard University Press, 1958), p. 116.

[2] Jawaharlal Nehru, *The Discovery of India* (New York: The John Day Company, Inc., 1946), p. 13.

IS THERE AN INTERNATIONAL MORAL CODE?

It should be apparent that the answer one gives to this question is crucial, for in the absence of agreed ways in which one is morally obliged to behave there are no criteria for judgment. True, each actor may have his own peculiar moral code in accordance with which he attempts to behave and to judge others. But these are particular codes rather than an *international* moral standard of conduct. Only an *international* code will be capable of mobilizing the informal pressures which support both moral and legal norms. There will be no international community to rally to the cause of "egocentric morality."[3]

The question of whether there is an international moral code is answered in various ways. Some deny that one exists. Others, while believing there is such a standard, disagree on its content. The latter fall roughly into two groups. Some identify the international moral code with that for interpersonal relations. Other hold that there are moral norms, but ones peculiar to international society. According to the latter view, these are variations of group norms, but somewhat different from those which regulate intergroup behavior within integrated national communities.

Denial of the Existence of an International Moral Code

Realists from the days of Kautilya in ancient India, through Machiavelli in fifteenth-century Italy, to the modern exponents of *Machpolitik*, tend to deny the existence of a moral code among nations. Statesmen, of course, speak in high moral terms to justify the pursuit of self-interest. According to the Preamble of the Holy Alliance, the sovereigns of Austria, Prussia, and Russia proclaimed their sole guide to be "the precepts of that Holy Religion, the precepts of Justice, Christian Charity and Peace, which, far from being applicable only to private concerns, must have an immediate influence on the councils of Princes, and guide all their steps." This is *moralism*, however, rather than morality. The result is generally deleterious. "National morale and international prestige are *casualties* of moral outlooks that are either too egocentric or too pretentious. A country's moral stock in the world rises and falls as its moral claims are plausible and convincing and its policies in line with its declarations."[4] Furthermore, "the periods of greatest decline in inter-

---

[3] The author is indebted for this term to Vernon Van Dyke, *International Politics* (New York: Appleton-Century-Crofts, Inc., 1957), pp. 306, 308.

[4] Kenneth W. Thompson, *Political Realism and the Crisis of World Politics* (Princeton: Princeton University Press, 1960), p. 135.

national morality have come when national purposes have been presented as pure and unsullied goals for acceptance or rejection by the rest of the world."[5]

It is sometimes contended that although from the seventeenth to the nineteenth century international morality had a more or less prominent part in guiding the affairs of states, it has since declined or disappeared altogether. Two factors account for this situation. Then the international moral code was primarily a personal one among monarchs. Likewise, there was a group of professional diplomats, men whose primary loyalty was to their professional counterparts and who felt perfectly at ease in offering their professional service in the international market place. With the disappearance of absolute monarchy and the growth of democracy and nationalism, international relations was transformed from personal into group relations. Instead of a common moral code, each nation now pursued its own interests which it dressed in the garb of universal morality. Diplomats served the national interest with the consequent severance of the ties of professionalism. Secondly, international relations was essentially European-centered, and there natural law was regarded as universal moral norm. By the nineteenth century the doctrine of positive law and moral relativity undermined the belief in natural law. Of perhaps greater consequence was the enlargement of the international system to encompass the varied cultures and beliefs of the entire world. With this extension there was no longer a common theological and philosophical basis for legal and moral norms. This difficulty was compounded with the growth of fascism and communism in the nineteen-twenties. Today, added to the cultural diversities and the "nationalistic universalism" is the dichotomy between the communist and the democratic worlds.

Under these conditions realists counsel the pursuit of the "national interest." They warn, however, that only if national objectives are strictly limited, similar interests of other nations respected, and the temptation to indulge in moralistic crusades avoided, will the compromises between nations necessary to prevent total war be possible. Contending that Americans need to abandon the concept of "total victory," which springs from their "legalistic-moralistic" approach to world affairs, George F. Kennan writes:

But it will mean the emergence of a new attitude among us toward many things outside our borders that are irritating and unpleasant today—an attitude more like that of the doctor toward those physical phenomena in the human body that are neither pleasing nor fortunate—an attitude of detachment and soberness and readiness to reserve judgment. It will mean that we will have the modesty to admit that our own national interest is all that we are really capable of knowing and understanding—and the courage to recognize that if

---

[5] *Ibid.*, p. 168.

our own purposes and undertakings here at home are decent ones, unsullied by arrogance or hostility toward other people or delusions of superiority, then the pursuit of our national interest can never fail to be conducive to a better world. This concept is less ambitious and less inviting in its immediate prospects than those to which we have so often inclined, and less pleasing to our image of ourselves. To many it may seem to smack of cynicism and reaction. I cannot share these doubts. Whatever is realistic in concept, and founded in an endeavor to see both ourselves and others as we really are, cannot be illiberal.[6]

While counseling pursuit of the national interest, modestly conceived, those who deny the existence of an international moral code contend that there is nothing immoral about a sole concern with national interest. As we have suggested above, the test of the morality of action is its purpose and consequences. If one's only values are those which are subsumed under the nebulous national interest, then to further them is the only moral course, for nothing else matters. But to the Christian, the Buddhist, the Hindu, and the followers of Islam, the nation is a false god. Likewise, the humanist believes that it is to the welfare of all men, rather than to the sovereign state, or even exclusively to his own fellow nationals, that loyalty is primarily due. Nevertheless, the pursuit of one's narrow interests is less dangerous, and probably more moral, than attempting to foist on others one's own narrow view of universal truth.

Personal Codes as
International Moral Standards

There is a large and distinguished group which contends that the moral standards that guide men in their personal behavior apply with equal force in their group relations, including those between states, international organizations, and dependent peoples. Lofty precepts applicable in private concerns must also "have an immediate influence on the Councils of Princes and Guide all their steps." President Wilson and Colonel House laid stress on the identity of private and state morality. In his 1917 address to Congress, calling for a declaration of war, Wilson proclaimed that "we are at the beginning of an age in which it will be insisted that the same standards of conduct and of responsibility . . . shall be observed among nations and their governments that are observed among the individual citizens of civilized states."[7] The first article of an early American draft of the League Covenant reads as follows: "The same standards of honor and ethics shall prevail internationally and in affairs

---

[6] *American Diplomacy, 1900-1950* (Chicago: The University of Chicago Press, 1951), pp. 102-03.

[7] Ray Stannard Baker and William E. Dodd, eds., *Public Papers of Woodrow Wilson: War and Peace* I, (New York: Harper & Brothers, 1927), II.

of nations as in other matters. The agreement or promise of a Power shall be inviolate."[8]

It is one thing for a person to feel that private individuals and statesmen should act "honorably, justly, and with forthrightness," and quite another to determine that a common code obligates all alike. Professor Herbert Butterfield, Cambridge historian, contends that there is a single ethic. Quite understandably, he believes it derives from a "higher law," according to which all values center in the human personality. This requires men to have "respect for the other man's personality, the other man's end."[9] Butterfield also holds that there is an international order to which the interests of states should be subordinated. Both morals and self-interest require that "national egotism" be "checked, superseded and transcended."[10]

Belief in a higher law and its moral content is an act of faith. Even if there be such it is of little use unless there is agreement on its essentials. Although men generally insist that international behavior is a fit subject for moral judgment, there is no reliable information available as to their criteria of assessment. It is uncertain to what extent they agree on the norms which should regulate interstate behavior, whether they believe these are based on a higher law, whether they are the same standard that they apply to personal behavior, or to what extent they are perfectionists or non-perfectionists. Perhaps UNESCO should undertake a world-wide inquiry into these questions of international morality.

A "Double Standard" of Morals

If there be an international moral code, i.e., common norms which most ordinary men as well as statesmen feel obliged to follow, but private norms are not applicable, then international standards must be of a somewhat different kind. Those who so contend usually argue that intergroup norms generally are different from interpersonal ones, and that the former are considerably less demanding. One possible explanation is that individuals, frustrated in their personal lives, and under social pressures to suppress their views, identify themselves with the collectivity. Lost in the group, individuals seek vicarious outlets for their vices which become collective virtues. With the growth of nationalism, even though a nation may be made up of men of good will toward their fellow men in general,

---

[8] Charles Seymour, ed., *Intimate Papers of Colonel House* (Boston: Houghton Mifflin Company, 1928), IV, 28.

[9] Herbert Butterfield, "Morality and Historical Process in International Affairs," unpublished manuscript for the June 12, 1956, meeting of the Columbia University Seminar on Theory of International Politics, p. 2, as cited in Thompson, *Political Realism and the Crisis of World Politics*, p. 139. See also Butterfield's *Christianity, Diplomacy and War* (London: Abingdon Press, 1954).

[10] "Morality and Historical Process," p. 10, as cited in Thompson, p. 142.

their collective loyalty to the nation-state requires their decision-makers
to disregard the rights of other nations. In a sense, the virtue of personal
willingness to sacrifice for the nation becomes a public menace.[11] In the
words of Cavour, "If we had done for ourselves what we did for the state,
what scoundrels we would have been."

Carried to its extreme, this tendency would leave no room for any international moral code, as contended by those discussed above. While
recognizing that group, and especially interstate moral norms are different, and when compared with those applicable to individual behavior,
depart further from an ideal code such as the golden rule, it is contended
that they nevertheless exist. If the international society is as lacking in the
features of a true community as we have pictured it throughout this study,
it seems reasonable to assume that however ordinary men think international decision-makers ought to behave, the standard is both different
and lower, in ideal terms, from the way they feel they ought to treat their
neighbors.

We are again confronted with the problem of determining the content
of international standards. If public proclamations—in speeches, treaties,
and charters—are to be taken at face value, we have evidence in
abundance of what they require. It is difficult, however, to determine how
and to what extent these differ from personal norms, in part because the
latter vary greatly among different societies. The problem of separating
the statements made for public consumption from those which serve as
guides to conduct is even more complex and indeed may be impossible
of solution. Even Genghis Khan, Hitler, Mussolini, and Stalin professed
to believe in certain minimum moral standards among all nations. The
UN Charter and the Declaration of Human Rights contain contemporary
evidence of publicly professed moral norms. Nations undertake moral,
and in some instances even legal obligations to "save succeeding
generations from the scourge of war . . . , establish conditions under
which justice and respect for the obligations arising from treaties . . .
can be maintained . . . , promote social progress and better standards
of life in larger freedom . . . , practice tolerance . . . , recognize the
principle that the interests of the inhabitants [of their dependent areas]
are paramount . . . , promote . . . [their] well-being . . . ," and to
treat everyone "without distinction of any kind, such as race, colour, sex,
language, religion, political or other opinion, national or social origin,
property, birth or other status." Professor Claude sees the "town meeting"
of the UN as a rudimentary institutional setting for the formulation of "a
not inconsiderable list of generally agreed international standards: prohibition of aggressive warfare, avoidance of forcible intervention except

---

[11] See R. Niebuhr, *Christian Realism and the Political Problem* (New York: Charles
Scribner's Sons, 1959).

under extreme provocation, respect for a minimum standard of human rights, recognition of the legitimacy of aspirations for self-government and economic development, etc."[12] He believes that the "validity and efficacy" of international moral restraint is "largely attributable to the functioning of the newly-institutionalized international forum."[13]

IS INTERNATIONAL BEHAVIOR IMMORAL?

To those who reject the notion of an international moral code, it is meaningless to inquire concerning its observance. But to others the question is as important as it is complex, and to many it is a source of profound dejection. In the popular view, international morality and law are breached more often than they are observed. Those who accept a single standard and a perfectionist concept are quite naturally inclined to view the scene as blacker than are those less exacting in their demands, especially if they accept the principle of extenuating circumstances. Whether one holds to an absolutist or relativist view seems to be of little significance with respect to this problem. The standard, a perfectionist or non-perfectionist viewpoint, and one's conception of how international decision-makers behave, are the factors which determine one's judgment of international morality, or the lack of it. Obviously, performance will depart further from high than from less lofty standards. If there be a single standard of norms, and conformance to it on the domestic scene be really as ideal as is sometimes pictured, and interstate behavior as black as it is painted, then international morals are deplorable. One may suspect, however, that this is a contrast between an over-idealized view of intra-state relations and an exaggerated picture of the immoral international politician. If a realistic view of business, pedagogical, and political ethics on the domestic scene were to be compared with how international statesmen actually behave, the differences in their shades of gray might indeed be difficult to discern, and in the eyes of the non-perfectionist they might disappear entirely. Both these propositions are disputable, and reliable evidence is admittedly hard to come by.

The non-perfectionist contends that most men are potential criminals, and that few are capable, come what may, of adhering to the moral standards they profess. There are two possible interpretations of non-perfectionist ethics. One is that there are certain moral norms which it is reasonable and just to expect men to follow under normal circumstances, but that extraordinary conditions call for and justify violations of the code. It may be equally if not more logical to conceptualize moral norms for each particular circumstance. For example, Claude maintains that

---

[12] Claude, *Swords into Plowshares*, p. 327.
[13] *Ibid.*, p. 328.

contemporary standards call for avoidance of forcible intervention *except under extreme provocation.* In other words, the norm permits such intervention in a situation of this kind.[14]

An extreme statement of this proposition is that necessity knows no law. It has even been contended that under certain circumstances statesmen act out of necessity, having no choice in the matter. Taken literally, this is a deterministic proposition, and therefore inappropriate for moral judgment. One does not condemn a nuclear bomb for destroying life; those who decide to drop the bomb, however, as long as they have any choice in the matter, *are* subject to moral judgments. Are men really compelled by the "necessities of state" to engage in "power politics"? Arnold Wolfers contends:

> It confuses the moral issue to state the case in this way. The "necessities" in international politics and for that matter in all spheres of life do not push decision and action beyond the realm of moral judgment; they rest on moral choice themselves. If a statesman decides that the dangers to the security of his country are so great that a course of action which must lead to war is necessary, he has placed an exceedingly high value on an increment of national security.[15]

In short, it may be necessary to pursue a course of action which will lead to war if certain values are to be pursued, but the choice of values still remains open. One may suspect that actions often justified by necessity are actually nothing of the sort. Rather they are taken because the values of a humane or Christian ethic pale into insignificance when placed against other ideological values, be they those of nationalism, communism, or fascism. This should not be difficult to believe when we recall that "Christians" have put to death their fellow men who failed to interpret the gospel in terms of the prevailing orthodoxy.

To the non-perfectionist, whatever his moral code, *morality consists of doing his best, under the circumstances.* He may believe, along with Nehru, that either action or inaction brings evil in its train. One must choose among the lesser evils.

The non-perfectionist's choice may be regarded with horror by righteous men. Yet who among us who are less than saints do not follow it? Most men are willing to kill other men in self-defense, and in "just" wars. Few will admit, at the time at least, that their country fights unjustly. And who does not believe that men should be punished for their crimes, perhaps even by taking their lives for their more horrendous ones? This

---

[15] "Statesmanship and Moral Choice," *World Politics,* I (January, 1949), 187. I wish to express my indebtedness to Mr. Wolfers for the stimulating ideas gained from this excellent article.

[14] Perhaps this second interpretation is really perfectionism, for it seems to imply that there is a different standard for each circumstance.

may be just and moral, but it hardly conforms to the tenets of "love thy enemies," and "recompense no man evil for evil."

Far from being an easy course, the non-perfectionist "ethic of responsibility," as Max Weber terms it,[16] places almost impossible demands on even the most wise and conscientious: who can really predict the consequences of his decisions? Assuming the existence of some kind of moral standards, should it have been clear in advance, or is it today, whether the British, French, and Israeli decision-makers acted morally or immorally in their invasion of Egypt in 1956? If the action were immoral, was the American intervention in the Lebanon two years later less so? What about the moral implications of the behavior of the United States in the successful Guatemalan intervention of 1954, or the ill-fated Cuban episode of early 1961? Were these essentially different morally from the Soviet part in the 1948 communist *coup d'etat* in Czechoslovakia, or intervention in Hungary in 1956? Were all of these events justified by "extreme provocation" or were the United States and the Soviet Union equally guilty of immorality? Or was the United States behavior moral, or at least less immoral, than was that of the Soviet Union? Is the national use of force inherently immoral? We have noted that under the prevailing decentralized international legal system peaceful change is in many instances impossible. It is widely assumed, especially among states satisfied with the international status quo, that it is immoral to use force to change it, but quite moral to defend with force that which exists. The proposition is advanced here that it may, although it depends on the circumstances, be more moral to use costly means, including a resort to war, to change an unjust status quo than it is to defend an unjust one. There are few Americans who believe that their ancestors acted immorally when they fought for "justice" in 1776, or wrested a continent from its previous possessors, and not always by peaceful means. Would it be immoral to use force to oust a communist regime from a legally constituted position in the Western Hemisphere? To the perfectionist the answers are relatively easy. The non-perfectionist, however, will search his mind and his heart for even tentative conclusions to knotty questions of this kind.

SANCTIONS OF INTERNATIONAL MORALITY

International decision-makers may observe international moral norms because of either internal or external pressures. Among the former are those which spring from their own consciences, as well as the sanctions of domestic public opinion. These we have termed "egocentric morality." Despite the fact that people in general are more likely to condemn other

---

[16] "Politics as a Vocation," in *From Max Weber: Essays in Sociology* (New York: Oxford University Press, Inc., 1946), p. 121.

governments than they are their own, the latter are not entirely immune. Preventive war, even against a powerful enemy, conquest and permanent occupation of weak countries short of "necessities of state" or as an incidental outcome of war, are largely ruled out in the Western world by the force of domestic public opinion. It is almost impossible to visualize any circumstances under which the American people would tolerate war against Canada, and almost as difficult to do so in the case of Mexico. Probable domestic repercussions to the use of American force against Cuba in 1961 seem to have had something to do with the fact that they were not employed directly. Perhaps considerations of this sort explain in part why nowadays nations fight only "defensive" wars, or in any case only "just" ones! Nor should it be overlooked that states, for various reasons, may prefer a stable world order. They may, therefore, decide to forego the satisfaction of certain lesser desires in the interests of a basic long-term goal. Wanton violation of an undesirable norm may weaken respect for norms in general.

The force of "world public opinion" must also be reckoned with. Otherwise why would nations be so concerned with the "image" they present to the world, and forever attempt to justify their actions within and outside the forums of the UN? Those who argue that power alone counts are likely to overlook this fact. We have contended that the capacity of a state depends on consent as well as power, and that the more it has of the former the less need there is for the latter. Neither the lack of power on the part of the United States, nor the fear of repercussions at home were the principal reasons for the American reluctance to use their own forces in Cuba in 1961, or in other areas in recent years where the provocations have been great. Rather, consideration was given to a "decent respect for the opinions of mankind," loss of which would reduce American capacity to realize its objectives.

It is not that countries simply want to be liked. Americans in general do, however, seem to want approbation, and feel incensed when other people do not respond with gratitude to acts of American "benevolence." Perhaps respect is a more valuable international asset than gratitude, and to be feared is preferable to being disregarded.

In any case, an unfavorable opinion of a country abroad must be counted a liability which carries with it certain relatively tangible consequences. The latter are basically similar to the informal sanctions behind legal norms.[17] Sanctions of this type may be referred to as self-interest, which means that the costs of probably retaliatory actions may outweigh the values of the ends to be achieved. A reputation for dependa-

---

[17] For a consideration of sanctions of law, which in most instances also serve to strengthen moral norms, see Morton A. Kaplan and Nicholas de B. Katzenbach, *The Political Foundations of International Law* (New York: John Wiley & Sons, Inc., 1961), Chapter 13.

bility is an asset not lightly to be cast aside by responsible statesmen. Otherwise nations would not clothe their most ruthless acts in the garb of righteousness. It may be argued that the United States could not afford to remain aloof from the Lebanon crisis of 1958, despite the risks involved, because of promises previously made. Perhaps a nation that "stands on principle" is less likely to be blackmailed than is one which acts out of temporary expediency.[18]

SUMMARY AND CONCLUSIONS

In view of the complexity of the subject of international morality, and the fact that very able and conscientious men have wrestled with it to no basic agreement, it would be reckless indeed for this writer to offer conclusions with an air of dogmatic finality. Yet here as elsewhere to decide not to take a position is also a decision.

Whatever be their content, and regardless of whether they be viewed as absolute or relative, simple or double standard, there do seem to be international moral norms on the basis of which international behavior is judged, and for violations of which informal sanctions are imposed. Whether they be viewed as absolute or relative is far less significant than the extent to which there is agreement that men are morally obliged to behave in certain ways. Their quality is perhaps more important, but a judgment on this point is largely a personal matter. In the ultimate resort, one's view of what is right can only rest on one's own values and assessment of the total consequences of action. The certainty of the absolutist is perhaps more satisfying than are the uneasy and tentative views of the relativist. On the other hand, the most brutal and total conflicts have not been between right and wrong, but between opposing forces each convinced that it battles for the Lord. Those who deny the existence of international moral standards altogether, provided they are humble enough to recognize their own moral limitations, are likely to be less eager than is the absolutist to engage in moralistic crusades.

The perfectionist position is an almost impossible one for those whose characters are less than flawless, with insights short of omniscience. Needless to say, very few of Plato's philosopher-kings have occupied seats of political power, and if such men existed they would be unlikely to gain or retain office in free elections. The argument that there are peculiar moral norms to fit each set of circumstances may be logically convincing, but it is too much of a rubber standard to serve as a useful guide to conduct. Yet it must be confessed that it is little less so than the concept that almost anything goes if "necessity" is great enough. But if there be no practical alternative, what are imperfect men to do? One answer may be that

---

[18] The author is indebted to Kaplan and Katzenbach, *ibid.*, p. 345, for this idea.

man has a basic duty to build an international order in which extenuating circumstances would be less likely to occur. Directing his remarks to those who would exclude morals from the "determinants of foreign policy," Professor Corbett maintains that they

. . . seem to forget, in their intense preoccupation with the State and its power, that the State is nothing more than a human device for satisfying the needs and enhancing the welfare of the individual. Among the needs of the individual I would argue that we must include his aspirations, even those directed to raising the moral level of national behavior. Not uncommon among those aspirations is that of serving a world larger than the national group. Statesmen themselves, who make decisions in foreign policy, are not immune from such urges. I submit that the desire to see the United States directly and systematically useful to the world at large is strong enough in American statesmen and the American public to operate as a substantial factor in foreign policy decisions, and that a State which did not attempt to implement such a desire would be failing to serve one of the purposes for which it exists. Granted that material prosperity and physical security are two of the primordial objects of political association, what prevents us, as civilization advances, from recognizing public purposes of less palpable content? Is it, indeed, quite realistic to deny that such objects are imposed upon some governments by their constituents?[19]

SUGGESTED READINGS

Acheson, Dean, "Morality, Moralism, and Diplomacy," *Yale Review*, XLVII (June 1958), 481-93.

Barraclough, Geoffrey, "History, Morals, and Politics," *International Affairs*, XXXIV (Jan. 1958), 1-15.

Butterfield, Herbert, *Christianity and History*. London: G. Bell & Sons, Ltd., 1949.

————, *History and Human Relations*. London: William Collins Sons & Co., Ltd., 1951.

————, *International Conflict in the Twentieth Century: A Christian View*. New York: Harper & Brothers, 1960.

————, "The Scientific *versus* the Moralistic Approach in International Affairs," *International Affairs*, XXVII (Oct. 1951), 411-22.

Fox, William T. R., "National Interest and Moral Principles in Foreign Policy: The Reconciliation of the Desirable and the Possible," *The American Scholar*, XVIII (Spring 1947), 212-16.

---

[19] Percy E. Corbett, *Morals, Law, and Power in International Relations* (Los Angeles: The Haynes Foundation, 1956), pp. 5-6.

Halle, L. J., "Foreign Policy and Whose Morality?" *Virginia Quarterly Review*, XXXIII (Winter 1957), 1-16.

Huizinga, J. K., "On the High Cost of International Moralizing," *The Fortnightly Review*, CLVI (Nov. 1944), 295-300.

Kennan, George F., "Foreign Policy and Christian Conscience," *Atlantic Monthly*, CCIII (May 1959), 44-49.

Merchant, Livingston T., "The Moral Element in Foreign Policy," *Department of State Bulletin*, XXXVII (Sept. 2, 1957), 374-79.

Morgenthau, Hans J., "National Interest and Moral Principles in Foreign Policy: The Primacy of the National Interest," *The American Scholar*, XVIII (Spring 1949), 207-12.

Nagle, William J., ed., *Morality and Modern Warfare*. Baltimore: Helicon Press, Inc., 1960.

Niebuhr, Reinhold, *Christian Realism and Political Problems*. New York: Charles Scribner's Sons, 1953.

————, *Moral Man and Immoral Society: A Study of Ethics and Politics*. New York; London: Charles Scribner's Sons, 1932.

Sterling, Richard W., *Ethics in a World of Power: The Political Ideas of Friedrich Meinecke*. Princeton, N.J.: Princeton University Press, 1958.

Thompson, Kenneth W., *Christian Ethics and the Dilemmas of Foreign Policy*. Durham, North Carolina: Duke University Press, 1959.

————, "The Limits of Principle in International Politics: Necessity and the New Balance of Power," *Journal of Politics*, XXX (Aug. 1958), 437-67.

————, "National Security and Morality: An American View," *International Journal*, XIII (Autumn 1958), 265-79.

————, *Political Realism and the Crisis of World Politics: An American Approach to Foreign Policy*. Princeton, N.J.: Princeton University Press, 1960.

Trivers, Howard, "Morality and Foreign Affairs," *Virginia Quarterly Review*, XXXII (Summer 1956), 345-60.

Weldon, T. D., *States and Morals: A Study in Political Conflicts*. New York: Whittlesey House, McGraw-Hill Book Co., Inc., 1947.

Wolfers, Arnold, "Statesmanship and Moral Choice," *World Politics*, I (Jan. 1949), 175-95.

20

Disarmament
and Arms Control

Historically, disarmament has been more a subject of special pleading by reformers than it has of hard-headed analysis by scholars, more a matter to be treated cavalierly by statesmen than to be negotiated with serious intent. "There is no more striking fact in the history of international relations than that so serious a question should have been treated with such amateurish simplicity as has been the case in the plans for armament reduction."[1]

Today there is a sense of urgency. Men best acquainted with the facts are most likely to believe that something must be done if civilization is not to be destroyed in a nuclear holocaust. They may not believe that "general and complete disarmament" is likely or even desirable; they nevertheless hold that there is some possibility, through control or reduction of national armaments, of less of a "balance of terror" and more of a "balance of prudence." This concern, coupled with a belief and faith that the problem is not completely intractable, has been expressed in a growing body of literature in which very able minds have grappled with the problem, and have attempted to unravel its complexities and to suggest workable plans which are also politically feasible. Far from being characterized by "amateurish simplicity," these writings reflect a high level of sophisticated scholarship.[2] Equally encouraging is the fact that the more

---

[1] J. T. Shotwell, *On the Rim of the Abyss* (New York: The Macmillan Co., 1936), p. 277.

[2] "Arms Control," *Daedalus*, Special Issue (Fall 1960), contains contributions by twenty-one authors and extensive annotations of seventy-three documents, books, and articles. Eighteen of the above papers are expanded and updated in Donald G. Brennan, ed., *Arms Control, Disarmament and National Security* (New York: George Braziller, Inc., 1961).

responsible members of the military forces are just as concerned as are the most ardent pacifists. In the early nineteen-sixties there was evidence that the work of the scholars was beginning to have an impact on United States policy. Only the unmitigated cynic rejects disarmament negotiations as completely useless, and likely to raise completely false hopes; only the perfectionist gives up in dispair when the millennium of general and complete disarmament seems impossible of attainment.

ARE DISARMAMENT, ARMS CONTROL, AND NATIONAL SECURITY COMPATIBLE?

Terminology is in a transitory stage. Disarmament is a traditional term. Taken literally, it means reducing or eliminating the matériel and human instrumentalities for the exercise of physical violence. But over the course of years it has come to mean anything having to do with the limitation, reduction, abolition, or control of such instrumentalities through the voluntary agreement of two or more states. Thus conceived, it excludes some things, unilateral disarmament for example, that are literally disarmament. On the other hand, it includes control which may not involve any reduction of arms.

"Arms control" is used by some writers as a generic term to include any kind of cooperation with respect to armaments which would curtail the arms race, reduce the probability of war, or limit its scope and violence.[3] It includes unilateral decisions of states, informal understandings among them, and formally negotiated and institutionalized agreements. The stress is on reducing the *incentives* rather than the *capacity* for war. This does not mean that it might not require substantial arms reduction; on the other hand, it might mean their increase, at least in certain categories. Likewise, the monetary cost might be more rather than less, for the costs of control measures could more than overbalance savings, even in the event of a measure of disarmament.

We prefer to distinguish between "disarmament" and "arms control." The former will refer to the reduction of war matériel and personnel in accordance with international agreements. Arms control will mean all international agreements and measures to regulate the use of arms which may be permitted, and to enforce the observance of prohibited actions, such as, but not confined to, the possession of any or certain types of weapons and military personnel. This distinction has become a source of propaganda in the Cold War, the Soviet Union charging the United States with wanting control without disarmament, and the latter counter-charging the Soviet Union with advocating disarmament without control. There is some truth and considerable distortion in these charges, judging from actual proposals made by both antagonists.

---

[3] See Thomas C. Schelling and Morton H. Halperin, *Strategy and Arms Control* (New York: The Twentieth Century Fund, 1961), pp. 2 ff.

What is the relationship between disarmament and arms control? First, control is a condition of disarmament. It is quite clear that the United States and its allies will not agree to disarm unless by inspection and other control measures they can have some assurance that the Soviet Union and the countries within the communist bloc will comply with the terms of the agreement. The Soviet Union has never denied the need for control. The controversy, rather, has been over its form and timing. Khrushchev has said on several occasions that he would agree to very strict measures of control once "general and complete disarmament" has been attained.[4]

Secondly, the basic objectives of disarmament and control are identical —to prevent, limit, or reduce the probability of the *illegitimate* use of force in international society. The use of force would be legitimate if employed under collective security provisions or by an international police force. In fact, if there were substantial disarmament, collective security might be a practical measure. Moreover, some kinds of international enforcement measures would in all probability be necessary to induce nations to agree to substantial disarmament, just as it would be essential to maintain the peace once they were disarmed. On the other hand, if the purpose of arms control is to stabilize the arms race, or to make mutual deterrence less risky, the use of force, or at least the threat of the use of national armed forces, is an essential part of the arrangement. Thirdly, disarmament and arms control may or may not be compatible. The prevention of war by deterrence, unilateral, or mutual, is obviously incompatible with its prevention by the elimination of armaments. Efforts to stabilize the military balance by maintaining armed forces at certain levels cannot be pursued simultaneously with their reduction below those levels. However, if stability can best be promoted by reduction, then deterrence requires the elimination of some armaments. Moreover, as we have noted, there may be *controlled disarmament* (or control to prevent rearmament) as well as *control of armaments*. Arms control, therefore, is perfectly consistent with, and even necessary to, a fully disarmed world. In short, the incompatibility is not between disarmament and arms control, but between *complete* disarmament as a means of controlling the use of force, and the reliance upon deterrence. For "stabilized deterrence as a concept is not committed in advance to any particular level of destructive power."[5]

Considerations such as these should be sufficient to set at ease those who feel there is an inherent contradiction between disarmament and arms control. Even more important, it should be equally plain that there is *not* a problem of disarmament and arms control versus military security. On the contrary, the former is a means to the latter. The military policy

---

[4] See *New York Times,* September 19, 1959, p. 9.
[5] Schelling and Halperin, *Strategy and Arms Control,* p. 59.

of a country can be "general and complete disarmament" in the interest of security. As a matter of fact, nearly all states are officially committed to that end, through UN resolutions and otherwise.

The international control, reduction, and elimination of armaments requires a major effort in international cooperation. Furthermore, it entails not alone, or essentially, cooperation among friendly states but between potential, or even actual enemies. For example, there may be agreement on attempts to control the use of arms in a war in order to keep it limited in its level of violence and localized in its scope. Do states have compatible objectives which will incline or permit them to agree on common methods to control the use of violence among them? The record of the past affords few grounds for optimism. Perhaps the principal new factor in the situation is the belief that the alternative to the uncontrolled armaments race is wholesale destruction or annihilation. Kant once suggested that a group of devils ought to be able to devise and agree on means to assure their survival, *provided* they were intelligent devils. Those who cope with the problem of armament are not devils, nor are they angels. They are rational men, but so far thy have not evidenced sufficient intelligence to insure human survival.

There is no reason to believe that all official proclamations, and all the thousands of hours spent around the conference tables, have been hypocritical concessions to the growing demands for doing something to control the arms race. It is true that "the concept of disarmament has achieved such ideological sanctity that international organizations are as likely to strike it off the agenda of debate as churches are to eliminate prayers from their Sunday Service."[6] Still, the problem of arms control and the reduction of armaments is taken seriously by informed men, including a growing number in the rank of the official international decision-makers. The Soviet Union seems to want disarmament, on its own terms of course, as does the United States. Both are motivated by economic considerations, the fear of destruction, and concern with the spread of nuclear weapons—the "N th" country problem. There are also grounds for believing that Soviet leaders are confident of their ability to achieve their ends, perhaps more expeditiously, and certainly with far less risk, if fear of nuclear-missile warfare could be eliminated or materially reduced.[7] If these assumptions are valid, and they are highly debatable, the problem is one of overcoming the obstacles, establishing the conditions, agreeing upon the methods, and implementing programs to reduce and control national armaments through international cooperation.[8]

---

[6] Inis L. Claude, Jr., *Swords into Plowshares*, p. 303.

[7] For an excellent discussion of Soviet attitudes toward disarmament and the forces which work both for and against Soviet agreement, see Richard J. Barnett, *Who Wants Disarmament?* (Boston: Beacon Press, 1960), pp. 56-98.

[8] See Robert R. Bowie, "Basic Requirements for Arms Control," and "Arms Control," *Daedalus*, Special Issue (Fall 1960), pp. 708-22.

GENERAL FACTORS IN
DISARMAMENT AND ARMS CONTROL

The possibility and probability of international agreement on disarmament and arms control, its nature and effectiveness, depend largely upon several key factors. Of these, two are favorable: (1) the fear of nuclear war, the desire for peace, and the belief that arms contribute to tensions and war; and (2) the instabilities and dangers growing out of the unregulated arms race. On the other hand there are serious obstacles: (1) nationalism and sovereignty; (2) the problem of the "ratio"; and (3) distrust among nations. Two additional factors: (1) the priority of disarmament or the settlement of political problems; and (2) economic considerations, work both for and against agreement.

Fear, Desire for Peace, and the
Belief that Arms Cause Wars

People the world over want peace; they believe disarmament would be conducive to peace; and they fear war and destruction unless there is disarmament. No statesmen of any country, therefore, dare proclaim that they disagree and refuse to negotiate to bring it about. To oppose disarmament is to be branded a warmonger. If for no other reason than to attain a propaganda advantage, negotiations for disarmament will continue. Although nothing is more difficult than to discover the real motives of statesmen, what they say seems to correspond to reality sufficiently to warrant the conclusion that many of them see the prevention of war as conducive to the realization of their interests, and some form of armament control as necessary to that end. Yet their views are diverse as to the possible and desirable forms it can and should take.

Scholars and statesmen disagree concerning the relationship between arms and peace. Some contend that wars cause arms whereas others believe arms cause war. We are concerned here with the question of the effects of general systems of armaments, arms races, and so forth. We are not concerned with whether unilateral disarmament or pacifism are conducive to peace. The question is: would war be less likely if arms generally were reduced or eliminated?

The negative argument is ardently, if not necessarily convincingly, advanced in the two following statements:

The international situation and the fundamental causes which sometimes lead to war cannot be altered substantially by intervention in the realm of military technology. A tool is nothing but a tool, and no amount of dialectical finesse has yet been able to adduce conclusive proof that weapons cause war and to disapprove that, on the contrary, it is war or the danger of war which produces the weapons.[9]

---

[9] Robert Strauz-Hupé and S. T. Possony, *International Relations in the Age of Conflict between Democracy and Dictatorship* (New York: McGraw-Hill Book Co., Inc., 1950), p. 591.

Although for centuries many peace advocates have believed that armaments cause wars,

in reality, the reverse is more nearly true: war machines are reduced only when peace seems probable, the expectation of conflict leads to competition in armaments, and armaments spring from war and from the anticipation of war. Yet men have long sought to put the cart before the horse—since the horse is intractable and best ignored, while the cart is moved about at will, even if to no effect.[10]

The opposite opinion is put quite as fervently and persuasively in the two following statements. The first represents the point of view of the American Friends Service Committee.

Can it be that rearmament, which we [the United States] have adopted in the interest of security, is itself contributing to our insecurity and to the insecurity of the world? . . . In the realm of arms, one nation's common sense is another nation's high blood pressure. Our arms create fear in Russia; Russian arms create fear in us. By seeking to deter the Russians by military might, we are inevitably forced to plunge the world into an arms race, and arms races are not conducive to security. Indeed, each new measure and counter-measure adopted by the principals in the name of defense has the effect of intensifying insecurity in both countries.[11]

The second statement is by Benjamin V. Cohen, former deputy United States representative on the United Nations Disarmament Commission.

Effective disarmament for peace should mean the elimination of mass armies as well as all instruments adaptable to mass destruction. Effective disarmament should relieve the world not only from the terror of all weapons of mass destruction but from the threat of mass armies without which no aggressor can accomplish his evil designs. A small militia with small arms is quite sufficient to cope with internal disorders.

If we knew of certainty that no nation was in a state of armed preparedness to undertake a war with any prospect of success or to accomplish an act of aggression by a quick, decisive blow, there would be a profound change in the climate of international relationships. . . . There would be much less danger of states seeking to strengthen and protect themselves in event of war by strategic settlements which themselves plant the seed of friction and war. Armaments aggravate tensions and fears among nations. By releasing tensions and fears, disarmament should facilitate and strengthen the process of peaceful settlement.[12]

---

[10] Frederick L. Schuman, *International Politics: The Western State System in Mid-Century*, 5th ed. (New York: McGraw-Hill Book Co., Inc., 1953), p. 230. See also Morgenthau, *Politics Among Nations*, pp. 326-30.

[11] *Steps to Peace: A Quaker View of U.S. Foreign Policy*, A Report Prepared for the American Friends Service Committee, 1951 (Pamphlet), pp. 13-14.

[12] Quoted from "Disarmament and International Law," address before the International Law Association, American Branch (New York: United States Mission to the United Nations, Press Release No. 1469, May 8, 1952), mimeographed, pp. 3-4. See also Ernest A. Gross, "Disarmament as One of the Vital Conditions of Peace," *Department of State Bulletin*, XXVIII (Mar. 30, 1953), 476.

The contention that arms are the fruits rather than the seeds of war was probably nearer the truth in a simpler age than the present. Then a smaller portion of a nation's resources were mobilized for war, weapons were less destructive, the rate of technological change slower, and, above all, the dangers of accident and miscalculation much less. As we noted in the previous discussion of "mutual deterrence," all this has changed in the modern period. Instability, a premium on a first strike, and the danger of pre-emptive war have increased immeasurably. Arms, or in any case the uncontrolled arms race, are presently, beyond any doubt, productive of tensions, conflict, and war.

To contend, however, that national armaments contribute to tensions and war is not to argue that they are their sole cause, and that with their elimination war would cease. To the easy argument that regardless of the causes of war complete disarmament would lead to peace by eliminating the means to fight, it may be replied with some levity that men could still use sticks and stones, nails and teeth. More seriously, the "prevention of war through the abolition of means" thesis overlooks the fact that complete disarmament would eliminate the hen but not the egg. Missiles and nuclear bombs might be abolished, but more could be hatched as long as the scientific and technological knowledge, and the factories and materials remain for producing instruments of war. Moreover, although complete abolition of armaments would reduce ready military capacity to zero, and thus place all states on an equal military status *for the moment*, disarmament alone would not eliminate *potential* unequal military power, any more than it would other forms of power. It would, however, certainly affect all of these. Effective international control measures would be particularly important to protect states lacking the eggs from replenishing their military arsenals in the event of the breakdown of a general disarmament agreement.

Nevertheless, if national armaments could be drastically reduced or eliminated, and effective international controls established, it appears probable that the effects on international society would be salutary, aside from the possible monetary savings. Certainly there is no example—and it is difficult to conceive of one—of a peaceful society even *with* government, in which individuals and contending groups were allowed the unlimited right to possess arms and armies. Order, law, and the outlawry of force and the instruments of force among contending parties are highly conducive, perhaps indispensable, to a peaceful society. Certainly they are necessary to real peace as contrasted with cold war.

The basic problem, however, is to determine whether there are possible conditions under which a disarmed world would be better than an armed one, to formulate proposals to realize these conditions, and to obtain the necessary agreements to establish them. To cite only one difficulty, there are some who argue that once a nation has a supply of nuclear weapons it would be virtually impossible, by any known inspection methods, to determine whether it had hidden, say fifty bombs, even though it had agreed to the abolition of all such weapons. If other nations acted in good faith, and disarmed completely, they would be at the mercy of the nation that cheated. But if each nation were allowed, let us say three hundred weapons, it would not matter greatly if one nation possessed an additional fifty hidden ones.[13]

Instability

The relative stability of military technology in past periods contrasts sharply with its instability in the present era, in which the very rate of change is one of its chief characteristics. This instability proceeds in two dimensions—the spread of nuclear weapons to more and more countries (the "N th" country problem), and a race for more and improved weapons by the present nuclear-missile powers.[14] At least a dozen countries, including Communist China, East Germany, and Czechoslovakia, will be capable of producing nuclear weapons in the near future. It is generally assumed that whereas the control of these weapons is technically manageable at present, when possessed by a dozen or more nations this would no longer be so. Even if, as some argue, very few of these nations have the capacity to maintain modern weapons systems, including missiles and possibly outer space vehicles, the situation would still be of great concern.[15] Undoubtedly fear of the spread of military technology is a factor conducive to agreement among the present nuclear powers. It is an especially important factor contributing to the possibility of success in nuclear test negotiations. Yet the very possibility that other powers will insist upon first attaining this new "symbol of nationhood" before agreeing to its control is not an optimistic prospect. France has certainly shown no interest in agreeing to a test ban.

A "stable" relationship between two or more nuclear powers has been defined as one "in which circumstances and influences conducive to and favoring the initiation of total nuclear war are countered and outweighed by opposing factors."[16] The validity of the argument for "nuclear deterrence" rests upon the proposition that no nation can, by a knock-out blow in a surprise attack, destroy the capacity of its victims to retaliate. It also assumes men will act rationally, and accidental war will be avoided. The

---

[13] See Henry A. Kissinger, "Arms Control, Inspection and Surprise Attack," *Foreign Affairs*, XXXVIII (July 1960), 557; Albert Wohlstetter, "The Delicate Balance of Terror," *Foreign Affairs*, XXXVII (Jan. 1959), 211-34.

[14] See Howard Simons, "World-Wide Capability for Production and Control of Nuclear Weapons," *Daedalus*, LXXXVIII (Summer 1959), 385-409.

[15] See above, p. 272.

[16] "Developments in Military Technology and Their Impact on United States Strategy and Foreign Policy," p. 6.

volatile nature of technology and the possibility of a surprise attack which might be decisive, mean that

> every country lives with the nightmare that even if it puts forth its best efforts its survival may be jeopardized by a technological breakthrough on the part of its opponent. It also knows that every invention opens up the prospect of many others. No country can protect itself against *all* the technological possibilities increasingly open to its opponents. Conversely, an advantage once achieved will produce a powerful incentive to exploit it, for the scientific revolution which made it possible also insures that it will be transitory.[17]

The fear of instability and the dangers and temptations inherent in it are major factors conducive to achieving some kind of an arms limitation agreement. At the same time, the increasing momentum of the extensive and intensive spread of military technology makes disarmament increasingly difficult. The fact that decision-makers have been deeply influenced by the widely accepted belief that no conceivable inspection system would prevent cheating by a power that possessed nuclear weapons prior to the inauguration of the inspection system, is a prime evidence of this contention. Although the belief that stability is possible is conducive to controlled disarmament, it is not necessarily favorable to a material reduction in armaments.

Nationalism and Sovereignty

Nationalistic attitudes, which place a high premium on state sovereignty, make it very difficult to obtain agreement on organs endowed with sufficient authority to control states in their use and possession of arms. Even inspection to prevent surprise attack, an important element in mutual deterrence, requires freedom of movement that every nationalist is bound to resent and resist. International plans and organs to apply sanctions in the case of violations, to interpret disarmament agreements, and perhaps to bring about peaceful change if forceful change is to be ruled out, inevitably run up against the obstacle of preferences for sovereignty over survival.

That nationalism and sovereignty are not insuperable obstacles, however, may be argued on at least two grounds. First, people able to believe that each of the fifty states of the United States is sovereign should find it possible to accomodate a considerable degree of centralization in international society and still feel that the nation has retained its sovereignty. Secondly, loss of the ability of states to perform their historical and basic protective function is due in considerable part to the fact that missile-nuclear weapons systems have destroyed the possibility of defense, and thus rendered the sovereign state system obsolete. If the fact were understood, would not people be willing to make the adjustment necessary to realize disarmament? A persuasive argument can be advanced that the

---

[17] Kissinger, "Arms Control, Inspection and Surprise Attack," p. 557.

degree of sovereignty retained after these changes were made, and the greater assurance of personal survival, would be preferable to the destruction of nations and individuals that appears possible, and to many probable, if changes are not made. In short, moderate reforms would have more conservative consequences, even for sovereignty, than would a continuation of the arms race.

The "Ratio"

The problem of the "ratio" among the parties to a disarmament treaty is that of agreeing to changes that leave no party relatively worse off than before the agreement, and, ideally, better off. Hence the terms "balanced" or "proportionate" reductions. As long as states rely on military force to obtain their objectives, since power is a *relationship* rather than a thing, each party to disarmament negotiations must of necessity give major attention to the effect of any change on its relative power position. There is always the suspicion, usually quite justified, that a state is trying to strengthen itself and weaken its opponents.

Salvador de Madariaga illustrates the problem vividly in his fable of the animals' disarmament conference, told at the Geneva Disarmament Conference in 1932 in response to a proposal by Litvinov.

> When the animals had gathered, the lion looked at the eagle and said gravely, "We must abolish talons!" The tiger looked at the elephant and said, "We must abolish tusks." The elephant looked back at the tiger and said, "We must abolish claws and jaws."
>
> Thus each animal in turn proposed the abolition of the weapons he did not have, until at last the bear rose up and said in tones of sweet reasonableness:
>
> "Comrades, let us abolish everything—everything but the great universal embrace."[18]

Certainly the 1946 atomic weapons proposals of the United States were as one-sided as were those of the Soviets for abolishing these weapons.[19]

It is technically difficult to determine the military needs of states, and to measure the effect on their power positions of any particular reduction or limitation. John Foster Dulles gave it as the principal reason for the United States rejection of any substantial disarmament.[20] There are two ways of bypassing the difficulty. One is complete disarmament of all states. The other is to provide international protection through collective security or an international police force. These solutions would, of course, be acceptable only to states not interested in altering the international status quo by forceful means. Furthermore, reliance cannot be placed upon either a police force or collective security without a drastic reduction of armaments, at least of the major powers. Therefore, the problem of

---

18 Cited in the New York *Times,* Sept. 19, 1959, p. 1.
19 See below, pp. 422-24.
20 See below, pp. 425-26.

the ratio must be faced, rather than bypassed, until and unless national armaments are reduced drastically.

Distrust

It is often argued that disarmament and arms control, as well as the solution of other political problems, is impossible in the face of distrust. Distrust is a matter of degree in most social relationships. If there were perfect trust between nations, arms would be unnecessary and disarmament would not be a problem. Given complete distrust, human relations would be Hobbesian.

Yet there is no doubt that the degree of distrust which exists between the Soviet and non-Soviet blocs is an impediment to agreement on disarmament, as it is on other matters. Still, it is possible that the solution of the armaments problem would contribute to agreement on political questions, and consequently reduce distrust.[21] This assumes, of course, that distrust and political difficulties are in part functions of the fear generated by the armaments race. Distrust works in two directions. It hampers initial agreement, and it might lead to the breakdown should a disarmament scheme be put into operation. Yet, to the extent that statesmen believe distrust grows out of the fear of mutual destruction, it serves as a force conducive to agreement.

Priority of Disarmament or the Solution of Disputes

The question of whether disarmament must await the solution of political problems, or *vice versa,* is very much a hen-and-egg proposition. It is hotly debated to no final and convincing conclusion. But if we are correct in assuming that armaments are a cause of disputes, then it follows that their elimination or control would reduce tensions, remove the causes of the difficulties, and contribute to an international atmosphere more amenable to peaceful settlement. But disarmament would not automatically remove, or lead to the settlement of all international difficulties, any more than it would eliminate all tensions and war. In any case, the practical approach seems to be to proceed simultaneously on as many fronts as possible, hoping that a breakthrough anywhere will contribute to progress elsewhere along the line.

Economic Problems

The approach of Americans to the economics of disarmament is ambivalent. On the one hand they look forward to vast savings and, on the other,

---

21 For an argument that an ineffective control plan would increase distrust, see Salvador de Madariaga, "Disarmament? The Problem Lies Deeper," *The New York Times Magazine,* Oct. 11, 1959, pp. 17, 72, 75.

fear its dislocating consequences. Both hope and fear are probably exaggerated. Expenditures on armaments were around $120 billion in the early sixties, with the United States (about $45 billion) and the Soviet Union (about $40 billion) accounting for approximately three-fourths of the total. General and complete disarmament conjures up dreams of the possible constructive uses of these vast sums. It is an especially appealing hope to the people of the underdeveloped countries, who have been promised time after time that at least a part of the savings from disarmament would go to improve their levels of living.

The savings resulting from disarmament would depend on its effect on total production. Although it has been a constant theme of Marxist doctrine, especially of the communist variety, that capitalism cannot survive without the artificial stimulus of expenditures for war, there appears to be no basis for this contention. Premier Khrushchev appears to have conceded as much in one of his several revisions of Marxism-Leninism. The postwar examples of West Germany and Japan are among the contemporary contradictions of the dogma.

It is acknowledged that there would be problems of adjustment of economies geared to a high level of expenditures for military defense. However, since it is highly probable that any substantial reduction of armaments would be spread over a period of years, adjustments would be gradual. For example, in the United States a reduction of expenditures for disarmament at an annual rate of one per cent of the gross national product would result in total disarmament in less than ten years.[22]

It is quite possible that both the hopes and fears of the economic consequence of disarmament are unrealistic. If military forces were stabilized at a high level, the costs of a control system might be as great or even greater than the savings. Nevertheless, the expectation of savings is a force favorable to disarmament. The manpower shortage of the Soviet Union, combined with its apparent desire to increase the level of consumption at home, and certainly to conduct the economic war abroad, are among the factors which appear to motivate the leaders of the Kremlin.[23] The pressure from the underdeveloped countries has been commented upon. It is difficult to estimate the effect of hope and fear on the relatively affluent Western societies, but it would seem that they are on balance favorable to disarmament.

THE PERENNIAL STRUGGLE

For those who believe that history repeats itself, there can be but one conclusion as to the prospects for the elimination and control of arma-

---

[22] For a discussion of this point, see Gerard Piel, "The Economics of Disarmament," *Bulletin of Atomic Scientists*, XVI (Apr. 1960), 117-22, 126.

[23] Robert Loring Allen, *Soviet Economic Warfare* (Washington, D.C.: Public Affairs Press, 1960), pp. 8-23.

ments: they are dim indeed. There are few "successful" attempts on record. The Rush-Bagot Treaty of 1818 between the United States and Great Britain, providing for naval disarmament on the Great Lakes, is of minor importance on the larger world scene. The Washington Naval Agreement of 1922, and its related Four- and Nine-Power Pacts, however one evaluates them, were shortlived. With these exceptions, the history of disarmament negotiations has been uniformly unsuccessful.

It is at least of passing interest that those assembled at the Hague in 1899 agreed unanimously to a resolution expressing "the wish that the Governments, taking into consideration the proposals made at the conference, may examine the possibility of an agreement as to the limitation of armed forces by land and sea, and of war budgets."[24] The Russo-Japanese, the Boer, and the Spanish-American wars all stimulated demands for disarmament, and various peace groups, especially in the Anglo-Saxon countries, increased pressures to that end. It was discussed for exactly twenty-five minutes at the Second Hague Conference of 1907, another innocuous resolution was passed, and the subject was laid to rest.

The League and Disarmament

Practically all proposals having international peace as their aim include disarmament as an ingredient, usually on the assumption that national armaments are a contributing cause of war and tension. It was natural, therefore, that the framers of the League Covenant and the UN Charter should have included disarmament among their multifaceted approach to peace. In his famous Fourteen Point address on January 8, 1918, Wilson called for national armaments to be reduced to the lowest point consistent with *domestic* safety. After various drafts by Wilson and Colonel House, and subsequent changes at Versailles, the key disarmament provisions of the League Covenant were set forth in Article 8:

1. The members of the League recognize that the maintenance of peace requires the reduction of national armaments to the lowest point consistent with national safety, and the enforcement by common action of international obligations.
2. The Council, taking account of the geographical situation and circumstances of each state, shall formulate plans. . . .

Here we find (1) the thesis that arms cause wars; (2) *domestic* changed to *national* safety, with all that this implied; and (3) the proposition that collective security required the retention of national armaments. Lord Davies has called the latter two provisions "an attempt . . . to square the circle, to combine . . . two incompatible principles, namely, the old doctrine of absolute self-defense, enshrined in so many prewar resolutions,

---

[24] Cited in Merze Tate, *The United States and Armaments* (Cambridge: Harvard University Press, 1948), p. 42.

and the alternative idea of a police function, 'the enforcement by common action of international obligations.' "[25]

The efforts of the League to achieve disarmament fall into two periods. The first, from 1920 to 1926, was primarily an effort to prepare the basis for disarmament or, more specifically, to satisfy the demands of France and her supporters for security, which they consistently maintained was its prerequisite. The conclusion of the Locarno treaties in 1925, one of the purposes of which was to "hasten in effecting disarmament provided for in Article 8 of the Covenant," paved the way for the second phase. It opened with the creation of the League Preparatory Commission, and ended with adjournment in 1934 of the Conference for the Reduction and Limitation of Armaments.

The Conference convened on February 2, 1932, with sixty-one governments represented. The detailed story cannot be told here. There was disagreement over both technical and political problems. Should limitation be direct—matériel and men under arms—or should it be budgetary? Should land, naval, and air forces be treated separately or together? Should there be inspection and control, or should observance of agreements be left to good faith? Could offensive and defensive weapons be distinguished? France insisted that disarmament was impossible without more adequate security guarantees; the British and Americans reasoned that disarmament would bring security; the Germans and Italians demanded equality; the Russians proposed complete disarmament and an inspection system. Various attempts were made to end the deadlock, including President Hoover's proposal to abolish certain weapons and to reduce others by a third. In October 1933, Germany withdrew from the Conference, which met for the last time on June 11, 1934. Thus ended the first major attempt at general disarmament.

The United Nations and Disarmament

In contrast to the League Covenant, the UN Charter does not reflect, at least directly, a belief that armaments cause war; their "regulation" rather than "reduction" is emphasized. Article 26 states the purpose of regulation as follows: "to promote the establishment and maintenance of international peace and security with the least diversion for armaments of the world's human and economic resources. . . ." The Charter authorized the General Assembly to consider the "principles governing disarmament and the regulation of armaments" (Art. 11). In contrast, the "Security Council shall be responsible for formulating, with the assistance of the Military Staff Committee . . . plans to be submitted to the members of the United Nations for the establishment of a system for the regulation of armaments" (Art. 26). Despite the Charter, the Military Staff Committee has never

---

[25] Lord Davies, *The Problem of the Twentieth Century: A Study in International Relationships* (London: Ernest Benn, Ltd., 1934), p. 227.

functioned in that capacity. Aside from the disarmament activities of the Council and Assembly, plans have been formulated by the various governments, and negotiated in several commissions established by the Council upon the recommendations of the Assembly, or by committees only tenuously related to the UN. Some have maintained that had the knowledge of the "ultimate weapon" been available to the delegates at San Francisco, the disarmament provisions of the Charter would have been considerably different and stronger. In any case, the atomic bomb, initially, and the "permanent revolution" in military technology subsequently, were important factors back of the early and continued consideration of disarmament by the UN.

Negotiations for the reduction or control of armaments since 1945 fall into three periods. The first, from 1945 to 1950 (there was no serious consideration of the subject between 1950 and 1954), was primarily concerned with "weapons of mass destruction," mainly the atomic bomb. This was the period of the comprehensive "Baruch" proposals by the United States, endorsed in their essentials by the UN, and rejected by the Soviet Union. During the second period, from 1954 to 1957, the scene shifted to London where a five-power subcommittee of the UN Disarmament Commissions considered nearly all aspects of the question. Proposals advanced by the Western powers were accepted in essence by the Soviet Union, only to see the United States reject most of those she had endorsed previously. The meeting collapsed in failure on September 6, 1957. The third period opened in 1958 and continued in some form as these lines were written in the winter of 1961. Two technical conferences were held, one dealing with the prevention of surprise attack and the other with cessation of atomic tests. These were followed by political sessions on the latter subject, and by a ten-nation committee which convened at Geneva on March 15, 1960. Its task was to consider "complete and general disarmament." It adjourned in acrimonious disagreement on June 27 of the same year.[26]

It was anomalous, on the surface at least, that the United States, with her atomic monopoly, should have been the leading advocate of atomic control, but apparently was relatively unconcerned with conventional weapons, while the Soviet Union, soon to be regarded as superior in conventional arms, and armed forces, should have sponsored the resolution for creating the Commission on Conventional Armaments. The Korean War furnished convincing evidence that conventional weapons were not obsolete, and that their control was inextricably linked with that of non-conventional ones. The result was the replacement of the two former commissions and the assumption of their responsibilities by a new

---

[26] For a brief historical analytical account of these negotiations through 1959, see Joseph Nogee, "The Diplomacy of Disarmament," *International Conciliation*, No. 526 (Jan. 1960).

Disarmament Commission in 1952. In the words of the General Assembly's resolution, its duty was "to prepare proposals . . . for the regulation, limitation, and *balanced* reduction of all armed forces and armaments . . . [and] for the elimination of all major weapons adaptable to mass destruction. . . ." [Italics mine—CPS] Although prodded by the General Assembly at successive sessions, the results of the Commission's work were as unpromising as its meetings were desultory.

The first Period—1945-1954. Prior to the consideration of atomic disarmament by the UN, there were a series of agreements and understandings among the United States, Great Britain, Canada, and the Soviet Union. In its first resolution on January 21, 1946, the General Assembly provided for the establishment of the Atomic Energy Commission by and under the Security Council. Composed of the same membership as the Security Council (plus Canada when she was not a Council member), it was charged with formulating plans for (1) the control of atomic energy to the extent necessary to ensure its use for peaceful purposes only; (2) elimination from national armaments of atomic weapons and of all other weapons adaptable to mass destruction; and (3) effective safeguards through inspection and other means to protect states against violation and evasions. The great urgency felt for atomic control, the view of the United States that agreement on conventional weapons would be impossible unless first achieved with respect to "weapons of mass destruction," and the belief that success achieved there would be transferable to the control of conventional armaments, account for the early neglect of the latter. Nevertheless, the Soviet Union had early advocated their simultaneous consideration. Yielding to its plea, the Commission for Conventional Armaments, identical in composition to the Atomic Energy Commission and also responsible to the Security Council, was established on February 13, 1947.

The Atomic Energy Commission, from its first meeting on June 19, 1946, until the end of 1949, was the principal arena for disarmament negotiations, although the Commission for Conventional Armaments was moderately active for a time. From mid-1948, however, when both commissions had reached an impasse, negotiations were largely *pro forma* until the Korean War, when they ceased entirely.

The so-called Baruch proposals made to the Atomic Energy Commission in June 1946, and subsequently endorsed by the UN General Assembly (but later abandoned) were indeed far-reaching. They called for an international atomic development authority which would own (or manage), operate, and control all facilities, except mines, for the production of atomic energy. National or private operations of non-dangerous activities would be permitted under strict licensing by the authority, which would also conduct a program of research for the development of atomic energy for peaceful purposes, as well as for the production of weapons. The basic assumptions back of this plan for the international socialization of atomic energy were that every step in the process must be controlled; that no *external* control would be an adequate safeguard, for the controlling organization must be as thoroughly informal as the actual operators; and that this was possible only if operations and controls were combined in a single agency.

Finally—and this we regard as the decisive consideration—we believe that an examination of these and other necessary preconditions for a successful scheme of inspection will reveal that *they cannot be fulfilled in any organizational arrangements in which the only instrument of control is inspection.*[27]

The Soviet Union called for national ownership and operation of atomic facilities, to be controlled by an international commission to insure the use of atomic energy for peaceful purposes. The majority plan was attacked as an infringement on the sovereignty of states, as indeed it was, at least potentially, and as a capitalistic conspiracy to prevent the economic development of the Soviet Union, which it was not. It is true, however, that no state, including the Soviet Union, would, under the plan, have been able to decide unilaterally on the use of atomic energy.

Aside from agreeing that the national possession and use of atomic weapons of mass destruction should be prohibited, there was a minimum of agreement between the contending parties. The problem of timing was crucial. The Baruch plan would have the development authority proceed by stages, assuming more and more authority as it demonstrated its capacity, and as national security increased. Only in the final stage would the national use of atomic weapons be prohibited, and the United States turn over its atomic monopoly. Meanwhile, the Soviet Union would be prohibited from atomic energy activities. Equally important, the United States would decide unilaterally when it was safe to move from one stage to another. The Soviet Union, on the other hand, proposed originally that the possession and use of atomic weapons be outlawed first, with their control to be provided for in a subsequent convention. Later (1949) they suggested simultaneous prohibition and control. They quite accurately charged that under the plan the United States would maintain an atomic monopoly over an indefinite period.

The issue of inspection was a central one, as it has continued to be. Both the United States and the Soviet Union reversed, or at least changed their prewar positions, the former now proposing thoroughgoing inspection and the latter taking an ambiguous position. The Soviet Union accepted inspection "in principle," but only if it did not interfere "in the domestic affairs of States." How this miracle could be accomplished was obscure. The majority plan was condemned as a conspiracy to place spies

---

[27] *A Report on the International Control of Atomic Energy*, Department of State Publication No. 2498 (Washington, D.C.: Government Printing Office, Mar. 1946), p. 6.

and saboteurs within the Soviet Union. Among the several reasons for Soviet reluctance to accept a liberal inspection system, none is more important than that the very nature of their "closed" society gives them an advantage over the relatively "open" society of their chief antagonist, an advantage they do not propose to lose. In short, the issue involves the "ratio," for the Western powers would stand to gain more by "free inspection" of the Soviet Union than would the latter by the additional information she would acquire about her antagonists. It is incorrect, however, to assume that without inspection nothing would be known about the military capacity of communist countries, or that the information revealed through inspections might not already be known through "clandestine" methods—a dignified term for spying. The important point is rather that information obtained through legitimate channels is far more useful in controlling armaments than that obtained by other methods. In the former case it may be freely used in discussions by the control organs with national authorities in order to induce them to comply with these international obligations. Regulating an arms agreement, of which inspection is only one aspect, requires judgment, interpretation, and negotiation, not just a look at the facts.

"It will involve continual administration and regulation, as well as argument and negotiation. The 'inspection' concept suggests an analogy with fraud rum-running; but if the analogy is tax evasion, regulation of monopolies, or enforcement of international-trade agreements, 'inspection' may be not only inadequate but somewhat off the central point."[28] For these and similar reasons, Schelling and Halperin conclude that "inspection has been overemphasized in most discussions of arms control.[29]

The last principal issue involved in the early atomic controversy was that of sanctions. It was agreed that the international authority would function within the framework of the Security Council, and that its day-to-day decisions would be made by majority vote. The majority plan proposed that the authority should have the right to enforce compliance with the terms of the agreements by both officials and private individuals, but the methods by which it would do so were never made clear. In any case, there was to be no Security Council veto over enforcement. The Soviet Union simply proposed that the control commission report violations to the Security Council, which would proceed according to the Charter with its requirement of unanimity of the permanent members on substantive measures.

The Second Period—1954-1957. The ending of the Korean War, the breaking of the atomic duopoly by Great Britain in 1952, the accumulation of a sizable stockpile of atomic weapons, and the explosion of a hydrogen weapon by the United States in 1952 and by the Soviet Union nine

---

[28] Schelling and Halperin, *Strategy and Arms Control,* pp. 107 ff.
[29] *Ibid.,* p. 91.

months later, set the stage for the next round of negotiations. These took place, however, not in the Disarmament Commission, but in its five-power (Canada, France, U.S.S.R., U.K., and U.S.) Sub-Committee, which negotiated at London in five series of closed sessions between May 13, 1954, and September 6, 1957. These discussions were apparently conducted, at least for a time, with extreme seriousness by all parties. Views were clarified and positions compromised as most phases of the disarmament question were considered. It was reported, with considerable evidence, that the negotiators were on the verge of signing an agreement. Hope rose, when on May 10, 1955, the Soviet delegates made major concessions to the Western point of view. The Sub-Committee then adjourned to meet again on August 29 after the 1955 Geneva summit conference. Then on September 6, the United States delegation placed "a reservation upon all of its pre-Geneva substantive positions. . . ." The reason given for the reversal was the "revelation" in the Soviet paper of May 10 that UN inspection might not be able to detect concealed nuclear weapons. The truth was that this had long been known.

From May 1955 to September 1957 the Western powers, having retreated from their "comprehensive" plan, urged "partial" disarmament instead. On paper at least, the Soviets seemed willing "to accept *much more disarmament, and much more inspection and control.*"[30] That the attitude of the United States was hardly favorable to disarmament is indicated in the following statement by President Eisenhower:

In numbers, our stock of nuclear weapons is so large and rapidly growing that we are able safely to dispense it to positions assuring its instant availability against attack and still keep strong reserves. Our scientists assure me that we are well ahead of the Soviets in the nuclear field, both in quantity and in quality. *We intend to stay ahead.* [Italics mine—CPS][31]

It appears that the Western proposals in the Sub-Committee, as of 1957, especially for the cessation of production of fissionable material, together with the retention of a "substantial part of nuclear stocks," was intended to allow the United States "to stay ahead." Under the conditions then existing, a proposal of this sort could not have been made with any serious expectation that the Soviet Union would accept it.

The "inside story" of what happened in the period between May 1955 and September 1957 has never been made public, as far as this writer is aware. Possibly it was because American officials had other "revelations" that the Western position was reversed. According to Secretary of State Dulles:

Past efforts have usually proceeded from the assumption that it is possible to establish and maintain certain defined levels of military strength and to equate

---

[30] Philip Noel-Baker, *The Arms Race* (London: Stevens & Sons, Ltd., 1958), p. 27.
[31] Broadcast on "Science and National Security," Nov. 1957.

these dependably as between the nations. *Actually, military potentials are so imponderable that this always has been and always will be a futile pursuit.* [Italics mine—CPS][32]

And Harold Stassen:

There was a time when there was in my country considerable thought of a very extreme form of control and inspection, and a very low level of armaments, armed forces, and military expenditure. We have concluded that that extreme form of control and inspection is not practical, feasible, or attainable.[33]

A more likely explanation, however, is that the right hand did not know what the left hand was doing. Relatively little thought had been given by the government to disarmament, and its relation to security and military policy. Other aspects of military policy were incompatible with those involving disarmament. Confronted by the possibility of Soviet acceptance of certain Western proposals, subjected to pressure by the Atomic Energy Commission and the Pentagon, and probably by both Britain and France who wanted to achieve "nuclear respectability" before agreeing to limitation and control, the Department of State simply gave in.

Third Period—1958-   . In 1957, the Soviet Union began to insist upon "parity" between the negotiating parties. The United States not only resisted this, but was reluctant to increase the number of negotiators. In its autumn session, the General Assembly enlarged the Disarmament Commission to twenty-five members; but since sixteen of these were United States allies, the Soviet Union boycotted it. At Soviet insistence, in 1958 it was further enlarged to include all UN members.

Nuclear Test-Ban and Surprise Attack Negotiations.   In the intense disarmament negotiations of 1958-1960, which took place in Geneva, the UN was even less involved than at London in 1954-1957. These negotiations originally grew out of exchanges between President Eisenhower and Premier Khrushchev in 1958, resulting in the holding of two conferences of scientific experts. At the first, on the prevention of surprise attack, five nations from each group were represented, thus meeting the Soviet demand for parity. Its efforts were abandoned after thirty fruitless meetings in which the West accused the Soviet-bloc delegates of injecting political issues. The second, the Conference of Experts to Study the Possibility of Detecting Violation of a Possible Agreement on Suspension of Nuclear Tests, consisting of experts representing four Soviet-bloc and four Western countries, met from July 1 through August 21, 1958. It concluded unanimously that it was "technically feasible to establish . . . a workable

---

[32] "Challenge and Response in United States Policy," *Foreign Affairs*, XXXVI (Oct. 1957), p. 34.
[33] Noel-Baker, *The Arms Race*, p. 29.

and effective control system to detect violations of an agreement on the world-wide suspension of nuclear weapons tests."[34]

Agreement among the experts led to the three-nation (U.S., U.S.S.R., U.K.) nuclear test ban conference which began in the autumn of 1959 and survived the collapse of the 1960 summit and ten-nation disarmament committee negotiations. The fact that these negotiations persisted, that there was substantial agreement on a number of points, and that inspection and control appeared to be less complicated and demanding than in most other areas of disarmament, led many observers to conclude for a time that agreement was probable.

The consensus of the experts as to the feasibility of detecting nuclear tests by the control scheme they had recommended, was disrupted by United States insistence that its 1958 "Hardtack" test series and subsequent studies had indicated certain underground nuclear explosions could not, by seismic devices, be distinguished from earthquakes. The Soviets at first rejected these findings, but eventually agreed to study the matter. The United States proposed, pending the development of more adequate means of detection of these explosions, that they be excluded from limitation and control. The issue was unresolved, although it was suggested that it might be solved by a more liberal provision for the dispatch of inspection teams to areas where the cause of disturbance was questionable, or by the improvement of means of detection.

Agreement had apparently been reached on the establishment of a control organ on which the three major nuclear powers would have permanent, and four others non-permanent representation. The Soviets demanded parity of representation with the West, but at first did not demand a veto right. But in 1961, having apparently decided that there were no neutrals who would be "objective," the Soviet Union insisted that, as in other UN organs, no decision be made without its concurrence. It was agreed that personnel of the mobile inspection teams and of the control posts would consist of both indigenous and foreign personnel, although the Western powers insisted on a larger proportion of the latter, and greater freedom for the mobile teams than was agreeable to the Soviet Union. Although the United States subsequently made certain concessions to the Soviet position, it appeared in the summer of 1961 that Khrushchev had lost interest in an atomic-test ban. At the Vienna Khrushchev-Kennedy talks held in June 1961, the former proposed that the atomic-test talks be adjourned, but that the problem be considered in the general negotiations to be resumed in late July of that year. The United States refused to agree to the suggestion for adjournment.

The Ten-Nation Committee. In 1960, the chief prospect for an agreement on disarmament, aside from that relating to atomic tests, seemed to depend upon the outcome of negotiations in the ten-nation disarmament

---

[34] United Nations Doc. A/3897 (Aug. 28, 1958), p. 20.

committee which convened at Geneva on March 15. This committee, agreed to by the foreign ministers in 1959, was composed of representatives of Canada, France, Italy, the United Kingdom, and the United States for the West, and Bulgaria, Czechoslovakia, Poland, Rumania, and the U.S.S.R. for the Soviet bloc, thus again conceding the Soviet demand for parity.

As in the case of the other negotiations from 1958 onward, these took place outside the auspices of the UN. Secretary-General Hammarskjöld was not entirely satisfied with these developments, however, as indicated by his statement of July 23, 1959, that disarmament "is one of those questions of which the General Assembly should always be seized." The Fourteenth (1959) session of the General Assembly passed a number of resolutions relating to disarmament, and thus indicated its intention to at least prod the major powers. It was also agreed that the Secretary-General should be represented at the ten-nation committee negotiations, which would be serviced by the UN Secretariat, and should report to the UN.

In a sense, the agenda for the committee had been set by the speech of Premier Khrushchev on September 8, 1959, before the General Assembly, in which he proposed "that, over a period of four years, all states should carry out complete disarmament and should divest themselves of the means of waging war." To assure compliance, he proposed an international control body "in which all states would participate." This plan, along with several others, was referred by unanimous vote to the ten-nation disarmament committee. All members of the UN were now committed to the principle of "complete and general disarmament."

Each side presented a comprehensive set of proposals before the committee when it met on March 15.[35] These were debated at length, but the general impression was that the committee was sparring pending instructions from the Heads of States scheduled to meet in Paris in May. When the conference reconvened, following the ill-fated Paris summit conference, the Soviets presented a revised plan.[36] The most important change, which seemed to be a concession to France, was that "nuclear weapons shall be eliminated from the arsenals of states, their manufacture shall be discontinued and all means of delivery of such weapons shall be destroyed . . ." in the first stage of disarmament. Coupled with this was the proposal that all foreign troops should be withdrawn from the territories of other states and all foreign military bases eliminated. This plan was rejected by the Western nations as an attempt to divide them and leave the Soviet Union, with her superiority in troops and conventional weapons, in a position of virtual hegemony in Europe.

Nevertheless, the Soviet proposals seemed to have attracted consider-

<hr>

[35] For a point-by-point comparison of the Western and Soviet position, see *NATO Letter*, Vol. 8, No. 5 (May 1960).

[36] For full text, see *New York Times*, June 3, 1960, p. 6.

able support. Perhaps because of this, the U.S. delegate, Frederick M. Eaton, returned to the United States for new instructions.[37] Prepared to present these on his return to Geneva, he was prevented from doing so by the walk-out of the representatives of the Soviet-bloc powers on June 27. Among the proposed changes, two appeared to be of considerable importance and designed to meet Soviet demands. The first related to the timing of each of the three phases through which disarmament would proceed; the second to the relationship of the disarmament control organization to the UN. Prior to this, the Western powers had never been willing to stipulate an exact period of time. Both of these points were provided for in the following statement of controlling principles: "General and complete disarmament shall proceed through three stages containing balanced, phased, and safeguarded measures with each measure being carried out in an agreed and strictly defined period of time, under the supervision of the International Disarmament Control Organization, within the framework of the United Nations." The International Disarmament Control Organization would verify the measures taken within each stage, and transition between stages would be initiated when the Security Council agreed that all measures in the preceding stage had been fully implemented, that effective verification was continuing, and that additional verification arrangements and procedures required for measures in the next stage had been established and were ready to operate effectively.

From the formal proposals of the two groups as of the summer of 1960, leaving aside the mutual charges of duplicity and insincerity, it was possible to conclude that there were large areas of agreement between the negotiators. The following points, based on the Soviet proposal of June 2, and those of the United States on June 27, 1960, represent an attempt to set forth the principal areas of agreement and disagreement:

1. General and complete disarmament is the ultimate goal.

2. It should be realized in three phases. The Soviets hold that it should be attained in four years, whereas the Western powers have not, until recently, been willing to talk in terms of specific time limits. As indicated above, however, the United States proposals of June 27, 1960, included the proposition that within each stage "each measure shall be carried out in an agreed and strictly defined period of time. . . ."

3. A control organization, consisting of representatives of all participating states, would be established within the framework of the UN. There would also be a control commission within the larger control organization. The Western proposals did not specify the composition or voting arrangements of the former, whereas the Soviet Union would have it composed of representatives of both blocs, plus neutrals, with substantive matters decided by a two-thirds vote and procedural ones by a simple majority vote.

---

[37] For full text, see *New York Times*, June 28, 1960, p. 11.

4. Inspectors, recruited on a wide geographic base, and functioning under the control commission, would be authorized to carry out the inspection functions. These inspections would begin simultaneously with the inauguration of each measure of disarmament. The Soviet proposals of June 2 with respect to inspection during the stages of disarmament reads as follows:

The control organization shall post its inspectors in the territories of states in such a way that they can proceed to put their disarmament measure into force. Each party to the treaty shall be required to allow control officers and inspection teams in their territories prompt and free access to *any place where disarmament measures subject to control are being carried out or to any area in which on-the-spot inspection of such measures is to take place.* [Italics mine—CPS]

The United States proposals of June 27 on the other hand provided that "verification shall include the capability to ascertain that not only do reductions of armed forces and armaments in agreed amounts take place, but also that *retained armed forces and armaments do not exceed agreed levels at any stage.*" [Italics mine—CPS] The chief Soviet delegate, V. A. Zorin, maintained that the West proposed to establish "controls without disarmament," and F. M. Eaton, head of the United States delegation, accused the Soviet Union of refusing "to accept, even in principle, that international inspectors would have the right to determine whether clandestine installations or hidden forces still existed." This appeared to be true during the disarmament process, but the Soviet statement did provide that after completion of the program of complete and general disarmament: "the Control Council shall have the right to send mobile inspection teams to any point and to any facility in the territories of states."

5. The disarmament plan should be embodied in a treaty, or treaties, open to all states. The Western powers would draw up a treaty to be signed by the ten nations represented on the committee, "embodying the first stage of the program," and later present an agreed draft covering the second and third phases to a world disarmament conference. Other states would also be asked to accede to the first-stage treaty. The Soviet Union, on the other hand, proposed that the complete plan be included in a treaty to be presented to and approved by a world-wide conference. The United States delegate maintained that the result would be "to postpone any useful action in the disarmament field to the indefinite future."

6. Any disarmament scheme, or agreed steps toward it, should not result in "obtaining any unilateral advantage for one side" (Soviet statement), but should "be carried out in such a manner that at no time shall any state, whether or not a party to a treaty, obtain military advantage over other states as a result of the progress of disarmament," (U.S. statement). Both sides have accused the other, quite truthfully, with violating

the principle. And herein lies the difficult, perhaps unsurmountable, problem of the "ratio," referred to by Mr. Dulles when he maintained that *"military potentials are so imponderable"* that to "equate these dependably . . . always will be a futile pursuit."* [Italics mine—CPS]

7. Violations of agreements should be subject to international military sanctions, within the UN, *once general and complete disarmament is realized.* Differences in views on this matter, however, are indicated by the following positions. The United States proposed that, beginning with the second stage, "an international police force, within the United Nations, should be progressively established and maintained with agreed personnel strength and armaments sufficient to preserve world peace when general and complete disarmament is achieved." The Soviets would begin *studying* the measures to maintain peace in stage two. After disarmament was completed, states would "undertake to place at the disposal of the Security Council as necessary formations from the contingents of police (militia) retained by them" in order to "maintain peace and security in accordance with the Charter of the United Nations."

In addition to broad issues of this nature, there were others relating to the stages at which each disarmament measure would take place. These appeared to be of lesser importance than those already considered, and most of them were probably subject to compromise.

When the negotiations collapsed on June 27, 1960, the Soviet Union declared it was "interrupting its participation in the ten-nation committee in order to raise at the next session of the United Nations General Assembly the question of disarmament. . . ." The United States took the issue before the Disarmament Commission, in advance of the Assembly meeting, but no action was taken there. Before the fifteenth (1960) regular session of the General Assembly acted on the general disarmament question the Soviet and American delegations had agreed to meet for considering the composition of a body to continue disarmament negotiations, and to resume the talks in the summer of 1961. The Assembly, therefore, simply took note of this fact, and decided to take up "for consideration at its sixteenth session the problem of disarmament, and all pending proposals relating to it."

SUMMARY AND CONCLUSIONS

Despite the seemingly unsurmountable obstacles in the path of effective and acceptable plans for disarmament and arms control, as evidenced by the failures of almost countless rounds of negotiations, hope persists that a way around them may be found. Some of the difficulties are "technical" in the physical and social sense, and inventions in both realms are needed to surmount them. The more intractable of these are rooted in the ideologies of nationalism and those which divide the closed and open societies.

The hopes and fears of the economic consequences of disarmament and arms control are largely unfounded. Distrust, political disputes, and similar impediments are partly cause and partly consequence of unregulated arms races, especially in the age of the continuous weapons revolution; and some of them would disappear or lend themselves to solution were the armaments problem brought under effective control.

Military policy, disarmament, and the control of armaments, far from being distinct or contradictory policies, are intimately related, and are, or may be, all directed to the same ends of peace and security. Nevertheless, there is an incompatibility between peace through deterrence by arms and peace by their total elimination or reduction below certain levels.

Effective disarmament and its control, or the control of armaments, will require greater intelligence than hitherto evidenced by peoples and their leaders. It will require more sincere efforts to disarm and fewer to gain a propaganda or power advantage, development of attitudes appropriate to an age of interdependence, and acceptance and support of institutional arrangements for international society suitable for a dangerous age—but one which could see a greater realization of man's aspirations and avoidance of more of his objects of fear. In the oft-quoted words of Salvador de Madariaga: "The solution of the problem of disarmament cannot be found within the problem itself, but outside it. In fact, the problem of disarmament is not the problem of disarmament. It really is the problem of the organization of the World-Community."[38]

SUGGESTED READINGS

Barnet, Richard J., *Who Wants Disarmament?* Boston: Beacon Press, 1960.

Blackett, Patrick M. S., *Atomic Weapons and East-West Relations.* Cambridge: Cambridge University Press, 1956.

Bolte, Charles G., *The Price of Peace: A Plan for Disarmament.* Boston: Beacon Press, 1956.

Bull, Hedley, *Disarmament in the Missile Age.* New York: Frederick A. Praeger, Inc., 1961.

Corey, Robert H., Jr., "International Inspection: From Proposals to Realization," *International Organization,* XIII (Autumn 1959), 495-504.

Cousins, Norman, *In Place of Folly.* New York: Harper & Brothers, 1961.

---

[38] *Disarmament* (New York: Coward-McCann, Inc., 1929), p. 56.

Daedalus, "Special Issue: Arms Control," LXXXIX (Fall 1960), entire issue.

Eaton, Frederick M., U.S. Representative to the Conference. Five powers present plan for general disarmament as Ten-Nation Disarmament Conference convenes: working paper on general disarmament released on March 14, 1960, by Canada, France, Italy, the United Kingdom, and the United States. *Department of State Bulletin*, XLII (Apr. 4, 1960), 511-15.

Freeman, Harrop A. and Stanley Yaker, "Disarmament and Atomic Controls: Legal and Non-Legal Problems," *Cornell Law Quarterly*, XLIII (Winter 1958), 236-62.

Frisch, David H., ed., *Arms Reduction: Program and Issues.* New York: The Twentieth Century Fund, 1961.

Frye, William R., *Disarmament: Atoms Into Plowshares?* New York: Foreign Policy Association—World Affairs Center, 1955.

Galay, Nikolai, "Khrushchev's Disarmament Proposal," *Institute for the Study of the USSR Bulletin*, VI (Oct. 1959), 3-10.

"Geneva Test Ban Negotiations; USSR, UK, and US Reports; Technical Working Group II," *Bulletin of the Atomic Scientists*, XVI (Feb. 1960), 38-48.

Gromov, L. and V. Strigachov, "Some Economic Aspects of Disarmament," *International Affairs*, (Mar. 1960), pp. 26-34.

Henkin, Louis, ed., *Arms Control: Issues for the Public.* Englewood Cliffs, N.J.: Prentice-Hall, Inc., 1961.

Inglis, David R., "Fourth-country Problem: Let's Stop at Three," *Bulletin of the Atomic Scientists*, XV (Jan. 1959), 22-26.

King-Hall, Sir Stephen, *Defense in the Nuclear Age*, 3d ed. Toronto: Doubleday Canada, Ltd., 1958.

Kissinger, Henry A., "Arms Control, Inspection, and Surprise Attack," *Foreign Affairs*, XXXVIII (July 1960), 557-75.

Madariaga de, S., *Disarmament.* New York: Coward-McCann, Inc., 1929.

———, "Disarmament? The Problem Lies Deeper," *New York Times Magazine* (Oct. 11, 1959), p. 171.

Melman, Seymour, ed., *Inspection for Disarmament.* New York: Columbia University Press, 1958.

Murray, Thomas E., *Nuclear Policy for War and Peace.* Cleveland, Ohio: The World Publishing Company, 1960.

National Planning Association, Special Project Committee on Security through Arms Control, *1970 Without Arms Control.* Planning Pamphlet No. 104. Washington, D.C.: National Planning Assn., 1958.

Noel-Baker, Philip J., *The Arms Race: A Programme for World Disarmament.* London: Stevens & Sons, Ltd., 1958.

Nogee, Joseph, "The Diplomacy of Disarmament," *International Conciliation*, No. 526 (Jan. 1960), 235-303.

Piel, Gerard, "The Economics of Disarmament," *Bulletin of the Atomic Scientists*, XVI (Apr. 1960), 117-22+.

Rosenfeld, Arthur H., "What About the Undetectable Tests?" *Bulletin of the Atomic Scientists*, XV (Mar. 1959), 98, 103-08.

Russell, Bertrand, *Common Sense and Nuclear Warfare.* New York: Simon & Schuster, Inc., 1959.

Schelling, Thomas C. and Morton H. Halperin, *Strategy and Arms Control.* New York: The Twentieth Century Fund, 1961.

Simons, Howard, "World-Wide Capabilities for Production and Control of Nuclear Weapons," *Daedalus*, LXXXVIII (Summer 1959), 385-409.

Tate, Merze, *The United States and Armaments.* Cambridge: Harvard University Press, 1948.

Thomas, Norman, "Toward Total Disarmament," *Dissent*, VII (Spring 1960), 163-66.

Thompson, C. L., "History of Disarmament Proposals," *Current History*, XXXVI (Jan. 1959), 38-41.

Toynbee, Philip, *The Fearful Choice: A Debate on Nuclear Policy Conducted by Philip Toynbee with the Archbishop of Canterbury (and others)*. London: Victor Gollancz, Ltd., 1958.

U.S. Senate, Committee on Foreign Relations, Subcommittee on Disarmament, "Control and Reduction of Armaments, Detection of and Inspection for Underground Nuclear Explosions," Replies from Seismologists to Subcommittee Questionnaire, Staff Study No. 10. Committee Print, 85th Cong., 2d sess., 1958. Washington, D.C.: Government Printing Office, 1958.

———, "Control and Reduction of Armaments, Disarmament and Security in Europe," Staff Study No. 5. Committee Print, 84th Cong., 2d sess., Dec. 11, 1956. Washington, D.C.: Government Printing Office, 1956.

———, "Control and Reduction of Armaments: Final Report." Report No. 2501, 85th Cong., 2d sess., 1958. Washington, D.C.: Government Printing Office, 1958.

———, "Disarmament and Foreign Policy," Hearings before Subcommittee, 86th Congress, 1st session. Hearing No. 6057, Part I, Jan. 28-Feb. 2, 1959; Hearing No. 7610, Part II, Feb. 4-26, 1959. Washington, D.C.: Government Printing Office, 1959.

———, "Hearings, Technical Problems, and Geneva Test Ban Negotiations." Committee Print, 86th Cong., 2d sess., 1960. Washington, D.C.: Government Printing Office, 1960.

Wolfe, Thomas W., "Khrushchev's Disarmament Strategy," *Orbis*, IV (Apr. 1960), 14-27.

VI

THE UNITED STATES
AND ITS
WORLD RELATIONSHIPS

INTRODUCTION

In Part VI we examine a series of international relationships, in each instance the United States being one of the parties. We begin with a consideration of the objectives and role of the United States in world affairs, her resources, various internal factors which influence American officials responsible for relations with other countries, and a brief account of American foreign policy since 1945.

Against this background we consider United States relations with Europe, the Soviet Union, East Asia, Southern Asia, the Middle East, Africa, and Latin America. The special contributors, who have written all the chapters except the first, concentrate on the aspects of the several areas necessary for understanding relationships of the countries therein with the United States. As you read each of these chapters you should try to determine to what extent the generalizations made with respect to international relations in the first five parts of this book agree with the empirical evidence set forth in these case studies.

21

America Faces the World

The illusion of American isolationism, with its accompanying dream of remaining aloof from world affairs, died with World War II. Although the form and extent of future participation was unclear in the early post-war period, Americans generally sensed that instead of its former role of observer and occasional intervener in world affairs, the United States would henceforth be actively involved.

The trying years since 1945 have witnessed a revolution in American foreign policy, as the United States has tried to adjust to and shape the course of events beyond her borders. What are the objectives of this new United States foreign policy and what kind of an international role does she now seek to play? What are her resources for conducting policies in pursuit of these aims? What are the attitudes of the American people which influence the decisions of officials responsible for foreign policy? And how well do American political institutions lend themselves to the effective conduct of foreign relations?

FOREIGN POLICY OBJECTIVES AND ROLE

American loyalty tends to center around institutions, from the family outward; around sections and scenery and ways of life; around personal freedom and enterprise; and around neighborliness. These interests may be loosely summed up as the much-vaunted American way of life which, for all its varieties of connotation and despite all abuses committed and selfish interests defended in its name, symbolizes a central core of experience, emotion, and attachment. It is not a statist concept; it is not identified with government; and, though it includes our political mores, it is not, in feeling, political.[1]

These and similar loyalties, values, and interests are the deeper sources of both the domestic and foreign policy objectives of the United States.

---

[1] Thomas I. Cook and Malcolm Moos, "The American Idea of International Interest," *American Political Science Review*, XLVII (Mar. 1953), 32.

They find expression through the political process where, along with other factors, they play a role in shaping both the ends and the means of foreign policy.

There is broad consensus among political leaders and the public on certain general and relatively abstract foreign policy goals. It is generally agreed that national security should be given the highest priority, and that individual welfare, especially "economic well-being," rates a close second. Beyond these there is less consensus. One difficulty is the problem of separating ends from means. Some argue that the "containment of communism" is the principal motivating force of American foreign policy, whereas others see it as a means to attain other objectives, especially that of national security. Likewise, assisting the people of the less developed countries through economic aid is viewed as either (or both) an expression of humanitarian concern and a method of preventing communist expansion. Is peace an objective itself or is it a condition ordinarily necessary for the realization of other objectives? Peace at any price is certainly not an objective of American foreign policy. Do Americans value power and prestige for their own sakes, or because they are useful and necessary to defend other values?

A narrow concentration on ends such as these, especially on national security and the containment of communism, may be self-defeating. By stressing national security, the emphasis, as in the case of *the* national interest, is on the particular nation and tends to repel rather than enlist the support of others in pursuing common aims. Containing communism, while necessary, is essentially negative. The underdeveloped nations have protested that American aid has been an instrument in the Cold War, with the elimination of poverty, disease, and illiteracy an incidental means to the end of containment. The development of a community of interest which many Americans see as a major purpose of aid policies has been slow.

This concentration has also injured the historical image of the United States as a liberal—even revolutionary—nation. "Stability" has become a prominent term in American pronouncements of the kind of political and social regimes desired in the non-communist nations. Although stability is probably meant to imply orderly change, very often change entails considerable disorder, especially in semi-feudal societies. And communism thrives on disorder. Under these circumstances stability very often means a preservation of the status quo. Thus the image of the United States abroad becomes one of an affluent, satisfied society uninterested in and afraid of change in a changing world. This contention is amply documented in subsequent chapters.

In a report prepared for the Senate Committee on Foreign Relations, the Council on Foreign Relations remarked that concentration on resisting the communist threat and meeting the demands of the cold war "have obscured many other demands which are bound to affect America's interests and role in the world of the future. They have also tended to divert attention from the formulation and pursuit of long-term policies without which we can see no clear outline of our future relations with other nations, and indeed no successful outcome of the cold war itself."[2] The Council, while recognizing that concern for the opinions of other free nations and the risk of war imposed severe limitations on the nature of policies the United States could adopt in a direct challenge to the communist bloc, nevertheless held that "clearly the United States could have more dynamic and positive policies in the free world itself, where it does have more freedom of action and opportunity for leadership."[3]

Is there an alternative approach to that which stresses United States interests, security, and containment? The study cited above,[4] as well as others in the series, suggests that such an alternative would be to regard United States interests

as directly dependent upon the creation of some form of world order compatible with our values and interests. The establishment and maintenance of such a system calls for a protracted and creative effort on the part of the United States—an effort including, but going beyond, mere holding operations against Communist encroachment. From this viewpoint, the object of policy is focused more directly on what it is we are trying to construct, and to defend while we are constructing it, rather than merely upon reaction to communist encroachments.[5]

Granted, the "blueprint" for this new world order is vague, if indeed it has even been sketched. However, given the desire of the United States to provide for the greatest possible expression of liberty and variety compatible with stability, and an inclination to rely on persuasion and consent in cooperative relationships rather than on power and conflict, some of the characteristics of the kind of a world order desired are reasonably clear. From the close of World War II to the outbreak of the cold war this vision of a new world order was in the forefront of American thinking. Afterward it became a victim of the cold war. If the analysis advanced here has validity, one of the principal tasks of American decision-makers is to raise the building of a new world order to top priority among the American foreign policy objectives.

Viewing the basic objective of the United States in these terms puts the

[2] "Basic Aims of United States Foreign Policy," A Study Prepared by the Council on Foreign Relations for the United States Senate Committee on Foreign. Relations, No. 7, Nov. 25, 1959 (Washington, D.C.: Government Printing Office), p. 7.

[3] *Ibid.*

[4] *Ibid.*, pp. 9-14.

[5] "Developments in Military Technology and Their Impact on United States Strategy and Foreign Policy," A Study Prepared by the Washington Center of Foreign Policy Research, The Johns Hopkins University, No. 8, Nov. 6, 1959 (Washington, D.C.: Government Printing Office), pp. 13-14.

contest with the Soviet bloc in a somewhat different perspective than does concentration on security and other similar interests. The issue becomes one of who will build the new world order. "Since 1946, we have been trying to resolve that question, whether or not we have always been fully conscious of it, by contesting with the Soviet Union and its allies whether it would be they, or we and our allies, who would succeed in constructing such a new system."[6]

Over and above, but closely related to the pursuit of particular aims, is the role which a country seeks to play in world affairs. India regards herself as the leader of the non-aligned nations; Japan would speak for Asia and serve as a mediator between East and West; de Gaulle would restore the grandeur of France so that she may be the initiator rather than the victim of events. The United States feels it is her duty to act as a leader of the "free world," and that it is a responsibility imposed upon her rather than one which she actively seeks. Although other countries, especially France and Great Britain, recognize that United States superiority in resources makes it inevitable that she should play a leading role, they regard themselves as more mature and experienced than the United States, and entitled to be heard and heeded in decisions affecting the grand coalition. France, in particular, feels that she is entitled to a more prominent role, and the smaller nations have frequently protested that there should be "no annihilation without representation." The problem of leading a diverse group of nations is a perplexing one. It is inevitable that in pleasing some the United States will antagonize others. A policy of friendship with and assistance to India or Pakistan, for example, is regarded by the other as an unfriendly act. There is also the problem of the subtle blending of power and persuasion, with the danger, if the former prevails, of domination replacing cooperation.

RESOURCES—MATERIAL AND HUMAN

The United States has vast resources which she can—although she may not necessarily do so—utilize in pursuit of her foreign policy aims. We reemphasize that these resources may be used to exert power or to engage in cooperative ventures, and that the United States prefers to use them in the latter way.

The gross annual national product of the United States with 6.2 per cent of the world's population in the early nineteen-sixties was estimated at 29.4 per cent ($515 billion) of the world's total.[7] The annual growth rate was about three per cent. Slightly over ten per cent, or $50 billion

---

[6] *Ibid.*, p. 14.
[7] See P. N. Rosenstein-Rodan, "International Aid for Underdeveloped Countries," *Review of Economics and Statistics*, XLIII (May 1961), p. 118.

plus, was spent for foreign policy purposes, of which military defense accounted for approximately nine-tenths of the total.[8]

The United States is richly endowed with a wide variety of natural resources necessary to sustain an industrial economy, and to maintain a costly military defense establishment. Nevertheless, she is deficient in certain essential items, and therefore relies increasingly on imports. As high-concentrate iron ores neared exhaustion, she turned to foreign sources, especially to Labrador and Venezuela, importing about twenty per cent of her total consumption of these ores. For certain other metals the United States depends heavily on imports from abroad: manganese (86%), chromite (94%), cobalt (79%), nickel (87%), tungsten ore (74%), aluminum (83%), tin (79%), platinum (87%), asbestos (94%), and mica (95%).[9] With a growing demand, not only in the United States but throughout the world, for raw materials of this kind, there was every prospect that their cost would rise and their procurement become increasingly difficult in the years ahead. In energy resources the United States is rather amply supplied, although she will probably have to rely increasingly on petroleum imports. Agricultural production, especially of food supplies, is a source of domestic embarrassment because of its very magnitude. As the surplus piled up in the nineteen-fifties and sixties, attempts were being made, with some degree of success, to convert a domestic problem into an international asset.

Although sheer size of population is not necessarily an asset, especially in a technological age, a country with a very small population cannot produce goods and services in quantities sufficient to exert significant power and influence in international society. With a population base of some 185 million in the early nineteen-sixties, and a relatively high level of income, education, and skills, the United States possessed vast human resources to pursue her foreign policy aim. At least in one respect, however, her population was "underdeveloped." There was a shortage of people with a knowledge of languages, understanding of other cultures, and skills in "human engineering" to carry out the task of working within other societies. Despite the high level of production in the United States, and a consequent high annual average per capita G.N.P. ($2,790 in 1961), there was considerable sluggishness in the economy, as evidenced by the low level of economic growth and an unemployment rate of over six per cent. Undoubtedly it was important that the rate of growth be increased and fuller employment attained. Nevertheless, there was no real shortage of either goods or manpower which could be devoted to foreign policy

---

[8] With 7.2 per cent of the world's population, the Soviet Union's G.N.P. was 12.1 per cent of the world's total, or $212 billion, about 41 per cent of that of the United States. Yet the Soviet Union probably devoted almost as much as did the United States—about 25 per cent of her G.N.P.—to international purposes.

[9] United States Department of the Interior, Bureau of Mines. *Yearbook, 1957*, I. (Washington, D.C.: Government Printing Office, 1958), 18-19.

objectives. The problem was one of willingness on the part of Americans to make the necessary allocation from their plenty. No real sacrifice was involved. Whether they would do so depended in considerable part on effective political leadership, and the adequacy of political institutions to deal with the problems of the times.

PUBLIC OPINION AND FOREIGN POLICY

Public opinion is an elusive term. Rather than attempting a definition, we shall simply consider the influence of the attitudes of the American people on foreign policy. Certainly not all of them exercise an equal voice. Young children and persons confined in "institutions" are politically inarticulate, as are many adults who are preoccupied, apathetic, and indifferent toward foreign affairs. Others, fairly well-informed but inactive, are the "attentive" public. Some who are well-informed, as well as others who are not, take an active interest, both "intellectually" and by attempting to influence policy-makers. These we may designate the leaders, the "politists," or the "elite."[10]

One study indicates that approximately 30 per cent of the American electorate is unaware of almost any event in American foreign affairs, and that although another 45 per cent is aware of important events in the field it is not really informed. Only about 25 per cent shows a consistent knowledge of foreign affairs.[11]

Yet the lack of knowledge, or the presence of apathy, indifference, and misinformation on many issues, does not necessarily mean that the influence of public opinion on foreign affairs is unimportant. People in mass may influence government in a positive or a negative way—i.e., serve as a goad or a brake. The sinking of the "Maine" in Havana Harbor in 1898 provoked a mass outcry for war against Spain. True, the "yellow press" was in part responsible, but it would have been ineffective had it not been for the mood and predisposition of the people. The Kellogg-Briand Pact of 1928 "outlawing" war, negotiated by a reluctant Secretary of State, resulted from a strong public sentiment. The "braking" power of the general public, however, is greater than is its power of acceleration. Policy formulators usually ask themselves what the public will stand rather than what it demands. This is quite understandable, since it is the leaders, not the general public, who are in a position to take the initiative. Fear or uncertainty as to how people will react is often an important consideration to both the executive and legislative branches of the govern-

---

[10] See Gabriel A. Almond, *The American People and Foreign Policy* (New York: Harcourt, Brace and World, Inc., 1950), especially Chaps. IV, VI, VII.

[11] Martin Kriesberg, "Dark Areas of Ignorance," in Council on Foreign Relations, *Public Opinion and Foreign Policy*, ed. Lester Markel (New York: Harper & Brothers, 1949), p. 51.

ment, especially when there is considerable public awareness of and concern with an issue. In the thirties President Roosevelt was greatly influenced by the general public opposition to the involvement of the United States in war. He therefore resorted to many subterfuges to save the American people from what he thought would be dangerous consequences of their bad judgment. Public attitudes toward China after 1949, and toward settlement of the Korean War, are among the instances in which definite limitations were placed on government action. Many routine decisions, however, as well as others of great importance, are made with little or no concern with public reaction.

The following are frequently noted as American attitudes which influence officials charged with foreign policy responsibilities. Although there are grains of truth in each of them, like all such generalizations they should be scrutinized with a critical eye.

1. Americans are impatient, demand direct answers to all questions and speedy solutions to all problems. The result is to generate tremendous pressure for action that experienced diplomats realize is unwise, and that embarrasses them in the conduct of delicate and complex negotiations for which time alone may provide a solution.

2. Closely related to the first quality is what has been called a "preference for dichotomies," or the attitude that the only solutions to problems are extreme ones—total peace or total war, complete involvement or total isolation. The attitude is said to be responsible for the view, now passing, that "neutrality" is immoral, and that a country which does not align itself with virtue and the grand alliance must perforce be in the camp of evil and communism.

3. Emotionalism is another characteristic of Americans. Their hates and loves are violent, though transient. They insist on policies in accord with their current feelings, while wise policy is stable and coldly objective.

4. Some "realists" view the "legalistic-moralistic" approach to foreign policy as the most serious fault of American policy formulation.

It is the belief that it should be possible to suppress the chaotic and dangerous aspirations of governments in the international field by the acceptance of some system of legal rules and restraints. . . .

It is the essence of this belief that, instead of taking the awkward conflicts of national interest and dealing with them on their merits with a view to finding the solutions least unsettling to the stability of international life, it would be better to find some formal criteria of a juridical nature by which the permissable behavior of states could be defined. . . . Behind all of this . . . lies the American assumption that the things for which other peoples in this world are apt to contend are for the most part neither creditable nor important and might justly be expected to take second place behind the desirability of an ordered world, untroubled by international violence.[12]

---

[12] George F. Kennan, *American Diplomacy, 1900-1950* (Chicago: The University of Chicago Press, 1951), pp. 95-96, passim.

On the moralistic side, with which legalistic notions are closely associated, it means "the carrying over into the affairs of states of the concepts of right and wrong, the assumption that state behavior is a fit subject for moral judgment."[13] It is contended that the legalistic approach, instead of doing away with war and violence makes violence more likely, terrible, and destructive. And "a war fought in the name of high moral principle finds no early end short of some form of total domination."[14]

5. Americans are said to deprecate the role of power in international relations, from which attitude flows a whole series of unfortunate consequences.[15] Among these may be listed the failure to keep power and commitments in balance; a tendency to regard conflict as abnormal and transitory; reliance upon the outlawing of war by treaty; military unpreparedness; a tendency to retreat into isolationism and to leave the world to its own fate, as well as the reverse—a crusade to eliminate power and evil from the world forever.

6. Good will and altruism toward others, with some exceptions, and a desire to be liked in turn, are often noted as elements of American national character. When such attitudes and actions are not forthcoming, Americans are disappointed and hurt. And when, as in the case of China, nearly a century of concern and protection is repaid by rapacious lies and deep animosity, the American reaction is likened unto the fury of the lover scorned.

7. Finally, perhaps in contradiction to several of the generalizations set forth above, it is said that in the end, but in time, the common sense of the American people prevails and rescues them from the dangers of emotionalism and other follies.

THE CONDUCT OF FOREIGN RELATIONS

Constitutional Allocations of Authority

The supreme, or highest law for the United States is international law. Sovereignty, i.e., the freedom of a state under international law, includes the right to conduct its foreign relations subject to that law. The Constitution contains several provisions concerning the conduct of foreign relations, including allocations of authority. These provisions, which are in most instances rather general and in several ambiguous, undergo interpretation as they are applied in specific situations. Yet there are several

---

[13] *Ibid.*, p. 100.

[14] *Ibid.*, p. 101.

[15] See in particular Walter Lippmann, *U.S. Foreign Policy: Shield of the Republic* (Boston: Little, Brown and Co., 1949).

unresolved and controversial issues concerning constitutional provisions relating to foreign affairs.

The two principal features of American government are federalism and the separation of powers. In providing for the first, the Constitution divides authority between the central government and the states, and for the second, between the three branches of the central government. Both of these features are important for the conduct of the foreign relations.

The Federal System and Foreign Relations. One of the major purposes of the framers was to endow the new central government with adequate authority to conduct foreign relations free from state interference. Thus the states were prohibited (Art. I, sec. 10) from making treaties and entering into alliances and confederations. The central government, therefore, has sole authority over foreign affairs.

What is the extent of and limitations on its authority? Although the Constitution does not provide a clear answer to these questions, the courts have done so in a number of cases over the years. A leading case was decided in 1796.[16] During the Revolution Virginia confiscated the property of British subjects in that state, but the peace treaty of 1783 provided for its restoration. The Supreme Court ruled that Article VI of the Constitution, which provides that treaties made under the authority of the United States are a part of the supreme law of the land, meant that the treaty took precedence over the state law. In every succeeding case when a treaty has conflicted with a state law or constitution the former has prevailed.

In 1920 the Supreme Court upheld a treaty and its implementing legislation bringing game birds that migrate from Canada into the United States under the protection of the central government. Justice Holmes, speaking for the Court, rejected the idea that the treaty-making power was limited by "some invisible radiation from the general terms of the Tenth Amendment." He went on to say: "It is not lightly to be assumed that, in matters requiring national action, 'a power which must belong to and somewhere resides in every civilized government' is not to be found."[17] In 1936 the Supreme Court made an even more sweeping statement. It held that a treaty was not necessary to enable the central government, when exercising its foreign affairs authority, to deal with matters reserved to the states. The central government's powers in this area, contended the Court, do not depend on affirmative grants of the Constitution, but upon the fact that the United States is a member of the family of nations. The powers to declare war and all its other foreign affairs powers, "if they had never been mentioned in the Constitution, would have been vested in the federal government as necessary concomitants of nationality."[18]

---

17 *Missouri* v. *Holland,* 252 U.S. 416 (1920).
18 *United States* v. *Curtiss-Wright Export Corporation,* 299 U.S. 304 (1936).

These cases all demonstrate that the central government has wide authority to conduct foreign relations despite the federal system. This could be used to undermine that system; on the other hand, it is desirable and necessary for the central government, in the conduct of foreign relations, to be able to deal with matters ordinarily reserved to the states.

Are there no limitations on the central government's authority in dealing with foreign affairs? The Court has asserted on several occasions that there are, and has implied that it would declare a treaty unconstitutional if it went too far. "It would not be contended that it [the power of the central government] extends so far as to authorize what the Constitution forbids, or a change in the character of the government, or in that one of the States, or a cession of any portion of the territory of the latter, without its consent. . . ."[19]

In summary, the authority of the central government is quite ample to deal with foreign affairs, but it is limited by the specific prohibitions and certain general principles of the Constitution.

The Separation of Powers and Foreign Policy. The separation of powers, unlike the federal system, presents problems especially acute for the conduct of American foreign relations. Although the Constitution seems to vest primary foreign affairs responsibility in the presidency, Congress has a number of powers in this field, and in several areas their powers overlap. It is especially important that the President and the Congress should be able to work together for common ends. Yet conflict and struggle for leadership between the two are more prevalent than are harmony and cooperation. A Woodrow Wilson Foundation Study Group stated that:

The lessons of history on the conduct of United States foreign affairs seems to show as more or less normal a kind of smoldering, occasionally open, warfare between the Executive and the Legislature. There are periods of truce, periods of "cold war," periods of peace. But some degree of legislative-executive struggle, often "hot," has been a persistent characteristic of this nation. This condition, always annoying, becomes more and more preposterous in a world in which "power tensions" require a far more prompt national response than is possible under legislative-executive "guerrilla warfare" habits of mind and patterns of behavior.[20]

The nature of the American political system contributes to this situation. Congressmen and senators are elected more on the basis of local and sectional issues than on national ones, especially those involving foreign policy. Once elected, they continue to reflect particular interests rather than those of the nation. Secure for a period of two or six years, and usually dependent for re-election upon small but powerful groups in their

19 *Geofroy* v. *Riggs*, 133 U.S. 258 (1890).
20 Woodrow Wilson Foundation, *United States Foreign Policy: Its Organization and Control*, report of a study group, William Yandell Elliott, Chairman (New York: Columbia University Press, 1953), pp. 6-7.

districts or states, all too often they go their ways with a minimum feeling of responsibility to party or country. Another cause of conflict is the absence of effective leadership in Congress. Finally, the strong committees and their chairmen, selected on a seniority basis, are little governments in themselves, frequently able to defy the will of the majority.

The fact that the executive and legislative branches of the government have independent tenures of office has a dual effect. First, there is no effective way to break a deadlock between them. Secondly, congressmen feel too free to defy the President, since he is unable to dissolve the Congress and to force the members to face a re-election.

These are by no means all the factors involved in a very complex situation; moreover, there are some factors which make for unity. Members of a party may have an important stake in the success of the President, since it will probably have a bearing on their own chances of re-election. In time of emergency and war there will be much greater cooperation, for Congress will be more likely to follow presidential leadership. Finally, there are a number of senators and representatives who surmount these obstacles and display commendable courage, vision, and statesmanship.

Most of the references to foreign affairs are found in Articles I and II of the Constitution, principally in the latter. Professor Corwin maintains that "Article II is the most loosely drawn chapter of the Constitution."[21] This ambiguity is itself conducive to conflict between the legislative and executive branches. Nevertheless, some of the constitutional provisions allocating foreign affairs authority between them are reasonably clear, or in any case a working interpretation has been firmly established through practice or judicial decisions. For example, the President is commander-in-chief of the armed forces; he (or persons authorized by him) is the sole *official* spokesman for the United States in international relations; he has exclusive power to receive, or to refuse to receive, diplomatic representatives of other countries; and only the President can decide on the recognition of states and governments, as well as the maintenance or severance of diplomatic relations.

Over most other matters, however, the President and Congress have joint or "cognate" powers in which there is an intermingling or overlapping rather than a separation of powers. For example, although only Congress can declare war, of ten wars fought by the United States, including that in Korea (1950-53), in only five has there been a declaration of war. Moreover, the courts have held that the President can use the armed forces to repel invasion without the consent of Congress. Even the authority of the President as commander-in-chief is a source of controversy. In 1950, when President Truman dispatched four divisions to Europe, it provoked a "great debate" in Congress, but the legal issue of whether an

---

[21] Edward S. Corwin, *The President: Office and Powers, 1787-1957*, 4th rev. ed. (New York: New York University Press, 1957), p. 3.

action of this nature required the approval of Congress was left unresolved. Only Congress can appropriate funds for the maintenance of the military establishment, but the President can refuse to approve their actual expenditure. Likewise, the Senate must approve a treaty before the President may ratify it, but the latter may refuse to carry through with the ratification. The treaty-making power, that to make certain kinds of executive agreements, and the general law-making and appropriating authority are all cognate powers. Powers of this nature are so broad, so overlapping, and so indefinite that it would be almost impossible for the courts to disentangle them even if they were willing to try. The so-called separation of powers thus turns out to be a built-in conflict of powers.

Despite all this, it is rather clear that in foreign affairs the role and power of the presidency is superior to that of Congress. As a general principle, we may conclude that *when the Constitution leaves powers unassigned, or unclear, Congress has the authority in domestic affairs, whereas in external affairs it resides in the presidency.* Nevertheless, the situation is unsatisfactory, and there is need for mutual trust and cooperation rather than for the customary tug-of-war between the two branches of the government entrusted with the joint responsibility for foreign relations.

How may this be promoted? One proposal is that a joint council consisting of the President and his principal foreign affairs advisers on the one hand, and appropriate congressional leaders on the other, be established to share information and to work out mutually acceptable programs. Another is that cabinet members be allowed to attend sessions of Congress where they would answer questions and participate in debates on foreign policy. While there might be advantages in these arrangements (and both are now used in some form), many doubt that they would be sufficient. Almost any more far-reaching change would require amending the Constitution. It has been suggested that members of the House of Representatives be elected for a four-year term. This might reduce the influence of local issues and make congressmen less subject to pressure groups. Along with this change, the President could be given the authority to dissolve the Congress once in each four-year period, in case of a serious deadlock between the two branches. The people would then resolve the issue. Most drastic of all, a considerable number of serious students of the problem see no effective solution short of a responsible cabinet system on the British model. Presumably, however, an elected President would be the "king."

Foreign Affairs Administration

The substance of American foreign policy, as well as the efficiency with which it is conducted, depends in large measure on the personnel and organization of the executive branch of the government charged with foreign affairs responsibilities. One study of this administrative problem concluded that

In their total complexity and weight, they are quite literally beyond the managerial capacity of the men and agencies responsible for conducting them. Manifestly requiring the best of public management, the world business of the U.S. in its sheer volume and variety daily defies the best efforts of good men to keep it under executive control. The fact that it is nevertheless kept under minimum control, and never quite defeats or overwhelms the agencies charged with managing it, is something of a continuing miracle.[22]

Although the President has the ultimate foreign affairs power and responsibility, he cannot, however astute and energetic he may be, perform the multitude of tasks inherent in the presidency. He is therefore forced to delegate most of these to subordinates, reserving for his own consideration only the more important ones. The wisdom of his decisions on these will depend heavily on how well his subordinates have marshalled and evaluated the pertinent data, and set forth feasible alternative courses of action.

Although the Department of State is supposed to be the right arm of the President in the discharge of his foreign affairs responsibilities, it is only one of several arms. The Hoover Commission task force on foreign affairs maintained that "the most striking present-day feature of the organization of the United States Government for the conduct of foreign affairs is the participation in all its phases of departments and agencies other than the State Department."[23] We shall consider (1) the President and his Executive Staff; (2) The Department of State; (3) the other administrative agencies; and (4) overseas administration.

The President and his Executive Staff. The President is free to draw on advice and assistance from any source within or without the government. His immediate official advisers and assistants are organized within the several divisions of the Executive Office of the President. First, there is the White House Office, in which his personal staff is assembled. Other divisions that play a significant role in foreign affairs are the Bureau of the Budget, the Council of Economic Advisers, the Office of Civil and Defense Mobilization, and the National Security Council. The Joint Chiefs of Staff, although not in the Executive Office, serve very much as do the divisions noted above.

The most important of these is the National Security Council (NSC), along with the Central Intelligence Agency (CIA) which is under the direction of the Council. The province of NSC is *national security*, and there is little that term does not embrace. Its functions are "to advise the

---

[22] John Osborne, "Is Our State Department Manageable?" *Fortune*, LV (Mar. 1957), 112.

[23] *Task Force Report on Foreign Affairs, Appendix H.*, prepared for the Commission on Organization of the Executive Branch of the Government (Washington, D.C.: Government Printing Office), p. 56.

President with respect to the integration of domestic, foreign, and military policies relating to national security so as to enable the military services and other departments and agencies of the Government to cooperate more effectively in matters involving the national security." The Council is composed, according to statute, of the President, the Vice President, the Secretaries of State and Defense, and the Director of Civil and Defense Mobilization. Others serve at the discretion of the President. The Council is served by an executive secretary and a deputy executive secretary. NSC is assisted by a "Senior Staff" which does much of the preliminary work, and in turn is assisted by a "working level" secretariat.

Although existing informally since 1945, CIA was authorized by statute in 1947 along with NSC. CIA is only the *central* organ concerned with intelligence, for the Department of State and several other agencies, including the military, have their own intelligence units. CIA gathers and coordinates data obtained by other agencies, and supplements them when necessary by obtaining additional information from domestic and foreign sources. Some of the data is obtained by "espionage," but for the most part the job is to make sense out of facts readily obtainable. Its "intelligence estimates," prepared regularly for NSC and the President, are simply conclusions reached by CIA. At best, policy is made on the basis of "educated" guesses; the more facts at hand and correctly "estimated," the more likely are the guesses to be accurate. CIA is also entrusted with very delicate "operational" responsibilities, as indicated by its role in the Cuban invasion episode of 1961, and its suspected hand in the Guatemalan adventure of 1954 as well as in others.

The Department of State. The functions of the Department of State fall into six categories: participating in the formulation of objectives and policies; furnishing information to the President and to other executive agencies; representing the United States abroad in the bulk of its relations with other governments; conducting foreign negotiations on a bilateral and multilateral basis; directing certain "operations"; and, when interdepartmental matters of principal importance for foreign relations are involved, assuming the initiative in seeing that action is properly coordinated.[24]

The Department has the total responsibility for none of these. The question of whether it should be an "operating" agency is especially controversial. It engages in certain operations, but it does not have the major responsibility for these. It administered the Greek-Turkish Aid program, and after 1949 it was responsible for the German Occupation, although its major operating responsibilities of the early postwar years were Point Four and the International Information Program. Both of these

---

[24] For a comprehensive and excellent discussion of the Department of State, see Don K. Price, ed., *The Secretary of State,* prepared for the American Assembly (Englewood Cliffs, N.J.: Prentice-Hall, Inc., 1960).

THE DEPARTMENT OF STATE

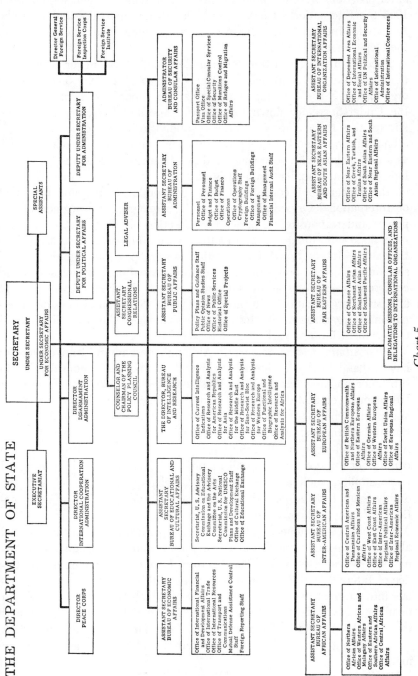

Chart 5.

latter programs were subsequently assigned to separate agencies, but after 1955 the International Cooperation Administration (ICA), and later the Agency for International Development, were autonomous agencies within the Department of State.

Since 1945 the Department has undergone several major reorganizations to make it a more effective agency. (See Chart No. 5, p. 451 for organization.) The Secretary and his various subordinates, ranging from the Under Secretary down through the Assistant Secretary level, constitute the top segment. Various subdivisions are concerned with administration. Another group of "functional" bureaus and officers, such as those dealing with economics, and intelligence and research, as well as long-term planning, have primarily staff and advisory functions. The core of the Department consists of five "geographical" bureaus plus that of International Organization Affairs. The geographical segments have power and responsibility, under the direction of the Secretary and his immediate subordinates, for all matters within their respective areas. The Bureau of International Organization Affairs provides "guidance and support for United States participation in international organizations and conferences, and acts as the channel between the Federal Government and such organizations. It prepares United States positions on international organization matters, and coordinates the overall Federal Government interest with respect thereto."

Other Administrative Agencies.   Although most administrative agencies have a hand in the foreign affairs pie, their role varies considerably in substance and importance. The President, his immediate staff, and the Department of State carry the major burden of formulating objectives and plans, whereas the primary task of the other agencies is administration and operations. In practice, however, it is impossible to separate these functions; all agencies therefore participate in varying degrees in the conduct of foreign policy "in all its phases." Some have only a marginal responsibility, such as the Securities Exchange Commission and the Smithsonian Institution. Others perform important foreign affairs functions, although their primary concern is with domestic affairs. The Agriculture Department establishes import quotas, assists in the disposal abroad of surplus agricultural commodities, and administers the International Wheat Agreement. The Treasury Department, which has an Office of International Finance, is concerned with the activities of the various international financial organizations of which the United States is a member, such as the World Bank, the International Monetary Fund, and the Inter-American Development Bank. It also participates in negotiations with foreign governments involving international financial and monetary matters.

Finally several agencies, in addition to the Department of State, are primarily involved in the conduct of foreign affairs. The Defense Department is concerned with the use of force in the promotion of foreign policy objectives. It also administers the military aspects of the Mutual Assistance Program. Through the National Security Council, the Joint Chiefs of Staff, and in other ways it shares in the development of foreign policy plans.

The United States Information Agency (USIA) established in 1953, took over responsibilities previously performed by the Department of State and the Mutual Security Agency. Through short-range propaganda and longer-range "information" programs USIA combats hostile propaganda and attempts to present a favorable image of the United States to foreign peoples and governments. It operates radio, television, and motion picture programs, and provides press and publication services to most of the countries of the world. Its United States Information Service offices abroad were located in ninety-four different states and dependent areas (1961), including one communist country, Yugoslavia.

Lastly, there are several agencies concerned with technical and economic aid to other countries. The chief of these is the Agency for International Development (AID), *in* but not really *of* the Department of State. It is responsible for technical assistance, for the principal grant and loan assistance programs, including defense support, and for various types of special assistance. Along with the Department of Agriculture, it administered the overseas surplus agricultural commodities program. The Development Loan Fund, created in 1957 as a part of ICA, became an independent corporate agency the following year. Its management was vested in a board of directors, of which the Under Secretary of State for Economic Affairs was chairman. Its principal concern was supplying long-term development capital to both governments and private enterprise in the less developed countries. The Export-Import Bank is also engaged in foreign lending, although its primary function is to stimulate United States exports.

The existence of several agencies responsible for one form or other of foreign economic assistance complicated the task of coordination, and was a source of confusion to the foreign countries concerned. Under the Democratic administration, which assumed office in January 1961, several of these agencies were consolidated in the new Agency for International Development.

Overseas Administration. The conventional view of the official overseas business of the United States being centered in a diplomatic mission acting as an arm of the Department of State has never been wholly accurate. Other agencies have long had personnel stationed in foreign countries. After World War II, the principle of "diplomatic mission monopoly" was more seriously breached, especially by the military agencies and the Economic Cooperation Administration responsible for the Marshall Plan. In the early nineteen-sixties fourteen civilian agencies, ranging from the

CIA (in numbers unknown but to a few) to the Department of State, employed more than 33,000 persons abroad. Of these, however, only some 12,000 were American citizens.

The Department of State (exclusive of AID) employed about 23,000 persons. Of these, 12,000 were American citizens, half of whom worked in the Department in Washington and the other half abroad in over 120 countries and territories. Some 10,000 foreign nationals accounted for the remainder. The AID had about 9,000 employees, 2,000 at home and 7,000 abroad, with the latter evenly divided between American citizens and nationals of other countries. The USIA employed most of the remainder—some eleven thousand—consisting of 4,000 American citizens, half of them at home and half abroad, and 7,000 others also stationed abroad.

There are different personnel systems, with different rates of pay, retirement systems, tenure, etc., for these different officers and employees. Until 1954, there were two personnel systems within the Department of State, one for the regular staff permanently stationed in Washington, and a second for the members of the Foreign Service. The first group, with the exception of the political appointees, were employed under the terms of the Civil Service Act. The Foreign Service personnel, regulated by a separate statute, was divided into Foreign Service officers, Foreign Service reserve officers, staff officers and employees, and aliens. The methods of selection, pay, and so forth were different for each of them.

The Foreign Service officers constituted the elite group. Nearly all of them entered by means of a stiff competitive examination at an early age and in the lowest grade, planning to make a career in the Service. There was a great deal of ill feeling and jealousy between the regular Department employees and the Foreign Service officers. More serious even was the fact that those stationed in Washington lacked overseas experience, while the Foreign Service officers, who spent most of their time abroad, lost touch with developments at home. Finally, after several years of largely unsuccessful attempts to "integrate" the officers of the Department and the Foreign Service officers, in 1954 a program of rapid integration began. The result was that most of the officers of the Department of State became Foreign Service officers, all of whom were henceforth subject to rotation between posts in Washington and the field. Foreign Service officers constitute, however, only about 4,000 of the 23,000 employees in the Department. The others are clerical and similar types of employees in Washington still on "civil service," those in the Staff Branch, Foreign Service reserve officers, and the foreign nationals.

There is no career service for either AID or USIA personnel, although the relative permanence of economic aid and information activities seems clear. In time, perhaps, the personnel of these agencies, with exceptions for persons with specialized skills hired on a short-term basis, will also be integrated into the Foreign Service.

FOREIGN POLICY SINCE 1945

Since 1945 Americans have compromised between trying to adjust to, withdraw from, or make over the kind of world they did not like. At times they were inclined to retreat within a shell of isolationism and at others to venture forth on crusades to transform the world into a model society, even at the risk of total war. In the end, however, they have tended to settle down to a middle course of living with an unsatisfactory situation, hoping that time would permit the passing or solution of these problems, and that total war could be avoided.

We shall trace in broad terms the evolution of postwar policy as background for the consideration of America's world relationships in subsequent chapters. First, however, a few words about the general world situation at the close of World War II are in order. Various meetings of heads of governments from the two or three big powers, as well as their lesser representatives, were held during the war and early postwar periods.[25] Although an attempt was made to avoid discussion of controversial matters that would interfere with unity and hamper victory, a number of important decisions were made, especially at Yalta and Potsdam. The essentials of the UN Charter were agreed upon at Dumbarton Oaks and Yalta. Germany was divided into zones of occupation and the Balkans split into spheres of influence between the Soviet Union and Great Britain, but not with the consent of the United States. Compromises were made with respect to the government of Poland; "temporary" divisions of territory were agreed to in Eastern Europe involving Poland, Germany, and the Soviet Union; and a declaration was issued that in "liberated" areas temporary governments would be set up "broadly representative of all democratic elements," to be followed by "the establishment by free elections of Governments responsible to the will of the people." At Yalta and Potsdam the Soviet Union promised to enter the war against Japan, contrary to the terms of the Soviet-Japanese neutrality pact of April 1941. Stalin agreed to continue recognizing the Nationalists as the government of China, and was promised the return of rights and territories taken from Russia by Japan in 1905, the Kurile Islands, and a free hand in Outer Mongolia. Japan was also to give up her outer territories in the Pacific and on the Asian mainland, including Korea and Taiwan, with the latter to be returned to China.

American postwar policy can be divided into three successive, although

---

[25] Roosevelt and Churchill met at the Atlantic Conference (Aug. 1941), in Washington (Dec. 1941, June 1942, May 1943), at Casablanca (Jan. 1943), in Quebec (Aug. 1943, Sept. 1944), and at Cairo (Dec. 1943). They were joined by Stalin at Teheran, Iran (Nov.-Dec., 1943), at Yalta (Feb. 1945). At Potsdam (July-Aug. 1945). Truman represented the U.S. and Attlee replaced Churchill midway through the conference.

hardly distinct, periods, characterized by (1) cooperation and accommodation; (2) patience and firmness with the Soviet Union; and (3) containment of the Soviet Union and the other communist bloc countries. The latter period, extending from 1947 to the present, falls in turn into a number of sub-periods.

Cooperation and Accommodation—
1945-August 1946

United States foreign policy, during the war and especially the early postwar period, was influenced by what was hoped and thought to be possible. It was characterized by participation in relief and reconstruction through UNRRA, formulation and establishment of the UN, withdrawal of the bulk of its troops from Europe and demobilization of military forces, proposals for the international control of atomic energy, attempts to bring Chinese Nationalists and Communists into a working coalition, conclusion of peace treaties with the former German satellite states and Italy, proposals for an International Trade Organization, the Yalta and Potsdam agreements, and the reform of Germany and Japan. It was based on the assumption that wartime collaboration was possible in the postwar period. The use of power, especially military power, was not only unnecessary, but would be positively dangerous, because large military forces would breed fear and suspicion.

Firmness and Patience—
August 1946-March 1947

The period of firmness and patience following the first phase, characterized by the cooperative approach, was one of transition. The problem of the Soviet Union came to the fore, where is has since remained. Even before the war ended the United States had become alarmed at Russian policy in Eastern Europe, especially at what was believed to be a violation of the Yalta agreement to permit the establishment of free governments there. Several controversies arose at the San Francisco United Nations Conference that put the policy of trust and cooperation to a severe test. In 1946 and early 1947, relations were strained by disagreement over the occupation of Germany, the unification of Korea, Soviet demands upon Turkey, and civil war in Greece. Negotiations over the international control of atomic energy were deadlocked.

Gradually the practice of making concessions to the Soviet Union was abandoned. Instead there was firmness on each specific issue. So far, however, there was no consistent policy of organizing general opposition to the Soviets, especially by an alliance network. The idea was not to play the game the Kremlin's way, but by firmness and patience get it to play according to American rules.

Cold War and Containment—1947-?

Beginning in 1947, the United States embarked upon a program known as "containment." Whether it was the Soviet Union, and later China, or communism in general that was to be contained has been unclear. In American eyes they have been identical, except in the case of Yugoslavia. The emphasis has been on military methods and the building of military strength at home and among allies abroad. Nevertheless, a program of economic aid was inaugurated, quite massive (but of short duration) in the case of Western Europe, and, while more limited among the under-developed areas, destined to extend over an indefinite period of time. Many members of Congress, however, and considerable segments of the American people, were unable to face the realities on this score. The result was unnecessary waste and inefficiency as "aid" was annually debated in Congress, and in the end reluctantly approved. There is no better example of the frustrations resulting from the nature of the American political system than this annual show. Information and propaganda made up the third facet of American foreign policy. Although its effects were difficult to measure, there was every evidence that the "image" of America abroad was hardly that which Americans had of themselves as a people and as a nation among nations.[26]

Averell Harriman, adviser to Presidents Roosevelt and Truman, and George F. Kennan, Soviet expert in the foreign service, questioned the validity of the assumption that the cooperative approach was the best way to deal with the men in the Kremlin, who, it was contended, understood and respected firmness and interpreted any other approach as evidence of weakness and vacillation. Secretary of State Byrnes returned from the Moscow Conference of December 1946 thoroughly disillusioned about the possibility of "horse trading" with the Soviets, as was his successor, George C. Marshall, following his experience at Moscow in the late winter of the following year. Yet President Truman, in his State of the Union message in January 1947, said that "whatever difficulties there may have been between us and the Soviet Union, however, should not be allowed to obscure the fact that the basic interests of both nations lie in the early making of a peace under which the peoples of all countries may return to the essential tasks of production and reconstruction."

During the transition period there was one group that would revert to cooperation and another that advocated containment. Vice President Henry Wallace was a representative of the first, and George F. Kennan of the second. Wallace believed then (he changed his mind after the Korean War) that the Soviet Union was motivated primarily by fear and needed

[26] Franz M. Joseph, *As Others See Us: The United States Through Foreign Eyes* (Princeton, N.J.: Princeton University Press, 1959).

assurance against a Western attack. In February 1946, Kennan, then serving in the American Embassy in Moscow, sent a long memorandum to the Department of State setting forth essentially the position taken in his famous "Mr. X" article.[27] Although hardly the architect of the containment policy, Kennan rationalized it and helped shape its development. After an analysis of the chief motivations of Soviet conduct he declared: "In these circumstances it is clear that the main element of any United States policy toward the Soviet Union must be that of a long-term, patient but firm and vigilant containment of Russian expansive tendencies."[28] Neither words alone nor sporadic acts of resistance would be effective, for the Soviets followed a long-range plan. A similar plan would have to be developed to contain them "by the adroit and vigilant application of counter-force at a series of constantly shifting geographical and political points, corresponding to the shifts and manoeuvres of Soviet policy, but which cannot be charmed or talked out of existence."[29] Applied over a period of ten to fifteen years, it might be expected to promote tendencies which "must eventually find their outlet in either the break-up or the gradual mellowing of Soviet power."[30]

Containment through Economic Aid—March 1947-April 1949. On March 12, 1947, two days before the Moscow Conference opened, President Truman made a dramatic appeal before Congress in which he proclaimed the Truman Doctrine. This was occasioned by the Greek Civil War and the British note declaring the intention to withdraw their military forces from that country. The President said:

I believe that it must be the policy of the United States to support free peoples who are resisting attempted subjugation by armed minorities or by outside pressures. . . .
I believe that our help should be primarily through economic and financial aid which is essential to economic stability and orderly political processes.

To implement this policy he called for an appropriation of $400 million to give economic and military aid to Greece and Turkey, which, after considerable delay, was approved by the Republican Congress. The Truman Doctrine marked the real turning point in American postwar policy. What has since followed is simply a logical development from the principle: "to support free people . . . resisting . . . subjugation by armed minorities or by outside pressure."

When Secretary Marshall returned from Moscow in the spring of 1947, he was impressed by the economic needs of Western Europe. Aid had hitherto been unplanned and piecemeal. On June 5, 1947, in a commence-

---

[27] See X, "The Sources of Soviet Conduct," *Foreign Affairs,* XXV (July 1947), 566-82.
[28] *Ibid.,* p. 575.
[29] *Ibid.,* p. 576.
[30] *Ibid.,* p. 582.

ment address at Harvard University, he invited the countries of Europe, including Russia,

> . . . to take the initiative and come to some agreement among themselves as to the requirements of the situation and the part these countries will take in order to give proper effect to whatever action might be undertaken by this Government. . . .
>
> Any assistance that this Government may render in the future should provide a cure rather than a mere palliative. Any government that is willing to assist in the task of recovery will find full co-operation, I am sure, on the part of the United States Government. Any government which maneuvers to block the recovery of other countries cannot expect help from us.

After conversations in Paris between French, British, and Soviet representatives, the Russians refused to go along. Eighteen European states subsequently accepted the U.S. invitation; the result was the Marshall Plan, or more formally, the European Recovery Plan, to which the United States contributed about $12 billion.

In addition to the Truman Doctrine and the Marshall Plan, a third program was initiated during this period. The fourth point of President Truman's inaugural address of January 1949 called for a "bold new program" of technical assistance to the underdeveloped countries. Slow to get under way, and supported by limited funds, this long-term program was felt to hold vast promise.

Three events which had great influence on the evolution of United States foreign policy took place during the period under consideration. These were the Communist seizure of power in Czechoslovakia in February 1948, the Russian blockade of Berlin, and the final conquest of the Chinese mainland by the Communist forces. The first convinced many people that the Soviets would destroy democratic governments whenever they could do so, and the second that they would use force to achieve their ends. The success of the Chinese Communists changed the whole basis of our Far Eastern policies. We found ourselves "waiting for the dust to settle."

Military Commitments and Limited Military Strength—April 1949-June 1950. During the early stages of the Marshall Plan, while it was still under consideration by Congress, it was argued that dollars for economic aid would be substitutes for arms and men. Then, before the Marshall Plan was approved, another development took place. In May 1948, the Vandenberg Resolution was approved by the Senate, sixty-four to four. The State Department called it a "new departure in American foreign policy," for it proposed that ". . . for the first time in the nation's history the United States associate itself in peacetime with countries outside the Western Hemisphere in collective security arrangements designed to safeguard peace and to strengthen our security." The result was the North Atlantic Treaty Organization.

One of the most important influences on United States military strategy was its temporary monopoly of the atomic bomb. Although it was assumed that other nations—the Soviet Union in particular—would eventually produce atomic bombs, it was also assumed that it would take considerable time for them to do so. In June 1945, James F. Byrnes expressed the belief that it would require at least seven to ten years. Respected thinking further proceeded along the following lines: any war involving the United States would be a general war in which strategic atomic bombing would play a major part; before Russia could produce the bomb, the threat of strategic bombing would be the essential deterrent against Soviet armed expansion. Hanson F. Baldwin, military editor of *The New York Times,* writes: "The freezing of our strategic concepts around the one-weapon theory in part explained the unpreparedness of the armed services for the Korean War; we were prepared for war but not for the war we had to fight."[31]

On September 23, 1949, President Truman announced that there had been an "atomic explosion" in the Soviet Union. The effect of this early development was to make the United States' leisurely timetable obsolete. The assumption had been that by the time the Soviets got the bomb Western Europe would be sufficiently strong to withstand a Russian attack, and American general superiority in other fields could be brought into play. Despite the surprising speed with which the Soviets developed atomic weapons, the immediate effect on American actions was hardly discernible. Reliance continued to be on atomic weapons and strategic bombing. The idea that the Soviets would soon achieve effective nuclear parity with the United States, that mutual would replace unilateral deterrence, and that the United States policy of massive retaliation would be obsolete to deter less than all-out aggression, was slow in penetrating the minds of the American people or their leaders.

Increased Emphasis on Military Strength—June 1950-1953. The Korean War which began in June 1950, aside from the fact that it witnessed the first application of military sanctions under the auspices of an international organization, did not lead to the adoption of new American policies; but it did give impetus to those already in existence. Appropriations for American military forces were increased more than threefold; assistance to Europe began to emphasize military strength, and Marshall Plan funds became "defense support funds." The Marshall Plan, NATO, and military assistance to Europe had been viewed by many as substitutes for American troops. In the autumn of 1950, however, President Truman, on his own authority, ordered four divisions to Europe to augment the military forces under NATO. The "Uniting for Peace" resolution of December 1950, designed to by-pass the Security Council veto and to enable the General Assembly to assume responsibility for the application of sanc-

---

31 *The New York Times Magazine,* May 17, 1953, p. 37.

tions, was another result of the Korean war. Finally, plans for the remilitarization of Japan and Germany, and the incorporation of the forces of the latter into a Western European army under NATO command, received strong support from the United States.

The New Look and Summitry: 1953-1961. The inauguration of a Republican Administration in January 1953, the death of Stalin, the Korean truce, peace gestures from Moscow, demands for tax reductions throughout the Western world, and jaded nerves, all combined in 1953 and for a time thereafter to bring about a cooling of the cold war and a relaxation of tensions.

Republicans had charged, from 1950 and through the election of 1952, that containment was a costly and unending policy leading nowhere. "Liberation" therefore should replace containment, and there would be a "new look" at the military establishment in order to adjust it to the "long haul" rather than build up to a crisis previously predicted for 1953 or 1954. The Republican administration was accused of fitting the military establishment to the size of the budget rather than *vice versa.* The new Secretary of the Treasury warned that unless government expenditures were reduced there would be a depression which would "make your eyebrows curl."

After the election the call for liberation was quietly dropped, since there appeared to be no means by which it could be accomplished short of war. It was declared that the American Seventh Fleet would no longer prevent the Chinese Nationalist Government from invading the mainland from their base on Taiwan; but since they were incapable of doing so in any case, and in 1954 promised to consult with the United States before making any such attempt, the American declaration was but a gesture.

As a part of the "long haul" program, greater emphasis was placed on airpower and strategic bombing as a deterrent against Soviet and Communist Chinese aggression. On January 12, 1954, Secretary of State Dulles stated that henceforth "local defenses must be reinforced by the further deterrent of massive retaliatory power. . . . The way to deter aggression is for the free community to respond vigorously at places and with means of its own choosing."[32] Whether correctly or not, the statement was widely interpreted as meaning that henceforth the United States would meet any aggression by the Soviet Union, or by countries within its orbit, with an all-out atomic blitz. There would be either no war or total war. Presumably the announcement also meant that total war would be the only kind of war the United States would prepare to fight. Following criticism at home and abroad, the "new" strategy was clarified and amplified. "It does not mean that if there is a Communist attack somewhere in Asia, atom or hydrogen bombs will necessarily be dropped on the great

---

[32] Dulles, Secretary of State, "The Evolution of Foreign Policy," Department of State *Bulletin*, XXX (Jan. 25, 1954), 108.

industrial centers of China or Russia. It does mean that the free world must maintain the collective means and be willing to use them in the way which most effectively makes aggression too risky and expensive to be tempting."[33] Conventional armaments would continue to be necessary and "local defense" would remain a part of the grand strategy.

Nevertheless, American capacity for waging conventional warfare was widely regarded as inadequate and as the Soviet Union developed thermonuclear weapons and long-rang missiles, it became less and less likely that "massive retaliation" would be used to deter aggression undertaken anywhere by conventional and covert means.[34]

During the eight years after 1953, the other aspects of the containment policy continued without substantial change. There were crises over Indo-China; the Communist Chinese bombardment of the Nationalist held off-shore islands; the Suez Canal and the British-French-Israeli attack on Egypt; and over Hungary, Berlin, the Congo, and Cuba. There was also a summit meeting in Geneva in 1955 at which no issues were settled; but declarations issued there were interpreted to mean that the era of "mutual nuclear deterrence" had arrived.

In September 1959, Premier Khrushchev visited the United States and met with President Eisenhower. The crisis over Berlin was eased, and the way supposedly paved toward a summit meeting in Paris the following May. Shortly before the meeting was scheduled to open, the Russians downed an American U-2 "spy plane" 1300 miles within Soviet territory. After considerable confusion and evasion in Washington, the truth was finally admitted and President Eisenhower assumed full responsibility. Although the principals assembled in Paris, the final steps to the summit were never mounted, for Khrushchev demanded and Eisenhower refused an apology over the U-2 incident as a condition for the opening of negotiations. Soviet-American relations were further strained during the remainder of the Eisenhower administration.

The New Frontier and American Foreign Policy—1961-? The new administration which took over in Washington in January 1961 was soon faced with a number of crises—Laos, Cuba, and Berlin—and with the perennial problems of the cold war. After a short "honeymoon" with the Soviet Union, this war resumed its familiar shape. Like the previous administration, the new one sought ways to seize the initiative, and to develop a "positive" foreign policy.

A number of trends were discernible during the first year. First, efforts were made to develop greater capacity to conduct conventional and

---

[33] John Foster Dulles, "Policy for Security and Peace," *Foreign Affairs*, XXXII (Apr. 1954), 359.
[34] See General Maxwell D. Taylor (Ret.), *The Uncertain Trumpet* (New York: Harper & Brothers, 1959), for a vigorous criticism of the doctrine of massive retaliation and U.S. military preparation.

guerrilla-type warfare. Secondly, the problem of disarmament and arms control, and their relation to general military policy and security, underwent a thorough re-examination in an effort to explore all possible avenues to international agreement on armaments. Thirdly, the foreign aid administrative apparatus was reorganized, and a renewed effort made to convince Congress that foreign economic assistance should be put on a long-term basis. Fourthly, greater attention was given to Latin America in order to overcome the feeling of neglect in that area, to prevent the spread of Castroism, and to remove the image of America as a friend of dictators. Fifthly, the vigorous young American President, after having decried summitry and suggested that more use would be made of conventional diplomacy, soon found himself traveling to the capitals of America's major allies, and even meeting with Premier Khrushchev in Vienna, where the two men could "size each other up."

Lastly, efforts were made to inject more vigor into American society through federal aid to education, various efforts to decrease unemployment and increase the rate of economic growth, and to insure civil rights for all Americans. If these efforts were successful, the political feasibility of persuading the people and the Congress to devote a larger share of production to the advancement of foreign policy goals would be enhanced, and the message of the "Voice of America" as a nation still interested in the ideals of the American Revolution would be more convincing abroad. Whether these efforts would meet with greater success than had those of the previous administrations was uncertain as these lines were written.

SUGGESTED READINGS

Acheson, Dean G., "The Premises of American Policy," *Orbis*, III (Oct. 1959), 269-91.

Almond, Gabriel A., *The American People and Foreign Policy*. New York: Harcourt, Brace & World, Inc., 1950.

Bastert, Russell H., "The Two American Diplomacies," *Yale Review*, XLIX (June 1960), 518-38.

Bell, Phillip W., "Colonialism as a Problem in American Foreign Policy," *World Politics*, V (Oct. 1952), 86-109.

Berle, Adolph A., Jr., *Tides of Crisis: A Primer of Foreign Relations*. New York: Reynal & Co., Inc., 1957.

Blake, Nelson Manfred and O. T. Barck, *United States in Its World Relations.* New York: McGraw-Hill Book Co., Inc., 1960.

Bloomfield, Lincoln P., *The United Nations and U.S. Foreign Policy: A New Look at the National Interest.* Boston: Little, Brown & Co., 1960.

Briggs, Herbert W., "The United States and the International Court of Justice: A Re-examination," *American Journal of International Law,* LIII (Apr. 1959), 301-18.

Brogan, Denis W., *America in the Modern World.* New Brunswick, N.J.: Rutgers University Press, 1960.

Carleton, William G., *The Revolution in American Foreign Policy: 1915-1954,* rev. ed. New York: Random House, 1957.

Cheever, Daniel S. and H. Field Haviland, Jr., *American Foreign Policy and the Separation of Powers.* Cambridge: Harvard University Press, 1952.

Cleveland, Harlan and others, *The Overseas Americans.* New York: McGraw-Hill Book Co., Inc., 1960.

Committee for Economic Development, *Economic Growth in the United States: Its Past and Future; A Statement on National Policy by The Research and Policy Committee.* New York: 1958.

Crabb, Cecil V., *Bipartisan Foreign Policy: Myth or Reality?* Evanston, Illinois: Row, Peterson & Company, 1957.

Cutler, Robert, "The Development of the National Security Council," *Foreign Affairs,* XXXIV (Apr. 1956), 441-58.

"The Department of State, 1930-1955: Expanding Functions and Responsibilities," *Department of State Bulletin,* XXXII (Mar. 21 and Mar. 28, 1955), 470-86; 528-44.

Elder, Robert Ellsworth, *The Policy Machine.* Syracuse, New York: Syracuse University Press, 1961.

Elliott, William Y. and others, *United States Foreign Policy: Its Organization and Control.* New York: Columbia University Press, 1953.

Finletter, Thomas K., *Foreign Policy: The Next Phase: the 1960's,* rev. ed. New York: Harper & Brothers for the Council on Foreign Relations, 1960.

Fuchs, Lawrence H., "Minority Groups and Foreign Policy," *Political Science Quarterly,* LXXIV (June 1959), 161-75.

Furniss, Edgar S., Jr., *American Military Policy: Strategic Aspects of World Political Geography.* New York: Holt, Rinehart & Winston, Inc., 1957.

Gange, John, *American Foreign Relations: Permanent Problems and Changing Policies.* New York: The Ronald Press Company, 1959.

Gelber, Lionel, *America in Britain's Place.* New York: Frederick A. Praeger, Inc., 1961.

Goldwin, Robert and others, eds., *Readings in American Foreign Policy.* New York: Oxford University Press, Inc., 1959.

Graebner, Norman A., *The New Isolationism: A Study in Politics and Foreign Policy since 1950.* New York: The Ronald Press Company, 1956.

Hero, Alfred O., *Americans in World Affairs.* Boston: World Peace Foundation, 1959.

Hilsman, Roger, "Congressional-Executive Relations and the Foreign Policy Consensus," *American Political Science Review,* LII (Sept. 1958), 725-44.

Hyde, Louis K., *The United States and the United Nations, Promoting the Public Welfare: Examples of American Cooperation, 1945-1955.* Prepared for the Carnegie Endowment for International Peace. New York: Manhattan Publishing Co., 1960.

Joseph, Franz M., ed., *As Others See Us: The United States Through Foreign Eyes.* Princeton, N.J.: Princeton University Press, 1959.

Kennan, George F., *American Diplomacy, 1900-1950*. Chicago: University of Chicago Press, 1951.

Kertesz, Stephen D. and M. A. Fitzsimons, eds., *What America Stands For*. Notre Dame, Indiana: University of Notre Dame Press, 1960.

Kust, Matthew J., "The Great Dilemma of American Foreign Policy," *Virginia Quarterly Review*, XXXIV (Spring 1958), 224-39.

Liska, George, *The New Statecraft: Foreign Aid in American Foreign Policy*. Chicago: University of Chicago Press, 1960.

Mangone, Gerard J., *A Guide to United States Foreign Policy*. Syracuse, New York: Syracuse University Press, 1959.

Martin, Edwin M., "New Trends in United States Economic Foreign Policy; with Questions and Answers," *Annals of the American Academy of Political and Social Science*, CCCXXX (July 1960), 67-76.

McCamy, James L., "The Administration of Foreign Affairs in the United States," *World Politics*, VII (Jan. 1955), 315-25.

Osgood, Robert Endicott, *Ideals and Self Interest in America's Foreign Relations: The Great Transformation of the Twentieth Century*. Chicago: University of Chicago Press, 1953.

Perla, Leo, *Can We End the Cold War? A Study in American Foreign Policy*. New York: The Macmillan Co., 1960.

Pratt, Julius W., *A History of United States Foreign Policy*. Englewood Cliffs, N.J.: Prentice-Hall, Inc., 1955.

———, "Anticolonialism in U.S. Policy," *Orbis*, I (Oct. 1957), 291-314.

Rockefeller Brothers Fund, *Foreign Economic Policy for the Twentieth Century*. Report of the Rockefeller Brothers Fund, Special Studies Project (Panel III). Garden City, New York: Doubleday & Company, Inc., 1958.

———, *The Mid-Century Challenge to U.S. Foreign Policy*. Report of the Rockefeller Brothers Fund Special Studies Project (Panel I). Garden City, New York: Doubleday & Company, Inc., 1959.

Rostow, Walt W., *The United States in the World Arena: An Essay in Recent History*. New York: Harper & Brothers, 1960.

Rostow, Eugene V., "American Foreign Policy and International Law," *Louisiana Law Review*, XVII (Feb. 1957), 552-71.

Sapin, Burton M. and Richard C. Snyder, *The Role of the Military in American Foreign Policy*. Garden City, New York: Doubleday & Company, Inc., 1954.

Steiner, Zara S., *The State Department and the Foreign Service: The Wriston Report: Four Years Later*. Princeton, N.J.: Center of International Studies, Princeton University, 1958.

Stephens, Oren, *Facts to a Candid World: America's Overseas Information Program*. Stanford, California: Stanford University Press, 1955.

Stevenson, Adlai E., "Putting First Things First," *Foreign Affairs*, XXXVIII (Jan. 1960), 191-208.

Strausz-Hupé, Robert and William R. Kinter, "A Forward Strategy Beyond Survival," *Orbis*, IV (July 1960), 141-58.

Swift, Richard N., "United States Leadership in the United Nations," *Western Political Quarterly*, XI (June 1958), 183-94.

Taylor, Maxwell D., *The Uncertain Trumpet*. New York: Harper & Brothers, 1960.

Truman, Harry S., *Memoirs*, 2 vols. Garden City, New York: Doubleday & Company, Inc., 1955-56.

United States in World Affairs. New York: Harper & Brothers for the Council on Foreign Relations: Annual, 1931 to date (Not published during war years).

U.S. Congress, Economic Joint Committee, Study Paper No. 18, "National Security and American Economy in 1960's," by Henry Rowen. Joint Committee Print, 86th Cong., 2nd sess., 1960. Washington, D.C.: Government Printing Office, 1960.

U.S. Senate, Foreign Relations Committee, *United States Foreign Policy: Compilation of Studies, Nos. 1-13*, 2 vols. No. 9. "The Formulation and Administration of United States Foreign Policy," by the Brookings Institution. Committee Print, 86th Cong., 2nd sess., 1960, pp. 791-990. Washington, D.C.: Government Printing Office, 1960

————, *United States Foreign Policy: Compilation of Studies, Nos. 1-13*, 2 vols. No. 6. "The Operational Aspects of United States Foreign Policy," by Maxwell Graduate School of Citizenship and Public Affairs, Syracuse University. Committee Print, 86th Cong., 2d sess., 1960, pp. 555-634. Washington, D.C.: Government Printing Office, 1960.

Westerfield, Bradford, *Foreign Policy and Party Politics: Pearl Harbor to Korea.* New Haven: Yale University Press, 1955.

Wriston, Henry M., *Diplomacy in a Democracy.* New York: Harper & Brothers, 1956.

22

Europe, the United States, and the Atlantic Community

S. Grover Rich
*Department of Political Science and Institute of
International Studies, University of Utah*

Western Europe, although stripped of its former great military power and no longer dominant in the world, remains the most valuable, dynamic, and potentially powerful piece of real estate on earth. Little larger than the eastern seaboard of the United States, it is populated by some 325 million of the world's most literate, urbane, skilled, and industrious people. It has a sea coast three times as long as Africa's, crowded with shipping and port facilities. Its fertile earth is elaborately cultivated, its rich store of minerals and other resources is fully exploited, and its industry, trade and finance are highly developed. It is the depository of Western culture, and the mother not only of America and the American way of life, but of all the great forces that are molding the present world: science, capitalism, socialism, democracy, humanism, fascism, communism, colonialism, nationalism, and imperialism.

The one *ism* that might restore its power and glory is federalism. For if Western Europe's twenty nations could be united politically and economically, the resulting state would rival the world's greatest powers. The Russians fully realize this, as do the Americans. Should Europe's vast human and natural resources be added to Russia's and come under the centralized totalitarian control of its Communist Party, freedom would be doomed. Of all the issues in the current world struggle between the Soviet Union and the United States, the future of Europe, therefore, remains the most important. And as it is often said that "as Germany goes, so goes Europe," the future of Germany probably holds the key to future United States-Soviet relations: indeed, Berlin is the symbol of the East-West struggle.

Writing in 1943, before the victory over fascism and the consequent struggle with the Soviet Union was in sight, Walter Lippmann contended that:

the question in Europe is whether Russia will seek to extend her power westward into Europe in such a way that it threatens the security of the Atlantic states. The question in the Pacific is whether as nearest neighbors by land, sea, and air, the United States and Russia will move towards rivalry or towards a common ground of understanding. The two questions are inseparable because, as the Russian statesmen have so often insisted, peace is indivisible. . . . the crucial question of the epoch that we are now entering is the relationship between Russia and that Atlantic Community in which Britain and the United States are the leading military powers.

. . .

If we fail to make peace after this war, we . . . shall be immediately forewarned that we must prepare for the next war . . . because the objective test of whether there is to be peace or war will be whether the borderland between Russia and the Atlantic states is settled by consent or by pressure, dictation, and diplomatic violence. . . . If in this region the effort to settle territorial boundaries and to decide what governments shall be recognized discloses deep and insoluble conflicts between Russia's conception of her vital interests and that of the Western Allies, then every nation will know that it must get ready and must choose sides in the eventual but unavoidable next war.[1]

BUILDING THE ATLANTIC COMMUNITY

Current American foreign policy in Europe, as elsewhere, has been molded to meet the challenge thrown up by Russian insistence on extending her dominion by "pressure, dictation, and diplomatic violence." United States reaction to this threat has been a series of bold policy actions designed to contain Soviet power. With regard to Europe, these were as follows:

The Truman Doctrine

The first step in the containment of Russia after World War II came unexpectedly soon, because of a British default. The eastern Mediterranean had long been a British sphere of primary interest. Greece, Palestine, Turkey, Cyprus, and Suez were British protectorates or allies. By a war-

[1] Walter Lippmann, *U.S. Foreign Policy: Shield of the Republic* (Boston: Little, Brown & Co., 1943), pp. 146-48.

time agreement, Stalin had agreed to the postwar domination of Greece by Britain in return for Churchill's acceptance of Soviet priority in Bulgaria and Rumania.[2] At Yalta Stalin demanded (unsuccessfully) a greater Russian voice in the control of the Turkish Straits, Russia's outlet to the Mediterranean. Following the war, Soviet troops remained in Northern Iran and attempted to establish a Red puppet regime there. Pressure applied through the UN induced their withdrawal. Russian diplomatic pressure against Turkey also failed when the Turks rejected Russian demands for an alliance and greater control of the Straits.

In Greece, however, it was a different story. The British had restored the Greek monarchy, but it remained unpopular and political stability was not achieved. Anxious for drastic reform, the people were discontent; with the aid of Marshal Tito a Red-led revolution soon threatened to overthrow the Greek government. Britain herself was exhausted by war, in the throes of economic depression, and unable to maintain her worldwide commitments. The Labour Government appealed to Washington in early 1947, and Truman quickly decided to fill the vacuum that would result from the British decision to abandon Greece. The result was the "Truman Doctrine," an American aid program designed to win the civil war, preserve the Dardanelles and the Eastern Mediterranean from Soviet control, and shore up Greece and Turkey against pressure from the Reds. The policy was a dramatic success, aided it is true by the Yugoslav expulsion from the Soviet bloc in 1948.

The Marshall Plan

In Greece, the Red threat was military and the instrument chosen to gain control was civil war. In Western Europe, although civil war was a possibility, the challenge was more thoroughly political and economic. Its economy was at a standstill, and its people demanded jobs and drastic social reform. Europe's communist parties, Russia's primary instruments of Soviet policy, were in the forefront of this movement. Over a third of the people of France and Italy were regular communist voters, and Red domination of several western European governments was not an unlikely possibility.

American military aid was a major factor in winning the war in Greece, and American economic aid the battle for Europe. The Marshall Plan poured over $12 billions into Western Europe in four years, and governments friendly to Washington remained in popular control. Building on this foundation, Western Europe experienced great prosperity, with its rate of economic growth surpassing that of the United States.

---

[2] Winston S. Churchill, *The Second World War: Triumph and Tragedy,* Vol. VI (Boston: Houghton Mifflin Company, 1953), pp. 226-28.

The North Atlantic Treaty Organization

The restoration of economic stability in Western Europe was only a partial answer to the Soviet threat. It was obvious that military security against Russia was also necessary. Europe therefore became not only a ward, but a protectorate of the United States. This was accomplished by the signing the North Atlantic Treaty (1949) by twelve states, and the prompt organization of a joint NATO military establishment, first commanded by General Eisenhower. Greece and Turkey became members in 1952, and Germany in 1955.

Whereas aid to Greece and Turkey had protected the Mediterranean flank, NATO protected the center and the north flank of Europe. With Western bases in Norway and Denmark, as well as in Turkey and Greece, Russian sea power could be kept out of the Mediterranean and the North Sea. With land and air power stretched across the heart of Europe, and with the Americans having a monopoly on atomic weapons and pledged to defend Europe, the Soviets would hesitate to use military force to expand westward.

Within a few years, NATO had become only one (though the key one) of a series of interlocking, mutually dependent, regional defense systems, built upon alliances with the United States.[3] Hence the United States had gone far toward ringing the Soviet Union with military bases and a complex of interrelated defense alliances. These have proved successful in their primary goal, and since their formulation the Kremlin has not resorted to outright military attack by Soviet troops to expand its control. Although the alliance system has been an important factor in successfully deterring Soviet military aggression, after Russia obtained atomic weapons and the ballistic missiles to deliver them, America's allies were less sure that they could rely upon her for protection. Finally, while the Soviets have not used their military power to expand, they have turned to psychological, economic, and political warfare with spectacular success. Against such tactics, military alliances were no defense.

Military Assistance

Complementing the creation of an alliance system, the United States carried out an elaborate program of military assistance to the non-communist world.[4] This was especially important in Europe, where her NATO allies could not afford large defense expenditures in the immediate postwar years. Their most urgent goal was economic revival, and buoyed up

---

[3] See Chapter 15.

[4] This began in 1950 with the Mutual Defense Assistance Program. In 1952 economic, military, and technical aid programs were combined into a single Mutual Security Program.

THE INSTITUTIONS OF THE EUROPEAN COMMUNITIES

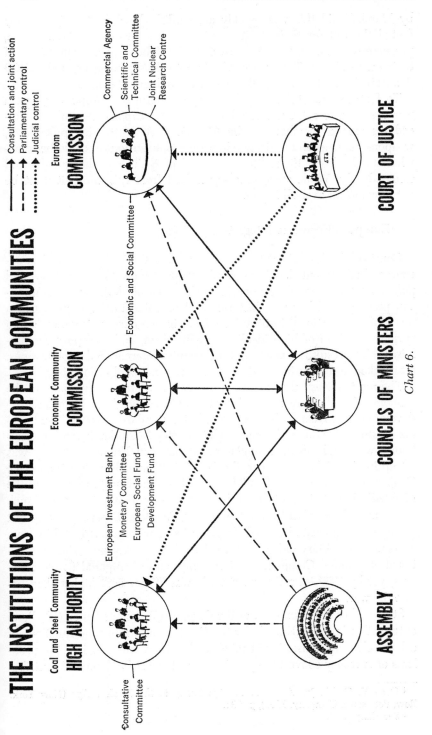

Consultation and joint action
Parliamentary control
Judicial control

Coal and Steel Community
HIGH AUTHORITY

Consultative Committee

Economic Community
COMMISSION

European Investment Bank
Monetary Committee
European Social Fund
Development Fund

Economic and Social Committee

Euratom
COMMISSION

Commercial Agency
Scientific and Technical Committee
Joint Nuclear Research Centre

COURT OF JUSTICE

COUNCILS OF MINISTERS

Chart 6.

ASSEMBLY

by Marshall aid this was quickly accomplished, while America largely footed the bill for their defense. Afterwards, the countries of Europe, prosperous as never before, were capable of bearing a larger share of their own defense. They were reluctant to do so, however, and NATO therefore failed to develop the necessary military strength.

To further strengthen NATO and the defense of Europe, a program was designed to achieve a standardization of weapons and military procedures among members of the Atlantic Pact. If training procedures, weapons, replacement parts, and logistic supply structures could be somewhat standardized, the military potential of NATO would be enhanced tremendously. While some success resulted from this effort, it must be put down as an over-all failure.

European Economic Integration

Consistently throughout the postwar period, the United States has encouraged movements looking toward the greater economic, military, and political integration of Europe. Europe's response, deriving from American pressure and her own historic ideal of unification, has produced a series of supranational institutions which, in one observer's views, "are a curious amalgam of high idealism, opportunism, and sweeping compromises."[5] The result is a crazy quilt of complex international organizations, interlocked and superimposed upon Europe's national economies.[6]

The most successful of Europe's unification ventures have been in the economic field, where national tariff barriers have long hampered the development of freer trade and higher living standards. In 1944, the Benelux Customs Union, embracing Belgium, the Netherlands, and Luxembourg, was established. A similar union between France and Italy was set up in 1949. The same year, the OEEC (Office of European Economic Cooperation) came into being. The OEEC was the European organ of the Marshall Plan, designed to plan the expenditure of American aid in such a way as to bring about the integration of Western Europe. It early lost the power to allocate Marshall funds to its members, and the shift from economic to military aid further weakened its control over Europe's national economies. Compromise after compromise hampered its effectiveness; yet by 1955 intra-European trade was 70 per cent higher than before the war.

Still another development was the European Payments Union (EPU), an outgrowth of proposals made by the OEEC. Performing the functions of a bank clearing house, it did much to facilitate and alleviate the problems of currency convertibility in Europe. Its most fundamental contribu-

---

[5] Cecil V. Crabb, Jr., *American Foreign Policy in the Nuclear Age* (New York: Row, Peterson & Company, 1960), p. 231.

[6] See Chapter 9.

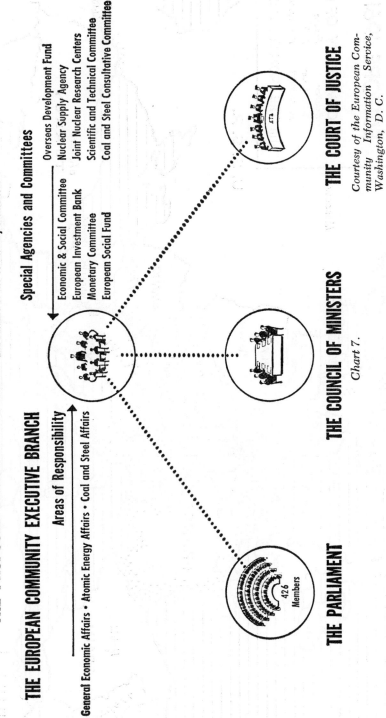

THE PROPOSED FEDERAL REVISION: How a Fusion of the Executive Branches Would Alter the Structure and Balance of the Community Institutions

THE EUROPEAN COMMUNITY EXECUTIVE BRANCH

Areas of Responsibility

General Economic Affairs • Atomic Energy Affairs • Coal and Steel Affairs

Special Agencies and Committees

Economic & Social Committee
European Investment Bank
Monetary Committee
European Social Fund

Overseas Development Fund
Nuclear Supply Agency
Joint Nuclear Research Centers
Scientific and Technical Committee
Coal and Steel Consultative Committee

THE COURT OF JUSTICE

Courtesy of the European Community Information Service, Washington, D. C.

THE COUNCIL OF MINISTERS

Chart 7.

THE PARLIAMENT

426 Members

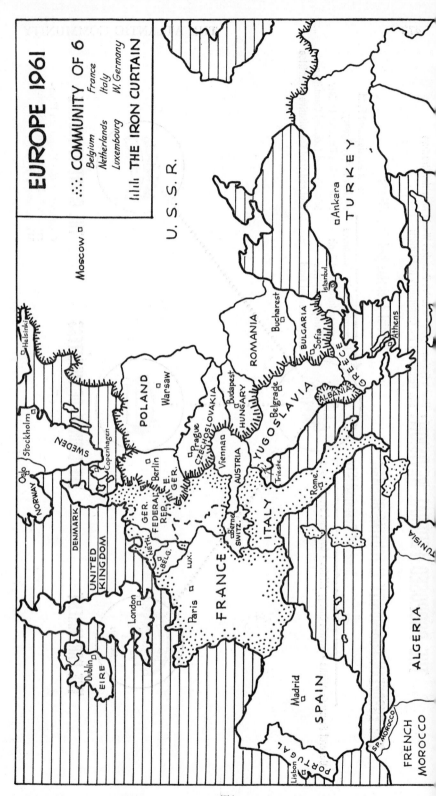

EUROPE 1961

COMMUNITY OF 6

Belgium — France
Netherlands — Italy
Luxembourg — W. Germany

THE IRON CURTAIN

U.S.S.R.

Moscow □

Helsinki □

Oslo □ Stockholm □

SWEDEN

NORWAY

DENMARK

Copenhagen □

POLAND

Warsaw □

Berlin □

E. GER.

FEDERAL REP. GER.

Prague □ CZECHOSLOVAKIA

Vienna □

AUSTRIA Budapest □

HUNGARY

Berne □ SWITZ.

ROMANIA

Bucharest □

YUGOSLAVIA Belgrade □

Trieste

BULGARIA

Sofia □

Istanbul

ALBANIA

GREECE

Athens □

TURKEY

Ankara □

London □

UNITED KINGDOM

Dublin □ EIRE

NETH.

BELG.

LUX.

Paris □

FRANCE

ITALY

Rome □

Madrid □

SPAIN

PORTUGAL

Lisbon □

ALGERIA

TUNISIA

SP. MOROCCO

FRENCH MOROCCO

tion, however, lay in preparing the way for the adoption of the European Common Market.

The potential of the Common Market is tremendous. If all goes well, it not only will eliminate trade barriers but eventually equalize wages, social conditions, taxes, and fiscal policies. Freight rates will be harmonized and restrictions on the free movement of labor and capital will be abolished. A new international bank, the European Investment Bank, will make loans to prevent temporary economic disruptions and will foster the development of underdeveloped areas such as Southern Italy. Price supports and similar programs will stabilize agriculture. It could well lead ultimately to full economic union and the adoption of a common currency.

As a counterbalance against the "Inner Six" of the Common Market, seven other European nations (Britain, Sweden, Denmark, Norway, Austria, Switzerland, and Portugal) organized a European Free Trade Area (EFTA). Led by Britain, the EFTA was a less comprehensive association, created by the "Outer Seven" largely as a defensive measure to strengthen their bargaining position with the Inner Six. Britain moved to join the Common Market in 1961, followed by other EFTA members. The outcome of these negotiations, and subsequent American policy if a successful merger results, will have a far reaching effect upon the future of the Atlantic Community leading to disintegration—or conceivably to an Atlantic Confederation.

European Political Unification

The dream of a United States of Europe is nearly as old as Europe itself, but with the emergence of the two super-powers the need to unify in order to maintain great-power status has made the dream a practical and urgent necessity. Following World War II, political union became the goal of practical men-of-affairs in nearly every western European country. Moreover, to bolster the policy of containment, the United States strongly encouraged the political integration of Europe.

Progress toward political union has been painfully slow. In 1948, the French Parliament called for the creation of a European constituent assembly to draft a constitution for a new European federation. This resulted in the establishment, the following year, of the Council of Europe. It was a purely consultative body, whose representatives had power only to "recommend" measures to their home governments. Nevertheless, it set the stage for more dramatic moves to come.

The creation of NATO and the American military assistance program marked a reversal of the policy of the United States and its European allies toward Germany. If NATO were to succeed, Germany had to become a member. This meant Germany's rearmament and the restoration of its sovereignty. A possible alternative was the incorporation of West

Germany into the Soviet bloc, which would place the West in a hopelessly inferior military position. Yet to many Europeans, a sovereign and rearmed Germany, possessing its own general staff and national army, was a greater threat than Russia. This was especially true of the French, who feared Germany's domination of Europe more than Soviet attack.

Efforts to reconcile French fears of German militarism with American insistence on German participation in NATO led to the proposal for a European Defense Community (EDC). This was the most ambitious plan for the political integration of Europe witnessed to that time, and was widely looked upon as the forerunner to genuine union. It aimed at establishing a common European army, a common military budget, and a supranational political organization. Germany would thus be denied a national army under its own control, and the continent would take a huge step in the direction of unity.

Before the treaty could be ratified, Stalin died and fear of a Russian attack abated; the British refused to associate with EDC; the increasing importance of atomic weapons seemed to lessen the need for land armies; and Europe's fear of Germany became more vocal. On August 30, 1954, the French National Assembly rejected the treaty, and Europe's most dramatic effort at political union died. It was ironical that the French, who had initiated the proposal, were the ones finally to kill it.[7]

The United States had counted heavily on ratification of the treaty and now talked of abandoning its other NATO allies as worthless and of "going it alone with Germany." Meanwhile, the occupation of Germany ended, but the British announced their willingness to station troops in Europe permanently, and America encouraged rapid German rearmament. These moves plus the continuing threat from Russia prompted Western Europe to try again on a less ambitious scale.

The substitute for the defunct EDC was called the Western European Union (WEU).[8] While more than a mere military alliance, it was hardly the political union envisaged by EDC. Plans for a unified European army were abandoned in favor of national armies committed to NATO. The elaborate administrative structure of EDC was also abandoned, and with it any hope of real political unity. In time, WEU's only meaningful function came to be the supervision of the arms controls imposed in the treaty (and directed largely at preventing German military hegemony). One cannot help but reflect on what the situation might have been if, as in the case of the Common Market, the European Defense Community had been successfully put into operation. Its defeat is one of the most important events in postwar European history.

---

[7] See Daniel Lerner and Raymond Aron, eds., *France Defeats EDC* (New York: Frederick A. Praeger, Inc., 1957).

[8] The signatories were: Britain, France, West Germany, Italy, Belgium, the Netherlands, and Luxembourg.

THE PROBLEMS OF THE SIXTIES

By the end of the nineteen-fifties, Russia had been contained—militarily at least—certainly in Europe, if not elsewhere. American-backed economic, military, and diplomatic support had given Western Europe political stability, military security, a degree of unity and cooperation, and a level of living and prosperity it had never before known. American foreign policy in Europe had met some severe setbacks, but on balance it was an overwhelming success.

The United States was, in fact, a victim of its own success. The circumstances under which the policies of containment were laid out changed drastically within a few years. Europe was no longer on the verge of chaos. Stalin was dead, and Russia now spoke of "peaceful coexistence" instead of threatening to conquer the continent. And finally, the United States no longer had a monopoly on atomic weapons, so that NATO, especially because it failed to build up conventional forces, no longer provided a reliable defense. American policy had become obsolete, and was in need of a drastic overhaul if it was to meet the new conditions of the sixties.

The Military Problem

The United States atomic monopoly originally provided the nations of Western Europe with a cheap and relatively certain protection against Russian conquest. NATO was, in effect, an American commitment to employ the Strategic Air Command and nuclear bombs in case of Soviet aggression; no sacrifice and little risk was imposed on the other signatories so long as the United States had an atomic monopoly. When the Soviet Union became equal to the West in nuclear power, and perhaps superior in delivery systems, NATO was no longer able to perform this role, and was in some ways a liability. Western Europeans knew there was little chance for them to survive a nuclear war, and many were inclined to the belief that what little chance there was might lie in not being too closely identified with the United States. Hence, the appeal of "neutralism" in Europe, with its talk of disengagement, peaceful coexistence, withdrawal from NATO, and compromise with the Soviet Union.

The end of the American atomic monopoly also posed another problem —the need to revamp NATO military strategy, and the task of footing the bill. Reliance on SAC and the A-bomb was obsolete, and NATO could no longer rely on a weapons system which could not meet the threat of limited war. Such a war might come as a result of provocative actions by Soviet satellites (e.g., an East German blockade of Berlin); it could come as a result of an uprising in Czechoslovakia or East Germany; or as a consequence of Soviet blunders (e.g., military moves against Berlin based on a miscalculation of Western intentions or capabilities). Moreover, if against Soviet pinpricks the West could only retaliate with the threat of nuclear suicide, the Russians would continue to call the bluff. They knew the United States was unwilling to cause the near-total destruction of Europe and itself as well in order to prevent, say, the imposition of East German customs controls on West Berlin, or the partial blockade of Western goods into Berlin. Thus, there was the danger that the Soviet Union would continue to eat away at the Western position, constantly demanding only minor changes, unless NATO developed a strategy of "graduated deterrence," which would permit the employment of the amount of counter force necessary to meet whatever threat arose. Then if the Russians employed military action on a limited scale, and with conventional weapons, it would be possible to retaliate in kind, rather than either to back down or fight an all-out nuclear war. It was urgent that NATO widen its range of capability so as to be able to counter the subtle and ambiguous weapons and techniques employed by the Soviet Union. Included among the needed Western capacity was the ability to employ para-military or guerrilla warfare tactics should the need arise. Otherwise, the two ugly alternatives were eventual surrender or total war.[9]

But who would pay for redesigning NATO defenses? Who would provide the troops and weapons? Britain—like the United States—felt that the continental countries should assume a larger share of the burden. It was easier to rely on the Americans, the A-bomb, and SAC. Thus in the early nineteen-sixties the Europeans were spending on defense only slightly more than half as much of their total expenditures as was the United States. The burden, however, was unevenly distributed among the European countries. Because of the excessively heavy defense burdens of France (waging war in Algeria) and Britain (with world-wide military commitments), their military expenditures were considerable. Other European allies almost completely shunned their responsibilities.

What kind of defense strategy and military establishment should NATO have? Should it possess primarily a nuclear capability, on the grounds, obviously false, that the West could not possibly match the Soviets man for man? If so, should NATO have "tactical" nuclear weapons (little ones, which might prevent a limited war from becoming a major one), or a "strategic" capability (big ones, on the grounds that Europe would therefore be less reliant on the whims of American policy)? The United States hesitated to grant her NATO allies an atomic arsenal for several reasons. It might cause Russia to give such weapons to China. It might also lead to less, rather than greater, cooperation with the United States. France, now that it had its own nuclear capability, had already shown distinct

---

[9] Henry R. Kissinger, "For an Atlantic Confederacy," *The Reporter* (Feb. 2, 1961), pp. 16-20.

signs of refusing to cooperate with NATO. Moreover, the thought of Germany with an independent nuclear capacity aroused deep fear among other allies of the United States. The problems of mutual deterrence are dealt with more exhaustively in Chapter 13, but posing some of them here serves to dramatize the acute and urgent need for a complete overhaul of NATO.

The Economic Problem

Not only had the end of America's atomic superiority lessened Europe's reliance upon the United States; the economic recovery of Western Europe had likewise diminished its dependence on its trans-Atlantic partner. No longer in need of American aid, the nations of NATO were searching for new markets, and looked longingly beyond the walls of containment for new outlets for their products. Meanwhile, Khrushchev held out the olive branch and talked of disarmament, expanding trade, and peaceful competition. At the same time, American businessmen were losing markets to their European competitors, which further complicated the problem of United States-European cooperation. Moreover, the return of prosperity was driving the Atlantic world into competing trading blocs, thereby increasing the dangers of greater political disunity. And finally, European colonial policy, coupled with complacency, seriously hampered the West's effort to cooperate in aiding the underdeveloped areas and winning their allegiance.

If the problems were great, the needs were clear. During the late nineteen-fifties Western Europe's rate of economic growth surpassed that of the United States. It became capable of making a greater contribution to its own defense, and of aiding the underdeveloped countries. In fact, Western Europe was the world's largest importer of raw materials, and its sales and purchasing power in Asia, Africa, and Latin America could prove far more decisive in the development and future political alignments of these areas than could any economic aid program.

The need, then, was for a new and vigorous effort at United States-European economic cooperation, either through American association with the Common Market, or through agencies like the Organization for Economic Cooperation and Development which replaced OEEC in the autumn of 1961, and of which both Canada and the United States were full members. The need to prevent further economic rifts within the alliance also dictated such an effort. As the Common Market reached the period when it would impose tariffs upon the outside world, the temptation was strong to discriminate against American and British goods. A renewed effort at economic cooperation among the Atlantic allies was necessary to continue the movement toward an Atlantic Community.

Finally, the new Soviet trade offensive posed a difficult problem. As

European industry expanded and its surpluses increased, Soviet trade offers became more attractive. It became vital for the NATO allies to coordinate their economic policies and maintain unity in the face of the Soviet trade challenge. Here again, a new American-led effort at economic cooperation, through NATO or otherwise, seemed to be called for.

The Problem of Political Unity

If the goal of the Atlantic nations was a real community, it required not only military and economic cooperation, but the building of political institutions. Moreover, these steps could not be pursued separately. Military security was not possible without economic strength, and both were impossible without cooperation in other areas as well. And while cooperation was the essential minimum, the ultimate expression of a real community would be outright political integration under common governmental institutions. As argued elsewhere in this volume, the age of the nation-state is drawing to a close, sovereignty is already an anachronism, and human survival may well depend on man's ability to integrate, at least with those with whom he has most in common. The strength of the West lies in its love of freedom. On the other hand, communist strength lies in its unity, which the Soviets place above all other values, including freedom. It may well be that the side which first learns to employ both freedom and unity will win the cold war and dominate the epoch ahead.

Thus far, integrative efforts in the Atlantic area have been functional and partial rather than political and universal. The Coal and Steel Community, Euratom, the Common Market, EFTA, NATO, and OECD are all cases in point, dealing with limited problems, in most instances in restricted geographic areas. The movement toward Atlantic unity lacks true leadership, a coherent doctrine, and mass support. This situation has been aggravated by circumstances which have arisen in the last decade. The economic chaos in Europe and the Soviet threat of the immediate postwar years compelled Western Europe and the United States to cooperate as never before in their history. Although there were tendencies in both directions in the nineteen-sixties, "business as usual" and several growing political forces threatened the unity of the incipient Atlantic community.

The first of these was resurgent nationalism, most notably in France, but apparent everywhere. Even Canada had elected a government dedicated to "freeing itself from bondage to Washington." General de Gaulle spoke of reviving French prestige, asserting French independence, and freeing French military policy from NATO domination. Germany grew prosperous, and with increased military strength was tempted to go it alone. Britain searched for a compromise with the Soviets, and for an equal voice with Washington in the formulation of policy. In short, as the nations of West Europe became less dependent on the United States, they also became more assertive of their own national interests.

Closely allied with resurgent nationalism was the growing mass popularity of various brands of "neutralism" in Europe. The balance of nuclear power between East and West means suicide for most Europeans should general war break out. There is a natural yearning to "sit the next one out," accompanied by a search for accommodation with the Soviet Union at almost any price. Manifestations of this search are various proposals for disengagement and for the demilitarization of Berlin, or Germany, or even larger areas in the heart of Europe. All historical evidence, however, indicates that political and military vacuums invite infiltration or conquest. Still the search went on, harmful as it was to Atlantic unity, and it would take a strong reassertion of United States leadership during the next decade to overcome a further growth of neutralist tendencies.

Another divisive force within the Atlantic community may be labeled "continentalism," i.e., the tendency of certain continental powers, led by France, to transform the present institutions of European unity into instruments of discrimination against other members of the alliance. Typical was the Common Market of the "Inner Six," which threatened to drive a wedge between itself and both the United States and the British-led "Outer Seven." This trend toward exclusive groupings of European nations was closely associated with their desire to be more assertive of their own interest and less dependent upon the United States. American tendencies during the postwar period to assign Great Britain a preferred position in the alliance was also partially to blame. Gradually, France, Germany, and Italy came to resent this Anglo-American alignment. The result was to open dangerous breaches in the Atlantic alliance, and only the reassertion of dynamic United States leadership and skillful diplomacy could recapture the movement toward allied economic integration and political unity.

Another serious obstacle to unity was the recurrent fear among her allies that the United States would become weary of the burdens of the cold war and seek some kind of *modus vivendi* with the Soviet Union. In short, while the United States dreaded neutralist tendencies in Europe, Europeans periodically experienced similar fear about the United States. The latter could help allay these fears by periodic assurances of her determination, the continued maintenance of American troops in Europe, willingness to consult with her allies *before* decisions of import to the Atlantic community were taken, by renewed efforts to strengthen the machinery of NATO, and by a clear statement of willingness to build strong and permanent institutions for a pooling of sovereignty.

The most devastating blow to Atlantic unity, however, was the "new look" in Soviet diplomacy. Russia's foreign policy under Stalin was in the classic tradition of power diplomacy. It was rigid, unimaginative, and placed almost sole reliance upon the use of military action. Especially after World War II, Russia seemed to present a threat to the independence of Western Europe. Western cooperation was regarded as a matter of self survival, and Stalin was, in fact, the author of the Atlantic alliance. But if Stalin gave it birth, Khrushchev planned to "bury" it. In place of military threats and armed conquest, Khrushchev appealed for a relaxation of East-West tensions, for coexistence, peaceful competition, and an end to the cold war. And while Soviet goals were unchanged, the substitution of psychological, economic, and other more subtle techniques for military threats had an adverse effect upon Western unity. The growth of nationalism, continentalism, and "neutralism" in West Europe coincide directly with the Soviet "peace offensive," another weapon in the Soviet arsenal, one that clearly aimed at the disunity and psychological disarmament of the West. Containment, while under the threat of armed aggression, was one thing, but the maintenance of unity, psychological awareness, and a military posture in the face of a Soviet call to end the cold war was something else again.

The fluctuations of European attitudes toward unity and cooperation clearly reflected the ebb and flow of Soviet aggressiveness. When threatened, Europeans banded together and sought American protection and leadership, but relaxation in response to the "soft" Soviet line threatened the very existence of the Western alliance.[10] The United States had spent billions of dollars, and the time and effort of a decade, to bolster the will of her allies and that of non-aligned countries to resist Soviet pressures. In effect, she had said: "Don't trust them, have as little as possible to do with them." But if the United States fell in with Khrushchev's coexistence line, she would then seem to be saying, "They really don't want to attack you, but only to compete with you; they are not so bad after all, and cultural exchanges, trade relations, and the like are perfectly in order." In short, "It is not necessary to resist the Soviet Union with the same degree of determination as before." It required astute diplomacy to cope with this problem. For while the United States was interested in a negotiated settlement of her differences with the Soviet Union, at the same time she had to cope with the new Soviet techniques of psychological warfare aimed at destroying Western unity. Europe could be conquered through apathy and subversion as easily as by arms.

Overriding these problems remained the rivalries, fears, conflicting national interests, and internal political struggles of the European nations themselves. Their partisan and ideological differences had a profound effect upon Western unity. Approximately one-fourth to one-third of the French and Italian electorate continued to vote communist. The

---

[10] An excellent discussion of this problem appears in Hans J. Morgenthau's "Khrushchev's New Cold War Strategy," *Commentary* (Nov. 1959), pp. 381ff.

Communist Party of Italy was the largest in the Western world, and that of France the wealthiest and best organized, owning real estate of inestimable value, publishing newspapers, and maintaining control over 85 per cent of organized labor in France. One answer to communism in Europe seemed to be to encourage the emergence of nationalist party leadership, free of Soviet control. The Soviet 1956 intervention in Hungary, somewhat encouraged this tendency.

The periodic call for "popular fronts" made it difficult to weaken communist party strength in Europe. This was the strategy adopted in the thirties against fascism, consisting of endeavors to form "coalitions" with other left and center parties, for the purpose of gaining office and influencing policy. It allowed the communists to parade as champions of "liberalism," and gave them a degree of respectability they would not otherwise have had. It also tended to undermine or capture the more moderate left.

The Social Democrats, the most important of Europe's non-communist parties of the left, posed another kind of problem. They comprised either the ruling party, or the major opposition, throughout most of northern Europe. Somewhat akin to Britain's Labour party, they were bitterly anti-communist. On the other hand, they generally leaned to "neutralism," appealed for more independence from Washington, and favored a *rapprochement* with the Soviet Union. Although this line appealed to voters on the far left and hence weakened the communist parties, it also hampered allied unity and a policy of firmness toward the Soviet Union. Over a period of time the left as well as the right will hold the reins of power in a democracy; therefore American leadership and policy had to appeal to both left and right if the long-range cooperation of her allies was to be maintained.

COUNTRY-BY-COUNTRY SURVEY
OF UNITED STATES-EUROPEAN RELATIONS

Quite apart from the partisan differences of the European democracies, other internal conflicts—as well as conflicting national goals—needed American attention. A brief survey of the United States relations with a number of European countries will point this up.

The United Kingdom

The major consequence of World War II for Britain was a clear revelation of what had long been under way—a rapid decline in her status as a world power. Since the war she has undergone a period of severe hardship, accompanied by a series of "austerity programs," the socialization of her major industries, and a program of drastic social reforms. Prosperity has returned fully, but it rests on delicate foundations.

Britain depends heavily upon foreign trade and investment. During the war she liquidated her foreign investments, and at war's end found herself in near bankruptcy, with worn-out plant equipment, depleted resources, and huge international debts. She had lost her traditional markets during the war, and now faced competition from enemy and ally alike. America, meanwhile, had become an industrial giant. Many formerly underdeveloped countries like India were now competitors. Other countries, such as Germany and Japan, had few debts, low defense costs, and new industrial plants paid for by American aid. Moreover, World War II meant the rise of the super-giants and the demand for independence by the colonial world.

Britain's answer to all of this has been a foreign policy which she insists is highly realistic. She has slashed her foreign and military commitments, withdrawn from Asia and the Middle East, and is liquidating her empire at a rapid pace. In Asia she has given independence to her former possessions, recognized the Chinese Communist government, and sought compromise and expanded trade relations with communist powers. In the Middle East her abandonment of Greece, Palestine, Suez, and Cyprus has led to a power struggle to fill the vacuum. The Truman Doctrine for Greece and Turkey, the Eisenhower Doctrine for the Middle East, and the stationing of the American Sixth Fleet in the Mediterranean are consequences of Britain's decline in the area.

In Europe, Britain's policy is not so clear. On the one hand she has stationed troops in Berlin and supported NATO. On the other, she refused to join EDC, the Common Market (until 1961), and other European integration agencies, on grounds that she was a "world power," not just a European one. She was also the foremost exponent among the major European allies of the United States of a policy of accomodation with the Soviet Union. This often appeared to be at the expense of Germany, whom she distrusted and feared. Hence, she was more willing than West Germany to accept the division of Germany between East and West as permanent, and she periodically toyed with the idea of "disengagement," "internationalizing" Berlin, and "neutralizing" Germany, any of which would directly conflict with West German goals, and would mean a reduction of Western troops and commitments in Europe.

Militarily, Britain's policies have also been indecisive. Reluctant to accept anything less than great-power status, she has developed her own A-bomb and has played a major role in NATO. More recently, however, she has slashed her defense expenditures, abandoned the draft, and decided to give up the arms race.[11]

---

[11] "Britain's Policy on Defense," *Political Science Quarterly*, XXXI (Jan.-Mar., 1960), 1-6.

This all bears heavily upon her relations with the United States, upon whom she must still rely. Yet she resents being a junior partner, and periodically lacks confidence in American leadership. Britain has become a "permanent aircraft carrier," and a wrong move by Washington would cause her destruction. This is why her citizens are attracted to neutralism, and why her government encourages "summit" meetings, the recognition of Peking, disarmament, and efforts to reach a solution of the German problem. Any move which will lessen tensions with the communist bloc is likely to get British approval. The question is, will a willingness to compromise bring peace—or will it strengthen the communist position and perhaps be more dangerous than a policy of firmness? To many critics, the British position is essentially one of "appeasement."

France

French policy since the war has been marked by realism, boldness, idealism, frustration, and despair.[12] After a brief period of pursuing her historic policy of enmity toward and keeping Germany weak, after 1950 she turned hesitantly, and later more firmly toward a policy of cooperation and limited integration with Germany. Europe was being crushed between the super-powers, France was no longer a great power, and Germany was rapidly recovering. Therefore, Germany and France should cooperate and Europe should unite. The result was French proposals for European integration: the Schuman Plan, the European Defense Community, and the Common Market. By these plans the hegemony of Europe by a revived Germany could be prevented. Germany could regain her sovereignty, remilitarize, and re-establish her industrial might, and yet her economic and military power would benefit France and be controlled by supranational organizations in which the French had a veto. At the same time, French-German cooperation could help a French-led Europe regain a voice among the great powers.

By her defeat of EDC, France lost her chance of leading Europe as a "third force" in world affairs. At the same time Germany has forged ahead, and threatens to play the role France envisaged for herself. German hegemony of Europe is far more likely than French.

Accompanying these events were others which added to France's humiliation and despair. Before the war France was the greatest military power in Europe and the cultural center of the world. French pride was deeply hurt by her ignominious defeat in 1940. To this was added the humiliation of defeat in a long series of costly colonial wars in Southeast Asia and Algeria. Internally, her failures have been just as acute. National unity was impossible because of deep divisions within France, and the

[12] Edgar S. Furniss, Jr., *France, Troubled Ally: De Gaulle's Heritage and Prospects* (New York: Harper & Brothers, 1960).

divisive nature of her political system. Under the constitution of the Fourth Republic French governments lacked the power to govern and rarely stayed in office beyond six months. France therefore lacked the power and prestige to conduct a successful foreign policy. Despite this, her economy, especially since 1954, has shown a remarkable vitality.

In 1958 France abandoned the Fourth Republic, and with it her traditional form of democracy.[13] General de Gaulle ruled virtually with the power of a dictator. A drastic monetary reform accompanied by other measures further bolstered the French economy. In foreign affairs, de Gaulle brought the Algerian war to a near-end, acquired an independent nuclear capability, strengthened ties with Germany, but weakened those with NATO and the United States.

Of most concern to the United States was his relationship to NATO. His insistence upon joining the British-American "nuclear club" was accompanied by a series of steps which seriously endangered the effectiveness of the Western alliance. The French fleet was no longer part of the NATO naval force; United States missiles and atomic weapons in France were rejected; and the French failed to supply their share of NATO troops.

All of this was aimed at restoring French prestige, and at enabling her to participate on equal terms in the councils of the West. Yet while France recovered her pride, this was accompanied by a revival of intense nationalism. Her relations with Britain suffered, and though the French distrust the Soviet Union, they also harbor fear of a reviving Germany. Although de Gaulle has courted close relations with Bonn, both he and Chancellor Adenauer are old men, and their successors may revert to form.

With regard to Franco-American relations, France has long been a center of anti-Americanism in Europe. This was partially psychological, due to humiliation caused by her rapid decline, and envy of American power and leadership. It was also due in part to American attitudes, which tended to write France off as a third-rate power while at the same time praising Germany and treating Britain as in a special category. Although greater American tact could help, France would probably continue to be a sensitive and restless ally.

Spain

Spain is neither a "neutral" nor a full partner in the Western alliance. Internally, Spain is a semi-fascist dictatorship, with its army, monarchist upper class, fascist party, and powerful Catholic heirarchy held together by General Franco and the common fear of a leftist revolution. Spain was a non-belligerent ally of Germany and Italy during the war and Spanish

---

[13] Philip M. Williams and Martin Harrison, *De Gaulle's Republic* (London: Longmans, Green and Co., Ltd., 1960).

volunteers fought on the Russian front. At the same time Franco never broke relations with the Western powers, and despite Nazi pressure he avoided steps which would lead to his downfall should the allies win. Following the war, he courted the West, abandoned the more obnoxious fascist aspects of his regime, and reminded the world of his staunch anti-communism. Still, as Europe's "last remaining fascist dictator," he has never been accorded full partnership in the Atlantic alliance. Spain never received Marshall aid, is not a member of NATO, and has not been a participant in the organizations of European integration.

Nevertheless, Spanish cooperation was deemed important in Washington. The United States therefore signed bilateral agreements with Franco, who, in return for economic and military aid, granted rights and territories necessary for the establishment of United States air and naval bases on Spanish soil. In this way Spain is, indirectly, already part of the NATO defense system.

With the passage of time the onus of fascism and Spain's role in World War II will pass. Franco is now a very old man, and with his death a regime more acceptable to the rest of Europe may emerge. If so, the Spanish people may once again take their rightful place among the European family of nations.

Europe's Non-Aligned Nations and the United States

In following a policy of compromise, Britain and the remainder of America's European allies were deeply influenced by the example of Europe's neutrals. Switzerland is the classic example, but Sweden, too, stayed out of both world wars, avoided occupation and devastation, and prospered by trading with the belligerents on both sides. She intends to do the same in World War III. Though sympathetic to the West and fearful of Russia, she has refused to join sides in the cold war and trades freely with all nations. This policy is especially attractive to the other Scandinavian nations, Norway and Denmark. They both joined NATO and received Marshall aid, but they have long and traditional ties with Sweden, have refused the establishment of American missile bases on their soil, and periodically toy with the idea of giving up NATO in favor of a neutralist Scandinavian alliance.

There are also two communist-oriented neutrals in Europe: Finland and Yugoslavia. Finland is Western by sentiment and ideology, but geographically she is in the Russian sphere of influence. Apart from demanding heavy reparations payments which tie her economically to Russia, the Soviets signed a rather maganimous treaty with Finland at the end of the war, and allowed her a high degree of independence in the conduct of her affairs. Finland is not a puppet, and in fact holds free elections. She also trades freely with the West, and so long as she does not make any moves harmful to Russian interests, is left quite free of Soviet control. In fact, Finland is Russia's "showcase," an example of what states in the West can expect if they turn neutral.

Yugoslavia is a different case. Marshal Tito, the present ruler of the country, is an avowed Communist. He is also highly cosmopolitan, as much European as Russian in his orientation. Moreover, like the Red leaders of China, his present power and position did not come with Soviet help. He organized his own resistance, cleared the country of Germans on his own, and organized his own government after the war. He also followed his own policies, which did not always coincide with those of the Soviet puppet governments of Eastern Europe. This led to a break with Stalin in 1948, after which he promptly received American aid. Since then, he has reached a *rapprochement* with Khrushchev, who is more amenable to neutralism than was Stalin, but he continues to play an independent role in European affairs. Internally, his regime is a benevolent dictatorship which admits Western periodicals, tolerates some freedom of thought, and recognizes peasant ownership of the land along with other small-scale "capitalistic" enterprise. In foreign affairs, Marshal Tito fluctuates between siding with the communist bloc and championing the cause of "neutralism." This allows him to receive aid and favors from both Russia and the United States, to trade with both East and West, and to curry the favor of the Afro-Asian bloc. He is on good terms with both Nasser and Nehru, and in fact vies with them for prestige and influence over the lesser uncommitted nations.

Germany

Finally there remains the key to the cold war and the most dangerous problem of all: the "German problem"; and at the heart of this powder-keg, the issue of Berlin. The national goals of West Germany have been to win its sovereignty, restore its economy, and regain its voice in world affairs. West Germany, therefore, became the world's great beneficiary of the cold war, which led the West to rebuild West German economic strength, grant it independence, and encourage it to rearm. This accomplished, West Germany's primary national goal was reunification.[14]

No political party, nor any government the West Germans might elect, can do other than give, or at least appear to give, top priority to this goal. Whether the governing elite of Germany is really as interested in German unification as they proclaim is doubtful. Unification poses a serious problem to the West, for with Poland in possession of former German

---

[14] K. W. Deutsch and Lewis J. Edinger, *Germany Rejoins the Powers: Mass Opinion, Interest Groups, and Elites in Contemporary German Foreign Policy* (Stanford, California: Stanford University Press, 1959).

areas east of the Oder-Neisse rivers, and with East Germany in the hands of a Soviet puppet, there are—to oversimplify—only two ways the country can be reunited: either by meeting Soviet terms or by war. This is the "German problem," deeply feared but rarely discussed openly by the statesmen of all nations.

First there is the problem of war. It is not inconceivable that at some point either the East or West German government might resort to force against the other. This could come by accident, miscalculation, or—as in Korea—by one side deliberately attempting to conquer the other. In any case both the Soviet and American alliance systems in Europe would quickly be involved. It is quite obvious that German disunity contains the seeds of World War III, and the possible destruction of the Western world.

On the other hand, there is another alternative. If Germany is not reunited through war, it can only be reunified as a result of diplomatic negotiation—i.e., a deal with the communists. The price demanded by the Soviet Union would be high indeed, perhaps too high for West Germany to accept. Russia's greatest national fear is of a rearmed militant Germany; her greatest national goal is to insure that her soil is never again invaded from the west. Hence it is not to be expected that the Soviets will readily agree to German reunification except on their own terms; it is more probable that they eventually will try to control all of Germany, West as well as East. Nevertheless, there is always the possibility that the Soviet Union would abandon the East German regime if she could thereby destroy the Western alliance and its ability to resist. Might not West Germany pull out of NATO, abandon her Western allies, and adopt some form of neutralism, in return for the recovery of East Germany and a neutrality pact with the U.S.S.R.? The possibility seemed remote in the early nineteen-sixties, but time and a change of circumstances might lead to such a move. This enhanced the importance of the European integration movement, which increasingly enmeshed German interests with those of the remainder of Western Europe, and consequently lessened the attraction of a Soviet accord.

Meanwhile, 110 miles within the Soviet-controlled area lies the traditional capital city of Berlin, the heart of Germany. Divided like Germany itself into eastern and western zones, it is militarily indefensible even though allied troops are stationed there. If the Soviets or their East German puppets demanded withdrawal of Western troops and applied military pressure, would the West resist—knowing the area could not be defended—or would it seek a compromise? Upon the answers to these problems the future of the Atlantic alliance, the outcome of the cold war, and in fact the very existence of Western civilization may rest. Berlin could be the starting point of the war that was truly the "war to end all wars."

Thus we close this chapter where we began, with the knowledge that Europe remains the key prize in the global struggle of our time. The ability of the Atlantic powers to unite and cooperate may determine the outcome of that struggle, and will have a strong bearing on the kind of world we live in for a century to come.

SUGGESTED READINGS

Baker, Joseph E., "How the French See America," *Yale Review*, XLVII (Dec. 1952), 239-53.

Bathurst, Maurice E. and J. L. Simpson, *Germany and the North Atlantic Community: A Legal Survey*. London: Stevens & Sons, Ltd., 1956.

Baumann, Carol Edler, "Britain Faces Europe," *Political Science Quarterly*, LXXIV (Sept. 1959), 351-71.

Bolles, Blair, *The Big Change in Europe*. New York: W. W. Norton & Company, Inc., 1958.

Brinton, Clarence C., *The United States and Britain*. Cambridge: Harvard University Press, 1945.

"Britain's Policy on Defense," *Political Quarterly*, XXXI (Jan.-Mar. 1960), 1-70.

Catlin, George E. G., *The Atlantic Community*. London: Coram Limited, 1959.

Dehio, Ludwig, *Germany and World Politics in the Twentieth Century*, trans. Dieter Pevsners. New York: Alfred A. Knopf, Inc., 1959.

Deutsch, Karl W. and Lewis J. Edinger, *Germany Rejoins the Powers: Mass Opinion, Interest Groups, and Elites in Contemporary German Foreign Policy*. Stanford, California: Stanford University Press, 1959.

————, and others, *Political Community and the North Atlantic Area: International Organization in the Light of Historical Experience*. Princeton, N.J.: Princeton University Press, 1957.

Diebold, William J., "The Changed Economic Position of Western Europe: Some Implications for United States Policy and International Organizations," *International Organization*, XIV (Winter 1960), 1-19.

Epstein, Leon D., *Britain: Uneasy Ally*. Chicago: University of Chicago Press, 1954.

————, "Partisan Foreign Policy: Britain in the Suez Crisis," *World Politics*, XII (Jan. 1960), 201-24.

Erler, Fritz, "The Reunification of Germany and Security for Europe," *World Politics*, X (Apr. 1958), 366-77.

Fitzsimons, Matthew A., "The Continuity of British Foreign Policy," *Review of Politics*, XXI (Jan. 1959), 300-22.

Furniss, Edgar S., Jr., *France: De Gaulle's Heritage and Prospects*. New York: Harper & Brothers for the Council on Foreign Relations, 1960.

Gellner, Marianne, "Relations Between the Six and the Seven: A Survey of Recent Developments," *The World Today*, XVI (July 1960), 278-87.

Grindod, Muriel, *The Rebuilding of Italy: Politics and Economics, 1945-1955*. London, New York: Royal Institute of International Affairs, 1955.

Grunbaum, Werner F., "The British Security Program, 1948-1958," *Western Political Quarterly*, XIII (Sept. 1960), 764-79.

Haas, Ernest B., "Persistent Themes in Atlantic and European Unity," *World Politics*, X (July 1958), 614-28.

Howard, Michael, *Disengagement in Europe*. Baltimore: Penguin Books, Inc., 1958.

Kohn, Hans, "The Difficult Road to Western Unity," *Orbis*, III (Oct. 1959), 297-312.

Lawson, Ruth C., "Concerting Policies in the North Atlantic Community," *International Organization*, XII (Spring 1958), 163-79.

Lerner, Daniel and Raymond Aron, eds., *France Defeats EDC*. New York: Frederick A. Praeger, Inc., 1957.

Macridis, Roy C., *The De Gaulle Republic: Quest for Unity*. Homewood, Illinois: Richard D. Irwin, Inc., 1960.

Massip, Roger, "De Gaulle, Europe and NATO," *Western World*, III (Feb. 1960), 13-16.

Northrop, F. S. C., *European Union and United States Foreign Policy: A Study in Sociological Jurisprudence*. New York: The Macmillan Co., 1954.

Price, Harry Bayard, *The Marshall Plan and Its Meaning*. Ithaca, New York: Cornell University Press, 1955.

Prince Hubertus zu Lowenstein and Volkmar von Zuhlsdorff, *NATO and the Defense of the West*. New York: Frederick A. Praeger, Inc., 1961.

Robertson, Arthur H., *The Council of Europe: Its Structure, Functions, and Achievements*, 2nd ed. New York: Frederick A. Praeger, Inc., 1961.

Schlamm, William S., *Germany and the East-West Crisis: The Decisive Challenge to American Policy*. New York: David McKay Co., Inc., 1959.

Speier, Hans and W. Phillips Davison, eds., *West German Leadership and Foreign Policy*. Evanston, Illinois: Row, Peterson & Company, 1957.

U.S. Senate, Foreign Relations Committee, *United States Foreign Policy: Compilation of Studies Nos. 1-13*, 2 vols. No. 3. "United States Foreign Policy: Western Europe," by Foreign Policy Research Institute, University of Pennsylvania. Committee Print, 86th Cong., 2nd sess., 1960, pp. 199-300. Washington, D. C.: Government Printing Office, 1960.

"West Germany as a World Power," *Current History*, XXXVIII (Jan. 1960), entire issue.

Williams, Philip M. and Martin Harrison, *De Gaulle's Republic*. London: Longmans, Green & Co., Ltd., 1960.

Wright, Richard, *Pagan Spain*. New York: Harper & Brothers, 1957.

23

Crucial Conflict:
the Soviet Union and the United States

Robert Loring Allen
Department of Economics and Institute of
International Studies and Overseas Administration,
University of Oregon

The central set of interrelationships in the world today is that between the United States and the Soviet Union. These two countries alone produce nearly two-thirds of total world goods and services, and with their allies have most of its military capacity. Even those countries not formally allied with one or the other of the power giants are nevertheless affected by their behavior. The Soviet Union and the United States each has the ability to destroy the world and all of its people. Only through their cooperation can the world even hope to maintain peaceful progress. When the history of the second half of the twentieth century is written, it will depend primarily upon how the Soviet Union and the United States, and the countries allied with each, adjusted to the mutually-imposed "balance of terror."

But let it not be thought that the conflict is solely or even primarily of a military nature. Military action, or the threat of it, is a central ingredient, but the contest itself embraces all forms of oppositional behavior. It is a total conflict of indefinite duration involving all aspects of life and all resources at the command of the contestants. It is carried on through diplomatic channels, by subversion, with propaganda tactics, with economic and military assistance to less developed areas, through limited military hostilities—by using almost every device and technique that promises to advance the aims of either contestant.

The Soviet Union, while expecting victory, does not expect it to be easy or quick. Nor does the United States, which expects its way of life to prevail in the end, anticipate that its opposition will soon disappear. The world has never before witnessed a contest of these vast dimensions and with such portentous consequences. Yet the Soviet Union and the United States both seem to want to avoid warfare because it would result in the frustration of the aims of each. As long as they are able do so, the homelands of both participants are not directly involved. In this kind of conflict, where military forces may never be brought into action, except on a limited scale, the absolute amount of military and even economic capacity of a country may not be wholly relevant. Countries refusing to align with either side frequently hold the key to the resolution of any particular element of the conflict and may hold the over-all margin of power.

The Soviet Union and the United States are each at the center of a system of thought and behavior. Each seeks to perfect, defend, and promulgate its own version of a world order by whatever resources are available. At many points Soviet aims are opposed to those of the United States, giving rise to issues which are the symptoms of the conflict. It would be mistaken to regard acrimonious exchanges of notes, heightened tensions, or military or quasi-military actions in peripheral areas as the center of the conflict. These are, on the contrary, only momentarily visible manifestations of a deep-seated and abiding struggle between the two competitors for a world order.

The Soviet Union has a well-developed and articulate strategy by which it means to accomplish its goals. Rooted in ideology, modified by circumstances and events, and subject to continual changes as developments indicate, Soviet strategy is reflected in a series of moves and postures calculated to extend the power and influence of the Soviet Union. In some cases its tactics are ill-suited and have elicited an unexpected counteraction which has hampered rather than furthered its aims.[1]

It is, of course, impossible to cover all events, circumstances, and issues that have divided the Soviet Union and the United States. Sometimes the problems are trivial, such as the controversy over the lend-lease indebtedness which the United States claims is still owed by the Soviet Union. Others are of vital significance and could possibly lead to war. Rather than discuss all of these matters, it is more appropriate to define certain categories of conflict. One category is the division of the world along lines acceptable to both the Soviet Union and the United States. The former also resists and strikes out against the establishment of

---

[1] David J. Dallin, *Soviet Foreign Policy After Stalin* (Philadelphia: J. B. Lippincott Co., 1961), pp. 443-88.

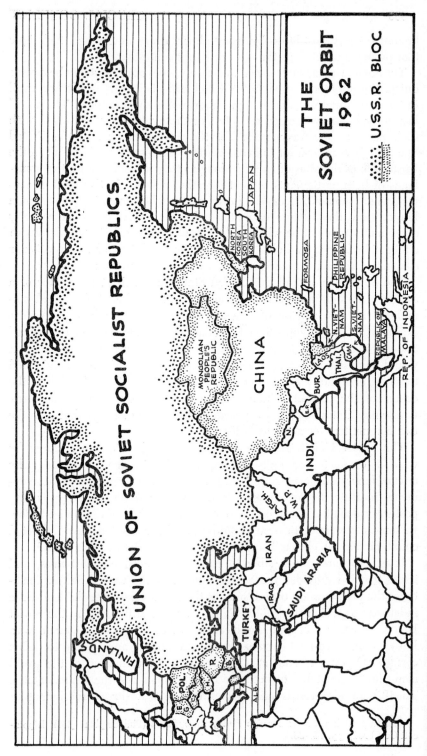

THE
SOVIET ORBIT
1962

U.S.S.R. BLOC

UNION OF SOVIET SOCIALIST REPUBLICS

MONGOLIAN
PEOPLE'S
REPUBLIC

CHINA

NORTH
KOREA
SOUTH
KOREA

JAPAN

FORMOSA

PHILIPPINE
REPUBLIC

N.VIET-
NAM

S.VIET-
NAM

LAOS

THAI.

CAM.

BUR.

REPUBLIC OF
MALAYA

REP. OF INDONESIA

INDIA

N.
P.

W.
PAK.

E.P.

IRAN

IRAQ

TURKEY

SAUDI ARABIA

FINLAND

E. GERMANY

POL.

CZECH.

H.

R.

B.

ALB.

alliances which it interprets as inimical to its aims while simultaneously endeavoring to erect an alliance system of its own. NATO, SEATO, and bilateral alliances involving the United States, come under unrelenting Soviet attack with periodic efforts to undermine them. The existence of these agreements frequently generates issues involving the Soviet Union and the United States.

SOVIET IDEOLOGY

It is impossible to understand Soviet-American relations without a consideration of the ideology which motivates the leaders and people of the Soviet Union. As a general problem in international relations, this topic is dealt with at length in Chapter 4. There is a long-standing controversy over the precise role of ideology in a country's foreign policy, but only a few would argue that the basic patterns of thought—religious and philosophical—are irrelevant in evaluating a nation's actions. In the case of a self-conscious ideology such as communism, which purports to offer a universal truth applicable in all nations, it is certain that the influence extends to the operational characteristics of the nation's foreign policies.

The intellectual support for modern communism comes from Karl Marx (1818-1883) and Nikolai Lenin (1870-1924). The former was the founder of a system of "scientific socialism" which supposedly underlies the Soviet economy. The latter was the founder of the present Soviet state and has extended Marxist thought, particularly in areas related to the practical problems of establishing and operating a socialist state. There have been and continue to be many modifications of communist doctrine. Two of the chief contributors to these changes have been Joseph Stalin (1879-1953) and Nikita Khrushchev (1894-   ). Despite many changes over the years, communist doctrine has displayed remarkable stability in its basic elements, and the ability to grow without destroying the foundations.

Early Additions to Ideology

Avoiding departure from Marxist principles, Lenin argued that the revolution in Russia was only the first of many throughout Europe. The new Soviet state could provide little support for promoting revolutions elsewhere because of a protracted civil war, a prostrate economy, and the need for effective mechanisms for operating the economy and government in the early years. In general, the new system conformed to the vision of Marx, largely because Marx left enough gaps in his analysis of socialism to make almost anything permissible.

When it became obvious that the capitalist countries were not going to join the new Soviet Union in revolution, a doctrinal rationalization and additional dogma were required. Thus, it came to be argued that socialism must be successful in one country first. The contrast between the peaceful progress of the Soviet Union and war-torn, crisis-ridden capitalist countries would impel other countries to follow suit. The Soviet Union, then, must realize the promise of socialism as rapidly as possible; it must become an example for the world, a bastion of socialist strength; other countries, observing the clear superiority of the Soviet Union, would naturally look to that country for leadership, and emulate its system.

In order to achieve these results, Soviet leaders became convinced that the Soviet Union must achieve great military, political, and economic power as rapidly as possible. After an initial period of consolidation and reconstruction, Stalin, following Lenin's recommendations, pursued vigorously and ruthlessly a course of forced-pace industrialization. Promising the people a higher standard of living later, Soviet leaders for nearly four decades invested 25 per cent of gross national product annually, while maintaining a large and expensive military establishment.[2]

Thus, almost from the very beginning communist doctrine began to be changed, a process which has continued since. The first steps were to isolate the Soviet Union from outside forces and to build Soviet power. Nationalism all but replaced internationalism, although the belief continued that other countries would join the Soviet Union in the socialist venture. It was apparent to Soviet leaders that their nation, as a nation, and not as an amorphous part of an international movement, would provide the leadership in an international socialist movement.

Ideological Developments Since 1945

Several important modifications in ideology have taken place in the period since the end of World War II and some of them have an important bearing upon Soviet international behavior. It is difficult to attribute them to any one man. Undoubtedly Stalin foresaw some of the world changes requiring ideological shifts, but it is clear that Khrushchev really introduced them and has made them an important part of communist thinking.

Nationalism. First and perhaps foremost is the continuation of the nationalistic trend which made it apparent that the Soviet Union would initially have to go it alone in a capitalist world. While internationalism has not been abandoned either in theory or in practice, Soviet ideology now recognizes the role of nationalism both in communist and non-communist states alike. Communism remains an international movement but it operates, according to present dogma, through existing nations.

Among communist countries the new emphasis on nationalism takes

---

[2] Georg van Rauch, *A History of Soviet Russia* (New York: Frederick A. Praeger, Inc., 1959), pp. 155-90.

the form of the recognition of national communism. By this is meant that each country will have a somewhat different economic and political system, which will be a variation of the communist theme. The basic core of communism is, of course, common to all such countries, but methods and institutions will differ. Thus, Poland and Yugoslavia may desire to rely more heavily on the price system, China may employ communes, all within the communist framework. The Soviet Union has made it clear, however, that not only is there a basic doctrine which must be accepted, but also that allegiance to the Soviet Union is mandatory.

The Soviet Union also has recognized the force of nationalism among non-communist countries. There has been a basic ideological decision that the national movements of the new and emerging countries are to be supported; that it is through these new governments that communist influence is to be felt. While subversive activities continue, and, if conditions and circumstances are appropriate, a communist revolution may receive assistance, the main emphasis has switched to support of the new national regimes. For example, economic and military assistance, as well as political assistance, is given to regimes which have little or no sympathy for communism and primarily respect and fear the Soviet Union.

The Soviet Union has in effect changed its brand of internationalism by recognizing the strength of nationalism. Whereas in earlier days its internationalism tended to be conspiritorial and extra-governmental, it has now emerged from its national isolation to engage in international political and economic affairs. The Soviet Union proposes to be a leader among nations, as well as the center of an international revolution. Specific conditions will determine its behavior in any given instance, but the ideological base of communism has been immeasurably broadened through the acceptance of the role of nationalism.[3]

Peaceful Coexistence. Accompanying this change has been the increasing emphasis on peaceful coexistence. There are two aspects to this strategy. One concerns the introduction of communism into non-communist countries. The other concerns the relations between communist and non-communist countries. On both levels peaceful coexistence implies a reluctance to accept violence and warfare, particularly nuclear warfare, as a necessary ingredient of the conflict between communism and capitalism. To the Soviet Union it means the continuation of a process of historical change which is operating to its benefit. It means a constant probing on the economic, political, psychological, and diplomatic level, seeking to find weaknesses and vulnerabilities which may be exploited without use of military forces.

No great showdown of power between communism and capitalism will

---

[3] Hugh Seton-Watson, *From Lenin to Khrushchev* (New York: Frederick A. Praeger, Inc., 1960), pp. 248-70, 291-329.

be necessary, as was indicated in the early strategy. Capitalism and communism can exist side by side peaceably and indefinitely, each competing for the allegiance of the people. Capitalist countries may make war on one another and there may be armed conflict between communism and capitalism—if forced upon the former by the latter—but peaceful change and evolution is possible and to be desired by the Soviet Union. The end result will be the triumph of communism without war.

All but jettisoned is the earlier ideological dictum that only through violent revolution can socialism and then communism be introduced into capitalist countries. The example of the Soviet Union and other communist countries, plus parliamentary procedures, can fulfill the same function. Revolutions there will be, but they can be peaceful, based on the natural superiority of communism.

SOVIET FOREIGN POLICY PROCESS

The Soviet Union is in form a federation of autonomous republics and territories. In fact, it is a highly centralized unitary government. It should be made clear at the outset that the Soviet Union does not employ democratic processes, despite having some of the trappings of democracy (such as a parliament and voting). The country is actually run by a small self-perpetuating oligarchy, operating simultaneously through the Soviet government and the Communist party. There is a written constitution and supposedly guaranteed rights and privileges.[4]

Public Influence

There is, however, no systematic method by which the people of the Soviet Union may express their will or influence their public officials. Civil, political, and minority rights and the right to dissent and to protest are narrowly circumscribed. Still, it cannot be said that the influence of the people is not felt in the Soviet Union. No matter how complete the control, the ruling group finds it convenient and certainly less expensive to accept the public will when it does not endanger the position of the group or jeopardize its goals seriously. Soviet leadership, for example, could conceivably deprive Soviet consumers of any increase in the level of living and there would be some advantages in doing so from the point of view of military and economic power. The leadership has found, however, that modest increases each year alleviate unrest, provide greater incentives, and make the job of running the Soviet Union much easier.

---

[4] Committee on Government Operations, U.S. Senate, *National Policy Making Machinery in the Soviet Union*, 86th Congress (Washington, D.C.: Government Printing Office, 1960), pp. 22-30.

Government and Party

The administration of state affairs in the Soviet Union is the dual function and responsibility of the government and the party. There are less than nine million members in the rigidly disciplined, hierarchial party machine. There is a branch in nearly every organization and institution in the Soviet Union, in plants, ministries, enterprises, universities, and so on. At the top of the Soviet administrative structure there is considerable overlapping between party and government functionaries. Members of the party Presidium are frequently ministers or deputy chairmen of the Council of Ministers, which is the executive branch of the government. Thus, the topmost leadership may have a specific functional responsibility, such as transportation or electric power, as well as a general party function in administering the affairs of state.

Foreign Policy Administration

The administration of Soviet foreign affairs is of central concern to Khrushchev and the party and government elite. The direct responsibility is in the hands of the Ministry of Foreign Affairs under the leadership of A. A. Gromyko, who does not happen to be a member of the party Presidium. It is likely that this Presidium and a small group within the Council of Ministers act as a sort of extra-ministerial policy-planning staff in foreign affairs, with power to make and implement policy. There are a number of other instrumentalities involved in foreign activities, not under the control of the Ministry of Foreign Affairs, but subservient to the Council of Ministers. These include the State Committee for Foreign Economic Relations, designed to establish and develop economic contacts with foreign countries and to supervise economic and technical assistance; the Ministry of Foreign Trade, constituting a complete state monopoly over all imports and exports; the Council of Mutual Economic Assistance, a consultative and coordinating body of all communist countries on economic matters, dominated by the Soviet Union; and communist parties in most foreign countries.

Stalin personally dominated the formation of foreign policy and brooked no interference. In the years immediately following his death a series of persons exercised some influence on Soviet international behavior and all of the top leadership seemed to be involved. As time passed the decision-making apparatus came to be more and more under the control of one man. By 1958, it became apparent that Khrushchev was the strongest single influence and by 1961 it was clear that Soviet foreign policy was in fact Khrushchev's policy. His views are no doubt modified by a consideration of the Presidium's views and those of the Council of

Ministers, but increasingly individuals appointed to these groups have been approved by Khrushchev.[5]

THE SOVIET ECONOMY

In implementing its international objectives the Soviet Union employs many devices. Propaganda activities and psychological warfare are used on a large scale. The Communist party is active in nearly every country. Diplomacy and occasionally force—usually indirectly through the supply of arms—are also used. Economic and technical assistance have become a major instrument of foreign policy. All of these techniques rely ultimately on the power of the Soviet state. Thus, the economic stature of the Soviet economy is of fundamental importance in Soviet international behavior. An elaborate administrative structure headed by GOSPLAN, the national planning agency, makes the basic economic decisions, directly under political authority.

Productivity and Growth

With a population about 20 per cent greater than that of the United States the Soviet Union produces approximately two-fifths as much goods and services. In terms of per capita consumption, the Soviet people are less than one-third as well off as those of the United States, but in such items as consumer durables and housing, they are woefully behind.

In allocating resources the Soviet Union spends nearly as much on the military as does the United States, which means a much higher proportion of its product. Capital formation proceeds at a rapid rate and much of the investment is in heavy industry. Consequently, consumption, light industry, and housing suffer.

The result of Soviet economic policy has been an unusually high rate of postwar growth for the economy as a whole, but more particularly in industry. The rate of growth of the Soviet gross national product has been 6 to 7 per cent; and of industry, about 8 to 9 per cent. These figures correspond to 3 per cent for American economic growth and 4 per cent for American industrial growth. It is not unlikely that in industrial production the Soviet Union may catch up with the United States in a generation. The Soviet Union is convinced that by the time this happens whatever American support exists in the world will have dissipated and even the United States will have to admit the superiority of the Soviet system.[6]

[5] Herbert McCloskey and John E. Turner, *The Soviet Dictatorship* (New York: McGraw-Hill Book Co., Inc., 1960), pp. 162-96.

[6] Robert W. Campbell, *Soviet Economic Power* (Boston: Houghton Mifflin Company, 1960), pp. 28-55.

The Economic Model

Several elements of the Soviet economy have a significant effect on its international behavior. The complete control exercised by political authority makes possible a very strong military posture and the supply of capital to other countries. It also facilitates economic growth, particularly in those sections of the economy which are useful for the promotion of Soviet international objectives. In May 1961, Khrushchev indicated that in the future light industry (consumer goods) would have equal rates of growth with heavy industry. This may be in part a response to a serious internal incentive problem, but it cannot fail to have escaped the Soviet leader that one of the reasons for the failure of the Soviet Union to sell its worker's paradise is that it provides an extremely limited amount, kind, and quality of consumer goods.

With a planned economy and planned foreign trade it is possible to isolate the internal economy from international disequilibrium. It is a proposition of no mean magnitude to be able to assert that the economy makes progress despite what is happening in the world. Domestic prices and costs, volumes of exports and imports, balance of payments problems, and other elements normally connected with the international economy in the Soviet Union are completely isolated and independent.

The system of state trading employed by the Soviet Union is a useful device for influencing other countries. Import and export prices may be manipulated to reward or punish. Particular trading partners may be selected with a view toward the political impact. With all foreign economic activities in the hands of the government, loans and other transactions may be undertaken to wield the greatest economic, political, or military influence.[7]

The Soviet Union relies heavily on the appeal of its economic system, particularly to the people of the less developed countries. If they adopt this economic model, the Soviet Union expects they will also borrow its ideological and political system. Emphasis on governmental activity and detailed planning, as well as isolation from external influence, are all factors which have great appeal in the less developed countries.

EVOLUTION OF
SOVIET INTERNATIONAL BEHAVIOR

Soviet international behavior has by no means remained static over the years; it has shifted as the world situation itself has altered. The Soviet Union has never wavered, however, in its almost single-minded purpose of promoting the cause of communism and maintaining leadership of the

---

[7] Symposium on State Trading, *Law and Contemporary Problems*, XXIV (Spring and Summer, 1959), 243-90, 398-481.

movement. What have changed have been various short-run outlooks, the way various problems have been faced, and tactics made possible by the growing power of the Soviet state.

War Communism and the New Economic Policy

In the period 1917-21 when the Soviet Union was being born, the principal aim was to make the revolution a success in Russia and extend it to Western Europe. This required an ignominious withdrawal from World War I and the ruthless exercise of power at home in order to quell the civil war. It became clear that capitalist countries were going to be hostile to the new regime: some, including the United States, even used their troops on Russian soil. It was in this period that the Soviet leaders developed a neurotic fear of encirclement, much as did earlier Russian rulers.

By 1921 the revolution was still shaky, although political power was in the hands of the communists. Civil war and intervention by capitalist states had left the country weak. The expected revolutions were further off than ever. Soviet leaders had made a mess of trying to operate the new economy. It was time to retrench, to back up, to reinstall limited capitalism at home and to try to mollify capitalism abroad. The period of the New Economic Policy (1921-28) was a breathing spell during which the Soviet Union could put its house in order and decide what to do next. In international affairs, it tried to become respectable, gain diplomatic recognition, and erase the bomb-carrying conspiritorial image of communism. Internally, it was a test of power between Stalin and Trotsky and a time of decision on the tempo and techniques of industrialization.

Soviet Policy in the Interwar Period

In 1928, Stalin was firmly in power and the New Economic Policy was superceded by the first Five-Year Plan, unbelievable in its harshness to the Russian peasant, with emphasis upon industrialization. Relations with capitalist countries were proper. Credit was obtained and repaid promptly. Large-scale imports of machinery, equipment, and technical assistance aided in the industrialization drive. The Soviet Union was preoccupied by its internal problems. The world was preoccupied with the Great Depression.

During the nineteen-thirties Soviet relations with the rest of the world gradually became normal. The United States, for example, recognized the regime in 1933 and diplomatic representatives were exchanged. Soviet-sponsored revolutionary activity in other countries diminished. The Soviet Union joined the League of Nations and became its most ardent supporter, seeking to gain acceptance among the great powers of the world.

In the late nineteen-thirties war clouds reappeared over Europe. In the middle of its third Five-Year Plan in 1938, the Soviet Union began preparing for war. The brief, ill-fated German-Soviet agreement of 1939, in which Poland was to be divided and the Soviet Union given a sphere of influence in the Middle East, was clearly indicative of its continued expansionist urge. When the Germans attacked, Western observers predicted the Soviet Union would not last long. But it held out, kept its army intact, and gave up nothing but battle-torn and scorched earth. Soviet performance during the war was a massive demonstration of the power of nationalism. Russians fought for their homes and homeland, not particularly for the regime; any lingering doubts within their leadership about the strength of nationalism were dispelled.

Having fortified itself by conquest and wartime agreements with a cordon of buffer states in the west, the Soviet Union, following World War II, chose to remain aloof from most postwar international efforts, although it joined the UN and participated in some of the specialized agencies. Attempting to take advantage of war-torn Europe, it endeavored to subvert West European governments. Confronted by increasingly stiff resistance in Western Europe, a participant in a military misadventure in Korea, and observing changes in the structure of the world, the present Soviet strategy began to be formulated in the early nineteen-fifties.

In the Korean War and through the mid-fifties the nature of the conflict came to be more clearly perceived by the United States and the lines of the cold war were firmly drawn. The death of Stalin in 1953 permitted the introduction of greater flexibility into Soviet international behavior. It also signalled the beginning of a period of greater interest and activity in the less developed countries. East European dissatisfaction was quelled in 1953 and 1956, and the Soviet Union made it abundantly clear that interference in its own bloc would not be permitted. At the same time the rise of Communist China injected a new element in its policy.

SOVIET STRATEGIC POSTURE

Stemming directly from its ideology and position in the world, the strategy of the Soviet Union is to maintain outward pressure at all points along the periphery of the area under its control and to seek weaknesses and vulnerabilities in areas beyond. It seeks change for the sake of change, expecting results favorable to itself from almost any kind of change in the non-communist world.

Soviet behavior in general tends to be adventuresome, bold, and unpredictable, even though the strategy is stable and predictable. It is not wholly new. Elements existed in earlier periods of the Soviet regime. Nor is it completely exclusive. Communist China has an even more reckless strategy than the Soviet Union, although basically the same one. The East European allies have a more conservative strategy, since trade is more important to them and they have a stronger affinity for West European countries. Hence, the Soviet Union, whose basic strategy dominates throughout the communist area, is impelled to less responsible behavior by the Chinese while tending to be held back by its European allies.[8]

Expansionist Pressure

The Soviet Union proposes to maintain constant pressure of every kind—political, economic, military, psychological—at numerous points along the boundary of the communist world, and by ideology and subversion beyond it. Every controversy between two countries, every existing or potential internal dissension, each weakness and vulnerability are suitable situations for probes by the Soviet Union. A military threat may weaken the determination of a country, economic aid may enlist the support of another, political assistance may be returned by political support, and taking sides with a country may heighten international tension. Such devices are used to divide and destabilize any and all parts of the non-communist world. In this manner the Soviet Union expects to add to its strength, detract from the strength of the United States, and gain support for its policies.

The size of the non-communist world is sufficiently large and its structure sufficiently diverse that at any given moment there is ample opportunity for the exercise of this strategy. For example, in early 1961 these situations were subjected to some degree of Soviet manipulation: civil war in Algeria, the Congo, Laos, and South Viet Nam; controversies between the United Arab Republic and other Arab states and Israel, India and Pakistan, Pakistan and Afghanistan; revolutions in South Korea, Angola, and Cuba (plus a bitter controversy between Cuba and the United States); internal racial difficulties in Kenya, South Africa, and the United States; stalled arms control negotiations in Geneva; and many other problems. As if these were not sufficient, there was the crushing burden of poverty, ignorance, and disease throughout the less developed countries of the world. Economic backwardness, dislocation, and instability, as well as tyranny and political unrest, constitute an open invitation for Soviet exploitation.

Soviet Initiative

Even though conditions in the world provide an adequate number of situations to manipulate, it is also a basic part of Soviet strategy to create

---

[8] Donald S. Zagoria, "Strains in the Sino-Soviet Alliance," *Problems of Communism*, IX (May-June, 1960), 1-11; and the same author's "Sino-Soviet Friction in Underdeveloped Areas," *Ibid.*, X (Mar.-Apr., 1961), pp. 1-13.

trouble for the United States. While the Soviet Union is convinced that historical processes are working in its favor, its leaders are not above giving history a push. Soviet initiative was exercised in some of the problems mentioned above. The rebels in Laos are supported militarily and politically by the Soviet Union. Communists have apparently captured the revolution in Cuba. The Soviet Union continues to threaten and make menacing moves concerning Berlin. It has launched a major attack on the structure and operations of the UN.

In addition to this fundamental posture the Soviet Union is endeavoring to create a favorable image of itself in the world. It does this by an apparent willingness to negotiate on any issue, by making grandiose disarmament proposals, by supporting the economic development aspirations of the less developed countries, by aligning itself with their political and economic policies, by sponsoring anticolonialism, and by undertaking all those actions which tend to make it appear as the progressive, peace-loving, helpful friend of the masses.[9]

Difficulty in Implementing Strategy

Soviet strategy has run into two difficulties. One arises from the nature of international relationships. In stimulating one country against another, the latter is naturally offended. Pakistan can hardly be expected to be happy with Soviet support of Afghanistan over Pushtoonistan. France is upset over the military arms going to the Algerian rebels. By attacking the UN the Soviet Union may lose the support of those who put great store in that institution. No country can please all countries simultaneously or all of the time. As the web of interrelationships increases, the opportunities for making everyone unhappy also increase. Despite an effort to distribute its supports and threats so that no country is pushed to the wall, the Soviet Union cannot expect to succeed in every element of its strategy.

The promotion of communism and subversion remains a basic element of Soviet strategy. No country likes to be host to a group which is a constant threat to its stability or even existence. Thus, to the extent that local communist parties are successful in stirring up trouble, they are also creating problems for the Soviet Union, which is in the awkward position of acting both as a nation and as the head of a revolutionary party which seeks to overthrow all existing regimes. As a nation it may be advantageous to work with the national regimes of other countries, but harmonious relations are sometimes difficult when the local communist party is continually attacking the existing regime.

In recent years the Soviet Union has tended to place more emphasis on

---

[9] Henry G. Aubrey, *Coexistence: Economic Challenge and Response* (Washington, D.C.: National Planning Assn., 1961), pp. 175-236.

its role as a nation rather than as head of the communist movement. This represents a calculation that its goals can best be accomplished by acting as a nation. If, as the Soviet Union seems fully convinced, the United States is the prime enemy of communism, then national strength and influence among nations is the way to reach the United States, since it seems impervious to subversion or ideological penetration. Therefore, working with and influencing national regimes, rather than trying to eliminate them, has been the principal strategic consideration. This does not mean that communist parties will not be used, as has been the case in Cuba and in other locations, but rather that this device is reserved principally for special situations in which this form of behavior appears to be decisively favorable.[10]

THE AMERICAN POSITION

Soviet international behavior is more clearly understandable when one examines the strategy of the United States. In general the United States has no territorial ambitions and does not seek to convert or subvert the remainder of the world to its way of thinking. Its principal preoccupation has been with its own defense and with the defense of those countries who do not want a communist society. American strategy is often a direct response to what it considers the communist threat, rather than the pursuit of an independent set of goals.

Following World War II it was hoped that the Soviet Union, having attained the status of a first-class power, would abandon its basic expansionist goals. When events proved this wrong (most notably the continued Soviet control of Eastern Europe, as well as the communist coup d'état in Czechoslovakia in 1948) American strategic policy bent itself toward containing the Soviet Union. By this is meant both physical containment within that area then under its control, and the restraint of the growth of Soviet influence in the free world.

Believing that communist doctrine is basically false, American leadership felt that if the Soviet area were isolated, the error of communist ways would eventually become evident and the people would throw off its yoke. At one time there was some thought given to the liberation of the peoples of Eastern Europe but it was clear that this could be done only by war; the best hope, then, was to prevent any further expansion and await the favorable outcome. To be certain of containment, a formidable military posture was required, as well as alliances and treaties which assured joint responsibility in the case of any Soviet expansion.

Conscious of the Soviet strategy of the selective probe, the American responsive strategy was to keep the unrest and weaknesses in the non-

---

[10] Milton Kovner, *The Challenge of Coexistence* (Washington, D.C.: Public Affairs Press, 1961), pp. 4-20.

communist world within bounds so that there would be little Soviet opportunity to exploit vulnerable spots. Whenever a difficulty arose in an
area not controlled by the Soviet Union, the United States has felt a
responsibility to assist in meeting it. If revolution threatened, the United
States tended to support the existing regime, fearing the successor might
fall under communist influence. If some issue created tensions between
two countries, the United States made an effort to mediate the issue. If
economic problems plagued a country, the United States endeavored to
give economic assistance. If a country felt that it might be threatened by
communism, either from within or without, the United States provided
military assistance.

In ways such as these, the United States has sought to maintain the
status quo, to resist change unless it were demonstrably favorable to
American interests, and to stop the expansion of communism everywhere
in the world. It was felt that so long as there was some chance of improvement, the situation was better than communist control, under which
a country ceased to determine its own fate. The inevitability of free men
choosing freedom was a basic postulate underlying American strategy
and justified all actions necessary to maintain freedom of choice. The
support of non-communist dictators was justified on two grounds: they
frequently were allied with American interests, and so long as the country
was not in communist hands there was an opportunity for a change
which would not impair American interests.

At the same time American policy-planners realized the necessity of
doing something to ameliorate the ravages of economic backwardness and
whenever possible the harshness of oppression and tyranny. Economic
and military aid as well as political support is given to countries and political groups who tend to favor the American position. There is a realization that such moves may initiate changes, including unrest and revolutions, which may be subjected to Soviet exploitation. It is a calculated
risk that sufficient economic and political improvement can take place to
forestall any substantial growth of communist influence.[11]

The American strategy has, for the most part, placed the initiative in
the hands of the Soviet Union. When a situation is quiescent, the United
States is disinclined to take action which will disturb the equilibrium.
Given some disturbance, the Soviet Union acts to exacerbate it and the
United States acts to heal over the wound and keep Soviet influence from
growing in the area. At various times the United States has sought to gain
the initiative, but largely without success. The basic posture of both
participants in the conflict probably gives the advantage to the Soviet
Union. The greatest opportunity for American initiative lies not in action
directed against it, but rather in fighting the age-old enemies poverty,

[11] James R. Schlesinger, *The Political Economy of National Security* (New York:
Frederick A. Praeger, Inc., 1960), pp. 222-68.

ignorance, and disease. To the extent that the United States is successful in eliminating these enemies, the Soviet Union will have less opportunity to exercise influence in the world.

ISSUES IN THE
SOVIET-AMERICAN CONFLICT

It would be possible to name literally dozens of specific issues in which there has been a difficult situation, a Soviet action, an American reaction, a period of interaction, and a few acceptable accommodations. Only in a few cases has the Soviet Union been in the position of reacting to American behavior. Rather than attempt to evaluate all of the issues, it will be possible here only to indicate the types of issues and to discuss some of the more important ones.

Border Issues

A significant number of issues concern areas which are on the borderlands of the communist world. The fact that these occur in peripheral areas is directly related to the strategies employed by the contestants. The Soviet Union, employing a fundamentally expansionist tactic, naturally probes first on its borders to find weaknesses. During and shortly after World War II the Soviet Union was largely unopposed in its move into the Baltic states, East Central Europe, and the Balkans. But similar thrusts in Turkey and Iran were resisted by the United States, and Soviet demands for control of Turkish Mediterranean ports and of Iran's Azerbaijan were dropped without becoming major issues.

Since the short-lived honeymoon immediately after the war, there have been issues involving countries on or close to the borders of the Soviet area, most of which have either been sponsored or supported by the Soviet Union. The Marshall Plan, for example, was a massive economic program designed in part to forestall Soviet progress in Western Europe. The status of Berlin and division of Germany remain major issues on which both the Soviet Union and the United States have taken strong positions. In Korea it was necessary to fight a minor war to prevent border expansion, although in this case mainland China succeeded the Soviet Union in the area shortly after the outbreak of hostilities. Turkey, Iran, and the West European countries have been subjected to military threats and the Asian borderlands have alternately been coaxed, converted, subverted, and threatened. The most recent issue is Laos, one of the small successor states to French Indochina. Rebel forces, supported militarily and politically by the Soviet Union, have threatened to take control of the entire country and not until 1961 was it possible to negotiate a shaky cease-fire and convene formal discussions over the issue.

Penetrating the
Noncommunist World

Not all expansionist issues have taken place at the border, however. In a few instances, the Soviet Union has vaulted over the countries immediately surrounding it and has begun to exercise substantial influence in countries within the noncommunist world. Communists gained substantial influence over the government of Guatemala in 1954, but were shortly thereafter unseated by an American-inspired and assisted counterrevolution. In Cuba a revolution was captured by communists and that country has informally aligned itself with the Soviet Union. In the Congo the Soviet Union backed the leader most sympathetic to communism. For a while in Iraq, Iran, and Syria, local communist movements made strong bids for power.

Tension, Influence, and Control Issues

Still another way of looking at Soviet-American interaction is in terms of what the Soviet Union hopes to accomplish. Some issues are raised simply for the purpose of creating increased tension, in the expectation that some favorable change may result. In other situations the Soviet Union definitely expects to increase its influence or prestige in the area. For example, the Soviet and Czech sales of arms to Egypt in 1955 was a trouble-making venture to curry favor with the Egyptians and cause trouble in that area's uneasy arms balance. When the United States and its allies used the arms deal as an excuse to deny economic assistance, the Egyptians retaliated by nationalizing the Universal Suez Canal Company. This was followed by hostile action by Israel, Great Britain, and France. The Soviet Union benefited substantially.

The Egyptian case also illustrates another form of Soviet behavior—actions undertaken to build Soviet influence in non-communist countries. Arms, economic and technical assistance, disarmament proposals, and activities in the UN demonstrate the desire of the Soviet Union to build prestige and influence throughout the world. On occasion an exercise of this sort brings it into conflict with the United States. The United States tends to regard its foreign economic assistance as a defense against communism. Disarmament and arms control negotiations go on interminably with little practical result as both the Soviet Union and the United States are vying for influence in the UN.[12]

In some cases the Soviet Union has been interested in far more than merely heightening tensions or building influence. It wants substantial

---

[12] Wladyslaw W. Kulski, *Peaceful Coexistence* (Chicago: Henry Regnery Co., 1959), pp. 203-300.

control over an area. Cuba is a case in point. In most cases, however, issues of control occur at the border of the Soviet area, as in the case of Turkey and Iran following World War II. In their immediate threat to peace, issues such as these involve the greatest risk of open conflict between the United States and the Soviet Union, since in most cases the former is as determined to avoid loss of an area as the latter is to gain it.

Berlin and Germany

Wartime agreements resulted in the partitioning of both Germany and Berlin. Berlin is deep in the Soviet Zone. The separated zones of the United States, France, and the United Kingdom were merged to become the Federal Republic of Germany. The Soviet Zone has been styled the German Democratic Republic. Almost from the beginning the Soviet Union regarded the Western-occupied zone of Berlin as an infringement upon its territorial rights, despite the agreement providing for such occupation until the postwar treaties were signed. In an effort to oust American influence deep in its German sector, the Soviet Union in 1948 prevented land entry into West Berlin. The result was the Berlin airlift, a period of nearly a year when the city was supplied by air.

Since the airlift West Berlin has been a major bone of contention between the United States and the Soviet Union. It is, in reality, a part of the larger problem of Germany, which the Soviet Union wishes to see united on terms acceptable to itself. The United States has vigorously opposed reunification of Germany except by free elections and has refused to budge from Berlin, regarding its presence there not only as a war-won right, but also as an obligation of the United States to the people of West Berlin. The Soviet Union is just as adamant in wanting to eliminate the Western enclave, not only because it is a glittering reminder of the prosperity of the Federal Republic and Western prosperity in general, but also because it is an all-too-easy center for East German defections which have been so numerous that the population of the area has actually declined in recent years. As the struggle over Berlin mounted in the late summer of 1961, the Soviet Union forbade East Germans to enter West Berlin, and limited Western access to East Berlin.

Khrushchev has told Western observers that Berlin is the most important single issue between his country and the United States and has made it clear that he intends to have his way. By concluding a treaty with the German Democratic Republic and turning over all authority to it, the Soviet Union feels it will have observed the original agreements, whether or not the United States recognizes the new treaty. The United States, for its part, has indicated that it will not tolerate a Soviet-dominated West Berlin, regardless of whether the Soviet Union or a puppet state attempts to exercise the control. In 1961 no solution seemed in sight as it appeared that the Soviet Union was girding its loins for another attempt to enforce its will on West Berlin and the United States was rallying its North Atlantic allies to its unconditional defense.

United Nations

Almost from the beginning of the UN the Soviet Union has been making an increasingly formidable bid for influence in the organization. Outvoted on most major issues, outnumbered by the United States, its allies, and other countries, the Soviet Union has tended to use the UN as a propaganda platform. As more countries joined who had little sympathy with the colonial powers and the United States, Soviet influence grew. The Soviet Union relied on the veto in the Security Council to bloc inimical moves, a circumstance which shifted power to the General Assembly. In 1960 the Soviet Union made its bid for more effective control over the UN. The immediate issue was the crisis in the Congo and the question of the performance of the Secretary-General. The Soviet Union proposed a tripartite secretary-generalship (*troika*), one man from the Soviet area, one "neutralist," and one from the Western countries. Most countries stood behind the secretary-general in resisting the Soviet proposal, which would extend Soviet control to the action arm of the organization. But it has initiated a major crisis in the UN and has to some extent impaired its effective operation. The situation has been further complicated by the sudden, tragic death of Secretary-General Hammerskjöld in September 1961, a situation the Soviet Union tried to exploit, but without much success.

Disarmament and Arms Control

The Soviet Union and the United States have been negotiating since 1945 on arms control and disarmament. Some of these negotiations have been under the auspices of the UN. In nearly every instance the Soviet Union has made a grand proposal for disarmament, abandonment of nuclear testing, or some arms control device. In every case the United States has found at least some important parts of the proposal unacceptable. Assuming good faith on the Soviet side, it is obvious that it wants a simple declaration of intent but does not wish to have any enforceable provisions relating to outside inspection or control, in any case short of "general and complete disarmament." The United States feels that without inspection and control and provisions for policing the agreement there can be no effective treaty.

The Soviet Union apparently holds the position that having outsiders with inspection and control functions within Soviet borders is in effect espionage and an infringement on sovereignty. No agreement has been reached on crucial problems of arms control. In 1958 a voluntary nuclear testing ban came into existence in anticipation of an early agreement on the subject. Despite earnest effort, apparently on both sides, no agreement has been forthcoming. Without doubt a genuine disarmament or arms control measure would be welcomed on both sides. Both are burdened with heavy armament expenditures. It also appears clear that neither side will agree to anything which does not either leave its relative position the same or improve it somewhat. The chances of finding such an accommodation seem remote.

The Problem of Economic Development

With a billion and a quarter of the world's people living on the edge of starvation, miserably housed, and poorly clothed, both the United States and the Soviet Union have vigorously undertaken programs which each hopes will gain or retain the allegiance of the people. Early in the postwar period the United States, with arms and economic assistance, bolstered Greece and Turkey, making them into effective allies. In subsequent years the same device was employed to strengthen alliances, pay for armies, and maintain friendly governments in power.

The Soviet Union was impressed with the technique and beginning in 1955 began to emulate it on a large scale. The first large transaction was an arms loan to Egypt which upset the arms balance in the Middle East. This has been followed by arms transactions with Morocco, Yemen, Syria, Iraq, Indonesia, Guinea, Cuba, Afghanistan, and others. Unlike American military aid, this aid was not to allies, but to countries professing non-alignment. In addition, the Soviet Union began an economic assistance program, made attractive by apparently favorable terms, for less developed countries. Between 1955 and 1960 the Soviet Union (with some assistance from Eastern Europe) agreed to loan $5 billion for arms and economic assistance and in 1960 was delivering at the rate of $800 million per year.[13]

It is clear that Soviet economic and arms assistance is not provided for self-protection and economic development purposes alone. Some of it is undertaken to increase tension, to initiate a change which the Soviet Union hopes will be favorable, or to increase its influence and prestige in the country. The pattern is amply illustrated by one of the more successful case studies, Cuba. Following the Cuban revolution, the Soviet Union offered economic and military assistance. This raised Soviet prestige and downgraded American influence. The United States became increasingly uneasy about Soviet arms, economic assistance, and trade. These factors, along with Cuban abuse and expropriation of American property, have

---

[13] Robert Loring Allen, *Soviet Economic Warfare* (Washington, D.C.: Public Affairs Press, 1960), pp. 110-43.

almost completely disrupted trade and have ruptured diplomatic relations. Partly because of local communists, partly because of Soviet influence through trade and economic and military assistance, Cuba now almost wholly supports Soviet policy.

THE FUTURE

There is no reason to be confident about the future of the world. The Soviet Union in general has been successful in its strategy and according to communist ideology, there is no reason for it to alter its behavior. The U.S. must counter Soviet actions and attempt to retain freedom of choice for people and governments throughout the world. Some issue may touch both sides so deeply that they may prefer to fight rather than give in. War could also come by accident or miscalculation, both increasing risks. It is also possible that if either side became convinced that it was losing, it might initiate hostilities. Whether or not it might be possible to limit the warfare, either in terms of weapons or in area, cannot be known.

Even assuming there is no war, it is certain that there will continue to be conflict in which every weapon short of physical force is employed. The Soviet Union, using economic aid, subversion, diplomacy, and every other means, must continue to thrust and probe. The U.S., with the same devices, must blunt these endeavors and parry the thrusts. The highest expectation is probably the maintenance of the present stalemate, with its hope that the Soviet Union will be increasingly occupied with internal affairs as its economy becomes more prosperous, and that the uneasy Soviet alliance with China will become a grievous worry to Soviet leaders.

SUGGESTED READINGS

Allen, Robert Loring, *Soviet Economic Warfare*. Washington, D.C.: Public Affairs Press, 1960.
Armstrong, John A., *The Soviet Bureaucratic Elite*. New York: Frederick A. Praeger, Inc., 1959.
Aubrey, Henry G., *Coexistence: Economic Challenge and Response*. Washington, D.C.: National Planning Assn., 1961.
Barghoorn, Frederick, E., *The Soviet Cultural Offensive*. Princeton, N.J.: Princeton University Press, 1960.

Bell, Daniel, "Ten Theories in Search of Reality," *World Politics*, X (Apr. 1958), 327-65.

Berliner, Joseph, *Soviet Economic Aid.* New York: Frederick A. Praeger, Inc., 1958.

Brumberg, Abraham, ed., *Communism After Stalin.* New York: Frederick A. Praeger, Inc., 1961.

Brzezinski, Zbigniew, *The Soviet Bloc: Unity and Conflict.* Cambridge: Harvard University Press, 1960.

Campbell, Robert, *Soviet Economic Power.* Boston: Houghton Mifflin Company, 1960.

Dallin, David J., *Soviet Foreign Policy After Stalin.* Philadlephia: J. B. Lippincott Co., 1961.

Dallin, Alexander, compiler, *Soviet Conduct in World Affairs: A Selection of Readings.* New York: Columbia University Press, 1960.

————, *The Soviet Union at the United Nations: An Analysis of Diplomatic Strategy and Tactics.* New York: Frederick A. Praeger, Inc., 1961.

Dinerstein, H. S., *War and the Soviet Union.* New York: Frederick A. Praeger, Inc., 1959.

Fischer, Louis, *Russia, America, and the World.* New York: Harper & Brothers, 1961.

Fitzsimmons, Thomas and others, *USSR: Its People, Its Society, Its Culture.* New Haven: Human Relations Area Files Press, 1960.

Gilney, Frank, *The Khrushchev Pattern.* New York: Duell, Sloan & Pearce, Inc., 1961.

Goldwin, Lerner, and others, eds., *Readings in Russian Foreign Policy.* New York: Oxford University Press, Inc., 1959.

Khrushchev, Nikita S., *For Victory in Peaceful Competition with Capitalism.* New York: E. P. Dutton & Co., Inc., 1960.

Kovner, Milton, *The Challenge of Coexistence.* Washington, D.C.: Public Affairs Press, 1961.

Kulski, W. W., *Peaceful Co-existence.* Chicago: Henry Regnery Co., 1959.

Marcuse, Herbert, *Soviet Marxism: A Critical Analysis.* New York: Columbia University Press, 1958.

McCloskey, Herbert C. and John E. Turner, *The Soviet Dictatorship.* New York: McGraw-Hill Book Co., Inc., 1960.

Pistrak, Lazar, *The Grand Tactician, Khrushchev's Rise to Power.* New York: Frederick A. Praeger, Inc., 1961.

Rauch, George van, *A History of Soviet Russia.* New York: Frederick A. Praeger, Inc., 1959.

Reshetar, John S., Jr., *Problems of Analyzing and Predicting Soviet Behavior.* Garden City, New York: Doubleday & Company, 1955.

"Resolving the Russian-American Deadlock," *Annals of the Academy of Political and Social Science,* CCCXXIV (July 1959), entire issue.

Roberts, Henry L., *Russia and America: Dangers and Prospects.* New York: Council on Foreign Relations, Inc., 1956.

Rubinstein, Alvin Z., ed., *The Foreign Policy of the Soviet Union,* (text and readings). New York: Random House, 1960.

Salisbury, H. E., *To Moscow and Beyond: A Reporter's Narrative.* New York: Harper & Brothers, 1960.

Schwartz, Harry, *The Red Phoenix: Russia Since World War II.* New York: Frederick A. Praeger, Inc., 1961.

————, *Russia's Soviet Economy.* Englewood Cliffs, N.J.: Prentice-Hall, Inc., 1954.

Seton-Watson, Hugh, *From Lenin to Khrushchev*. New York: Frederick A. Praeger, Inc., 1960.
Simmons, Ernest J., ed., *Continuity and Change in Russian and Soviet Thought*. Cambridge: Harvard Universiy Press, 1955.
Taylor, Overton H., *The Classical Liberalism: Marxism, and the Twentieth Century*. Cambridge: Harvard University Press, 1960.
Tomasic, Danko A., *National Communism and Soviet Strategy*. Washington, D.C.: Public Affairs Press, 1957.
Treadgold, W. Donald, *Twentieth Century Russia*. Chicago: Rand McNally & Co., 1959.
Ulam, Adam B., "Expansion and Coexistence: Counterpoints in Soviet Foreign Policy," *Problems of Communism*, VIII (Sept.-Oct. 1959), 1-6.

24

United States Relations
with East Asia:
Hope and Disappointment

Paul S. Dull
Department of History, University of Oregon

American isolationism has never been interpreted to mean aloofness from East Asia. In the early days of the Republic, American clipper ships sailed the China seas. The United States also participated in trade with China, and insisted on equal commercial opportunities when that country was opened to Western influence in the eighteen-forties. American warships helped to open Japan in the fifties, and to set that country on the path of modernization. From this period on, the United States took part in the international relations of the area, always taking considerable pride in her "protector role," especially of China. Although Americans are prone to overlook the fact, until the deterioration of United States-Japanese relations in the first half of the nineteenth century, these were also generally friendly.

Disappointments have often been deeper because of former high hopes and expectations. In no instance has this been better exemplified than in reactions to the "loss" of China when the Communists took over the mainland in 1949. After that debacle, American policy shifted to containment of Communist China by attempting to create and maintain a perimeter of military bases and military allies from Japan through South Korea, Formosa, and the Philippine Islands, to Southeast Asia. However, the new American position has been an awkward one. From such a stance, it has been difficult to maintain initiative against Communist China by offering hope to the nationalistic and anti-colonial East Asians. It has also been difficult to make efficient military partners of states where national free-

516

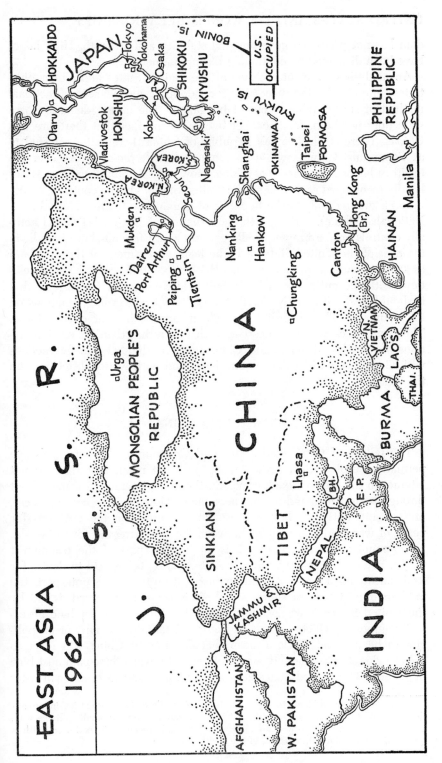

EAST ASIA 1962

U. S. S. R.

MONGOLIAN PEOPLE'S REPUBLIC

Urga

SINKIANG

TIBET

Lhasa

NEPAL

BH.

E. P.

JAMMU & KASHMIR

AFGHANISTAN

W. PAKISTAN

INDIA

CHINA

Nanking

Hankow

Chungking

Canton

Hong Kong (Br.)

HAINAN

BURMA

THAI.

LAOS

N. VIETNAM

Mukden

Dairen

Port Arthur

Peiping

Tientsin

Shanghai

N. KOREA

S. KOREA

Seoul

Vladivostok

HONSHU

Kobe

Osaka

Nagasaki

KIYUSHU

SHIKOKU

Otaru

HOKKAIDO

JAPAN

Tokyo

Yokohama

OKINAWA

RYUKYU Is.

BONIN Is.

U.S. OCCUPIED

Taipei

FORMOSA

PHILIPPINE REPUBLIC

Manila

dom has not produced governmental stability and strength. High hopes have been displaced by continuing disappointment.

An analysis of the interactions of the United States and China illustrates graphically the necessity for adopting an efficient, functional method of study. What is meant by China? The classic definition of a state does not help, for it cannot overcome the fact that there are two Chinas. There is the People's Republic of China (hereinafter referred to as Communist China), whose government has *de facto* control over the territory historically known as China. However, Communist China is not legally recognized as a state by the United States. On the contrary, recognition is granted only to the Republic of China (hereinafter referred to as Nationalist China). Although the government of Nationalist China actually controls only Formosa, the Pescadores and a few off-shore islands, in the eyes of the United States it is the legal government of the mainland as well. It would seem to follow that the United States could have no relations with the authorities who in fact rule Communist China, and that it should deal with the Nationalist government concerning situations on the mainland. The absurdity of such an approach is at once evident. Therefore, since we are concerned with fact rather than fiction, interactions of the United States and China must be divided into interactions with Communist China on the one hand and with Nationalist China on the other.

COMMUNIST CHINA

The failure of the United States and Communist China to exchange permanent diplomatic representatives does not mean that they do not interact in the international arena. Further, this interaction comes about through both official and private personnel.[1] Moreover, the consequences, present and potential, have far-reaching effects upon the decisions for peace or war (and the shadings between the two extremes) for the world.

Communist China, first of all, is an integral part of the communist world. Being so, it is drawn into the attempts by this world to devise for itself an organization to defend against or to attack its counterpart, the anti-communist bloc of states, which, it is commonly agreed, is led by the United States. This does not imply that the communist bloc necessarily agrees on which states shall exercise internal hegemony or on policies to be pursued. It does mean that Communist China will react to policies directed by the anti-communist world toward the communist bloc in general. The United States is in a comparable situation and will react

---

[1] It is, of course, difficult to differentiate between these two categories in an authoritarian state; it may be argued that it is also becoming more difficult to make such a differentiation among American citizens when their business is endowed with a quality of interaction with enemies of the United States.

to policies directed at the anti-communist bloc by Communist China. Second (and it should be understood that these categories of interaction are not mutually exclusive), what Communist China does in relation to other states (the Congo, Cuba, Laos, Tibet or India) may very well involve reaction by the United States; while American policy toward other states (Japan, Indonesia, Laos, or Formosa) may also bring reaction by Communist China.[2] Third, American participation in international organizations such as the UN and SEATO, and Chinese Communist participation in the Warsaw Pact, surely engender interaction. Fourth, Chinese Communist or American (generally through Nationalist China) influence upon overseas Chinese may cause interaction. Fifth, interaction may be accomplished by relations between one government and private personnel of the other, as was the case when relatives visited Americans held in Chinese prisons. American reception and use of Chinese refugees from the mainland is another such example. Last, the fiction that nonrecognition precludes intergovernmental relations is disproved by *de facto* interaction in official negotiations at Geneva in 1954 and 1961, in the conversations between Joseph Beam and Wang P'ing-nan at Warsaw, by negotiations relative to an exchange of newsmen, as well as by those carried on through the good offices of third states.

The Actors

If it be accepted that considerable interaction exists, the next step is to examine the characteristics of the personnel involved. The leadership of Communist China has remained relatively unchanged since the founding of the People's Republic in 1949. Mao Tse-tung has been the real, if not always the nominal head of state. Chu Teh, while aging, has remained in over-all command of the armed forces. Chou En-lai and Liu Shao-ch'i have been but a step below Mao. Other less well-known but important policy-makers have retained their positions in the ruling elite.[3]

Perhaps the primary characteristics of these men have been the result of conditioning to which they were subjected by the fight for existence in the revolution against the Kuomintang.[4] Although they are intelligent, rational men, there is evidence that their revolutionary experience created lasting emotional reactions which affect their decisions. This element of behavior has made it more difficult, if not at times impossible, for tensions

---

[2] Whether these third states are communist or non-communist does not affect reaction itself but only the kind of reaction.

[3] See Robert C. North and Ithiel De Sola Pool, *Kuomintang and Chinese Communist Elites* (Stanford, California: Stanford University Press, 1952).

[4] It is interesting to try to apply, *mutatis mutandis*, the theories of Crane Brinton's *Anatomy of Revolution*, rev. ed. (Englewood Cliffs, N.J.: Prentice-Hall, Inc., 1952) to an analysis of the behavior of the Chinese Communist leaders. The results suggest that patterns of revolution tend to transcend cultural boundaries.

with noncommunist states to be solved easily. It may even have impeded good relations between Communist China and other communist states. As history has so often disclosed, it has been difficult to negotiate with a Robespierre. Perhaps a second generation of leaders can be expected to be less rigid in its obsessions and compulsions.

A second behavioral factor has been the dedication of the Chinese Communist leaders to Marxist-Leninist ideology. This, too, follows the historical pattern that the closer leaders have been to their revolution, the more zeal and blind faith they have evinced in their revolutionary ideology and the less sophistication and accommodation they have shown to it. However, zeal and dedication to the ideology has not made the Chinese slavish subjects of the word as pronounced by the Kremlin oracle, for the revolution was in good part also inspired by nationalism. The Chinese communists have not been willing to gain independence from foreign domination politically and economically to lose it again to Russian ideological imperialism. Particularly Mao and Liu Shao-ch'i have exhibited the ambition to define communism not only for China but also at times for the rest of the communist world.

A third factor in the Chinese communist leaders' behavior has been the nature of their knowledge about the world outside China. From 1921 to 1949, they were preoccupied with domestic politics. What knowledge came to them about the outside world came *via* communist intelligence sources, with the result that it was incomplete and to a degree distorted. Continued oppression by the noncommunist states, fancied or real, after 1949 has given them little opportunity or reason, from their viewpoint, for a re-evaluation. The leaders of Communist China have done little or no traveling outside the communist bloc, and even little within it. Thus, if they possess a *Weltanschauung*, it suffers from distortion and narrowness.[5]

Below the elite, it is more difficult to reconstruct the behavior component of the Chinese, communist or not. Chinese throughout their long history have seldom been xenophobic. Moreover, before 1949, the United States and Americans were undoubtedly well liked by many Chinese. This could be attributed to the milder kind of imperialistic policy toward China, American aid during World War II, the good works of American missionaries, and perhaps the lesser assumption of attitudes of superiority by Americans resident in China. However, two factors have operated

---

[5] See Edgar Snow, *Red Star Over China* (New York: Random House, 1958); Robert C. North, *Moscow and the Chinese Communists* (Stanford, California: Stanford University Press, 1953); Robert Payne, *Mao Tse-tung; Ruler of Red China* (New York: Abelard-Schuman Limited, 1950); Nym Wales (pseudonym for Mrs. Edgar Snow), *Red Dust, Autobiographies of Chinese Communists* (Stanford, California: Stanford University Press, 1952) for evidence to support this interpretation. The subjectivity of the autobiographies in Snow and Wales and the biography by Payne is an asset as evidence in this case.

since 1949 to dry up this reservoir of good will and perhaps to engender active hatred. Official Chinese communist policy has pictured the United States as China's greatest danger and enemy, Americans as exploiters and agents of imperialism. It has portrayed American marines, or Kuomintang forces backed by American military power, as on the point of invading mainland territory. In addition, for the first time the minds of practically all Chinese are being reached by information supplied by the state through extensive education, newspapers, magazines, posters, public speakers, and omnipresent radios—information which emphasizes the "evil" role of the United States.

The attitudes of American officials involved in interaction with Communist China are somewhat more variable. However, though official personnel has changed and policy has been somewhat modified, there has been continuity. Identification of communism as a threat to world peace and American security since 1917, and with increasing conviction since World War II, has heavily influenced American officials. Such attitudes made Adlai Stevenson in the Security Council behave much as did his predecessor, Henry Cabot Lodge, although in other political arenas their behavior was dissimilar. Negotiations regarding Communist China have received priority in the UN (with Communist China excluded) because a majority there has supported American policy. Conversely, exclusion of Communist China from negotiations has been considered one element of containment. Injection of morality or moralistic phrases into international issues also has influenced American behavior. Other attitudes have included: belief that the Americans have been well liked by Chinese and that if Chinese are hostile now it is because they are either misled or brainwashed; a reluctance to face the fact that China, in recent history a militarily weak state, can possibly thwart American power; confidence that allies against Communist China can be secured by helping other states become economically and politically strong; and the assumption that non-communists will not be attracted to communism, and therefore will be willing to fight it actively. American officials followed similar policies toward Communist China during and since the Truman administration.

It is not only American officials who influence American policy. The Christian churches, Protestant and Roman Catholic, have long carried on extensive missionary activity in China. Many church members have resisted stoutly the expulsion, and at times arrest, of American missionaries. They have urged overthrowing the People's Republic. At the same time, however, a counter group of churchmen, perhaps motivated by the idealism inherent in Christianity, have reacted positively to the proposed goals of Communist China, and have stood as critics of a militant American policy that assists Nationalist China and withholds recognition from the mainland government. Both groups influence American public opinion which in turn exerts pressure on Congress. The "China Lobby" is another group that has attempted seriously to influence American policy. Its membership has never been precisely ascertained, nor has the amount of money at its command or the methods by which it acts. Generally speaking it is composed of Chinese Nationalists. Its funds come from their considerable wealth, held outside Formosa, and it tries to influence American policy-makers, legislative and executive, and to project before the American people a good Nationalist China image.

Finally, it should be remembered that the China issue has been an emotional one in American politics. The partisan question of whether the United States caused Mao's victory over Chiang K'ai-shek broke into the open when the late Senator Joseph McCarthy began his attacks on the Truman administration. Though the violence has now mostly gone from the debate, sides have been taken with such emotional bias that it is still difficult for most Americans to argue the question with objectivity.

The Issues

The issues between the United States and Communist China are many, varied, and complex. Most, however, stem from a single problem: the attempt by the United States to bring down the People's Republic of China, or to contain communism in Asia within its present boundaries. The problem, as seen by the Communist Chinese, is a struggle, motivated by nationalism as well as by communist ideology, to extend Chinese hegemony beyond the boundaries of the traditional Chinese state. Every clash between the two states has led to mounting tension, and the conflicts have been many.

It is difficult to mark precisely the genesis of the quarrel. Mao's communists have been from the beginning orthodox in pragmatically exploiting whatever situation they faced to bring about the victory of international communism. This has, of course, always directly implied the defeat of capitalist states. Thus, one finds consistency starting with Mao's debate with Chang Kuo-t'ao in 1937 which initiated the policy of cooperation with the Kuomintang in order to bring "defeat for all." This policy envisaged the defeat of an imperialist Japan in a world war, which would lay the groundwork for the later defeat of the Kuomintang. During World War II, hostility toward the United States was not overt. The Chinese communists needed the United States to destroy Japan, to restrain the Kuomintang from attempts to crush the Chinese Red Army, and to obtain war matériel from Nationalist China by utilizing American attempts to distribute these proportionately.[6] During the first part of World War II,

---

[6] The myth of the damage inflicted upon the Japanese army in North China by the Eighth Route Army was dispelled when Japanese army operational records were made public at the Tokyo War Crimes Trial.

the United States was preoccupied with the European theater. In addition, American officials generally were ignorant about the state of affairs in China, particularly in Yenan and in areas infiltrated by the Eighth Route (Communist) Army. Moreover, Americans were subjected to communist tactical propaganda which helped create the myth that Mao's communism was "Jeffersonian democracy" and merely agrarian reform. However, when in 1949, General Wedemeyer began training thirty-nine Kuomintang divisions and arming them with American equipment, Mao's new enemy began to take shape.

During the last year of World War II in China, both the Kuomintang and the Chinese Communists began to think ahead to the civil war which would decide who ruled China. Extensive and prompt American aid to the Nationalist government, putting the Kuomintang in control of the major seaboard cities, merely confirmed what ideology told the Chinese Communists would happen.

Despite the ill-fated attempt of General Marshall to solve the insoluble by mediating the civil war in 1946, continued American support through advisory army officers and war matériel brought about an open break between Mao's forces and the United States.[7]

The United States helped Nationalist China by giving war matériel valued at $2 billion—enough to earn hostility from the Chinese Communists but in itself not enough to bring about Mao's defeat. American policy-makers had foreseen a united and strong Nationalist China replacing Japan as East Asia's major power. As early as 1944, however, State Department foreign service officers had warned that a communist China would probably emerge from the war. As a communist state, it would be aligned with the U.S.S.R.[8] Nevertheless, America continued to back what in retrospect can be seen as a totally inept, corrupt and moribund government. Support was lacking in the one essential of victory for Nationalist China: the commitment of American troops.

When the People's Republic came into being in 1949, American officials were expelled by the government that the United States would not recognize. In the context of their ideology, the United States became the Chinese Communists' primary foe. Communist China was now committed, ideologically and pragmatically, to the defeat of the United States as the last necessary step to insure the victory of the Chinese revolution and of international communism.[9]

With two Chinas, the question immediately arose as to which would be accepted by the UN for the permanent seat in the Security Council

---

[7] Department of State, *United States Relations with China* (Washington, D.C.: Government Printing Office, 1949).

[8] *Ibid.*, pp. 564-76.

[9] H. Arthur Steiner, "Mainsprings of Chinese Communist Foreign Policy," *American Journal of International Law*, XLIV (Jan., 1950), pp. 69-99.

and representation in other UN bodies. American commitment to recognition of Nationalist China as the *de jure* government of China and refusal to grant even *de facto* recognition to Communist China entailed, unless a legal absurdity be admitted, support for the acceptance of Nationalist China as the China of the UN. The American position was sustained.

The invasion of South Korea by Communist North Korean troops further strained relations with the United States and the noncommunist members of the UN. During the first part of the war, Communist China's support of North Korea was primarily moral. However, when the UN "police" army under General Douglas MacArthur drove the North Koreans to the Yalu River (the boundary between Korea and Manchuria), the Chinese communists entered the hostilities under the guise of "volunteer" units. For the first time the two governments were engaged in war, the casualties of which were not the least reduced by the combat's being legally phrased by the UN as a "police action" against now both North Korea and the People's Republic.

The Eisenhower administration brought an end to the conflict after a stalemate had been reached. The UN and the North Korean and Chinese communists agreed upon an armistice at Panmunjom in 1953. Failure to settle the Korean question has continued the armistice; the UN has not rescinded its original action against Communist China. Thus the war left a legacy of more unresolved issues.

Today, a major issue continues to be whether the United States will recognize the Communist government and will agree to the seating of its delegates in the UN. As succinctly pointed out in the *Conlon Report* prepared for the United States Senate Foreign Relations Committee, the possibilities facing the United States are three: a policy of containment through isolation, a policy of normalization of relations, or a policy of exploration and negotiation which would try to find grounds for increased interaction and "test the willingness of Communist China to coexist with us." The last proposal would also foresee "cooperative thinking" with American allies and with neutrals in Asia to bring about a re-examination of the China problem.[10] Until the Kennedy administration, American policy was one of containment through isolation. During the first months of 1961, attempts were made to try a new policy as recommended in the *Conlon Report* to bring about the exchange of newsmen. Communist China answered by saying that no exchange could be effected until the United States withdrew its support, including the extensive military establishment, from Formosa. Mao's answer shows several disabilities in American thinking about the problem. The Chinese Communists do not desire recognition by the United States to the degree that Americans

---

[10] "Asia," A Study by Conlon Associates, Ltd., for the Committee on Foreign Relations, United States Senate, No. 5 (Washington, D.C.: Government Printing Office, November 1, 1959), p. 153, hereafter cited as *Conlon Report.*

expected. They may not even desire representation in the UN except on their own terms. Nor do they grant the United States the initiative, at its own whim and choice of time, in changing relations with them or with America's allies. It is still difficult for Americans to comprehend the degree to which the officials of Communist China hate the United States, or the pragmatic and ideological reasons for it.[11] The dilemma facing the United States, indeed, seems to be how to abandon the policy of containment through isolation without capitulation in a policy of establishing relations on Communist China's terms.[12]

The emergence of Communist China as the most powerful state of East Asia, if not all Asia, presents another set of problems for the United States. If American policy has not brought forth isolation, neither has it brought about containment. Chinese "volunteers" drove the UN armies south of the Yalu, and while, in turn, they were forced to retreat, a stalemate was reached at the thirty-eighth parallel. Today, the Chinese Communists are quite influential in North Korea.[13] To the south, Chinese communist support given Ho Chi Minh produced the Republic of Viet Nam. This new communist state carved out of that part of Indochina north of the seventeenth parallel was confirmed at Geneva in 1954. Despite the Geneva Agreement, Chinese Communist pressure has continued against South Viet Nam, Cambodia, and Laos. Civil war in Laos in 1960 led to a new crisis in which the United States provided military assistance and military advisers to the government in power. In turn, the Viet Namese Communists gave aid to the Laotian Communists. This aid was later reinforced by Russian and Chinese Communist matériel with the threat of Chinese Communist "volunteers" again creating international tension. After consideration by the UN, a truce commission composed of representatives of Canada, Poland, and India was established to try to neutralize Laos, and a conference to consider the question met in Geneva in 1961. Illustrating the complex nature of relations among states, the U.S.S.R. faltered in bringing about such a neutralization, as much or more to prevent the Chinese Communists from gaining hegemony there to the exclusion of Russian influence as to thwart the United States.

Communist China's suppression of the native government in Tibet and later border trouble with India did not cause direct official interaction with the United States. It did, however, influence American policy toward other non-communist states in Asia because, in their reaction to this aggression, they became psychologically more willing to support the American contention of the dangers posed by Communist China. Burma,

---

[11] Steiner, "The Mainsprings of Chinese Communist Foreign Policy."
[12] *Conlon Report*, p. 152.
[13] Russian hegemony in North Korea was supplanted by Chinese control after Communist China's entrance into the war.

too, has not been complacent about the integrity of her Chinese border. Moreover, the Asian states containing numbers of Chinese residents have begun to fear the influence and pressure exerted upon them by Communist China.[14] In varying degree, this problem is present in Burma, Thailand, Malaya, Indonesia, and the Philippines; thus, these states interact with the United States. The appearance of Chinese Communists in Iran, Iraq, the UAR, the Congo, and Cuba has been met by American reaction. The problem again is not always a clear communist vs. non-communist issue, for the Soviet Union has given ample evidence of displeasure at losing control of native communist parties to the Chinese in North Korea and Iran, and the possibility of further losses elsewhere. Such rivalry at once affects American-Soviet relations. It is not asserted that the U.S.S.R. and Communist China are enemies or that even the potential of enmity is as yet great. However, pragmatically, this possibility must at times temper the overt rivalry between the United States and the Soviet Union.

NATIONALIST CHINA

The United States officially interacts with Nationalist China through its diplomatic mission, as a fellow member of the UN and other international organizations, and as a military partner in the defense of the territory still under the jurisdiction of the Kuomintang. Interaction between them is often influenced by pressure groups and attitudes of private individuals. Thus, activities by the "China Lobby" affect American policy; Americans criticizing or praising Nationalist China arouse the anger or lessen the anxiety of the Chinese Nationalists.

The Actors

In analyzing the capacity of the personnel of Nationalist China, it must be noted that the elite group of rulers has not changed appreciably, except in age. Nor has their behavior changed much in a changing world. Chiang K'ai-shek still does not rule completely the government or party. He has become the symbol upon which the Kuomintang depends (often to its disadvantage outside Formosa), but he also remains not as a ruler but as a mediator between rival Kuomintang factions. Despite constant American pressure, the government still is based in reality upon a single party which effectively excludes non-Kuomintang Chinese and native Formosans from any real positions of influence. While economic reforms have stabilized Formosa's economy, there is still evidence of nepotism and some corruption. Moreover, there is no evidence that Chiang has

---

[14] Pressure is exerted on the overseas Chinese by means of threats to the safety of their relatives who remain in Communist China.

abandoned his essentially Confucian approach to political, economic, and social matters. The dream of the inevitability of Nationalist Chinese armies returning to the mainland to reinstitute Kuomintang rule there has not been dispelled by the realities of the situation. Even American disavowal of aid has not caused the dream to be abandoned. Chiang still hopes that a war, with the U.S.S.R. and Communist China pitted against the United States, will bring about his return. It would not be unfair to say that he would approve of such a war with a narrow disregard for the hideous possibilities of its becoming one employing nuclear weapons.[15]

When one goes below the level of official personnel, one finds a varied picture. The Chinese, in Formosa, are exiles from their beloved homeland. Their emotional reaction affects their behavior in proportion to their inability to face reality. One group is resigned to permanent exclusion from China and willing to make a new way of life on Formosa or elsewhere. Herein are found Chinese industrialists and intellectuals, who in many cases, if they have left Formosa, have abandoned the Kuomintang cause. The other group, more strongly emotional, tries to bring about return to the mainland. Officially, all the Kuomintang are pro-American. In reality many causes for nascent enmity exist. The officials have resented the failure of the United States to save them in China or to bring about reconquest. Pressure to reform has been galling to people who, too, are not immune to feelings of nationalism. The presence of considerable American personnel in Formosa, both civilian and military, has exacerbated Chinese feelings in many ways. This is particularly so when Americans bring with them their higher standard of living, which sharply contrasts with the native level, or when American personnel adopt attitudes of superiority or act with violence toward Chinese. The potential for eventual anti-American feeling is high. Last, the Formosans, the forgotten people in the tragedy of the two Chinas, have little influence on interrelations; they, too, are ambivalent. Their hope for eventual independence for themselves lies with the United States, which they try to influence. Yet they, too, share the Chinese resentment of Americans resident in Formosa.

Behavior of American decision-makers in conducting relations with Nationalist China is not uniform. High American civilian officials do not always act toward Nationalist China opposite to the way they act toward Communist China. This is understandable if one examines their behavior in the context of over-all policy. With American military leaders it is often different. To them, Formosa is a military problem, and their behavior is often predicated on a technical military situation and therefore may be more restricted. The American public displays feelings to-

---

[15] Chiang K'ai-shek, *Soviet Russia in China; A Summing Up at Seventy* (New York: Farrar, Straus & Cudahy, Inc., 1957).

ward Nationalist China which are often the reverse of feelings toward Communist China. As yet, Americans, official and civilian, have reacted little in awareness of the plight of Formosans.

The Issues

Issues between the United States and Nationalist China are centered on continued American recognition, continued American support in the UN, American pressure to secure reforms in Formosa, American economic aid, the possibility of aid to return the Kuomintang to the mainland, and defense of Nationalist Chinese territory. The last issue seems the most difficult to resolve. Nationalist China still holds Matsu and Quemoy and has committed a considerable portion of its armed strength to their defense. This has raised complicated legal and military issues between the United States and Nationalist China, Communist China, and third states. Matsu and Quemoy, lying off Fukien province, are within Communist China's territorial waters. Therefore, Communist China lays claim to them and has subjected the Nationalist Chinese garrisons to years of artillery fire from the mainland. The question raised for American policy-makers is whether these islands are included in the agreement to protect Nationalist China's territory. During 1958 and 1959, when it appeared that Communist China would essay an invasion attempt, American naval and air forces helped break the tight blockade imposed by the bombardment. Paradoxically, American forces, while under fire, scrupulously avoided returning that fire.[16] A policy of bringing pressure on Chiang to abandon the islands to avoid the consequences of an awkward military position has been sharply debated in the United States. Proponents of continued American support in defense of Matsu and Quemoy have claimed that the islands are the first step in an invasion of Formosa itself, that their loss would weaken the Kuomintang army if Nationalist Chinese troops were allowed to be entrapped on them, and would lower American prestige by giving way to communist pressure. Opponents have claimed that the military position of the islands is unimportant, that American prestige would be lowered if Chinese Nationalists lost the islands in battle, that their defense against an all-out communist attack is impractical if not impossible, and that possible American involvement in defense of Matsu and Quemoy might spark war with Communist China. This, in turn, might start World War III if the U.S.S.R. should honor its Military Assistance Pact with Mao's government.[17]

---

16 Matsu and Quemoy are more than a legal problem to Communist China too. In the hands of hostile troops, they are used to interdict shipping into Amoy and Swatow.

17 The issue was debated at length in the 1960 presidential campaign. Although Kennedy opposed defense of the islands, the first months of his administration brought forth no public renunciation of American commitment to do so.

Ends and Means

The last step in the examination of the interaction between the United States and the two Chinas is the identification of policy ends and an analysis of the possible means to them. In the examination of power theoretically available to realize goals, an analysis of the practical limitations on the use of this capacity is essential.

Defeat of the United States by military action, or conversely the destruction of Communist China's government by United States military power, are policy goals considered by the two governments. Mao's government does not now possess the power to achieve directly the defeat of the United States, nor will it in the foreseeable future. The consideration of power must, therefore, be broadened to include the entire communist bloc. Theoretically, the communist world might possess enough military capacity to defeat the United States in a world war. However, at once limitations are placed upon Communist China's use of that capacity. The Soviet Union seems committed to victory through economic rivalry, internal subversion among American allies, and proselytization among non-aligned countries in underdeveloped areas. It seems to have rejected Mao's thesis that World War III, fought with nuclear weapons, is necessary. In addition, the Soviet Union has ceased assistance to Communist China which would aid that country in producing its own nuclear weapons. It would follow, then, that Communist China could not utilize Russia's military power to defeat the United States unless the Chinese Communist leaders precipitate, by independent action, a global war. Given the present state of Communist China's industrial capacity, it is also improbable that a successful invasion of Formosa could be thrust through the shield of American military forces.

From the American standpoint there are similar problems. American power to defeat Communist China is limited by the realization that war with mainland China might bring the Soviet Union into World War III. Thus, application of military power to mainland China is limited in proportion to the caution of American military leaders or becomes involved in larger military considerations. Nationalist China has, of course, the weakest position. It is only through American military power that the Kuomintang can hope to fight Communist China. It follows, therefore, that Nationalist China's most logical solution to the problem of defeating Mao's armies is by involving the United States in war with Communist China, and in this Nationalist China is limited by its lack of means to influence American policy-making.

The application of power through war, however, is not the only method by which national capacity may be applied to defeat another country. Communist China has used other means. One has been the attempt to gain physical strength through expansion of national boundaries. Tibet and border disputes with India and Burma are cases in point. However, this has serious limitations. It has tended to alienate neutrals and has reinforced the position of the United States in seeking allies in Asia. A second device has been to subvert internally or to oppose the governments of states allied with the United States. Greatest success has been achieved in Laos and Viet Nam. Such means are being used in other Asian states. However, this also involves a limitation, for it has aroused the opposition of Russian officials who dislike to see hegemony over Asian communist parties pass to Communist China. In turn, this has tended to lessen tensions between the U.S.S.R. and the United States on certain specific issues, such as the nuclear disarmament negotiations and the Laotian truce negotiations.

The United States, of course, has utilized these means in reverse, attempting to forge alliances which, if they cannot be used to attack Communist China directly, can be used to try to contain it. Thus the United States has brought SEATO into being and has urged larger military establishments upon such countries as Japan, Thailand, Viet Nam, and the Philippines. The limitations upon the full use of this technique have come from several sources. Military assistance given to reactionary regimes has not created military strength that is constant, reliable, or permanent. Failure of American policy-makers to understand and to make accommodations for Asian nationalism in general, and in separate Asian countries in particular, has severely constrained the growth of ancillary American power. In general, the limitations upon these techniques have stemmed primarily from American ignorance and ineptitude.

A second approach that the United States has attempted to utilize to save countries from Chinese Communist domination has been to supply aid to promote healthy economies that can furnish military strength and can alleviate the poverty in which communism flourishes. What has been good in theory in America's aid program to underdeveloped countries has not always been good in practice. The limitation again has arisen from American ignorance and ineptitude as well as from the basic complexity of the economic problems. Ignorance of native languages and customs, allowing aid programs to benefit the reactionary elite instead of the suffering general population, and the difficulties inherent in industrializing agrarian communities have seriously failed to produce economic health and strength in underdeveloped Asian countries.[18] Formosa has witnessed the greatest American success in economic reform and there only to a limited degree. A variant of these techniques that some argue would not have the same difficulties would entail greater cooperation

---

[18] Thomas S. Loeber, *Foreign Aid: Our Tragic Experiment* (New York: W. W. Norton & Co., Inc., 1961).

with the UN in the latter's financing and administering of economic aid programs.[19]

Still another means of containing Communist China has been through the imposition of an embargo on trade in strategic supplies (CHINCOM) applied by the United States and imposed upon her allies. Inasmuch as this has meant pressure by threats to withhold American aid, it has led to resentment and offended nationalism, which has seriously impaired the over-all containment policy.

Finally, the United States has attempted to use the UN to isolate Communist China. This has been at the expense of a favorable American image in many parts of the world, and, as the margin of support for excluding Communist China from the UN has decreased, American prestige has depreciated. If the representatives of Communist China are seated in the UN in the near future, as seems inevitable, then American prestige will sink lower if that seating takes place with the United States still in active opposition.

When one looks at the achievements of the policies of Communist China to gain strength by expansion, influence over Asian states, and full admission into the family of nations in contrast to the achievements of the American policy of containment, on balance the power of Communist China seems to be slowly but steadily asserting itself over the power of the United States.[20]

Theoretically, policy goals in the interactions of the two countries need not necessarily be concerned with the tension engendered by rivalry to emerge victorious. Ideally, another policy goal of both states would be to reduce friction and promote unity. At present, however, both find fixing this as a goal and gaining the means of attaining it extremely difficult. Communist China's insistence upon the withdrawal of the American military establishment from Formosa limits Communist China's ability to develop normal relations either immediately or as a long-range program. American power is likewise limited. Withdrawal from Formosa would vitiate American military power in East Asia, would tend to drive American allies into positions of neutrality or alliance with Communist China, would break American treaties with Nationalist China, and would abandon Formosans to probable Chinese Communist rule.[21] The ability of the American government to bring about immediate normal relations would also be limited by the activities of the China Lobby, and by large sectors of adverse American public opinion. The ability to attain normal relations is as yet not possessed by either protagonist. An alternative has been the program recommended in the *Conlon Report:* a policy of ex-

---

[19] There is evidence that the Kennedy administration has been studying this new approach.
[20] *Conlon Report,* pp. 145-51.
[21] *Ibid.*

ploration and negotiation starting with the exchange of newsmen. This policy seeks the same goal as immediate normalization of relations. It also suffers the same disabilities. As long as Communist China places withdrawal from Formosa as the *sine qua non* of negotiation, the ability to institute negotiations is severely restricted.

American policy toward Communist China remains, after a decade of tension, on dead center. Communist China has not been destroyed; it has barely been contained; and the solution of issues between the two countries has not begun. It would seem incumbent upon both American officials and the American public to reassess goals and means to achieve them. This would involve clear identification of the goal of containment of communist power by short-range military and economic plans. It would also attempt to remove obstacles to achieving a long-range goal of easing tensions by establishing normal relations directed to a solution of quarrels. It would involve flexibility in keeping the short-range policy from blocking the long-range one. In theory, it is possible to construct a multi-faceted policy that minimizes limitations upon power to achieve both policy goals.

KOREA

The Republic of Korea (South Korea) has relations with the United States on a variety of levels. First, the UN police action against North Korea and Communist China has not been liquidated and in the period of armistice that still exists, Korean military leaders participate in armistice negotiations at Panmunjom and in the military command of UN forces in South Korea. South Korea furnishes the great bulk of UN armed "police" forces in Korea, and the United States furnishes the greatest foreign portion of it. Thus, military considerations form the top level of relations with the United States. Despite a strong nationalistic desire for complete independence and dislike of any American pressure upon the government, Korean leaders must undergo the restraint of this situation. It is difficult to separate diplomatic relations from the military situation; thus relations at the diplomatic level are undertaken by Korean officials under direction of Korean military men and by Americans who are either military officers or diplomats advised in many aspects of policy by American military officers.

The United States has provided a great amount of economic aid to the Republic of Korea, and in the implementation of this program a corps of American civilians has resided in South Korea. Again, this aid has represented a form of American direction of Korean policy. When the aid has been used by corrupt Koreans to form a wealthy and dictatorial elite, general Korean resentment against the United States has resulted. Dislike has been compounded by the glaring disparity in standards of living when Americans in South Korea have created a "little America" in their living accommodations. Another area of tension has resulted within the body of Korean officials whenever the United States has aided Japan or has attempted to ameliorate issues between South Korea and Japan. It is a rare Korean, official or private citizen, who can as yet quench the fire of hatred for Japan.

The presence of a considerable body of American troops in Korea has had ambivalent results. The American GI's emotional response to the lot of Koreans, especially children, has often resulted in good works for Korean orphanages and other philanthropic organizations. At the same time, the American soldier's dislike of his military duty in Korea, his contempt for Koreans in general, and his invidious comparison of Korea with Japan, often expressed overtly, have led to further tension. On balance, the presence of American military personnel in South Korea has probably led to a worsening of relations.

The Issues

The Republic of Korea has been a difficult country to work with in a short-range policy of defense against communism and in a long-range policy of founding future friendship. The fault has been not so much with the Korean people as with their tragic history. Centuries of misrule by the Yi dynasty which led to a pauperization and demoralization of the populace were followed by thirty-five years of complete Japanese domination. When Korea emerged from World War II into the freedom of national independence, a trained elite both in governmental affairs and in economic activities simply did not exist. National politics became characterized almost at once by a multiplicity of parties, exploitation by the group in power, and quarreling with a constant overtone of violence. Korea needed a period of tranquility to develop patterns of responsible self-rule. That period was denied when she became a pawn in the cold war. By 1948, Korea was divided at the thirty-eighth parallel, with two governments, each claiming jurisdiction over the entire country. The 1950 invasion added war devastation to the Republic of Korea's miserable lot. The armistice in 1953 brought an end to fighting, but not to the division of the country or the necessity for maintaining a large army or the presence of a foreign army in Korea. The Republic of Korea has existed under a Damoclean sword and has been subject to U.S. domination.

The character of the administrations under which Korea has been ruled has done little to help Korea or make its relations with the United States easier. Despite strong and repeated pressure from the American government, Syngman Rhee's government became more corrupt, more oppressive, and more inefficient until the Koreans themselves overthrew it in 1960. The downfall of the Rhee government only emphasized, however, the disunity of the country and the ineptness of its rulers. The succeeding government of John Chang corrected the positive evils of Rhee's regime but could not muster the skill or the unity necessary for good administration. Thus, even in the fact of American policy, opposition as expressed by General Magruder, Chang's government was toppled in turn by a *coup d' etat* of army men led by Colonel Chang Do Yung in 1961. All pretense of democratic government thereafter was abandoned.

Ends and Means

The United States seeks, primarily, for South Korea to remain one of the strong bastions against communism in East Asia. The means to this end have been the stationing of large numbers of American military forces in South Korea, the strengthening of the ROK defense capacity, the strengthening of the weak economy, the prevention of proselytizing by communists among the population by nurturing a democratic form of government, and the lessening of friction between South Korea and Japan to prevent a disastrous quarrel between allies. These policies have been carried out, on the military side primarily under the aegis of the UN, on the civilian side by unilateral action. Deterrents to the realization of American ends have been the failure to solve major issues in the cold war with the Soviet Union and Communist China, the ineptitude of South Korean officials, the severity of South Korea's economic and political problems, growing resentment of American domination, and the implacable hatred of Korea towards Japan. However, failure to solve problems has not rested wholly with the Koreans. The ignorance of American officials of Korean culture and the realities of the situation have caused mismanagement of aid programs so that despite the great amount of money expended, South Korea's economic and political situation was as acute as ever in the early nineteen-sixties. The American position in South Korea was on an almost day-to-day basis of survival, with the threat of internal collapse accompanied by renewed communist invasion an ever-present possibility. In truth, the problem of South Korea seems incapable of solution except as part of a general solution of the problems of East Asia undertaken by the United States with the U.S.S.R. and Communist China.

JAPAN

The governments of the United States and Japan interact as friendly nations and allies (although the realities of the alliance place the United States in the dominant position). The interactions include state-to-state relations carried out between official personnel, relations as members of international organizations, relations created by the United States-Japan Security Treaty and Administrative Agreement of 1960, and those established by Japan's participation in the anti-communist bloc led by the United States. In the last instance, American policy to give material manufactured in Japan to SEATO countries coincides with the Japanese policy of trying to improve political and economic relations with Southeast Asia. Also involved are the interactions created by the United States' attempt to enforce an embargo against Communist China, and by American efforts to create better relations between American allies who themselves are not friendly, e.g., Japan and the Republic of Korea. However, Japan belongs to the Afro-Asian bloc. In these interactions policies are pursued with acts which are not those of an ally. Japanese officials of all political coloration have identified themselves with the Afro-Asian bloc because of race (non-white), a political position of inferiority in the family of nations, and psychological motivation to assume leadership in some area of the international scene.[22] While a potential of less friendly official relations exists (as it does between any two states), at present Japan, the former bitter enemy of the United States, has become an amicable and trusted junior partner in East Asia.

The shift in popular attitudes toward each other has been created by individual, private relationships as well as those between the governments and private citizens. Contrary to expectations based on historical experience, the military occupation of Japan, undertaken primarily with American troops, created a preponderance of good will between the American occupying forces and the population of defeated Japan. From utter enmity in World War II (a war having distinct racial-conflict overtones) behavior during the occupation by both Americans and Japanese led to an atmosphere of mutual respect and cordiality.[23] The fairly large number of Japanese brides who have come to the United States with their American servicemen husbands has also led to intercultural understanding. Since the end of the military occupation in 1952, a considerable number of Japanese students and businessmen have come to the United States. In turn, American students, businessmen, and a flood of tourists have visited Japan. These contacts have further improved friendship between the two states. They now understand each other better than at any previous moment in history. While it is commonly agreed that Japan has borrowed extensively from American culture since 1945, the opposite, while not so commonly understood, has also been true. The understand-

[22] Iizuka Koji, "New Southeast Asian Problems: The Economic Development of Underdeveloped Countries," (title translated into English), *Sekai* (May 1958).

[23] This statement is made despite anti-United States demonstrations in Japan since 1952. Such demonstrations have been in response to internal political differences over the position Japan should assume in the cold war. The demonstration, moreover, did not disclose hostility to Americans as distinguished from the entity the United States.

ing of each other's cultural characteristics, often thought to be so disparate, has made friendly formal interaction easier.

The Actors

The behavior of Japanese officials is fairly easy to understand, if not to influence. Japan has been ruled by conservative politicians since V-J Day, with the exception of the short-lived Katayama government in 1948. Ideologically these officials are committed to an anti-communist program internationally and to an anti-renovationist program internally.[24] However, there is no unanimity of opinion among the conservatives over methods. Thus, not all conservatives automatically agree with the anti-communist policies of the United States. Japan's precarious position in a world threatened by nuclear warfare poses for them a Hobson's choice between strength through military alliance with the United States, and a neutralist position with reliance on the UN. Pressure from Japanese businessmen who would like to expand trade with Soviet Russia and Communist China constitutes a second factor in the conservatives' position as all-out American allies.[25] Finally, the Japanese conservative politician in his internecine intra-party quarrels has not been above subordinating ideological conviction to personal political advantage by cooperating with renovationist forces to emasculate the foreign policy of his party's "main-current" faction.[26] The conservatives, too, are not agreed upon how to live with the renovationists. Opinions range from a desire to remove them legally or otherwise from the political scene to opposing them only through scrupulously democratic methods.

It is not only the behavior of the ruling conservatives that affects the nature of American-Japanese interactions. Consideration must also be given to the renovationist politicians, because, in the strength of their numbers and the variety of their techniques of opposition, they have influenced Japanese policy. The conservatives and renovationists operate within a wide range of political processes. The ruling Liberal-Democratic party (*Jiminto*) has consistently held close to two-thirds of the seats in the House of Representatives in the Japanese Diet. The renovationists in the large Socialist party, in the splinter Democratic Socialist party, and in the small Communist party, fear the conservatives will revert to their prewar behavior and destroy them. They also fear that the conservatives

---

24 The term "renovationist" is used in Japan to describe those political forces who would renovate Japanese society. The term includes the shades of political belief from the right-wing Socialist party to the Japanese Communist party. In many ways, the term is preferable to the word "leftist."

25 Takasuki Tatsunosuke, "The Prosperity of Asia and the Destiny of Japan," (title translated into English), *Chuo Koron* (Jan. 1958).

26 Japanese political parties are still faction-ridden. The Japanese use the term "main current" to describe the faction or combination of factions in power in a party, the term "anti-main current" to describe the minority opposition faction or factions.

will gain the necessary two-thirds-plus-one seats in the House of Representatives, which would permit amendment of the constitution to their disadvantage. The renovationists, too, resist the passage of any legislation that they think will undermine their political position. This latter has included opposition to laws giving the police more power, to preventing teachers (organized in the communist-dominated Japan Teachers' Union) from engaging in political activities, and to the United States-Japan Security Treaty of 1960.[27]

In a situation where Japanese politicians are divided into a group that would preserve a capitalistic status quo and a group determined to change Japan permanently into a socialist state, there must exist, if democracy is to be practiced, some political mores by which the minority (the renovationists) can protect itself from extinction. These mores have not been developed by the politicians within Japan's legal political institutions. In consequence, the renovationists, to the degree they have felt threatened, have responded by physical obstructionism in the Diet, boycott of the Diet, and by calling out masses of demonstrators primarily from the ranks of members of the General Council of Labor Unions (Sohyo). The conservatives have very often reacted to these "illegal" maneuvers by accepting them as part of the political process and as a measurable aspect of public opinion. In consequence, they have dropped legislation which they could legally have passed through the Diet. The passage of the United States-Japan Security Treaty of 1960 by Kishi's government was an exception to this phenomenon. Nevertheless, this behavior of the renovationists definitely affects the capacity of Japanese officials in carrying out relations with the United States. In reality, Japan's foreign relations must be carried on under seemingly constant threat of civil war.

The behavior, too, of the Japanese public which affects relations with the United States is varied. There is no undercurrent of anti-Americanism among the vast majority of Japanese. However, when the public is subdivided, differences and shadings of opinion are apparent. An anti-United States attitude exists among Japanese students, professors, and other intellectuals—hostility engendered by zealous belief in Marxism. Anti-United States activity has been participated in by laborers with Sohyo membership in metropolitan centers. However, these acts are not always based on an anti-United States feeling and often not genuinely based on anti-American feeling. In other words, mass supporters of the renovationists follow their leaders' convictions without always understanding or sharing them. Supporters of the conservatives are less militant politically, thus leaving the arena of public demonstrations to the renovationist minority. It follows, then, that the number and frequency of overt

[27] For the renovationist viewpoint, see Endo Shokichi, Fujiwara Hirosato, Narita Tomomi, Matsumoto Schchiro, "Socialists! How to Fight Against the Liberal-Democratic (Party) Government," (title translated into English), *Chuo Koron* (Feb. 1958).

anti-United States acts are not necessarily the correct indices of Japanese public reaction. However, in another area of reaction to international affairs, the Japanese public shows more personal and unified conviction. It has shown that it still is anti-militaristic and has displayed uneasiness about providing military bases to the United States and standing as an American ally in East Asia. The Japanese remember Hiroshima and fear any act which might draw retaliatory communist nuclear attack. It is probably true that the majority of the Japanese emotionally embrace neutralism. Neutralism also is more compatible with the national pride that Japanese still evince.

There is one last segment of the Japanese public whose behavior affects the capacity of personnel charged with relations with the United States: the ultra-rightist organizations which, acting secretly and with a prewar ultra-nationalistic and pro-Japan mystic ideology, have resorted to force ranging from action squads demonstrating publicly to political assassination. Any Japanese politician must consider how his official acts will be judged by this small but violent minority.

The behavior of American officials affecting relations with Japan is more uniform. There is no great division between American political parties over Japanese policy. Neither is there any recognizable amount of anti-Japanese feeling. Perhaps the behavior that affects American capacity the most is the inclination to regard Japan patronizingly. This has been countered by the appointment in 1961 of Edwin Reischauer as Ambassador to Japan. Reischauer, a Harvard professor of Japanese history, was born in Japan, and during his boyhood learned to speak and read the language with the facility of a native. He is married to a Japanese—the granddaughter of *Genro* Matsukata. Japanese were pleased with the attention given their problems by such an appointment. However, the selection of Reischauer raised fear among Japanese conservatives, for during the hectic days of June 1960, he wrote an article warning American officials that they could not ignore or fail to understand the Marxist motivation of Japanese professors and students and the probable consequences of their ideological conviction.

The American public has varying attitudes. Businessmen whose profits are hurt by Japan's aggressive program to increase export trade are offset by businessmen who make profits by trading with Japan. There is little evidence of a significant amount of bigotry among the American public against the Japanese as a race. The occupation of Japan and the Korean war placed many servicemen in Japan. Consequently Japan is no longer an exotic land of mystery to many Americans.

The Issues

The issues that involve interaction between the two countries stem mostly from the post-World War II occupation and the desire to make

Japan a strong ally in the cold war. The original objectives of the occupation regime, hereinafter referred to as SCAP (Supreme Commander Allied Powers), were to remove Japan forever as a threat to the United States and world peace, and to allow the Japanese to form a government by their freely expressed will. The latter objective disclosed an American belief that may or may not be susceptible to verification: that such a government would be both peaceful and democratic. In implementing these objectives, SCAP, personified by General Douglas MacArthur, destroyed Japan's military power and war industry potential, punished Japanese war criminals, and disbanded those organizations that had advocated ultra-nationalism and policies of aggression. SCAP then set about positively to make a new Japan. This included the drafting of the 1947 constitution and the creation of a middle class out of which democracy could evolve. This entailed the destruction of the industrial combines (*Zaibatsu*), the undertaking of agrarian land reform, and the granting of various liberties. To have accomplished the remaking of Japan, SCAP would have needed a generation, but it had only three years before the exigencies of preparing for a possible new war to combat communism took precedence over the original objectives. After 1948, the United States wanted a strong, armed Japan to counter the emergence of Communist China as the great power in East Asia. To achieve this, SCAP halted the dissolution of the *Zaibatsu* to bring about resurgent economic strength through those who know how to achieve it. During the Korean War, Japanese industry was turning out war matériel for UN forces. Despite the fact that Article IX of the Japanese constitution forbade Japan to make war as a national policy and to have armed forces, the United States began to place pressure upon the Japanese government to rearm. The occupation came to an end in 1952, when the San Francisco treaty came into force. However, the United States realized that Japan did not have the power to stand alone, and moreover, the American government had learned the bitter consequences in Korea of creating a political vacuum. Therefore, Japan's independence was not complete: the San Francisco treaty was accompanied by an administrative agreement wherein the United States reserved the right to have Japanese bases where American military forces might be stationed to resist external aggression against Japan. Japan's midget military force under the agreement had the responsibility of protecting Japan against internal aggression.

This was not enough for the United States; the assumption of the military defense of Japan was costly and inefficient. The answer, as American policy-makers saw it, was to make Japan assume a larger burden of defense of increasing Japanese armed forces. This policy was received with mixed reactions by the Japanese conservatives; it was strongly opposed by the renovationists. It took, therefore, a combination of cajoling, bullying, and diplomacy by the United States to prod Japan into forming larger military forces.[28] In 1954, the Mutual Defense Assistance Agreement was consummated. Japan agreed to establish a Self Defense Force (*Jieitai*), its size being within the limits of Japan's economic potential,[29] and to collaborate with the United States in efforts "to preserve peace in line with the spirit of the United Nations Charter." Japan also agreed to honor the American CHINCOM embargo against Communist China. In return the United States gave military and economic aid to Japan and agreed to withdraw American troops as the Self Defense Force grew.[30] On July 1, 1954, the Self Defense Force came into being. Japan had an army, navy, and air force despite Article IX of the constitution.[31]

Neither the United States nor Japan was completely satisfied. American officials wanted greater military effort by Japan; Japanese officials disliked the continuation of American military bases in Japan and the fact that the 1952 Administrative Agreement was to continue indefinitely. By 1959, details were worked out to negotiate a new treaty and administrative agreement which would be limited to a ten-year period. Japan's military forces would be worked into a plan to defend East Asia against aggression and Japan would continue to receive American military assistance. On the other hand, prior consent by the Japanese government would have to be secured by the United States for use of Japanese bases in any military attack and Japan denied itself the right to send troops abroad. The attempts of the Kishi government to secure passage of the agreements, however, were met by the stoutest resistance ever put up by the renovationists. Violence in the Diet, boycott of Diet proceedings by the Socialists, huge mass demonstrations led by *Sohyo* and *Zengakuren* (All-Japan University Students' Federation) and rioting brought Japan close to civil war, and cancelled President Eisenhower's trip to Japan. All this did not deter Kishi, however, from his determination to secure passage of the pacts. The new United States-Japan Security Treaty and Administrative Agreement went into effect June 23, 1960.[32]

Ends and Means

Many other issues exist between the two countries, but most seem susceptible to a mutually agreeable solution. Politically, Japan seems to be a stable ally, but not a janissary. The conservative government has not embraced the violence to the rightists that led to the assassination in 1960

---

[28] This even included a statement by Vice-President Nixon to the Japanese that the United States had been wrong in demanding a disarmed Japan.

[29] The United States had wanted Japan to boost the military establishment to 350,-000 at once. Japan insisted that the force could not eventually rise to much more than 200,000 and won on this point. *Asahi* (Mar. 9, 1954). In 1961, the Self Defense Force stood at 230,000.

[30] For full text of MDA agreement, see *Nippon Times* (Mar. 9, 1954).

[31] *Asahi* (July 2, 1954).

[32] *Ibid.* (June 23, 1960).

of Asanuma Jiro, secretary-general of the Socialist party. Nor, on the other hand, has it given way to the demands of the Socialist party that would lead either to neutralism or to putting Japan in the communist bloc. The conservatives have stood firm without abandoning the devices of democratic government. Thus, cooperation with Japan has not led to the embarrassment of an alliance with a rightist dictatorship. As long as the conservative Japanese government can continue the rapid growth of its gross national product (about 8 per cent in 1960 and 13 per cent in 1961), there seems nothing in the Japanese scene to prevent the realization of the conservatives' goals of continued friendship and alliance with the United States. Danger of loss of rapport lies more with the United States. If internal pressures on American officials result in barring Japanese goods from American markets and in preventing Japan's seeking new markets in East Asia, then the capacity to continue friendship may become limited. At the same time, to keep tensions low, the responsibility lies with Americans to understand Japan's desire to replace protection by the United States with effective protection by the UN, and Japan's psychological need to try to lead in Afro-Asian affairs. Japanese leaders, even if they so desired, would be limited in their ability to change these two basic goals.

That the United States is blocking Japan's desire to secure markets in Communist China has been a subject of much American discussion, the consensus being that this places limits upon American ability to keep Japan friendly. The issue, as it exists among Japanese, is more psychological than economic. Moreover, the ability to secure such trade lies more with Communist China than with either of the other countries and, therefore, depends on the settlement of problems between the United States and Communist China. It is true that there has been pressure in Japan to trade with mainland China and there has been resentment against the CHINCOM embargo. However, there have been annual private barter agreements between Communist Chinese and Japanese traders, and in no year has the agreed upon amount of goods been exchanged. The Chinese have no intention of aiding Japan's economy or of falling victim to an economic imperialism that would jeopardize Communist China's industrialization. Mao Tse-tung in 1958 warned the Japanese that economics were always subordinated to politics (in a communist state) and that the price of trade with Communist China was breaking Japan's treaty relations with the United States and entering the communist orbit. The use of trade as an economic weapon was illustrated the same year, when, in retaliation against the Japanese government, Communist China dumped competitive goods throughout Southeast Asia. The move cost Japanese traders the equivalent of $200 million in foreign trade.

Finally, the United States could improve relations with Japan by evincing special regard for Japanese national pride. Official and private interactions which ignore this factor can limit the capacity of the American government to realize its objectives. However, it can be said in general that nothing in the international scene or in Japan at present limits seriously the realization of either Japanese or American policy goals.

For Japan to realize friendship with the United States depends upon the former's ability to maintain prosperity, to curb by democratic methods Socialist obstructionism, to prevent the reappearance of rightist terrorist societies, and to prevent civil war. For the United States to maintain friendship and alliance with Japan, it will be necessary for America to understand Japan's problems, fear of involvement in a nuclear war, and national pride.

SUGGESTED READINGS

Barnett, A. Doak, *Communist China and Asia*. New York: Harper & Brothers for the Council on Foreign Relations, 1960.

Brant, Conrad, *Stalin's Failure in China*. Cambridge: Harvard University Press, 1958.

Dening, Ester, *Japan*. New York: Frederick A. Praeger, Inc., 1961.

Fairbank, John King, *The United States and China*, 2d ed. Cambridge: Harvard University Press, 1958.

Hudson, G. F. and others, *The Chinese Communes*. London: Soviet Survey, 1959.

———, "Russia and China: The Dilemmas of Power," *Foreign Affairs*, XXXIX Oct. 1960), 1-10.

Ike, Nobutaka, *Japanese Politics*. New York: Alfred A. Knopf, Inc., 1957.

Kawai, Kazuo, *Japan's American Interlude*. Chicago: University of Chicago Press, 1960.

Mao Tse-tung, *Selected Works of Mao Tse-tung*, 4 vols. London: Lawrence & Wishart, Ltd., 1954.

Moraes, Frank, *The Revolt in Tibet*. New York: The Macmillan Co., 1960.

North, Robert C., *Moscow and the Chinese Communists*. Stanford, California: Stanford University Press, 1953.

Reischauer, Edwin O., "Broken Dialogue with Japan," *Foreign Affairs*, XXXIX (Oct. 1960), 11-26.

———, *The United States and Japan*. Cambridge: Harvard University Press, 1950.

———, *Wanted: An Asian Policy*. New York: Alfred A. Knopf, Inc., 1955.

Schwartz, Benjamin I., *Chinese Communism and the Rise of Mao*. Cambridge: Harvard University Press, 1951.

Skinner, G. William, "Overseas Chinese In Southeast Asia," *American Academy of Political and Social Sciences*, No. 321 (Jan. 1959), 136-47.

Tang, Peter S. H., *Communist China Today: Domestic and Foreign Policies*. New York: Frederick A. Praeger, Inc., 1957.

U.S. Senate, Committee on Foreign Relations, "United States Foreign Policy: Asia, Study No. 5," by Conlon Associates, Ltd. Committee Print, 86th Cong., 1st sess., 1959, pp. 85-155. Washington, D.C.: Government Printing Office, 1959.

Yanaga, Chiroshi, *Japanese People and Politics*. New York: John Wiley & Sons, Inc., 1956.

25

The United States
and Southern Asia

Richard L. Park *and* Russell H. Fifield
*Department of Political Science and
the Center for Southern Asian Studies,
The University of Michigan*

South and Southeast Asia have become focal points in foreign relations of the United States. Modern communications and jet-age transportation have made it possible for the great powers to influence the political and economic changes that have arisen in the region since the transfer of power from imperialist to nationalist hands. Ideological struggles, social change, programs for rapid economic development, and new outlooks in foreign policy are the rule rather than the exception in the countries of the area. The Soviet Union from a distance, and Communist China from the heart of the Asian continent, encourage these urgent demands for change in the direction of the communist world system. In response, and more positively in support of free governments, it is imperative that the United States give high priority to the concerns of Southern Asia.

South and Southeast Asia constitute the vast extensions of the continent, both mainland and offshore, from Pakistan in the west to the Philippines in the east (see map on page 550). India and Pakistan alone encompass a subcontinent. Either Burma or the old Indochinese area is larger than France. The islands from the Philippines to Indonesia cover a territory that, if joined together, would make up a small continent. Communist China is a neighbor common to the whole area, not only for the countries of the mainland, but also for island territories bordering the South China Sea. Communications in the past were mainly by sea because of formidable mountain barriers and the generally difficult nature of the terrain. The densely inhabited coastal plains, river valleys and deltas, and a few populous islands such as Java and Luzon, contain most of the region's 750 million people. In between areas of population concentration lie wide stretches of ocean as well as mountains, deserts, dusty plains of low fertility, and jungle swamps less densely inhabited. Religious and cultural differences—folk religions among the Chinese, Hinduism, Buddhism, Islam, Christianity, and Animism—characterize the heterogeneity in values of the peoples of Southern Asia, and histories that stretch back for many centuries attest to the maturity of their ancient cultures.

Since the close of World War II, a new problem of international relations has arisen in South and Southeast Asia with the appearance of ten newly independent states—India, Pakistan, Ceylon, Burma, Indonesia, the Philippines, Viet Nam, Laos, Cambodia, and the Federation of Malaya. Thailand and Nepal alone were independent before the war. (See Table 1, page 40, for statistics on these countries.) Even in those areas still under partial or full European control, such as Singapore, British Borneo, and Netherlands New Guinea, the international circumstances of remaining European activities have changed significantly. Experimentation with new governments would have been sufficiently challenging. But the seizure of power by the communists in China in 1949, the bifurcation of Viet Nam under conditions of war, and continuing influence by the communists throughout the region since the end of World War II have made of Southern Asia a major battleground of the cold war. Traditional British power based on India has disappeared, and the channeling of the relations of colonial peoples toward their respective metropolitan powers has given place to a much broader pattern of world-wide associations in which the United States increasingly has become a senior associate.

THE IMPERIAL LEGACY

Before World War II, South and Southeast Asia were essential parts of an imperial political and economic system that had been built from the seventeenth century and that had provided much of the strength of the industrial revolution in Western Europe. The resources of the area included natural rubber, tin, jute, hemp, rice, tea, iron ore, manganese, spices, medicinal plants, and numerous other raw materials that were in demand in Europe. The exploitation of these products brought substantial profits to investors, shippers, bankers, and—through direct and indirect taxation—to the mother country governments as well. Systems of preference linked colonies and home countries together. Only imperial systems with near monopolies over given products, such as that of the Netherlands East Indies, seemed interested in the advantages of free trade.[1] Although increases in the volume of production and trade pro-

---

[1] John S. Furnivall, *Colonial Policy and Practice: A Comparative Study of Burma and Netherlands India* (New York: New York University Press, 1956), pp. 1-22; 217-75.

vided more employment and thus higher national incomes in the colonies, the greater economic advantage rested with the home countries from which had come most of the entrepreneurial capital. Thus as the industrial revolution, aided by colonial resources, advanced the standards of living in Western Europe and in North America, the colonies developed economically but at a much slower pace.[2]

It was characteristic of nineteenth-century Southern Asia for British, French, and Dutch managers to control most of the banking, shipping, warehousing, plantation agriculture, servicing professions, and industrial functions in their own colonies. Even in India, where a small business class emerged late in the eighteenth century, British managing agents held contractual control over the larger native entrepreneurs. Chinese and a few Indian merchants in Southeast Asia efficiently managed most of the petty internal trade, thus discouraging the development of similar skills among the indigenous populations. The Japanese plan for an Asian co-prosperity sphere offered a means for breaking the European economic hold on South and Southeast Asia. But, as became obvious during World War II, Japan's intent was to replace European economic hegemony with Japanese, with no apparent advantage accruing to the nations of Southern Asia.

The skillful balance of power maintained by Great Britain on a worldwide scale up to the time of World War I had its Asian sector. One of the stabilizing elements of the prewar years in South and Southeast Asia was the predominant strength of the British in the region. The Indian Empire was the center of British power. But outposts of strategic importance from Gibraltar, Malta, Cairo, and Aden to Bombay, and beyond India through Colombo, Singapore, and Hong Kong to Shanghai gave the British a lifeline of Empire in the defense of British interests and, by her powerful presence, made her an inhibitor of cross-imperial warfare or of localized nationalist growths that might threaten the delicately ordered European involvements in the region.

Although the expansion of United States interests in the Pacific at the end of the nineteenth century threatened to upset British designs for Asian political balance, the United States confined its approaches largely to the Philippines, Japan, and China, and accepted the dominance of the European powers in most of Southern Asia. Some American commerce and industry had infiltrated into British, French, and Dutch territories. But compared with European commitments, United States' interests were primarily trade, commerce, banking, and industry on a relatively small scale. World War II, however, brought tens of thousands of American soldiers and sailors into direct contact with the lands and peoples of

---

[2] Norman S. Buchanan and Howard S. Ellis, *Approaches to Economic Development* (New York: The Twentieth Century Fund, 1955), pp. 126-74.

Southern Asia. India, despite protests from Indian nationalists, was made the center of the China-Burma-India Theater of War. Military supply bases were established in many parts of India, and air warfare against Japan in its early stages was launched substantially from India. As the Japanese were thrown back from Burma and from the islands of Indonesia and the Philippines, Americans joined their European allies in the broad attack.

With Japan defeated, with Western Europe devastated and at a low economic ebb, and with nationalist demands at a high pitch throughout Southern Asia, the United States had an historic role to play in helping to establish new political balances in Asia. No other state was in a position to assume these responsibilities. Unfortunately, leaders in the United States, to say nothing of the general citizenry, were ill-prepared to accept these responsibilities; the United States defaulted in the early postwar years under the pressures at home for rapid demobilization. Only the disaster involved in the communist capture of China in 1949 awakened the United States to its stake in the Asian world.

Thus before World War II, the United States had little political interest in Southern Asia except for the Philippines. Even with the rise of nationalist movements in the area, its official policy, expressed usually in silence, supported by passive acquiescence the imperialist status quo. Unofficially, of course, many American individuals and groups aided the various nationalist causes. But such personal and individual preferences did not affect United States policy to any measurable degree.

The civil and military institutions, architecture, traditions of law and administration, and urban language usage in Southern Asia today reflect the region's recent colonial history. Wherever British control has been predominant, one finds a measure of political sophistication, continuing strands of the common law heritage, civic buildings symbolizing the pomp and circumstance of the Victorian era, plus efficient, methodical administrative techniques, and English spoken by the ruling classes. In their former territories, the French bestowed the gift of their beloved language, plus artistic remnants of high European culture, but they left also an ill-equipped political and administrative cadre and economies that were unprepared for internal growth once the imperial tie was broken. The Dutch, much like the French, stubbornly refused to recognize the nationalist demands, and plodded on to the last with policies in the Indies that ignored the inevitable in the service of The Netherlands home interests. Needless to say, Dutch became a second language in Indonesia. As for the United States in the Philippines, educational and governmental institutions, an emphasis upon economic growth in the American capitalistic image, and an exaggerated positive value given to modern sewage disposal and sanitary water supply result in making most visiting Americans feel at home in Manila, particularly since they can use Americanized English and can express themselves in Christian value terms without fear of hurting local feelings.

DEVELOPMENT OF NATIONALISM AND INDEPENDENCE

The struggle between imperial interests and nationalist demands arose in the late nineteenth century, came to a head in the interwar years, and was resolved in favor of independence for most of the Southern Asian nationalist groups following World War II. India was in the vanguard of Asian nationalist movements.[3]

India was a large and heavily populated land with a modern culture resting upon a great and ancient civilization. The sheer size of the country and its citizenry led to the early growth of industry, commerce, and banking to facilitate the provision of essential consumer goods. Educational institutions from primary schools to universities were developed from the mid-nineteenth century as a means for training assistants to man the organs of British rule. But education along liberal British lines, and experience in the conduct of economic enterprise, hastened and enlivened the Indian nationalist cause. Perhaps most important, India produced many leaders of excellence who spoke eloquently for India's freedom and in turn for national freedom for all colonial peoples. The voices of Indian nationalism were shared throughout Southern Asia, and were augmented by national leaders like Aung San and U Nu in Burma, Sukarno in Indonesia, and Ho Chi Minh in Indochina.

Perhaps the most significant of all the nationalist leaders in Southern Asia was Mohandas K. Gandhi, the saintly and politically adept leader of the Indian National Congress from 1919 until his death in 1948.[4] Gandhi developed techniques of non-violent resistance to tyranny in South Africa before World War I. He translated his unique resistance methods into what he called *satyagraha* (literally, holding fast to truth), and thus created a method of action that enabled the nationalist effort in India to expand from a small, urban, intellectuals' endeavor to a mass, rural movement. Gandhi chose to live and work with the poor and to identify with their interests. Once he was accepted by the many, Gandhi introduced social changes, revolutionary in their implications, that would have been rejected if they had been presented by city-bred outsiders. Gandhi's political genius was broad: he raised the sense of self-respect of the Indian people; he lived the simple life and yet demanded the best of essentials

---

[3] William L. Holland, ed., *Asian Nationalism and the West* (New York: The Macmillan Co., 1953).

[4] P. Gopinath Dhawan, *The Political Philosophy of Mahatma Gandhi*, 2nd rev. ed. (Ahmedabad, India: Navajivan Publishing House, 1951); Joan V. Bondurant, *Conquest of Violence: The Gandhian Philosophy of Conflict* (Princeton, N.J.: Princeton University Press, 1958).

for India, including self-government (*swaraj*); he urged the development of India's indigenous crafts and industries, and demanded that home products be used exclusively (*swadeshi*); he gave his people a peaceful weapon to use in their own national struggle (*satyagraha*); he honored his heritage by daily devotion to the good and truthful life.

British responses to nationalist demands were to provide constitutional structures in which Indian representatives played an increasingly active role, from the passage of the Acts of 1909 and 1919 through the Constitution of 1935. The latter provided for provincial autonomy, but the central government and the governors in the provinces retained ultimate political control. Constitutional advances always were inadequate to meet nationalist expectations. By the time of World War II, only complete independence was acceptable to the nationalists.

The drama of the fight for independence in India was matched in the other British territories of Burma, Ceylon, and Malaya, although at a slower rate of growth.[5] By 1947 the gap in nationalist preparedness had closed, and independence for Burma and Ceylon came at about the same time as it did for India. Malaya's case took longer, and some British ties still remain in nearby Singapore. Pakistan, of course, was founded in 1947, carved from the eastern and western Muslim-majority sectors of the subcontinent.

The American promise of independence for the Philippines was made good in an orderly fashion in 1946. But the French and Dutch had to be forced out of their Asian colonies under conditions of bitter warfare. They had failed to calculate accurately the strength of nationalist demands and the implications raised by the devastations of war on the capacities of The Netherlands and France to maintain far-flung empires.

Japan's rapid economic advance before World War I and its successful wars against China and Russia contributed to the esteem in which Japan was held in the eyes of other Asian nationalists. European imperial rule throughout most of Southern Asia was demoralizing to the local inhabitants. The Asian people were led to believe that European military and political power was matched by superior social and cultural systems as well. Japan's dramatic economic and military successes led many in Asia to question the inevitability of the success of European power when pitted against Asian resistance, and in turn European civilization as such was lowered to a less exalted status in the hierarchy of cultures. But the Japanese symbol was abstract and impersonal since few in Southern Asia knew the Japanese except as traders and diplomats. The war against China waged by Japan from 1937 was watched anxiously in Southern Asia, and public opinion certainly favored the Chinese. As Japan's might

---

[5] Robert Aura Smith, *Philippine Freedom 1946-58* (New York: Columbia University Press, 1958); John F. Cady, *A History of Modern Burma* (Ithaca, New York: Cornell University Press, 1958).

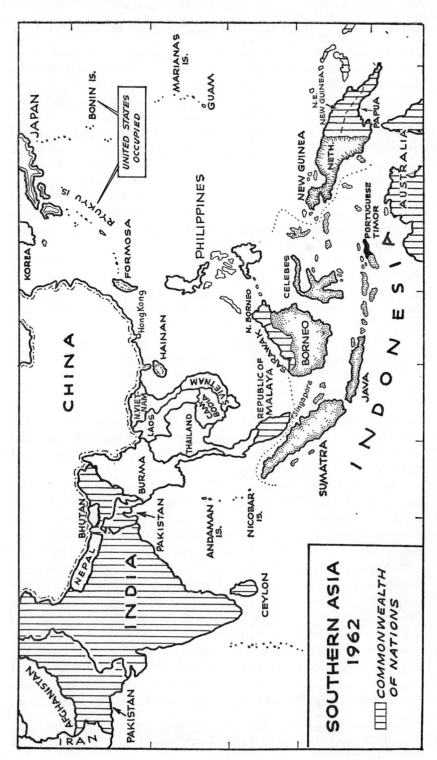

SOUTHERN ASIA
1962

▦ COMMONWEALTH
OF NATIONS

UNITED STATES
OCCUPIED

expanded up to December 1941 and the attack on Pearl Harbor, nationalist opinion about the Japanese in Southeast Asia wavered between a
fear of Japanese aggression and a hope of ultimate liberation from European control under the military blanket of the Japanese.[6]

Japan's promise of a co-prosperity sphere in Asia was put to the test
following Pearl Harbor. The Japanese overran Southeast Asia rapidly and
occupied most of the area up through Burma, including the Philippines
and the Dutch East Indies (Indonesia), by early 1942. Japan's military
success broke the prestige of the European colonial powers irreparably.
The Japanese selected local puppet regimes to carry on the essentials of
government, and thereby gave governmental experiences to a good many
Southeast Asian leaders who never before had tasted political power. Although Japanese military leaders interfered in local affairs continuously
and permitted little real freedom in the occupied countries, nationalism
in Southeast Asia was given a severe stimulus. Independence alone would
satisfy nationalist aspirations at the end of the war.

SOUTH ASIA

South Asia includes India, Pakistan, Ceylon, Bhutan, and Nepal; Afghanistan is considered to be a part of South Asia when its interests inter-
sect with those of neighboring Pakistan or India. In a sense South Asia
is a region. All of this area was at one time either under British rule, or—
as in the cases of Nepal and Afghanistan—under British influence. Over
200 years of British dominance left behind similar approaches to political,
economic, and social problems. The similarities in institutional behavior
remain to tie the several independent countries into an historical con-
tinuum. Educational institutions are much alike throughout, as are legal,
medical, commercial, and industrial methods. Moreover, although Islam
predominates in Pakistan, Hinduism in India and Nepal, and Buddhism
in Bhutan and Ceylon, representatives of these faiths inhabit most of the
region's countries in substantial numbers. Geographically and economically, South Asia tends to possess complementary factors, although policies pursued since independence have ignored these and have favored
competition.

But the regional nature of South Asia did not impress itself upon
United States policy-makers in the post-World War II years. In Europe,
the Marshall Plan, NATO, and the European Coal and Steel Community
as components of America's policy gave impetus to interstate and inter-
functional cooperation on a broad scale. But in Southern Asia, SEATO
linked together only a few of the countries, and left aside its non-aligned
opponents to carry on as they pleased. Bilateral military defense arrange-

---

[6] Willard H. Elsbree, *Japan's Role in Southeast Asian Nationalist Movements,
1940-45* (Cambridge: Harvard University Press, 1953).

ments such as the United States-Pakistan Defense Pact (1954) were negotiated even though they were opposed strongly by neighboring governments. Economic aid under Point Four was organized unevenly on a
country-by-country basis. The Colombo Plan, sponsored by the Commonwealth of Nations, attempted to draw the Southern Asian region together
through mutual economic interest. But inadequate financing resulting
from lukewarm American support prevented the plan from flowering as
it had been conceived.

Adjustments in America's Asian policies in the early nineteen-sixties
appeared to be more sensitively alert to the need for mutual support
among the Southern Asian nations, even if "neutralism" should gain
somewhat in stature and if direct United States influence should thereby
be lessened. The future of South and Southeast Asia promised to become
more stable and secure as the countries of the region turned to themselves
for cooperative defense and economic growth, and turned against outside interference, whether from the communists or from the anti-com-
munists.

India's Foreign Policy

India is the pivot country in South Asia. All of South Asia, and much
of Southeast Asia as well, are influenced by trends there. The capture of
this large country by the communists probably would spell the end of
free governments throughout Asia: where the communists did not take
over the other governments directly, authoritarian regimes of some sort
would have to be devised to maintain the independence of the state
against increased communist subversion or aggression. In any event, free
governments would expire. Thus what takes place internally in India, and
what policies India devises for its foreign policy, are of the utmost importance to the United States. We are here concerned primarily with
matters of foreign policy.[7]

The principles that have guided foreign policy in India since 1947 were
developed over the years since 1926 by Jawaharlal Nehru. Long experience with colonial status and involuntary involvement in British imperial
affairs underlie the Indian policy of "non-alignment" or of "positive neutralism." Rather than become a middle power subordinate to a great
power's influence, India has chosen to ride the middle line between the
two super-powers and to try to influence both. Mr. Nehru's policy has
not been directed towards withdrawal from world affairs, but rather aims
at a form of mediating involvement that may help to resolve differences,
reduce tensions, and thus make more feasible the peaceful pursuit of programs in India for social change and economic development. Without

---

[7]Jawaharlal Nehru, *Independence and After: A Collection of Speeches, 1946-49*
(New York: The John Day Company, Inc., 1950); Werner Levi, *Free India in Asia*
(Minneapolis: University of Minnesota Press, 1952).

military or political commitments abroad, India believes that its advice may be taken more seriously by all parties at dispute.

India's world policies center around its wish to construct a neutral but active base of diplomacy which will enable India to help create conditions favoring world peace. Such a neutral role has made it possible for India to "decide international issues on their merits," and to deal with all sides in attempting to resolve disputes. India has endeavored with some success to attract a UN following for these views among the Afro-Asian states.

These basic principles of India's foreign policy have directly defied the world-views both of the United States and the Soviet Union. For both of these, the question was: Would the communists advance or not? All parties should choose sides for the struggle. India has not altered its position of non-alignment since 1947, nor, indeed, have the United States and the Soviet Union changed their fundamental strategies. As a matter of tactics, first the Soviet Union and more recently the United States have found it advantageous to recognize the principle of non-alignment and each has attempted to gain the support of India by economic and other constructive means. The result has been vastly increased economic aid from the United States (exceeding $4 billions in loans and grants by 1961) and a lesser but still substantial (about $1 billion) amount from the Soviet Union.[8]

Indian leaders have had great respect for the economic achievements of the Soviet Union. They have been impressed that its program of economic development has raised a backward area to a point where it was able to withstand the power of Hitler's armies. India and other countries in Southern Asia believe that they have much to learn from Soviet experience. They also remember Soviet support given to Asian national aspirations in the nineteen-thirties when others, like the United States, were mum. Though the postwar years brought disillusionment regarding Moscow's alleged benevolent intentions toward the new states of South and Southeast Asia, India realized that the Soviet Union was a powerful neighbor with whom it would be folly to pick a quarrel.

India generally has maintained friendly relations with the United States, especially on economic matters where American assistance is greatly needed. India has noted, however, that Washington, in its prosecution of the cold war, has tended to support any government which could be classed as anti-communist. Distrust of American policy is underscored by Washington's continued support of Chiang Kai-shek and its refusal to recognize Peking as the *de jure* government of China, and as the appropriate representative of China in the UN. Time has tended to lessen the distrust. Disagreements over matters such as Taiwan or Jammu-Kashmir

---

[8] Charles Wolf, Jr., *Foreign Aid: Theory and Practice in Southern Asia* (Princeton, N.J.: Princeton University Press, 1960).

now are accepted as legitimate disagreements, rather than as bitter and personal centers of hostility.

India's desire to follow a friendly policy toward China was put to its first severe test in Korea. The Indian representative at the UN joined with the majority of the Assembly in condemning North Korean aggression. However, after China entered the war, New Delhi noted that China had reason to fear General MacArthur's approach to the Yalu River boundary. India's conciliatory policy towards Communist China has been sorely tried since China has pressed claims for territory on India's northern borders, and has occupied substantial portions of the area claimed.

New Delhi is friendly to Japan as a fellow Asian nation, and hopes to obtain from Japan both capital goods and technical assistance for India's own economic development.

Other aspects of India's foreign policy include support for nationalist movements throughout the Afro-Asian world; opposition to discrimination based on race, color, sex, or creed; opposition to all military pacts; the encouragement of disarmament; opposition to nuclear testing; and encouragement given to bridging the economic gap between the developed and underdeveloped worlds. On these policies, the United States and India are generally in agreement, except on questions of military policy.

Indian-Pakistani Relations
in the Postwar Period

Britain's transfer of political power to India was complicated by a series of crises growing out of antagonisms between the Hindu majority and the large Muslim minority in the country. The partition of the subcontinent in August 1947 created problems which have since been among the major concerns of the foreign policies of the two newly independent states.

Muslim opposition to Hindu-majority rule and the determination of Mohammad Ali Jinnah, president of the Muslim League, ended all possibilities for a compromise solution that would sustain the unity of India. Leaders of the rival parties under the British Cabinet Mission Plan of 1946 were associated temporarily within the same interim government, but attempts at political cooperation between the communities were abandoned early in 1947 amid increasing violence to both persons and property in Punjab and elsewhere. When it became evident that a unified India could be preserved only at the cost of civil war, the party leaders in May 1947 conceded that the partitioning of India was necessary if not inevitable.

The division of the subcontinent was filled with tragedy for the refugee inhabitants. The flight in both directions (Hindus and Sikhs to India and

Muslims to Pakistan) across the newly formed boundaries involved upwards of twelve million persons. The completion of the process of the transfer of power to the two states was accomplished by Independence Day, August 15, 1947.

The problems of Indo-Pakistani relations can be outlined here only in summary fashion. The immediate difficulties occasioned by the partition concerned the disruption of normal transportation and communications services between the two states and the care of millions of destitute refugees. Incoming refugees could not easily be fitted into the places in the economy left by the evacuees. Hindus and Sikhs who fled from Pakistan's Punjab area left behind much more property in land and goods than did the Muslims going in the opposite direction. Compensation for such losses has never been arranged, except in nominal amounts for the smaller claims. The interruption of normal trade patterns included the cessation of Indian coal exports on which Pakistan's industries and railways were dependent. India's textile industries, on the other hand, required long-fibre cotton and raw jute grown in Pakistan. It took more than ten years after partition for India and Pakistan to adjust their economies to the new political circumstances.

In the political field, serious controversies developed over the accession of the princely states of Junagadh, Hyderabad, and Jammu-Kashmir. The first was a small Hindu-majority state, surrounded by Indian territory, with a Muslim ruler who had acceded to Pakistan; the second was a large Hindu-majority state, completely encircled by Indian territory, headed by the Nizam, a Muslim ruler; the third, Jammu-Kashmir, was a Muslim-majority state with a Hindu ruler. In Junagadh, India's military forces intervened and India absorbed the state after a referendum favorable to India. In Hyderabad, after "police action" undertaken by India, the state acceded to India. In Jammu-Kashmir, an invasion by armed Pathan tribesmen from the North West Frontier in Pakistan created such chaos and fear in the state that the Maharaja was compelled to accede to India. Indian troops flown into the Vale of Kashmir at the behest of the Maharaja saved the area from ruination in the hands of the rapacious tribesmen. Although the formal accession of the state to India was accepted subject to eventual confirmation by a referendum, no agreement has been reached on the conditions requisite for holding it. The ensuing "civil war" within Jammu-Kashmir was halted in late 1948 on the basis of a cease-fire, which left all but a small western and northwestern sector under control of Indian forces. The problem has defied solution by direct negotiation and by the patient efforts of the UN. Pakistan continues to argue that a plebiscite should be held to decide the case; India asserts that the state is an integral part of India, and that elections held since in the state constitute the promised referendum.

The United States has been caught in the crossfire of Indo-Pakistani relations in establishing its own position with the countries of South Asia. India and Pakistan tend to judge a third country's fundamental friendship by its stand on Jammu-Kashmir. By attempting to be impartially sympathetic, the United States is held in suspicion by both India and Pakistan. For India, the United States defense agreement with and military aid to Pakistan was a clear indication of United States support for Pakistan in Indo-Pakistani disputes. For Pakistan, extensive United States economic aid to India was seen as favoritism shown to a nearby enemy—and a "neutral" enemy at that.

Other questions of importance are involved in the Jammu-Kashmir dispute. One of these concerns the distribution of the waters of the Indus river valley system, the headwaters of which lie partially within Kashmir. The water from these rivers is vital to the irrigation systems of West Pakistan, and water from the same source is needed for new irrigation works in India as well. With the extension of United States military aid to Pakistan in 1954, the importance of the area was enhanced, and a solution to the dispute rendered more difficult. However, after years of negotiation with the International Bank, an agreement was reached in 1960 to divide the Indus valley waters between India and Pakistan, and to construct the necessary diversionary canals, dams, and other controls to make such a division possible, with International Bank and multi-national assistance.

India's policies of non-alignment and mediation between the communist and noncommunist worlds contrast sharply with Pakistan's policy of cooperation in mutual defense against communist expansion and internal subversion. Although the demand raised by Communist China for over 50,000 square miles of Indian territory in the Tibetan border region initially suggested the urgency of Indo-Pakistani plans for joint subcontinental defense, other disputes, especially those centering upon Jammu-Kashmir, have prevented such cooperation.

India and Pakistan both remain members of the Commonwealth of Nations and cooperators in the Colombo Plan. But the Commonwealth tie is only one of several international connections of importance maintained by the two countries. Economic aid is of such crucial significance to each country that relations with the United States (as the most generous of the international sources to both countries) tend to outweigh in significance the club-like political linkages of the Commonwealth.

Afro-Asian Relations

An attempt to demonstrate India's cultural leadership in Asia was made in early 1947 when Jawaharlal Nehru, then head of the interim government, convened at New Delhi the Inter-Asian Relations Conference. India again took the lead in the summer of 1947, following the first Dutch "police action" in Java, in championing the Indonesian nationalist cause before the UN Security Council. When the Dutch made their second attack on central Java in December 1948, Premier Nehru called an emergency conference to mobilize a regional protest against the Dutch.

Prime Minister Nehru has been particularly concerned with maintaining friendly relations with Burma. He earlier refused to press the protests of Indian moneylenders against Rangoon's cancellation of land titles and mortgages to millions of acres of Indian-owned paddy lands, and he consented to a postponement of the payment of principal and interest on Burma's public debt to India. A settlement of the latter was reached in 1954.

With respect to Africa, India's representatives at the UN forced a review by the Assembly of racial discrimination policies in South Africa, which adversely affected the interests of Indian residents as well as those of the Negroes. The departure of South Africa from the Commonwealth in 1961, an action encouraged by both India and Pakistan, was a final, formal step reflecting Commonwealth opposition to South Africa's policies of *apartheid*. Indians from time to time have also indicated an unofficial interest in Kenya, Tanganyika, Nigeria, Angola, Ghana, and countries elsewhere in Africa where nationalist movements or Indian traders have been parties to controversy.

The Bandung Conference of 1955, convened by several states, including India, was expected in New Delhi to be a first step towards greater accord within the Afro-Asian-Middle Eastern region. Nehru did not see his hopes achieved; Chou En-lai took the center of the stage. The proceedings revealed the serious differences in outlook that separated the participating countries, rather than the ties that bound their interests together.

Whether India aspires to a position of leadership in Asia or not, India is incapable of taking over Britain's former leading role. India lacks a powerful air force, navy, merchant marine, and industrial potential capable of maintaining such a stance of power. The collapse of Britain's strategic position in the Middle East (especially at Suez) is adverse to the security interests of India as it is to the countries of Western Europe. Perhaps most important, India, being a large and potentially powerful country in a region populated with small and weak states, is itself feared by its neighbors. The smaller states of Southern Asia, jealous of their sovereignty and assertive of their own values, reject hegemony from India or any other country. This fact is well understood in New Delhi today.

With respect to maintaining the security of the northern approaches to India's borders, New Delhi takes very much the same attitude that it did under the British. Thus, when Communist China laid claim to substantial segments of India's Himalayan borders in 1957, and since then actually occupied over 12,000 square miles of Indian territory, India protested vigorously and re-assigned its defense forces on the borders. Soviet or Chinese infiltration into neighboring or near-neighboring countries arouses concern in India. Kashmir's strategic importance to India has already been pointed out. To forestall communist infiltration of Nepal, India intervened politically first in 1951-52 to liberalize the country's outdated feudal government, and since then has been Nepal's guide in matters of defense, communications, and security.

The Sino-Indian border dispute has led to a debate over foreign and domestic policy in India that reflects an increased sophistication toward the nature of communist world strategy in relation to India's national interests. Taking into consideration also the enormous hard currency aid needed for the Third and Fourth Five Year Plans, India now turns more regularly to the United States for consultation and assistance. While India's foreign policy aims have not been altered substantially, the balance of decision more and more favors shared objectives with the United States.

Ceylon

Since the end of the war Ceylon has been accorded independent sovereign status, and it remains a member of the Commonwealth, but its international relations have been narrowly circumscribed. It was denied membership in the UN for a number of years by Soviet veto. Because of Ceylon's financial position and its proximity to the Indian subcontinent, the authorities at Colombo were content to postpone attempts to develop their own means of security. More recently, under the governments of the late S.W.R.D. Bandaranaike and his widow (the present Prime Minister), an independent policy in foreign affairs has been developed which is generally sympathetic to the "neutralist" doctrines of India. Ceylon's most intimate cultural relations are with the Buddhist countries of Burma and Thailand. Barter arrangements with Communist China (exchanging Ceylon's rubber for Chinese rice) have complicated United States economic aid to Ceylon. But barter and aid co-exist at present.

SOUTHEAST ASIA

In the formulation and execution of American policy in Southeast Asia, officials of the United States must take into consideration the importance of the area to the United States, the problems posed by the region's instability both in terms of domestic politics and international security, and the need for sound objectives and realistic programs.[9]

---

[9] George McT. Kahin, ed., *Governments and Politics of Southeast Asia* (Ithaca, New York: Cornell University Press, 1959).

Strategic, Economic,
and Demographic Significance

Southeast Asia is a strategic area of great importance. It commands the shortest water passageway between the Pacific and Indian Oceans; its peninsular and insular territories provided steppingstones between continental Asia and Australia. Not by accident did Great Britain develop Singapore into one of the great seaports and naval bases of the world. Air transportation routes parallel to a considerable degree those by sea, adding to the regions strategic importance. The Kra Isthmus in Thai territory possesses a location of considerable politico-geographic value. On the eastern shores of the South China Sea, the Philippines afford civil and military facilities that can influence the future of Southeast Asia. If the region fell to a power or combination of powers hostile to the United States, not only would American interests suffer, but also those of allied countries such as Australia, New Zealand, and Pakistan, and non-aligned states such as India and Ceylon.

Southeast Asia also has a number of exports whose significance must not be underestimated. Among these items may be singled out rice, tin, rubber, and petroleum, each having its own importance depending upon the needs of customers and varying circumstances of trade. Burma, Thailand, and Viet Nam have long been called the rice bowl of Asia because of extensive exports to rice-deficient countries in East Asia. Around 60 per cent of the world's output of tin and 90 per cent of natural rubber come from Southeast Asia, with Indonesia and Malaya being outstanding producers. About 2.5 per cent of the world's production of crude oil originates in Indonesia and British Borneo. If Communist China could get full control of the products of Southeast Asia, it could regulate their export to suit its own needs, and at the same time exert pressure at will on other powers. Western countries such as the United States and Great Britain, and Asian ones such as Japan and India, have a substantial economic stake in the future of Southeast Asia.

The region also is important in terms of demography; over 192 million people inhabit an area smaller than half that of the United States. Although certain areas of Southeast Asia are densely populated such as central Luzon and the Red River delta, the region as a whole could sustain a much larger number of people. At present the rate of population growth is around 1.8 per cent each year, a significant figure but below that of some other Asian states such as China. Southeast Asia contains ample space for settlement by large numbers of outside people. The 15 million Chinese living in the area testify to their adaptability in what they call the *Nan Yang*.

Problems of Instability and Insecurity

Instability in Southeast Asia arises from a complex of factors having their matrix in political, economic, and social conditions before and since independence. In most of the countries ample preparation was not made for *Merdeka* (independence); it came in the aftermath of the destruction and dislocation of World War II. The revolutionary nationalists often proved unable to cope with the grave problems of leadership in making government a going concern in the twentieth century. The administrators also found themselves generally ill-prepared to carry out the essential functions of government. In some countries of Southeast Asia the military elite came to occupy a position of prominence in an effort to forestall a collapse of law and order. It is clear that western parliamentary democracy must be adapted to the Asian environment and to Asian needs if it is to be successfully transplanted.

In the economic field, the newly independent countries inherited an economy from the colonial powers wherein the former served as producers of certain raw materials, as places for capital investment, and as markets for manufactured goods in the interests of the latter. Independence in Southeast Asia brought a mounting desire for development and modernization; a steel mill, for instance, became a symbol of status, regardless of its real value to the current economy. The "revolution of rising expectations," made possible by the expansion of communications and mass media, helped to create a situation wherein government leaders were under pressure to improve the standard of living. At the same time they did not have in their countries the capital and expertise essential to meet the growing demands.

Social instability, related to political and economic conditions, was aggravated by the existence of a pluralistic society in transition. The departure of Western rulers and administrators, the rise to power of indigenous leaders, and the readjustment of the Chinese and Indian middle class to the new environment contributed to social instability. Moreover, the phenomenal rise in urban population created widespread unemployment, bad living conditions, and security problems, all taxing the abilities and resources of municipal authorities. The growing numbers of youth and their tendency to move to urban areas should not be underestimated in ultimate effects upon the future of the respective states.

The countries of Southeast Asia are able for the most part to maintain a relatively high degree of internal security, but they do not have the ability to withstand alone or together a Chinese military assault. Moreover, several of them have not yet indicated any desire to support collective defense arrangements in the region. The Philippines, Thailand, the Federation of Malaya, and the Republic of Viet Nam are allied formally or informally to one or more countries of the western alignment; the People's Republic of Viet Nam is a member of the Sino-Soviet bloc; Cambodia, Indonesia, and Burma are unaligned; and Laos in the early sixties with its rival governments reflected the confrontation of the Peking-Moscow axis and the western alliance. Southeast Asia, to use a popular phrase, is a "power vacuum," the existence of which under the present circumstances of intense international rivalry menaces the peace of the region, of East Asia, and of the world.

International communism is a clear-cut threat to both internal stability and international security in Southeast Asia. On the domestic front the local communist parties, aided and abetted in varying degrees by the People's Republic of China and the Soviet Union, take full advantage of all the conditions conducive to instability. Militant nationalism, economic unrest, suspicion of former colonial rulers—these and many others, are utilized. Although the threat of overt military aggression on the part of Communist China in Southeast Asia seems less pronounced at present, the tactics of indirect aggression through subversion and infiltration constitute a grave menace to the independence of the states of the area.

American Objectives and Policies

In view of the interests of the United States, the conditions in Southeast Asia, and the threat to its security, what are the American objectives in the region? What are the policies and programs that have been formulated in an effort to translate objectives into accomplishments? What measure of success or failure has been evident?[10]

The United States, in the ultimate analysis, seeks to strengthen internal stability and to enhance international security in Southeast Asia. It wants the countries of the area to progress along the road of modernization under conditions responsive to the needs of the people by evolutionary means. It seeks to use its margin of influence, varying from country to country, to advance stability in a noncommunist and nontotalitarian framework. The United States realizes that internal stability cannot be achieved or long endure in an environment where local governments are subject to the daily threat of foreign invasion from outside the area. It therefore seeks to assist in removing this threat from Southeast Asia. At the same time it wants the countries of the region to be responsible members of the world community.

American objectives are implemented through political, military, economic, information, and cultural programs, all, it is hoped, contributing to desired goals. The programs are instruments of national policy to

---

[10] Russell H. Fifield, *The Diplomacy of Southeast Asia, 1945-1958* (New York: Harper and Brothers, 1958).

maintain the political independence and territorial integrity of the states of Southeast Asia.

The division among the countries of the region between western-committed and "neutralist" states—except for North Viet Nam with its ties to the communist bloc—poses serious problems for American policy-makers. Relations with allies being different from those with unaligned nations, a policy on a truly regional basis is difficult to maintain. Among the nations of Southeast Asia, the United States is a formal ally only of Thailand and the Philippines. These two, along with Pakistan, Great Britain, France, Australia, New Zealand, and the United States are joined in the Southeast Asia Collective Defense Treaty signed in 1954. This Manila pact, with its subsequent Southeast Asia Treaty Organization (SEATO), was principally designed to deter overt communist aggression in the treaty area. Here SEATO has been successful; at least international communism has not provoked a Korean-type war. On the other hand, the SEATO pact has not proved very effective in coping with indirect aggression. Communist expansion in Laos reached a stage in 1961 where most optimists joined the pessimists in predicting a communist takeover. SEATO's accomplishments in the fields of economic and cultural cooperation have been noteworthy but not outstanding.

Even before the Manila Pact, the United States was formally allied with another Southeast Asian state, namely, the Philippines. The mutual defense treaty of 1951 along with the presence of American bases in Luzon reflect the security ties between the two republics. In fact, the Filipinos place more faith in the mutual defense treaty than they do in SEATO. The security links of the United States with the Republic of Viet Nam exist formally through the latter as a designated protocol state under the Manila Pact.

American policy toward the "neutrals" of Asia shifted from a posture of criticism to one of tolerance and then of genuine understanding. In fact, some of the allies of the United States are beginning to question the advantages of commitment as compared with those of neutrality. It can be argued that a genuinely "neutral" Laos, whose neutrality is truly recognized and respected by all interested powers, is preferable to a western-aligned Laos if under the latter circumstance that country would be a pawn in power politics and a threat to world peace. But it is doubtful whether international communism would accept neutrality as an end in itself; it is more likely that it is considered a tactic by which conditions can be created conducive to an eventual takeover. Under such circumstances genuine neutrality is an ideal that can never be achieved.

Through its military and economic aid programs in Southeast Asia, the United States is able to exert a measure of influence. Military assistance is needed more in the area than in a number of other places, for the communist threat is both internal and external. It is clear that the countries themselves can never develop a military potential strong enough to withstand Communist China. Nevertheless, if they were militarily stronger, they would be in a better position to preserve their internal security and in some cases to exercise a delaying operation against a communist onslaught.

Economic aid can be used in emergencies requiring stopgap measures, but its effectiveness over a period of years is dependent upon long-range planning and financing. The recipients must be prepared to make necessary reforms if the assistance is to benefit the many in a country instead of the few in power. Economic development is a process that calls for sustained effort and sacrifice over many years on the part of the leadership and people of a country. The United States can help to provide the margin of necessary capital and the essential expertise in human resources—even in some cases to achieve an early breakthrough to self-sustained growth; but the recipients must bear the main burden. Modernization, moreover, is a complex process that affects not only the economic, but also the social and political foundations of the state. Through its contributions to modernization the United States can help produce a better community of nations in the developing, newly independent areas of the world.

CONCLUSIONS

Relations between the United States and the countries of South and Southeast Asia are certain to be the subjects of many headline stories in the nineteen-sixties and beyond. The power of Communist China, early tested in Korea, probes the extensive Chinese perimeter from Ladakh in Kashmir to the South Korean border, and is influential politically in the islands from Indonesia to Japan. No country in Southern Asia can escape the consequences of China's perspectives on Asia's future condition. While maintaining independence, each of the countries concerned strives to build its economy and to create a stable political order that can respond adequately to the rising expectations of its people. In resisting communist forces from within or without and in developing modern, productive states, Southern Asia needs the help of the United States.

Military aid for defense no longer seems to hold the key to the security of South and Southeast Asia, at least in the minds of those somewhat distant from China's borders. But budgets for the armed forces necessarily remain high, in the non-aligned as well as in the committed countries of the region. Prudence, in the local national interest for security, dictates that these budgets probably should increase rather than decrease over the coming decade. The requirements for civil expenditure at the same time rise sharply as the preparatory stages of economic development move into the stage of more rapid expansion. With limited local resources, under these demanding circumstances external assistance becomes a sheer necessity. One of the results of substantial economic assistance, such as United States aid to India, is the relief given to India's central budget in releasing greater internal financial resources for defense. The Asian SEATO powers, on the other hand, are recipients both of defense and economic aid. The crucial questions in the SEATO cases involve the balance that results between total defense spending and total civil expenditure, and the effectiveness with which civil funds are used. An imbalance favoring the military, as in Laos or Viet Nam, does not seem to have provided the desired results. But one cannot ignore the military requirements of the area, whether defense policies are for the moment popular or not. One of the crucial elements in the future relations between Southern Asia and the United States will be the skill with which balanced and responsible economic and military aid agreements are renegotiated. Countries such as India, Burma, and Indonesia, favoring policies of non-alignment, nevertheless have severe military defense problems. The costs are no less onerous because of non-alignment. Since non-alignment is likely to become more widespread, United States policies on economic aid must contain careful calculation of the military defense implications of given levels of economic aid.

It is in these realms of defense and economic assistance that the relations between the United States and Southern Asia are bound to settle in the nineteen-sixties. Cultural and educational exchange, trade and commerce—plus private assistance in encouraging the process of industrialization—also will be present. But public assistance in producers' goods, food, finance, credit, and considerate advice constitutes the critical minimum that is needed, except where crisis situations demand direct or indirect military aid.

It is not likely that regional cooperation in Southern Asia will increase in significance over the coming decade without encouragement. Competition for scarce resources in external assistance and for export markets outweigh cooperative ventures for economic growth such as the Colombo Plan. But cooperation, at least to the extent developed in Western Europe since the end of World War II, would appear to be advantageous to all concerned if such a process of interrelationships could be organized effectively.

SUGGESTED READINGS

GENERAL

East, W. Gordon and O. H. K. Spate, eds., *The Changing Map of Asia*, 3d rev. ed. New York: E. P. Dutton & Co., Inc., 1958.

Farley, Miriam S., *United States Relations with Southeast Asia: with Special Reference to Indo-China, 1950-1955*, rev. ed. New York: Institute of Pacific Relations, 1955.

Fifield, Russell H., *The Diplomacy of Southeast Asia, 1945-1958*. New York: Harper & Brothers, 1958.

Furnivall, John S., *Colonial Policy and Practice: A Comparative Study of Burma and Netherlands India*. New York: New York University Press, 1956.

Ginsburg, Norton, ed., *The Pattern of Asia*. Englewood Cliffs, N.J.: Prentice-Hall, Inc., 1958.

Hall, D. G. E., *A History of South-East Asia*. New York: St. Martin's Press, Inc., 1955.

Holland, William L., ed., *Asian Nationalism and the West*. New York: The Macmillan Co., 1953.

Kahin, George McT., *The Asian-African Conference: Bandung, Indonesia, April 1955*. Ithaca, New York: Cornell University Press, 1956.

———, ed., *Governments and Politics of Southeast Asia*. Ithaca, New York: Cornell University Press, 1959.

King, John K., *Southeast Asia in Perspective*. New York: The Macmillan Co., 1956.

Pauker, Guy T., "Southeast Asia as a Problem Area in the Next Decade," *World Politics*, XI (Apr. 1959), 325-45.

U.S. Senate, Committee on Foreign Relations, "United States Foreign Policy: Asia, Study No. 5," by Conlon Associates, Ltd. Committee Print, 86th Cong., 1st sess., 1959. Washington, D.C.: Government Printing Office, 1959. [Section on South Asia: Richard L. Park. Section on Southeast Asia: Guy Pauker. Section on East Asia: Robert A. Scalapino.]

Vandenbosch, Amry and Richard A. Butwell, *Southeast Asia among the World Powers*. Lexington, Kentucky: University of Kentucky Press, 1958.

Wolf, Charles, Jr., *Foreign Aid: Theory and Practice in Southern Asia*. Princeton, N.J.: Princeton University Press, 1960.

Zinkin, Maurice, *Asia and the West*, rev. ed. New York: Institute of Pacific Relations, 1953.

INDIA

Berkes, Ross N. and Mohinder S. Bedi, *The Diplomacy of India: Indian Foreign Relations in the United Nations*. Stanford, California: Stanford University Press, 1958.

Bowles, Chester, *Ambassador's Report*. New York: Harper & Brothers, 1954.

Brecher, Michael, *Nehru: A Political Biography*. New York: Oxford University Press, Inc., 1959.

————, *The Struggle for Kashmir*. New York: Oxford University Press, Inc., 1953.

Brown, W. Norman, *The United States and India and Pakistan*. Cambridge: Harvard University Press, 1953.

Harrison, Selig S., ed., *India and the United States*. New York: The Macmillan Co., 1961.

Karunakaran K. P., *India in World Affairs: 1947-1950*. New York: Oxford University Press, Inc., 1952.

————, *India in World Affairs: 1950-1953*. New York: Oxford University Press, Inc., 1958.

Menon, V. P., *The Transfer of Power in India*. Princeton: Princeton University Press, 1957.

Nehru, Jawaharlal, *Independence and After: A Collection of Speeches, 1946-1949*. New York: The John Day Company, 1950.

Overstreet, Gene D. and Marshall Windmiller, *Communism in India*. Berkeley, Calif.: University of California Press, 1959.

Park, Richard L. and Irene Tinker, eds., *Leadership and Political Institutions in India*. Princeton, N.J.: Princeton Universiy Press, 1959.

Talbot, Phillips and S. L. Poplai, *India and America: A Study of Their Relations*. New York: Harper & Brothers, 1958.

PAKISTAN

Ahmad, Mushtaq, *The United Nations and Pakistan*. Karachi: Pakistan Institute of International Affairs, 1955.

Callard, Keith B., *Pakistan: A Political Study*. New York: The Macmillan Co., 1957.

————, *Political Forces in Pakistan, 1947-1959*. New York: Institute of Pacific Relations, 1959.

Korbel, Joseph, *Danger in Kashmir*. Princeton, N.J.: Princeton University Press, 1954.

Palmer, Norman D., "The United States and Pakistan," *Current History*, XXXIV (Mar. 1958), 141-46.

CEYLON

Rao, P. R. Ramachandra, *India and Ceylon: A Study*. Bombay: Orient Longmans, 1954.

Wriggins, W. Howard, *Ceylon: Dilemmas of a New Nation*. Princeton, N.J.: Princeton University Press, 1960.

BURMA

Cady, John F., *A History of Modern Burma*. Ithaca, New York: Cornell University Press, 1958.

Christian, John L., *Modern Burma: A Survey of Political and Economic Development*. Berkeley, Calif.: University of California Press, 1942.

Tinker, Hugh, *The Union of Burma: A Study of the First Years of Independence*, 2d ed. New York: Oxford University Press, Inc., 1959.

THAILAND

Blanchard, Wendell and others, *Thailand: Its People, Its Society, Its Culture*. New Haven: Human Relations Area Files Press, 1958.

MALAYA

Ginsburg, Norton and Chester F. Roberts, Jr., *Malaya*. Seattle, Washington: University of Washington Press, 1958.
Mills, Lennox A., *Malaya: A Political and Economic Appraisal*. Minneapolis, Minnesota: University of Minnesota Press, 1958.
Pye, Lucian W., *Guerrilla Communism in Malaya: Its Social and Political Meaning*. Princeton: Princeton University Press, 1956.

INDONESIA

Hatta, Mohammad, "Indonesia's Foreign Policy," *Foreign Affairs*, XXXI (Apr. 1953), 441-52.
Kahin, George McT., *Nationalism and Revolution in Indonesia*. Ithaca, New York: Cornell University Press, 1952.

VIET NAM, CAMBODIA, LAOS

Buttinger, Joseph, *The Smaller Dragon: A Political History of Vietnam*. New York: Frederick A. Praeger, Inc., 1958.
Fall, Bernard B., *The Viet-Minh Regime: Government and Administration in the Democratic Republic of Vietnam*, 2d ed., rev. New York: Institute of Pacific Relations, 1956.
Hammer, Ellen, *The Struggle for Indochina*. Stanford, California: Stanford University Press, 1954.
Steinberg, David J., *Cambodia: Its People, Its Society, Its Culture*. New Haven: Human Relations Area Files Press, 1957.

THE PHILIPPINES

Grunder, G. A. and W. E. Livezey, *The Philippines and the United States*. Norman, Oklahoma: University of Oklahoma Press, 1951.
Smith, Robert Aura, *Philippine Freedom. 1946-1958*. New York: Columbia University Press, 1958.

26

The United States and the Middle East

Richard W. Cottam
Department of Political Science,
University of Pittsburgh

Extending from Turkey and the United Arab Republic on the west to Afghanistan on the east, the Middle East stands as a great barrier separating the Soviet Union from the open seas to the south. To reach the Mediterranean from Black Sea ports, Soviet shipping must pass through the Bosporus and the Dardanelles, which are under virtual Turkish control. The Middle East also separates Europe from the rich markets of South and Southeast Asia. The Suez Canal, through which passes the bulk of European-Asian shipping, is controlled by the UAR. Both the Soviet Union and the European powers, therefore, in their efforts to maintain the security of their vital commercial lifelines, must interest themselves deeply in Middle-Eastern affairs. Furthermore, its military position is of the utmost strategic significance in conventional warfare planning.

Approximately one-half the world's known oil resources are in this area, and it is Europe's chief petroleum source. Middle-Eastern oil is also important for the Soviet Union, but because the latter has substantial supplies of its own, its chief concern is to be in a position to deny the oil to Europe in the event of a major crisis. Although oil is concentrated in Iran, Iraq, Saudi Arabia, Kuwait and other Arab sheikdoms, its transportation through the Suez Canal and through the pipe lines crossing several countries including Syria, Lebanon and Jordan, and the Elath-

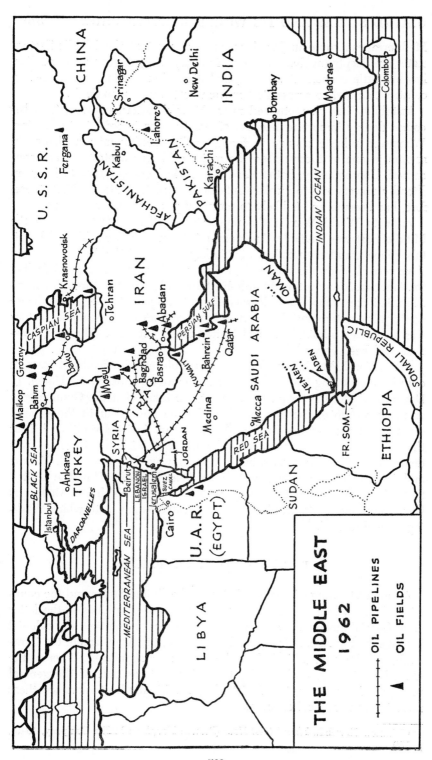

THE MIDDLE EAST
1962

-|-|-|- OIL PIPELINES

▲ OIL FIELDS

Mediterranean route in Israel, means that most of the Middle-Eastern states are deeply involved in the oil industry. Only Afghanistan and Turkey are little concerned with oil, and it has been seriously proposed to construct a pipeline across Turkey from northern Iranian fields.

Instability has characterized many Middle-Eastern regimes. This becomes doubly important because of great-power interest in the region. Whenever a basic change in foreign policy accompanies a change in regime in one of these states, the major cold war contestants are concerned. Consequently, both sides have worked energetically to buoy up friendly powers and to weaken unfriendly ones. The Middle East, therefore, has become and is likely to remain a primary cold war arena.

Prior to World War II the reputation of the United States in the Middle East was enviable. American missionaries had established hospitals, schools, and even colleges in Turkey, Iran, and the Arab areas, and their record of public service had done much to generate good feeling for America. Many future Middle-Eastern leaders passed through American missionary schools and learned there to appreciate the liberal democratic value system and their own cultures. America's anti-colonial history was also much admired. Official United States activity in the area, however, had been very slight.

After World War II the United States could avoid official involvement only by reconciling itself to the loss of the area to the Soviet Union. In November 1940, the Soviet government had asked that the German government recognize the area south of Batum and Baku in the general direction of the Persian Gulf as the center of Soviet aspirations.[1] That these aspirations were unaffected by the war with the Germans was demonstrated by the aggressive campaign waged against both Turkey and Iran in the immediate post-World War II years. Thus the United States became involved intimately in an area about which few Americans knew anything and in problems as complicated as any with which Washington had to deal.

BACKGROUND OF CONFLICT

An understanding of relations between the United States and the countries of the Middle East requires a knowledge of conditions in the latter area. Crucial among these are the social-political revolution, the colonial heritage, and intra-area conflicts. Of the latter, the Arab-Israeli, the intra-Arab, and the Iranian-Turkish-Arab are the most significant. Whereas the United States views Middle East developments as part of the general problem of containing the Soviet bloc, the Middle-Easterners see these more in terms of local concerns.

---

[1] Winston Churchill, *Their Finest Hour* (Boston: Houghton Mifflin Company, 1949), p. 589.

The Socio-Political Revolution

The stark contrast between the great metropolitan centers such as Istanbul and Beirut and the timeless, primitive Arab sheikdoms along the Persian Gulf and the Indian Ocean, tells a good deal about the Middle East. The entire area is in the process of taking a giant lurch forward from the medieval to the modern world. Such a profound transition cannot be made smoothly, and the interactions of this fundamental social and political revolution with the great-power struggles are the primary determinants of international relations involving the Middle East.

Although the generalization is warranted that the entire area is in a state of rapid transition, the rate of change differs from section to section. Israel is in many respects more European than Middle Eastern in political behavior, and Turkey has gone far along the road of modernization. At the other end of the spectrum stand the Yemen and the Arab Sheikdoms which only now are beginning to awaken. Probably no other factor is as important in explaining the striking variations in the international political behavior of Middle Eastern states as is the stage of transitional development in any particular state.

In a period of rapid transition there will inevitably be elements of the population applauding and encouraging change, while others seek to preserve the status quo. Generally speaking, in the Middle East those in the first category include most of the professional people, the commercial middle class (when members of this group are not also members of minority groups) and some intellectual, reform-minded religious leaders. The traditional groups include large landowners, tribal chiefs, and most religious leaders, as well as the members of old dynasties and their advisers. The great mass of peasants, tribesmen, and urban laborers have been politically unaware until recently and in general could be counted on to follow the traditional leaders with whom they were in daily contact. Since the large majority of the population is to be found in these latter categories, traditional leaders throughout much of the transitional period could count on majority acquiescence. Indeed, were it not for the fact that the mass of the population is disinterested and politically passive, the minority of modernizers would have been doomed to failure.

Throughout the transitional process, the central domestic political struggle takes place between the aspiring modernists and the once-firmly-entrenched traditionalists. The modernists universally have embraced nationalism and identify the restoration of their national dignity with the replacement of the traditional leaders. Many modernizers, especially those educated in American and European institutions, have embraced a liberal democratic ideology, but others doubt the applicability of liberal concepts to the Middle East; and a vocal if numerically small group accepts communism. The traditionalists rarely follow any particular ideology, but they usually stand in opposition to both liberal democracy and communism since both would fundamentally alter the old order.

Colonial Heritage

During the past century the entire Middle East has experienced some form of European control. For the northern tier of states—Turkey, Iran, and Afghanistan—it was informal and indirect. Turkey, despite open intervention by British, French, and Russian ambassadors during the nineteenth century, has few permanent scars. By 1922, the great modernizing leader Ataturk was in full control of the Turkish government and foreign interference was minimal. In Iran and Afghanistan the scars are deep and abiding. Foreign interference there has been so extensive that at times the two states could better be described as semi-colonial than as independent.

Since the British and the pre-Bolshevik Russian empires met at their borders, Iran and Afghanistan constituted a delicately balanced buffer zone. Neither great power could invade without risking war, and yet each wished to gain control over this vital area. Due to the nominal independence of the two states, this control could only be achieved by establishing a semi-covert relationship with important Iranians and Afghans. Both the Russians and the British found many collaborators willing to accept some foreign direction in return for political support, and these were almost entirely from among the traditional elements. Because of the semi-covert nature of this relationship, it could not be known with certainty through whom the foreign powers were working. For the increasingly nationalistic modernizers, the conviction grew that almost all of the traditional leaders had become willing tools of European imperialism and hence were traitors. This view so colored the attitude of the nationalistic groups in Iran and Afghanistan that it became and remains even today a prime determinant of their domestic and international behavior.

With the exceptions of the Yemen, which was largely ignored by the great powers, and Saudi Arabia, which felt little foreign interference, foreign control over Arab states was far more direct. Today, however, such control is to be found only in the sheikdoms, where the British are the avowed protectors of the traditionalist sheiks. But the memory of colonial rule is very strong.

In Iraq and Jordan the parallel with the Iranian attitude is a close one. Both states had been British mandates in the interwar period and in both the British had ruled indirectly through traditional leaders; in Iraq through the royal family and the remarkable conservative leader Nuri as-Said, and in Jordan through the Emir Abdullah. Formal independence was granted Iraq in 1932 and Jordan in 1946, but for the modernists these dates were without significance. In their eyes formal British rule was replaced by informal control since the men the British have always worked through remained in power. However, in July of 1958 the traditionalist rule came to a violent end in Iraq. Each year had seen a steady increase in the number of people who shared the anti-British attitude of the modernists and the conviction that the traditional leaders were traitors. So great was popular resentment, in fact, that the young King Faisal, the Crown Prince, and Nuri as-Said were murdered and the bodies of the latter two mutilated by furious mobs.

Developments in Jordan were similar. The Arab Legion, a military force officered, equipped, and trained by the British had helped make Jordan a tranquil outpost. But at the close of the Arab-Israeli War in 1948, Abdullah incorporated a section of Palestine into the newly independent Kingdom of Jordan, and in so doing he prepared the ground for his own destruction. The Palestinian Arabs in Jordan outnumbered the old population two to one and included a significant number of modernists, who viewed Jordan's traditional leaders as British lackeys. In 1951 Abdullah was assassinated, but the modernists have yet to gain complete control of Jordan.

The pattern in Egypt was significantly different from that of Iraq and Jordan. In the first, British rule (1882-1922) had been direct. There had been no serious attempts to rule through an alliance with any section of the Egyptian population, and the politically aware Egyptian, whether landowner or professional man, shared a common goal: to drive out the British. After World War I the great Egyptian nationalist leader, Saad Zaghlul, was almost universally popular among the politically aware, and when the British permitted a relatively free election in 1924, Zaghlul and his Wafd party won overwhelmingly. But the British had no intention of surrendering the Suez Canal, and although they gave Egypt formal independence in 1922, they inaugurated what amounted to indirect rule.

At first the British were able to work only with Turkish-speaking traditionalists; but in 1936 and again in 1942 they were able to persuade the successor of Saad Zaghlul in the Wafd party, Nahas Pasha, to cooperate with them. For nationalists in Egypt Nahas was thus discredited, as had been King Farouk and most of the traditional leaders. Egyptian politics did not crystallize, therefore, into the Iranian-Iraqi pattern of a traditionalist-British alliance against the modernists. Instead, political forces splintered, with the religio-political Muslim Brotherhood and the fascistic Egyptian Socialists of Ahmad Hossein attracting many dissillusioned modernists. As later events were to prove, the most significant of the political groups was the Free Officers Movement. Anti-British attitudes and the belief that many Egyptian leaders, both traditionalists and modernists, had sold out to the British was the one common characteristic of these groups.

Syria and Lebanon were under French mandate, and although the

French had also hoped to rule indirectly, they proved to be temperamentally incapable of doing so. Their rule was, in fact if not in form, direct. The result for Syria was similar to that for Egypt prior to World War I. No Saad Zaghlul emerged to unite Syria, but traditionalists and modernists did work together in the common cause. Furthermore, when in 1945 the French were compelled to give up their claim to Syria and Lebanon, the break was a clean one. Later, however, when conservative Syrians and Lebanese sought to ally themselves with Nuri as-Said of Iraq, they became, in modernist eyes, infected with the same pro-British virus that was endemic among Iraqi traditionalists.

In Lebanon the situation was seriously complicated by the country's deep sectarian divisions. Whereas ninety per cent of the people of the Middle East are Muslims, Lebanon is divided evenly between Muslims and Christians. Furthermore, within both of these communities there are deep divisions. The largest of the Christian sects, the Maronites, has a long history of close relationships with French missionaries and traders. Under the French mandate, many of them were perfectly content, and naturally enough served as a mainstay of support for the mandate. Among the pro-French element were many who refused to regard themselves as Arabs and who argued instead that they had a distinctive Mediterranean culture. Such an attitude could only be anathema to those Lebanese who looked forward to the formation of a great Arab nation. Once again the question of treason was raised. Lebanese politics became a web of interacting conflicts of which the modernist-traditionalist struggle was only one part. Included also were the bitter sectarian struggle and the widely-differing attitudes toward Britain and France.

The interaction of the domestic modernist-traditionalist conflict with the anti-colonial struggle has done much to color Middle-Eastern attitudes. Herein lie many of the roots of current anti-western sentiment which is of so much concern to the United States. But the conclusion should not be made, as it is so often, that Middle-Eastern modernizers generally are philosophically distant from the West.[2] In their value system nationalism and resentment of the old colonial powers are constants, while an attachment to liberal democracy is a variable. But a very common attitude in the Middle East is a combination of nationalism, dislike of Western powers, and adherence to liberal democracy.

The Arab-Israeli Struggle

The third of the basic elements necessary for a comprehension of United States and Middle-East relationships is the Arab-Israeli conflict. There are three major Middle-Eastern ethnic groups: Iranians, Turks,

---

[2] Walter Z. Laqueur, *Communism and Nationalism in the Middle East* (New York: Frederick A. Praeger, Inc., 1957), p. 7.

and Arabs. The three most important minorities are the Jews, the Armenians, and the Kurds. The Arab-Israeli conflict involves intimately only the two Semitic peoples of the Middle East, the Arabs and the Jews. There is without question much sympathy for the Arabs among Iranians and Turks but this is as much due to their anti-imperialism as to their being co-religionists.

The background to the Arab-Israeli conflict is a compound of competing interests and misunderstandings arising out of World War I. In the interest of winning the war in the Middle East the British made a series of agreements with other European states, with the Jews and with the Arabs. Several of these agreements were mutually incompatible but none more so than those that touched on the area of Palestine. In return for rebelling against the Ottoman Turks, in 1915 the Arabs were promised postwar independence. Excluded from this promise was the area of primary French interest, the eastern Mediterranean coast from the Turkish southern border south to a line running west from Damascus. Quite clearly the area known as Palestine was not to be excluded. A few months later in an agreement with the French, the British promised to help France gain the area later known as "Syria and the Lebanon," and to turn Palestine over to international control. Then in 1917, by the Balfour Declaration, the British agreed that Palestine should become a Jewish homeland. Thus Palestine was promised to the Arabs, to an international administration, and to the Jews all at one time.

At the peace conference the Arab voice was not heard. Faisal, later king of Iraq, went to Paris and London to demand Arab rights; but little attention was paid him. The French were given Lebanon and Syria as mandates, and the British were given Iraq, Transjordan and Palestine. In the latter case, the Conference at San Remo was even more explicit than the Balfour Declaration and changed "*a* Jewish homeland" to "*the* Jewish homeland." Naturally enough the Arabs felt deceived, and due note was taken of statements by some British officers that a Jewish state would be helpful for the British imperial lifeline.[3] The Arabs concluded that the Jewish homeland was essentially a creation of Western imperialism to maintain Western control over an increasingly assertive Arab world. But the simple fact was that Chaim Weizmann and other Zionist leaders had more influence in London and Paris in 1917-1920 than did the Arab leaders.

The interwar period witnessed energetic Jewish efforts to create a homeland in Palestine, increasing Arab bitterness, and a wildly fluctuating British policy.[4] When World War II approached, however, the Arab

---

[3] For the classic account of the Arab treatment in this period and also for some interesting documents, see George Antonius, *The Arab Awakening* (New York: H. Hamilton, 1938).

[4] The best account of this period is found in J. C. Hurewitz, *The Struggle for Palestine* (New York: W. W. Norton & Company, Inc., 1950).

bargaining position improved markedly. The Arab conviction that they were the victims of an Anglo-French-Jewish imperial plot helped German and Italian propagandists greatly in this vital war arena. In order to counter this propaganda advantage, the British adopted a harsh policy toward a Jewish homeland in Palestine, one which remained in effect until after the war.

Despite this British policy, the Arabs could not separate the Arab-Israeli dispute from the struggle against Western imperialism and the modernist-traditionalist conflict. The general Arab assumption was and is that there is a working alliance of Arab traditional leaders, the old colonial power representatives, and the increasingly powerful Zionist leaders. On the domestic level the conservative status quo leaders are struggling against Arab nationalism just as surely as are the British, French, and Zionists on the international level.

The British announced their intention to withdraw from Palestine in 1948, and turned over to the youthful UN a very complex, emotion-ridden issue. Accepting this difficult problem, the UN set up a committee (UNSCOP) to prepare a recommendation for a solution to the Arab-Jewish conflict. After carefully considering the alternatives a majority of the committee came out in favor of partitioning Palestine into Jewish and Arab states and the internationalizing of Jerusalem. The General Assembly, over violent Arab objections, accepted this plan. Open warfare was already being waged on a minor scale but the termination of the British mandate on May 14, 1948, marked the beginning of all-out warfare. Participating against Israel were Lebanon, Syria, Iraq, Jordan, Saudi Arabia, Egypt, and the Palestinian Arabs. On the face of it, such an array of states committed to destroying Israeli independence would seem to have been assured of success. But the Israelis, because of their superior morale and leadership and because of Arab disunity and corruption, emerged victorious. The impact of this defeat on the Arab world was profound. Arab nationalism had been wounded and the Arab nation humiliated. Public opinion turned feverishly to seek out the villains in the case. In every Arab state the leadership, everywhere predominantly traditional, was discredited. At best the charge was corruption, at worst treason.

From January to July 1949, armistice negotiations were concluded between Israel and each of the Arab combatants except Iraq, which lacks a common border with Israel. But peace did not return to the area. Israeli shipping could not pass through the Suez Canal or into the Gulf of Aqaba, and the Arabs organized an economic boycott of Israel. Raids by Arabs against Jews were a daily occurrence. Most of these, however, seemed to have been spontaneous attacks by individual Arabs, usually displaced farmers, nursing grievances against Israel.

No section of Israel is more than a few miles away from an Arab border, and consequently all Israel was on edge from the continuous raiding.

In an effort to force the Arab governments to restrain the raiders and possibly even to persuade the Arab states to formalize the armistice agreements, Israel, at Ben-Gurion's urging, adopted a retaliation policy.[5] Four major raids were conducted against the Arabs between October 14, 1953, and December 11, 1955. Of these, by far the most significant was the Gaza Strip raid of February 28, 1955. Destroyed in the raid was the Egyptian headquarters on this tiny strip of land jutting up along the Mediterranean Sea on Israel's southwestern border and populated by Arab refugees. If Ben-Gurion expected to quiet the Arabs by this show of force, he made a major miscalculation. Arab public opinion was inflamed and demanded redress. Nasser's response was to organize the *Fedayan*, a trained corps of cross-border raiders, and to make a major effort to purchase more arms. Failing with the West, he turned to the Soviet bloc and in late 1955 concluded an agreement for the purchase of Czechoslovak arms. A deadly chain of events had been set into motion that led to the British-French-Israeli attack on Egypt.

The success of Israeli arms on the Sinai Peninsula in 1956 was not without solid returns for Israel despite its having been compelled by United States and UN pressure to withdraw behind the old armistice lines. *Fedayan* raids ceased and the Gulf of Aqaba was opened to shipping. The Suez Canal remained closed to Israeli shipping, however. On the debit side, Arab hostility to Israel and the conviction that Israel had every intention of expanding her borders at Arab expense were strengthened. Eventual Arab-Israeli understanding was farther away than ever.

Intra-Arab Relations

Even before World War I Arab intellectuals were calling for a unification of the so-called Arab nation. As Arab political activity expanded this call was heard with increasing frequency. Today hardly an Arab political organization exists that does not refer to the unification of the Arab nation as a primary goal. But there is little unity of viewpoint on the form of union. Some would like to see a centralized Arab state; others envision a confederacy; and still others have no desire to go much beyond the present Arab League, a loose association of independent states entered into after World War II.

Within the Arab world there are very strong local differences which would make a centralized union difficult to form and to hold together. Historical dislikes and conflicting ambitions for pre-eminence in the union stand in the way of unity. The chief obstacle to Arab unity and the chief determinant of intra-Arab relations, however, has been the modernist-traditionalist conflict. The battle was joined on an international plane in 1955 when Colonel Gamal Abdul Nasser effectively destroyed his tradi-

---

[5] George Lenczowski, *The Middle East in World Affairs* (Ithaca, New York: Cornell University Press, 1958), p. 360, referring to an article by Harry Gilroy in the *New York Times*, Dec. 18, 1955.

tional opposition in Egypt and was ready to lead the modernist, nationalist crusade in the rest of the Arab world. His chief opponent was Iraq's Nuri as-Said and the battle raged both within and without the level of intra-Arab conflict until the summer of 1958.

Syria was the first of the Arab states to join Egypt in the modernist camp. In fact, by 1956 the main domestic political conflicts within Syria were among competing modernist groups, including a small but extremely active communist group. Incongruously, Egypt and Syria were joined in this alliance by Saudi Arabia, the most traditionalist of important Arab states. Ibn Saud, the king of Saudi Arabia, preferred this alliance to one with the traditionalist states of Iraq and Jordan since these were ruled by members of the Hashemite dynasty, the historic enemy of the Saud dynasty.

In late 1955, serious rioting broke out in Jordan against the Baghdad Pact and the traditionalist Jordanian government. This revelation of anti-traditional strength led to a rapid retreat on the part of King Hossein and the Jordanian government which was climaxed by the dismissal of the chief British adviser to the Arab Legion, the famous Glubb Pasha, and Jordan's dramatic move into the Syria-Egypt-Saudi Arabian camp. In the spring of 1956, relatively free elections were held in Jordan which resulted in a smashing victory for the modernists.

In Lebanon an opposite trend was underway. A coup d'état in 1952 resulted in a substantial improvement for the modernist forces. But very quickly the new president, Camille Chamoun, demonstrated that he was far more in sympathy with the traditional elements, and since parliament was in traditional hands, the Lebanese government from 1953 until 1958 moved steadily in the direction of strengthened traditionalist control. Internally, however, the social trend was moving in the opposite direction, and Lebanon moved toward the inevitable explosion.

The situation in October 1956 when Israeli troops launched their attack was one in which Egypt, Syria, and Jordan had modernist governments and were in alliance with the traditionalist Saudi Arabian government. Iraq was the bedrock of the traditionalists and the government of Lebanon scarcely concealed its anti-Nasser attitude. The Suez war strengthened the belief that Israel was a tool of Western imperialism and the modernist suspicion that traditionalist Arab leaders were traitorous. Therefore the traditionalist-modernist struggle became increasingly bitter, and those traditional leaders who had attempted to compromise with the modernists realized that any such compromise could only be temporary and that domestic modernists would doubtless seek their overthrow. By early 1957 both Ibn Saud and Jordan's King Hossein fully understood the threat to their positions. Jordanian nationalist leaders made little secret of their desire to see Jordan give up a precarious independence and pass into a broader Arab union. Hossein, therefore, in the spring of 1957, led a royalist coup d'état and established a dictatorial control under traditionalist direction. Jordan, therefore, left its alliance with Egypt and Syria and moved back into a quiet understanding with Lebanon and Iraq. Ibn Saud at the same time brought his disenchantment with Nasser into the open and, swallowing his dislike of the Hashemites, entered into the formless Iraq-Jordan-Lebanon association.

Very much encouraged by their victories in early 1957, the traditionalist forces joined battle in modernist-dominated Syria. Here, however, they suffered the first of a series of stinging setbacks. An effort to overthrow the Syrian government failed, and the failure was accompanied by the charge of American involvement.[6] Coming on the heels of the Syrian fiasco, an alleged plot against Nasser's life financed by Ibn Saud was announced to a shocked and credulous public.[7] Evidence for this, as for the Syrian charge, is unconvincing, but Ibn Saud's position was weakened to the point that he was compelled to surrender effective power to his modernist-minded brother, Prince Faisal. A few weeks later Syria and Egypt formed the United Arab Republic and it was rumored that this was done because of the headlong flight Syria was making toward communism. Unity with Egypt seemed the only way to stop it.

The center of the stage then shifted to Lebanon. Camille Chamoun's term of office was about to come to an end, and by law he was ineligible for a second term. However, Chamoun made little secret of his belief that he alone could save Lebanon from disaster and that a means had to be found to give him a second term. Open civil war broke out in the spring of 1958 between Arab nationalists and the traditionalists with their Maronite allies. With all eyes focused on this civil conflict, few were prepared for the news that within a matter of hours the supposed "bulwark of the West," the Nuri as-Said government of Iraq, had fallen. Within weeks the victory of the Iraqi modernists was consolidated.

At this point the intra-Arab conflict moved dramatically to the cold war level. Although no effort was made to reverse the Iraqi developments, Western intervention did take place in both Jordan and Lebanon. In the former British troops were flown in to bolster the regime. In the latter, American forces were landed at the request of President Chamoun. But when the American troops left, a few weeks later, Lebanon had a coalition modernist-Maronite government with a rebel nationalist leader as premier. By the fall of 1958, therefore, only Jordan remained solidly in the hands of the traditional leaders and Jordan was no threat to anyone. Modernist Arabs were confident that the days of traditional rule were sharply numbered even in the primitive south.

Having consciously or subconsciously identified the modernist, nationalist movement in the Arab world with President Nasser of the UAR,

---

[6] *New York Times,* Aug. 14, 1957, p. 1; Aug. 17, 1958, p. 10.
[7] *Ibid.,* Mar. 16, 1958, p. 4.

the world was surprised to find that a major split had developed in modernist ranks. The primary challenge to Nasser's leadership came from the leader of the Iraqi coup d'état, General Abdul Karim Kassem. Since Nasser had been extremely popular among Iraq's noncommunist intellectuals and commercial middle class, Kassem turned for support to anti-Nasser communists, the politically unsophisticated lower classes, and the Kurdish tribal leaders. For a time Kassem moved dangerously close to communism, but after mid-1959 he reversed that trend. General Kassem has lacked the popular appeal of Nasser, and his effort in 1961 to absorb the Sheikdom of Kuwait attracted little support among Arabs. Kassem has demonstrated, however, the limits of Nasser's appeal.

A second challenge to Nasser was even stronger. In September, 1961, a remarkably swift and effective coup succeeded in splitting Syria from the UAR. Nasser promptly announced that this was a temporary victory for the imperialist-traditionalist alliance. This argument carries little weight, however, since the new Syrian leaders, although conservative, are clearly of the modernist camp. On the contrary, the very defeat of the Arab traditionalists paved the way for the Syrian defection. With the removal of the cohesive force of a common enemy, the divisive forces operating within the UAR were much too strong for the union to hold.

Iranian-Turkish-Arab Relations

In 1959, when the UN General Assembly was attempting to choose the successor to Japan on the Security Council, Poland and Turkey fought a bitter battle for the vacancy. Turkey, as the most powerful and the most modern of Middle-Eastern states, would seem logically to have been the natural leader of the Middle East and should have been able to count on the solid support of its brother Muslim states. Actually, most of the Arab delegations voted against Turkey. The explanation for this was partly historical; of more importance was the fact that the modernist Arabs regarded Turkey as an ally of the traditionalists. Ironically, Turkey's modernist-traditionalist battle had been won in the nineteen-twenties by the modernists, and all Turkish political factions, conservative and liberal, claimed to be direct descendants of the modernist forces. Turkey's alliance with traditional Middle-Eastern regimes was a fact, however, and was due to Turkey's attitude regarding international affairs, an attitude which in many respects resembled that of the United States and Western Europe. Having been subjected to a military-political-psychological onslaught by Stalin's government at the close of World War II, the Turks were very much aware of the threat posed by the Soviet Union. The Turkish government sought, therefore, to construct a defense frame by which Turkey would be tied to the United States and Western Europe through NATO and also by which Turkey could lead the Middle East into a defensive alliance interlocking with NATO. To this latter proposal the Menderes government of Turkey found the governments of Iraq and Iran openly receptive, the government of Egypt hostile, and the others divided. Very quickly the pattern developed by which traditional-ist-dominated regimes looked with favor on an alliance with Turkey and modernists looked with suspicion on it. By playing such a central role in an effort which was so closely identified by Arab and Iranian modernists with Western imperialism, the Turkish government placed itself (in modernist eyes) in a position essentially similar to that of the traditionalist Nuri regime. Not unnaturally, many Arabs and Iranians assumed that the internal political situation of Turkey resembled that of the Arab states and Iran, with Premier Menderes a Turkish Nuri as-Said. This was not true, however, and although Menderes was conservative and was de-spised by major elements of the Turkish population, the Turkish opposi-tion approved of the general lines of his foreign policy.

In the summer of 1958, at the time of the Iraq revolution, a strong rumor swept the Middle East that Turkish troops would attempt to restore traditionalist rule in Iraq. At this point opposition spokesmen in Turkey argued that Turkey was already being isolated from other Middle-Eastern states and that this action would further estrange Tur-key from the dominant Arab leaders.[8] Two years later, Turkey had its own revolution, but the successor government remained firmly on the side of the West in the cold war. Some effort was made to improve rela-tions with the Arab governments, but Turco-Arab relations are still characterized by mutual suspicion and little understanding of each other's objectives.

Iranian involvement in Middle-Eastern politics is due overwhelmingly to the demands of the cold war. There is little love lost between the Iranians and the Turks or the Iranians and the Arabs, and commerce within the area is sluggish. However, the Iranians are acutely interested observers of Arab political developments and to many modernist Iranians, Nasser's struggles with his foreign and domestic enemies parallel very closely the lost battles in which Iran's very popular premier, Dr. Mo-hammad Mossadeq, struggled with a foreign-supported traditionalist group. For this reason Nasser is popular in Iran with the nationalists and extremely unpopular with the traditionalist government.

UNITED STATES-MIDDLE-EASTERN RELATIONS AND THE COLD WAR

After the Bolshevik Revolution in Russia, the communist leaders re-nounced the old Russian imperialistic policies in the Middle East. At a conference in Baku in 1920 it was agreed that the progress of world com-munism called for the support of bourgeois nationalist and anti-colonial

---

[8] *Ibid.*, July 29, 1958, p. 3.

movements in the Middle East.[9] In the years that followed, however, Soviet policy reflected more the needs of the Soviet economy than of advancing communism. Only after World War II did Stalin turn seriously to the Middle East. Apparently assuming that the United States would once again withdraw from active participation in world affairs, and that the power status of Great Britain had declined drastically, the Soviet Union began preparation in 1944 for a major military-political move. In 1946 the Soviets engineered the taking over of the northern Iranian province of Azerbaijan by local communists and the setting up of a puppet regime. A considerable amount of Soviet military equipment poured into Azerbaijan and moved toward the Turkish border.[10] The move into Azerbaijan coincided with a massive propaganda attack on Turkey which included a demand for Soviet control of the Straits and the cession of two border areas of Turkey to the Soviet Union. Stepped up operations of the pro-communist Greek guerillas occurred simultaneously.

This was the moment of decision for the Truman administration. Instead of following the old isolationist pattern, United States representatives in the Middle East and in the UN asserted strong support for the Iranians and for the Turks, and the Truman Doctrine of 1947 provided the military and economic means to back up the verbal support of Greek and Turkish independence. Rather surprisingly, the Soviets responded to the hard line from Washington by retreating. Soviet troops were withdrawn from Iran and the propaganda assault on Turkey was eased.

From this point until after Stalin's death, Soviet policy in the Middle East was far less obtrusive. Much ground had been lost in Turkey and Iran and to a lesser extent in the Arab lands where brief Soviet support for Israel was bitterly resented. But the Middle East had been placed on notice that it was a prime Soviet target area and as the leadership of Khrushchev was consolidated the tempo of Soviet Middle-Eastern operations was steadily increased.

United States and
the Arab-Israeli Conflict

With the exception of the small communist minorities, the United States policy of standing firmly against the Soviet challenge won the approval of the entire Middle East. But another policy decision of the Truman administration did not fare so well. American sympathy for the Jewish people as a result of Hitler's genocide was extremely strong, and the proposition that the Jews should be permitted to resettle their an-

---

[9] For a good treatment of the theoretical discussions in the Soviet Union concerning their Middle-Eastern policy, see George Lenczowski, *Russia and the West in Iran* (Ithaca, New York: Cornell University Press, 1949), chap. 5.

[10] Robert Rossow, Jr., "The Battle of Azerbaijan," *The Middle East Journal* (Winter 1956), pp. 17-32.

cestral homeland seemed to many Americans simple justice. The Truman administration accurately reflected this sentiment and gave full support to Jewish immigration into and to the creation of an independent Israel. With little or no understanding of the Middle East, Americans generally were simply not concerned with the repercussions of their pro-Zionist attitude in this Muslim area. However, from the Arab point of view, by taking the side of the Jews the United States had associated itself with the traditional Arab-colonial Jewish-power alliance. Whereas previously Americans had been regarded as the natural defenders of the modernists, particularly those of liberal persuasion, the United States had suddenly moved over to the other camp, and a new and radically different image of the United States began to form.

The Anglo-Iranian Dispute

Although the Western powers agreed that the Soviet challenge in the Middle East could best be met by encouraging the creation of stable, noncommunist regimes in the areas, there was growing disagreement as to how this could best be done. The British formula, although never formally pronounced, was apparently to give support to conservative, status quo elements. United States opposition to this line was sporadic and never well formulated, but almost from the beginning there seems to have been a strong current of opinion among concerned United States officials that long-range stability could only be achieved by modernist regimes.

This issue was first joined in Iran in 1951. There the modernist government of Dr. Mohammad Mossadeq sought a fundamental break with the past and believed, as did its supporters, that such a break could only be made if the old Iranian traditionalist-colonial combine was destroyed for all time. Since a major point of its program was the nationalizing of the British government-controlled Anglo-Iranian Oil Company, Iran's new government was of instant and vital concern in the cold war. The British, seeing a very unhealthy precedent being set with regard to Middle-Eastern oil production, toyed with the idea of reversing the situation by force. They were dissuaded from this, in part at least by American pressure, and the suspicion grew into conviction that Mossadeq had the support of the United States. The communist press throughout 1951 referred to Mossadeq as an American agent.[11] Without question the United States did look on the Mossadeq government with some favor. Economic and military aid programs, previously negotiated, were continued during the Mossadeq regime, and even as late as 1953 President Eisenhower told Anthony Eden that Dr. Mossadeq was essential to the task of keeping

---

[11] For example, see *Besuye Ayendeh*, Sept. 26, 1951.

communism out of Iran.[12] The Soviet response to Mossadeq, judging from the tenor of the communist press, was one of intense hostility.

In 1952, however, the United States government became increasingly impatient with Dr. Mossadeq because his preoccupation with the negative goal of destroying British power in Iran was so complete that he was failing to attack constructively Iran's overwhelming problems and was therefore weakening his nation's ability to meet the Soviet challenge. In 1953, United States-Iranian relations deteriorated further until, in August, a coup d'état, which all Iranians believe had American support, ousted Mossadeq.[13] The successor governments were openly anti-communist, but they were also unpopular. For Iranians who regarded Mossadeq as a great patriot, the Shah-dominated government was little better than an Anglo-American puppet regime.

This experience set a pattern for American behavior in dealings with the Arab states. Here, too, an initially favorable response to the appearance of a modernist regime was gradually replaced by hostility and an increasing identification with traditional leaders. The explanation for this behavioral pattern is to be found in the opposite demands of short- and long-range stability. Traditional regimes in the short-run had a real advantage: they understood and opposed the communist threat and sought to establish internal stability. But their long-run stability was seriously to be questioned, and the United States, by permitting itself to be identified with the traditionalist-colonial alliance, ran the risk of incurring the hostility of successor modernist regimes.

The Baghdad Pact and CENTO

For a period of two years after the Free Officer Movement triumphed in Egypt, the United States dealt very sympathetically with the Nasser-dominated government.[14] This policy indicated a realization of the force of the social revolution in Egypt and the necessity for accomodating Western policy to the political manifestations of this revolution, particularly that of Arab nationalism. However, the United States also had a high-priority goal of bringing the Middle East into a Western-supported defensive alliance to mobilize the area against communist expansion. In 1953, Egyptian leaders had told Western statesmen plainly that historic suspicions of Western intentions were too strong and that any Arab government responsive to Arab public opinion could not associate itself with a Western-inspired and supported defense pact.[15] But this was an era of

---

[12] Anthony Eden, *Full Circle* (Boston: Houghton Mifflin Company, 1960), p. 235.

[13] See the extraordinary article by Richard and Gladys Harkness in the *Saturday Evening Post*, Nov. 6, 1954, pp. 66-68.

[14] George E. Kirk, *Contemporary Arab Politics* (New York: Frederick A. Praeger, Inc., 1961), p. 29.

[15] Lenczowski, *The Middle East in World Affairs*, p. 428.

Western thinking in which the creation of defensive alliances ringing the Sino-Soviet bloc was almost a dogmatic compulsion. Consequently the United States and Britain refused to follow Egyptian advice and pressed for a Middle East defense pact with or without Egyptian participation. In 1955, the so-called Baghdad Pact, subscribed to by Turkey, Pakistan, Iran, Iraq and Great Britain, came into existence.

For Nuri as-Said a Middle East defense pact was in many ways ideal. He had to have British military support if his regime was to endure, and the Baghdad Pact, as an international defense agreement, was far more palatable than a bilateral arrangement. The argument that the Baghdad Pact was directed against Soviet aggression and subversion convinced few Arab modernists who came to regard it as nothing more than the latest Western effort to perpetuate the traditionalist-colonial alliance.[16] Iran joined the Baghdad Pact in October 1955, but public opinion was unenthusiastic. In Teheran the pact was seen as a crutch for the traditionalist-supported dictatorship of the Shah. It was immediately and violently denounced in Egypt, and efforts made to bring Syria and Jordan into the pact not only failed but resulted in discrediting the political right in both states. Then finally, after the 1958 coup, the government of Iraq withdrew from the pact, thereafter known as the Central Treaty Organization.

Although Secretary of State John Foster Dulles had fathered the idea, the United States did not formally join the Baghdad Pact. Opposition from Israel and Egypt was so strong that American adherence would have severely damaged American influence in those two areas. However, the United States government associated itself so closely, both militarily and economically, with the pact that failure to sign was only of psychological importance.

The Suez Crisis

The Soviet role up to this point had been remarkably passive, and a Soviet breakthrough did not occur until September of 1955 when the Egyptian arms agreement with Czechoslovakia was concluded. With this agreement the cold war in the Middle East gained momentum, and in the nine months following the United States made an effort to reverse Soviet diplomatic gains. For the Egyptians these were happy months, in which they could watch the United States and the Soviet Union compete for the privilege of financing the construction of the Aswan Dam on the Nile River, an immensely expensive enterprise which was Nasser's answer to the overpopulation problem. But Washington became increasingly annoyed with what it regarded as the arrogance of Nasser's diplo-

---

[16] Caractacus (Pseud.), *Revolution in Iraq* (London: Victor Gallacz, 1959), p. 102.

macy (which culminated in the recognition of the Communist Chinese regime).

On July 19, 1956, shortly after the Egyptians had decided to accept the Western offer to finance the Aswan Dam, Secretary Dulles announced curtly that the deal was off. A good case could be made for this refusal. The cost of its Czech arms purchase was placing a severe strain on Egyptian financial resources; the Senate was unhappy with the arrangement; those Middle-Eastern regimes closely allied with the West argued that the huge grant to Egypt was in effect a reward for neutralism. But the timing and manner of the rejection argue strongly that personal pique on the part of Dulles had much to do with the rejection. Nasser's response was violent. In a furious speech he denounced the West and announced the immediate nationalization of the Suez Canal Company, an internationally owned but Egyptian incorporated concern. By this stroke Nasser apparently hoped to restore some of his damaged prestige.

Nasser's actions placed Secretary Dulles in a difficult position, and although he refused to admit that his withdrawal of the Aswan Dam proposal had precipitated the Suez crisis,[17] he could not ignore the fact that the British and the French held him responsible and were demanding United States assistance to rectify the situation. Dulles, who had been trying to avoid the polarization of the Middle East into modernist-Soviet and traditionalist-Western camps, made a major effort to avoid a showdown. But the British and French, tiring of the endless delays and chafing at what seemed to them a lack of candor on Dulles' part, decided to go their own way. Israel understandably was delighted with the improvement Nasser's difficulties had brought to its international position; but whether the attack Israel launched against Egypt on October 29, 1956, was the result of collusion with the British and French has not been revealed. The time sequence, however, argues strongly in favor of this conclusion. Very shortly after the invasion, Britain and France sent an ultimatum to Egypt and Israel calling for the withdrawal of both parties from a zone ten miles on either side of the Canal. Israel accepted but Egypt would not, and the British and French began bombing Egyptian military targets. At this point the United States and the Soviet Union joined in the UN to denounce the Anglo-French-Israeli action and to demand that Israel withdraw and the British and French cease their attack. This incident furnishes the classic example of the power of the UN when two great powers agree on a course of action. The British and French ceased their attack and withdrew, and a UN force took their place.

The Eisenhower Doctrine

Consequences of the Suez crisis were portentous. Hatred of Israel was intensified; the image of Britain and France as powerful states was weak-

17 Eden, *Full Circle,* p. 486.

ened; and the Soviet Union, despite its actions in Hungary, gained in respect and prestige. With regard to the United States, opinions were mixed. There was general admiration among modernist Arabs and Iranians for the placing of principle before the demands of close allies. But there was confusion as to the real American attitude toward Arab nationalism and Nasser. This confusion was well-justified. Quite clearly Washington was greatly perplexed and uncertain as to what was called for in this period. The administration wished to prevent the Soviets from solidifying their alliance with Nasser and Arab nationalism generally. But at the same time the United States wished to give full backing to the anti-communist, anti-Nasser traditional regimes of Iraq and Iran. With some fanfare, a policy was announced known as the Eisenhower Doctrine. But this doctrine stated only that the United States would assist any Middle-Eastern state requesting assistance against an attack from the Soviet Union or a Soviet-dominated state. Since the Soviet Union was most unlikely to launch a direct attack, and since no Middle-Eastern state was under Soviet control, the doctrine appeared to be virtually meaningless. It was silent on the critical modernist-traditionalist intra-Arab struggle, on the Arab-Israeli conflict, and on communist subversion.

Although the text of the Eisenhower Doctrine offered few clues to American policy in the Middle East, events rapidly defined this policy. Noting that the weak link in the Egypt-Jordan-Syria-Saudi Arabia bloc was the latter state, the administration made the most of the 1956 visit of Ibn Saud to the United States in a fairly obvious effort to widen the breach between Nasser and Saud. Since Saud was by now well aware of the threat posed by Nasser to his traditionalist regime, success for this effort seemed assured. On April 13, 1957, the royalist coup d'état took place in Jordan. Eleven days later the United States announced that preserving the new regime's independence was in tune with the doctrine. The Sixth Fleet was dispatched to Beirut and an airlift of supplies was flown into Jordan over Israeli territory (a fact which Arab nationalists found significant). Ibn Saud now openly associated himself with Iraq and Jordan against Egypt and Syria.

Washington seemed to feel at this point that its policy had met with great success. Of the three allies of Egypt two had now defected. In fact, however, Washington had succeeded in doing precisely what it had attempted to avoid doing in previous years. By associating with the traditionalist Iraqi regime and by helping traditionalists come out on top in both Jordan and Saudi Arabia, the United States was now firmly committed to the traditionalist side. As such, in modernist Arab eyes, it merely took the place of Britain and France in the traditionalist Arab-colonial powers-Israel combine.

The Soviet Union made the most of its opportunities arising from the growing antagonism between the United States and the Arab modernists. Soviet gains in Syria approached the spectacular. With Egypt the domestic gains were few owing to the Nasser dictatorship's tighter controls. But on an international plane Soviet-Egyptian relations were very cordial. A trip by Nasser to the Soviet Union was most successful from the Soviet point of view.

On August 13, 1957, the Syrian government asked that three American officials in Syria leave the country immediately. Ostensibly these men were part of a plot to effect in Syria a coup d'état that would take that country out of the pro-Nasser camp and that would halt Soviet penetration. Whether true or false, this episode marked the turning-point of United States fortunes in the Middle East. Syria moved sharply to the left, and Arab opinion throughout the area became increasingly hostile to the United States. Then only a few months later another defeat was suffered when Ibn Saud had to give up his power. But the climax came in July of 1958 when Nuri as-Said was murdered. With him died United States hopes of building an anti-Nasser, anti-communist bloc in the Arab world. The United States did intervene in the Lebanese civil war, but in the negotiations that followed, President Chamoun's departure was called for and a major shift in power to the opposition nationalists resulted.

Paradoxically, the Iraqi revolution, which brought into power a regime that veered dangerously close to communism, was not without its embarrassing features for the Soviet Union. As long as the Soviets were able to play the role of defender of the modernist Arabs against the United States-traditionalist Arab assault, the relations of the Soviet Union with the UAR were very good. But the internal communist threat in Iraq opened many eyes in the UAR. Gone suddenly was the virulence of the traditionalist threat and in its place was a frightening pro-communist Arab-Soviet combine. President Nasser responded by denouncing strongly the threat of communist subversion. With this Nasser's relations with the Soviet Union cooled and those with the United States quickly improved.

After the Iraqi regime began moving away from communism, Soviet-Nasser relations improved, and the Soviet government did agree to give major financial assistance for the construction of the Aswan Dam. But the cordiality of the pre-1958 period did not return, and in 1961 a significant anti-Nasser propaganda campaign was inaugurated in the communist world. United States relations with Nasser suffer always from the friendship of the United States government, and of individual Americans, with Israel. Also, the policy of the United States in the Congo, Laos, and Cuba have all been denounced by Cairo as old-style Western imperialism. However, the United States in the nineteen-sixties is far more tolerant of "neutralism" than it was in the nineteen-fifties, and may even wish Nasser well in his efforts to give leadership to a neutral third force,

United States Aid
to the Middle East

United States military, economic, and technical aid policies for the Middle East have mirrored the political policies. Turkey, which is the mainstay of the United States defense program in the area, has received the most military and economic aid, with Iran a distant second. Furthermore, aid to Iran increased dramatically after the overthrow of the Mossadeq government. Israel has received more financial aid than all of the Arab states combined, and Jordan in 1960 received $47 million, which is more than double the total given all the other Arab states. Egypt was treated fairly generously from 1952 to 1954, but assistance declined sharply when Egypt moved toward neutralism. Similarly, aid to Iraq stopped after the 1958 coup.

Despite the frequently voiced claim that the United States turns its back on its friends and treats generously the neutrals, the evidence in the Middle East is quite the contrary. The primary criterion for granting aid, except for the special case of Israel, seems to have been a willingness to side with the United States in the cold war. Traditionalist regimes commonly have come close to institutionalizing corruption, and the returns from economic aid to such regimes are modest. Modernist regimes are far less likely to be corrupt and far more likely to engage in really fundamental social and political reform; but since modernist regimes in the Arab and Iranian Middle East are rarely close friends of the United States they have received little assistance.

United States foreign policy in the Middle East has followed some clear patterns. Close ties have been maintained with Turkey and Israel and with traditionalist Arab and Iranian governments. But the traditionalist regimes in the Middle East have now either been replaced or are shaky, and the challenge for the United States in the nineteen-sixties is to assure that the successor modernist regimes, whether neutral or ally, remain on this side of the Iron Curtain.

SUGGESTED READINGS

Adams, Michael, *Suez and After: Year of Crisis*. Boston: Beacon Press, 1958.

Antonius, George, *The Arab Awakening*. Philadelphia: J. B. Lippincott Co., 1939.

Campbell, John C., *Defense of the Middle East: Problems of American Policy*, rev. ed. New York: Frederick A. Praeger, Inc., 1960.

Caractacus (pseudonym of F. S. Snell), *Revolution in Iraq: An Essay in Comparative Public Opinion.* London: Victor Gollancz, Ltd., 1959.

Elwell-Sutton, Lawrence Paul, *Persian Oil: A Study in Power Politics.* London: Lawrence & Wishart, Ltd., 1955.

Fraser-Tytler, Sir William Kerr, *Afghanistan: A Study of Political Developments in Central Asia.* New York: Oxford University Press, Inc., 1950.

Glubb, John Bagot, *A Soldier with the Arabs.* New York: Harper & Brothers, 1958.

Harris, George L. and others, *Iraq: Its People, Its Society, Its Culture.* New Haven: Human Relations Area Files Press, 1958.

Hay, Sir Rupert, *The Persian Gulf States.* Washington, D.C.: Middle East Institute, 1959.

Hourani, A. H., *Syria and Lebanon.* New York: Oxford University Press, Inc., 1946.

Hurewitz, J. C., *Middle East Dilemmas: The Background of United States Policies.* New York: Harper & Brothers, 1953.

———, *The Struggle for Palestine.* New York: W. W. Norton & Company, Inc., 1950.

Johnson, Paul, *The Suez War.* Philadelphia: The Chilton Co., 1957.

Karpat, Kemal H., *Turkey's Politics: The Transition to a Multi-Party System.* Princeton, N.J.: Princeton University Press, 1959.

Kedourie, Elie, *England and the Middle East.* London: Bowes and Bowes Publishers, Ltd., 1956.

Khadduri, Majid, *Independent Iraq: A Study of Iraqi Politics since 1932.* New York: Oxford University Press, Inc., 1952.

Kirk, George, *Contemporary Arab Politics.* New York: Frederick A. Praeger, Inc., 1961.

———, *A Short History of the Middle East.* London: Methuen & Co., Ltd., 1955.

Lacouture, Jean and Simone, *Egypt in Transition.* New York: Criterion Books, Inc., 1958.

Laqueur, Walter Z., *Communism and Nationalism in the Middle East.* New York: Frederick A. Praeger, Inc., 1956.

———, ed., *The Middle East in Transition: Studies in Contemporary History.* New York: Frederick A. Praeger, Inc., 1958.

———, *The Soviet Union and the Middle East.* New York: Frederick A. Praeger, Inc., 1959.

Lenczowski, George, *The Middle East in World Affairs,* 2nd ed. Ithaca, New York: Cornell University Press, 1956.

———, *Oil and State in the Middle East.* Ithaca, New York: Cornell University Press, 1960.

———, *Russia and the West in Iran: 1918-1948.* Ithaca, New York: Cornell University Press, 1949.

Lewis, Geoffrey L., *Turkey.* New York: Frederick A. Praeger, Inc., 1955.

Little, Tom, *Egypt.* New York: Frederick A. Praeger, Inc., 1958.

Marlow, John, *Arab Nationalism and British Imperialism: A Study in Power Politics.* New York: Frederick A. Praeger, Inc., 1961.

Nuseibeh, Nazem Zaki, *The Ideas of Arab Nationalism.* Ithaca, New York: Cornell University Press, 1956.

Polk, William R. and others, *Backdrop to Tragedy: The Struggle for Palestine.* Boston: Beacon Press, 1957.

Rondot, Pierre, *The Changing Patterns of the Middle East.* New York: Frederick A. Praeger, Inc., 1961.

591   THE UNITED STATES AND THE MIDDLE EAST

Royal Institute of International Affairs, *The Middle East: A Political and Economic Survey*, 3rd ed., rev. London: Oxford University Press, Inc., 1958.

Sayegh, Fayez, *Arab Unity: Hope and Fulfillment*. New York: The Devin-Adair Company, 1958.

Shwadran, Benjamin, *Jordan: A State of Tension*. New York: Council for Middle Eastern Affairs Press, 1959.

Thayer, Philip W., ed., *Tensions in the Middle East*. Baltimore: The Johns Hopkins Press, 1958.

Thomas, Lewis V. and Richard N. Frye, *The United States and Turkey and Iran*. Cambridge: Harvard University Press, 1951.

Twitchell, K. S., *Saudi Arabia*, 3d ed. Princeton, N.J.: Princeton University Press, 1958.

Upton, Joseph M., *The History of Modern Iran: An Interpretation*. Cambridge: Harvard University Press, 1960.

Wheelock, Keith, *Nasser's New Egypt*. New York: Frederick A. Praeger, Inc., 1960.

Wynn, Wilton, *Nasser of Egypt: The Search for Dignity*. Cambridge: Arlington Books, 1959.

Yale, William, *The Near East: A Modern History*. Ann Arbor, Michigan: University of Michigan Press, 1958.

Ziadeh, Nicola, *Syria and Lebanon*. New York: Frederick A. Praeger, Inc., 1957.

27

The New Africa and
the United States

Hilton B. Goss
Director, Social Science Division
General Electric Company,
Santa Barbara, California

Africa, the world's second largest continent, became a major concern of the United States only in recent years. Before that it had long been largely a European colonial preserve, guarded with jealous zeal. There was very little American interest in Africa, almost no direct official relations with it, and no United States policy toward the area. Africa was regarded as a place apart, as a region in which the United States had little stake and which could and should be left to Western Europeans to deal with as their political and economic interests dictated.

Nevertheless, relations with specific African areas date back in a few instances to the early days of the United States as a nation. The fledgling American navy fought the Barbary pirates of the North African coast during the first decades of the Republic. The first modern republic in Africa, Liberia, was established in 1847 on the Gulf of Guinea by former slaves who after 1821 had been returned from the United States by the American Colonization Society. The United States was represented at the Berlin conference in 1885, where several European nations agreed on spheres of influence in Africa; territorial partitions were arranged without much consideration of the African peoples; and the Congo Free State was assigned to the personal direction of Leopold, King of the Belgians. Again, at the Algeciras meetings of 1906, the United States was involved in decisions which further clarified European divisions of interest on the African continent. But in the main the United States kept aloof from the European scramble for African territories and the subsequent colonial exploitation of African manpower and material resources. Even in the Middle East, where geographically a connection with the African continent across the Isthmus of Suez might have aroused interest, the involvement of the United States was spasmodic and often indirect—taking place through activities of religious groups, engineers and petroleum resource developers, financial advisers to native rulers, archeologists, and educators.

All this did not mean that some Americans as individuals were not aware of Africa. Through the efforts of explorers, naturalists, humanitarians, missionaries, industrialists, and others, there was considerable interest in and knowledge of this great continent and of its actual and imagined resources. Henry M. Stanley, the journalist-explorer; John Hays Hammond, the mining promoter; Richard Harding Davis, foreign correspondent; Harvey S. Firestone, the rubber magnate; Carl Akeley, the naturalist, and scores of other pioneers brought to Americans factual and intriguing information about the mysteries of the African scene. Nevertheless, for the average American of the nineteenth and early twentieth centuries, Africa was an exciting, distant, and often romantic land, better known in the fiction of Rider Haggard and of the later Hollywood versions from Tarzan to Beau Geste and the exaggerations of "The Sheik" and "White Cargo" than in the facts of world affairs. The fact that approximately ten per cent of Americans had had a common African ancestry made little impression either upon that minority or upon the other ninety per cent.

Africa contains about 11,500,000 square miles, exclusive of some offshore islands, but including the larger islands of Madagascar and Zanzibar. Its population is estimated at approximately 220 million. The increase is 1.8 per cent annually, which, if continued, would mean a doubling of the population in thirty-five to forty years. Africa is as varied in climate as can be imagined, except that it does not extend into the polar zones. It is not well endowed with evenly distributed resources, although it has potentials of water power and minerals. Some areas are rich and productive; others are barren and unpopulated. Some of the continent is overcrowded, and much of it cannot support new settlements. But there are areas of great promise, where the introduction of scientific techniques in agriculture and the use of local labor for light manufacturing might raise living standards appreciably. With many new urban and suburban centers appearing on the African map, and improvements in transportation and communication altering the old ways, the primitive economies of most African areas have been undergoing rapid change. Along with a political revolution in much of Africa, the period since World War II has been characterized by an economic evolution that has its revolutionary aspects as well. Unfortunately, the aspirations of many of the Africans for economic betterment and industrialization will be difficult to satisfy. But in spite of the difficulties, the Africans of the emerging free nations have great faith in the future of their countries.

There is no general agreement on how the African continent should be subdivided for purposes of discussion. The Mediterranean coast of North Africa is in some respects an extension of Southern Europe, although the predominantly Muslim population of the nations from Morocco on the west to Egypt on the east give a color and culture to the region that are distinctly its own. South of this coastal strip, the Atlas Mountains and the vast Sahara in past ages posed barriers to large-scale intercourse between the peoples of the Mediterranean littoral and those of the equatorial belt—where river valleys, rain forests, jungles, and semi-arid plateaus further isolated tribal groups. Today, as in much of the rest of Africa, air transportation and expanding road networks are erasing these barriers, but sub-Saharan Africa is still regarded as a fairly well-defined portion of the continent in terms of political development, economic status, and cultural background, as well as geographic identity.

Within both North Africa and Africa South of the Sahara there are many diversities of topography, climate, political and cultural heritage, and other factors. For the most part, when present-day events in Africa are reported and analyzed, it is important to differentiate among the various territories. While it is still possible to generalize about Africa and African affairs in survey discussions, the danger lies in confusing what few and isolated characteristics the continent and its people have in common with the marked differences that continue to prevail. Although it is true that the most spectacular advances toward political self-rule have recently occurred in tropical Africa, the developments in Morocco, Algeria, and Tunisia have been just as striking in their way, and so have those in the quite dissimilar territories of the Union of South Africa and the Rhodesias. All together, the diverse countries of Africa comprise one of the world's least homogenous entities. Separately they merit and require attention as individual units each with problems, potentialities, and places in the study of international affairs peculiarly their own.

UNITED STATES AND AFRICA: 1940-1955

With the 1935 Italian invasion of the remote and feudal kingdom of Ethiopia (or Abyssinia as it was likewise known), Africa, as well as Europe and Asia, became an area to watch for signs of the coming storm. Americans read and heard of the Italian conquest, with its atrocities and its uneven pitting of modern weapons against the spears and primitive shields of the Abyssinian tribesmen. Air-bombing of civilians became commonplace. The plight of Haile Selassie as he toured the European capitals and sought assistance from the League of Nations aroused sympathy in the United States. But as the Italians swiftly conquered Ethiopia, and European imperialists continued to look on Africa as a place for expansion, the United States, while concerned, regarded all this as relatively insignificant in view of the threats to world peace that followed in rapid succession in Spain, China, Austria, and Czechoslovakia, and climactically, in Poland in 1939.[1]

World War II Awakens American Interest in Africa

The campaigns of World War II for the first time acquainted thousands of Americans with the realities of African problems. While the bulk of American personnel was concentrated along the northern rim of the continent—from the Atlantic shores of Morocco to the delta of the Nile—considerable numbers in uniform or as civilian adjuncts to the military effort were stationed in such remote areas as the Belgian Congo, Eritrea, the Union of South Africa, Kenya, and the Anglo-Egyptian Sudan—to name but a few of the regions.

During these war years many mistaken judgments were formed on both sides, yet there was widespread recognition on the part of the Africans that the United States was somehow different from the European colonial powers, and, on the part of the Americans, that the Africans were individuals with aspirations for freedom and with talents for self-expression in terms of skills and arts. From World War II onward American involvement in African affairs, although it developed slowly in the next decade, was a reality. And the revolution that the war generated in Africa had real impact upon the foreign policies of the United States.

America's Economic Stake in Africa

American economic interests in Africa up to the war years had been slight: rubber plantations in Liberia (just beginning to be productive), mining enterprises in South Africa and the Rhodesias as well as minority investments in the copper mines of the then Belgian Congo, and some commercial activities where the sale and distribution of American products were competitively advantageous.

Between the close of the war and 1950, United States private investments in Africa more than doubled, although they still remained relatively small, amounting to about $300 million—or 2.3 per cent of total American direct investments abroad.[2] Moreover, they were concentrated geographically, about two-thirds of the total being in South Africa and Liberia. There was almost no American investment in the dependent territories, and the processing and sale of petroleum products accounted

---

[1] The Spanish Civil War (1936-39) had some of its beginnings in the African Spanish protectorate of Morocco across the Straits of Gibraltar from the Iberian peninsula.

[2] A brief analysis of American-African economic relations is contained in "The African Economy and International Trade" by Andrew M. Karmack, a chapter in *The United States and Africa* (New York: The American Assembly, Columbia University, 1958).

for at least one-half of this amount. In Liberia, the Bomi Hills iron ore deposits attracted American developers and the improvement of the harbor at Monrovia during the war led to increased trade with the small republic. Motor roads were constructed and a railroad—the country's first—was built to carry ore to the seacoast. In Morocco several American enterprises began operations. And, mainly in the English-speaking territories, American products and representatives of American industries appeared with increasing frequency. In spite of European domination of most of Africa, American trade was beginning to penetrate the continent's markets, partly because of the inability of war-ravaged colonial powers to supply the accelerated demands of the African economy for the machinery, tools, and utilitarian products required by an advancing civilization.

Africa's Political Links with Europe

Because of the political ties existing between the European colonial powers and the African territories most of the public funds spent on technical assistance and economic development in the years just before the wave of independence came from the parent nations. Particularly notable examples were the Colonial Welfare and Development Fund offered by the United Kingdom and the *Fonds d'Investisement pour le Développement Economique et Social de France d'Outre-Mer*, its French counterpart. The direct contribution of the American government to economic growth was slight, although beginnings were made in Liberia and Ethiopia during this period with programs that expanded as the nineteen-fifties passed. The United States government also spent large sums to develop military bases in Morocco, Libya, and to a lesser degree in Eritrea, thereby affecting the economies of those territories, especially in the localities immediately surrounding the defense installations.

At the close of World War II there were only four independent African countries—Liberia, Egypt, Ethiopia, and the Union of South Africa. The remainder of the continent was under the protection, domination, or control of non-African powers. Italy had lost its colonies—Libya, Eritrea, Somaliland, and the conquered nation of Ethiopia. But under subsequent trusteeship arrangements with the UN the Italians administered Somaliland, while Britain and the United States jointly served as temporary guardians for Libya, and Eritrea was administered by British occupation forces.[3] All the other European colonial nations—Great Britain, France,

---

[3] The tangled situation of the former Italian possessions is too complex to chronicle here. John Gunther treats the subject journalistically in *Inside Africa* (New York: Harper & Brothers, 1955). Professor A. A. Castagno has written numerous scholarly articles on the former Italian colonies, and Henry S. Villard, "Libya: Experiment in Independence," *Current History*, XXXVII, (July 1959), 7-12, serves as an introduction to his publications on that part of the Italian empire.

Belgium, Portugal, and Spain—retained the territories they had held at the outbreak of the war.

Thus, the United States could deal directly only with the four independent nations. Matters relating to the other areas of Africa first had to be taken up in London, Paris, Brussels, Lisbon, or Madrid. This consider-

TABLE 3

POLITICAL STATUS OF AFRICAN TERRITORIES: 1945

Independent Nations

Egypt	(1922)	Liberia	(1847)
Ethiopia	(1896)*	Union of So. Africa	(1910)

* Under Italian rule, 1936-41.

International Rule

Anglo-Egyptian Sudan	(UK-Egypt)	Italian Somaliland	(UN)**
British Cameroons	(UN)*	Libya	(UN)**
British Togoland	(UN)*	Ruanda-Urundi	(UN-Belgium)*
Eritrea	(UN)**	Southwest Africa	(UN)***
French Cameroon	(UN)*	Tanganyika	(UN-UK)*
French Togoland	(UN)*	Tangier	(International Comm.)

* UN trusteeship territories, formerly League of Nations mandates.
** Former Italian colonies under UN guardianship pending treaty of peace between Allies and Italy.
*** League of Nations mandate retained by Union of South Africa through refusal to accept transfer of territory to UN trusteeship administration.

Belgian Rule

Belgian Congo

French Rule

Algeria*	French Somaliland
Comoro Islands	French West Africa
French Equatorial Africa	Madagascar
French Morocco (Protectorate)	Tunisia (Protectorate)

* Integral part of French Republic.

*Portuguese Rule**

Angola	Portuguese Guinea
Cape Verde Islands	Principe
Mozambique	Sao Tome

* All regarded after 1954 as Overseas Territories and integral parts of the Portuguese nation.

Spanish Rule

Spanish Guinea	Ifni
Spanish Morocco (Protectorate)	Spanish Sahara

United Kingdom Rule

Basutoland	(P)*	Northern Rhodesia	(P)
Bechuanaland	(P)	Nyasaland	(P)
British Somaliland	(P)	Sierra Leone	(C/P)
Gambia	(C/P)	Southern Rhodesia	(C)
Gold Coast	(C)	Swaziland	(P)
Kenya	(C/P)	Ugandi	(P)
Nigeria	(C/P)	Zanzibar	(Protected Sultanate)

* Designation P = Protectorate, C = Colony, C/P = Colony and Protectorate contained in one territory.

ably obstructed rapid action, understanding (since three parties were initially involved), and a clear interchange of views. When questions did arise in Washington concerning African matters, the United States was unable to secure information readily, even though relations at the time might be quite friendly with the parent power in Europe. In like manner, native African leaders had no direct way of bringing to the attention of the United States government the problems facing their peoples, or, in fact, of officially soliciting the aid of the United States in their quest for freedom. But as various African territories attained independence during the fifteen years after 1945, it became possible for American officials to work directly with their leaders. These, briefly, were the conditions under which the United States developed a relationship with the Africa of the years after 1945.

Emerging Relationships

Much of African knowledge of the United States at this time was acquired during the war and from doubtfully reliable sources. However, a very few African natives had come to the United States in search of education. Mainly they had studied at small sectarian schools and seminaries. Kwame Nkrumah, later President of Ghana, received some of his college education in the United States, as did Nnamdi Azikiwe, Governor General of Nigeria, and Dr. Hastings Banda, nationalist leader working for the independence of Nyasaland. A number of younger members of the various African independence movements have studied at American colleges and universities in recent years, as have many junior educators and technicians who are providing strength to the developing African nations. In addition, Africans who went from British colonies to the United Kingdom or from French colonies to Paris for study, political training, or technical proficiency, became aware of America's position in the world. But this slight exposure did not cause any great impact upon the masses of Africans—at least not for some time.

During this same period American academic institutions gave increased attention to Africa. This was partially an outgrowth of the "area study" programs so popular during and after World War II. Whereas previously a few anthropologists, archeologists, historians, economists, geographers, or political scientists had specialized in particular aspects of the African scene in terms of their disciplinary interests, there now sprang up a number of "institutes."[4] Leading newspapers and periodicals gave more space to news and views about Africa and books about that continent began to

---

[4] Those at Northwestern University, Boston University, the Johns Hopkins School of Advanced International Studies, Duquesne University, and the University of California at Los Angeles are characteristic examples.

appear in respectable numbers.[5] By 1958, sufficient interest had been displayed by scholars and government officials in the interchange of knowledge on African subjects to justify the organization of an African Studies Association similar in concept and function to those professional groups devoted to other geographical areas or subject fields.

Still, the bulk of the American people were not very interested in Africa or its problems. As a general position, Americans were against "colonialism." Their own experience with it had been an unhappy one and they were proud of their record in helping Cuba win her freedom and in granting Philippine independence. Those who thought about the dilemma faced in the contradictions of the alliance system and beliefs in "self-determination of all peoples" were few in comparison to the many who wished to ignore or forget the whole matter.

If the United States had any basic policy toward Africa, it was difficult to discover; it certainly had not been put into any form for statesmen to voice. Occasionally some event in that far-off continent would arouse a momentary interest on the part of the few who knew of the gathering tensions. Perhaps those most acutely aware of the significance of what was happening in Africa between 1945 and the early nineteen-fifties were to be found in the military services, in a few places in the State Department, and among the academicians doing research at home or in the field. Among the first two groups security considerations limited their abilities to bring the problems into the open. And the academicians were still too few in numbers to gain the attention of citizens who were being bombarded by warnings of perils in Europe, the Far East, the Soviet Union, India, the Middle East, and Southeast Asia, not to mention those closer at home in the Congress, the administration, and in the colleges and universities themselves. Africa was not yet a "crisis area," and until it became so the publicists and the public had plenty to keep their attention constantly shifting elsewhere.

PROBLEMS AND ISSUES
IN CONTEMPORARY RELATIONSHIPS

Aside from the instance of Libya, which was granted independence by UN action in 1951, the United States has had very little direct part in the rush toward freedom that has characterized the African scene in recent years. In those cases where independence came as the result of a promise

---

[5] John Gunther's *Inside Africa* perhaps did most to make Americans aware of African problems. The report of the trip made in the autumn of 1955 by Representative Frances P. Bolton (R., Ohio) to twenty-four territories of Africa south and east of the Sahara, and the many showings of the films of her journey also had considerable influence. See *Report of the Special Study Mission to Africa, South and East of the Sahara,* 84th Cong., 2d sess., House of Representatives, Committee on Foreign Affairs (Washington: Government Printing Office, 1956). Committee Print.

by the UN, the United States can be said to have participated. Partially because the United States had not been a member of the League of Nations there was no direct role for her to play in Africa when the old mandate system was transformed into the UN trusteeship arrangements. In most of the actions that created new nations in Africa the parties involved were the European colonial powers and the subject territories. Thus the United States was virtually compelled to accept a series of *faits accomplis.*

It is not possible to say at this time what influence the United States, through diplomatic or other means, may have exercised upon the European power or the African territory. Some commentators have professed to see the handiwork of Americans in behind-the-scenes actions that hastened the independence of the former Belgian Congo, or in the arrangements the French made to relinquish their protectorate over Morocco. Likewise, certain Europeans have indicated that they believe pressures were brought to bear upon British government officials to accelerate the timetables for granting independence to their colonies in Africa. Flat denials of such accusations can never convince everyone who wishes to believe that nations operate through means of this sort. Nor is it easy to identify what is a pressure and what is merely a re-emphasis of something that is already, without any ulterior motive, exerting its weight on a given situation.

It does seem evident that the United States, in common with much of the remainder of the world, was not prepared for the pace with which colonial territories in Africa gained their independence between 1955 and 1960.

Certain Americans knew and said that freedom was coming, but their time sense was as far wrong as was that of other people. Or, if they were somewhat more prescient, their voices were not heard above the clamor over more immediate crises. The vote of the Sudanese for independence was not regarded as much of a weather-vane, for the deterioration of the British position in the Nile country was a fact taken into account ever since the disorders in Egypt had forced the British to withdraw from the area they had dominated for so many years. Nor were the French agreements with Morocco and Tunisia seen as significant straws in the wind, for there also the European position had been somewhat tenuous because of French weakness during and after World War II.

What really brought the United States—and, in fact, much of the rest of the world—to a realization that the days of "colonialism" in Africa were numbered was the outright grant of independence to the Gold Coast colony by the British government.[6] Here, for the first time, a predomi-

---

[6] The Gold Coast had never been heavily colonized by the British, mainly because of the unhealthful climate. In 1955, out of a population of 4,500,000, only 10,000 Europeans (whites) lived there.

TABLE 4

CHRONOLOGY OF AFRICAN INDEPENDENCE: 1951-1961

Year		Territory Achieving Independence
1951	Libya	(Tripolitania, Cyrenica)
1956	Sudan	(Anglo-Egyptian Sudan)
	Morocco	(French and Spanish Morocco, Tangier)
	Tunisia	
1957	Ghana	(Gold Coast)
1958	Guinea	(French West Africa)
1960	Cameroon	(French trust territory)
	Togo	(French trust territory)
	Togoland	(British trust territory, added to Ghana)
	Niger	(French West Africa)
	Chad	(French Equatorial Africa)
	Central African Republic	(French Equatorial Africa)
	Ivory Coast	(French West Africa)
	Voltaic Republic	(French Equatorial Africa)
	Senegal	(French West Africa)
	Mali	(French West Africa)
	Dahomey	(French West Africa)
	Gabon	(French Equatorial Africa)
	Congo Republic	(French Equatorial Africa)
	Malagasy Republic	(Madagascar)
	Somalia	(British Somaliland and Italian trust territory)
	Republic of the Congo	(Belgian Congo)
	Nigeria	(British West Africa)
	Mauritania	(French West Africa)
1961	Sierra Leone	(British West Africa)
	Tanganyika	(British East Africa trust territory)

Note: This table should be compared with Table 3, page 597. The designation in parentheses indicates the identification of the territory before independence.

nantly African nation was established. A native African people had persuaded their European "masters" that they should be free. And this was accomplished not with violent revolutionary conflict or long and costly military effort, but mainly with parliamentary debate, voting, and friendly negotiation. This had happened elsewhere in the world, but never in Africa.

Official opinion in the United States welcomed the news. The Gold Coast—or Ghana, as the country was named when it became independent in March 1957—provided the first example of a basic American principle applied to modern Africa—the right of peoples to achieve freedom through orderly political processes. As a revolutionary nation itself, the United States could cite many parallels, not all of them exact or appropriate, in rejoicing over the admission of Ghana to the UN, hopefully as an added adherent to the cause of the "Free World" in its containment of the Soviet threat. Initial United States reactions were instinctive and, in the main, praiseworthy. But they were scarcely based on an appreciation of what Africans were like or on a knowledge of the forces Ghanian independence would most certainly let loose throughout what the French call *L'Afrique Noire*. The presence among the Commonwealth Prime Ministers of a colorfully robed Nkrumah delighted the press photographers and reflected credit on the liberality of the British Conservative party. But the fire set by Nkrumah's ascent to the first minister's place has blazed throughout most of Africa ever since and gives no indication of dying down for a long time to come.

An American Dilemma

One of the most troublesome and delicate issues to vex the United States in the postwar period has been the conflict between its desire to support the self-determination of peoples and to remain on good terms with its European allies, several of whom were colonial powers. The conflict has been particularly acute as Africa has moved toward freedom and NATO has been regarded as the cornerstone of the American alliance system.[7]

Of the fifteen members of NATO, five were deeply committed in Africa. And even Spain was brought into the NATO orbit through arrangements whereby the United States was given air and naval base privileges on Spanish soil. Therefore, any action that upset European control of African territories could have serious repercussions upon the strength and unity of NATO. Just as seriously, whenever the NATO structure was weakened, either because of domestic affairs within one of the member nations or because of quarrels between them, one of the first manifestations of this weakness was likely to appear in the temper of unrest in the African possessions of the major NATO powers—France, Britain, or Belgium.

Examples of this are the effect upon NATO's fortunes of the Moroccan, Algerian, Congo, and Suez crises, and the Portuguese troubles in Angola. French military commitments to NATO forces have several times been weakened or unfulfilled because of the French government's decision to use troops in Algeria to combat native rebels. Belgium withdrew some support from NATO as a show of displeasure with UN actions—including those in which the United States took part—during the most acute phases of the Congo troubles following the achievement of Congolese

---

[7] One of the earliest American symposia on modern Africa was held in 1953 at the University of Chicago. To the published collection of papers Professor Hans J. Morgenthau contributed an essay on "United States Policy Toward Africa," which recognized the dilemma stressed above while Africa was largely a colonial domain. See Calvin W. Stillman, ed., *Africa in the Modern World* (Chicago: University of Chicago Press, 1955), pp. 317-25.

independence in the summer of 1960. The opposition expressed by the Portuguese to the 1961 vote of the United States in the UN on the issues of colonialism and Angola was reflected in their dissatisfaction with NATO arrangements. Likewise, African independence leaders have used economic and political turmoil in the European nations then controlling their territories to press for freedom.

Two of the earliest instances of the advantages taken by African nationalist movements of political developments in Great Britain were the Egyptian pressures to force the British out of their military positions in the Nile delta country at the close of World War II, and the strikes promoted by the native leaders in the Gold Coast in 1948. Both of these actions capitalized on the postwar disorganization of the British economic and social structure as well as upon the existence in Britain of a Labour government in which opposition to colonialism was strong. The weakness of the Fourth Republic at home and in Indochina during the nineteen-forties and early nineteen-fifties encouraged nationalist leaders in French Africa to press for concessions, many of which were included in the arrangements offered by General de Gaulle when he assumed power in 1958. And the failure of the Franco-British military effort at Suez in the autumn of 1956 indicated to many Africans that they could proceed with a boldness that was previously impossible or impolitic.

On many occasions during the past decade, the United States has been faced with a dilemma—either in UN balloting or in its relations with its NATO partners—of whether to support the independence movements in Africa and thus embarrass or alienate its European allies, to support its allies and antagonize the Africans, or to abstain from voicing its choice and thus anger both. Officially, abstention has often been the course. Early in 1961, the United States took a somewhat different stand in the UN by voting on several questions involving Africa rather than abstaining. These votes—on the condemnation of colonialism, and on the disapproval of policies pursued by Portugal and the Union of South Africa, for example—appeared to put the United States on the side of the new African nations and in opposition to its NATO allies. Although the anti-colonial Africans were pleased, many of the Europeans were antagonized. One of the facts of the alliance system was that it weakened the American position in the eyes of many Africans seeking independence, however much it may have strengthened the United States and its allies in their military stand against the communist bloc. The "dilemma" of the United States in dealing with these problems is illustrative of an important truth: it is the nature of international relations, as in society generally, that decisions can rarely, if ever, be satisfactory or popular all around.

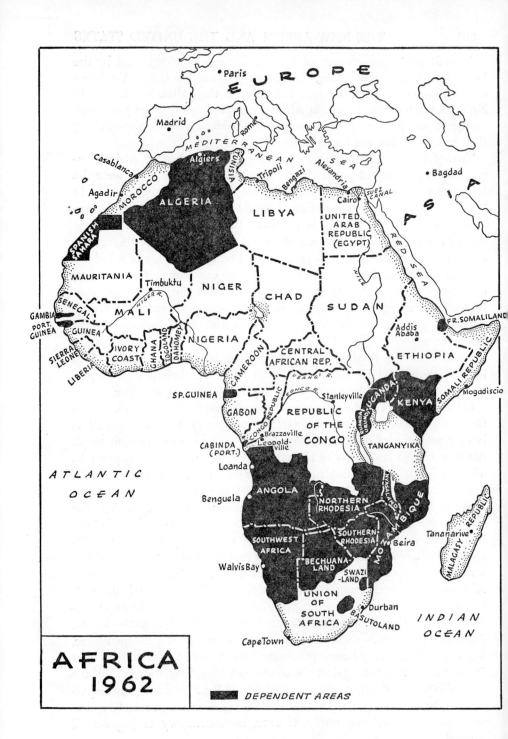

THE POWERS OF A AND THE UNITED STATES

• Paris

EUROPE

Madrid

MEDITERRANEAN SEA

Casablanca

Agadir

MOROCCO

Algiers

TUNISIA

Tripoli

Bengazi

Alexandria

Cairo

SUEZ CANAL

• Bagdad

ASIA

ALGERIA

LIBYA

UNITED
ARAB
REPUBLIC
(EGYPT)

RED SEA

SPANISH SAHARA

MAURITANIA

Timbuktu

NIGER

CHAD

SUDAN

NILE

Addis
Ababa

FR. SOMALILAND

GAMBIA

PORT. GUINEA

SENEGAL

NIGER R.

MALI

GUINEA

SIERRA LEONE

LIBERIA

IVORY
COAST

GHANA

TOGOLAND

DAHOMEY

NIGERIA

CAMEROON

CENTRAL
AFRICAN REP.

UBANGI R.

ETHIOPIA

SOMALI REPUBLIC

Mogadiscio

SP. GUINEA

GABON

CONGO REPUBLIC

CONGO R.

Stanleyville

REPUBLIC
OF THE
CONGO

UGANDA

KENYA

CABINDA
(PORT.)

Brazzaville

Leopold-
ville

TANGANYIKA

ATLANTIC

OCEAN

Loanda

Benguela

ANGOLA

NORTHERN
RHODESIA

NYASALAND

MOZAMBIQUE

Beira

SOUTHERN
RHODESIA

Tananarive

MALAGASY REPUBLIC

SOUTHWEST
AFRICA

WalvisBay

BECHUANA-
LAND

SWAZI-
LAND

UNION
OF
SOUTH
AFRICA

BASUTOLAND

Durban

INDIAN

OCEAN

CapeTown

AFRICA
1962

DEPENDENT AREAS

604

Objectives Toward the New Africa

As has been indicated, so long as most of Africa was controlled by European powers, American policy-makers had first to consider what effect any policy toward Africa might have upon relations with their NATO partners. Now the situation had changed materially. As new nations were created, the United States could deal with them directly. Thus, it becomes appropriate to examine the objectives of the United States toward this quite different situation in Africa. These secondary objectives should, of course, further the more basic foreign policy objectives of the United States, discussed previously in this volume—building a new world order, security, economic, humanitarian, etc.

Basically, American policies for Africa will be concerned with: (1) political stability, since without this little hope exists for future peace and development in the area; (2) technical, social, and economic advances, wherein the pace of growth will be determined as much by the desires of the African people as by their resources; (3) involvement of African countries in the cold war, with the possible creation of an Afro-Asian bloc in international affairs.

American policies and objectives toward Africa, therefore, will, or should be

(1) to help the African nations achieve political stability, without attempting to dictate the forms of government that would be acceptable to the United States;

(2) to provide opportunities for Africans to obtain educational advantages through exchange of persons and ideas, and to support their educational systems by providing economic assistance and capital;

(3) to cooperate in efforts to improve standards of health and social welfare;

(4) to stimulate economic development, consonant with the promotion of economic systems that afford the Africans the best chances to become self-sustaining;

(5) to employ the prestige and influence of the United States to persuade its European allies still ruling territories in Africa to prepare them for orderly and eventual self-determination of their future status;

(6) to assure the new African nations that the United States will strive to prevent Africa from becoming an arena of combat in the cold war competition.

In expressing and implementing these objectives, the United States should be aware of the dangers. To avoid misunderstandings and misinterpretations, American leaders could call upon the reservoir of good will already existing wherever the record of their dealings with under-developed areas is known. And more use could be made of agencies, such as the UN, presently engaged in assistance to new countries.

Mixed with these objectives, of course, is the "image" the United States wishes to present to the newly emergent African nations. It should be clear that the American intent, ever since it began recognizing the fact of African independence, was to show itself as the friend of the Africans. This has not always been easy. The violence attending efforts to desegregate schools in the Southern states, racial discrimination, official American treatment of racial minorities in the past, the support given by the United States to the colonial powers in the UN—all receive much publicity in Africa and do incalculable harm to the image the government prefers to project. But where it was possible—through the work of the United States Information Agency, other governmental offices, and the variety of private and semipublic efforts—some small successes have been registered. The task of explaining United States attitudes and policies to Africans offers one of the most demanding challenges for future good relations between the peoples of the two continents.

Need for Stability

Problems of political stability were at the base of the American policy toward Africa. The events of the latter half of 1960 and 1961 in the former Belgian Congo were adequate testimony to the need for such stability before anything else of much consequence could be accomplished to build up the effectiveness of a new nation. Wherever political instability persists, there is considerable danger that tensions will involve both great and small nations in open conflict. Therefore, it is to the interest of the United States that every possible effort be made to help these new African states establish sound and workable governmental systems. This does not mean that the United States should intervene to dictate the form of government or to put too much pressure on the official decision-makers. But it does require alertness to the opportunities to assist these new countries toward political maturity.

It would seem that such an end could be achieved in several ways. As already suggested, one of these is collective effort through the UN. Another is through American offers to provide training and education for governmental administrators. And a third might be the encouragement of well-designed moves to unite several African nations into viable federations where existing talents—slim as they are—could be made available for a wider sharing by those who need help in carrying out the ordinary governmental public service functions. The paucity of native experience in staffing post offices, tax bureaus, public health administrations, educational facilities, river, harbor, and transportation improvements, labor pools, agricultural programs, police forces, etc., is commonplace in the new African states. Without a firm foundation for carrying on these and other necessary operations, political stability is not likely to be achieved in time to prevent unsettling conditions leading to disorders, revolutions, or collapse.

Consideration should also be given to the ways in which the United States might make direct contributions through programs of foreign aid. A number of requests for technical assistance and economic aid have been presented to Washington by the African governments and some have been answered through development loan funds, dispatch of technical advisers and instructional teams, and promises to study the needs of the newly independent nations. In addition, the United States has cooperated in the activities of the United Nations Economic Commission for Africa. The first project approved for President Kennedy's Peace Corps was a survey and building program for roads in Tanganyika on the eve of that territory's independence in 1961. Gradually the United States might become involved in a series of programs, on both local and inter-country scales, where American technical and managerial skills could help to promote stability in the new African states so that private capital would find conditions safe and attractive for investment. Congressional attitudes in recent years toward long-term foreign aid commitments have been uncertain or hostile. As a result, American efforts to work out aid policies with continuity have been hampered. Something has been accomplished in spite of difficulties both in Washington and in the field. But the United States has faced the added task of trying to convince its European allies that they should take up a larger share of the burden of assisting underdeveloped areas. However, all factors contributing to instability—whether they are political, economic, or social—must be looked at together so that policy determinations may be reached as intelligently and speedily as possible.

In looking at United States objectives toward Africa, one can see many areas of concern. It is not likely that the United States will ever have a fully enunciated policy for each African nation, or for all the individual African situations in the years to come. Only in 1958 did the State Department appoint an Assistant Secretary for African Affairs. Before that time Africa had been lumped, in State Department organizational concerns, with the Middle East and Southeast Asia. Between 1950 and 1960 the number of foreign service posts in Africa grew from twenty-one to forty. This demonstrates how recently Africa has become a concern for United States policy-makers. Such speed does not make for an orderly development of well-thought-out policy positions. Even deep consideration given to what United States national policies toward modern Africa should be must result in some indefiniteness.[8]

As a central factor in American relations with Africa it must be borne in mind that the attractions of non-alignment for the Africans will pull strongly during the coming decade. The views of administration leaders, as expressed in public statements and in actions in the UN—especially after the succession to office of Secretary of State Christian Herter and the advent of the new administration in January 1961—indicated an abandonment of the effort to entice the new African nations, as well as others in similar circumstances, into joining the noncommunist alliance system. The price of gaining African support for American objectives becomes incalculably high if the United States demands military bases, mutual defense treaties, and anti-communist solidarity within and outside the UN. As does the rest of the world, the United States recognizes that Africa could become a battleground for a struggle between opposing power blocs and that, once the fight was joined, it would be difficult to confine the weapons employed to non-lethal varieties. In the cold war, Africa affords a tempting place for testing economic, political, and psychological maneuvers, much as did Spain for deadlier devices during 1936-39. This in itself would be dangerous enough, but in addition Africa has to some degree become the scene of the first skirmishes in a war between the races. While the interracial troubles in South Africa, the Congo, Angola, Kenya, and elsewhere on the continent have had more than one cause, in each instance "whites" (or Europeans) and "blacks" (or Africans) have clashed in serious affrays. It is apparent, therefore, that the United States should have as an overriding objective the prevention of such a catastrophe. To avoid this danger, American interests—both selfish and altruistic—lie in assisting the Africans to develop their own institutions and inherent potentials to the end that Africa shall become an area of cooperation, rather than a prize to be won or a continent to be fought over by the "new" imperialists.

African Expectations of the United States

With twenty-nine independent nations in Africa at the end of 1961 (as contrasted with four a decade earlier), it is impossible to present a de-

---

[8] This is shown by the conclusions of the study group at Northwestern University which in 1959 provided the Senate Committee on Foreign Relations with a series of recommendations. See "United States Foreign Policy: Africa," A Study by Program of African Studies, Northwestern University, for the Committee on Foreign Relations, United States Senate, No. 4. Government Printing Office (Oct. 1959). This study suggests that United States policy toward Africa still tends to be vague, contradictory, and, where it is less indefinite, based upon reactions to Soviet bloc initiative. The difference between the 1959 Northwestern study and the study made the previous year (*The United States and Africa*) in terms of policy suggestions is indicative of the advances made in thinking about Africa in the space of a single year.

tailed examination of the attitudes of each toward the United States. This will become even more difficult, because there will likely be a dozen or more new African nations before another decade has passed. The differences between these nations are often greater than are those between the countries of the Western Hemisphere. Certainly it is hardly possible to conceive of a truly compatible alignment between Ghana and the Union of South Africa, although both were until recently fellow members of the Commonwealth. And the fact that Tunisia and the UAR are both Arab nations scarcely unites them in a mutually trustful embrace. However, limitations of space allow only some over-all views on the objectives African nations may have with respect to the United States.

Perhaps the overriding objective is the most obvious—that African nations wish, one and all, to be free to develop their own ways of life without outside dictation or coercion. Therefore, they will regard with distaste any attempt on the part of the United States to say what shall be their goals and methods. In most cases, the United States has avoided doing just that and the Africans are grateful for her forbearance. If the United States can maintain this policy, and can resist the temptation to want to set everything and everyone "straight," much good will can be generated in Africa.

In the slightly more developed countries, such as the Union of South Africa, and, to a lesser degree, the coastal rim of Morocco, Tunisia, Egypt, and a future autonomous or independent Algeria, relations with the United States rest on a different basis than with the tropical African nations. Industry, commercial contacts, shipping, and the presence of an influential (if small) class of individuals trained in the fields of international economic intercourse enable these countries to view the United States as just another member of the world's association of traders—more fortunate, perhaps, than European or Asian counterparts, but a segment of the same system.

Among this class it is probably true that there is less concern with political objectives than with the maintenance of good business relationships. This is why South African business leaders are distressed when the bad publicity engendered abroad by the Union government's policy of *apartheid* disrupts the pleasant associations they have had for many years with businessmen in New York, Chicago, or San Francisco, and discourages American investment in South Africa. Likewise, Cairo merchants and bankers who have dealt with the international houses of Wall Street are uncomfortable under a Nasser who enters into arrangements with the Czechs, Russians, and with fellow African leaders who lean toward friendlier relations with Moscow. Yet, the voices of those who would stress the necessity to keep on good terms with Americans are not easily heard by the nationalist political rulers.

African Nationalist Leadership

In most of Africa today nationalism is the dominant theme, and those who represent its manifestations are taking over the seats of power. Although African nationalism is in many respects different from the historic nationalism of the older states of Europe, North America, and even Asia, there can be no question but that millions of Africans are well on their way to a real identification of themselves with "nations" as opposed to tribes, villages, families, or other more traditional groupings.[9] Whereas colonial Africa in a political sense was a creation of European map-makers who often set boundary lines with only the most rudimentary knowledge of their appropriateness, the new African countries have already made progress toward unifying the inhabitants of what are still illogically designed "nations." Although divisive trends continue, it is now possible for an individual to identify himself as a Ghanian, a Kenyan, a Nigerian, a Sudanese, or a Tanganyikan—probably at first in addition to (but eventually instead of) an Ewe, a Kikuyu, a Fulani, a Shilluk, or a Masai. The nationalist leaders see the value of encouraging this identification with the new flags, the new anthems, and the new status, for such attributes of nationalism bring the leaders authority abroad and at home.

Since it is largely the voices of the nationalist leaders that will be heard in the immediate future, their objectives toward the United States are most likely to affect relationships over the indefinite future. In many instances their pronouncements are characteristically friendly toward the United States. They profess an admiration of the American ideals of freedom and democracy. They identify themselves in some measure with great American leaders—especially those who struck blows against colonialism, slavery, tyranny, and economic backwardness. This identification, of course, varies with the circumstances and the sophistication of the leaders. But there is a general reservoir of good will.

Some observers claim to see in this admiration of America and things American a devious intent to play off against American näiveté toward Africa a threat to take sides in the cold war. If, these individuals intimate, the United States demurs or delays in affording aid to the new African states, then the nationalist leaders will turn to the Soviet bloc. Some cynical and opportunistic African politicians may operate in this manner. But many African nationalists are strongly committed to an anti-communist position and they would hold to this ground without pressure or largesse from the United States.

---

[9] Beginning with such classics as Raymond L. Buell, *The Native Problem in Africa* (New York: The Macmillan Co., 1928) and Lord Malcolm Hailey, *An African Survey,* revised and rewritten (London: Oxford University Press, Inc., 1957) down to George H. T. Kimble, *Tropical Africa,* two vols. (New York: The Twentieth Century Fund, 1960), the problems of African tribalism and nationalism have received scholarly treatment.

What does seem evident is that the emerging Africa is looking to the United States for a type of moral as well as material assistance. African aspirations are not beyond the comprehension of Americans if they re-examine their own past. The "revolution of rising expectations," includes a desire on the part of illiterate, but not unintelligent, Africans to be regarded as individuals striving for the blessings of liberty. In many corners of Africa the knowledge has spread that the United States threw off the bonds of colonialism and fought two world wars in part to extend the principle of self-determination. Many Africans have come to regard the United States as a source of power and influence that could be ex-erted on behalf of African independence and African development. The American "dream" has been translated into terms that are understandable to many levels of African society. Whether the interpretation is realistic or not, the leaders of African independence movements—and many of their followers—are counting upon the United States to provide the lead-ership that will enable the underdeveloped areas of the world to realize the fulfilment of their own version of this dream.

Not all African nationalist movements hold the United States in this high esteem. Some regimes prefer a "go-it-alone" policy, as in the case of the Union of South Africa, which has chosen to withdraw from mem-bership in the Commonwealth. And Guinea has certainly oriented her policies toward the Communist bloc. Others, while having a high regard for American material progress, prefer to base their political institutions on British, French, or other European models. Yet, even in these areas a common attitude prevails and American leadership, so long as it is dis-played and offered without dictation, would be acceptable. Perhaps the African attitude can best be expressed by saying that Africans conscious of the position of the United States as a world power would be most sat-isfied with a two-fold American approach to the problem: (1) a policy that would present to all nations of the world the fact of a United States that carried out in practice, without arrogance or condescension, the prin-ciples on which the nation was founded; (2) a concurrent policy that dealt individually with each African nation, on a basis of dignity and tolerance, with a view toward assisting that nation to achieve its inherent potential as a contributor to the common welfare of all of Africa and of mankind.

Need for Patience Toward Africa

Such an ideal, most African leaders would recognize, demands a ma-turity and responsibility their people are not yet ready or able to assure. These leaders therefore hope that the United States will be lenient in respect to African shortcomings. In the way of the insecure and uncertain everywhere, some African leaders try to cover by bluster and boast their fancied "independence" of American opinion and counsel. Nasser, Nkrumah, Touré, Verwoerd, Mboya, and others display these tendencies. Yet, others such as Bourguiba, Nyerere, Balewa, and Sylvanus Olympio show that they accept and respect responsibilities. Even some of the more flamboyant nationalists exhibit a calm and reasonable demeanor when they are away from home, in contrast to political representatives of supposedly experienced nations. Likewise, in the way of the strong everywhere, there are expressions of impatience from the United States and elsewhere with the slowness or deviousness of African developments. Such impediments to a mutual understanding of each other's problems are a part of the complexity of international relations.

National capacity, as noted in a previous chapter, is composed of several factors, one of the most important being consent. In the General Assembly of the UN, African votes can prevail over that of the United States by a wide margin. With the admission of Sierra Leone, Tanganyika, and Mauritania to the UN in 1961, all the African states—twenty-nine in number—were now members. Mauritania and Outer Mongolia were admitted through a "package deal" arrangement. So long as the UN is operated on the basis of "one nation, one vote," the United States, for all its prestige and authority, must reckon with the voting strength than can be aligned against it. No African statesman, however, believes that his nation's vote is an accurate gauge of his country's power. While American capacity continues to reside in many moral and material factors, the emerging African nations—and in the sense of political maturity all African nations from the Cape of Good Hope to the Mediterranean are quite young—ask that American preponderance of wealth, experience, and good fortune be employed *for* rather than against them as they struggle to improve their lot. The Africans argue that to help them is not to dilute America's capacity. Whether they will also demonstrate that sharing responsibilities in a competitive world is within their capacities is the greatest question posed by the entry of the free nations of Africa into world affairs.

SUGGESTED READINGS

Adams, Thomas R., *Government and Politics in Africa South of the Sahara.* New York: Random House, 1959.

Africa Report. Washington, D.C.: Issued as Africa Special Report, 1956-1960, monthly. Contains current news on African developments as well as feature articles, book reviews, maps, etc.

Almond, Gabriel and James S. Coleman, eds., *The Politics of the Developing Areas*. Princeton, N.J.: Princeton University Press, 1960.

American Assembly, *United States and Africa*. New York: The American Assembly, Graduate School of Business, Columbia University, 1958.

Bartlett, Vernon, "The Re-Awakening of the Afro-Asian Nations," *African Affairs*, LIX (Apr. 1960), 105-11.

Carter, Gwendolen M. and William O. Brown, eds., *Transition in Africa: Studies in Political Adaptation*. Boston: Boston University Press, 1958.

Castagho, Alphonso A., Jr., "Somalia," *International Conciliation*, No. 522 (Mar. 1959), 339-400.

Coleman, James S., *Nigeria: Background to Nationalism*. Berkeley, Calif.: University of California Press, 1958.

Duffy, James, *Portuguese Africa*. Cambridge: Harvard University Press, 1959.

Gallagher, Charles F., "Toward a Settlement in Algeria," *Foreign Affairs*, XXXVIII (Jan. 1960), 273-84.

Gunther, John, *Inside Africa*. New York: Harper & Brothers, 1955.

Hailey, William H., *An African Survey: A Study of Problems Arising in Africa South of the Sahara*. London, New York: Oxford University Press, Inc., 1957.

Haines, Charles G., ed., *Africa Today*. Baltimore: The Johns Hopkins Press, 1955.

Hance, William A., *African Economic Development*. New York: Harper & Brothers for the Council on Foreign Relations, 1958.

Hatch, John C., *Africa Today and Tomorrow: An Outline of Basic Facts and Major Problems*. New York: Frederick A. Praeger, Inc., 1960.

Henry, Paul M., "Pan-Africanism: A Dream Come True," *Foreign Affairs*, XXXVII (Apr. 1959), 443-52.

Hodgkin, Thomas, *Nationalism in Colonial Africa*. London: Muller, 1956.

Houphuet-Boigny, Félix, "Black Africa and the French Union," *Foreign Affairs*, XXXV (July 1957), 593-99.

Kilby, Peter, "American Aid to Emerging Africa," *New Leader*, XLIII (Aug. 29, 1960), 16-19.

Kimble, George H. T., *Tropical Africa*, 2 vols. New York: The Twentieth Century Fund, 1960.

Kitagawa, Daisuke, "The West and the Afro-Asian World," *Political Quarterly*, XXX (Apr. 1959), 157-70.

McConnell, Grant, "Africa and the Americans," *Virginia Quarterly Review*, XXXVII (Winter 1961), 34-50.

McKay, Vernon, "United States Policy for the New Africa," *Current History*, XXXVII (July 1959), 1-6.

Merriam, Alan P., *Congo: Background of Conflict*. Evanston, Illinois: Northwestern University Press, 1961.

Nkrumah, Kwame, *Ghana: The Autobiography of Kwame Nkrumah*. New York: Thomas Nelson & Sons, 1957.

Penfield, James K., "Africa: A New Situation Requiring New Responses," *Department of State Bulletin*, XLII (June 6, 1960), 918-23.

————, "African Nationalism and United States Foreign Policy," *Department of State Bulletin*, XLIII (Dec. 26, 1960), 951-58.

Rothchild, Donald S., *Toward Unity in Africa: A Study of Federalism in British Africa*. Washington, D.C.: Public Affairs Press, 1960.

Satterthwaite, Joseph C., "The United States and the New Africa," *Department of State Bulletin*, XL (Feb. 9, 1959), 190-96.

————, "The United States and West Africa: A Survey of Relations," *Department of State Bulletin*, XL (May 25, 1959), 744-49.

Scott, John, *Africa: World's Last Frontier*. New York: Foreign Policy Association, 1959.

Segal, Ronald, ed., *Political Africa*. New York: Frederick A. Praeger, Inc., 1961.

Shepherd, George V., "The Conflict of Interests in American Policy on Africa," *Western Political Quarterly*, XII (Dec. 1959), 996-1004.

Stillman, Calvin W., ed., *Africa in the Modern World*. Chicago: University of Chicago Press, 1955.

Thompson, Virginia and Richard Adloff, *The Emerging States of French Equatorial Africa*. Stanford, California: Stanford University Press, 1960.

U.S. Senate, Foreign Relations Committee, *United States Foreign Policy: Compilation of Studies, Nos. 1-13*, 2 vols. No. 4. "United States Foreign Policy: Africa," by Program of African Studies, Northwestern University. Committee Print, 86th Cong., 2nd sess., 1960, pp. 301-90. Washington, D.C.: Government Printing Office, 1960.

28

Relations Between Unequal Neighbors: Latin America and the United States

Morton Kroll
Department of Political Science,
University of Washington

A familial designation—let us say "Big Brother"—sometimes seems more appropriate than "neighbor" to characterize relations between the United States and the twenty nations to the south. This Western Hemispheric community has, for better or worse, existed for more than a century and a quarter. History and geography, economics and intercultural influences have made for a complexity of relationships at times intimate, distant, friendly, hostile, haughty, but never really detached.

Since 1800 the nations of Latin America have moved from colonialism to pawnship to independence and now, as is increasingly evident, to interdependence. The evolution has been slow, uneven, and not without hardship and bloodshed; vestiges of the past remain. There are still nations whose wealth is controlled by landed oligarchical aristocracies. A shrinking number of Latin-American countries are run by *caudillos*—military dictators. Foreign economic influence in the area is still strong, though it no longer has the former overtones of reckless exploitation and imperialism. Latin America is today a sub-continent of ever-accelerating economic, political, and social change, wrapped securely in a package of resurgent nationalism, always strong, but particularly virile in the mid-twentieth century.

It is difficult to generalize about Latin America. Each nation has developed its unique pattern of life and politics. They vary in size, wealth, population, and resources. There are nevertheless common denominators. First, most of them have a common Spanish cultural, political, and linguistic heritage, although one must not overlook the influence of the Portuguese in Brazil, the French in Haiti, and the indigenous Indian cul-

LATIN AMERICA

CUBA
JAMAICA
HAITI
DOMINICAN REP.
PUERTO RICO

MEXICO

BR. HONDURAS

GUATEMALA
EL SALVADOR
COSTA RICA
PANAMÁ
COLOMBIA
GALÁPAGOS IS.
ECUADOR

HONDURAS
NICARAGUA

TRINIDAD
VENEZUELA

BR. GUIANA
SURINAM
FR. GUIANA

PERÚ

BOLÍVIA

PARAGUAY

CHILE

BRAZIL

URUGUAY

ARGENTINA

FALKLAND IS.

LEGEND
MINERAL FIELDS
C - COPPER
I - IRON
L - LEAD
O - OIL
S - SILVER
T - TIN

616

tures in Peru, Chile, Mexico, and elsewhere. Second, many have a common colonial, liberation, and independence experience. Third, nothing has been so important to their common international experience during the past century and a half as living in the proximate presence of the "Colossus of the North." Fourth, most are "developing nations." Tremendous progress has been made towards industrial development, urbanization, improved agricultural techniques, and the diversification of single commodity economies. But the economic, as well as social and political dislocations during this period of change have been severe, and many nations are now badly in need of financial and technical assistance.

PHYSICAL AND HUMAN
GEOGRAPHY OF LATIN AMERICA

Physical Geography

To the North American, Latin America is a rugged land with impassable terrain and impossible climate. Customarily the principal regions are designated as Middle America, the Caribbean, and South America. Middle America includes Mexico and Central America. Northeast of Middle America lies the Caribbean Sea, with its conveniently placed rim of the West Indies separating it from the Atlantic. Here intense nationalism rubs shoulders with colonialism, making the Caribbean a caldron of conflicting ideas and movements.

The dominant physical feature of South America is the tremendous *cordillera* of the Andes running from the Caribbean to Tierra del Fuego. Though these mountains lie predominantly to the west, they nonetheless form an historically important east-west division and account for the shoestring shape of Chile, three thousand miles long and one hundred miles wide. The Orinoco, Amazon, Paraguay-Parana-Plata river systems, their basins and plains, constitute important regions. Geographically, as well as culturally, because of their Hispanic background it has always been easier for Latin Americans to look to Europe than to the United States. During World War II, for example, an armada of allied aircraft maintained a round-the-clock schedule from Natal, near the eastern-most tip of Brazil, to Dakar, on the west coast of Africa, about 1,800 miles away.

Population

The population of Latin America is about 190,000,000, approximately ten million more than that of the United States. It is growing at a more rapid rate than any other area in the world and may well reach more than

300,000,000 by 1975.[1] Racial diversity characterizes the area. The three major population groups are European, Indian, and Negro, and there is every conceivable combination of these. There are sharp differences within these broad groupings. In a number of nations the native Indian cultures have been absorbed into the national life and have become important factors in shaping national policies. In addition, there is a substantial Oriental minority. While Latin Americans are generally tolerant, racial discrimination is not unknown, especially in those nations with a predominantly white population.

Economic Dependence and Monoculture

In most nineteenth-century Latin-American nations the predominantly agrarian economies, as well as political institutions, were controlled by small landholding oligarchies whose members were European in their orientation and sympathies. These groups owned most of the land, generally consisting of large estates. The landowners were mainly concerned with maintaining a feudal status quo in the highly stratified society they controlled. There was almost no middle class.

The enforced dependency of the colonial economies was transferred at the turn of the century from Spain to the major European powers, especially Britain and France. These industrial nations found a rich wellspring of natural resources and a large manipulative market for capital and goods. Latin America also provided ripe pickings for rampant, often unscrupulous British speculators who deceived investors by organizing and selling bonds on the indebtedness of Latin-American governments, which subsequently defaulted.

At the turn of the century foreign firms owned all oceanic transportation connecting Latin America with the other parts of the world. Most railroads, communications facilities, and many banks, mines, and agricultural enterprises were wholly or partially foreign-owned. In this atmosphere of foreign economic domination, exploitation, and dependence, Latin-American nations nonetheless increased their commerce from an estimated $50 million in 1825 to $1 billion in 1900.

The twentieth century opened with a continuation of the pattern of the nineteenth, with the added participation of the United States—which had been gradually increasing its trade with its southern neighbors.[2] After

---

[1] "United States-Latin American Relations: Problems of Latin American Economic Development," a study prepared at the request of the Subcommittee on American Republics Affairs of the Committee on Foreign Relations, United States Senate, by the University of Oregon Institute of International Studies and Overseas Administration, No. 6 (Washington, D.C.: Government Printing Office, Feb. 11, 1960), p. 3.

[2] J. Fred Rippy, *Globe and Hemisphere* (Chicago: Henry Regnery Co., 1958), pp. 30-35.

1898 these economic relations were not without political consequence. Five times the United States militarily and economically intervened in Central America and the Caribbean, in part for economic reasons.

The reliance of a nation for its economic sustenance on its capacity to export a single commodity is called *monoculture*. The principal Latin-American exports were, and are, foodstuffs and raw materials. Many nations produced one major exportable commodity such as coffee, sugar, nitrates, or tin, and thus became the victim of world-wide market fluctuations over which they had little or no control. Many Latin-American countries have tried to solve this problem by improving the efficiency of handling their major commodity, by diversifying their exports, and by developing processing and manufacturing plants at home.

Especially since World War II, economic development has been promised by Latin-American leaders. Spurred on by nationalism, accelerating population growth, and the "revolution of rising expectations" of their people, Latin America has struggled to achieve a level of independence and economic stability. The gross national product has bolted ahead, increasing in the 1950-57 period about thirty-five per cent. Table 5 indicates the rate of growth in specific economic sectors.

TABLE 5

ECONOMIC GROWTH IN LATIN AMERICA: 1950-1957

Increase in Percentages

Agricultural Production	26
Mining	70
Manufacturing	37
Construction	28
Transportation	50
Services	31

Source: Reynold E. Carlson, "The Economic Picture," *The United States and Latin America* (New York: The American Assembly, 1959), pp. 117-22.

The current economic condition has elements of grimness which have obvious implications for the role of this region on the world scene. From 1955 to 1960 the economic expansion slowed, especially in relation to population growth. "The rate of per capita increase in all production in 1960 over 1959 was negligible . . . agricultural production per capita in Latin America dropped 2 per cent."[3] In fact, the population is growing at a faster rate than is the economy. Over-all, less food was produced per capita in 1960 than in 1938. The strong current of nationalism has not encouraged foreign investment, especially for important capital development. Ninety per cent of such funds come from indigenous sources. Japan, West Germany, Italy, and France have been increasingly active

---

[3] *New York Times*, Jan. 11, 1961, p. 49.

along with the United States, especially in exports and services. France exported manufactured equipment worth $230 million to Latin America in 1959 and imported some $225 million in raw materials.[4]

We have given some emphasis to the economic environment because it is a major variable in motivating Latin-American behavior in relations with the United States. It is not the only factor, however, which explains why Latin-Americans react as they do at world council tables and towards their northern neighbor. The influence of the Hispanic environment, the resurgence of national spirit, and the strained history of Latin America's relations with the major world powers must be considered in conjunction with economics.

UNITED STATES RELATIONS WITH LATIN AMERICA: THE HISTORICAL PERSPECTIVE

Citizens of the United States tend to relegate what happened fifty or a hundred years ago to the dim recesses of historical ambiguity, feeling that it has no bearing on the present. This is a cultural attribute and is related to American ideas of material progress and pace of growth. Other nations view history in an entirely different light. To Latin-Americans the past is part of the present, part of their national being. A small, economically impoverished country may have little more than the past upon which to live. Unlike North Americans, their neighbors to the south remember their history well, with a mixture of national pride and international bitterness.

In its historical perspective the pattern of relations between the United States and Latin America is hardly a happy one. In many respects the most glorious moments were those at the beginning (in the early part of the nineteenth century) when the United States provided a beacon for republican ideas and ideals, as opposed to monarchical institutions and colonial controls. To the Latin-Americans the United States was the revolutionary force in the world, a symbol of independence which helped sever the umbilical cord that for several centuries had bound the Spanish colonies to the mother country. Independence was probably more important to the colonies in rebellion than were Anglo-American concepts of liberty and representative institutions, which really did not lend themselves to easy adaptation by Hispanic societies.

Early policies of the United States towards the New World were based on anxious self-interest. The "shoe-string republic" had much to fear from the colonial powers of monarchical Europe, which appeared to be blocking "natural paths of expansion," especially towards the south and west. Spain conspired in the Floridas, as did Britain to the north. France,

---

[4] *Ibid.*, Feb. 23, 1961, p. 7.

especially under Napoleon, held illusions of developing a vast empire in North America.

Napoleon's invasion of the Iberian peninsula provided the rationale for the colonial break with Spain in Latin America. The sympathies of the United States were with the independence movements, exemplifying all that was new and progressive—values that nations struggling for identity easily could adopt. There were material reasons for supporting the struggle. After purchasing Louisiana from France, the United States was interested in acquiring East and West Florida from Spain, as it was feared that the areas might be gained by Great Britain. In 1811 Congress passed a resolution stating that the United States could not, "without serious inquietude see any part of the said territory pass into the hands of any foreign Power."[5] This "No-Transfer Resolution" was the harbinger of the Monroe Doctrine, though its immediate significance was not very great. Of prime significance was the kernel of the idea of American concern for the sovereignty of territories within an area it regarded as its orbit.

The Monroe Doctrine

The United States was the first nation outside Latin America to recognize the newly independent states. Recognition was followed in 1823 by the enunciation of what was to become known (though not until 1853) as the Monroe Doctrine, the classic expression of American policy in the Western Hemisphere.[6] It contained three elements of vital importance: First, the powers of the Holy Alliance were warned against extending colonization to the New World. Second, the United States would oppose any interference in the political affairs of the American states. Third, it had no intention of meddling in the affairs of Europe.

The ideological effect of the Monroe Doctrine—and no doubt such was the intent of its framers—was to separate the republican New World from the monarchical alliances of the old. Its *de facto* base, however, rested on British sea power. While the British could under no circumstances be considered anti-monarchical, they had gained trade advantages with the rebelling colonies, and the future appeared brighter for British merchants under independence than under the closed system of Spanish colonialism.

The Doctrine was cynically received by the Holy Alliance. It ran counter, as well, to prevailing concepts of international law concerning the rights of powers to unoccupied territory and the right of intervention. Latin-American reaction, such as existed, was generally favorable. The

---

[5] Samuel Flagg Bemis, *The Latin American Policy of the United States* (New York: Harcourt, Brace & World, Inc., 1943), p. 29.

[6] James W. Gantenbein, ed., *The Evolution of Our Latin American Policy* (New York: Columbia University Press, 1950), pp. 323-25.

United States, despite formal neutrality, was the major outside "friend" of the new nations.

The Doctrine was a unilateral declaration. The United States did not seek support from its new neighbors and it rejected the idea of a joint declaration with Great Britain. This unilateral aspect did not prove easy to dilute; attempts through the Pan-American movement to make non-intervention a multilateral concern have proved only moderately successful. The superior force of the North American "partner" was to make itself felt too often to provide the basis for genuine mutual trust. There was nothing in the Doctrine to guarantee that the United States had denied itself authority to intervene, and intervene it did, repeatedly. Furthermore, there were times in the nineteenth century when the Europeans ran rampant in a number of nations while the United States stood by, helpless or preoccupied with its own troubles. At other times, however, it warded off threatening and actual European interference. The Monroe Doctrine not only was, but remains dependent upon the strength of *a major power*. Once the United States blossomed as a world naval power at the end of the nineteenth century, it succeeded Britain as the enforcer of the Doctrine. The Clayton-Bulwer treaty of 1850, a compromise at best, prevented exclusive British hegemony over a proposed Nicaraguan Canal. American readiness to intervene on Mexico's behalf, once the Civil War was concluded, was a contributing factor to the withdrawal of French occupation of that country, which had lasted from 1861 to 1865. Several times (in 1829, 1830, 1840) the United States warned Spain and other powers that it would not countenance the transfer of Cuba from Spain to another non-hemispheric power.

We can only conclude that in the nineteenth century the United States was not entirely consistent in its role as guardian of non-intervention. Much depended upon time, circumstance, and the capacity of the prime actors to move either towards or away from doctrinal policy. During the last century, Latin-American nations were plagued by the devastating partnership of external exploitation and internal corruption. It was a short step for the United States, once its citizens became heavy investors and entrepreneurs in Latin America, to conceive of the idea of intervening to prevent intervention. Small wonder that Latin-Americans are ambivalent about the Doctrine and alternately regard it as a rationale for United States intervention and as a guardian of their independence.

Corollaries to the Doctrine

The numerous statements made by American governmental leaders in the nineteenth century to give expression to the Doctrine—indeed to extend it—were varied. On the whole they did not contribute to either the elaboration or diminution of the central thesis of non-colonization and non-foreign governmental intervention. Presidents Polk and Johnson were strongly belligerent in their tone and it was during Polk's administration that the United States, as a result of the Mexican war and the Gadsden Purchase which followed, acquired about half Mexico's territory. Grover Cleveland heralded the age of American imperialism with the enunciation of his "doctrine of paramount interest," which asserted the right of the United States to intervene on behalf of its own interests. His administration further suggested that this nation "is practically sovereign upon this continent." Cleveland's doctrine of paramount interest was not inconsistent with the Roosevelt Corollary that followed it. The latter declared that the United States could interpose its forces and resources to prevent conditions from arising which might result in non-hemispheric intervention. The Roosevelt Corollary was written into the Hay-Bunau-Varilla Pact of 1904 with Panama so that in defense of the Canal the United States could intervene in that country to "preserve order." Panama had been virtually seized from Colombia and established as a "sovereign" state.

Thus the "Era of Protectorates" was launched. The Dominican Republic was occupied from 1905 until 1924. American marines landed in Nicaragua in 1911 to "protect the life and property of Americans"; although they were withdrawn in 1924, they returned again to remain until 1933. Haiti was occupied in July 1915, originally at the request of the Haitian government, although by the time the marines landed there virtually was no government. The United States remained a dominant partner in Haitian politics and administration until 1934. The general impact of all this was negative: dictatorships were established in Nicaragua and the Dominican Republic; Haiti continued to live in penurious chaos; Panama resented the pre-emption of the Canal Zone. Cuba, which had gained its independence from the mother country with the help of the United States was, nonetheless, not permitted a life of its own. The Platt Amendment deprived her of her autonomy in the conduct of foreign relations and severely limited her in domestic affairs. All told, the Roosevelt Corollary did little more than pay for satisfying the egos of American jingoists and, not too incidentally, helped American enterprise develop favored positions in these countries. The price of embittered historical remembrance has proved dear in establishing good relations between the United States and Latin America.

Under the thesis of national self-determination, implied in the original statement of President Monroe, the Caribbean and Central American protectorates could not be continued. Professor Dexter Perkins, the foremost American authority on the Monroe Doctrine, referred to this period as "imperialism with an uneasy conscience."[7] The "Good Neighbor Policy" was an attempt to restore confidence in the United States. In his famous inauguration address of March 4, 1933, President Franklin D. Roosevelt proclaimed that the policy of the United States was to be a "good neighbor—the neighbor who resolutely respects himself and, because he does so, respects the rights of others—the neighbor who respects his obligations and respects the sanctity of his agreements in and with a world of neighbors."[8] The refrain had been heard before in Latin America and the Good Neighbor Policy required action to gain support. Some steps had already been taken; marines had been withdrawn from Nicaragua and negotiations had been made to remove them from Haiti. President Hoover's pronouncements as well as those of a number of Republican secretaries of state stood as take-off points.

The actions of the New Deal in accomplishing its program were sweeping. In 1934 the Platt Amendment was abrogated and the Cubans were thus free to follow their own stormy pursuits. That same year the United States surrendered its right to intervene in the internal affairs of Panama. It also subscribed to the principle of non-intervention in a protocol concluded in 1936. When, in 1938, the government of Mexico expropriated foreign-owned oil properties in that country, the United States decision not to intervene was applauded by many Latin-Americans.

During World War II, with varying degrees of enthusiasm, the United States was supported by Latin America, with the exception of Argentina. The extent to which the Monroe Doctrine was regionalized was made firmly evident when in 1945, having been virtually ignored at Dumbarton Oaks, the hemispheric nations (excluding Canada and Argentina for entirely different reasons) proclaimed the obligations of hemispheric defense and regional arrangements at the Chapultapec conference.

The deeds of the American Good Neighbor Policy could not in themselves undo a half-century of events which had wrought attitudes of resentment, suspicion, and mistrust. Yet, because of the pro-UN identifications of the leaders of most Latin-American nations, when World War II ended the United States had a limited reservoir of good will. At the same time, as we shall see in the section on contemporary relations, the increase or resumption of friendship resulted in an increase in the expectations of cooperation and aid, and, in this, the other American nations were to be sorely disappointed.

---

[7] Quoted in Hubert Herring, A History of Latin America (New York: Alfred A. Knopf, Inc., 1955), p. 760.

[8] Quoted in Gatenbein, The Evolution of our Latin American Policy, p. 159.

Pan-Americanism

In one respect Pan-Americanism has served as the antidote for the unilateralism of the Monroe Doctrine; in another it is the logical historical concomitant of American policy. If the Monroe Doctrine implied a separate, regional community of nations of the Western Hemisphere, the Pan-American movement attempted to give structure to this idea. Counterposed to the Pan-American idea are numerous programs which have ranged from intense nationalism to Pan-Hispanicism and Pan-Latinism. There have always been articulate elements among Latin-Americans who have argued that their ties are basically European and that they have nothing to gain from association with the United States.

Every movement has its instrumentality, and Pan-Americanism's first *modus operandi* was the hemispheric conference. The numerous conferences convened by the Latin-Americans themselves prior to 1889 and those held under American auspices after that year record the concerns of the nations and the region. There was no dearth of candor, particularly in the twentieth century. Despite suspicion and disharmony one finds in these conferences a search for a community of security and economic interests as well as cultural understanding.

Prior to World War I their major organizational achievement—although not so regarded—was the Commercial Bureau of the American Republics, established in 1890, which after numerous reorganizations, emerged in 1910 as the Pan-American Union. Many Latin-Americans regarded it as a tool of American policy. The American secretary of state was ex-officio chairman of the Union's governing board until 1923. Not until 1947 was the Union's director general a person other than an American citizen.

From 1923 through 1938 numerous agreements were reached at the successive conferences on matters ranging from aircraft communications to copyright conventions and the status of armed merchant vessels. Latin-American delegates to a number of these candidly criticized the United States. During this period the United States unveiled and activated its Good Neighbor Policy. International instruments for peacemaking and non-intervention were reaffirmed. Beginning in 1938, the major concern of the conferences became the determination of methods of reacting to the increasingly grave world situation. The foreign ministers conference was established to consider special and emergency problems. Three "Meetings of Consultation of Foreign Ministers" were held between 1939 and 1942 and mark the transition from neutrality to hemispheric security in World War II.

After World War II, two major developments took place: (1) the establishment of the Organization of American States and (2) the framework and structure for inter-American security.

The Pan-American movement is very much a child of historical and geographic circumstance. Inevitably it seems the nations of the hemisphere have grown together. The ties which bind them remain tenuous, however, and no one, least of all the United States, can take them for granted.

RELATIONSHIPS IN THE
CONTEMPORARY ERA: PERSISTENT ISSUES

Several major trends are of paramount importance in understanding relations between the United States and Latin America. First, economic and social change are accelerating within the Latin-American republics, as they move rapidly, if at different rates, in the direction of urbanization and industrialization. Secondly, in an age of jet aircraft and electronics, the vast distances which have separated them from each other as well as from their northern neighbor, have shrunk appreciably. Third, there is a growing interdependence between the United States and Latin America. In particular, the area needs economic and technical assistance. In the raw aspects of its power struggle with the Sino-Soviet bloc, especially at the council tables in international organizations, the United States as the leader in the Western democratic coalition requires the voting and moral support of Latin America.

Viewed against the backdrop of domestic political development as well as the history of inter-American relations, the problems of today are not dissimilar from those of the past. Tensions have increased because of accelerating change and the impact of the world scene. Yet the misunderstandings, and mistrust, as well as the lack of positive appreciation between the United States and Latin-American nations for each other's culture and politics remains as a dominant conditioning force.

One can hope for a growing sense of mutual understanding and appreciation as the nations of the Western Hemisphere become increasingly interdependent. Certainly there are signs in many Latin-American nations of a growth of liberal noncommunist groups which are politically and economically sympathetic to the United States, especially in its competition against the communist nations. It is through a brief analysis of major policy perspectives that we can judge the effectiveness of the United States in establishing a community of support based on these groups.

Political Relations: The Modern
Monroe Doctrine and Pan-Americanism

The United States de-emphasized the Monroe Doctrine in the late forties. Mutual defense and regional security were more important. During the nineteen-fifties the purposes of the Doctrine took on a different aura. The United States' major concern was to prevent communism from gaining a foothold in the hemisphere. Could the communist parties of Latin America be regarded as *prima facie* evidence of Moscow (or Peiping) inspired aggression in the hemisphere or were they indigenous movements? The whole question of how to cope with the rapid and often revolutionary changes exploded in sharp relief in the last decade. Nor were there any black-and-white answers. Vice President Richard M. Nixon, who came perilously close to being assaulted in Lima and Caracas in May 1958, acknowledged that the hostility he experienced could not be wholly attributed to communist inspiration.

The association of the Monroe Doctrine with combatting communism established in 1948 was reaffirmed by Secretary of State Dulles when he pressed hard for anti-communist resolutions in Caracas in 1954. At that time the regime of President Jacopo Arbenz in Guatemala was regarded as pro-communist and the evidence is that the United States played an active part in overthrowing it. Most Latin-American representatives at the conferences of this period were more interested in getting American help to alleviate their economic plight than in promulgating anti-communist resolutions.

The Cuban Revolution of 1958 and the emergence of Fidel Castro fomented the most recent articulation of the Monroe Doctrine. When in mid-April 1961 a small army of Cuban exiles, supplied and trained by the United States, embarked on an ill-fated expedition against the Cuban mainland, President Kennedy, while denying that the United States would take direct action in support of the rebels, told a conference of American newspaper editors that:

. . . any unilateral American intervention in the absence of any external attack upon ourselves or an ally, would have been contrary to our traditions and to our international obligations. But let the record show that our restraint is not inexhaustible.

Should it ever appear that the inter-American doctrine of noninterference merely conceals or excuses a policy of nonaction—if the nations of this hemisphere should fail to meet their commitments against outside Communist penetration—then I want it clearly understood that this government will not hesitate in meeting its primary obligations which are to the security of our nation.[9]

This statement asserted the right of any state to take unilateral action in defense of its security, despite the Organization of American States and UN Charters. More significant, however, was the inference that the United States would judge whether the nations of the hemisphere were meeting their commitments against external aggression. The effect of the President's remarks was to bring back the unilateral image of the Monroe Doctrine. National security was an objective which the nations of the Western Hemisphere could and did accept. But the passing of judgment upon the obligations of other sovereign states was not calculated to gain

---

[9] *Christian Science Monitor,* Apr. 22, 1961, p. 1.

firm support and there was no dearth of criticism of United States policy.

The Monroe Doctrine stands, for better or worse, as the backbone of American policy towards Latin America. If it adjusted to the twentieth century it would have to do so through the process of multilateralization. The struggle between the communist and noncommunist worlds placed a severe strain on the formal processes of international relations. The strength of the Doctrine lay in its guarantee of national self-determination. Conflict and its resolution in the nineteen sixties has become infinitely more subtle and complex than state-to-state relations. Indeed, the difficulty of the United States in dealing with Cuba in the dark days in the spring of 1961 was that it was trying to win a battle with the weapons of a bygone era.

The Pan-American movement entered a period of diversification in the late nineteen-forties and fifties. Most important in developing a common bond was the establishment of the Organization of American States.[10] The framework for inter-American collective security, established at the Chapultepec conference in 1945, had been reinforced at Rio De Janeiro in 1947. At Bogotá, Colombia, in 1948, amidst the gunfire and rioting of a bona fide revolution, the Organization of American States was forged. The Tenth International Conference of American States was held in Caracas, Venezuela, in May 1954. The United States preoccupation with the communist menace—at least so it seemed to many Latin-American delegates—led to a "Declaration of Solidarity . . ." the heart of which was as follows:

The Tenth Inter-American Conference declares . . .
That the domination or control of the political institutions of any American state by the international Communist movement, extending to this hemisphere the political system of an extra-continental power would constitute a threat to the sovereignty and political independence of the American states, endangering the peace of America, and would call for a meeting of consultation to consider the adoption of appropriate action in accordance with existing treaties.[11]

The Latin-American nations put through a number of resolutions designed to gain assistance in meeting their economic problems. The conference was not precisely a victory for the United States. A number of delegations were concerned that on the one hand the United States condemned communist totalitarianism, and on the other seemed to approve the right-wing dictatorships of such men as Trujillo in the Dominican Republic and Batista in Cuba.

The Eleventh Conference was to have been held in February 1960 in Ecuador, but was twice postponed. There was strong feeling among the leaders of the American nations that it was unwise to convene the conference until relations between the United States and Cuba had reached

---

10 See above, pp. 192-97.
11 *Department of State Bulletin,* XXX (Apr. 26, 1954), 638.

a stage where it might produce something more than propaganda, vitriol, and increased tensions.

Pan-Americanism reflects the degree to which the several nations can identify their interests with a common hemispheric policy. The major bases of a Pan-American community are coldly pragmatic, which is not surprising in view of the intensity of national spirit in the hemisphere. The United States is committed to developing this community. The extent of its success will depend upon convincing the nations of Latin America that the Pan-American movement is an instrument of hemispheric cooperation and not a pawn in cold war international politics. Despite a certain social and economic inevitability no one, in the mid-twentieth century, could take the Pan-American movement for granted.

Cooperation in academic and artistic endeavors involving the exchange of ideas, works, and individuals has been increasing steadily between the United States and Latin America. Reciprocal translation programs, music festivals, art exhibits, and exchange programs have worked well for all involved. A recent study on the effectiveness of hemispheric cultural activity reported that the OAS "tends to succeed in implementing its goals in economic, social, and cultural activities when the content of its activities is more technical and less directly political and when the execution of its decisions depends more on persons, acting as professionals and individuals, and less on governments acting as sovereign states."[12]

Military Cooperation

Hemispheric defense has been a perennial concern of the makers of United States foreign policy. In gaining domination of the Caribbean during the latter part of the nineteenth and early twentieth centuries, the United States took strong measures to insure its supremacy. Certainly the Roosevelt Corollary can be seen in this light. When, on the eve of World War II, the United States took stock of its resources the role of the hemisphere took on more than passing importance. Once the mantle of neutrality was shed, it sought to bring Latin America into its orbit of defense and, finally, make it an effective partner in waging war. The record of assistance in World War II is far more impressive than the standoffishness of World War I, when only nine of the Latin-American nations declared war.

The structure for military coordination was provided by the Inter-American Defense Board (IADB), which was established at the Third Meeting of Consultation of Foreign Ministers in January 1942 and given

---

[12] "United States-Latin American Relations: The Organization of American States," A study prepared at the request of the Subcommittee on American Republics Affairs of the Committee on Foreign Relations, United States Senate, by Northwestern University, No. 3 (Washington, D.C.: Government Printing Office, Dec. 24, 1959), p. 27.

permanent status at the Chapultapec meeting of 1945. That same year the IADB proposed that efforts be made to standardize military technology and organization on the United States model. Its effectiveness has been uncertain. Its recommendations in 1945 led to the introduction, at the behest of President Truman, of a bill for inter-American military cooperation which would have permitted the United States to continue equipping Latin-American military machines, to exchange old implements of war for new, and to train Latin-American forces. Congress did not pass this bill. After the outbreak of the Korean conflict the United States once again pressed for hemispheric support, and the IADB was given a greater planning role.

The United States obviously stands at the center of hemispheric defense. Title IV of the Mutual Security Act of 1951 authorized military assistance to Latin America. Prior to this, as a result of the Fourth Meeting of Consultation of Foreign Ministers in March-April 1951, Congress appropriated $38 million for military aid to the area. In 1952, Mutual Defense Assistance Agreements were concluded with Ecuador, Cuba (under Batista), Colombia, Peru, and Chile. Twelve countries are now involved in such agreements which link their systems of defense and the provision of strategic materials to those of the United States. Table 6 indicates the cost of the program under these agreements.

TABLE 6

MILITARY ASSISTANCE PROGRAM SHIPMENTS TO LATIN AMERICA

Fiscal Year	Millions of Dollars	Fiscal Year	Millions of Dollars
1952	0.2	1956	21.2
1953	65.2	1957	32.0
1954	37.9	1958	56.8
1955	36.9	1959	67.0

Source: "United States Latin-American Relations: Post World War II Developments in Latin America" (Washington, D.C.: Government Printing Office, 1959), p. 33.

Hemispheric defense cannot be divorced from the global scene. A number of serious questions must be raised in this context. Is military invasion by an extra-hemispheric force likely? Given the nature of modern military technology, can Latin America make very much of a contribution in the near future? Many Latin-American leaders feel that the United States has placed too great an emphasis on military concerns and too little on economic development for peaceful purposes where the Western Hemisphere is concerned. There is a strong anti-militarist movement among Latin-Americans who see hope in disarmament and economic and social development. Certainly, there is little likelihood that either the Soviet Union or Communist China will seek direct territorial aggrandizement in the New World. There is a strong feeling that under the Rio treaty and the Bogotá Pact (yet to be ratified) sufficient machinery exists to handle security matters of concern to the hemisphere, including intra-hemispheric problems. Latin-Americans can point with justified pride to their growing capacity to put out their own fires of war. Of particular promise has been the mediating work of the Inter-American Peace Committee (IAPC) whose origins date back to 1940, but which was not put into full use until 1948. The Council of the OAS appoints the members of the IAPC which acts as a standing, trouble-shooting mediator. Twenty times between 1948 and 1960 the IAPC considered problems including territorial disputes, disputes over the jurisdiction of nations, and an allegation of an "imminent attack." It has been reasonably effective, enough so to provide promise for the future peaceful settlement of disputes it may be called upon to mediate.

Finally, the fundamental difference in attitude towards hemispheric defense between the United States and Latin America is one of perspective between a major world power and smaller nations. The United States tends to evaluate its relations with all nations in the context of its global concern in its competition with the communist world. The Latin-American states, struggling to meet the demands and exigencies of economic and social transformation, are not so concerned with global competition. Historically, they have seen in the United States, especially in the Caribbean area, as much of a threat as that of the great European powers. There is a justified grain of cynicism in the Latin-American's reaction to the moral platitudes and pleas for support against the current menace which are posed by "Big Brother" to the north. Americans must understand this attitude if they are to appreciate and cope with Latin-America in the international arena.

Economic Relations and the "Alliance for Progress"

The United States has almost since independence provided a major market for the raw materials and products of its neighbors to the south. In the twentieth century it became a key investor in many Latin-American countries, to the extent of over $5 billion by 1914. In a few instances American corporations became dominant features of the economic and political life of a country; this was especially the case with the United Fruit Company, established in 1899, which was (and is) active in the Caribbean and much of Central America.

Private investment is a vital part of the economic relations between the United States and the area. Direct investment there by United States individuals and firms increased from $2.7 billion in 1943 to $9 billion in

1959. The exports of United States companies from Latin America in 1957 accounted for one-third of their total exports. Over twenty per cent of all taxes collected there was paid by American firms. Thus the economic ties between most of the Latin-American countries and the United States are intimate.

The major concern of the United States government in providing economic assistance to developing areas throughout the world has been primarily to meet what the International Cooperation Administration termed in one of its reports the "immediate threat of large-scale external Communist aggression." Latin America, before the Cuban Revolution of 1958, seemed at least geographically remote from such a threat. Nevertheless, as noted above, considerable sums in military assistance were being poured into the area.

Whereas the United States government, until the nineteen-sixties at least, insisted that Latin-American nations rely primarily on private economic aid, the latter preferred government assistance. The pattern of this economic and technical assistance to Latin America defies pat descriptions. The United States has been directly involved in programs of public health and sanitation, agriculture, education, science, housing, and general economic progress. It has worked on a country-to-country basis, making use of the World Bank and the Inter-American Development Bank.[13] In September 1960, the United States subscribed along with eighteen other members of the OAS to the Act of Bogotá, which proposed a sweeping program of social and economic reform for Latin America.

United States governmental grants for technical and economic assistance varied from year to year from 1950 to 1959 (see Table 7 below).

TABLE 7

NET LONG-TERM FLOW OF CAPITAL FROM THE UNITED STATES
TO LATIN AMERICA: 1950-1959
(Millions of Dollars)

Years	Grants	Credits	Total
1950	19	35	54
1951	17	93	110
1952	22	65	87
1953	27	343	370
1954	42	36	78
1955	68	5	73
1956	82	−26	56
1957	110	162	272
1958	113	391	504
1959	105	226	331

Source: Committee for Economic Development, *Cooperation for Progress in Latin America* (New York: Committee for Economic Development, 1961), p. 38.

---

[13] "United States-Latin American Relations: Problems of Latin American Economic Development," Chap. 6.

In March 1961, President Kennedy announced his "Alliance for Progress" program to a group of Latin-American diplomats. This was followed by a message to Congress in which he outlined a ten-point program to develop a policy of cooperation and assistance for the next decade, in fulfilment of the Bogotá pledge. He asked that the Latin-American nations work at a long-range plan for economic and social development. Expansion of technical training programs, intensifying the U.S. goverment's Food for Peace Program, commodity market analyses, scientific exchange, and economic integration were among the steps he advocated. Congress, especially in view of the Cuban crisis, appropriated the $500 million it had previously authorized to assist "social progress" (which involved land use programs, educational support, housing, and so forth).

In August, 1961, the Inter-American Economic and Social Conference convened at Punta Del Este, Uraguay, to consider the new American proposals. The results were embodied in the Charter of the Alliance for Progress signed by representatives of all the American Republics, with the exception of Cuba. The United States pledged $20 billion in long-term financing, announced willingness to join a world coffee agreement, and to study an international system designed to stabilize prices of primary commodities. The Latin-American nations in turn pledged to undertake major programs in housing, health, and agriculture, including land reforms. The Secretary General of the Organization of American States was instructed to organize, within six months, task forces of experts to formulate national programs of social reforms in these areas.

UNITED STATES
RELATIONS WITH CUBA: A CASE STUDY

Several underlying facts must be taken into account in any analysis of United States relations with Cuba. First, the United States is less than one hundred miles from the "Pearl of the Antilles." Secondly, the United States was the primary agent of its independence. Thirdly, from the end of the Spanish-American war until 1934, Cuba was under the official tutelage of the United States. The instrument of this domination was the Platt Amendment, a rider to the United States army appropriations bill of 1901, which in 1903 was embodied in a treaty between the two countries.[14] The Platt Amendment (1) guaranteed the right of the United States to lease land for naval bases and put its military forces on Cuban soil; (2) forbade Cuba to enter into a treaty with a foreign power that would impair its sovereignty; and (3) prohibited Cuba from incurring indebtedness beyond its capacity to repay. Most distasteful to Cuba was

---

[14] Gatenbein, *The Evolution of Our Latin American Policy*, pp. 488-91.

that section of the edict which permitted the United States to intervene "for the preservation of Cuban independence, the maintenance of a government adequate for the protection of life, property, and individual liberty, and for the discharging of obligations. . . ."

The United States intervened in Cuba on three major occasions between 1906 and 1934. No matter how enlightened and well-meaning these interventions may have been, they carved deep scars in the Cuban national psyche. It was no coincidence that one of the first major steps taken by the administration of President Franklin D. Roosevelt in demonstrating his Good Neighbor Policy was to abrogate the Platt Amendment.

Economically Cuba has been closely tied to the United States. By 1960 American corporate wealth in Cuba had grown to over one and a half billion dollars. Nearly all of her sugar was grown for American refining and consumption, and sugar was her major export commodity, vital to her economic well-being. American sugar quotas were generous to Cuba until the break with Fidel Castro. By 1958 Cuba was importing $543 million worth of commodities from the United States. Many Americans profited through these extensive commercial relations.

Early in 1959 the dictatorial regime of Fulgencio Batista was toppled and Fidel Castro became the leader of the new revolutionary government. Castro promised to redistribute the land by breaking up the large estates. He promised adequate housing, education, and economic opportunity. There would be enough food for all Cubans. The socialist economy that Castro and his advisers planned fitted in well with the anti-Americanism of the revolutionary movement. A national plan rigidly controlling the economy was established, and business and industry were nationalized. There was some discussion, which grew increasingly vague as the revolution became established, that free elections would one day be held.

The United States was quick to recognize the new regime, but the honeymoon was short-lived. The first major bone of contention was the nationalization of property owned by United States firms and citizens. Land, oil refineries, sugar processing plants, utilities, and retail establishments were involved. United States protests against inadequate compensation for expropriated properties fell upon incensed Cuban ears. It was a tenet of the revolution that Cuban workers had been exploited by Americans and that any compensation at all for nationalized properties was more than was deserved. The Cubans also turned hungry eyes to the huge American naval base at Guantánamo which had been held by the United States under a treaty dating back to 1903. In 1961, the Cuban government seized the privately owned reservoir which supplied water to the base. The United States replied to Cuban threats by virtually eliminating its importation of Cuban sugar and by cutting off all exports to that country except food and medical supplies. In January 1961, President Eisenhower severed diplomatic relations.

The United States has taken the position that Cuba has become, in effect, a Communist nation and, as such, is a threat to hemispheric security. The Cuban government has claimed that the United States sought to intervene in Cuba to overthrow the Castro government. Cuba turned to the communist bloc countries for trade, and also received arms shipments from them. In April 1961, the United States government published a "white paper" on Cuba, a thirty-six-page pamphlet charging that Castro's regime was linked with the international communist movement. It argued that the revolution had been betrayed and expressed confidence that the Cuban people would continue their struggle for liberty. Evidence of this struggle was not long in coming. The *New York Times* reported that from five to six thousand Cuban exiles were being trained in Louisiana and Guatemala.[15] The phrase used to describe the United States government's position was "active cooperation."

At dawn, April 17, 1961, a "task force" estimated at about 1,200 to 1,500 Cuban exiles, having taken off from their Guatemalan base, landed at Cochinos Bay, in the "soft underbelly" of the island. Within forty-eight hours the forces of Fidel Castro had annihilated the invaders, taking many prisoners. A few escaped to the Escambray mountains; a very few made it back to the American mainland.

At the UN the Cuban foreign minister charged American aggression, which the American delegate denied. Many Afro-Asian and Latin-American representatives were sympathetic to the Cubans. Presidents Quadros of Brazil and Frondizi of Argentine, who had been meeting in South America, did issue a statement condemning "external aggression" in the hemisphere, but the reaction from other nations was generally favorable to Castro. The Soviet Union strongly supported the Cuban position. Twice, Soviet Premier Khrushchev, on April 18 and 22, sent messages to President Kennedy demanding that the United States call off the Cuban intervention. A sharply worded Soviet note even intimated reprisals on the American mainland.[16]

The position of the United States government was that it had not officially intervened or taken part in the ill-fated invasion. Both the President and Secretary of State Dean Rusk denied military involvement. President Kennedy, however, in replying to the first message of Premier Khrushchev, declared that the United States can "take no action to stifle the spirit of liberty."[17]

Putting the case in its barest essentials, the attempt to overthrow Fidel Castro failed and the United States was held responsible, blamed by the

---

[15] *New York Times,* Apr. 9, 1961, p. 1.
[16] *Congressional Quarterly,* XIX (week ending Apr. 28, 1961), 705, 740.
[17] *Ibid.*

supporters of the exiled Cubans for not providing enough support, blamed as well by many Latin-Americans for intervening in Cuba. Newspapers reported that the President had acted on the advice of the CIA and the Joint Chiefs of Staff, who had urged American support, maintaining that there would be mass defections inside Cuba as soon as the invasion took place and that many Cubans would flock to support the invaders. These agencies also argued that it was "now or never." If the invasion did not take place, Castro, who was becoming militarily stronger, would soon be virtually impossible to dislodge. If President Kennedy had received contrary advice he overruled it. As a consequence of this fiasco the President ordered a full-scale inquiry into his intelligence services.

No doubt there was a communications failure in the high intelligence echelons of the United States. But the Cuban "miscalculation" was based on the American failure to perceive the strength of social change in Latin America. Any intelligence service is, by definition, nationalistically myopic. Americans may strongly disapprove of Fidel Castro. But it does not follow that he is similarly unpopular in Cuba. American public opinion, as expressed in American newspapers, was influenced largely by interviews with Cuban exiles living in Florida, most of whom were middle-class and upper-middle-class people whose property had been seized and who were only a small segment of the Cuban population. To many Cubans, however, Fidel Castro in the early nineteen-sixties symbolized a very basic freedom, freedom from hunger and want. The United States government quite obviously failed to recognize the strength of this force. If there was disenchantment inside Cuba, the April invasion probably helped to close ranks. The consequence of United States policy was thus the very antithesis of its intent. Castro was stronger. Latin-Americans liked the United States less, though Castro's cavalier treatment of captured invaders in May 1961 evidently lost him some support in Latin-America. Many informed leaders throughout the world regarded the bungle as comparable to the Franco-British Suez fiasco of 1956.

THE UNITED STATES, LATIN AMERICA, AND THE FUTURE

In Latin America the United States must substitute understanding, tolerance, and cooperative assistance for the single-minded anti-communism it professed in the nineteen-fifties. Indeed, an enlightened development and extension of the Good Neighbor Policy in mid-century terms would prove far more potent in combatting inroads of international communism than would pressures for votes and resolutions at international council tables.

There is a new image ablaze in Latin America, the image of modern, national self-sufficiency, the image of an urban industrial society. If anything, this should bring the United States and Latin America closer than ever. But there is a turbulent history to overcome and a cornerstone of most Latin-American foreign policies is suspicion, if not downright fear, of the "Yanqui." Many Latin-Americans are well aware of their inferior position in relation with the United States. At the same time, they are proud of their heritage and their achievements.

It is important for the United States to understand this new image and to appreciate what economic and social change means to the different national societies. The "revolution of rising expectations" has far outdistanced the capacity of most of the Latin-American nations to meet the new needs. The old problems remain in many countries. Maldistribution of wealth and property; the related problems of large, illiterate, poverty-stricken populations; political instability; and resistance to change on the part of many groups wielding economic and political power—all co-exist and block easy transition or evolution. The basic fact, however, is that Latin America is changing and is moving towards, rather than away from, the socio-economic pattern of the Western world.

United States policy must be sensitized to this new dynamism. Economic necessity and existing governmental and administrative patterns have moved most Latin-American nations towards social democracy. Catholic, democratic-socialist nations might well be the outcome of current turmoil. It is doubtful whether any Latin-American nation, Cuba included, will become communist, except temporarily, to meet the exigencies of a national crisis.

The United States must seek in Latin America friends and allies whose differences it can appreciate and from whom it can learn. Only through peaceful, intelligently helpful association can the United States hope to win Latin-American support. Economic and technical assistance, people-to-people programs in all fields of endeavor, and non-paternalistic understanding and appreciation are needed in large quantities.

SUGGESTED READINGS

Adams, Richard N. and others, *Social Change in Latin America Today: Its Implications for United States Policy.* New York: Harper & Brothers for the Council on Foreign Relations, 1960.

Bailey, Helen Miller and Abraham P. Nasatir, *Latin America: The Development of Its Civilization.* Englewood Cliffs, N.J.: Prentice-Hall, Inc., 1960.

Committee for Economic Development, *Cooperation for Progress in Latin America*. New York: Committee for Economic Development, 1961.

Dozer, Donald M., *Are We Good Neighbors? Three Decades of Inter-American Relations, 1930-1960*. Gainesville, Florida: University of Florida Press, 1959.

Duggan, Laurence, *The Americas: The Search for Hemispheric Security*. New York: Holt, Rinehart & Winston, Inc., 1949.

Fenwick, Charles G., "The Organization of Central American States," *American Journal of International Law*, XLVI (July 1952), 509-12.

Fitzgibbon, Russell H., "Dictatorship and Democracy in Latin America," *International Affairs*, XXXVI (Jan. 1960), 48-57.

Gantenbein, James W., ed., *The Evolution of Our Latin American Policy: A Documentary Record*. New York: Columbia University Press, 1950.

Gomez, Rosendo A., *Government and Politics in Latin America*. New York: Random House, 1960.

Guerrant, Edward O., *Roosevelt's Good Neighbor Policy*. Albuquerque, New Mexico: University of New Mexico Press, 1950.

Herring, Hubert, *A History of Latin America from the Beginnings to the Present*. New York: Alfred A. Knopf, Inc., 1955.

Houston, John A., *Latin America in the United Nations*. New York: Carnegie Endowment for International Peace, 1956.

Humphrey, John, *Inter-American System: A Canadian View*. Toronto: Macmillan Company of Canada, Ltd., 1942.

"Latin America in Revolution," *Current History*, XXXVIII (Mar. 1960), entire issue.

Lieuwen, Edwin, *Arms and Politics in Latin America*. New York: Frederick A. Praeger, Inc., for the Council on Foreign Relations, 1960.

Madariaga de, Salvador, *Latin America Between the Eagle and the Bear*. New York: Frederick A. Praeger, Inc., 1961.

Martz, John D., *Central America: The Crisis and the Challenge*. Chapel Hill, North Carolina: University of North Carolina Press, 1959.

————, *Communist Infiltration in Guatemala*. New York: Vantage Press, 1956.

Matthews, Herbert L., ed., *The United States and Latin America*. New York: The American Assembly, Graduate School of Business, Columbia University, 1959.

Mezerik, A. G., ed., *Cuba and the United States: Record of Revolution, USSR-China, UN and OAS Action*. New York: International Review Service, 1960.

Padilla, Ezequel, "The Meaning of Pan-Americanism," *Foreign Affairs*, XXXII (Jan. 1954), 270-81.

Palmer, Thomas W., *Search for a Latin American Policy*. Gainesville, Florida: University of Florida Press, 1957.

Perkins, Dexter, *A History of the Monroe Doctrine*, rev. ed. Boston: Little, Brown & Co., 1955.

————, *The United States and Latin America*. Baton Rouge, Louisiana: Louisiana State University Press, 1961.

Pike, Frederick, B., "Guatemala, the United States, and Communism in the Americas," *Review of Politics*, XVII (Apr. 1955), 232-61.

Rieser, Carol, "Latin America: The Pains of Growth," *Fortune*, LVII (Feb. 1958), 112-19ff.

Rippy, James Fred, *Globe and Hemisphere: Latin America's Place in the Post-War Foreign Relations of the United States*. Chicago: Henry Regnery Co., 1958.

Schneider, Ronald M., *Communism in Guatemala, 1944-1954*. New York: Frederick A. Praeger, Inc., 1959.

Stokes, William S., *Latin American Politics*. New York: Thomas Y. Crowell Company, 1959.

Stuart, Graham H., *Latin America and the United States*, 5th ed. New York: Appleton-Century-Crofts, Inc., 1955.

Tannenbaum, Frank, "The Political Dilemma in Latin America," *Foreign Affairs*, XXXVIII (Apr. 1960), 497-515.

Thomas, Ann Van Wynen and A. J. Thomas, Jr., *Non-Intervention: The Law and Its Import in the Americas*. Dallas, Texas: Southern Methodist University Press, 1956.

Travis, Martin Bice, Jr. and J. T. Watkins, "Control of the Panama Canal: An Obsolete Shibboleth," *Foreign Affairs*, XXXVII (Apr. 1959), 407-18.

U.S. Senate, Committee on Foreign Relations, Subcommittee on American Republics Affairs, "United States-Latin American Relations. No. 1 Post World War II Political Developments in Latin America," by University of New Mexico School of Inter-American Affairs. Committee Print, 86th Cong., 1st sess., 1959. Washington, D.C.: Government Printing Office, 1959.

Whitaker, Arthur P., *The Western Hemisphere Idea: Its Rise and Decline*. Ithaca, New York: Cornell University Press, 1954.

Wright, Theodore P., Jr., "Free Elections in the Latin American Policy of the United States," *Political Science Quarterly*, LXXIV (Mar. 1959), 89-112.

Index

Index

Index